Corporate Governance

TOPK 1

D0879107

Analogy

Like a team of climbers facing a mountain peak, those responsible for governing organizations today face an uphill challenge. In many sectors around the world, tough conditions prevail, calculated risks have to be taken, and above all strong, strategic leadership is vital.

Corporate Governance

Principles, Policies, and Practices

THIRD EDITION

Bob Tricker

OXFORD

UNIVERSITY PRESS

UNIVERSITY PRESS

Great Clarendon Street, Oxford, OX2 6DP,
United Kingdom

Oxford University Press is a department of the University of Oxford.
It furthers the University's objective of excellence in research, scholarship,
and education by publishing worldwide. Oxford is a registered trade mark of
Oxford University Press in the UK and in certain other countries

© Bob Tricker 2015

The moral rights of the author have been asserted

First edition 2009
Second edition 2012

Impression: 4

All rights reserved. No part of this publication may be reproduced, stored in
a retrieval system, or transmitted, in any form or by any means, without the
prior permission in writing of Oxford University Press, or as expressly permitted
by law, by licence or under terms agreed with the appropriate reprographics
rights organization. Enquiries concerning reproduction outside the scope of the
above should be sent to the Rights Department, Oxford University Press, at the
address above

You must not circulate this work in any other form
and you must impose this same condition on any acquirer

Published in the United States of America by Oxford University Press
198 Madison Avenue, New York, NY 10016, United States of America

British Library Cataloguing in Publication Data
Data available

Library of Congress Control Number: 2014950236

ISBN 978-0-19-870275-7

Printed in Italy by L.E.G.O. S.p.A.

Links to third party websites are provided by Oxford in good faith and
for information only. Oxford disclaims any responsibility for the materials
contained in any third party website referenced in this work.

Dedicated to academic colleagues, board-level experts, and students of corporate governance whose experiences have enlivened my knowledge and understanding of the subject over the years, including contributors and reviewers for Corporate Governance: An International Review *and thousands of board chairmen, directors, auditors, regulators, and other board-level advisers.*

Acknowledgements

I owe a considerable debt to the many who, over the years, have contributed to my knowledge and understanding of corporate governance. Gratitude is clearly owed to the directors of the ten organizations who supported my original research in the Corporate Policy Group at Nuffield College, Oxford, from 1979 to 1983, which led to the publication of *Corporate Governance* in 1984. Since then, a long and fascinating road has led me to the present work.

Sir Adrian Cadbury has made a special contribution. His internationally influential report *The Financial Aspects of Corporate Governance* was published in 1992. Subsequently, he graciously commented that 'your 1984 book introduced me to the words *corporate governance*'.

Colleagues who have been influential include Alan Au, Raymond Chan, Thomas Clarke, Lex Donaldson, Robert Gibson, Jim Gillies, Fred Hilmer, Simon Ho, Bill Judge, Richard Leblanc, Gregg Li, Jay Lorsch, Chris Mallin, Bob Monks, Fred Neubauer, Bernard Taylor, Shann Turnbull, and many, many more.

Many thanks are also due to the faculty, students, and directors of client companies who contributed to the development of these ideas. Contributors to *Corporate Governance: An International Review*, both during my editorship and subsequently, also added much to my understanding. Kirsten Shankland and her colleagues at the Oxford University Press have been a constant source of support, and the anonymous reviewers made suggestions that significantly improved the book. I am grateful to them all. The opportunity to draw material from the websites of companies, regulators, and other institutions is also much appreciated.

Chapter 1 has been adapted by permission of the publishers from *Corporate Governance*, seminal readings in the History of Management Thought series, R. I. Tricker (ed.), Ashgate, Aldershot, UK, and Burlington, Vermont, USA, 2000.

Figures (2.1, 2.5, 2.6, 2.7, 2.8, 2.9, and 13.1) and case studies (Tyco, Drexell Burnham Lambert, HIH Insurance, and Robert Maxwell,) are based on material that first appeared in The Economist Essential Director, by Bob Tricker, Profile Books, 2003, and reproduced with kind permission. I also acknowledge the approval of Routledge to include some new cases (RBS and Fred the Shred, LIBOR rate rigging scandal, The corporate culture at Goldman Sachs, Board failings at Olympus Japan, and The collapse of HBOS bank), which appeared in Tricker, Bob and Gretchen, *Business Ethics —A Stakeholder, Risk, and Governance Approach*, Routledge, 2014.

Finally, thanks to my wife, Gretchen, not only, as so many authors say, for her support during the writing, but for her direct contribution. Being an editor and writer herself—among other things she wrote the centennial history of the Hong Kong Stock Exchange—she has undoubtedly made this script more readable.

Bob Tricker, 2014

Preface

This edition has had to be extensively rewritten to reflect changes since the second edition was published in 2012. Corporate governance around the world continues to develop and grow in importance. Principles, policies, and practices have all been extended. New theoretical insights have occurred. In many jurisdictions, the global financial crisis brought changes in company law and new corporate regulation, while some stock exchanges have extended their corporate governance reporting requirements. Boards' responsibility for the governance of risk has been emphasized. Levels of director remuneration have caused public dissatisfaction, and various schemes to increase transparency and obtain approval have emerged. Creating the company's ethical culture, determining its corporate social responsibility, and integrating economic, social, and environmental performance are increasingly recognized as part of boards' corporate governance responsibilities.

The previous editions were derived from material produced over the years for courses involving post-experience Master's degree students and corporate governance practitioners (company directors, company secretaries, auditors, corporate lawyers, and so on). Experience shows that the book has been used in various graduate, undergraduate, and professional courses and as a set text for professional examinations. So, although the original three sections—principles, policies, and practices—remain, the sequence of some chapters has been changed.

The book takes a comprehensive and international perspective on a subject that is of ever increasing significance—the way power is exercised over corporate entities. Public companies, family firms, public bodies, and many other types of corporate institutions are covered. The financial crisis, which saw some major institutions in the United States, the United Kingdom, and Europe threatened with collapse, government bail-out, and nationalization, focused attention on the culture of these organizations and their directors' attitude to risk. Significant developments have occurred in the past two or three years in some of these cases. Institutional investors and an investigative media increasingly challenge board-level decisions. Investor relation activities have increased in response. Further recent developments, such as growing concerns about business ethics and the role of business leaders, aggressive tax avoidance, alleged excessive executive remuneration, whistle-blowing, relations with auditors, corporate social responsibility, attitudes to risk, women on boards including ideas around the world on quotas, shareholder involvement, and the governance of corporate entities that do not have shareholders, highlighted the need for new material.

There have also been some changes in presentation. Colour has been introduced and the case studies now appear at the end of each chapter.

To assist the learning process, each chapter has a set of self-test questions (with answers at the end of the book), which enable readers to see what knowledge they have gained. For teachers wanting exercises that develop a critical analytical perspective, most of the case studies raise questions for discussion, as do the projects at the end of each chapter. More case studies and supportive material can be found on the Online Resource Centre.

Bob Tricker, Devon, 2014

Contents

List of case studies

Introduction

What the book is about

This book will enable readers to:

- appreciate the nature, functions, and realities of boards of directors and other governing bodies;
- analyse board structures, systems, and procedures, including board committees, chairmen, and chief executives, board remuneration, board leadership, and board effectiveness;
- understand major aspects of corporate governance, including:
  - corporate governance principles and codes of practice;
  - the board's performance roles: strategy formulation and policymaking;
  - the board's conformance roles: executive supervision and accountability;
  - the board's responsibility for handling corporate risk;
  - assessment of board and director performance;
  - corporate governance rating systems;
- understand various theories of corporate governance;
- appreciate corporate governance processes around the world, including:
  - adopting an international and comparative perspective on the subject;
  - contrasting corporate governance regimes around the world;
  - understanding the cultural aspects of different approaches to governance;
- recognize the issues that are influencing corporate governance and board thinking, including strategic risk management, corporate social responsibility, sustainability, and business ethics.

Who the book is for

The book will be useful for students studying for:

- Master's degrees in corporate governance, directorship, and related topics;
- MBA degrees;
- degrees in law, accountancy, and business studies.

It will also be relevant at the professional level for:

- directors of companies and potential directors;
- members of the governing bodies of other corporate entities;

- managers working with boards and other governing bodies;
- corporate secretaries, auditors, lawyers, and corporate governance consultants advising boards and directors.

The book has been adopted by universities and colleges for director training and board development. At least one professional body has adopted the text for its professional qualifying examinations. Of course, the book will also be relevant to academics teaching and researching corporate governance.

The book recognizes that the subject of corporate governance is changing and expanding all the time. Consequently, readers are encouraged to explore developments through the many references to relevant websites and further reading. The book also combines detailed text and explanations with case studies.

The basis of the book

The book is based on material that the author has developed over the years for directors' courses at the Institutes of Directors in London and Sydney, the MBA programme at the Australian Graduate School of Management, executive Masters at Hong Kong University, Melbourne University, Hong Kong Baptist University, and an open-learning course for Hong Kong Open University, as well as corporate governance courses for Russian university teachers sponsored by the Canadian Government at the Schulich School of Business in Toronto.

Some of the material has been adapted from previous publications with the approval of the copyright-holders, including:

- *Business Ethics—a stakeholder, risk, and governance approach*, Bob and Gretchen Tricker, Routledge, Abingdon, 2014;
- *Corporate Governance: An International Review*, Blackwells, Oxford;
- *Corporate Governance*, seminal readings in the History of Management Thought series, R. I. Tricker (ed.), Ashgate, Aldershot, UK and Dartmouth USA, 2000;
- *The Economist Essential Director*, Profile Books, 2009;
- *Governance* (InfoAustralia).

How the book came to be written: a personal note from the author

My initial work in the field was sponsored by Deloittes, the international accountancy firm, in the 1970s. The aim of the project was to examine the growing use of audit committees in the United States and to explore the possibility of introducing them into British companies. Audit committees were standing subcommittees of the main board, made up mainly of outside independent directors, acting as a bridge between external audit firm and board. Unfortunately, it quickly became clear that the concept of the audit committee would not work in British listed companies because there were not enough independent directors to staff them. Worse, while the concept of non-executive directors was understood, the notion of director independence was not.

Power in British boards at that time was the prerogative of executive directors. The conventional wisdom in the United Kingdom was that non-executives could be useful in board deliberations; about a third of the board was probably a good balance, but never as many as half. The notion that non-executive directors should be independent of the company was not part of conventional wisdom. The resultant book explained that audit committees without independent directors would be ineffective; it was entitled *The Independent Director*.[1]

My interest in boards and their behaviour was really kindled, however, in the 1970s, when I was head of the Oxford Centre for Management Studies, subsequently to become Templeton College, and then part of the Saïd Business School, Oxford. The Management Centre was incorporated as a company limited by guarantee and its large governing council comprised heads of Oxford colleges and leaders of major British companies. The council outnumbered the academic staff. Its divisive cliques, political power plays, and unpredictable interpersonal relations astounded me. This was not the behaviour of the classical organization theories, analytical decision-making, and basic management concepts that we were teaching in the Management Centre.

It occurred to me that governance was different from management. Throughout the 20th century, the focus had been on management. But where was the board on the management organization chart? Clearly, the governance of corporate entities and the processes of their governing bodies was a subject that deserved study. The subsequent opportunity to research at Nuffield College, Oxford, then led to a paper, *Perspectives on Corporate Governance: Intellectual Influences in the Exercise of Corporate Governance*, that was published in 1983 in a collection of essays.[2]

Over thirty years later, that paper's first sentence, which linked John Maynard Keynes, John Stuart Mill, and Karl Marx, seems unbearably pretentious. But the paper did manage to introduce the subject and the phrase 'corporate governance'. It identified some issues that remain pertinent to this day: the structure of boards; the role of non-executive directors; the governance of complex groups; the board's supervision of management; accountability; corporate regulation; and corporate social responsibility. In those days, board-level participation by employees was also an important topic.

The ideas in my paper in the Earl collection were developed in the book, *Corporate Governance*, published in 1984.[3] I remember agonizing over the term 'corporate governance' in the title. Although 'governance' was an ancient concept, *corporate* governance was not a phrase then in use. Indeed, I had named the trust that funded my research at Nuffield College the Corporate *Policy* Group, not the Corporate *Governance* Group. Subsequently, of course, the subject has moved centre stage. Indeed, it may well be that the social historian will see the 21st century as the era of corporate governance, just as the 20th century had been that of management.

Bob Tricker, Devon, 2014

[1] Tricker, R. I. (1978) *The Independent Director*. Tolley, London.
[2] Earl, Michael (ed.) (1983) *Perspectives on Management: A Multidisciplinary Analysis*. Oxford University Press, Oxford.
[3] Tricker, R. I. (1984) *Corporate Governance: Practices, Procedures, and Powers in British Companies and their Boards of Directors*. Gower Publishing, Aldershot, UK.

Part One

Principles

Corporate Governance: A subject whose time has come

 Learning Outcomes

In which we see how corporate governance has evolved:

- All corporate entities need governing
- Corporate governance is old, only the phrase is new
- The early days: merchants and monopolists
- The invention of the limited-liability company
- The separation of ownership from operations
- Developments in the 1970s: audit committees, two-tier boards and corporate responsibility
- Developments in the 1980s: corporate collapses
- Developments in the 1990s: corporate governance codes arrive
- Developments early in the 21st century: reactions to more corporate collapses
- Corporate governance implications of the global financial crisis
- New frontiers for corporate governance

All corporate entities need governing

The 20th century saw massive growth in serious management thought. Organization theories acquired new significance, although the board of directors did not appear on most organization charts. Strategic management has made great strides, but the contribution of the board seldom received a mention. Important theories and practices were developed for the management of finance, marketing, and operations, although little concern was shown for the role of the directors. This was the era of management theories, management consultants, management gurus, and management teaching, all reflecting a preoccupation with management.

However, if management was the focal point for the 20th century, corporate governance is set to be the primary focus for the 21st. Almost all advanced and advancing economies have introduced corporate governance codes or enacted new company laws, as in the United States following the Enron debacle.[1] The global financial crisis starting in 2007 added further

[1] The classic Enron case is in Chapter 4.

strands to corporate governance policy and practice. We will be studying these developments later in this chapter.

All corporate entities, including profit-orientated companies, both public and private, joint ventures, co-operatives, and partnerships, and not-for-profit organizations such as voluntary and community organizations, charities, and academic institutions, as well as governmental corporate entities and quangos,[2] have to be governed. All need a governing body. In the case of a company, this is its board of directors. Other corporate entities may call their governing body a council, a court, a committee, a board of governors, or, in the case of some Oxford colleges, just the governing body. To avoid repetition, from now on we will refer to all governing bodies as 'boards' and their members as 'directors', since many of the essential principles and practices apply, whatever names are used.

Essentially, corporate governance is about the way power is exercised over corporate entities. It covers the activities of the board and its relationships with the shareholders or members, and with those managing the enterprise, as well as with the external auditors, regulators, and other legitimate stakeholders.

Corporate governance is different from management. Executive management is responsible for running the enterprise, but the governing body ensures that it is running in the right direction and being run well. Directors are so-called because they are responsible for setting the organization's direction, formulating strategy and policymaking. Further, the board is responsible for supervising management and being accountable. Overall, the board is responsible for the organization's decisions and its performance.

Corporate governance is old, only the phrase is new

The idea of governance at the level of government is ancient. Chaucer (c.1343–1400), the English writer, philosopher, and courtier, used the word, although he could not decide how it should be spelt ('gouernance', 'governaunce'). But the phrase 'corporate governance' did not come into use until the 1980s. However, it has been quickly adopted worldwide. In 1988, Cochran and Wartick published an annotated bibliography of corporate governance publications; it had 74 pages. Today, Google accesses over 110 million references to corporate governance. Research into corporate governance also began to develop in the late 1980s. The research journal Corporate Governance—An International Review was founded in 1992.

Yet, although the theoretical exploration of the subject is relatively new, the practice of corporate governance is as old as trade. Shakespeare (1564–1616) understood the problem. In his play The Merchant of Venice, Antonio the merchant agonized as he watched his ships sail out of sight, with his fortune entrusted to others.

Whenever a principal has to rely on agents to handle his or her business, governance issues arise. This agency issue has long been recognized and has become a central challenge in the running and regulating of modern enterprise today. With a sole trader or in a small family firm, there is seldom any real separation between management and governance; changes in strategic direction merge with the day-to-day running.

[2] An acronym meaning quasi-autonomous non-governmental organization.

In this chapter, we trace the evolution of corporate governance ideas and practices over the years from the governance of merchant ventures, through companies set up by trading empires, to the brilliant invention of the limited-liability company in the 19th century, which opened the door to the bludgeoning ambiguity, complexity, and rapid changes in corporate governance today. The underlying ideas and concepts of corporate governance have been slow to evolve, with the underpinning legal frameworks still owing more to mid-19th-century thinking than to the realities of complex modern business. We shall also see how changes are often responses to critical situations rather than developments in theory.

The early days: merchants and monopolists

In medieval Europe, craft guilds for each trade, such as weavers, tailors, and wheelwrights, enforced standards, regulated prices, and controlled training and entry to their trade. Guilds were incorporated by legal processes, usually a charter, by cities and states. Only masters of the trade could be members of the guild and only guild members could practise that trade. Guild members elected the guild's governing body.

By the 17th century, economic, political, and military competition was growing between the empires of Britain, Holland, Portugal, and Spain. Companies, created by charter from the monarch or the state, pursued trading interests under rules set in the charter. In 1600, England's Queen Elizabeth I granted a royal charter to the East India Company, giving it a monopoly over all trade between England and Asia. The Company was a joint-stock company, with over 1,000 stockholders, who elected a governing board of 24 directors each year. The company traded principally with India and China in cotton, silk, tea, and opium, at one time administering parts of the British Indian Empire with a private army. The Dutch East India Company was granted a charter by the Republic of the Netherlands in 1602 to run Dutch colonies and to trade with Asia. The Dutch West India Company was chartered in 1621 to run the slave trade between Africa, the Caribbean, and North America. The Hudson Bay Company received its royal charter in 1670, when Prince Rupert, cousin of King Charles II, saw the opportunities for fur trading in the Hudson Bay area of what is now Canada.

As we shall see, the story of corporate governance has many overambitious and dominant businessmen with unrealistic expectations, leading to corporate collapses and, sometimes, fraud. The South Sea Company was incorporated in 1711 to trade with Spain's South American colonies, mainly in slaves. In 1718, King George I of England became governor of the company, bringing prestige and confidence. Then, in 1720, the British House of Lords gave a monopoly to the company on the understanding that the company undertook to guarantee the British national debt at a fixed interest rate. Massive speculation in its stock followed: stock prices went from £100 to over £1,000. Then the bubble burst. The Chancellor of the Exchequer was found to have taken bribes to inflate the stock. Many of the British gentry lost their fortunes, banks failed, while directors of the company were imprisoned and their wealth confiscated.

There was an outcry about such corporate excesses and risk-taking, very much as happened following the recent global financial crisis, when banks collapsed and had to be bailed out by governments. Adam Smith (1723–1790), a moral philosopher at the University of Glasgow, argued that society benefits when individuals pursue their own self-interest, because the free market then produces the goods and services needed at low prices. He is considered by many to be the father of modern economics.[3] But he was suspicious of businessmen, as many academics are to this day. His oft-quoted comment on their behaviour offers a classic corporate governance perspective:

> The directors of companies, being the managers of other people's money rather than their own, cannot well be expected to watch over it with the same anxious vigilance with which (they) watch over their own.
>
> (Adam Smith, *The Wealth of Nations*, 1776)

The invention of the limited-liability company

At the start of the 19th century, apart from corporations created by the crown or the state, there were basically three ways in which people could engage in business: as a sole trader, in a partnership, or as an unincorporated body in which some managed the firm while sleeping partners just provided finance. In each case, if the business became insolvent, the creditors could pursue their debts with any and all of those involved until ultimately they became bankrupt. In those days, not paying your debts was a crime leading to debtors' prison, with the possibility of your wife and children being sent to the parish workhouse. This was quite a disincentive to invest unless people were directly involved in the management activities. But this was a period of great economic growth, generated by the Industrial Revolution. Firms needed external capital to expand faster than ploughed-back profits would allow. Moreover, the emerging business and middle classes had funds available.

The French were the first to create a form of corporate incorporation, which restricted shareholders' liability. From 1807, the *Société en commandité par actions* limited the liability of external investors, but executive directors, who managed the enterprise, still remained personally exposed to their companies' debts. Meanwhile, in Britain, the need for companies to access capital without exposing external investors to the threat of bankruptcy was debated in Parliament. Some members of Parliament called for a form of incorporation that mirrored the French system. But in the event, the British Companies Acts of 1855 and 1862 gave limited liability to *all* shareholders, whether they were involved in the management of the company or not.

It proved to be one of the finest systems ever designed. The key concept was the incorporation of a legal entity, separate from the owners, which nevertheless had many of the legal property rights of a real person—to contract, to sue and be sued, to own property, and to employ. Yet the shareholders were no longer responsible for the company's debts. The company had a life of its own, giving continuity beyond the life of its founders, who could transfer their shares in the company. Nevertheless, ownership remained the basis of power. Shareholders elected their directors, who owed a stewardship duty and reported to them. The concept of ownership and shareholder rights still underpins modern company law, although the reality of power over many large companies is now very different.

During the 19th century, some states in the United States passed legislation allowing the incorporation of companies. In New York, Wall Street financial institutions were financing

---

[3] Adam Smith ([1776] 1976) *The Wealth of Nations*, revised edn., George J. Stigler (ed.), University of Chicago Press, Chicago.

and trading the shares of companies formed to build railways and to develop industry in the growth years that followed the American Civil War (1861–1865). But legislators were suspicious of limiting shareholders' responsibility for their companies' debts. Moreover, the objectives of each company and its life span were defined, and one company could not own another. The industrial age brought great wealth to some American companies and their owners. Subsequently, state constitutions were amended and laws rewritten to be more amenable to these powerful companies. Shareholder limited liability was introduced. Charter battles were fought to allow conglomerates, in which companies owned other companies. Eventually, corporate charters ceased to limit companies' activities and their life spans.

In 1918, the right of individual states to regulate their companies was challenged at the federal level. The court in the state of New Hampshire had revoked the royal charter given to Dartmouth College by the English King George III, but the US Supreme Court overruled the lower court. Many states saw this as a federal attack on state sovereignty and rewrote their laws to circumvent the Dartmouth ruling (see Friedman, 1973). To this day, companies in the United States are incorporated at the state not the federal level.

The concept of the limited-liability company spread throughout the British Empire of the late 19th century. The company laws of Australia, Canada, some Caribbean islands that are now tax havens, India, Malaysia, New Zealand, Singapore, South Africa, and other African countries still reflect those origins, although they have subsequently developed to reflect local circumstances. However, although these countries' laws evolved to reflect their changing situations, in many cases Commonwealth case law can provide precedents. Hong Kong, while now a special administrative region of China, still retains its British-orientated company law and legal system.

The notion of the limited-liability company was elegantly simple and superbly successful, leading to huge industrial growth around the world, and the creation of untold employment and wealth. Unfortunately, the simplicity of the mid-19th-century model now bears about as much relationship to reality as a hang-glider does to a fleet of jumbo-jets. Nevertheless, the original corporate concept remains the essential basis of contemporary company law.

Initially, though, all joint-stock, limited-liability companies were public companies—that is, they could invite the public to subscribe for their shares. Their main purpose was to raise capital from the public, who would not be responsible for their company's debts. By the early 20th century, however, business people saw that the model could be used to give limited liability to family firms and other private businesses, even though they did not need access to capital from outside investors. Such private companies, incorporated in jurisdictions around the world, now far outnumber public companies which can invite the public to subscribe for their shares.

The separation of ownership from operations

In the early days, limited-liability companies were relatively small and simple. Shareholders were drawn from the wealthier classes and could attend or be represented in annual general meetings of the company. They were relatively close to the companies in which they had invested. In those days, there were no chains of financial institutions, pension funds, hedge funds, brokers, or agents between the investor and the boardroom.

But by the early years of the 20th century things were changing. In the United States, the United Kingdom, and other economically advancing countries, many companies had become large and complex. Their shareholders were now numerous, geographically wide-spread, and differed in both their time horizons and their expectations about dividends and capital growth. Shares in most public companies were now listed on stock exchanges. Chains of financial institutions and other intermediaries stood between companies and the votes of their shareholders in company meetings. Links between management and investors in their companies were becoming distant.

Using data from companies in the United States, Berle and Means (1932) drew attention to the growing separation of power between the executive management of major public companies and their increasingly diverse and remote shareholders. They realized the significance of corporate power, observing that:

> The rise of the modern corporation has brought a concentration of economic power which can compete on equal terms with the modern state—economic power versus political power, each strong in its own field. The state seeks in some aspects to regulate the corporation, while the corporation, steadily becoming more powerful, makes every effort to avoid such regulation . . . The future may see the economic organism, now typified by the corporation, not only on an equal plane with the state, but possibly even superseding it as the dominant form of social organization.

> (Berle and Means, 1932, revised edn 1967)

This was a seminal work of corporate governance (although that was not a phrase Berle and Means used), and is still one of the most frequently cited works in corporate governance writing today. The recognition of issues raised by this work was instrumental in the creation of the US Securities and Exchange Commission (SEC). Berle and Means left a vital intellectual inheritance for the subject. It is surprising that it was so long before it was taken up.

For the next forty years, the work of directors and boards remained the province of jurisprudence, enlivened by anecdote and exhortation. In 1971, a pioneering work by Mace, based on research in US companies, sought to discover what directors really did and, in the process, challenged the conventional wisdom:

> In most companies, boards of directors serve as a source of advice and counsel, serve as some sort of discipline, and act in crisis situations if the president dies suddenly or is asked to resign because of unsatisfactory management performance.
>
> The business literature describing the classical functions of boards of directors typically includes three important roles: (1) establishing basic objectives, corporate strategies, and board policies; (2) asking discerning questions; and (3) selecting the president.
>
> (Instead) I found that boards of directors of most large and medium-sized companies do not establish objectives, strategies, and policies however defined. These roles are performed by company management. Presidents and outside directors generally agreed that only management can and should have these responsibilities.
>
> A second classical role assigned to boards of directors is that of asking discerning questions—inside and outside the board meetings. Again it was found that directors do not, in fact, do this. Board meetings are not regarded as proper forums for discussions arising out of questions asked by board members.
>
> A third classical role usually regarded as a responsibility of the board of directors is the selection of the president. Yet it was found that in most companies directors do not in fact select the president, except in . . . crisis situations . . .

> (Mace, 1971)

Developments in the 1970s: audit committees, two-tier boards, and corporate responsibility

Three significant developments occurred in corporate governance thinking in the 1970s. In 1972 in the United States, the SEC required listed companies to create audit committees, as standing committees of the main board comprising independent outside directors. These audit committees were to provide a bridge between the external auditor and the main board, ensuring that directors were made aware of any issues that had arisen between the auditor and the company's finance department. In Europe, two-tier boards were promoted, and on both sides of the Atlantic debates arose around board duties towards other stakeholders.

An increasingly litigious climate in the United States, with shareholders of failed companies seeking recompense from directors, boards, and, in particular, auditors (whose indemnity insurance was seen to provide a 'deep pocket' to be emptied for shareholders' benefit) led to more emphasis on checks and balances at board level. Auerbach (1973) wrote of the audit committee as a new corporate institution. Mautz and Neumann (1970, 1977) discussed the practicalities of audit committees. In the United Kingdom, Tricker (1978) undertook a study of British board structures, membership, and processes, intending to advocate audit committees in the United Kingdom, but concluded that, although many listed-company boards did have non-executive directors, the concept of director independence was not understood in Britain. Sir Brandon Rhys-Williams, a member of the British Parliament, also called for non-executive directors and audit committees in the United Kingdom, a proposal that led to a Green Paper *The Conduct of Company Directors* (1977) and a parliamentary Bill calling for audit committees, which ultimately failed.

The European Economic Community (EEC)[4] issued a series of draft directives on the harmonization of company law throughout the member states. The EEC Draft Fifth Directive (1972) proposed that unitary boards, in which both executive and outside directors were responsible for seeing that the business was being well run and run in the right direction, be replaced by the two-tier board form of governance practised in Germany and Holland. In this form of governance, companies have two distinct boards, with no common membership. The upper, supervisory board monitors and oversees the work of the executive or management board, which runs the business. The supervisory board has the power to hire and fire the members of the executive board.

The idea of the two-tier board was not well received in Britain—partly because it would replace the unitary board, which was seen, at least by directors, as a viable system of governance.

Moreover, in addition to the separation of powers, the directive included co-determination ideas then practised in Germany, in which the company was seen as a social partnership between capital and labour with the supervisory board made up of equal numbers of representatives of the shareholders and employees. The United Kingdom's response was the report of the Committee chaired by Lord Bullock. *The Report of the Committee of Inquiry on Industrial Democracy* (1977) and the research papers (1976) associated with it reflected the first serious

---

[4] Subsequently renamed the European Union.

corporate governance study in Britain. The Committee's proposal, for a continuation of the unitary board, but with some directors representing the employees, was not well received in Britain's boardrooms either.

The 1970s also saw a questioning of the role of the major corporation in society. Broadly, the argument was made that public companies have responsibilities beyond their prime legal duty to their shareholders. Given the scale and significance of such companies, boards should report and, some argued, be accountable to a range of stakeholders who could be affected by board decisions—customers, suppliers, and others in the added-value chain, employees, the local community, and the state. In the United States, there was an important dialogue between the American Bar Association, looking for an alternative basis of power over companies, and the Corporate Roundtable representing directors' convictions of the value of the existing model. Consumer advocate Ralph Nader offered a specification for a model corporation rooted in stakeholder thinking. Jensen and Meckling (1976), whose work was subsequently to become crucial to the development of agency theory, asked whether the original concept of the company could survive.

The debate was picked up in the United Kingdom. A committee of the Confederation of British Industries, chaired by Lord Watkinson (1973), reported on the wider responsibilities of the British public company. A report by Fogarty (1975) discussed companies' responsibilities and stakeholder participation. The Accounting Standards Steering Committee produced *The Corporate Report* (1975), which called for all economic entities to report publicly and accept accountability to all those whose interests were affected by the directors' decisions. The political implications of these proposals for the widening of accountability and control over companies, and the related erosion of managerial power, soon consigned this report to the archives.

Meanwhile, a number of corporate governance problems featured in the reports of inspectors appointed by the UK government Department of Trade. The inspectors at Pergamon Press (1971) concluded that owner Robert Maxwell[5] should not again run a public company—advice that was subsequently ignored, enabling him to build a media empire that collapsed dramatically twenty years later. Other inquiries, which examined board-level problems at Rolls Royce (1973), London and County Securities (1976), Lonhro Ltd (1976), and others, all added to the interest in the way companies were governed, although commentators still spoke of the way they were managed.

Developments in the 1980s: corporate collapses

In the 1980s, broader stakeholder concerns became overshadowed by the market-driven, growth-orientated attitudes of Reaganite and Thatcher economics. Directors' responsibility to increase shareholder value was reinforced. The profit performance model became the basis for the privatization of state-run entities—rail, coal, electricity, gas, and water enterprises were all privatized in the United Kingdom and, gradually, around the world. The threat of predator takeover bids (the market for control) was presented in Anglo-American circles as an essential incentive for strong board-level performance. Hostile bids, at this time, were often financed through the newly available high-risk, high-rate 'junk' bonds.

---

[5] The Robert Maxwell case is at the end of this chapter.

By the late 1980s, the downside of such thinking was becoming apparent. In the United States, the names of Ivan Boesky, Michael Levine, and Michael Milken were to go down in the annals of corporate governance with the massive, junk-bond-financed, insider information deals through Drexal, Burnham, and Lambert.[6] In Australia, the names of Alan Bond, Laurie Connell of Rothwells, and the Girvan Corporation were being associated with questionable governance practices. In Japan, Nomura Securities was accused of having too close links with its regulator, having offered well-paid sinecures to senior bureaucrats on retirement (called *amakudari*—literally 'descent from heaven'). Lavish payouts to major institutional clients to cover losses and links with a *yakuza* underworld syndicate were also alleged. The presidents of Nomura Securities and Nikko Securities resigned; so did Nomura's chairman, who also stood down from vice-chairman of the *Keidanren*, the federation of Japanese economic organizations.

In Australia, a 1989 report from the National Companies and Securities Commission[7] on the collapse of Rothwells Ltd, a listed financial institution, commented that 'at no time did the board of Rothwells perform its duties satisfactorily'. The company was dominated by an entrepreneurial figure, Laurie Connell, who expanded the company with acquisitions providing loans to many companies on the second board of the Western Australia Stock Exchange that were newer, smaller, and more entrepreneurial than those on the main board. Many were also riskier, but Connell financed them, acquiring the title 'Last Chance Laurie' in the process. The stock-market collapse in 1987 provided the catalyst that finally brought the company down, although earlier the auditors had refused to sign the 1988 accounts, and the official report disclosed 'massive private drawings by Connell and the rearrangement of affairs so that no disclosure of loans to directors had to be made'.

In the United Kingdom, it was the Guinness case and, subsequently, the collapse of Robert Maxwell's companies.[8] Boards dominated by powerful executive directors were now seen to need checks and balances, particularly where the posts of chief executive and chairman of the board were combined and the outside directors were weak. The concepts of corporate governance were at last to become the focus of attention; indeed, the phrase itself was about to appear.

In the mid-1980s, research into corporate governance expanded: for example, Baysinger and Butler (1985), using the phrase 'corporate governance', looked at the effects on corporate performance of changes in board composition, and Mintzberg (1984) posed the question 'Who should control the corporation?' But the subject came centre stage less as the result of academic, research-based deliberations, and more as a result of official inquiries set up in response to the corporate collapses, perceived board-level excesses, and apparently dominant chief executives in the later part of the 1980s.

In the United States, boards and their directors were coming under pressure. Institutional investors became increasingly proactive in corporate governance. Drucker (1991) drew attention to the potential governance power in shareholders' proxy votes. Companies needed to influence their share prices and to tap the ever-increasing pension funding and savings around the world. Expectations of institutional investors for performance improvement grew, along with pressure to end corporate governance practices that benefited incumbent boards

---

[6] The Drexel, Burnham, Lambert case is at the end of this chapter.
[7] Now the Australian Securities Commission.   [8] See case study 1.1.

and reduced the probability of the company being subjected to hostile bids. Investigative media and the threat of litigation added to the pressure on directors. The directors of American Express, General Motors, and IBM all had cause to regret the power of institutional fund managers to vote their shares against incumbent members of boards whom they considered to be performing badly.

The US Treadway Commission had been formed in 1985 to consider fraudulent corporate financial reporting. Its first report (1987) led to the creation of the Committee of Sponsoring Organizations of the Treadway Commission (COSO),[9] a private-sector initiative to encourage executive management and boards towards more effective business activities.

Developments in the 1990s: corporate governance codes arrive

In the 1990s, corporate governance codes arrived. The first was the United Kingdom's Cadbury Report (1992), produced by a committee chaired by Sir Adrian Cadbury, on the financial aspects of corporate governance. Based on what was considered good practice, the code called for:

- the wider use of independent non-executive directors, with 'independence' defined as being 'independent of management and free from any business or other relationship which could materially interfere with the exercise of independent judgement, apart from their fees and shareholding';
- the introduction of an audit committee of the board with independent members;
- the division of responsibilities between the chairman of the board and the chief executive, or, if the roles were combined, strong independent directors;
- the use of a remuneration committee of the board to oversee executive rewards;
- the introduction of a nomination committee with independent directors to propose new board members;
- reporting publicly that the corporate governance code had been complied with or, if not, explaining why.

Some critics of the Cadbury Report argued that it went too far—the emphasis on the importance of non-executive directors would introduce the controls of the European two-tier supervisory board by the back door, they said. Others felt that the report did not go far

---

[9] Originally formed to sponsor the National Commission on Fraudulent Financial Reporting, the Committee of Sponsoring Organizations (COSO) of the Treadway Commission is a voluntary private-sector organization dedicated to guiding executive management and governance participants towards the establishment of more effective, efficient, and ethical business operations on a global basis. It sponsors and disseminates frameworks and guidance based on in-depth research, analysis, and best practice. The following organizations take part: the American Accounting Association; the Institute of Management Accountants; the American Institute of Certified Public Accountants; the Institute of Internal Auditors; and the Financial Executives International.

enough—it lacked teeth by proposing delisting for defaulters rather than legally enforce-able sanctions.

In the United States, companies must follow the company law of the state in which they are incorporated, and comply with US generally accepted accounting principles (GAAP). In addition, companies must meet the demands of the SEC, and the rules of any stock exchange on which their shares are listed. In 1997, the US Business Roundtable, which takes a pro-business perspective, produced a Statement on Corporate Governance, which was updated in 2002, listing the following guiding principles of sound corporate governance:

- The paramount duty of the board of directors of a public corporation is to select a chief executive officer (CEO) and to oversee the CEO and other senior management in the competent and ethical operation of the corporation on a day-to-day basis.
- It is the responsibility of management to operate the corporation in an effective and ethical manner in order to produce value for stockholders.
- It is the responsibility of management, under the oversight of the board and its audit committee, to produce financial statements that fairly present the financial condition and results of operations of the corporation.
- It is the responsibility of the board and its audit committee to engage an independent accounting firm to audit the financial statements prepared by management and to issue an opinion on those statements based on GAAP.
- It is the responsibility of the independent accounting firm to ensure that it is in fact independent, is without conflicts of interest, employs highly competent staff, and carries out its work in accordance with generally accepted auditing standards (GAAS).
- The corporation has a responsibility to deal with its employees in a fair and equitable manner.

But corporate governance in the United States tends to be based on mandatory compliance with regulation and law,[10] rather than the discretionary 'comply or explain' approach of codes elsewhere.

The Cadbury Report became significant in influencing thinking around the world. Other countries followed with their own reports on corporate governance. These included the Viénot Report (1995) from France, the King Report (1995) from South Africa, the Toronto Stock Exchange recommendations on Canadian Board practices (1995), the Netherlands Report (1997), and a report on corporate governance from the Hong Kong Society of Accountants (1996).[11] As with the Cadbury Committee Report (1992), these reports were particularly concerned about the potential for abuse of corporate power. Similarly, they called for greater conformance and compliance at board level, recommending the use of audit committees as a bridge between board and external auditor, the wider use of independent outside, non-executive directors, and the separation of the role of chairman of the board from that of chief executive. The theme was more checks and balances to

---

[10] This was reinforced by the 2002 post-Enron Sarbanes-Oxley Act.

[11] We will study these codes in detail in Chapter 5.

avoid executive domination of decision-making and to protect the rights of shareholders, particularly minority shareholders. An Australian Committee on Corporate Governance (1993), chaired by Professor Fred Hilmer of the Australian Graduate School of Management, however, advanced a view that added a new dimension to the conformance and compliance emphasis of the Cadbury and the other reports. Governance is about performance as well as conformance, his report argued: 'The board's key role is to ensure that corporate management is continuously and effectively striving for above-average performance, taking account of risk.' It adds, almost as an afterthought, 'this is not to deny the board's additional role with respect to shareholder protection'.

The committee gave its report the splendid title *Strictly Boardroom*—after the film *Strictly Ballroom*, which portrays the world of competitive ballroom dancing, in which originality, creativity, and innovation had been sacrificed to inflexible and inhibiting rules and regulations. This is the danger facing current governance practices, argued Hilmer, with conformance and compliance overshadowing improved corporate performance.

In 1998, the Organisation for Economic Co-operation and Development (OECD) proposed the development of global guidelines on corporate governance and encouraged states to introduce such guidelines. The report usefully emphasized the contrast between the strong external investment and firm corporate governance practices in America and Britain and those in Japan, France and Germany, which had less-demanding governance requirements. In these countries, other constituencies, such as employees, receive more deference, the regulatory structures are less obtrusive, directors are seldom truly independent, and investors seem prepared to take a longer-term view. Some dismissed the proposals as 'pointless'; others saw merit in establishing some core principles of good corporate governance. Then, the Commonwealth countries also produced a code of principles of good corporate governance, which made recommendations on good corporate governance practice at the level of the company.

In the United States, Institutional Shareholder Services and the Investor Responsibility Research Center emerged to inform institutional fund managers on governance issues. In the United Kingdom, the Association of British Insurers and the National Association of Pension Funds also actively advised their members on proxy voting issues. In Australia, it was the Australian Investment Managers' Association. The Californian State Employees Pension Fund (CalPers) was particularly active, producing global principles for corporate governance, intended to benchmark corporate governance practices in companies in its portfolio around the world. In response, some companies, such as General Motors (1996), published their own board governance guidelines on significant governance issues.

However, probably the most telling driver of change in corporate governance in the 1990s was the dynamic, flexible new corporate structures, often global, that were now replacing the stable, often regional, corporate groups of the post-war years—massively complex networks of subsidiary companies and strategic alliances with cross-holdings of shares, cross-directorships, chains of leveraged funding, and dynamic and ever-changing operational and financial linkages throughout the added-value chain. These were networks that operated in multiple jurisdictions, cultures, and currencies—groupings with voracious appetites for growth. Top management of major corporations around the world was now wielding enormous power. While claiming to reflect owners' interests, directors were seen to be pursuing their own agendas and expecting huge rewards—privileges reserved in earlier generations for kings and their courtiers.

Developments early in the 21st century: reactions to more corporate collapses

As the 21st century dawned, corporate governance seemed to be developing well around the world. The importance of good corporate governance was well recognized. Codes of principles or best practice in corporate governance for listed companies were in place in most countries with stock markets. Many of the corporate governance codes now called for director appraisal, training, and development, and for board-level performance reviews. Many felt that markets were offering a premium for shares in well-governed companies. This was particularly the case in the United States. Indeed, there was a widespread expectation in the United States that the rest of the world would gradually converge with the American approach to corporate governance and the US GAAP, not least because the world, it was felt, needed access to American funds.

But the new century had scarcely begun when disaster struck. Enron, one of the largest companies in the United States, collapsed on the back of heavy, unreported indebtedness and dubious corporate governance attitudes among the executive directors. In addition to Enron, Waste Management, Worldcom, and Tyco also collapsed. So did their auditor, Arthur Andersen, one of the big five global accounting firms, as their clients changed auditors and partners changed firms. Corporate governance problems appeared in companies in other parts of the world as well. In the United Kingdom, Marconi, British Rail, Independent Insurance, and Tomkins faced governance problems, as did HIH Insurance[12] in Australia, Parmalat in Italy, and Vodaphone Mannesmann in Germany.

The US GAAP were now pilloried as being based on rules that could be manipulated, rather than on the principles of overall fairness required in international accounting standards. Financial transparency, governance processes, and, most significantly, attitudes toward corporate governance were questioned. Confidence in the financial markets was shaken. Suddenly, from being the leaders of economic success, entrepreneurial risk-taking, and sound corporate governance, directors were depicted as greedy, short-sighted, and more interested in their personal wealth and share options than in creating sustainable wealth for the benefit of the shareholders. The response was more legislation.

In 2001, in the United States, a Blue Ribbon Commission, set up by the National Association of Corporate Directors (NACD), published a report *Director Professionalism*, the key recommendations of which were as follows.

- Boards should be composed of a substantial majority of independent directors.

- Boards should require that key committees—including, but not limited to, audit, compensation, and governance/nominating—be composed entirely of independent directors, and be free to hire independent advisers as necessary.

- Each key committee should have a board-approved written charter detailing its duties. Audit committee duties, at a minimum, should include two key elements:

  a. oversight of the quality and integrity of financial reports and the process that produces them; and

  b. oversight of the management of risk.

[12] See the case at the end of this chapter.

Compensation committee duties should include performance goals that align the pay of managers with the long-term interests of shareholders. Governance/nominating committee duties should include setting board and committee performance goals and nominating directors and committee members with the qualifications and time to meet these goals.

- Boards should consider formally designating an independent director as chairman or lead director.

- Boards should regularly and formally evaluate the performance of the CEO, other senior managers, the board as a whole, and individual directors. Independent directors should control the methods and criteria for this evaluation.

- Boards should review the adequacy of their companies' compliance and reporting systems at least annually. In particular, boards should ensure that management pays strict attention to ethical behaviour and compliance with laws and regulations, approved auditing and accounting principles, and with internal governing documents.

- Boards should adopt a policy of holding periodic sessions of independent directors only. These meetings should provide board and committee members with the opportunity to react to management proposals and/or actions in an environment free from formal or informal constraints.

- Audit committees should meet independently with both the internal and independent auditors.

- Boards should be constructively engaged with management to ensure the appropriate development, execution, monitoring, and modification of their companies' strategies. The nature and extent of the board's involvement in strategy will depend on the particular circumstances of the company and the industry or industries in which it is operating.

- Boards should provide new directors with an orientation programme to familiarize them with their company's business, industry trends, and recommended governance practices. Boards should also ensure that directors are continually updated on these matters.

A year later, the American Law Institute published a set of general principles on corporate governance, which generated a debate on the regulation of boards and directors. In November 2003, the SEC approved new listing requirements reflecting many of the NACD's recommendations.

In 2002, the US Sarbanes-Oxley Act was rushed through, placing new stringent demands for the governance of all companies listed in the United States. This Act, now nicknamed 'SOX' or 'Sarbox', significantly raised the requirements and the costs of corporate governance. The New York Stock Exchange and Nasdaq reflected the changes in their listing rules. Only independent directors could now serve on audit and remuneration committees, shareholders had to approve plans for directors' stock options, and subsidized loans to directors were forbidden. A new institution was created to oversee audit firms, which must rotate their audit partners, to prevent an over-familiarity between auditor and the client's finance staff. Auditors were also forbidden to sell some non-audit services to audit clients, and audit staff were to serve a cooling-off period before joining the staff of an audit client—all of which had happened in Enron.

Towards the end of the 20th century, the main emphasis in the field of corporate govern-ance had been on listed companies. But a parallel development had occurred during the 1990s, accelerating into the 2000s: the concepts and principles of corporate governance developed for listed companies were also seen to be relevant to unlisted private companies and to many other corporate entities. Corporate governance policies and procedures were developed for charities, educational, sports and medical bodies, professional institutions, government corporations, and quangos. In some cases, corporate governance codes and best governance practices were published.

Corporate governance implications of the global financial crisis

In 2007, in the United States, after more than a decade of substantial growth, house prices began to fall, leaving some owners in negative equity, their mortgage loans greater than the value of their homes. Worse, it emerged that many of these loans had been made to peo-ple who were not good credit risks—the so-called sub-prime market. Foreclosures escalated, driving house prices down further.

For a decade, lax monetary policies, cheap money, and massive liquidity had produced a lending-and-asset bubble in the Western world. Companies used low-interest loans to lever-age their financial strategies. World trade had boomed, with some countries facing vast trade imbalances. Personal borrowing soared, some secured on inflating house prices, some on extended credit card debt.

The catalyst for the subsequent chaos was financial engineering. Financial institutions had bundled their loan assets into securities, which they then sold on to other financial institu-tions. This securitization of debt spread the risk around the world's financial systems, but, because these instruments were complex and sophisticated, there were problems matching exposure to security. Moreover, not all bank directors appreciated the extent of their banks' exposure to risk. Rumours of banks' overexposure to sub-prime debt circulated, lowering confidence, which is the basis of every financial system: confidence that credit will be avail-able when needed and trust that debts will be repaid when due. Facing uncertainty, banks began to tighten their lending policies. Funds became scarce. Central banks had to make special arrangements to provide money to meet some institutions' liabilities.

In 2007, the first run on a UK bank for over a century occurred at the Northern Rock bank,[13] which had to be taken over by the British government. In the United States, Bear Stearns, a financial institution, was bailed out by the US government. Then, dramatically, the two huge American mortgage organizations, Fannie Mae and Freddie Mac, which account for a large part of all mortgages to homeowners in the United States, were given government guaran-tees of up to US$5 trillion. Next, American International Group (AIG), the world's biggest insurer and provider of hedging cover to the banking system, imploded. The US government, believing that it could not countenance the adverse economic effects of the failure of AIG, provided a loan facility of US$85 billion to protect the interests of its taxpayers, secured on AIG assets, taking an 80% equity stake in the company. Lehman Brothers was not so fortunate:

[13] We will study the Northern Rock case in Chapter 8.

the Federal Reserve System refused to provide support and, after 158 years, the firm became bankrupt, which drove down market confidence still further.

In September 2008, the US Federal Reserve and the US Treasury tried to restore confidence. They proposed a bailout in which the American government would take on banks' bad debts, including the sub-prime loans, with the underlying collateral security. Some complained that this would allow the financial executives, whose reckless investments had caused the crisis in the first place, to unload their risky assets and then walk away with their bonuses and golden parachutes intact.

Other countries around the world also experienced liquidity problems. In September 2008, there was a run on the Bank of East Asia in Hong Kong, which was quickly met by reassurances from Hong Kong's financial authorities. In October 2008, all of the banks and the stock exchange in Iceland were closed when depositors' demands for cash could not be met. Iceland, a country of around 300,000 people, which had previously relied on fishing and tourism, had been led by a handful of financial entrepreneurs to engage in international finance way beyond its economic potential.

In the United States, plans were announced for the government to take a US$700 billion equity stake in its banks. In the United Kingdom, the government effectively nationalized three banks—Royal Bank of Scotland, HBOS, and Lloyds TSB. Some bank bosses lost their jobs. In both the United States and the United Kingdom, the government had now become the largest provider of mortgages. Iceland, meanwhile, its banks and stock exchange still closed and its currency untradable, appealed to the International Monetary Fund for help.

The global financial crisis raised some fundamental corporate governance issues.

- Where were the directors of the failed financial institutions—particularly the independent outside directors who were supposed to provide a check on over-enthusiastic executive directors? Did they really understand the strategic business models and sophisticated securitized instruments involved? In other words, did they appreciate the risk inherent in their companies' strategic profile?

- Where were the banking regulators? Although the extent of the crisis was unprecedented, the regulators seem to have been beguiled into complacency, perhaps taken over by the industry they were there to regulate. New rules followed.

- Where were the auditors? In approving the accounts of client financial institutions, did they fully appreciate and ensure the reporting of exposure to risk?

- Did the credit agencies contribute to the problem by awarding high credit ratings to companies overexposed to significant risk?

- Government bailouts also raised the question of so-called moral hazard—by protecting bankers from their past reckless decisions, would others be encouraged to take excessive risks in the future?

- Will the experts who designed the sophisticated loan securitization vehicles and other financial engineering systems be held to account? Are their ideas and enthusiasms now under control?

- Were any of the financial institutions' activities illegal? Compare the situation with Enron, in which some top executives continued to believe that nothing they had done was illegal, even after they were in jail.

- Finally, did excessive bonuses and share options encourage short-term and unrealistic risk-taking with shareholders' funds? The news that some bankers had lost their fortunes as share prices collapsed was cold comfort to mortgagees who lost their homes, shareholders who lost their savings, and employees who lost their livelihoods.

Predictably, regulatory authorities sought to improve corporate regulation to avoid further problems. In the United States, the SEC proposed changes to regulatory procedures for listed companies including obligatory (although non-binding) shareholder votes on top executive remuneration, the annual election of directors, and the creation of board-level committees to focus on enterprise risk exposure. The separation of the CEO role from that of the board chairman, as called for in corporate governance codes in other countries, was suggested.

In the United Kingdom, although the Financial Review Council did not find evidence of serious failings in the governance of British businesses outside the banking sector, it did propose changes to the UK Code to improve governance in major companies. The proposed changes were intended to enhance accountability to shareholders, to ensure that boards are well balanced and challenging, to improve a board's performance and to deepen awareness of its strengths and weaknesses, to strengthen risk management, and to emphasize that performance-related pay should be aligned with the company's long-term interests and risk policy.

In 2010, the existing UK Combined Code was renamed the UK Corporate Governance Code, a name some thought might have been more appropriate all along. The main proposals for change were:

- annual re-election of the chairman or the whole board;
- new principles on the leadership of the chairman, and the roles, skills, and independence of non-executive directors and their level of time commitment;
- board evaluation reviews to be externally facilitated at least every three years;
- regular personal performance and development reviews by the chairman with each director;
- new principles on the board's responsibility for risk management;
- performance-related pay should be aligned to the company's long-term interests and its risk policy;
- companies to report on their business model and overall financial strategy.

The corporate governance principles published by the OECD were designed to assist countries to develop their own corporate governance codes.[14] The OECD's Steering Group on Corporate Governance re-examined the adequacy of these principles in light of the global economic problems. The real need, it felt, was to improve the practice of the existing principles. In two seminal papers,[15] four broad areas were identified as needing attention: board practices; risk management; top-level remuneration; and shareholder rights.

---

[14] OECD (2004) Principles of Corporate Governance. Available at: www.oecd.org/daf/corporateaffairs/principles/text

[15] Grant Kirkpatrick (2009) The Corporate Governance Lessons from the Financial Crisis. February. Also, Corporate Governance and the Financial Crisis: Key Findings and Main Messages. June 2009. Both publications are available at www.oecd.org

New frontiers for corporate governance

Corporate governance thinking and practice continue to evolve. We will be exploring these new frontiers throughout this book, but for now let us consider some of the more significant.

Growing corporate complexity

Research from the Harvard Business School,[16] following the global financial crisis, concluded that recent boardroom failures differed from the previous corporate failings, such as Enron, World-Com, and other corporate collapses, which were rooted in management malfeasance and led to the US Sarbanes-Oxley Act. Recent corporate governance problems, the researchers found, were primarily attributable to the growing complexity of the companies that boards governed. The research also found a strong consensus among directors that the key to improving boards' performance was not government action, but action by each board. Moreover, it emphasized the differences between companies and concluded that each board needed to develop structures, processes, and practices to fit its needs. The notion that 'one size fits all' was viewed with scepticism. The Harvard research identified six areas for improvement at board level:

- clarifying the board's role;
- acquiring better information and deeper understanding of the company;
- maintaining a sound relationship with management;
- providing oversight of company strategy;
- assuring management development and succession;
- improving risk management.

Changes in ownership patterns

In the early days of the corporate concept, the shareholding owners of the company were just one removed from the board of directors they elected to run their company. This can still be the case in small companies and start-up situations. But elsewhere the position has become strikingly different. A complex chain of intermediaries and agents can lie between investors and the company in which they are ultimately investing. For example, an individual might invest in a pension fund, which invests in a highly geared hedge fund, which invests in an index-tracking fund, which invests in the shares on a given stock market index. Moreover, shares in the chain could be lent to cover other transactions of the financial institution involved. Consequently, it can be difficult for the ultimate owner to exercise any influence over the governance of the company in which his or her funds have been invested, which was the original intention of the corporate concept. Further, private equity deals, in which financial institutions take major stakes in listed companies, often with highly leveraged financial positions, have added to corporate governance issues, particularly accountability and transparency.

[16] Jay Lorsch with Joe Bower, Clayton Rose, and Suraj Sriinivasan (2009) *Perspectives from the Boardroom.* Harvard Business School, Cambridge, MA.

Board responsibility for enterprise risk management and business continuity

Companies add value in different ways to achieve their corporate goals. In some businesses, added value might lie in the global upstream supply chain, their technological expertise, product uniqueness and brand image. In other cases their market position, the downstream distribution network, access to finance, managerial expertise, or reputation might be the foremost consideration. Failure in a critical area can expose a company to strategic risk and even threaten business continuity. Consider the case of the catastrophe at BP's Deepwater Horizon oil rig.[17]

Surprisingly, studies have shown that some outside directors do not know where value is added in their company. Consequently, they cannot know whether the company is exposed to strategic risk. So the most significant risks that companies face may be the least well understood by boards. In the global financial crisis, it was apparent that many directors of financial institutions did not understand their firms' exposure to strategic risk.

Directors need to understand how value is added within their business, where the company is critically exposed to risk, and what policies are in place to manage those risks. Identifying and assessing critical risk needs to be a board-level activity. The handling of operational and managerial risk can be delegated to management, with the board ensuring that the enterprise risk management policies and systems are working. But decisions about risks at the strategic level should not be delegated. They are fundamentally part of the board's responsibility for formulating strategy. Corporate governance involves creating business value while managing risk. Of course, senior management plays an important part in the process, but the responsibility ultimately belongs to the board.

Corporate governance be by rule or principle

Many commentators have referred to the 'Anglo-American' approach to corporate governance. They contrast the Anglo-American governance traditions of the unitary board, which has both executive and non-executive directors, with the continental European two-tier, supervisory board and executive board. They compare the company law approach of the Anglo-American common law jurisdictions with that of civil law countries. But actually a schism has appeared between American and British concepts of corporate governance. The former is built on a prescriptive rules-based legal approach to governance; the latter prefers a non-prescriptive, principles-based, more self-regulatory approach.

The underpinning of American corporate governance has become mandatory governance determined by regulation and law, such as the SOX Act. In other words, 'obey the legal requirements or risk the penalties', which can include unlimited fines and jail. China is following a similar legal orientation. By contrast, the basis of corporate governance in Britain and many other countries,[18] whose company law has been influenced over the years by UK common law traditions, involves a discretionary approach to governance by principle. In other words, 'comply with the code or explain why you have not'. This frontier is really a fundamental philosophical debate of considerable significance for the future of the subject.

---

[17] The case of the BP Deepwater disaster is covered in Chapter 8.
[18] Including Australia, Canada, New Zealand, Hong Kong, India, Malaysia, South Africa, Singapore, and Hong Kong.

The European Union is again reviewing the basis of corporate governance in member states and may opt for the more rule-orientated continental European model of company law. The dilemma remains unresolved.

Boards marking their own exam papers

Another dilemma concerns the workings of the unitary board, in which directors are responsible for both the strategic direction of the business and overseeing the activities of executive management. In other words, the board is expected to be involved in strategy formulation and planning while also supervising management performance. It has been suggested that this means the unitary board is effectively trying to mark its own examination papers. Of course, the two-tier board structure avoids this problem by having the executive board responsible for performance and the supervisory board for ensuring conformance, common membership between the two boards being forbidden.

To overcome this dilemma, corporate governance codes call for independent outside (non-executive) directors to play a vital role. Independence is precisely defined to ensure that these directors have no interest in the company that might, or might be seen to, adversely affect genuine independent and objective judgement. The minimum number or percentage of independent board members is usually specified. The definition of independence in most corporate governance codes is typically exhaustive. To be considered independent, a director must have no relationship with any firm in the upstream or downstream added-value chains, must not have previously been an employee of the company, nor must he or she be a nominee for a shareholder or any other supplier of finance to the company. Indeed, the definition of independence is so strict that an independent director who has served on the board for a long period is often assumed to have become too close to the company and is no longer considered independent. But this can create another dilemma.

Independent directors who do not know enough about the business

The more independent directors are, the less likely they are to know about the company and its industry. The more non-executive directors know about a company's business, organization, strategies, markets, competitors, and technologies, the less independent they may become. Yet the knowledge and experience of such people are exactly what top management needs to contribute to its strategy, policymaking, and risk assessment.

The New York Stock Exchange (NYSE) sponsored a Commission that published ten core principles of corporate governance.[19] While the Commission supported the NYSE's listing requirements, which call for a majority of independent directors, it also pointed out that companies can have additional non-independent outside directors so that there is an appropriate range and mix of expertise, diversity, and knowledge. The Commission pointed out that while independence is an important attribute for board members, the NYSE's Listing Standards do not limit a board to just one non-independent director, and boards should seek an appropriate balance between independent and non-independent directors.

[19] New York Stock Exchange: Sponsored Commission on Corporate Governance, 10 Core Principles of Corporate Governance, October 2010—a commission representing investors, issuers, broker-dealers, and governance experts.

The ten core principles were as follows.

1. The Board's fundamental objective should be to build long-term sustainable growth in shareholder value for the corporation.

2. Successful corporate governance depends upon successful management of the company, because management has the primary responsibility for creating a culture of performance with integrity and ethical behaviour.

3. Good corporate governance should be integrated with the company's business strategy and not viewed as simply a compliance obligation.

4. Shareholders have a responsibility and long-term economic interest to vote their shares in a reasoned and responsible manner, and should engage in a dialogue with companies in a thoughtful manner.

5. While legislation and agency rule-making are important to establish the basic tenets of corporate governance, corporate governance issues are generally best solved through collaboration and market-based reforms.

6. A critical component of good governance is transparency, because well-governed companies should ensure that they have appropriate disclosure policies, and practices, and investors should also be held to appropriate levels of transparency, including disclosure of derivative or other security ownership on a timely basis.

7. The Commission supports the NYSE's listing requirements generally providing for a majority of independent directors, but also believes that companies can have additional non-independent directors so that there is an appropriate range and mix of expertise, diversity, and knowledge on the board.

8. The Commission recognizes the influence that proxy advisory firms have on the markets, and believes that it is important that such firms be held to appropriate standards of transparency and accountability.

9. The SEC should work with exchanges to ease the burden of proxy voting, while encouraging greater participation by individual investors in the proxy voting process.

10. The SEC and/or the NYSE should periodically assess the impact of major governance reforms to determine if these reforms are achieving their goals.

Board Diversity

Diversity in board membership has become a major interest around the world in recent years, particularly gender diversity, driven by a concern for greater equality between men and women at the top of large corporations. In 2014, Denmark had a relatively high percentage of women serving on the boards of listed companies and state corporations: around 41%. In Sweden and Finland it was over 25%, in the United Kingdom around 20%, and in the United States about 17%. In France the percentage was 18%, in Germany 14%, and Australia 12%. In Japan and the United Arab Emirates, however, it was only slightly over 1%, and In Saudi Arabia barely 0.1%.

To redress the gender imbalance, some countries have advocated quotas for women to be appointed to boards. Norway introduced a quota in 2005. India, Malaysia, and South Africa have also called for quotas. In 2009, the US regulator, the SEC, passed a rule that required companies to explain their policies on nominating directors; in other words, companies had to explain their own attitudes towards diversity. In 2011 in the United Kingdom, a government-commissioned report by Lord Davies called for 25% women on boards by 2015 and also called for listed companies to explain their policies. The European Union has taken steps towards equality between men and women by requiring 30% board representation by women by 2015 and 40% by 2020. However, not all member states have accepted the requirement. Many companies are also opposed to quotas, arguing that they do not guarantee that the most appropriate people become directors and, if mandated, the women board members could become 'token directors,' with decision-making powers held outside the board room.

Calls for more women on boards and the use of quotas have tended to come from governments, regulators, and interest groups. Board members and shareholders, including institutional investors, have tended to be unenthusiastic, despite the obvious missed talent and opportunities for the female perspective.

In addition to gender diversity, some commentators have called for greater diversity by business experience and skills, for boards to reflect stakeholders' interests, and even to mirror the diversity of society. We will explore the implications of such notions in the next chapter.

Shareholders' changing expectations of directors and boards

Once upon a time, a directorship was a sinecure—an occasional meeting between friends, maybe a few supportive questions, then a fee and probably lunch. Not now. Today, more is expected of company directors, indeed of the members of all governing bodies, than ever before. In listed companies, shareholders are no longer compliant. They expect their directors to increase shareholder value, but not at the price of accounting distortions, excessive director remuneration, or misleading financial disclosure. Institutional investors in these companies—the insurance companies, pension funds, and financial institutions—can put pressure on poorly performing boards, complain publicly about allegedly excessive directors' remuneration, and demand high standards of corporate governance. The requirements on listed companies and their directors, from financial regulators, stock exchanges, and an increasingly investigative media around the world, have also increased. The threat of litigation against companies, boards, and individual directors has introduced the risk of serious financial exposure as well as the potential for public derision.

Directors of private companies, that is, those without public investors, including entrepreneurial businesses, subsidiary companies, joint venture entities, and family firms, can also find themselves under the corporate governance spotlight. The interests of minority shareholders must be protected. In certain circumstances, directors can become personally responsible for their company's debts. They can also be fined heavily if the company fails to meet its statutory obligations. Moreover, like their public company counterparts, shareholders in private companies now expect their directors to set high standards of governance and to deliver improving corporate performance.

Members of the governing bodies of not-for-profit institutions, including hospital trusts, charities, professional bodies, co-operatives, colleges, and community organizations, also face demands for better governance. Members of their governing bodies are expected to act professionally, and to be accountable, with their activities transparent.

Society's changing expectations of directors and boards

Society's expectations of companies, boards, and directors are changing, too. The movement we saw in the 1970s, expecting more of companies than just making a profit for their shareholders while remaining within the law, has reappeared with new force. Company collapses in the late 20th and early 21st centuries and growing criticism of directors' behaviour, reinforced by the trauma caused by the global financial crisis, have led to renewed concern about business ethics. The original 19th-century concept of the limited-liability company was founded on trust and stewardship. But the ethical framework enshrined in the original concept has been overshadowed as power shifted from owners to directors. Now pressures for sound governance, director-level stewardship, and ethical business behaviour are emerging.

In a world affected by global finance, trading, and services, the need for socially responsible behaviour by companies has acquired new momentum. Calls have increased for companies to show concern for the effects of their actions on all stakeholders including the communities they affect. Corporate social responsibility, or CSR as it is now widely known, has become a major concern of many companies, as we shall see. The interest in ecology and the conservation of the planet's resources, taking corporate decisions that do not deplete the world's resources to the detriment of future generations, has brought sustainable development to the corporate governance agenda. Corporate governance has acquired some new dimensions.

Cultural considerations affect corporate governance

As we saw earlier in this chapter, significant developments in corporate governance have come from the unitary board countries, principally the United States and the United Kingdom, while continental European countries provide a counterpoint with their two-tier boards. But, subsequently, some unique aspects in other countries that affect the way in which corporate governance develops have become apparent. For example, the way in which business is done, the extent to which legal contracts or interpersonal trust form the basis for business decisions, the sources of capital, the legal traditions, the state of company law, the reliability of the courts, the existence of relevant institutions, the standing of the accountancy, audit, and legal professions, the powers of the regulatory authorities, and overall the traditions of the country and the expectations of its people, all influence the way in which corporate governance develops. Later, we will explore the relevance of culture to corporate governance, reviewing governance in Brazil, China, India, Japan, Russia, countries in which Islamic *sharia* law affects governance, and those in which the traditional Chinese-led family business dominate.

Some classic corporate governance cases

 Case study 1.1   Robert Maxwell

Robert Maxwell, then Jan Ludvik Hoch, was born in Czechoslovakia in 1923, grew up in poverty, fought with the Free Czech army in the Second World War, and received the British Military Cross. He became an international publishing baron. In the early 1970s, inspectors appointed by the UK government led an inquiry into the failure of his company Pergamon Press and concluded that he was not 'a person who can be relied on to exercise stewardship of a publicly-quoted company'. Nevertheless, he subsequently succeeded in building a media empire including two public companies—Maxwell Communication Corporation and Mirror Group Newspapers. Following his death in 1991, in mysterious circumstances at sea, it was alleged that he had used his dominant position as chairman of the trustees of the group's pension funds to siphon off funds to support his other interests and that he had been involved in an illegal scheme to bolster the price of companies in the group. Eventually, the lead companies were declared insolvent, banks called in loans that could not be repaid, and the group collapsed. Investigators estimated that £763 million had been plundered from the two public companies and their pension funds to prop up Maxwell's private interests.

There are many lessons for directors in the Maxwell affair. Maxwell's leadership style was dominant: he reserved considerable power for himself and kept his top executives in the dark. An impressive set of independent non-executive directors added respectability to the public company boards, but they were ill-informed. Maxwell threatened litigation to prevent criticism of his corporate affairs: many investigative journalists and one doctoral student received writs. The complexity of the group's organizational network, which included private companies incorporated in tax havens with limited disclosure requirements, made it difficult to obtain a comprehensive overview of group affairs. The auditors were criticized. In a revealing internal memo, the senior partner of CoopersLybrandDeloittes wrote: 'The first requirement is to continue to be at the beck and call of Robert Maxwell, his sons, and his staff, appear when wanted, and provide whatever is required' (discovered by Persaud and Plender, 2006). The failings of the trustees of the Maxwell group pension fund and the regulatory bodies were all recognized.

Involvement with his father's empire left Robert Maxwell's son Kevin bankrupt. Two decades later, in 2011, he was disqualified as a director for eight years by the UK Department for Business Innovation and Skills. According to its findings, he and two other directors had diverted more than £2 million out of the bankrupt construction company Syncro Ltd ahead of liquidation. He had also failed to preserve accurate records in a 'disregard for a director's duty'.

Discussion questions

1. What would you say are the crucial questions in the Maxwell affair?

2. How might they have been answered?

 Case study 1.2   Drexell, Burnham, Lambert

This Wall Street securities trading firm was at the heart of the predator takeover market in the 1980s, using high-return, high-risk 'junk' bonds. It provided the base for the insider dealing activities of Ivan Boesky, and provided the setting for the nefarious activities of Dennis Levine and Michael Milken.

Dennis Levine, then in his twenties, discovered that insider trading was easy and apparently foolproof. In his job, he had access to information about prospective financial deals. If he exchanged that knowledge with an executive in another bank who knew about *that* bank's deals, traded the shares under a pseudonym in the Bahamas, then transferred the profit to an account in a Swiss bank; bingo, the compliance authorities would never know.

Later, he grew overconfident—some might say greedy. He took a position in a company, for which his own company was preparing a bid, and made US$1.3 million. But he underestimated the capabilities of government investigators, acting with the co-operation of securities regulators (particularly IOSCO[20]). Levine pleaded guilty, gave evidence against his colleagues, and was sentenced to two years' imprisonment and a fine of US$362,000. Further, he had to make restitution to the SEC of US$11.6 million in insider trading profits and was barred from employment in the securities business for life.

Michael Milken was charged with racketeering and securities fraud. He agreed to plead guilty to six felonies, paid US$600 million in restitution, and was sentenced to ten years in prison. One of the effects of these activities was a growing interest in corporate governance.

In 1988, the Drexel firm pleaded guilty to six securities felonies and paid a record US$650 million in retribution. In 1990, it filed for the protection of the Bankruptcy Court.

Discussion questions

1. Milken had to make restitution to the SEC of US$11.6 million in insider trading profits. Who had suffered as Milken made these insider trading profits?

2. Why is insider trading considered a crime by the regulatory authorities?

[20] International Organization of Securities Commissions.

 Case study 1.3   HIH Insurance

HIH Insurance Group was Australia's largest insurer. When it collapsed in 2001, the £1.9 billion loss left many policyholders and investors bereft. Some lost their homes.

A royal commission questioned the founder and chief executive, Ray Williams. Observers commented on a tale of 'spectacular munificence' and that 'it was like the last days of Pompeii'. Mr Williams enjoyed a millionaire's lifestyle. His secretary travelled first class. A corporate adviser was given round-the-world air tickets for himself, his wife, four children, and a nanny to compensate for working over Christmas. A director, Rodney Adler, whose FAI insurance company had been taken over by HIH for more than £200 million, received a £2.3 million termination payment and a £350,000-a-year consultancy fee.

Mr Williams, a philanthropist who had donated millions to medical research, claimed that his own life savings were in the company and that he had not sold any shares. The problems, he claimed, were due to errors of judgement—in particular the failure to undertake a due diligence study on FAI, which was discovered to have gaping holes in its finances.

Discussion questions

1. What was the board doing while this saga was going on? What should it have done?

2. Whose fault was it that FAI had been acquired without a due diligence study and with 'gaping holes in its finances'?

3. What is your opinion of the reward given to a corporate adviser (round-the-world air tickets for himself, his wife, four children, and a nanny) to compensate for working over Christmas?

References and further reading

Accounting Standards Steering Committee (1975) *The Corporate Report: A Discussion Paper*. London.

American Law Institute (1984) *Principles of Corporate Governance*, in three parts. Philadelphia, PA.

Auerbach, Norman E. (1973) 'Audit Committees: New Corporate Institution', *Financial Executive*, September, pp. 96–97, 102, 104.

Baysinger, Barry D. and Henry N. Butler (1985) 'Corporate Governance and the Board of Directors: Performance Effects of Changes in Board Composition', *Journal of Law, Economics and Organization*, 1, pp. 101–124.

Berle, Adolf A. and Gardiner C. Means (1932) *The Modern Corporation and Private Property*. Macmillan, edn revised by Adolf Berle (1967) Columbia University, Harcourt, Brace and World, New York.

Bullock, Lord (1977) *Industrial Democracy: A Report of the Committee of Inquiry on Industrial Democracy*. HMSO Cmnd. 6706, 1977 [with European Experience—reports prepared for the Industrial Democracy Committee (1976) Eric Batstone and P. L. Davies, HMSO].

Cadbury, Sir Adrian (1992) *The Financial Aspects of Corporate Governance: A Report of the Committee on Corporate Governance*. Gee & Co., London.

Chaucer, Geoffrey (c.1483 and 1476) *The Canterbury Tales*. Caxton.

Cochran, Philip L. and Steven L. Wartick (1988) *Corporate Governance: A Review of the Literature*. Morristown, Financial Executives Research Foundation.

Corporate Governance: An International Review. Wiley-Blackwell, Malden, MA.

Cruver, Brian (2002) *Enron—anatomy of greed, the unshredded truth from an insider*. Random House, London.

Dimma, William A. (2006) *Tougher Bards for Tougher Times—corporate governance in the post-Enron era*. John Wiley, Ontario.

Drucker, Peter F. (1991) 'Reckoning with the Pension Fund Revolution'. *Harvard Business Review*, March–April, pp. 106–114, .

Earl, Michael J. (ed.) (1983) *Perspectives on Management*. Oxford University Press, Oxford.

Estes, Robert M. (1973) 'Outside Directors: More Vulnerable than Ever'. *Harvard Business Review*, January/February, pp. 107–114.

European Economic Community (1972) *Proposal for a Fifth Directive on the Structure of Companies*. Strasbourg.

Fogarty, Michael P. (1975) *Company Responsibility and Participation: A New Agenda*. PEP Broadsheet Number 554, Volume XLI, London, August.

Friedman, L. M. (1973) *A History of American Law*. Simon and Schuster, New York.

Friedman, Milton (2002) *Capitalism and Freedom*. University of Chicago Press, Chicago.

Friedman, Milton (2008) *Milton Friedman on Economics: Selected Papers*. University of Chicago Press Journals, Chicago.

Greenbury, Sir Richard (1995) *Directors' Remuneration: The Report of a Study Group*. Gee & Co., London.

Hadden, Tom (1972) *Company Law and Capitalism*. Weidenfeld & Nicolson, London.

Hampel, Sir Ronald (1998) *Committee on Corporate Governance: Final Report*. Gee & Co. London, January.

HMSO (1977) *The Conduct of Company Directors*. White Paper, UK Cmnd. 7037 presented to Parliament.

Hilmer, Frederick G. (1993) *Strictly Boardroom: Improving Governance to Enhance Company Performance*. Information Australia, Melbourne, Australia.

Jensen, Michael C. and William H. Meckling (1976) *Can the Corporation Survive?* Centre for Research in Government Policy and Business, University of Rochester, USA, May.

Mace, Myles L. (1971) *Directors: Myth and Reality*. Graduate School of Business Administration, Harvard University, Boston, MA.

Mautz, R. K. and F. L. Neumann (1970) 'The Effective Corporate Audit Committee'. *Harvard Business Review*, November/December.

Mautz, R. K. and F. L. Neumann (1977) *Corporate Audit Committees: Policies and Practices*. Ernst and Ernst, New York.

Mintzberg, Henry (1984) 'Who Should Control the Corporation?', *California Management Review*, XXVII, pp. 90–115.

National Association of Corporate Directors (1996/2001/ 2005) *Report of the NACD Blue Ribbon Commission on Director Professionalism for Public Company Governance*. Washington, DC.

Persaud, Avinash D. and John Plender (2006) *All You Need to Know about Ethics and Finance*. Longtail Publishing, London.

RSA (The Royal Society for the Encouragement of Arts, Manufactures and Commerce) (1995) *Tomorrow's Company the Role of Business in a Changing World*. London.

Securities and Exchange Commission (1972) 'Standing Audit Committees Composed of Outside Directors', Release No. 123, March, *SEC Accounting Rules*.

Shakespeare, William (1596/8) *The Merchant of Venice*, Act 1 Scene 1, first folio.

Smith, Adam (1759) *The Theory of Moral Sentiments*.

Smith, Adam ([1776] 1976) *The Wealth of Nations*. Revised edn, George J. Stigler (ed.), University of Chicago Press, Chicago.

Tricker, R. I. (1978) *The Independent Director: A Study of the Non-executive Director and of the Audit Committee*. Tolley with Deloitte, Haskins & Sells, London.

Tricker, R. I. (1984) *Corporate Governance*. Gower Publishing, Aldershot, UK.

Watkinson, Lord (1973) *Responsibilities of the British Public Company: Report of the Company Affairs Committee of the Confederation of British Industry*. London, September.

Projects and exercises

1. Prepare a report on why the underlying ideas and concepts of corporate governance were slow to evolve. Why was the phrase 'corporate governance' not used until the 1980s and the subject scarcely studied during the later half of the 20th century when the study of management was at its height?

2. Research one or more of the cases of early corporate collapses mentioned in the text: in Australia, Alan Bond, Laurie Connell of Rothwells, and the Girvan Corporation; in Japan, Nomura Securities and the Recruit Corporation; in the United States, Ivan Boesky, Michael Levine, and Michael Milken of Drexal, Burnham, and Lambert; in the United Kingdom, Guinness and the Robert Maxwell companies. Prepare a report or class presentation outlining the case(s). What was the underlying reason for the failure? Would today's corporate governance codes, rules, and regulations have prevented these outcomes?

3. Explore the cases of corporate collapse mentioned in the text. Is there an underlying explanation for their failure? Prepare a report or a class presentation

4. Explore the collapse of financial institutions mentioned in the chapter. Prepare a report or a class presentation on corporate governance implications stemming from the global financial crisis.

Self-test questions

To confirm your grasp of the key points in this chapter, try answering the following questions.

1. Define corporate governance.

2. What are the main attributes of the limited-liability company?

3. What is the basis of corporate power?

4. What did the classical Berle and Means (1932) study emphasize?

5. What was the response of the UK Bullock Committee Report (1977)?

6. What did the Corporate Report (1975) from the UK Accounting Standards Committee propose?

7. Name some corporate collapses in the 1980s that led to the first studies of corporate governance.

8. What was the first official report on corporate governance and why was it commissioned? What were the major recommendations of the Cadbury Report?

9. Name some financial institutions in the United States that failed during the global financial crisis.

10. What additional dimension did the Australian Hilmer Report add to the conformance and compliance concepts of corporate governance?

2 Governance and Management

 Learning Outcomes

In which we recognize:

- Definitions of corporate governance
- The scope of corporate governance
- The significance of constitutions for corporate entities
- The difference between governance and management
- The performance and conformance aspects of governance
- Alternative board structures
- Board diversity

Definitions of corporate governance

In the last chapter, we suggested that corporate governance is concerned with the exercise of power over corporate entities. While this is true, it is an overarching view that does not help in understanding the boundaries, levels, and processes of the subject. We now need to explore other definitions of corporate governance. Notice how the different definitions reflect alternative viewpoints on the subject.

An operational perspective

The definitions adopted by some authorities focus on governance structures, processes, and practices. The first corporate governance report, Sir Adrian Cadbury's *Report on the Financial Aspects of Corporate Governance* (1992), took such a view. This report defined corporate governance as 'the system by which companies are directed and controlled', and further explained that boards of directors are responsible for the governance of their companies, while the shareholders' role in governance is to appoint the directors and the auditors, and to satisfy themselves that an appropriate governance structure is in place. Hilmer (1993), writing in the Australian context, emphasized the strategic responsibility of the board, suggesting that 'the board's key role is to ensure that corporate management is continuously and effectively striving for above average performance, taking account of risk, (which) is not to deny the board's additional role with respect to shareholder protection'. The operational perspective was also adopted in the corporate governance code developed by the Organisation for Economic Co-operation and Development (OECD) (2001): 'Corporate governance is about the procedures and processes according to which an organization is directed and controlled.'

The operational perspective, focusing on the shareholders, the board, and the management, has been the basis for much work in corporate governance. Notions of best practice in the interactions between them is fundamental to the corporate governance codes.

A relationship perspective

However, the OECD report strengthened the operational perspective by including the relationship among various participants: 'The corporate governance structure specifies the distribution of rights and responsibilities among the different participants in the organization—such as the board, managers, shareholders, and other stakeholders—and lays down the rules and procedures for decision-making.' The Corporate Library (now GMI Ratings), an influential website (www3.gmiratings.com), described corporate governance as 'the relationship among the shareholders, directors and management of a company, as defined by the corporate charter, by-laws, formal policy, and rule of law'. This relationship perspective was reinforced by the California Public Employees Retirement System (CalPers), a significant institutional investor, which included in its definition 'the primary participants are: shareholders, company management (led by the chief executive officer), and the board of directors'. Monks and Minow (1995) agreed, but added the employees: 'Corporate governance involves the relationship among various participants, including the chief executive officer, management, shareholders, and employees, in determining the direction and performance of corporations.'

A stakeholder perspective

Notice that the OECD definition above includes 'other stakeholders', as well as the shareholders, board, and management. It takes a wider view of those involved in and affected by corporate governance. In the last chapter, we adopted this wider relationship perspective: 'Corporate governance is about the activities of the board and its relationships with the shareholders or members, and with those managing the enterprise, as well as with the external auditors, regulators, and other legitimate stakeholders.' Demb and Neubauer (1992) also took the stakeholder view: 'Corporate governance is the process by which corporations are made responsive to the rights and wishes of stakeholders'. We will consider later who the stakeholders in a modern corporation might be.

A financial economics perspective

Financial economists tend to see corporate governance through a different lens from that of the lawyer and management expert. 'Corporate governance deals with the way suppliers of finance assure themselves of getting a return on their investment' wrote Shleifer and Vishny (1997). Their principal concern was with the ownership concentration in corporate governance systems around the world and the legal protection available to investors. Nevertheless, financial economics has been the dominant contributor of scholarly research into corporate governance, applying agency theory to board-level activities.

A societal perspective

Finally, we come to a perspective that places the corporate entity in society. In 1995, Blair set corporate governance in this context as 'the whole set of legal, cultural, and institutional arrangements that determine what public corporations can do, who controls them, how that control is exercised, and how the risks and return from the activities they undertake are allocated'. Many would now include all corporate entities, as well as 'public corporations'.

Sir Adrian Cadbury, addressing the Global Corporate Governance Forum of the World Bank in 2000, took such a viewpoint when he said:

> Corporate governance is concerned with holding the balance between economic and social goals and between individual and communal goals. The corporate governance framework is there to encourage the efficient use of resources and equally to require accountability for the stewardship of those resources. The aim is to align as nearly as possible the interests of individuals, corporations and society.

Such a perspective sets corporate governance at a high level of abstraction. It includes all of the stakeholders involved with the company, including the contractual stakeholders such as the shareholders, managers, and other employees, suppliers, customers, consumers, bankers, but also other stakeholders outside the company whose interests could be affected by corporate behaviour, including the local, national, and international societal interests. Such a perspective can raise interesting philosophical issues about relationships between the individual, the enterprise, and the state. The societal perspective is reflected in the growing interest in stakeholder theory, which we will consider in the next chapter, and corporate social responsibility.

Of course, these different perspectives are not mutually exclusive; they overlap. None are all-inclusive; each can be relevant in context. The vital issue is to adopt the perspective that is appropriate to the matter under review.

The scope of corporate governance

Figure 2.1 shows schematically the parties involved in the various perspectives on corporate governance.

Central to corporate governance thinking and practice are the shareholders, the board of directors, and the management. The corporate governance codes focus on this set of players, as does much company law. External auditors play a crucial role in corporate governance, although they are not often presented as central to its study. In the original 19th-century concept of the corporation, the shareholders appointed some of their own members to act as auditors, to check on the reports presented to them by their directors. Subsequently, they were replaced by professional auditors, as the accounting profession developed in the later years of that century. Later, we shall consider the implications of audit in the modern, global world, with just four massive, international firms of accountants, following the demise of the fifth, Arthur Andersen, after the Enron debacle, which we will study in Chapter 4. The importance of audit committees—standing committees of the main board, which are now required by all the codes of good practice in corporate governance—will also be studied in depth.

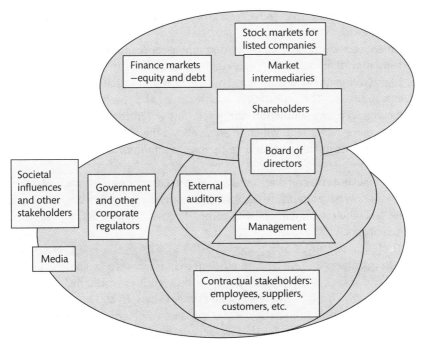

Figure 2.1 The scope of corporate governance

For public, listed companies, the stock markets and their listing rules are, clearly, vitally significant to corporate governance. The rules that govern the stock market on which the company's shares are listed and in particular the requirements laid down for listing are fundamental to the effective governance of listed companies. Stock markets around the world also play an important role in the creation and policing of corporate governance codes.

Another perspective focuses on the interrelations between the company and its shareholders, including any dominant owners, and institutional investors, minority shareholders, and stock exchanges where a company is listed. The governance interests of any providers of non-equity debt capital also need to be included. In public companies, market intermediaries play an increasingly important role in modern corporate governance. In the original model of the corporation, shares were held by individual shareholders who interacted directly with their company. Today, although individual investors do have a significant share in some markets, institutional investors play a very significant part in most. The institutional investors may include an array of financial institutions such as pension funds, investment funds, life assurance funds, unit trusts, hedge funds, and other investment houses. There can be a raft of intermediary institutions between the company and the ultimate investor in its shares. Investment bankers may act as underwriters in launching shares in an initial public offering (IPO) of shares. Brokers, merchant bankers, and other institutions can hold shares on behalf of others. A further complication can arise if the financial institution holding shares lends them as security for other transactions. This situation can make it difficult for companies to know who their voting shareholders are, and for those shareholders to exercise their proxy votes and to take part in the governance of the company.

Governments obviously provide the underpinning for corporate governance by enacting the legislation that facilitates, regulates, and constrains the activities of corporate entities registered in their jurisdiction. The creation and updating of Companies Acts are obvious examples. The registration of companies and the filing and access to corporate documents is also a function of the relevant government department. The relationship between government, which in effect allows the corporate entity to be created and to operate in its jurisdiction, and companies is an important element of corporate governance.

Corporate regulators play an ever-increasing role in corporate governance. Many company jurisdictions now have a separate regulatory authority that monitors stock market activity, determines and requires compliance with corporate governance codes, and has the power to ensure compliance.

In the United States, the US Securities and Exchange Commission (SEC) exists to protect investors, to maintain fair, orderly, and efficient markets, and to facilitate capital formation. The SEC oversees the key participants in the securities world, including securities exchanges, securities brokers and dealers, investment advisers, and mutual funds. Crucial to the SEC's effectiveness in each of these areas is its enforcement authority, being able to take legal action against insider trading, accounting fraud, and the provision of false information.

Some commentators and researchers widen the focus of corporate governance to include contractual stakeholders—that is, those with whom the company has contractual relations, including employees, suppliers, and all those in the upstream and downstream added-value chains from suppliers of original goods and services, other contractors and supply firms, through distributors, wholesalers, and retailers, to the final customer and consumer. Government and other corporate regulators are also basic components of the corporate governance system. This includes the effect of the company law, the legal institutions, and the regulatory mechanisms of the country concerned. Previously, the press showed little interest in business affairs unless there were major catastrophes. But, in recent years, the media has shone a spotlight on corporate activities, and the investigative media now play a useful role in the corporate governance process and have to be considered by practitioners.

Finally, the growing importance of societal influences and other stakeholders in corporate governance needs emphasis. In earlier days, companies tended to be left alone to carry on their activities in the pursuit of profit without interference, provided that they abided by the laws of the jurisdictions in which they operated. This is no longer the case. Today, many people expect companies to adopt a socially responsible attitude to their activities, for example by not doing objectionable things, such as exploiting workers, polluting the environment, or wasting energy.

Corporate social responsibility (CSR) reflects what some commentators see as companies' obligations to everyone who might be affected by the company's activities (the stakeholders): not only contractual stakeholders, such as employees, suppliers, and customers, but local neighbourhoods who could be affected by a plant closure, cities and states affected by the loss of jobs and tax revenues by a company's strategy to move activities elsewhere, and even larger international society for companies' employment policies, environmental impacts, or marketing policies around the world.

At this stage it may be useful to consider the role of regulatory bodies such as the US Securities and Futures Exchange, the UK Companies House, the listing requirements of the Australian Stock Exchange, and the role of the Hong Kong Securities and Futures Commission. This information, in the boxes that follow, will give you an insight into the regulatory process and encourage you to explore the way the regulatory institutions operate in your own country,

Corporate governance in action 2.1 The role of the US SEC and EDGAR and XBRL reporting

The SEC was created following the Great Crash of 1929. Previously, there was little support for federal involvement in corporate matters. During the 1920s, over 20 million shareholders set out to make their fortunes on the stock market. Of around US$50 million in new securities issued, half became worthless. Countless fortunes were lost. Many banks failed. Depression followed and confidence in the markets collapsed.

Congress passed the 1933 Securities Act to restore investor confidence. The SEC was set up to enforce the new laws designed to promote security in the market by requiring public companies to tell the truth about their business, their securities, and the risks involved, and requiring security dealers to treat investors fairly and honestly.

The mission of the SEC is to protect investors, to maintain fair, orderly, and efficient markets, and to facilitate capital formation. Unlike the banking world, where deposits are guaranteed by the federal government, stocks, bonds, and other securities can lose value. The laws and rules that govern the securities industry in the United States derive from a simple and straightforward concept: all investors, whether large institutions or private individuals, should have access to certain basic facts about an investment prior to buying it, and as long as they hold it. To achieve this, the SEC requires public companies to disclose meaningful financial and other information to the public. This provides a common pool of knowledge for all investors to use to judge for themselves whether to buy, sell, or hold a particular security.

The SEC oversees the key participants in the securities world, including securities exchanges, securities brokers and dealers, investment advisers, and mutual funds. Crucial to the SEC's effectiveness in each of these areas is its enforcement authority. Each year, the SEC brings hundreds of civil enforcement actions against individuals and companies for violation of the securities laws. Typical infractions include insider trading, accounting fraud, and providing false or misleading information about securities and the companies that issue them.

To support investors, the SEC provides a mass of information, including the EDGAR database of disclosure documents that public companies are required to file with the Commission. From 2011, the SEC required filings of all necessary corporate documents to be XBRL-based. XBRL (eXtensible Business Reporting Language) is an open, free, global standard system covering financial data and facilitates the creation, distribution, and use of business reports.

The SEC is the primary overseer and regulator of the US securities markets, and works closely with many other institutions including Congress, other federal departments and agencies, the self-regulatory organizations (e.g. the stock exchanges), state securities regulators, and various private sector organizations. In particular, the Chairman of the SEC, together with the Chairman of the Federal Reserve, the Secretary of the Treasury, and the Chairman of the Commodities Futures Trading Commission, serves as a member of the President's Working Group on Financial Markets.

(For more information, see www.sec.gov and www.xbrl.org.uk)

Corporate governance in action 2.2   Companies House: the UK company registration service

In the United Kingdom, Companies House is the central registry for all companies registered in the United Kingdom—private, public, and limited by guarantee. All companies in the United Kingdom have to be formally incorporated through Companies House, and must file the required documents and financial accounts, annually and whenever changes occur. These documents are then available for public scrutiny.

Companies House requires companies to file online, using XBRL (eXtensible Business Reporting Language), an electronic reporting system.

Companies House provides a free searchable index of company names and addresses on over 2 million companies registered in the United Kingdom. Companies House WebCheck is an online search tool, for accessing and downloading company information from over 250 million company documents including company accounts. Copies of a company's latest accounts and annual return and some company reports can be bought online.

(For more information, see www.companieshouse.gov.uk)

Corporate governance in action 2.3   The role of the Australian Stock Exchange (ASX)

The ASX has two basic functions, as follows.

1. To operate Australia's primary national stock exchange for equities, derivatives, and fixed-interest securities, including settlement facilities. It also provides comprehensive information on the Australian stock market, including share prices. Under the Australian Corporations Act, ASX is required to operate markets that are fair, orderly, and transparent.

2. To supervise the market, including monitoring participants' conduct and enforcing compliance with the rules. To protect the integrity of the market, ASX sets standards for the behaviour of listed companies through its Listing Rules.

In 2006, to overcome concerns about conflict between its regulatory and commercial functions, and to provide greater transparency and accountability, ASX placed its supervisory function in a separate subsidiary called ASX Markets Supervision, with its own board. ASX Market Supervision processes applications for listing on the ASX, monitors compliance with the Listing Rules, and reviews proposals from listed entities for significant restructures, reorganizations, and new issues.

The ASX Corporate Governance Council has developed a set of guidelines: Principles of Good Corporate Governance and Best Practice Recommendations.

(For more information, see www.asx.com.au)

Corporate governance in action 2.4   The Listing Rules of the Australian Stock Exchange

To protect the integrity of the market, ASX sets standards for the behaviour of listed companies through its Listing Rules. These Listing Rules cover the following matters.

- Admission of companies to the ASX Official List
- Market quotation

- Continuous disclosure of relevant information
- Periodic disclosure of specific information
- Additional reporting for mining and exploration firms
- Securities trading
- Changes in capital and new issues of shares
- Transfers and registration of share transactions
- Restricted securities
- Transactions with persons in a position of influence
- Significant transactions
- Ongoing requirements
- Additional requirements for trusts
- Meetings required
- Documents required
- Fees
- The halting of trading, suspension, and removal of companies
- Application of the listing rules

The ASX Listing Rules, Appendices, and Guidance Notes are available in electronic format.

(For more information, see www.asx.com.au)

Corporate governance in action 2.5   The role of the Hong Kong Securities and Futures Commission

The Securities and Futures Commission (SFC) is an independent non-governmental statutory body outside the civil service, responsible for regulating the securities and futures markets in Hong Kong, for administering the laws governing the securities and futures markets in Hong Kong, and for facilitating and encouraging the development of these markets.

The statutory duties of the SFC are:

- to maintain and promote the fairness, efficiency, competitiveness, transparency, and orderliness of the securities and futures industry;
- to promote understanding by the public of the operation and functioning of the securities and futures industry;
- to provide protection for members of the public investing in or holding financial products;
- to minimize crime and misconduct in the securities and futures industry;
- to reduce systemic risks in the securities and futures industry;
- to assist the Financial Secretary in maintaining the financial stability of Hong Kong by taking appropriate steps in relation to the securities and futures industry.

As the statutory regulator of the securities and futures markets in Hong Kong, the Commission places great importance on corporate governance: 'We always strive to enhance our accountability to the public and the transparency of our work. We adopt and implement corporate governance practices commensurate with the best standards applicable to public bodies.' All important policies and decisions are discussed and approved by the board, which meets regularly every month and holds additional meetings as necessary. Divisional staff attend board meetings to explain policy proposals, reporting on important operational matters and regulatory issues. Members are also briefed on the financial positions of the Commission and provided with monthly financial statements.

(For more information, see www.sfc.hk)

The significance of constitutions for corporate entities

Every corporate entity needs a constitution

A corporate entity is formed whenever a group of members organize a company, institution, society, association, or other entity to serve their purpose. Being artificial, corporate entities have to be created. For that, they need some form of constitution, which may be formal under the law, for example under company law or the law registering co-operatives, or it can be informal, consisting of little more than a name, a purpose, and a set of rules. As the name indicates, corporate governance is about the way in which these corporate entities are governed.

In each case, the entity has an existence separate from its members, runs activities, and needs to keep separate financial accounts. Its constitution should define the rights and duties of its members, and lay down the rules about the way in which it is to be governed. Typically, the constitution will define the nature of the governing body, its role, and how its members are elected or chosen.

Figure 2.2 provides some comparisons of corporate entities, showing the separation between corporate entities and their members, with examples of different constitutions and governing bodies.

The governing body usually wields governance power over the corporate entity. However, in the case of companies, particularly public companies, other drivers of governance power can include shareholder activists, institutional investors, corporate raiders, and holders of blocks of shares, as well as threats of hostile takeover bids.

Corporate entity	Members	Constitution	Governing body
Limited liability company	Shareholders	Memorandum and articles of association	Board of directors
Professional organization	Qualified members of the profession	Charter and membership rules	Council
Local football club	Club members	Rules	Committee
Trades Union	Registered members	Constitution and Branch rule books	General Executive Council
Oxford College	Fellows of the College	Founding statute or Royal charter	The Governing Body

Figure 2.2 Examples of the governance arrangements in different corporate entities

Whether the constitution is formal, as required under law, or an informal set of rules, it is a fundamental underpinning of the corporate entity and, hence, its governance. Yet, amazingly, many people appointed as directors of limited companies or elected to councils or committees of other bodies have never read that entity's constitution. An important part of the induction of every company director should be to study and understand the company's articles of association, particularly the rules about its governance.

Incorporating a joint-stock limited-liability company

The incorporation of a limited-liability company involves the registration of formal documents, in line with the company laws of the jurisdiction in which the company is to be incorporated. Typically, the founding members (shareholders) of the company have to prepare and submit the articles of association for the proposed company to the companies' registrar. In some jurisdictions a memorandum is also required stating the company's name, share capital, registered office and, sometimes, its purpose. Alternatively, the promoters of the company may buy a company 'off the shelf', from a business that specializes in setting up companies, and simply change the name of the company to the one they want.

The companies' registrar will check the proposed company name to ensure that there is no duplication and that the name is not undesirable (for example, in the United Kingdom, names that suggest a connection with the royal family or involvement with unacceptable activities are not allowed). On incorporation, the company's name is entered on the companies' register and the articles of association become public documents, available for scrutiny by anyone.

Other statutory documents, such as an annual return with the details of the shareholders, officers, and directors, changes to company details and changes to the capital structure have to be filed together with, in some jurisdictions, financial accounts.

In the United States, companies are incorporated under the laws of a specific state. As we saw in Chapter 1, unlike most other countries, there is no provision for the formation of a company at the federal level in the United States, although the Securities and Exchange Commission provides federal-level oversight of public companies listed on US stock markets. Many public companies, with shares listed on a US stock market, are incorporated in the state of Delaware, where corporate laws offer more flexibility in conducting business than in many other states. Delaware also has a highly respected business court, the Delaware Court of Chancery, which is considered by some to be sympathetic to boards of directors.

In Europe, however, it is now possible to incorporate companies not only in the country of origin, but also at the European level. The European company, known by the Latin term *Societas Europaea* (SE), enables companies incorporated in different member states of the European Union to merge or to form a holding company at the European level. In other words, it provides firms with the option of incorporating in other member states. Formation of an SE holding company is available to both public and private companies with registered offices or branches in different member states. One-tier or two-tier boards are permitted. Provisions also call for the participation of employees in company matters.

Companies incorporated for profit-making purposes with shareholders who have limited liability can be classified, broadly, into two groups—public and private.

1. The public limited company may offer its shares to the general public. Shareholder members are not liable for the company's debts. In the United Kingdom, public limited companies must add the designation plc' to their names; elsewhere, they are required to add the word 'limited' or 'incorporated' to their name, so that those contracting with them understand that the shareholders' liability is limited. Not all public companies are listed on a stock exchange, but all listed companies must be public companies. To obtain a listing on a stock exchange, a company must meet the listing requirements of that exchange. In most jurisdictions, the company must also pass the scrutiny of the securities regulatory authority. Typically, a listing requires the preparation of a prospectus, which is a legal document that reviews the company, and its history, business, and financial situation. The prospectus provides prospective investors with the information that they will need to decide whether they wish to risk their funds.

2. The private limited company cannot offer its shares to the general public. This is by far the most common form of incorporation. Private limited companies are required to add 'Limited' ('Ltd') or 'Incorporated' (Inc.) to their names. In most jurisdictions, the number of members of a private company is limited and the requirements for filing documents with the registrar are not as demanding as those for public companies.

A third category covers corporate entities created for the public benefit or community interest rather than private advantage and profit-making. In the United States, public benefit corporations are incorporated within states for the delivery of public services, for example transportation authorities, port authorities, and community organizations. Such entities have no shareholders, and raise their funds through bonds that pay interest, which is a charge against profits, rather than pay dividends, which would take a share of profits. In the United Kingdom, private companies incorporated by guarantee have guarantor members whose liability is limited to the amount they agree to contribute on a winding-up, often quite a nominal sum. A 2004 UK Act created the community interest company (CIC) for activities that benefit the community rather than private interests. Examples include companies limited by guarantee, charities, and other not-for-profit entities, National Health Service foundation trusts, companies providing services with an element of public subsidy (see Case study 3.2 Network Rail in Chapter 3), as well as organizations linking the public and private sectors, such as regeneration projects. A state regulator ensures that the CIC has been established for community benefit and that all assets and profits are used for these purposes.

We will study subsidiary and associated companies, joint ventures, public interest companies, and complex groups of companies in a later chapter.

The memorandum and articles of association

A company's memorandum is a short document that states the company's name, outlines the purposes for which it has been created, gives the address of its registered office, lists the nominal amount and classes of shares with which it is being formed, and states that the liability of its members is limited to the equity capital subscribed. In most jurisdictions, details of the initial subscribing members are included. A registered office is needed because the company is not a person and anyone dealing with the company needs to know where to find it. The objects clause in a memorandum defines its purposes. In the early days, this was, in effect, a constraint imposed by the community for allowing the company to trade with limited liability. Action taken by a company outside its objects would be invalid. Subsequently, this clause has often been drawn very widely, so that the company is free to carry on a wide range of activities. Because of the breadth of activities now included, some company laws no longer require an objects clause, and some no longer call for a memorandum.

The articles of association are, in effect, the rules by which the company is governed. Companies Acts in many jurisdictions contain a draft memorandum for guidance. Corporate governance in action 2.2 provides an example of the contents of a simple set of articles. Memorandum and articles are public documents and anyone may request copies. Many companies now make them available on their websites. Most jurisdictions require companies to file registration documents, periodic financial and other reports to help investors, creditors, and other interested parties find relevant information. For links to a complete list of filings and instructions for searching the EDGAR database, go to: www.sec.gov/edgar/searchedgar/webusers.htm

Corporate governance in action 2.6   Example of the contents of articles of association

A typical set of articles might contain detailed rules on the following.

Share capital

Details of the share capital, including any class of shares with special rights, such as voting rights or being preferential in dividends, also the means of varying such rights; if the shares are not fully paid up on issue, the way in which calls may be made; the way in which shares may be transferred from one shareholder to another; the type of meeting and resolution of the members required to alter the company's capital.

General meetings of the company

The requirement to hold an annual meeting of the shareholder members; the rules governing special or extraordinary meetings of members; the notice required for meetings; proceedings at general meetings, including the necessary quorum, the appointment of the chairman, and voting on resolutions by a show of hands of those present or by a poll based on shareholdings.

Directors

The number of directors, any shareholding qualification for directors, the determination of the remuneration of directors; the powers and duties of directors; the disqualification of directors, for example by becoming bankrupt, of unsound mind, missing meetings, or prohibited by the courts or companies registrar from acting as a director; the length of service and the rotation of directors, for example with one third retiring every year (known as a staggered board); the proceedings at directors' meetings, including notice of meetings, quorum, election of chairman, delegation of powers to committees of the board.

Officers of the company

The board's power to appoint a managing director or chief executive officer, a company secretary, and other officers such as a chief finance officer.

Dividend policy and reserves

The powers of the members in general meeting to agree policies on reserves and the payment of dividends. (Typically, on such matters, the general meeting will follow the proposals put before it by the board.)

Requirements for accounts and audit

The requirement for the directors to keep proper financial records for the company and to provide regular accounts, including a profit and loss account and balance sheet to the members periodically; the appointment of auditors in line with the Companies Acts.

Provisions for winding up the company

The procedures for winding up the company with the members' agreement or on enforced liquidation.

Other forms of incorporation

We have looked at the incorporation of limited-liability companies (private companies limited by shares, private companies limited by guarantee, and public company limited by shares) under the Companies Acts of the jurisdiction in which the companies are registered. But there are other ways in which corporate entities can be formally created, as we saw in Figure 2.2.

Some sectors—for example, savings and loan associations in the United States, building societies in the UK and Commonwealth countries, co-operatives for farmers and other suppliers in Canada, and consumer co-operatives in the United Kingdom—are incorporated under legislation designed to facilitate and regulate that specific sector.

Incorporation of specific corporate entities by the state is also common in many countries. The legislature provides the new organization with its own facilitating legislation, which defines and creates the entity and determines its governance processes, including its mission and accountability, the form of its governing body, and how the directors are appointed, which is often by the government or state agencies. For example, the Federal National Mortgage Association (Fannie Mae) was created by the US government to provide government backing for financial products and services that make it possible for low- and middle-income families to buy homes of their own. Such entities are sometimes referred to as quangos, which is an acronym for quasi-autonomous non-governmental organization, because, although they have a life and mission separate from the state, the state maintains an arm's-length interest in them. Indeed, during the global financial crisis, Fannie Mae and its sister institution, Freddie Mac, had to be bailed out by the US government.

To add a degree of confusion, 'quango' is also used, particularly in the United Kingdom and Australia, as an acronym for quasi-autonomous *national* governmental organization to describe organizations to which governments have devolved power, but in which they retain a direct influence. Examples include the Risk Management Agency of the US Department of Agriculture, the Adult Learning Inspectorate of the UK Department of Education and Skills, and the Australian Communications and Media Authority.

Charities are often set up as not-for-profit, incorporated bodies and registered under the charities law in the relevant jurisdiction. Most of the principles and practices discussed in this book apply to the governance of such entities, although those serving on their governing bodies may also be trustees and subject to additional requirements of trust law. In some countries, the charity and other not-for-profit sector bodies have developed their own corporate governance principles, codes, and best practice guidelines, as we will see later.

Partnerships provide another form of corporate entity. Typically, in a partnership, all partners are liable for the partnership debts in line with the agreement between the partners. But in some jurisdictions it is now possible to incorporate limited-liability partnerships, which have proved attractive to some audit firms to provide a cap to an individual partner's liability.

Professional bodies provide some interesting cases of alternative approaches to incorporation and governance. In some countries, professional bodies are incorporated under their own statute by the state authorities. In the United Kingdom and some other Commonwealth countries, many professional bodies have been created by a royal charter. Such chartered professional bodies have sovereignty over their own affairs, including the examination and admission to membership, the maintaining of standards, and the disciplining of members.

The engineering profession in both the United States and the United Kingdom has developed with constitutionally separate professional bodies to represent the interests of the various branches—electrical, civil, and mechanical and so on. Subsequently, in Britain, the Engineering Council was created by royal charter to oversee an effective federation of the separate bodies. Unlike the engineers, the UK accountancy profession has not managed to agree a federation and has a number of separate professional bodies. In the United States, criticisms following the collapse of Enron and Andersen, its auditor, led to the creation of the Public Company Accounting Oversight Board (PCAOB). In Canada, by contrast, there are provincial institutes of chartered accountants with a Co-ordinating Council of Institutes of Chartered Accountants of Canada. The governance of professional bodies, many of which have relatively large governing bodies (often called councils), can be intriguing.

Finally, we should note that a vast number of small corporate entities are created simply by agreement between interested parties. Sports clubs, drama groups, arts societies, and religious organizations all provide examples. Nevertheless, all such entities need governing as well as managing, and, consequently, need some form of constitution, which should be written if unnecessary disputes are to be avoided.

In this chapter, we have distinguished many different forms of incorporation. The principles and practices of corporate governance apply to them all, although obviously they need adapting to the circumstances. This book focuses on the governance of companies, recognizing that all other corporate entities need corporate governance, and that the methods of governing companies can be adapted to the not-for-profit and other non-company sectors.

The difference between governance and management

As we saw in the first chapter, professional management was the major focus in business throughout the 20th century. Today, the way companies are governed has become more important than the way they are managed. Yet some people fail to make the distinction

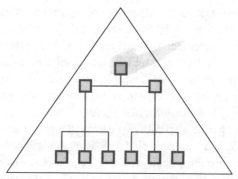

Figure 2.3 The classical depiction of management

between governance and management. The notion of management as a hierarchy is commonplace—as in the classical pyramid of Figure 2.3.

A chief executive officer, or managing director, has overall managerial responsibility, with other managers reporting to him or her and so on down the management hierarchy. Authority and responsibility are delegated downwards, with matching accountability expected upwards in return. The classical theory enables functional departments to be shown, and distinctions drawn, between line management responsible for executive action and staff management responsible to advise the line. We understand that this is an inadequate picture of the realities of management, but we generally accept that management operates through hierarchies. We know who reports to whom in the organization.

But where is the board in classical management theory? Boards seldom appear on organization charts. The board is not part of the management structure; nor is it a hierarchy. Each director has equal responsibility and similar duties and powers under the law. There is no executive 'boss' of a board.

In Figure 2.4, the board has been superimposed on the management structure.

In a unitary board—that is, a board with both executive and non-executive outside directors—the executive directors hold a managerial role in addition to their responsibilities

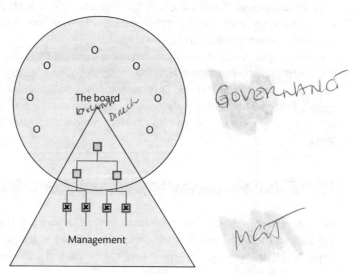

Figure 2.4 The board and management

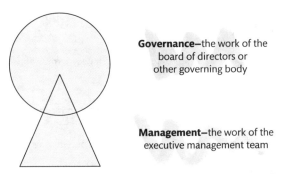

Governance–the work of the
board of directors or
other governing body

Management–the work of the
executive management team

Figure 2.5 Governance distinguished from management

as members of the board of directors. Shown in the figure, they sit in both the board circle and the management triangle. As executives, they are employees of the company and covered by employment law. Directors, as such, are not employees and are subject to company law. The other directors, shown in Figure 2.4, are the non-executive or outside directors–members of the board circle, but not part of the management hierarchy. Other managers, who are not on the board, are also shown with a cross.

A further important distinction can be drawn between non-executive directors who are independent of the entity, and non-executive directors who, although they are not executives of the company, have some link with it. Independent non-executive directors have no relationship with the company that could affect the exercise of independent and objective judgement. Those who are not independent have some link with the company, such as close family ties to the chairman, being a representative of a dominant shareholder, having previously served as an executive of that company, having links with major trading partners of the company, and so on.

Such connections raise questions about these directors' independence. There may be good reasons for having them on the board, but we shall refer to them as 'connected' non-executive directors. These issues will be explored in more depth later. In the United States, the common practice is to refer to non-executive directors as 'outside directors'. For consistency, we will use the abbreviations INED (independent non-executive director) and CNED (connected non-executive director). Some authorities refer to a CNED as an affiliated non-executive director.

We now have a model that enables us to distinguish governance from management: see Figure 2.5.

Management runs the business; the board ensures that it is being well run and run in the right direction.

The performance and conformance aspects of governance

Board responsibilities

We can now explore what the board does. Overall, the board's task is to direct the company, which is why directors are so-called. This activity can be seen to involve four basic elements–strategy formulation; policymaking; supervision of executive management; and accountability to shareholders and others.

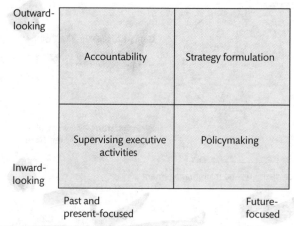

Figure 2.6 The basic board perspectives and processes

In fulfilling their duties, directors have to consider the future of the company as well as its present position and recent results. They also need to look inwards at the organization and its component parts, and externally at the company in its competitive market position and in its broader economic, political, and social context. These basic perspectives and processes are shown in Figure 2.6.

In formulating strategy, the board works with top management, looking ahead in time and seeing the firm in its strategic external environment. Strategies then need to be translated into policies to guide top management action and to provide plans for subsequent control. The board then needs to monitor and supervise the activities of executive management, looking inwards at the current managerial situation and at recent performance. Accountability involves responding externally, reflecting corporate activities and performance to the shareholders and other stakeholders with legitimate claims to accountability. Of course, a simple 2x2 matrix inevitably presents a simplified view of board processes—but at least by looking forwards and backwards in time and internally and externally in space, it is all-embracing!

The Cadbury Report (1992) supports this framework, commenting that 'the responsibilities of the board include setting the company's strategic aims, providing the leadership to put them in effect, supervising the management of the business and reporting to shareholders on their stewardship'.

Boards vary in the extent to which the board as a whole engages in these functions or delegates work to the CEO and the management team, while ensuring that the necessary monitoring and control processes are in place. An extension of the basic quadrant of board processes recognizes this by introducing a central cell showing that boards work with management, through their chief executives or managing directors.[1] Figure 2.7 depicts this process. Boards can choose the extent of their delegation of functions to the management. In some cases, for example, boards play a major part in the formulation of the company's strategy; in others, this is delegated to top management, with the board receiving, questioning and finally approving management's strategic proposals.

---

[1] Hilmer, Frederick G. (1993) *Strictly Boardroom: Improving Governance to Enhance Company Performance.* Information Australia, Melbourne, Australia.

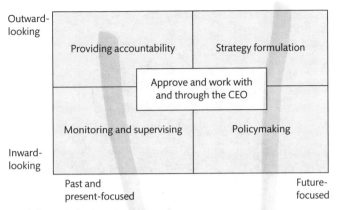

Figure 2.7 Framework for analysing board activities

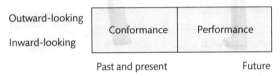

Figure 2.8 The performance and conformance aspects of a board's work

Figure 2.7 can also highlight a potential dilemma for the unitary board. The roles in the right-hand column—strategy formulation and policymaking—are performance roles, concerned with the board's contribution to corporate direction. Those on the left—executive supervision and accountability—are essentially concerned with ensuring conformance. Figure 2.8 shows this important distinction.

As Lord Caldecote, a very experienced board chairman, once commented, 'a problem with the unitary board is that directors are marking their own examination papers'. In a two-tier board the roles are separated with the executive board responsible for performance and the supervisory board responsible for conformance.

Alternative board structures

Unitary boards

When a company has a single governing body, the board is known as a 'unitary board', in contrast to the two-tier board. The formal structure of such boards has been widely written about in corporate governance. What is the appropriate balance between executive and non-executive members? What is the appropriate size for the board? Intuitively, there are four possible structures: a board with only executive directors; a board with a majority of executive directors; a board with a majority of non-executive directors; and a board with only non-executive directors.

In the *all-executive director board,* the top managers are also the directors. There are no outside, non-executive directors (see Figure 2.9). This structure can be found in many small

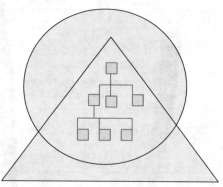

Figure 2.9 The all-executive director board

family firms and start-up businesses. Typically, the company has not reached the stage at which it needs non-executive directors. Directors on such boards seldom draw a distinction between their duties as directors and their roles as managers. In their minds, the company is a legal convenience, perhaps with taxation advantages and limiting personal liability, rather than a distinct legal entity. Bankers providing finance to such companies often require personal guarantees from individual directors to cover loans made to the company. As we will see later, the all-executive director board is also found frequently in the board structures of subsidiary companies operating in corporate groups.

In the *majority-executive director board*, some non-executive directors have been invited to join the board, although they remain in the minority (see Figure 2.10). The addition of non-executive directors to a board can arise for various reasons. The executive directors of a successful, growing company may feel the need for additional expertise to back up their own experience, perhaps as they enter new markets, get involved in new technologies, or face more complex managerial or financial issues. The price of accepting significant growth capital from an outside source may also result in the requirement to allow a non-executive director to represent the interests of the lender. A family firm moving into the second generation may find that, while some family members continue to be directly involved in the management of

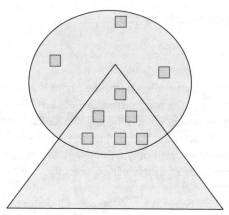

Figure 2.10 The majority executive director board

the firm, others are now outside the firm and shareholders only. Calls for non-executive directors to represent the non-management family shareholders on the board may now arise. The challenges of governance in family firms will be discussed later.

However, in the majority-executive board, the executive directors are in the majority and typically continue to exercise considerable power over the company. Some authorities refer to such boards as 'executive boards'. This model reflected the typical structure of the British public listed company until the 1970s. Research has shown that, at that time, the boards of even major companies had a majority of executive directors. The conventional wisdom was that non-executive directors could be quite useful on a board, adding additional experience, perspective, and insight to discussions, that about a third non-executive directors was about right, but that the non-executives should never be in the majority. In those days, executive directors wielded the power over what they perceived as 'their' company.

However, in the United States, the United Kingdom, and similar advanced economies, the boards of most significant listed companies now have a *majority of non-executive directors* and many of these non-executive directors are likely to be independent directors. Indeed, as we shall see, many corporate governance codes now demand this structure for listed companies.

Clearly, when non-executive directors are in the majority, the culture of the board, its internal relationships, and, indeed, its activities are likely to be different from those of boards dominated by executive directors. Some authorities refer to such boards as 'professional boards' (see Figure 2.11).

The typical board of a company listed in the United States will have only one or two executive directors—the chairman (CEO), the chief finance officer (CFO), and perhaps the chief operating officer (COO)—with three or four times that number of outside directors. Nevertheless, the chairman/CEO continues to wield considerable power, because in the United States these roles are often combined in a single person. Consequently, the outside directors are expected to provide oversight and supervision of executive activities, the achievement of corporate objectives, and assurance of compliance with corporate governance requirements. Since independence criteria require outside directors to have no relationship with the company, other than the directorship (which can mean that such directors have relatively little knowledge of the company's industry or markets), the formulation of strategy has to be led by the CEO supported by the top management team, with the board questioning to ensure that strategic developments are in an appropriate direction and that business risks have been appropriately assessed. Critics of this type of board structure suggest that, in practice, it gives too much power to the executive directors by making them responsible for strategy as well as the day-to-day running of the enterprise. The outside directors, they suggest, are inevitably pushed into a conformance and compliance mode, rather than contributing positively to the performance aspects of strategy formulation and policymaking. 'Such board structures are pushing us towards the European two-tier board system' one experienced director of a British public company argued.

Finally, there is an obvious fourth category of board structure: the *board composed entirely of non-executive directors* (see Figure 2.12). Such board structures are seldom found in listed public companies, but frequently in the boards of not-for-profit entities, such as charitable organizations, arts, health, and sports organizations, and quangos. Frequently, the constitutions of such organizations call for a proportion of the board members to be drawn from

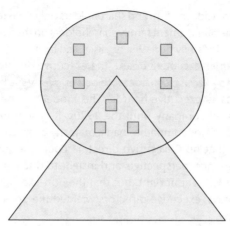

Figure 2.11 The majority non-executive director board

interest groups involved; in a hospital, for example, this means medical staff, administrators, funding bodies, patients, and the local community. Some authorities refer to such boards as 'stakeholder boards'.

The boards of some subsidiary companies in corporate groups may also have such a structure, in which the board consists of senior executives from elsewhere in the corporate organization. When boards have this structure, the chief executive and, perhaps, members of the management team typically attend board meetings, but are there to provide information and to answer directors' questions, not to be formally involved in the taking of decisions. Indeed, in most cases, the constitution will provide for the board to invite managers to attend meetings, either for the entire agenda or for specific items, but reserving the right to ask them to leave and for the board to take decisions in camera.

Two-tier boards

It is apparent that, conceptually, the all non-executive board has the same structure as the European two-tier or supervisory board architecture.

Figure 2.12 can be redrafted to show this, as in Figure 2.13.

In the German approach to corporate governance, large and public companies are required to have a two-tier board structure: the upper, supervisory board, called the *Aufsichtsrat*, and the lower, management board or committee, called the *Vorstand*. The supervisory board is comprised entirely of outside directors and the management board entirely of executive directors.

Germany has long believed that the management of large companies should involve a close relationship between the workers and the company, an informal partnership between labour and capital. This process, referred to as 'co-determination', is enshrined in law. As a result, half of the members of supervisory boards represent the interests of the employees and are appointed through the trades' union organizations. The remaining supervisory board members represent the interest of the shareholders and are appointed by them. In Germany financial institutions are major shareholders and their representatives are often members of supervisory boards.

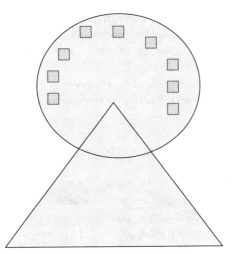

Figure 2.12 The all non-executive director board

In practice, members of the management board attend meetings of the supervisory board, but have no vote. The executive members present their strategies, management plans, and budgets to the supervisory board for comment and approval. If necessary, the supervisory board refers matters back to the executives for further consideration. The supervisory board can then review and assess subsequent managerial performance. The power of the supervisory board lies in its ability to appoint to and remove members from the executive board.

The German Corporate Governance Commission launched a code of best practice (Kodex) in 2002, which provided supervisory boards with more powers over management and external audit, required details of directors' remuneration (including the criteria for performance-based rewards), and gave investors more timely information. While technically voluntary, some of the provisions have been enshrined in company law. Since 2003, German companies have had to issue an annual statement published online, showing whether they have complied with the code and explaining any discrepancies.

The corporate governance architecture of Dutch companies also adopts the two-tier board. But the structure of the Dutch supervisory board is tripartite—one third representing capital, one third employees, and the other third society at large. A companies' court resolves questions about the suitability of members to represent the three interest groups.

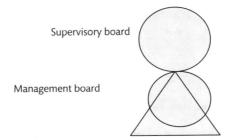

Figure 2.13 The two-tier or supervisory board

As we saw earlier, at one time the Commission of the European Union (or European Economic Community as it then was) believed that the two-tier board should be adopted in all member states, but subsequently adopted a more adaptable approach reflecting practices in the member states. The legal framework in those countries that adopt the two-tier board model is typically based on continental European Napoleonic civil law, which is based on abidance with the rule of law. By contrast, in the United States, the United Kingdom, and many Commonwealth countries with law derived originally from British law, the legal framework is rooted in common law that evolves as decided cases set precedents. Corporate governance in action 2.7 shows the practical effects of a two-tier board.

Taiwan also uses two-tier boards. In mainland China, the authorities, in creating the corporate governance structures and processes for their newly privatized and listed companies, require a two-tier board with a supervisory board and a main board, but, quite unlike the continental European model, also called for independent outside directors on the main board.

Table 2.1 compares corporate governance board structures in various countries.

Table 2.1 Comparison of corporate governance board structures

Country	Chairman/CEO separation	Average board size	% outside directors
Unitary board model			
Australia	Very high	8	High
Belgium	High	15	High
Brazil	Low	6	Moderate
Canada	High	13	Very high
France	Nil	13	High
Hong Kong[2]	Very low	8	Low
Italy	Total	11	High
Spain	Low	12	High
Sweden	High	9	Very high
Switzerland	High	5	Very high
UK	Very high	12	High
US[3]	Very low	13	Very high
Two-tier board model			
France	Total	12	Very high
Germany	Total	15	Total
Netherlands	Total	7	Total
Business network model			
Japan	Total	large	Very low

[2] Although this is changing as the Hong Kong Stock Exchange lists companies incorporated and operating in mainland China.

[3] In the United States, the separation of the roles of board chairman and CEO is under review, and some listed companies now separate the roles.

Corporate governance in action 2.7   Volkswagen's supervisory board

German company Volkswagen, Europe's largest car-maker, had a supervisory board. Institutional investors demanded that the chairman of the supervisory board, Herr Piëch, resign because of alleged conflicts of interest. They claimed that Herr Piëch and his family held significant shares in Porsche, which held a near 20% stake in Volkswagen.

German's voluntary corporate governance code states that conflicts of interest should result in the termination of a supervisory board member's mandate. Herr Piëch claimed that the conflict would be managed by him leaving the room whenever any Porsche-related matter was discussed. Some American institutional investors called this 'naive'. Herr Piëch was strongly supported by the ten employee representatives on the 20-strong board.

Advisory boards

Advisory boards, sometimes called advisory committees, may be created by companies operating in various parts of the world, to give advice to the corporate directors about matters in overseas places. Typically, business leaders, influential politicians, and other prominent figures from the region are invited to serve, but are not given executive powers. Advisory boards were more prevalent in the 1970s and 1980s. Subsequently, companies found that the advice they needed could be obtained more cheaply from consultants, who may be retained only as long as their advice is wanted. Some also found that advisory boards, although they had no formal executive authority, assumed an independence that created complications by making policy recommendations, which were inconsistent with group-wide needs. An advisory board might, for example, call for more investment in a given country, when the board's global strategy called for disinvestment there.

Business start-up entrepreneurs and small companies may also create advisory boards to get advice and counsel from an impartial and experienced group. Again, such advisory boards have no executive power.

Board diversity

As we noted in Chapter 1, the predominant interest in the diversity of board membership has been in gender diversity. But some commentators also call for a broader representation of different interests on boards. Such concerns cover a wide range of ideas and a careful definition of board diversity is then needed. The various notions can be divided into concerns for:

Diversity for business effectiveness

This perspective calls for boards with a balance of experience, knowledge and skills relevant to the company's business and industry, plus an appropriate mix of functional abilities in, for example, accountancy and finance, human relations, marketing and so on. This idea has a lot of intuitive validity. Of course, the more diverse the experiences and knowledge of board members, the more the board chairman may have to handle conflicts of opinion: but that is what good chairmanship involves.

Stakeholder diversity

This rationale calls for boards to have representatives of those with contractual links to the company, such as customers, contractors and distributors, suppliers, shareholders and other sources of finance, and so on. Such a notion, of course, also includes employees of the company. This suggestion was discussed *ad nauseam* in the United Kingdom in 1977 when the EEC (as it then was) in its draft 5th directive, called for two-tier boards with worker appointed members on the supervisory board,. This was followed by Lord Bullock's report on industrial democracy in Britain, which argued that unitary boards were perfectly adequate but proposed that they should include worker representatives. In the event neither proposal got off the starting line. Such board membership could promote conflicts of interest between the different interest groups.

Societal diversity

This idea believes that board members should reflect the impact a company might have on society at large, and should include representatives by age, gender, nationality, political interest, environmental and safety concerns, and so on. The intention would be for boards to balance corporate decisions with the interests of society. Inevitably such a governance system would result in competing and potentially conflicting goals, and would effectively challenge the concept of the joint-stock limited liability company and free market capitalism.

The arguments for each of these alternatives are tenable but the nature and culture of the resultant board would be very different in each case, varying from a closely-knit team devoted to sound corporate governance (both performance and conformance) to a sort of adversarial parliament. Which is desirable is a philosophical issue hinging on what we expect companies to be and to do.

Some classic case studies

 Case study 2.1   Long-term Capital Management (LTCM)

LTCM was a hedge fund founded in1994 by John Meriwether, and included board members Myron Scholes and Robert Merton, who had shared the Nobel Prize in economics. Initially, the fund was highly successful and became an example for the hedge fund industry.

The company developed mathematical models to arbitrage deals in American, Japanese, and European government fixed-interest bonds. Profit was made by buying some bonds and short-selling others as prices narrowed. As the firm prospered, it generated more investment than could be used for these arbitrage opportunities and began to undertake trading decisions beyond its experience, including options and merger arbitrage.

The 1997 East Asian financial crisis produced significant losses. Then, in 1998, the Russian government defaulted on its bonds. Holders of European and Japanese bonds, fearing further defaults, transferred to US Treasury bonds and the previous arbitrage opportunities used by LTCM reversed. The firm lost nearly US$2 billion of its capital.

Fearing a chain reaction in the financial markets, the Federal Reserve Bank organized a bailout by major creditor institutions of over US$3.5 billion. The banks participating in the bailout received 90% of the hedge fund and an independent supervisory board was created. The LTCM fund was wound up in 2000. Some of the positions formerly held by LTCM were eventually liquidated at a small profit to the bailout institutions. The fear remained, however, that the intervention by the Federal Reserve might encourage other institutions in the future to assume risks in the belief that they would be bailed out.

Discussion questions

1. Should the Federal Reserve Bank have arranged the bailout of LTCM?

2. Compare and contrast the 2008 case of Northern Rock Bank in the United Kingdom (in case study 8.1 in Chapter 8).

 Case study 2.2   Lord Black and Hollinger International

Conrad Black, a Canadian who took British citizenship to enter the British House of Lords, was an international media mogul, famed for his business strategies, his arrogance, and for bringing legal actions against any one who challenged him. But he eventually appeared in a Chicago court accused of money laundering, racketeering and obstructing justice.

Black controlled an empire of publications through a chain of companies:

- *Chicago Sun-Times* and local newspapers
- UK national newspapers
- Canadian regional publications

Notice two classic corporate governance devices used to leverage Black's control: an ownership chain with outside investors in two listed companies; and dual-class shares with voting rights greater than their equity value. In other words, Black was able to control Hollinger International, which owned Canadian, British and US publications, even though he held less than 16% of the chain's equity.

Black was also known for his ostentatious life style, with corporate jets, a fleet of vintage cars, apartments, and domestic staff paid for by the company. His wife memorably commented to *Vogue* magazine that 'I have an extravagance that knows no bounds', which prompted some institutional investors and the chairman of the audit committee to look more closely at the Black empire.

Like Robert Maxwell, his predecessor in the international media business and other corporate governance case-studies, Black filled his board-room with prestigious names, including Henry Kissinger, the former US Secretary of State, and Richard Pele, a former Pentagon adviser, as well as friends—mainly chairmen of other companies.

Black and some colleagues were charged with diverting over $80 million from Hollinger International from the sale of newspapers in the United States and Canada. It was also alleged that Black's company Ravelston had charged Hollinger International multi-million dollar fees for management and for agreeing not to compete with regional newspapers that had been sold.

Allegedly the directors had approved these payments without question or independent advice. Nor had they queried the personal use of company assets. They allowed Black to treat the company as his private empire. As Black said: 'this is my company and I decide what the board knows, and when they know it.'

Judge Amy St Eve told Black that she believed he had not accepted his guilt, had abused the trust of shareholders, and had engaged in sophisticated schemes that required more than minimal planning. He was sentenced to 6 1/2 years in prison and fined $125,000. Protesting his innocence to the end, Black claimed that he was the victim of 'corporate governance zealots.'

In June 2011, after a year on bail mounting a partially-successful appeal, Black was told that he must serve a further year in jail. 'It's not that I don't have remorse,' he said, 'but I regret my scepticism about corporate governance zealotry which made my shareholders suffer.'

Discussion questions

1. Black was able to control Hollinger International through an ownership chain with outside investors in two listed companies; and dual-class shares with voting rights greater than their equity value, although he held less than 16% of the chain's equity. What is your opinion of that situation? Remember that no one forced the outside shareholders to buy into his companies and the ownership structure was in the public domain.

2. Black filled his boardroom with prestigious names. What are the pros and cons of such a situation?

3. How can a successful entrepreneurial character, like Lord Black, be controlled in order to protect outside investors, whilst still allowing reasonable profit-generating risk?

 Case study 2.3   The Sunbeam Corporation

In 1996, Sunbeam, a US appliance manufacturer, was in serious financial trouble. Al Dunlap, known as 'Chainsaw Al' for his approach to cutting staff, was appointed to save the company. Over the next two years, the business reported dramatically improved results. Investors chased after the shares as the price rocketed. There was talk of a bid, which would make the investors, and particularly Dunlap and his colleagues, a lot of money. But no bid came.

By 1998, some outside directors were uneasy and launched an inquiry. They did not like what they found and Mr Dunlap was fired. The SEC subsequently charged him, other senior executives, and the audit partner at Arthur Andersen, who had approved the accounts, with fraud. The SEC alleged that, on his arrival, Mr Dunlap identified massive previous losses, which he wrote off, giving him a 'cookie jar' to dip into to inflate subsequent results.

Then he shipped out more goods through his distribution channels than they could possibly sell, taking credit for the revenues, but pushing forward the problem to the next financial year. Returned goods were overlooked. Other efforts were made to boost sales artificially: record numbers of outdoor barbecues were reported sold during the winter months.

In 2001, Andersen agreed to pay US$110 million to the Sunbeam shareholders in settlement of a lawsuit alleging that the auditors had failed to identify the problem.

Discussion questions

1. Directors have a fiduciary duty to protect the interests of shareholders. In this case, they apparently failed. Why?

2. When good results were posted and there was talk of a bid, the share price rocketed. But some of the independent outside directors were uneasy and launched an inquiry, which discovered a disastrous situation. How could this have been avoided?

3. Can directors rely on the report of the independent outside auditors?

References and further reading

Clarke, T. (2004) *Theories of Corporate Governance.* Routledge, London and New York.

Colley, John L. et al. (2003) *Corporate Governance?* McGraw Hill Executive MBA series, New York.

Colley, John L. et al. (2005) *What is Corporate Governance?* McGraw Hill, New York.

Davies, Adrian (1999) *A Strategic Approach to Corporate Governance.* Gower, London.

Demb, Ada and Frederick Neubauer (1992) *The Corporate Board: Confronting the Paradoxes.* Oxford University Press, New York.

Hilmer, Frederick G. (1993) *Strictly Boardroom: Improving Governance to Enhance Company Performance.*

The Sydney Institute and Information Australia, Melbourne, Australia.

Mallin, Chris (2004, 2010) *International Handbook on Corporate Governance.* 3rd edn, Edward Elgar Publishing, London.

Monks, Robert A. G. and Nell Minow (1995, 2011) *Corporate Governance.* 4th edn, Wiley, Chichester, UK.

Nordberg, Donald (2011) *Corporate Governance: Principles and Issues*, Sage Publications, London.

Shleifer, Andrei and Robert W. Vishny (1997) 'A survey of corporate governance', *The Journal of Finance*, Vol. LII, No. 2, June.

Projects and exercises

1. The European Union has passed legislation permitting the incorporation of a 'European company' transcending the borders of its member states. Would it be a good idea if companies were able to be incorporated in the United States at the Federal level?

2. Chart the governance and management structure of a corporate entity with which you are familiar, using the circle and triangle schematic. Academic, sporting, or professional bodies could be covered, as well as public or private companies. Does the diagram help to depict the potential to exercise power in that organization?

3. Consider the scope of corporate governance outlined in Figure 2.1. In your opinion, does this adequately cover the extent of the subject? What would you add or change to give a better perspective?

4. Research the state of gender diversity around the world. What are the pros and cons of moves towards greater equality between men and women on the boards of listed and government corporations?

Self-test questions

To confirm your grasp of the key points in this chapter, try answering the following questions.

1. Why does a corporate entity need a constitution?
2. What is the principal difference between a private and a public company?
3. Explain the difference between governance and management.
4. What are the two aspects of the board's work that can provide a paradox for the unitary board?
5. Describe the scope of corporate governance.
6. Where can one inspect company accounts, annual returns, and other documents filed under the UK Companies Acts?
7. What led to the creation of the US Securities and Exchange Commission? When? What is its mission?
8. What sort of companies might have an all-executive board?
9. What is the typical structure of the board of companies listed in the United States?
10. What is a two-tier board? Outline how it works in Germany.

3 Theories and Philosophies of Corporate Governance

 Learning Outcomes

In which we consider:

- The agency dilemma
- Agency theory
- Transaction cost economics
- Stewardship theory
- Resource dependency theory
- Managerial and class hegemony
- Psychological and organizational perspectives
- The societal perspective: stakeholder philosophies
- Enlightened shareholder theory
- Differing boundaries and levels: systems theory
- A subject in search of its paradigm

This chapter is important for students studying corporate governance theory. Directors seeking information to improve their board-level contributions and those studying for professional examinations in corporate governance may not need this level of theoretical background.

The agency dilemma

A fundamental challenge underlying all corporate governance affairs is not new.

> The directors of companies, being managers of other people's money, cannot be expected to watch over it with the same vigilance with which they watch over their own.
>
> (Adam Smith, *The Wealth of Nations* (abridged), 1776)

This is the agency problem. In its simplest form, whenever the owner of wealth (the principal) contracts with someone else (the agent) to manage his or her affairs, the agency dilemma arises. How to ensure that the agent acts solely in the interest of the principal is the challenge. In the 18th and 19th centuries, many contracts were, indeed, between a single principal and a single agent—involving trading ventures, construction projects, running a factory, and so on.

The arrival of the joint-stock limited-liability company in the mid-19th century increased the number of principals (shareholders) and their agents (directors). The number and increasing diversity of the shareholders in public companies meant, moreover, that the interests of shareholders were no longer homogeneous. As Berle and Means (1932) showed in their influential analysis, as listed companies grew and their shareholders became more diverse, the separation between owners and directors increased and power shifted towards the directors.

Today, agency relationships in public companies can be complex. For example, an individual owner might invest his or her funds through a financial adviser, who invests the funds in a mutual fund or investment trust, which in turn seeks to gear its portfolio by investing in a hedge fund, which invests its resources in a range of equities, property, commodities, and other hedge funds. Tracing the agency chain in such cases can be difficult, and establishing the exposure to agency risk well nigh impossible. However, the agency dilemma potential exists throughout the chain. The demands for transparency, reporting, accountability, audit, independent directors, and the other requirements of company law and securities legislation, plus the requirements of regulators and stock exchange rules, and the demands of the corporate governance codes, are all responses to the agency dilemma. Indeed, the conceptual underpinning of corporate governance codes around the world and the demands of company law for checks and balances is the need to respond to the agency problem.

The practice of stock borrowing, used by sophisticated investors such as hedge funds, means that not only can the fund benefit from a fall in a share's value, but it can also use the share's voting rights. It can thus build up a significant stake, in fact up to the level at which it, and any other fund acting in concert with it, would be required to make a public offer for the company. In other words, it is possible to acquire voting rights in a company without owning or investing in its stock. This is a long way from the original concept of the joint-stock company. It also raises a potential dilemma for directors: are they the stewards of the interests of the long-term traditional shareholders, or short-term activist institutions? Their interests are unlikely to be the same.

Nor is the agency problem limited to relations between investors in listed companies and their agents. The agency dilemma can occur in private companies, joint ventures, not-for-profit organizations, professional institutions, and governmental bodies. Wherever there is a separation between the members and the governing body put in place to protect their interests and to deliver the required outcomes, the agency dilemma will arise and corporate governance issues occur. The members could be the shareholders in a company, the members of a professional institution or a trade union, a group of owners in a co-operative, or the holding company in a corporate group; the governing body might be called the board of directors, the council, the committee, the governing body, or the holding company. But whatever names are used, whenever responsibility for activities and assets is delegated by those in the principal position to those in the agent situation, the agency dilemma will occur.

For example, consider a pyramid group of companies. The board of the holding company decides to operate the group with profit-responsible subsidiary companies in organizational divisions. The board believes that motivation and commitment will be maximized if the directors of each subsidiary are held responsible for generating profits and are measured by their company's annual return on investment (ROI). The opportunities for the subsidiary company directors to take decisions beneficial to the subsidiary, but detrimental to the group, are legion—for example by postponing longer-term decisions on research and development, management development, or maintenance to improve the short-term profit, or by manipulating the asset base in the ROI calculation. If the subsidiaries inter-trade, the opportunities multiply. Take a simple example: subsidiary company A manufactures a component that is incorporated into subsidiary company B's product. Company A needs a transfer price at which to sell to company B. Of course, A wants the highest price to maximize its profits, while B wants the lowest to maximize its returns. If they cannot agree, company B may buy in the open market, leaving A with under-recovered overheads. Conversely, company A may sell to the market, leaving B with an insecure supply. Referring the transfer price decision to the holding company might resolve the dilemma, but at the cost of removing the decision-making authority of the directors of A and B. This situation is typical in decentralized groups and is called 'sub-optimization' by some authorities. In essence, it reflects the agency dilemma.

The agency problem can also arise in not-for-profit entities. Consider the British National Health Service (NHS): the responsible government ministry contracts with the providers of medical services to deliver them through local doctors, hospitals, and other institutions. The authorities set standards and targets to measure achievement. For example, they might call for a hospital to improve its bed occupancy rate, thus encouraging the hospital governors to keep patients in for longer than is really necessary. Conversely, the authority might call for a speedy return of patients to the street, resulting in rising emergency readmissions. In fact, the NHS promulgates a large list of performance measures with quantifiable outputs in an attempt to reduce the agency dilemma. But success is only partial because agents always find ways of benefiting their entity to the detriment of the system as a whole.

Essentially, in agency situations, the parties have asymmetrical access to information. The directors know far more about the corporate situation than the shareholders, who must trust them. Indeed, shareholders have to rely on the directors to decide what information they should have, over and above the minimum required by regulation and company law. This is the underpinning concept of the joint-stock limited-liability company: the shareholders trust the directors to be stewards of their funds. The agency theory of corporate governance takes a less sanguine view of directors' behaviour.

Agency theory

Agency theory, or principal–agent theory as some writers refer to it, looks at corporate governance practices and behaviour through the lens of the agency dilemma. In essence, the theory perceives the governance relationship as a contract between shareholder (the principal) and director (the agent). Directors, it is argued, seek to maximize their own personal benefit, to take actions that are advantageous to themselves, but detrimental to the shareholders (see Figure 3.1).

As the early proponents of agency theory, Jensen and Meckling (1976), explained:

> agency theory involves a contract under which one or more persons (the shareholders) engage other persons (the directors) to perform some service on their behalf which includes delegating some decision-making authority to the agent. If both parties to the relationship are utility maximizers there is good reason to believe the agent will not always act in the best interests of the principal.

Anecdotal evidence of such behaviour is not hard to find. There are myriad cases in which directors treat a listed public company as though it were their own property, exploiting their position, receiving unsanctioned benefits, and taking remuneration unrelated to their

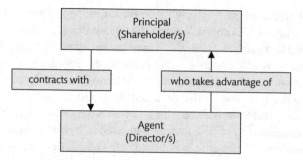

Figure 3.1 The governance relationship

performance to the shareholders' detriment. Bob Monks (2008), a shareholder activist, reckoned that trillions of dollars of shareholders' wealth have been wrongly extracted from US corporations over the years by directors abusing their power.

Directors may also take a different view from their shareholders on corporate risk. After all, it is not their money they are risking. Of course, successful management involves taking controlled risks. But directors might hazard corporate funds on riskier ventures, a hostile take-over bid for example, than many of their shareholders would expect or want. Potential investors can only judge the ability of the board-level decision-makers and their risk profile from the company prospectus, reports, and past performance.

Most scholarly research into corporate governance has used agency theory, which has been developed within the discipline of financial economics (Fama and Jensen, 1983). Looking at corporate governance through the agency lens, researchers have explored links between corporate governance processes and corporate performance. In other words, they have looked for causal links between governance systems and their effects. For example, a study might test whether there is a correlation between board structure (the proportion of independent directors to executive directors) and long-term corporate performance.

Agency theory focuses at the level of shareholders and boards as entities. Board-level processes, political activities and interpersonal relations between directors are outside their scan.[1] Consequently, researchers do not need access to the boardroom or to individual directors. Most agency theoretical research uses data about governance practices and company performance that are readily available in the public domain using, for example, directors' reports and audited company accounts. Agency theory offers a statistically rigorous insight into corporate governance processes. Because of its simplicity and the availability of both reliable data and statistical tests, agency theory has provided a powerful approach to corporate governance theory building.

Criticisms of agency theory

Some critics of agency theory emphasize its relatively narrow theoretical scope. To study the intricacies of corporate governance in terms of contracts between principals and agents, they

---

[1] Some authorities refer to this as being treated as a 'black box', but that can confuse since the black box on an aircraft contains all of the vital data.

argue, is naive. They criticize the focus on purely quantitative metrics, such as board structure or corporate compensation packages, or on the building of a governance index through a 'box-ticking approach' where compliance with governance criteria mechanically feeds into a broad governance index, which is then compared with some measure(s) of corporate performance. Such critics believe that board behaviour does not consist of sets of contractual relationships, but is influenced by interpersonal behaviour, group dynamics, and political intrigue. They question whether the subtle and complex dynamics of board behaviour lend themselves to measurement and numerical analysis. As Ada Demb wrote in 1993, 'statistical methods will not explain the reality of the boardroom'.

Other contemporary scholarship has discovered that not only does increasing governance conformance and compliance not necessarily add to corporate performance, but it can actually detract from it. Muth and Donaldson (1997) challenged the findings of other agency theoretical research. Boards with well-connected, executive directors perform better, they found, than those that followed corporate governance codes on the use of independent directors.

Other critics have challenged the shareholder/director agency model as simplistic in practice. These days, they suggest, pension funds, hedge funds, and other institutional investors can behave like imperial traders, even corporate raiders, rather than the long-term investors perceived by the agency paradigm. Also, the short-term outlook of stock markets in the United Kingdom and United States may produce different agency relationships from the longer-term and bank-related investment seen in countries such as Germany and Japan.

But there is also a deeper issue: inherent in agency theory is a philosophical, moral assumption about the nature of man. The theory assumes that people are self-interested, not altruistic; they cannot be expected to look after the interests of others. In other words, directors cannot be trusted. The legal concept of the corporation, and the basis of stewardship theory, as we shall see, takes the opposite view.

In summary, critics of agency theory argue that it has been erected on a single, questionable abstraction that governance involves a contract between two parties, and is based on a dubious conjectural morality that people maximize their personal utility. Nevertheless, agency theoretical research has remained the mainstay of published papers in corporate governance. An interesting research frontier of the subject bridges the disciplines of economics and law, applying the agency theoretical insights of economics to the legal context of the corporation.

Does good corporate governance produce better corporate performance?

Agency theoretical research has shown some linkages between company performance and various attributes of governance, such as women on boards, board structure and size, or audit committee activities. However, it has to be said that, so far, most conclusions are weak.

Indeed, in some cases in which a positive relationship has been shown between good governance and better performance, other scholars have reworked the data to draw contrary conclusions. More convincing evidence of a relationship between good corporate governance practices and company performance comes from the behaviour of institutional investors who are prepared to pay a premium for companies they judge to have good governance because they feel it reduces their exposure to risk.

However, a significant study was published by the Association of British Insurers (ABI) in 2008 (Selvaggi and Upton, 2008), which suggests that there *is* a robust causal relationship between good corporate governance and superior company performance. ABI represents the interest of insurance companies in the United Kingdom, which tend to invest long-term, reflecting their need to meet long-term obligations. The ABI Institutional Voting Service database shows the extent to which listed UK companies comply with the provisions of the UK Combined Code, and adds expert judgements on other aspects of governance practices. A point is awarded for every governance failure, producing a numeric score, with a zero score being ideal up to a theoretical maximum of 42 if a company were to fail on every criterion. The ABI uses a colour code: blue-top companies have no areas of concern; amber-top companies have some concerns, such as abnormal salary increases; and red-top companies show major concerns, for example where non-executive directors did not meet the independence criteria, or where an executive director serves on the audit committee.

Drawing on the governance scores of 361 companies between 2002 and 2007, and using return on assets and 'Tobins Q'[2] as the performance criteria, the study showed a clear connection between good governance and both good company performance and share price levels.[3] Companies with poor governance showed a strong negative impact on performance. Moreover, companies that were red-topped repeatedly underperformed by 2–5% a year in terms of industry-adjusted return on assets. The study also suggested that it was good corporate governance that led to better performance, not the other way around. Further, well-governed companies delivered higher returns when adjusted for risk, and the volatility of their share price returns was lower. The study also discovered that the impact of governance on performance was long-term. Lags of between two and three years between poor governance and inferior performance were found. This study clearly suggested that sound governance does have a positive effect on profitability and boosts share price. In other words, it shows that governance expenditure can be cost-effective.

However, the issue is not yet determined, as Bhagat, Bolton, and Romano (2007) explain, citing methodological shortcomings in existing papers:

> Financial economists and commercial providers of governance services have in recent years created measures of the quality of firms' corporate governance . . . there is no consistent relation between governance indices and measures of corporate performance. Namely, there is no one 'best' measure of corporate governance: the most effective governance institution appears to depend on context, and on firms' specific circumstances.[4]

Transaction cost economics

Closely related to agency theory, transaction cost economics was derived from original work in 1937 by Coarse. He recognized that a firm could save costs by undertaking activities within

---

[2] That is, the market value of a company divided by the accounting replacement value of its assets. A result between 0 and 1 indicates that the market value of the company fails to reflect the accounting value of its assets.

[3] Regression analysis was used to test relationships between the corporate governance criteria and corporate performance. The multivariate econometric methodology used allowed the determination of relationships between various factors simultaneously.

[4] We will review various indices of corporate governance later.

the organization rather than externally. In other words, the firm would get goods or services at a lower price than in the marketplace. However, as a firm grows, there comes a point at which the external market becomes cheaper. Williamson (1975 and 1988) built on Coarse's work, arguing that large corporate groups could overcome disadvantages of scale by 'the choice of governance structures'.

Transaction cost economics, therefore, focuses on the cost of enforcement or check-and-balance mechanisms, such as internal and external audit controls, information disclosure, independent outside directors, the separation of board chairmanship from CEO, risk analysis, and audit, nomination and remuneration committees. The argument is then advanced that such enforcement costs should be incurred to the point at which the increase in costs equals the reduction of the potential loss from non-compliance.

Stiles and Taylor (2001) observed that 'both transaction cost economics and agency theories are concerned with managerial discretion and both assume that managers are given to opportunism (self-interest seeking) and moral hazard, and that managers operate under bounded rationality'. In other words, directors and top management act in their own best interests, not necessarily in those of the shareholders. But transaction cost analysis focuses on governance structures and mechanisms, whereas agency theory sees the firm as a set of contracts.

The underlying discipline of transaction cost economics, like agency theory, is financial economics. Although the focus is different, the level of abstraction is similar, being at the level of the firm and its governance structures rather than board-level behaviour. Again, research results have been inconclusive, possibly because the complexity within organizations is ignored. For a seminal review of the earlier contributions of financial economics to corporate governance knowledge, see A. Shleifer and R. Vishny (1997) 'A survey of corporate governance', *Journal of Finance*, Vol. 52, No. 2, June, pp. 737–783.

Stewardship theory

Stewardship theory looks at governance through a different lens from agency theory, reflecting the original legal view of the corporation. The joint-stock company with limited liability for its shareholding investors was a simple and eminently successful development of the mid-19th century. The limited-liability company has provided capital, encouraged business growth, secured employment, provided innovation in industry and commerce, and created untold wealth over more than 150 years. This model proved robust and adaptable. Indeed, its great flexibility has led to the huge proliferation, diversity, and complexity of corporate types and structures today.

In essence, each company is incorporated as a separate legal entity. The shareholding members of the company nominate and appoint the directors, who then act as stewards for their interests. The directors report to them on the results of that stewardship, subject to a report from an independent auditor that the accounts show a true and fair view. Ownership is the basis of power over the corporation. Directors have a fiduciary duty to act as stewards of the shareholders' interest. Inherent in the concept of the company is the belief that directors can be trusted.

Stewardship theory reflects the classical ideas of corporate governance. Directors' legal duty is to their shareholders not to themselves, nor to other interest groups. Contrary to

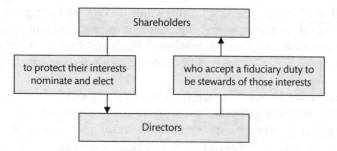

Figure 3.2 The shareholder/director relationship

agency theory, stewardship theory believes that directors do not inevitably act in a way that maximizes their own personal interests: they can and do act responsibly with independence and integrity. Of course, some fail, but this does not invalidate the basic concept.

Stewardship exponents recognize that directors need to identify the interests of customers, employees, suppliers, and other legitimate stakeholders, but under the law their first responsibility is to the shareholders. They argue that conflicts of interest between stakeholder groups and the company should be met by competitive pressures in free markets, backed by legislation and legal controls to protect customers (monopoly and competition law), employees (employment law; health and safety law), consumers (product safety law; consumer protection law), suppliers (contract law; credit payment law), and society (environmental law; health and safety law; taxation law). We will explore so-called stakeholder theory later in this chapter, and the growing interest in corporate social responsibility and a wider range of responsibilities for boards later.

The underpinning disciplines in stewardship theory are legal and organizational studies. By reflecting the legal model, stewardship theory provides precise boundaries for the company, clearly identifying its assets and liabilities, its shareholders and its directors. Stewardship theory emphasizes the responsibility of boards to maximize shareholder value sustainably in the long term.

Criticisms of stewardship theory

Critics of stewardship theory point out that the *de facto* situation in modern corporations is quite different from the 19th-century model. They argue that the concept of a set of shareholders owning a single company and appointing its directors is naive in modern circumstances, except for smaller companies. In listed companies, they point out, shareholders have become remote from the company and do not nominate the directors. Financial reports, they suggest, have become intelligible only to experts. Consolidated group accounts, recording the finances of modern entities, complicate rather than explain complex groups. Complex corporations lack transparency and their directors are not readily accountable to shareholders.

Other critics of stewardship theory point out that because the theory is rooted in law, it is normative. It emphasizes what should be done, or even exhorts. It is not, they argue, predictive and is unable to show causal relationships between specific behaviours and corporate performance. Mallin (2004) made a further important point on the relevance of stewardship thinking. The fundamental concept of the joint-stock, limited-liability company provides the conceptual underpinning of company law in the United States, the United Kingdom, and many other jurisdictions around the world where common law prevails—that is, law based on legal principles enhanced by the precedents of case law and relying on independent judges and juries. As a result, the rights of shareholders, particularly minorities, have been protected and in these countries the shareholder base in many public companies is diversified. In other countries, in continental Europe and Latin America for example, civil law prevails, which has less flexibility, does not learn from precedent, and is often administered by judges who are civil servants. As a result, laws are more codified and there is less protection for minorities; consequently share ownership is less widespread, with many companies still influenced by dominant shareholder and family interests.

After major corporate collapses in the late 20th and early 21st centuries, many commentators felt that the trust directors owed under the stewardship model had been undermined, and that this erosion of trust had adversely affected the well-being of investors, employees, and communities. Questions about the commitment of boards to members' interests surfaced. Nevertheless, stewardship theory remains the legal foundation for companies' legislation all around the world.

The global financial crisis and the resultant dissatisfaction with companies and their boards led to calls for shareholder empowerment. A return to shareholder democracy, it was suggested, could redress the balance of power in favour of owners. Investors, particularly pension funds, hedge funds, and other institutional investors, should be more active. Such shareholder activism could include, for example, individual negotiations with management, or working collectively to develop strategies to influence companies with specific proposals and, if necessary, litigation, while voting all of the shares they held.

Sceptics of shareholder empowerment have argued that boards, elected by investors, should still have primacy. Only the directors are in a position to take into account relevant factors in business decisions. Giving more power to investors, the sceptics suggested, would increase investor costs and reduce returns. Involvement by investors in the governance of companies changes relationships and no longer being at arm's length might limit freedom to deal in the shares. Moreover, involvement could lead investors to advance special interests, promote narrow self-interests, and realize short-term gains. Further, they pointed out that the interests of pension fund members and investors in other funds are not homogeneous; they may have diverse needs, and could disagree with decisions of the fund.

A recent theoretical development recognizes the naivety, in the modern investment world, of the 19th-century model of shareholder capitalism in which joint-stock, limited-liability companies are owned by a handful of individual shareholders. Referred to as a theory of universal ownership, this view of fiduciary capitalism recognizes that modern listed companies, particularly in liquid markets such as the United States and the United Kingdom, are typically held by a highly diversified set of equity holders, including holdings concentrated in the hands of a few large institutional investors.

In the United States, the hundred largest financial institutions hold over 50% of all publicly held equity. In the United Kingdom, there is a similar concentration of ownership. Since these large institutions have massive funds to invest, they need to buy shares across the board, effectively indexing the market as a whole. They are also likely to be investing in a wide range of equities, across geographical and emerging markets, and through a range of investment instruments, including hedge funds. Consequently, such institutional investors, the theory argues, now play an essential role in corporate governance and should assume a responsibility for overseeing governance issues, and abide by principles of responsible investment, including collective action if necessary. Critics of this approach point out that institutional investors such as pension funds are run by trustees whose accountability is not always apparent and is seldom challenged, whose interests do not align with those of fund beneficiaries, and who may use investment funds to protect themselves from claims for negligence.

Resource dependency theory

Resource dependency theory takes a strategic view of corporate governance. It sees the governing body of a corporate entity as the linchpin between the company and the resources it needs to achieve its objectives. These resources could include, for example, links to relevant markets including potential customers and competitors, access to capital and other sources of finance, provision of know-how and technology, and relationships with business, political and other societal networks and elites. The directors are viewed as boundary-spanning nodes of networks able to connect the business to its strategic environment. Studies from this perspective focus on the interdependence of companies in a market and can serve to reduce uncertainty in corporate decisions. The theory finds its roots in organization theories, for example Pfeffer (1972).

The theory of social networks recognizes that those involved in corporate governance processes are often linked through networks. Individuals at the nodes may have things in common including, perhaps, social standing, class, income, education, institutional or corporate links and so on. Lifestyle theory, focusing on the backgrounds of key players, has also been used. Some individuals in the networks, such as the chairman or CEO, may be pivotal nodes in a number of networks, increasing their communication leverage. Such social networks can enhance or adversely interfere with independent and objective governance activities. Identifying such networks and monitoring their activities provides another insight into governance processes and powers.

Managerial and class hegemony

This perspective on the governance of companies focuses on the view that directors have of themselves and its impact on their behaviour and corporate governance implications. Directors in some companies perceive themselves as an elite group. This self-perception encourages them to behave in an elite way, dominating both the company organization and its external linkages. Top management appointments ensure that newcomers fit into that elite and sustain its image. Similarly, new independent directors are likely to be nominated and appointed only if they sustain the dominance of the ruling group. Calls for more representative boards, including quotas to increase the number of women directors, challenge such attitudes, and will be discussed later.

Class hegemony recognizes that directors' self-image can affect board behaviour and performance. Further, executive directors, with their own self-image bolstered by access to information, knowledge of ongoing operations, and decision-making power, may dominate board decisions.

The theories of managerial and class hegemony are rooted in the socio-political disciplines, but have used case research, allied with biographical analysis, to produce some penetrating insights into corporate governance. Essentially, these studies see corporate governance as an interpersonal, political process.

Research using this approach requires access to individual directors. In one of the few books that successfully explored board behaviour through interviews, LeBlanc and Gillies (2005) *Inside the Boardroom* provided sets of quotations from different directors, grouped by topic. Earlier works focusing on realities that are not illuminated by either agency or stewardship theories include Lorsch and McIver (1989), Demb and Neubauer (1992), Monks and Minow (1995), and Monks (1998).

Critics of the case approach to the study of corporate governance complain that the evidence is statistically irrelevant, largely anecdotal, and can be influenced by prejudice, self-centred reporting, and biased insights. The counter-argument is that corporate governance involves a political process, not a statistically controlled group activity.

Psychological and organizational perspectives

Both agency and stewardship theories view corporate governance at the level of the firm, being concerned with relationships between owners and directors. Resource dependency and class/managerial hegemony theories again take a firm-level focus. Individual players, with their different mindsets, personalities, and foibles, do not appear in these theoretical paradigms.

But practitioners recognize that knowing what goes on in the boardroom and during interactions between directors is vital to understanding corporate governance. Empirical investigation is obviously needed. But access to directors and boards can be difficult. Directors may believe that secrecy is vital to protect strategic plans, to guard trade secrets, and, for the listed company, to avoid a leak of stock-market price-sensitive information. Some boards may also resist access from investigators to preserve interpersonal relationships within the board, to prevent the presence of an outsider changing board-level interactions, and to avoid unwanted media interest. Individual directors might also be concerned to prevent damaging information leaking out, affecting their reputations or, worse, generating law suits.

Corporate governance research from a psychological perspective seeks to understand how individual directors perceive their board-level work and what they believe leads to effective performance. Cognitive maps, produced by repertory grid techniques (Kelly, 1955, 1963), can be used to chart directors' mindsets. Constructs of language, using the language of the director not words imposed by the researcher, can help to describe and interpret board-level experiences. If words such as 'involvement', 'leadership', 'participation', 'reputation', or 'teamwork' are used by the director, or moral values such as trust, harmony, or ethical standards mentioned, these become the frame of reference for the researcher. Psychological theories have yet to make a significant impact in understanding corporate governance, but the relevance of individuals at board level in the overall governance process suggests that this field has potential.

Viewing corporate governance from a longitudinal perspective has also provided some insights. Filatotchev and Wright (2005) collected material looking at the evolution of corporate governance practices over the life cycles of enterprises and institutions. Further light has been thrown onto corporate governance from the perspective of political economics. Roe (2003), writing about political and social conflict in corporations and the institutions of corporate governance, showed how a nation's political economy interacts with its legal structures and financial markets. Game theory has also been applied to corporate governance issues.

The societal perspective: stakeholder philosophies

Finally, we turn to perspectives on corporate governance at a societal level: so-called stakeholder theory. 'Stakeholder', a word coined to stand in juxtaposition to 'shareholder', recognizes the interests of *all* those affected by companies' decisions, including customers, employees, and managers, partners in the supply chain, customers, bankers, shareholders, the local community, broader societal interests for the environment, and the state. Companies, stakeholder advocates suggest, owe a duty to all those affected by their behaviour. Some advocates go further and call for directors to be accountable and responsible to a wide range of stakeholders far beyond companies' current company law responsibility to shareholders. Such responsible behaviour, the stakeholder advocates argue, should be the price society demands from companies for the privilege of incorporation, granting shareholders limited liability for the company's debts.

Stakeholder thinking is concerned with values and beliefs about the appropriate relationships between the individual, the enterprise, and the state. It involves a discourse on the balance of responsibility, accountability, and power throughout society. It is not a predictive theory. Consequently, this societal view of corporate governance is probably better thought of as a philosophy rather than a theory.

In 1975, the UK Accounting Standards Steering Committee produced a discussion paper, the *Corporate Report*, which recommended that all large economic entities should produce regular accountability reports to all stakeholder groups whose interests might be affected by the decisions of that entity. The political implications of such a heroic idea quickly relegated the report to the archives.

In the United States, proposals for new company ordinances, including stakeholder accountability, came from Ralph Nader, who tussled with the boardroom-orientated Business Roundtable in 1970. In 1980, Nader and Green argued, emotively, that:

(Giant corporations) can spend decisive amounts to determine which towns thrive and which gather cobwebs, corrupt or help overthrow foreign governments, develop technology that takes lives or saves lives . . . (The giant corporation) is largely unaccountable to its constituencies—shareholders, workers, consumers, local communities, taxpayers, small businesses, future generations.

Stakeholder thinking faded in the free-market, 'growth and greed' attitudes of the 1980s. But in the more environmentally and socially concerned world of the late 20th and early 21st centuries, corporate social responsibility and sustainability reporting were taken seriously again. The interest is also reflected in socially aware mutual funds, which limit their investment to companies deemed to adopt suitable business strategies, for example by not dealing in tobacco, gambling, or armaments. The Royal Society of Arts in England published a report in 1999 entitled *Tomorrow's Company,* which advocated wider recognition of corporate responsibility to stakeholders such as suppliers, customers, and employees. The chairman of the committee producing this report, Sir Stuart Hampson, who was also chairman of the John Lewis Partnership—a company run as an employees' partnership—wrote:

> Shareholder value is the imperative commanding a lot of attention, but you cannot create shareholder value by talking to your shareholders. You create it by looking at the four drivers of a successful business: how good you are at involving and motivating your staff; how close you are to your customers; how good you are at removing wastage from the supply chain and maintaining good relations with suppliers; what your reputation is in the community at large. We don't believe that the board is there purely to create shareholder value. I'm sure nobody leaps out of bed in the morning and says 'I want to create shareholder value!' It's unrealistic.

The challenge to boards trying to adopt a stakeholder approach is that they no longer have a single constituency, the shareholders, to satisfy, but need to balance the potentially conflicting interests of a diverse set of stakeholders.

Sternberg (2000) argued that stakeholder ideas are fundamentally flawed, strongly advocating the ownership rights perspective. Potential conflicts between the expectations of different stakeholders were irreconcilable, she argued: boards need a single responsibility—to their shareholders. Turnbull (1997: 2) took the opposite view, calling for a systems perspective that included all of the components in the corporate situation. Expectations of companies around the world are changing, with growing demands for better consumer, environmental, and societal behaviour.

The 1998 UK Hampel Committee dismissed stakeholder notions, saying 'directors are responsible for relations with stakeholders, but are accountable to the shareholders'—a view reflecting the conventional wisdom in boardrooms in both the United Kingdom and the United States. Roberto Goizuetta, a former head of Coca-Cola, captured the issue:

> Saying that we work for our shareholders may sound simplistic—but we frequently see companies that have forgotten the reason they exist. They may even try to be all things to all people and serve many masters in many different ways. In any event they miss their primary calling, which is to stick to the business of creating value for their owners.

But overshadowing agency, stewardship, stakeholder, and the other theoretical perspectives are also some basic unresolved issues at a meta-philosophical level. Every theory of corporate governance needs to be founded on a view on the legitimate relationship between the individual and society. Where does the desirable balance lie between the rights, responsibilities, and powers of the individual, the enterprise, and the state? Opinions vary significantly by culture, political context, and social system. Moreover, they have been evolving throughout history. All systems of governance must seek an appropriate balance between the interests of self and society. That applies to corporate governance just as it does to governance in other areas of society.

Enlightened shareholder theory

The stakeholder approach to corporate governance calls for boards to take into account the interests of a diverse and wide range of stakeholder groups, including shareholders, rather than to act solely in the interest of the shareholders, as called for in stewardship theory. Critics of stakeholder ideas say that dual legitimacy—meeting the needs of stakeholders and shareholders—is not feasible because:

- the interests of stakeholders are potentially in conflict—what benefits one group disadvantages another (e.g. higher wages, lower selling prices, or community contributions reduce the funds available for the other stakeholders, including the shareholders);
- it is impossible to maximize all stakeholder interests simultaneously;
- within stakeholder groups, interests vary (e.g. some employees may prefer higher wages, others better pension conditions);
- who establishes the interests of each stakeholder group is undefined;
- if directors represent stakeholder interests, they face conflicts of interest between constituencies.

A recent theoretical development has attempted to go beyond this shareholder versus stakeholder debate. *Enlightened shareholder theory* recognizes that the satisfaction of stakeholder needs and interests is crucial to corporate success and the creation of long-term wealth. The theory recognizes that companies generate profits and increase shareholder wealth only by satisfying stakeholder needs and responding to their interests. Shareholders benefit when boards satisfy stakeholder interests, because profits are made and they are primary stakeholders. The theory is grounded in continuing shareholder primacy, but differs from classical stewardship theory because boards are required to take stakeholder interests into account, explaining their actions to all stakeholders, including the way in which their decisions have exposed the company to risk.

In Chapter 9, on corporate social responsibility, we will see how the call for directors to recognize stakeholders is being pursued in statutory requirements (UK Companies Act 2006), in exhortatory guidance (the UN Principles for Responsible Investment), and in initiatives from institutional investors.

Differing boundaries and levels: systems theory

The disciplines contributing to the study of corporate governance to date include financial economics, law, accountancy, management studies, organizational behaviour, sociology, politics, and, perhaps, philosophy. The two dominant contenders for theoretical insight, agency and stewardship theories, are properly based on bounded models of reality: agency theory on an economic perspective; stewardship theory on a legal one. Inevitably, each perspective is limited. Each theory sees the world through a different lens.

Changing the metaphor, each of the various theoretical perspectives on corporate governance can be visualized as a spotlight lighting up part of the stage on which the corporate governance action is being played (Figure 3.3). Some spotlights illuminate one part of the stage; others throw light on other areas and from different angles. Each theoretical spotlight leaves some players and part of the action in darkness.

Some theories focus on the shareholders and the board as a whole with its standing committees, perhaps including the external auditors; other theories focus on individual directors

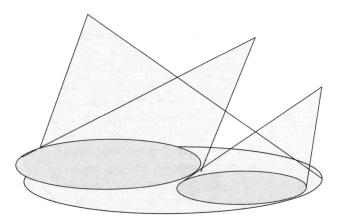

Figure 3.3 Spotlights on the corporate governance stage

on the board and the interactions between them; yet other theories take the perspective of the stock markets, investors, and regulators; at the highest level, the political situation, the economic impact, and the cultural context come into view, along with legislatures, states, and international agencies. As yet, there is no theoretical floodlight that adequately lights the whole stage, illuminating all of the players, and showing their relationships and the action.

Systems theory takes a similar approach to understanding situations. All phenomena can be thought of as a hierarchy of systems. Take a car, for example: there are molecules in the steel washer, which is a component of the carburettor, which is part of the engine, which is a feature of the car, which can also be viewed as part of a traffic system. Each is useful in context; none tells the whole story.

Systems theory offers a useful way of looking at a situation. The classical view of systems uses three criteria to identify a system:

- the system's boundaries—that is, determining what is to be considered as within the system itself and what in the system's environment (systems are man-made artefacts to help us to understand a situation; moreover, each system can be further broken down to suit the needs of the user);

- the system's level of abstraction—that is, the level at which the system is perceived and the amount of detail treated within it;

- the system's function—that is, what occurs between the system's inputs and outputs.

So what are the boundaries of corporate governance? Cochran and Wartick, in the first bibliography of corporate governance published in 1988, suggested that:

> Corporate governance is an umbrella term that includes specific issues arising from interactions among senior management, shareholders, boards of directors, and other corporate stakeholders.

Earlier, we adopted the simple expedient of defining corporate governance as being about the way power was exercised over corporate entities. In this way, we did not have to identify the players, nor define boundaries for their action. In Chapter 2, we saw how different author-ities had produced other definitions of corporate governance. But what should be in the system and what should be its boundaries? We have a choice—individual directors, corporate entities, their owners or members, their governing bodies, intermediaries in the governance chain, auditors, regulators, laws, culture, national and international organizations, and all of the other stakeholders affected by the actions of those corporate entities.

Judging from the reams of academic literature, views clearly differ on the scope of cor-porate governance. As we have seen, for some, it is about principles and good practice on matters such as board structures and membership, the independence of directors, the use of audit, remuneration and nominating committees, and generally about board-level effective-ness. For others, corporate governance is about the relationship between owners and corpo-rations, about the exercise of power by shareholders, particularly institutional investors who, in recent years, have shown themselves capable of removing dominant executive directors, restructuring boards, and influencing strategic direction. For still others, corporate governance is about the social responsibilities that corporations owe to a wide set of stakeholders beyond the board's classical fiduciary duty to the shareholders—responsibilities and accountabilities to employees, customers, lenders, suppliers, the local community, and society at large.

Some researchers have gone beyond the use of systems theory as a convenient analogy, by applying systems analysis techniques to corporate governance processes. Such analytical tools have proved useful in describing governance activities with some rigour. Cybernetics—the study of communication and control in man and machine, which distinguishes adaptive and mecha-nistic feedback and regulation, and adds the concept of requisite variety in the design of effec-tive systems—has also proved a valuable adjunct to systems approaches. A potentially significant law of cybernetics is the law of requisite variety, which recognizes that control in a complex sys-tem needs sufficient levels and number of regulating devices. So it is with corporate governance.

The approach we adopt in this book is well described by Clarke (2007) when he suggested that theoretical perspectives on boards and governance can best be seen as 'multiple theo-retical lenses' with which to view the subject.

A subject in search of its paradigm

Agency theory is rooted in the belief that agents are utility maximizers, and therefore cannot be relied on to act in the best interests of their principals. Put simply: directors cannot be trust-ed. Stewardship theory is rooted in the belief that directors accept a fiduciary duty to act in the best interest of the owners who have entrusted their funds to them. In other words: directors can be trusted. Which is true? Karl Popper, in his influential work on scientific proof, argued that a scientific proposition could not be proved to be absolutely true, but a single contrary result would show it to be false. Both agency and stewardship theories fail the Popper's test of scientific truth because each can readily be shown to be false in specific circumstances.

Corporate governance, as yet, does not have a single widely-accepted theoretical base, nor a commonly accepted paradigm. In the words of Pettigrew (1992): 'Corporate governance lacks any form of coherence, either empirically, methodologically or theoretically with only piecemeal attempts to try and understand and explain how the modern corporation is run.' The subject has progressed some way since 1992, but is still in search of its paradigm.

In the original concept of the corporation, as we have seen, directors were appointed by, and were usually in direct contact with, their shareholders. Shareholder democracy had meaning and shareholders could participate. (Admittedly, some rogue entrepreneurs took advantage of their shareholders, but investment always involves risk.) But the concept of the corporation no longer works in that way. Directors in many large companies have become distant from the ultimate owners. Layers of brokers, agents, share-holding companies, institutional investors, pension funds, mutual funds, and banks come between boards and their companies' ultimate owners. In Western cultures a new governing elite has emerged. Self-enriching and self-perpetuating, these corporate directors wield the power, and reap the rewards, that were previously reserved for ruling monarchs and their aristocracy.

The 1990s saw a dramatic surge in academic interest in corporate governance. Unfortunately, research has so far failed to offer a convincing explanation as to how corporate governance works and has not contributed much to the *practice* of the subject. Significant professional developments have been responses to corporate corruption and collapse, not to research findings and theory building. The Sarbanes-Oxley Act of 2002 in the United States, the corporate governance codes in all economically developed nations, and the corporate governance institutions formed in many emerging economies have been based on the experience and conventional wisdom of company directors and their advisers, not on the conclusions of rigorous academic research.

Part of the problem, from a theoretical perspective, is the lack of clearly articulated understanding and definition of various governance-related terms. For example, the discussion of the 'Anglo-American' approach to corporate governance, usually meaning one based on common law, becomes woolly when the underlying philosophies of governance in the two systems are seen to be significantly different: one being principles-based; the other rules-based. Another example is in the use of the term 'outside' director, when the incumbent could be totally independent of the company (and may thus know little about it!), independent as defined by various governance codes, or connected with the company in some way.

Today, the frontiers of corporate governance are being pushed out rapidly. The importance of good governance is recognized by investors and regulators. Governance now affects global finance markets. The significance of governance for the long-term success of enterprise, in addition to sound management, is understood by business leaders. Directors and boards are facing up to the challenges.

Both agency theory and stewardship theory reflect the Anglo-Saxon case-law-based legal situation and financial markets with widely dispersed shareholders providing relative management autonomy. Some jurisdictions and markets do not have these characteristics. A more general theory of corporate governance would need to recognize the reality of company law, and ownership and control, in relevant jurisdictions and markets.

Corporate governance codes reflect the conventional wisdom of best practice in listed companies in that jurisdiction. There is a paucity of new conceptual thinking about corporate governance. Scholars need to break out of their preconceptions of corporate entities seen as legal entities or in terms of relationships between corporate entity and stakeholders, or of man as a utility-maximizing contract-maker, and build a theory that adequately reflects the world experienced by those actually involved at board level.

To present a comprehensive and coherent view of governance arrangements and structures around the world, corporate governance theory first needs a taxonomy of organizational types—public, private, family, subsidiary, associate, joint venture, non-profit, and so on—and complex ownership structures—pyramids, chains, nets, and the rest—to distinguish very different power bases and governance systems. Systems theory and cybernetics-based control system concepts such as networks, system boundaries, goals, and sub-optimization might provide insights.

The creation of a general theory of corporate governance is certainly premature and probably over-optimistic, but such a theory would need to embrace:

- the relationship between individual, enterprise, and state;
- a broader definition of corporate entities to cover every organization in which governance and management are separate from the members;
- a mapping of the elements affecting/affected by the governance of such organizations;
- the expectations, requirements, and demands of each participant;
- the duties and responsibilities of each participant;
- the powers, sanctions, and accountabilities of each participant.

At the moment, various theoretical insights cast light on different aspects of the play, highlighting some and leaving others in shadow. We need a viewpoint that will light up the entire stage, all of the players, and the entire action.

To return to our earlier traffic-system analogy, the overall operation of such a system depends on controls at three levels.

- Level 1—the regulatory level, with laws, regulations, and rules

At this level, conformance is mandatory: for example, in the United Kingdom, 'keep to the left of the road and at a roundabout give way to traffic coming from the right'. The actions of those involved are policed. There are sanctions and penalties for failing to obey.

Notice the legal and cultural dependency at this level: for example, in the United States, a reader might say 'keep to the *right* of the road' and 'what is a roundabout?'

- Level 2—the advisory level involving voluntary codes of conduct

At this level, the responsibility becomes a matter of generally accepted responsible behaviour, for example 'respect other road users' and 'look out for hazards—children, dogs, or obstacles in the road'.

- Level 3—the personal level, concerning individual beliefs and behaviour

At this level, personal value systems are involved, including courtesy, concern for others, socially aware behaviour, and trust.

The practice of corporate governance needs controls at similar levels. But to date the emphasis has been on levels 1 and 2:

- the regulatory level—laws, regulations, mandatory rules;
- the advisory level—voluntary codes of conduct, corporate policies.

What has been missing is any focus on personal behaviour rooted in basic values—morality, honesty, integrity, decency, concern for others, respect, and trust. The challenge for research and writing on corporate governance, while extending knowledge at the regulatory and advisory levels, is to break into the black box of the boardroom and to focus on board-level activities, directors' behaviour, and board leadership.

Case Studies

 Case study 3.1   The Walt Disney Company

Roy Disney, Walt Disney's nephew, was the last remaining member of the Disney family on the board of the famous Walt Disney Company. He was vice-chairman of the board and an executive director as chairman of the Animated Features Division. He was often paraded as the last survivor of the founder's family serving in the company.

However, in November 2003, he had a shock. The governance and nomination committee of the board lowered the mandatory retirement age for directors to 72. Roy was 73. Moreover, John Bryson, who was chairman and CEO of Edison International, an outside director of the Walt Disney Company and a member of its nomination and compensation committee, told him that, since he was past mandatory retirement, the committee had decided to make no exceptions and had agreed that he should not run for the Disney board at the next AGM.

Roy's response was: 'You'll regret this . . . ' But he was not really surprised: for a few years, relations between him and Michael Eisner, the chairman and CEO of Disney, had been poor. Indeed, by 2003, they were scarcely speaking.

Michael Eisner, who previously had a highly successful career with ABC and Paramount Pictures, had been appointed to Disney in 1984 by Roy Disney himself. In his early years, the company was highly successful in both animated and main films, videos, theme parks, and merchandise. The company's financial performance and its share price had improved significantly. In 1988, Eisner was the highest paid executive in America, with a salary, a bonus on profits, and the exercise of stock options amounting to some US$40 million. In 1992, he earned over US$200 million.

But as the 1990s progressed, problems arose. Financial performance fell off. Critics complained that Disney had lost its creative energy. The Euro World theme park in Paris faced a massive overspend and below-budget revenues: the strategies that had worked in the United States did not work in Europe.

Roy Disney was not alone on the board in criticizing Eisner. Stanley Gold, an independent outside director, questioned why, when profits had fallen 25% and the Disney share price was low, Eisner had been given a US$5 million bonus by the compensation committee. Gold had been chairman of that committee, but had been replaced by Judith Estrin just before this bonus was awarded.

Another outside director, Andrea van der Kamp, was also told in 2003 that she would not be re-appointed to the board. She wrote complaining that:

> I was asked to serve on this board to be an independent director, and now I'm not being re-nominated because that is just what I am—an independent director . . . The performance of this company has not been wonderful. I, along with some employees and shareholders are concerned. Michael Eisner has cost this company a lot of money . . . We have terrible relations with creative people in Hollywood because of Michael Eisner's arrogance. Many of the best executives have left the company. We've just fired all these people and yet Michael Eisner is getting a $5 million bonus . . .

Other directors on the board of 18 directors supported Eisner, approving the decisions of both the compensation committee and the nomination committee.

At the September 2002 board meeting, which approved new appointments to the nominating and governance committee, Eisner claimed: 'Today, we furthered our commitment to ensure that Disney remains among the progressive boards in America on governance issues.'

After John Bryson had told Roy Disney that the governance and nomination committee's decision was final, Roy realized that it would still need board confirmation. But Bryson and Eisner had then contacted the other directors to brief them and to confirm they would support the decision.

As James B. Stewart wrote: 'Obviously, Eisner controlled the Disney executive directors. But he maintained that the rest were independent. But he was defining independence so narrowly as to be meaningless.' Outside director Irwin Russell, for example, was Eisner's personal lawyer and had negotiated his lucrative contract: an obvious conflict of interest between a lawyer's duty to his client and a director's duty to the shareholders. Robert Stern, another outside director, was Eisner's personal architect, whose firm relied on Disney contracts.

In the end, Roy Disney decided that he should resign, making public his concerns for the future of the company. He wrote to Eisner:

It is with deep sadness and regret that I send this letter of resignation from the Walt Disney Company both as Chairman of the Animated Features Division and Vice-Chairman of the Board of Directors.

You know well that you and I have had serious differences of opinion about the direction of the company and style of management . . . you have driven a wedge between me and those I work with, even to the extent of requiring some of my associates to report my conversations and activities back to you. I find this intolerable.

Finally you discussed with the Governance and Nominating Committee its decision to leave my name off the slate of directors to be re-elected.

Michael I believe . . . that after 19 years at the helm you are no longer the best person to run Walt Disney Company . . . It is my sincere belief that it is you who should be leaving and not me . . . The company deserves fresh, energetic leadership.

With sincere regret, Roy E. Disney

Eisner and his associates felt that Roy's letter raised corporate governance issues. They decided to present his opinions as an attack on the company and the board, with him trying to block necessary governance reforms, not as a criticism of Eisner's management.

Over 4,000 present and past members of the staff of Roy's animation division wrote to support him. A few weeks later, Eisner shut down the Orlando animation unit.

Then Gold offered his resignation, too, writing:

. . . I am proud of my more than 15 years of service and my role in reshaping the company . . . I do however, lament that my efforts over the past three years to implement necessary changes has only succeeded in creating an insular board of directors servings as a bulwark to shield management from criticism and accountability . . .

On the decision to oust Roy from the board, he commented:

This is yet another attempt by this board to squelch dissent by hiding behind the veil of 'good governance'. What a curious result. The board seems determined to devote its time and energies to adopting policies that . . . only serve to muzzle and isolate those directors who recognize that their role is to be active in shaping the company and planning for executive succession. Further, this board isolates those directors who believe that Michael Eisner (when measured by the dismal results of the last seven years) is not up to the challenge.

Institutional investors, such as CalPers, also raised objections to Disney's performance and the lack of succession planning for Eisner. The 2004 annual general meeting of Disney shareholders was going to be crucial.

In February 2004, an influential shareholder advisory firm, Glass Lewis, interviewed Roy Disney and Gold, as well as Eisner and his supporters. It asked why the mandatory retirement age had been chosen as 72 and not, say, 75. The subsequent Glass Lewis report to shareholders was unequivocal: 'The Disney Board has been notoriously insular, famously gullible and blindly loyal to Mr. Eisner . . . Given the control Mr. Eisner is accustomed to, we are troubled that he still wields tremendous power over the operation of this board . . . Our concerns are substantial.'

The report also questioned the independence of Bryson (head of the governance committee), whose wife was a senior executive of a Disney joint venture.

Roy Disney and Gold launched a campaign to undermine and unseat Eisner, with a website (www. SaveDisney.com), which claimed that: 'Shareholder democracy, while lauded as the centrepiece of democratic capitalism, has in fact become an oxymoron, with the vast majority of corporations firmly in the grip of their chief executives and acquiescent boards.'

Other institutional shareholders joined the revolt, citing poor financial performance, loss of creative leadership, and poor board accountability. CalPers announced that it would vote with Gold and Roy Disney against Eisner. The state pension funds in Connecticut, Massachusetts, New Jersey, and New York followed. The T. Rowe Price Mutual Fund, which held 19 million shares, also called for Eisner to go. There were suggestions as well that the roles of chairman and CEO should be separated.

ISS, another shareholder advisory group, recommended that shareholders withhold their vote for Eisner to demonstrate their dissatisfaction, although under the US corporate voting system, it is almost impossible for shareholders of widely held public companies to evict directors, because of shareholder inertia, problems in identifying owners, and since many mutual funds, brokers and others automatically support incumbent management.

Just prior to the AGM in March 2004, Gold and Roy held a rally for shareholders opposed to Eisner's leadership, calling for a rediscovery of the original Walt Disney Company values.

The AGM produced a major rebuke from shareholders, with 43% voting against Eisner's renewal. Subsequently, the board decided to separate the positions of chair and CEO, creating a new role of chairman of the board. George Mitchell, the former senator, was appointed chairman, who assured the *Wall Street Journal* that corporate governance reforms were already in place. Eisner stayed as CEO.

At the June 2004 board meeting, Eisner announced his successor as CEO—Bob Iger—but the choice was not made public. Then, at the September 2004 board meeting, Eisner announced that he would stand down as CEO in September 2006 when his present contract ended. The board thanked him for his twenty years' service and looked forward to his continuing leadership throughout his remaining tenure. Gold and Roy called it window dressing.

But criticisms of Eisner intensified and, in March 2005, he announced that he would step down as CEO a year before the end of his contract, which he did on 30 September 2005. His successor was Bob Iger.

Discussion questions

1. Identify the issues raised by this case.

2. Andrea van der Kamp, an independent outside director, complained that she was not re-nominated to the board because she had been too independent. What can a director, who has criticized corporate culture, do if he or she is then not re-nominated?

3. What is your opinion of the following statement made in the case? 'Shareholder democracy, while lauded as the centrepiece of democratic capitalism, has in fact become an oxymoron, with the vast majority of corporations firmly in the grip of their chief executives and acquiescent boards.'

Primary source: James B. Stewart (2005) *Disney War*. Simon & Schuster, New York.

Case study 3.2   Network Rail

Before 1948 the railways in Britain were run by different public companies. Then they were nationalized and run by the state enterprise British Railways. In 1994, the United Kingdom's Conservative government privatized the railway system again. New companies were incorporated with the right to run train services over various routes. The government recognized that some public subsidy would be needed to cover unprofitable services and routes, but believed that with financial incentives and private sector managerial efficiencies, services would improve. Railtrack plc, a public company listed on the London Stock market, was incorporated to control the entire railway infrastructure (tracks, signals, bridges, tunnels and some stations), with the Rail Regulator setting charges for access to the tracks by the franchised train operating companies.

Over the following years, Railtrack was criticized for the spiralling costs of new projects, its poor performance in maintaining and developing the rail infrastructure, and particularly on its poor safety record. Fatal crashes occurred. Railtrack's use of contractors on maintenance work allegedly had led to loss of control and lower safety. The strategy of having a single company run the entire rail network, used by all the train operators, was questioned. In the old days, each railway company ran on its own tracks.

Following a major crash with many fatalities, the Railtrack board of directors was said to have panicked. Emergency tests showed dangerous faults on many lines and speed restrictions were imposed around the system, causing long delays for passengers and major losses to the train operators. The Railtrack board launched a massive investment programme, but by 2001 the company's debts were so large that the company needed repeated subsidy from the taxpayer to remain financially viable. Controversially, some government funding was used to pay a dividend to Railtrack shareholders.

But now the government changed, the Conservatives were replaced by New Labour. In October 2001, the new Secretary of State for Transport, Stephen Byers, called for Railtrack to be put into administration, claiming it was insolvent. Critics accused the government of deliberately bankrupting the company to begin the re-nationalization of the railway system, bringing the infrastructure back under state control. The government replied that the private sector would continue to run the railways but offered no compensation to Railtrack shareholders, arguing that the company was bankrupt.

In October 2002, the government created a new company to run Britain's rail infrastructure. Called Network Rail, it was incorporated as a private company limited by guarantee, although the government claimed that governance would meet the standards of a plc. Although the bulk of its funding would come from public funds, it was free from interference by government ministers. Moreover, it was exempted from the Freedom of Information Act, applicable to all public bodies.

The company's constitution provided for 'guarantor members' (not shareholders), who would receive the annual report and accounts, attend the AGM, and approve the appointment of directors and auditors. The members could also remove top executives. Over 100 members were appointed representing various stakeholders such as the railway industry, the Department of Transport, and the public. The company explained that it operated as a commercial business directly accountable to its members, but that it was a 'not for dividend company', any profits being ploughed back into investment. Its board of directors had twelve members—five executives, six outside non-executives, and a non-executive chairman.

A consulting firm, Coucher Pender (founded in 1999 by Iain Coucher and Victoria Pender) was retained by the Strategic Rail Authority to set up the new company for an undisclosed fee with a further £484,000 paid by Network Rail. In 2004, Coucher was employed by the company as deputy chief executive. Pender was subsequently appointed director of corporate and government affairs.

Some of the weaknesses of the new company's governance were seen in 2008 when significant overruns on maintenance work left hundreds of thousands of travellers stranded over the New Year holidays. Governing members complained that management was not really accountable to anyone.

'There is a democratic deficit' wrote Lord Berkely, a member representing the rail freight industry. He called for a new board with fewer 'governors' who would have wider powers to supervise management. Further complaints were that members had conflicting interests, those drawn from the travelling public wanted low fares and improved services, employee representatives wanted better wages and employment terms, whilst those representing the public interest wanted lower subsidies from taxpayers.

In 2009, the chief executive, Iain Coucher, was said to be the highest paid public official in Britain, with remuneration of over £1 million. In his defence, it was argued that Network Rail was independent of the state; although others pointed out that the company was publicly funded. Highlighting a turn round in safety and punctuality, Coucher said 'my priorities are to drive further a culture of safety, to get even better value for money for the British people and to be more attuned to the needs of customers. I want people to associate these words with Network Rail: transparent, accountable, and responsive.'

Subsequently, it was claimed that Coucher and Pender had received £180,000 every three months for 'unspecified services' on top of their other remuneration. Coucher was accused of leading a 'James Bond lifestyle', with an Aston Martin DB9 and a flat overlooking London's Regent's Park supported by corporate housing and car benefits. An internal inquiry by the audit committee found no evidence of wrongdoing, but an independent inquiry paid for by the company was set up in 2011 led by Anthony White, a leading Queen's Counsel, to investigate allegations of the misuse of state funding, of up to £4 billion a year. Further claims were made that cases of alleged sexual harassment and race discrimination from ex-employees had been silenced with huge pay-offs before the complaints could be heard by an employment tribunal.

Coucher left the company in October 2010 after eight years, three years as chief executive and five as deputy. He received a £1.6 million 'golden goodbye,' which the press described as a 'reward for failure'. The incoming chairman, Rick Haythornthwaite, suggested that Coucher was secretive and had a 'militaristic' management style. In May 2011, the official inquiry dismissed allegations of the misuse of public funds and 'serious financial impropriety.'

Strategic proposals for another reorganization of the British rail industry surfaced in 2011. A 'vertical re-integration' was suggested, with train operating companies owning and running tracks and stations. Such a strategy, it was suggested, would make the companies more profitable, and might attract capital from international asset management companies and private equity funds. In February 2011, newly appointed chief executive, David Higgins, said 'now we start a new chapter . . . as Network Rail seeks to build trust'. Unhappily, that month an inquest into the deaths of two schoolgirls on a level crossing found that Network Rail, trying to protect its safety record, had failed to provide a public inquiry with a risk assessment that had exposed the dangers years before.

In April 2014, the leader of the opposition party in parliament, Ed Miliband, said that if the Labour party was returned to power at the next general election in 2015, it would consider taking back control of the railway system, including Network Rail and the railway operating companies.

See www.networkrail.co.uk

Discussion questions

1. Identify the corporate governance issues in this case. Which corporate governance theories could be used to explore each of them?

2. What ethical issues, if any, arise in this case?

3. What is your opinion of the various British government strategies over the running of the railways?

4. Was the British government right to offer no compensation to the shareholders of Railtrack plc, arguing that the company was insolvent?

5. How would you organize the British railway system and its corporate governance?

References and further reading

Aoki Masahiko (2001) *Toward a Comparative Institutional Analysis*. MIT Press, Cambridge, MA.

Berle, Adolf A. and Gardiner C. Means (1932) *The Modern Corporation and Private Property*. Macmillan, edn revised by Adolf Berle (1967) Columbia University, Harcourt, Brace and World, New York.

Bhagat, Sanjai, Brian J. Bolton, and Roberta Romano (2007) 'The Promise and Peril in Corporate Governance Indices', 7 October, ECGI working paper No. 89/2007, Social Science Research Network (www.ssrn.com/abstract=1019921).

Clarke, Thomas (2004) *Theories of Corporate Governance: The Philosophical Foundations of Corporate Governance*. Routledge, New York.

Clarke, Thomas (2007) *International Corporate Governance: A Comparative Approach*. Routledge, London and New York.

Coarse, Ronald H. (1937) 'The Nature of the Firm', *Economica* N.4, reprinted in Stigler, G. J. and K. E. Boulding (eds) (1952) *Readings in Price Theory*. Irwin, Homewood, IL

Cochran, Philip L. and Steven L.Wartick (1988) *Corporate Governance: A Review of the Literature*. Financial Executives Research Foundation, Morristown, NJ.

Demb, Ada and Frederich Neubauer (1992) *The Corporate Board: Confronting the Paradoxes*. Oxford University Press, New York.

Demsetz, Harold (1988) 'The Theory of the Firm revisited', *Journal of Law, Economics and Organization*, Vol. 4, Spring.

Donaldson, L. and J. H. Davis (1992) 'Stewardship Theory or Agency Theory: CEO Governance and Shareholder Returns', *Australian Journal of Management*, Vol. 16, No. 1.

El-Mahdy, Dina Faisal and Carolyn Strand Norman (2011) *Corporate Governance and the US Firm: A Review and Directions for Future Research*. MWA Publishing, Swindon, UK.

Fama, Eugene and Michael Jensen (1983) 'Separation of Ownership and Control', *Journal of Law and Economics*, Vol. 26, June.

Filatotchev, Igor and Mike Wright (eds) (2005) *The Life Cycle of Corporate Governance*. Edward Elgar Cheltenham, UK and Northampton, MA.

Gomez, Pierre-Yves and Harry Korine (2008) *Entrepreneurs and Democracy: A Political Theory of Corporate Governance*. Cambridge University Press, Cambridge, UK.

Huse, Morten, Boards (2007) *Governance and Value Creation: The Human Side of Corporate Governance*. Cambridge University Press, New York.

Jensen, Michael C. (1986) 'Agency Costs of Free Cash Flow, Corporate Finance and Takeovers', *American Economic Review*, No. 76, May.

Jensen, Michael C. (2000) *A Theory of the Firm: Governance, Residual Claims and Organizational Forms*. Harvard University Press, Cambridge, MA.

Jensen, Michael and William Meckling (1976) 'Theory of the Firm: Managerial Behavior, Agency Costs and Ownership Structure', *Journal of Financial Economics*, No. 3 /4, October.

Kelly, G. A. ([1955] 1963) *The Psychology of Personal Constructs (A Theory of Personality)*. Norton, New York.

Lan Luh Luh and Loizos Hereacleous (2010) 'Rethinking Agency Theory: The View from Law', *Academy of Management Review*, Vol. 35, No. 2.

LeBlanc and Gillies (2005) *Inside the Boardroom*. Wiley, Canada.

Lorsch and McIver (1989) *Pawns or Potentates: The Reality of America's Corporate Boards*. Harvard Business School Press, Boston, MA.

Mallin, Christine A ([2004] 2007) *Corporate Governance*, Oxford University Press, Oxford.

Millstein, Ira M. and S. M. Katsch (1981) *The Limits of Corporate Power: Existing Constraints on the Exercise of Corporate Discretion*. Macmillan, New York.

Mintzberg, Henry (1983) *Power In and Around Organizations*. Prentice-Hall, Englewood Cliffs, NJ.

Mintzberg, Henry (1984) 'Who Should Control the Corporation?' *California Management Review*, Vol. XXVII, Fall.

Monks, Robert A. G. (1998) *The Emperor's Nightingale: Restoring the Integrity of the Corporation*. Capstone Publishing, Oxford.

Monks, Robert A. G. (2008) *Corpocracy: How CEOs and the Business Roundtable Hijacked the World's Greatest Wealth Machine*. Wiley, Hoboken, NJ.

Muth, Melinda M. and Lex Donaldson (1998) 'Stewardship Theory and Board Structure: A Contingency Approach', *Corporate Governance: An International Review*, Vol. 6, No. 1, January.

Nader, Ralph, Mark Green, and Joel Seligman (1976) *Taming The Giant Corporation*. W.W. Norton Co. Inc., New York.

Norberg, Donald (2011) *Corporate Governance: Principles and Issues*. Sage Publishing, London.

Pettigrew, Andrew (1992) 'On Studying Managerial Elites', *Strategic Management Journal*, Vol. 13.

Pfeffer, Jeffrey (1972) 'Size and Composition of Corporate Boards of Directors: The Organization and its Environment', *Administrative Science Quarterly*, 17, 218.

Roe, Mark J. (2003) *Political Determinants of Corporate Governance*, Clarendon Lectures in Management Studies Series, Oxford University Press, Oxford.

Shleifer, A. and Vishny, R. (1997) 'A Survey of Corporate Governance', *Journal of Finance*, Vol. 52, No. 2, June, pp. 737–L 783.

Selvaggi, Mariano and James Upton (2008) *Governance and Performance in Corporate Britain*, ABI research paper 7, Association of British Insurers, Gresham Street, London, February.

Smith, Adam ([1776] 1976) *The Wealth of Nations*. Revised edn, George J. Stigler (ed.), University of Chicago Press, Chicago.

Sternberg, Elaine (2000) *Just Business: Ethics in Action*. 2nd edn, Oxford University Press, Oxford.

Stewart, James B. (2005) *Disney War*. Simon & Schuster, New York.

Stiles, P. and B. Taylor (2001) *Boards at Work: How Directors View Their Roles and Responsibilities*. Oxford University Press, Oxford.

Thomsen, Steen (2008) *Introduction to Corporate Governance*. DJOF Publishing, Copenhagen.

Tirole, Jean (1996) *The Theory of Corporate Finance*. Princeton University Press, Princeton, NJ.

Tricker, R. I. (ed.) (2000) *Corporate Governance: History of Management Thought*. Ashgate, Dartmouth, UK.

Turnbull, Shann (2000) *Corporate Governance: Theories, Challenges and Paradigms*, Macquarie University, Sydney, see UK Social Science Research Electronic Paper collection.

Useem, M. (2006) 'How Well Run Boards Make Decisions', *Harvard Business Review*, November, pp. 130–138.

Williamson, Oliver E. (1975) *Markets and Hierarchy*. Free Press, New York.

Williamson, Oliver E. (1988) 'The Logic of Economic Organization', *Journal of Law, Economics and Organization*, No. 4, Spring.

Williamson, Oliver E. (1996) *The Mechanisms of Governance*. Oxford University Press, New York.

Projects and exercises

1. Prepare a paper or presentation analysing the various theories that have been applied to an understanding of corporate governance. Are they in conflict or are they, rather, different perspectives on the basic phenomena?

2. It has been suggested that: 'All major developments in the field (of corporate governance), including the codes of good practice and the American SOX Act, have been responses to corporate crises. The codes and principles of corporate governance have been created by business leaders based on their experience and conventional wisdom about what counts as good practice.' Do you agree? Is this a sound approach? What might be the drawbacks?

3. Do you agree or disagree that Roberto Goizuetta, a former head of Coca-Cola, captured the issue, when he said the following? '[S]aying that we work for our shareholders may sound simplistic—but we frequently see companies that have forgotten the reason they exist. They may even try to be all things to all people and serve many masters in many different ways. In any event they miss their primary calling, which is to stick to the business of creating value for their owners.'

Self-test questions

1. What is a fundamental difference between agency theory and stewardship theory?

2. What is a fundamental difference between stewardship theory and stakeholder philosophy?

4

The Governance Partnership: Investors, companies, and directors

 Learning Outcomes

In which we study:

- Shareholder rights
- Shareholder stewardship and activism
- Shareholder information
- Different types of director
- Directors' legal duties and rights
- The board leadership role of the chairman
- The corporate officers

A central concern of corporate governance is the relationship between members and the corporate entities of which they are members. In limited-liability companies, that is the relationship between the shareholders and the boards of the companies in which they invest. In not-for-profit corporate entities, professional bodies, and trades unions, for example, the crucial relationship is between the voting members and the governing body of the organization. In this chapter, we consider these essential relationships.

Shareholder rights

Shareholder rights are determined by the company's articles of association and company law, predominantly the Companies Acts or ordinances. With the ownership of shares come rights: the right to receive notice, attend and vote at shareholders' meetings, the right to inspect the shareholder register and the register of directors and officers, and the right to regular statutory information. But, having elected directors to govern the company, shareholders do not have the right to be involved in the day-to-day management of the business, nor to inspect company records or management accounts.

Obviously, the more voting shares held, the greater the potential power of the shareholder. Typically, a holding of more than 50% provides majority control, with the ultimate right to nominate and elect directors, and to influence the direction of the business. However, companies must respect the rights of any minority shareholders.

In the 19th-century model of the joint-stock limited-liability company, shareholders had the right to nominate and elect the directors of their company. This is still the case in most small companies. But in listed public companies, the scale and diversity of shareholders means that it is difficult to exercise such rights. Consequently, company law in many jurisdictions has laid down rules for the election of directors, which differ between jurisdictions.

In the United States, the incumbent board has considerable influence in the election of directors, sending a list of its preferred candidates to shareholders prior to voting at the shareholders' meeting. If shareholders want to nominate alternatives, they have to bear the cost of distributing the rival nomination forms themselves, which can be prohibitively expensive in a large company. Consequently, contested elections are rare, although internet communication may reduce costs. Proposals for companies to cover the costs of dissident shareholders wanting to nominate their own candidates have been around for many years. The Scott Report[1] (2004) from the Committee on Capital Markets Regulation called for 'majority voting' in which directors are elected with a majority of votes cast and for shareholders to put forward candidates for the board of directors by simply having their names added to the company's nomination proxy form. The US Securities and Exchange Commission (SEC) has tried to make it easier for shareholders to nominate their own candidates, but implementation has been delayed by pressure from business groups and directors, arguing that companies are protecting their shareholders from vested interests such as trades unions, hedge funds, and single-issue lobbyists who might want to have their representatives on the board. Attempts to force companies to change through class-action lawsuits on behalf of the shareholders, notably by Bob Monks, the founder of Institutional Shareholder Services,[2] also failed.

The European Union introduced the Shareholder Rights Directive in 2009, which aimed to encourage effective shareholder control in EU listed companies. Member states were required to incorporate the Directive into their national law. The United Kingdom, for example, passed the Companies (Shareholder Rights) Regulations[3] in 2009, which amended the Companies Act 2006 regarding resolutions, voting, and calling meetings. The use of electronic means of shareholder voting, the appointment of proxies, and the use of websites to communicate with shareholders were covered. Holders of 5% of the voting shares can now require the directors to call a shareholders' general meeting (previously it was 10%). A simple majority is all that is needed to remove a director or, indeed, the entire board.

The right of shareholders to have questions answered at shareholders' general meetings was also codified. The company must answer any questions relating to the business put by a member, unless it can be shown that it is not in the interests of the company, for example because it would mean disclosing confidential information, against the good order of the meeting, or that the question has already been answered on the company's website. Shareholders also acquired a new right to have matters included on the agenda of the annual general meeting if they hold 5% of the voting shares or have the support of 100 members entitled to vote. The company must bear the cost of circulating such requisitioned resolutions.

The EU also tried to rule that companies in all member states should apply the principle of 'one share, one vote', but failed to obtain agreement. Opposition came from countries such as Sweden, which permit dual-class shares, with different voting rights Even the United Nations has principles for responsible investment.

---

[1] Chaired by Harvard University Law School Professor Hal S. Scott.
[2] See www.issgovernance.com
[3] Guidance on the implementation of the Shareholder Rights Directive can be found online at www.icsa.org.uk

Corporate governance in action 4.1   Protecting minority shareholders' rights in Hong Kong

A Hong Kong-based company, which produced and marketed artificial Christmas trees, was listed on the Hong Kong Stock Exchange. The board proposed the sale of almost all of its business to parties linked with the majority shareholders, through a management buyout. A group of minority shareholders felt that the sale price was unreasonably low and tried to block the deal. Hong Kong is a common law country with well-established principles and a regulatory mechanism for the protection of minority shareholders from domination by majority shareholders, with the rights of minority shareholders codified in the Hong Kong Companies Ordinance (2014). However, in the event, the authorities decided that the rights of the minority shareholders had been met.

But some parts of the world have moved a long way away from the original notion of shareholder democracy. In the original limited-liability model, the company was in effect the shareholders acting together in a properly convened meeting. They could select the directors, influence the company direction, and agree directors' remuneration, termination, and severance pay. Some commentators call this 'shareholder democracy'. But today, in companies with many shareholders, these rights cannot be exercised. Many companies have attempted to improve communication with shareholders. But real shareholder democracy, in large companies with many and diverse shareholders, has not yet proved feasible.

Shareholder stewardship and activism

Advocates of shareholder democracy believe that with the rights of share ownership should come corporate governance responsibilities. Shareholders, particularly institutional shareholders, they argue, have a duty to act as watchdogs over corporate activities and possible excesses. Such shareholder stewardship sounds desirable, for example challenging excessive director remuneration, opposing schemes to protect the company and the incumbent directors from predators, and highlighting unsatisfactory performance. Indeed, some corporate governance codes call for such a commitment.

Shareholder pressure has been shown to be effective: in 2006, the CEO of Home Depot in the United States, Bob Nardelli, nicknamed 'Home Despot', was ousted; Hewlett-Packard had to amend its poison pill protection against predators; and McGraw Hill and other companies had to eliminate 'staggered boards', in which a third of the directors were elected every year, in favour of a system that forced every director to stand for election each year, thus making the replacement of the entire board easier.

But shareholder activists can also leave the company in a worse position than before. With control, activist shareholders are able to dictate the direction of the company for their own advantage. In underperforming companies, they can press management to sell corporate assets, cut costs leading to redundancies, or divest subsidiaries at a profit. The intention of such activism is short-term, trying to engineer a rise in the share price before selling out at a profit. Although such activities are damaging to the incumbent board and may disadvantage long-term investors, advocates argue that the market for control provides a desirable force for change and that all shareholders benefit from a rising share price.

The need to differentiate between shareholders with a short-term profit-orientated inter-est in a company and genuine long-term investors has been recognized. An advisory commit-tee in the Netherlands suggested loyalty bonuses, such as higher dividends, for those holding their shares for four years. In the United Kingdom, Lord Myners, a government adviser, has suggested that share voting rights should be related to the time for which the shares have been held. Another suggestion is that investors who bought their shares after the announcement of a takeover bid should not be able to vote their shares on that issue. The argument behind such proposals is that those who hold their shares for the long term are likely to behave as owners, concerned about shareholder stewardship, rather than as short-term speculators, benefiting from movements in share prices.

However, an unintended consequence of changes to tax law and corporate regulation in the United Kingdom has been a shift from a longer-term owners market to a shorter-term traders market. In the past, institutional investors owned up to 80% of the shares in the London market. Pension funds and insurance companies have been heavy sellers of equi-ties to overseas institutional investors, hedge funds, and sovereign wealth funds. Now, they account for less than 30% of UK share ownership. At this point, their leverage over compa-nies' behaviour begins to wane. However, some foreign hedge funds can be supportive of well-managed companies, continuously keeping in touch, whereas some British investment houses have taken their compliance responsibilities too lightly, voting only for management resolutions.

Should shareholders in listed companies, particularly institutional investors, take a more proactive role in corporate governance? The danger for the investor might be that they become locked into the company, unable, as the Americans say, 'to do the Wall Street walk' or, as the English say, 'to vote with their feet'. But if an institution is tracking a stock exchange index, it may need to hold shares in specific companies anyway: better that it engages with the board to improve long-term shareholder value. As Anne Simpson, of the US CalPers Fund, has commented: 'Shareholders do need more say in the way that boards are run, but that should be balanced out by shareholders being held responsible for their actions—just as directors are. International discussion about shareholder rights and responsibilities needs to be taken forward on a balanced ticket.'

In 2010, the UK Financial Reporting Council (FRC) introduced an institutional investor Stewardship Code (see Corporate governance in action 4.2). The Stewardship Code should be applied on a 'comply or explain' basis. In other words reporting how the principles of the Code have been applied or explaining why if they have not been met. The FRC emphasizes that compliance with the Code is not an invitation to manage the affairs of companies or preclude a decision to sell a holding, if this is considered in the best interest of investors.

Corporate governance in action 4.2   The UK Financial Reporting Council (FRC) Stewardship Code

Principle 1

Institutional investors should publicly disclose their policy on how they will discharge their stewardship responsibilities.

The disclosure should include:

- how investee companies will be monitored. In order for monitoring to be effective an active dialogue may, where necessary, need to be entered into with the investee company's board;
- the strategy on intervention;
- internal arrangements, including how stewardship is integrated with the wider investment process;
- the policy on voting and the use made of, if any, proxy voting or other voting advisory service, including information on how they are used; and
- the policy on considering explanations made in relation to the UK Corporate Governance Code.

Principle 2

Institutional investors should have a robust policy on managing conflicts of interest in relation to stewardship and this policy should be publicly disclosed.

An institutional investor's duty is to act in the interests of all clients and/or beneficiaries when considering matters such as engagement and voting.

Conflicts of interest will inevitably arise from time to time, which may include when voting on matters affecting a parent company or client.

Institutional investors should put in place and maintain a policy for managing conflicts of interest.

Principle 3

Institutional investors should monitor their investee companies.

Investee companies should be monitored to determine when it is necessary to enter into an active dialogue with their boards. This monitoring should be regular, and the process clearly communicable and checked periodically for its effectiveness.

As part of this monitoring, institutional investors should:

- seek to satisfy themselves, to the extent possible, that the investee company's board and committee structures are effective, and that independent directors provide adequate oversight, including by meeting the chairman and, where appropriate, other board members;
- maintain a clear audit trail, for example, records of private meetings held with companies, of votes cast, and of reasons for voting against the investee company's management, for abstaining, or for voting with management in a contentious situation; and
- attend the General Meetings of companies in which they have a major holding, where appropriate and practicable.

Institutional investors should consider carefully explanations given for departure from the UK Corporate Governance Code and make reasoned judgements in each case. They should give a timely explanation to the company, in writing where appropriate, and be prepared to enter a dialogue if they do not accept the company's position.

Institutional investors should endeavour to identify problems at an early stage to minimise any loss of shareholder value. If they have concerns they should seek to ensure that the appropriate members of the investee company's board are made aware of them.

Institutional investors may not wish to be made insiders. They will expect investee companies and their advisers to ensure that information that could affect their ability to deal in the shares of the company concerned is not conveyed to them without their agreement.

Principle 4

Institutional investors should establish clear guidelines on when and how they will escalate their activities as a method of protecting and enhancing shareholder value.

Institutional investors should set out the circumstances when they will actively intervene and regularly assess the outcomes of doing so. Intervention should be considered regardless of whether an active or passive investment policy is followed. In addition, being underweight [having a low investment] is not, of itself, a reason for not intervening. Instances when institutional investors may want to intervene include when they have concerns about the company's strategy and performance, its governance, or its approach to the risks arising from social and environmental matters.

Initial discussions should take place on a confidential basis. However, if boards do not respond constructively when institutional investors intervene, then institutional investors will consider whether to escalate their action, for example, by:

- holding additional meetings with management specifically to discuss concerns;
- expressing concerns through the company's advisers;
- meeting with the chairman, senior independent director, or with all independent directors;
- intervening jointly with other institutions on particular issues;
- making a public statement in advance of the AGM or an EGM;
- submitting resolutions at shareholders' meetings; and
- requisitioning an EGM, in some cases proposing to change board membership.

Principle 5

Institutional investors should be willing to act collectively with other investors where appropriate.

At times collaboration with other investors may be the most effective manner in which to engage. Collaborative engagement may be most appropriate at times of significant corporate or wider economic stress, or when the risks posed threaten the ability of the company to continue.

Institutional investors should disclose their policy on collective engagement.

When participating in collective engagement, institutional investors should have due regard to their policies on conflicts of interest and insider information.

Principle 6

Institutional investors should have a clear policy on voting and disclosure of voting activity.

Institutional investors should seek to vote all shares held. They should not automatically support the board.

If they have been unable to reach a satisfactory outcome through active dialogue then they should register an abstention or vote against the resolution. In both instances, it is good practice to inform the company in advance of their intention and the reasons why.

Institutional investors should disclose voting records publicly and if they do not explain why.

Principle 7

Institutional investors should report periodically on their stewardship and voting activities.

Those that act as agents should regularly report to their clients details of how they have discharged their responsibilities. Such reports will be likely to comprise qualitative as well as quantitative information. The particular information reported, including the format in which details of how votes have been cast are presented, should be a matter for agreement between agents and their principals.

Transparency is an important feature of effective stewardship. Institutional investors should not, however, be expected to make disclosures that might be counterproductive. Confidentiality in specific situations may well be crucial to achieving a positive outcome.

Those that act as principals, or represent the interests of the end-investor, should report at least annually to those to whom they are accountable on their policy and its execution.

Those that sign up to this Code should consider obtaining an independent audit opinion on their engagement and voting processes . . . The existence of such assurance certification should be publicly disclosed.

Shareholder information

Most company law and corporate governance codes encourage transparency in corporate matters and require the reporting of specific information. For example, the OECD corporate governance principles call for timely and accurate disclosure of all material matters regarding the company, its financial situation, performance, ownership, and governance. Such transparency requires accurate accounting methods, full and prompt disclosure of information regarding the company, and the disclosure of conflicts of interest that directors or controlling shareholders might have.

Investor relations is a fundamental responsibility of the board of listed companies, one often delegated to the finance director or CFO. The primary vehicles for communication with shareholders and potential shareholders are a company's reports and shareholder members' meetings. Annual reports and, in some jurisdictions, half-yearly or quarterly reports provide the chairman and board with the opportunity to report on company operations, significant developments, and its financial position. Company law and stock exchange listing regulations require the disclosure of specific matters of corporate and financial information. Under the UK Corporate Governance Code (2008), companies also have to explain the company's business model and overall financial strategy, and show that remuneration incentives are compatible with the company's risk profile. Most listed companies now use websites as well as hard-copy reports to convey shareholder information.

Concern has been expressed recently that financial statements have become too complex for many users to understand. A bulletin from the European Financial Reporting Advisory Group and the national standard setting authorities in France, Germany, Italy, and the United Kingdom, in 2014, recognized that some of this complexity arose from increasingly complex transactions, but noted that other possible causes was the increasing complexity of international financial reporting standards.

In the United Kingdom, listed companies are required to present shareholders with an enhanced business review. The board is responsible for reporting on the company's strategy, risk management, and governance procedures. Companies do not need to follow a specific template in their presentation. Their reports should offer an honest and open description of the company's exposure to risk, explain how they are identified, and outline the risk management systems in place. Companies can report operational performance in terms of their key performance indicators against industry benchmarks. The business review should also note any contractual relations that are essential to the business, including key licences to operate, significant financial arrangements, and reliance on dominant sources of supply or crucial customers.

The regulations for holding company meetings are provided by company law and companies' articles of association. Some companies now use road shows, conference calls, webcasts, and other opportunities provided by social media to communicate with shareholders and the public. A few have developed sophisticated online tools that allow readers to build their own reports. Others have realized that regularly updated standing information about the company, its activities, and its personalities can be used to declutter and simplify the annual company report. An online stock exchange announcement by a company can now trigger email alerts, media feeds, and the updating of Facebook, YouTube, and Twitter pages.

Unlike corporate reports, which are a one-way means of communication, these alternative methods provide opportunities for many-way communication, enabling the company to communicate genuinely, listening to its shareholders, the market, and the public, as well as telling them what the company wants them to hear. Shareholder relations becomes shareholder engagement.

Most companies provide more than the minimum information required by the regulations, going beyond mere compliance to voluntary disclosure that enhances the company image. Various annual competitions have been launched to encourage better disclosure, such as the ICSA Hermes Transparency in Governance awards in the United Kingdom and the Hong Kong Institute of CPAs Best Corporate Governance Awards.

There is also potential hazard in disclosing information to shareholders and the market. Insider dealing—that is, buying or selling shares on the basis of information that is not in the public domain—is wrong and a criminal offence in most jurisdictions. Companies need to take care that they do not disclose confidential information to one party that is not available to others. Stock exchange regulations typically require all significant company announcements to be filed with them before being made public.

A relatively new problem for companies in communicating with their shareholders is identifying who they are. Electronic share transfers through nominee accounts can cloak the ultimate beneficiaries. Companies do not know whether the intermediaries have passed on the information they want to give to their ultimate shareholders. Nominee accounts also prevent companies from knowing the scale and composition of their shareholder base. The company law in some jurisdictions has been extended to respond to this issue.

Corporate governance in action 4.3   On the annual accounts of financial institutions

A letter to the UK *Financial Times* following the global financial crisis:

A review of the published annual reports of the banks that have imploded and showered us with toxic debris shows that the accounting sleights of hand of the 1980s have been replaced by a thick, glossy catalogue of useless puffery, where mindless box-ticking compliance and endless committees stupefy the reader with page after page of irrelevant disclosure and really important information such as the CO_2 output of bank branches and details of the water-saving toilet flushing system installed in head office. Of the impending maelstrom, there was not a whisper.

It is time for the regulators, auditors, and companies to put a halt to this farce and return the annual report to its rightful place as a source of meaningful information for investors.

(A former investment banker with Dresdner Kleinwort Wasserstein)

Different types of director

We turn now to the other side of the governance partnership—the company, as represented by its board of directors. The architecture of corporate governance is concerned with the design and style of governance and the way in which its structures match form with function. But before we proceed, we should note that the title 'director' needs to be used with care.

Company law in most jurisdictions refers to 'directors', but does not distinguish between different types of director. In company law, all directors have similar roles and responsibilities. Moreover, any person occupying the position of director may be treated in law as a director, although given another title, such as 'governor'. A director *de jure* has been duly nominated and appointed as a director, in line with the company law. A director *de facto* acts as though he or she is a director, without having been so appointed. Whether a person is a *de facto* director depends on the circumstances, but if so, all of the duties and responsibilities of a director apply. But there are other potentially confusing uses of the title 'director'.

An *executive director* is a member of the board of directors who is also an executive manager of the company. In the wording of our governance and management model introduced in Chapter 2, an executive director is a member of both the board circle and the management triangle. The chief executive officer (CEO), sometimes known as the *managing director* in commonwealth law jurisdictions, is likely to be a member of the board, but does not have to be. Similarly, the chief finance officer (CFO), the chief operating officer (COO), and other members of what is sometimes called the 'C' suite of top executive officers may or may not also be executive directors.

Corporate governance in action 4.4   Lord Caldecote's advice to executive directors

Lord Caldecote, when he was chairman of Delta Metal, called newly appointed executive directors to meet him and reminded them that:

Executive directors have two hats—the hat of the executive and the hat of the director. When you come into my boardroom I want you to be wearing your director's hat. Each director is equally responsible with me for directing the company. You are not there to represent your function or your divisional company. Nor are you there to defend your executive performance or bid for resources for your executive activities. You are there to help me govern the company overall.

By contrast, a *non-executive director* (NED), is a member of the board who does not hold any executive management position in the company. He or she is in the board circle but not the management triangle. In recent years, a further distinction has crystallized between those NEDs who are independent of the company and those who, although not executives of the company, have other connections with it.

The *independent non-executive director* (INED) is a director with no affiliation or other relationship with the company, other than the directorship, that could affect, or be seen to affect, the exercise of objective, independent judgement. The definition of independence in a director is clarified in the codes of good practice in corporate governance. The International Finance Corporation has adopted definitions of independence (see Corporate governance in action 4.5), which list criteria reflected in many codes. In reality, however, independence is a state of mind. As well as meeting the independence criteria, the successful INED needs to be capable of thinking independently, making a stand, and, if necessary, being tough-minded in board-level deliberations.

On the other hand, the affiliated or *connected non-executive director* (CNED) is a director who, although not a member of the management team, does have some relationship with the company. The connection might be that the director is a retired executive of that company, is a close relative of the chairman or the chief executive, was nominated by a large shareholder, is linked with an important supplier, distributor, or customer, is a representative of a major financial partner, or is even a retired partner of the firm's external audit firm. Of course, there may be good reasons for appointing people with such experience or connections to the board, but they should not be seen as independent. The significance of the distinction between INED and CNED will become clear when we see, in codes of good corporate governance practice, that independent directors are needed to serve on various board committees.

The term *outside director* is widely used in the United States and jurisdictions influenced by US practices to refer to a non-executive director, as previously noted. Unless there is evidence

---

Corporate governance in action 4.5   An Independent Director defined by the International Finance Corporation (IFC)

IFC is an international body, which defines an 'independent director' as follows.

The purpose of identifying and appointing independent directors is to ensure that the board includes directors who can effectively exercise their best judgment for the exclusive benefit of the Company, judgment that is not clouded by real or perceived conflicts of interest. IFC expects that in each case where a director is identified as 'independent' the board of directors will affirmatively determine that such director meets the requirements established by the board and is otherwise free of material relations with the Company's management, controllers, or others that might reasonably be expected to interfere with the independent exercise of his/her best judgment for the exclusive interest of the Company . . .

'Independent Director' means a director who is a person who:

1. has not been employed by the Company or its Related Parties in the past five years;

2. is not, and has not been affiliated with a company that is an advisor or consultant to the Company or its Related Parties;

3. is not affiliated with a significant customer or supplier of the Company or its Related Parties;

4. has no personal service contracts with the Company, its Related Parties, or its senior management;

5. is not affiliated with a non-profit organization that receives significant funding from the Company or its Related Parties;

6. is not employed as an executive of another company where any of the Company's executives serve on that company's board of directors;

7. is not a member of the immediate family of an individual who is, or has been during the past five years, employed by the Company or its Related Parties as an executive officer;

8. is not, nor in the past five years has been, affiliated with or employed by a present or former auditor of the Company or of a Related Party; or

9. is not a controlling person of the Company (or member of a group of individuals and/or entities that collectively exercise effective control over the Company) or such person's brother, sister, parent, grandparent, child, cousin, aunt, uncle, nephew or niece or a spouse, widow, in-law, heir, legatee and successor of any of the foregoing (or any trust or similar arrangement of which any such persons or a combination thereof are the sole beneficiaries) or the executor, administrator or personal representative of any Person described in this sub-paragraph who is deceased or legally incompetent, and for the purposes of this definition, a person shall be deemed to be 'affiliated' with a party if such person (i) has a direct or indirect ownership interest in; or (ii) is employed by such party; 'Related Party' shall mean, with respect to the Company, any person or entity that controls, is controlled by, or is under common control with the Company.

(For more information, see www.ifc.org)

to the contrary, outside directors are typically perceived to be independent. Under US federal law,[4] independence requires a director not to accept any consulting, advisory, or other compensatory fee from the company or to be an affiliated person of the company or any of its subsidiaries.

A *shadow director* is a person who, although not formally a member of a board, is able to exert pressure on the decisions of that board. In many jurisdictions, a shadow director can be held liable as though a legally appointed director of the company.

The constitutions of some companies allow for the appointment of *alternate directors*, a person who can take the place of another director if that director cannot attend meetings. Alternate directors are often named for directors who live in different countries and cannot

Corporate governance in action 4.6   Shadow directors identified

When the company law in Hong Kong was changed to require the regular publication of individual directors' remuneration, a number of prominent directors resigned. Many of them held major shareholdings in successful family businesses, which had been listed, and wanted to preserve the secrecy of their personal finances. However, where it was apparent that the board continued to be strongly influenced by their thinking, they could be recognized as shadow directors, and held responsible as though they were directors.

[4] The Sarbanes-Oxley Act of 2002, §301.

attend every board meeting. An alternate is a director in his or her own right, not an agent for the director whom he or she is replacing. When acting as a director, the alternate has all of the rights and duties of any other director under company law.

A *nominee director* is a director who has been nominated to the board by a major shareholder or other contractual stakeholder, such as a significant lender, to represent its interests. Nominee directors can find themselves in tricky situations because of their inevitable dual loyalties. As directors, they owe a duty to the company—that is, to all of the shareholders equally. In board deliberations, they should be representing the interests of all shareholders and contractual stakeholders equally, not representing one set of interests alone. Moreover, they may not divulge sensitive information to an outside party. Yet that is precisely why the nominator had the director appointed in the first place.

A *governing director* is a title used mainly in Australia to describe a director with dominant powers in a private company. Although the Australian legislation requires such companies to have two directors, the statutes do not prevent companies from framing their articles of association to give virtually all powers to one person: the governing director.

Company law in some jurisdictions permits the appointment of a *corporate director*—that is, another company, not a human being—as a director. Subject to such law, and a company's own constitutions, those exercising control of the corporate director company have the powers of any other director, but it is the corporate director company that is the director, not the individual exercising that power.

A phrase that is sometimes heard, particularly in Europe, is *worker director*, or *employee director*. Proponents of industrial democracy argue that, since governing a major company requires an informal partnership between labour and capital, employees should participate in corporate governance. In the German supervisory board, one half of the members are chosen under the co-determination laws through the employees' trades' union processes. In the 1970s, the Draft Fifth Directive of the European Economic Community (now the European Union) proposed supervisory boards with employee representation for all large companies in all member states. The British Bullock Report, written in response to the EEC Directive, proposed unitary boards, but including some worker directors. Neither proposal became law. Since then, the company law harmonization process in the European Union has been overtaken by social legislation, including the requirement that all major firms should have a works council through which employees can participate in significant strategic developments and changes in corporate policy.

Finally and significantly, we come to the person who has the title of director, but who is not legally a member of the board at all. Many companies create titles including the word 'director' for senior executives who are not, in fact, members of either the main board or, indeed, the board of a subsidiary company, for example 'director of operations', 'risk and compliance director', or 'director of customer relations'. Such people are sometimes referred to as *associate directors*.

Why do companies give executives an associate director title? There seem to be three basic reasons—prestige, reward, and status. The title 'director' tends to convey a level of standing and respect that some clients, customers, or other authorities dealing with the company expect. Other companies use the title 'director' as a form of reward: in other words, recognition for success. Finally, in some communities, the title 'director' is a mark of distinction, with important social implications.

Associate directors do not have the rights or responsibilities in law of a formal director, unless those dealing with them reasonably believe they are dealing with a member of the board with the authority to speak for the company, in which case the associate director might be held personally responsible.

While discussing the concept of directorship, we should mention *cross-directorships*, which are directorships held by a set of directors in various companies. In the simplest form, director A of company A is made a director of company B, while director B of company B joins the board of company A. Most cross-directorships form more complex networks. Various studies have plotted cross-directors within a network of companies, identifying the key nodes—the directors who wield real power. In some countries, the network of cross-directorships highlights surprising concentrations of power within a relatively small circle of people. The arguments for cross-directorships are, obviously, that the network of linkages brings economic benefits to the companies concerned, and enables the rare talents of experienced and well-connected directors to be more widely available. The counter-argument is that such concentration of power is undesirable because it is not readily transparent and not the focus for accountability. Cross-directorships are typically legal, provided that there is nothing in a company's constitution preventing them and that the companies are not competing, in which case anti-monopoly rules might come into play.

Corporate governance in action 4.7   On Associate Directors

An international insurance broker based in London has a group devoted to writing airline insurance policies. Every member of the senior staff of that group has the title 'executive director'. None of them is a member of the board of directors. The reason for their title is that their airline clients expect to be dealing with a person at director level.

An Australian commodities firm had a long-serving security officer. He began his career as a uniformed guard at the gates. He had been promoted to sergeant, with a smarter uniform, then security officer, with a gold-braided cap, and finally was created 'security director' wearing a suit. Sceptics in the company said that all of this promotion was in lieu of pay increases. The man himself was well pleased. But he was not, legally, a director of the company.

In a major French organization, the title *directeur* was much sought after, even though directors were not members of the board, nor did the title bestow any financial benefit. But *directeurs* were entitled to use the directors' dining room, which boasted superb cuisine, and gave convivial access to members of top management.

Directors' legal duties and rights

Although company law varies in detail from jurisdiction to jurisdiction, the essence of directors' duties are similar. Directors' responsibilities derive from the nature of the joint-stock limited-liability company and are enshrined in statute law, case law, and stock exchange and other regulations. Essentially, directors' duties are twofold:

- a duty of trust—to exercise a fiduciary responsibility to the shareholders;
- a duty of care—to exercise reasonable care, diligence, and skill.

The duty of trust, or fiduciary duty, requires directors to act with integrity, behaving honestly and fairly for the benefit of the shareholders equally, recognizing the interests of any minority shareholders; they should also promote the aims of the company to ensure its success, and act solely within the powers delegated to them in the company's constitution. Directors of companies incorporated in the United States owe a specific fiduciary duty to any minority shareholders. British Commonwealth-based common law (Australia, Canada, Hong Kong, India, New Zealand, Singapore, South Africa, and so on) allows directors to determine the best interests of the whole company, subject to the right of appeal to the courts.

In other words, the primary duty of a director is to act honestly in good faith, giving all shareholders equal, sufficient, and accurate information on all issues affecting their interests. The underlying (and universal) principle is that directors should not treat a company as though it exists for their own personal benefit, unless of course they own all of the shares and, even then, they have to recognize the legal rights of creditors and other stakeholders.

In fulfilling their duty of trust, directors should avoid conflicts of interest, declare an interest in any proposed transaction or arrangement, and should not make a secret profit or take any unapproved benefit from their positions as directors.

The duty of care requires directors to exercise independent judgement with care, skill, and diligence. In earlier days, this duty was not particularly onerous, because courts tended to call for a level of care that could be expected of any reasonable person. In many jurisdictions today, however, courts demand a duty of care that is expected of a person capable of serving as a director. Moreover, that duty of care also takes into account the knowledge, skill, and experience that the director should actually have: if a director is an accountant, lawyer, or engineer, he or she is expected to bring those skills to bear as a director. The standard of professionalism now expected of directors around the world is significantly higher than was expected a few years ago.

Broadly, courts recognize that business decisions involve risk and will not second-guess board-level decisions, taken under normal business circumstances, if they subsequently prove to have been ill-judged. This is frequently referred to as the 'business judgement rule'. Courts can act, however, if negligent or fraudulent behaviour is alleged, or where an apparent abuse of power or suppression of minority shareholders' interests has occurred. For example, courts can give a ruling if it is alleged that the directors have negotiated a contract that is detrimental to the interests of minority shareholders.

Every director is a statutory officer of the company and is bound by the requirements of the company law of the state in which the company is incorporated. A company must, of course, also abide by the laws of all other states in which it operates. Directors can face penalties should the company fail in its legal obligations. In some jurisdictions, company directors may also find themselves exposed under other legislation, such as health and safety laws, environmental protection law, or anti-monopoly rules. A recent legal development in the United Kingdom raises the possibility of directors being charged with corporate manslaughter.

All directors on a unitary board have the same legal duties and potential liabilities. In most unitary-board jurisdictions, company law does not distinguish between executive and non-executive directors. In a two-tier board structure, on the other hand, the responsibilities of the executive board members to run the enterprise are fundamentally different from those of supervisory board members to monitor and supervise the executive board.

There is widespread misunderstanding about the liability of directors. In a limited-liability company, it is the shareholders' liability for the company debts that is limited, not the directors' liability. Directors are not automatically liable for the debts of their company, provided that they have not acted negligently, nor made it appear that they accepted personal liability. In some jurisdictions, a director can be personally liable for the firm's debts if he or she knew that the company was insolvent and allowed it to continue to trade.

Directors can also be charged if they mislead auditors or fail to file various documents with the companies' registry. Most company law jurisdictions provide for the disqualification of directors if they are found unfit to be a director. Causes can include bankruptcy, theft, fraud, and failure to meet the requirements of the companies' legislation, or running a company that has traded while insolvent and without a reasonable chance of paying its creditors.

The board leadership role of the chairman

Although many commentators refer to the 'chairman of the company', the 'company chairman' is in fact chairman of the board of directors, not of the company. Company law has relatively little to say about the specific role of the chairman. It is the company's constitution that determines the way in which the chairman of the board is appointed (typically by a simple decision of the board), the duties of the chairman, and other aspects of the role.

In the past and in some companies today, the chairman does little more than arrange and run directors' meetings. But, in recent years, the chairman's role has taken on a much wider responsibility as the leader of the board team. Not only do chairmen plan and run directors' and shareholders' meetings, they also need to ensure that the induction of new directors, the training and development of existing directors, and the performance evaluation of the board, its committees, and individual directors is sound, that the structure and membership of the board is appropriate, and that the strategic direction of the company is viable.

In many companies, the chairman is an independent non-executive director, serving on a part-time basis. But occasionally the post is described as 'executive chairman' to indicate that the chairman is devoting a substantial part of his or her time to the company, even though the role is separate from that of the chief executive. In any case, the chairman is not a member of management, whereas the chief executive (called 'managing director' in some cases) is an employee of the company and, as we saw in the last chapter, a member of management as well as the board.

The relative roles of chairman and chief executive continue to be among the contentious and unresolved dilemmas in corporate governance. A key question in contemporary corporate governance is whether the chairmanship and chief executive roles should be separate or combined in one person. The view of all of the codes of good practice in corporate governance is that the roles should be separate.

> The roles of chairman and chief executive should not be exercised by the same individual. The division of responsibilities between the chairman and chief executive should be clearly established, set out in writing and agreed by the board.
>
> (Principle A2.1, UK Combined Code on Corporate Governance)

The argument is that separation, providing duality at the top of the company, produces a check-and-balance mechanism, avoids the potential for abuse if power is concentrated in a single person, and enables the chief executive to concentrate on managing the business while the chairman handles the running of the board, relations with shareholders, and other non-contractual stakeholders, such as the government, the regulators, and the media.

Despite the well-honed recommendation around the world that the chairmanship and CEO should be separate, in American listed companies the roles are frequently combined. The arguments in favour of combined roles are that a dynamic enterprise needs just one leader, that spreading leadership duties between two people leads to conflict, and that this is the way in which American companies have been run very successfully for generations. In recent years, however, following a number of dramatic and heavily reported company collapses in the United States, many of them apparently due to the abuse of power by the head of the company, there have been calls from institutional investors for the roles to be separated. Not surprisingly, these views have been resisted by many incumbents of the combined position, because separation would erode some of their power. Such views are often supported by their outside directors, because many of them hold similar combined roles in their own companies. Interestingly, however, in the most dramatic collapse of all—Enron—the roles *were* separated.

There is no doubt that, where the roles of chairman and CEO are separated, the relationship between the chairman and the CEO is particularly important. Where it works well, as Sir Adrian Cadbury explains in his book on chairmanship, it can be a subtle, productive, and personally rewarding relationship. Where it fails, it can lead to major corporate problems and considerable personal stress.

This raises a related contentious issue: should a retiring CEO be reappointed as chairman of the company's board? Those in favour point out the years of experience, knowledge, and connections that the retiring top executive can bring to the board as its chair—experience that would otherwise be lost. Those questioning the move point out potential difficulties for the new CEO. It is a rare person, having been a successful CEO, who can pass on the executive decision-making reins to a new CEO without interfering in the day-to-day running of the business. Some codes of good practice in corporate governance oppose the retiring CEO becoming chairman in that company.

The corporate officers

The officers of a company are defined by the company laws of each jurisdiction. Typically, they include all of the directors and the company secretary, who might also be a director. In some countries, the term embraces officers who may not be on the board, such as the general manager, the treasurer, the comptroller, and the general counsel (Canada Business Corporations Act).

Company law stipulates the duties of the company officers. In the United Kingdom, these duties were previously defined by case law, but the Companies Act 2006 confirmed that company directors are responsible for ensuring that their companies are well managed, for promoting their success, and for benefiting the shareholders. The Act further confirmed that directors also have responsibilities to the company's employees, its trading partners, and the state. Company law, too, lays down penalties for failure to carry out these duties.

The company secretary has a formal role in corporate governance. In most jurisdictions, the company secretary is responsible for maintaining the records required by the law, such as the register of members, filing annual returns to the companies' registrar, and notifying changes to the company's registered address. Despite the title, the company secretary is a legal office of considerable importance, not a secretarial, clerical function. In the United States, the role is usually referred to as the *corporate secretary* and filled by the company's general counsel—that is, by the in-house lawyer.

The Cadbury Report (1992) emphasizes the significance of the job:

> The company secretary has a key role to play in ensuring that board procedures are both followed and regularly reviewed. The chairman and the board will look to the company secretary for guidance on what their responsibilities are under the rules and regulations to which they are subject and on how those responsibilities should be discharged. All directors should have access to the advice and services of the company secretary and should recognize that the chairman is entitled to the strong support of the company secretary in ensuring the effective functioning of the board.

Company law in most jurisdictions requires all companies to have a company secretary. In the United Kingdom, public companies must have one, who must hold a recognized legal, accountancy, or company secretarial qualification. But, unlike most other countries, in the United Kingdom private companies need not have a company secretary unless the members so require. In some countries, Australia for example, and public companies in the United Kingdom, the company secretary must be a real person, but elsewhere the purely legal function can be delegated to a specialist company or an outside agent such as the company's lawyer, but not auditor. In Hong Kong, for example, under the Companies Ordinance, every company must have a company secretary but the secretary may be an employee of the company or an agent providing services to the company. The company secretary may be a director, but need not be. But under the Listing Rules of the Hong Kong Stock Exchange, a listed company must have a secretary who is a person (not another company) ordinarily resident in Hong Kong. An exception is made in the case of mainland China companies listed in Hong Kong, but incorporated in the People's Republic of China.

Case studies

 Case study 4.1   Foreign and Colonial Asset Management plc

In February 2011, Edward Bramson, aged 59, founder of the US-based group Sherborne Investors and a veteran corporate raider, had reason to be pleased. His six-month battle for control of London-based F&C Asset Management plc (F&C) had succeeded. The shareholders voted convincingly for the removal of the existing chairman, Nick MacAndrew, and another independent board member, while electing Bramson and two of his nominees to the board.

F&C was a diversified investment management group, which could trace its origins to the launch of the Foreign & Colonial Investment Trust in 1868. The Group managed over £100 billion of assets for insurance clients, institutional investors, wealth managers, and private individuals, and operated from offices in eleven countries. While many asset managers are owned by financial services conglomerates, such as banks or insurance companies, F&C was an independent group, listed on the London Stock Exchange and a constituent of the FTSE 250 Index.

When Sherborne Investors GP, LLC acquired 5% of F&C in August 2010, paying £15.6 million, the share price jumped. Bramson had a history of corporate acquisitions. In 2003, he took over the chair of 4Imprint, a UK-based producer of promotional products. The shares rose from 42p to 110p in two years. In 2005, he gained control of Elementis, a UK-listed global speciality chemicals company, improving results to a near 150% return. The following year, he ousted the chairman of Spirent Communications plc, a leading communications technology company, and became executive chairman. By 2010, the share price had increased from 44p to 125p. But not all of his interventions had been successful. In 2007, he took control of Nautilus International, the share price of which subsequently dropped 80%.

The battle for control of F&C had been bitter. The incumbent board had called Bramson an 'interloper who was trying to hijack the fruits of the management'. Bramson claimed that the company was poorly managed and had excessive administrative staff, and he accused the board of buying overpriced assets.

At the shareholders' extraordinary general meeting in February 2011, a few small shareholders raised questions, claiming that they had been left in the dark: 'What were Bramson's plans for the company? There seemed to be little or no strategy.' Although called on to speak, Bramson was reticent. Not once did he attempt to outline his plans for the company he was intent on controlling. Calling for a poll vote, chairman MacAndrew was clear: 'The board believes you should vote against all of the Sherborne resolutions.' But the meeting showed its discontent with the incumbent team, with 70% voting to remove chairman MacAndrew and independent non-executive director Brian Larcombe, and to appoint Edward Bramson, Ian Brindle, and Derham O'Neill as directors. Sherborne held 18% of the shares. Institutional investors, led by Aviva Investors, which held nearly 9%, decided that Bramson was a risk worth taking.

Bramson had taken control. He subsequently said that he intended to run F&C as non-executive chairman from Sherborne's New York offices for a few months. He hoped that the existing chief executive Alain Grisay would stay in post. Although Grisay, a French-speaking Belgian, had been a leading figure in the management's opposition, Bransom said 'we have had a friendly and constructive conversation'.

After the meeting, Bramson said:

Sherborne welcomes the result of today's vote. The new directors are grateful for the support shown by shareholders and very much look forward to working with our new board colleagues to bring a fresh perspective to the Company's strategic direction, to the benefit of all shareholders, clients, and staff.

Grisay commented:

Shareholders have spoken clearly and we respect their decision. I look forward to working with all my board colleagues to ensure the continuing success of the business. Throughout this process our staff have remained focused on our clients. With the uncertainty around the general meeting now behind us, my priority is to ensure that we continue to deliver strong investment performance and the high quality service our clients have come to expect of F&C.

And Keith Bedell-Pearce, the remaining senior independent director of F&C, said:

The executive and non-executive directors who continue in office will work constructively with the newly elected directors in the best interests of F&C and its stakeholders. On behalf of all at F&C, I should like to thank Nick MacAndrew and Brian Larcombe for their highly valued contributions to the development of the business.

Discussion questions

1. Why did the institutional investors in F&C support Bransom's bid for power?

2. Some authorities believe that corporate raiders like Sherborne Investors should be required by law to hold their shares for a given period, say two years, before being able to table resolutions at shareholder meetings. What do you think?

3. Bransom asked the CEO Grisay to stay in post after the boardroom coup, despite Grisay's significant role in defending the company against him. Why was this, do you think?

 Case study 4.2   Enron—a classic corporate governance case

The merger of Houston Natural Gas and InterNorth in 1985 created a new Texas energy company called Enron. In 1989, Enron began trading in commodities—buying and selling wholesale contracts in energy. By 2000, turnover was growing at a fantastic rate, from US$40 billion in 1999 to $101 billion in 2000, with the increased revenues coming from the broking of energy commodities. The rapid rate of growth suggested a dynamic company and Enron's share price rocketed. Top executives reaped large rewards from their share options. The company's bankers, who received substantial fees from the company, also employed analysts who encouraged others to invest in Enron. But the cash flow statement included an unusual item: 'other operating activities $1.1 billion'. The accounts for 2000 were the last Enron was to publish.

The chief executive of Enron, Joseph Skilling, believed that old asset-based businesses would be dominated by trading enterprises such as Enron making markets for their output. Enron was credited with 'aggressive earnings management'. To support its growth, hundreds of special purpose entities (SPEs) were created. These were separate partnerships that traded with Enron, with names such as Cayman, Condor and Raptor, Jedi and Chewco, often based in tax havens. Enron marked long-term energy supply contracts with these SPEs at market prices, taking the profit in its own accounts immediately. The SPEs also provided lucrative fees for Enron top executives. Further, they gave the appearance that Enron had hedged its financial exposures with third parties, whereas the third parties were, in fact, contingent liabilities on Enron. The contemporary American accounting standards (GAAP) did not require such SPEs to be consolidated with partners' group accounts, so billions of dollars were kept off Enron's balance sheet.

In 2000, Enron had $100 billion in annual revenues and was valued by the stock market at nearly $80 billion. It was ranked seventh in *Fortune*'s list of the largest US firms. Enron then had three principal divisions, with over 3,500 subsidiaries: Enron Global Services, owning physical assets such as power stations and pipelines; Enron Energy Services, providing management and outsourcing services; and Enron Wholesale Services, the commodities and trading business. Enron was the largest trader in the energy market created by the deregulation of energy in the United States.

The company had many admirers. As the authors of the book *The War for Talent* (2001, Harvard Business School Press) wrote, 'few companies will be able to achieve the excitement extravaganza that Enron has in its remarkable business transformation, but many could apply some of the principles'.

Enron's auditor was Arthur Andersen, whose audit and consultancy fees from Enron were running at around $52 million a year. Enron also employed several former Andersen partners as senior financial executives. In February 2001, partners of Andersen discussed dropping their client because of Enron's accounting policies, including accounting for the SPEs and the apparent conflicts of interest by Enron's chief financial officer, Andrew Fastow, who had set up and was benefiting from the SPEs.

In August 2001, Skilling resigned 'for personal reasons'. Kenneth Lay, the chairman, took over executive control. Lay was a close friend of US President George W. Bush and was his adviser on energy matters. His name had been mentioned as a future US Energy Secretary. In 2000, Lay made £123 million from the exercise of share options in Enron.

A week after Skilling resigned, Chung Wu, a broker with UBS Paine Webber US (a subsidiary of Swiss bank UBS) emailed his clients advising them to sell Enron. He was sacked and escorted out of his office. The same day Lay sold $4 million of his own Enron shares, while telling employees of his high priority to restore investor confidence, which 'should result in a higher share price'. Other UBS analysts were still recommending a 'strong buy' on Enron. UBS Paine Webber received substantial brokerage fees from administering the Enron employee stock option programme. Lord Wakeham, a former UK cabinet minister, was a director of Enron and chairman of its nominating committee. Wakeham, who was also a chartered accountant and chairman of the British Press Complaints Council, was paid an annual consultancy fee of $50,000 by Enron, plus a $4,600 month retainer and $1,250 attendance fee each meeting.

A warning about the company's accounting techniques was given to Lay in mid-2001 by Sherron Watkins, an Enron executive, who wrote: 'I am nervous that we will implode in a wave of accounting scandals.' She also advised Andersen about potential problems. In October 2001 a crisis developed when the company revised its earlier financial statements revealing massive losses due to hedging risks taken as energy prices fell, which had wiped out $600 million of profits. An SEC investigation into this restatement of profits for the past five years revealed massive, complex derivative positions and the transactions between Enron and the SPEs. Debts were understated by $2.6 billion. Fastow was alleged to have received more than $30 million for his management of the partnerships. Eventually, he was indicted with 78 counts involving the complex financial schemes that produced phantom profits, enriched him, and doomed the company. He claimed that he did not believe he had committed any crimes.

The FBI began an investigation into possible fraud at Enron three months later, by which time files had been shredded. In a subsequent criminal trial, Andersen was found guilty of destroying key documents, as part of an effort to impede an official inquiry into the energy company's collapse. Lawsuits against Andersen followed. The Enron employees' pension fund sued for $1 billion, plus the return of $1 million per week fees, seeing the firm as its best chance of recovering some of the $80 billion lost in the Enron debacle. Many Enron employees held their retirement plans in Enron stock: some had lost their entire retirement savings. The Labour Department alleged that Enron illegally prohibited employees from selling company stock in their '401k' retirement plans as the share price fell. The Andersen firm subsequently collapsed, with partners around the world joining other 'big four' firms.

In November 2001, Fastow was fired. Standard and Poor's, the credit rating agency, downgraded Enron stock to junk bond status, triggering interest rate penalties and other clauses. Merger negotiations with Dynergy, which might have saved Enron, failed.

Enron filed for Chapter 11 bankruptcy in December 2001. This was the largest corporate collapse in US history up until then: Worldcom was to surpass it. The New York Stock Exchange suspended Enron shares. John Clifford Baxter, a vice chairman of Enron until his resignation in May 2001, was found shot dead. He had been one of the first to see the problems at Enron and had heated arguments about the accounting for off-balance-sheet financing, which he found unacceptable. Two outside directors, Herbert Weinokur and Robert Jaedicke, members of the Enron audit committee, claimed that the board was either not informed or was deceived about deals involving the SPEs.

Early in 2002, Duncan, the former lead partner on Enron's audit, who had allegedly shredded Enron files and been fired by Andersen, co-operated with the Justice Department's criminal indictment, becoming whistle-blower and pleading guilty to charges that he did 'knowingly, intentionally and corruptly persuade and attempt to persuade Andersen partners and employees to shred documents'.

Why did it happen? Three fundamental reasons can be suggested: Enron switched strategy from energy supplier to energy trader, effectively becoming a financial institution with an increased risk profile; Enron's financial strategy hid corporate debt and exaggerated performance; US accounting standards permitted the off-balance-sheet treatment of the SPEs.

What are the implications of the Enron case? First, important questions are raised about corporate governance in the United States, including the roles of the CEO and board of directors, and the issue of duality; the independence of outside, non-executive directors; the functions and membership of the audit committee; and the oversight role of institutional shareholders. Second, issues of regulation in American financial markets arise, including the regulation of industrial companies with financial trading arms like Enron, the responsibilities of the independent credit-rating agencies, the regulation of US pension funds, and the effect on capital markets worldwide. Third, there are implications for accounting standards, particularly the accounting for off-balance-sheet SPEs, the regulation of the US accounting profession, and the convergence of American GAAPs with international accounting standards. Last, auditing issues include auditor independence, auditors' right to undertake non-audit work for audit clients, the rotation of audit partners, audit firms or government involvement in audit, and the need for a cooling-off period before an auditor joins the staff of a client company.

Some British banks were caught in the Enron net. Andrew Fastow, the former CFO, produced an insider account of how the banks had helped to prop up the house of cards. Three British bankers were extradited to the United States to stand trial, under legislation designed to repatriate terrorists.

Jeffrey Skilling, the former CEO, was sentenced to twenty-four years' imprisonment and to pay $45 million restitution in October 2006. Claiming innocence, he appealed. Kenneth Lay (aged 64) was also found guilty, but died of a heart attack in July 2006, protesting his innocence and believing he would be exonerated.

Although Enron collapsed with such dramatic results, international corporate governance guidelines had in fact been followed, with a separate chairman and CEO, an audit committee chaired by a leading independent accounting academic, and a raft of eminent INEDs. However, the subsequent collapse owes more to abuse of their power by top management and their ambivalent attitudes towards honest and balanced corporate governance.

Discussion questions for Enron

1. Should a company's bankers, who receive substantial fees from that company, also employ analysts who encourage investment in that company?

2. Enron's external auditor, Arthur Andersen, earned substantial consultancy fees from the company as well as the audit fee. Enron also employed several former Andersen partners as senior financial executives. Could the external auditors really be considered independent?

3. What does this case suggest about corporate governance in the United States at the time? Consider the roles of the CEO and board of directors, the duality of chairman and CEO; the independence of outside, non-executive directors; the functions and membership of the audit committee; and the oversight role of institutional shareholders.

References and further reading

Barker, Roger M. (2010) *Corporate Governance, Competition and Political Parties.* Oxford University Press, Oxford.

Bishop, Matthew and Michael Green (2011) *The Road from Ruin.* A. & C. Black, London.

Cadbury, Sir Adrian (1992) *The Financial Aspects of Corporate Governance: A Report of the Committee on Corporate Governance.* Gee & Co., London.

Cadbury, Sir Adrian (2002) *Corporate Governance and Chairmanship: A Personal View.* Oxford University Press, New York.

Carter, Colin B. (2004) *Back to the Drawing Board: Designing Corporate Boards for a Complex World.* Harvard Business School Press, Boston. MA.

LeBlanc, Richard and James Gillies (2005) *Inside the Boardroom.* Wiley, Canada.

Lorsch, Jay W. and Elizabeth McIver (1989) *Pawns or Potentates: The Reality of America's Corporate Boards.* Harvard Business School Press, Boston, MA.

Mallin, Chris (2006) *International Corporate Governance* (cases), Edward Elgar Publishing, Cheltenham.

Projects and exercises

1. In the 2013 Excellence in Governance Awards, run by the UK Institute of Chartered Secretaries, the award for the Best Sustainability and Stakeholder Disclosure among FTSE 100 companies was won by Unilever plc. The judges noted that:

   Sustainability is presented from the outset as key to Unilever's strategy, with excellent recognition that value creation for shareholders comes from prioritising the interests of its key stakeholders. From the start, the chairman discusses the integration of the Sustainable Living Plan, and the CEO's introduction actively paints the company's past and future success in the company's sustainability initiatives, with its importance to the strategy clearly laid out. Sustainability KPIs are presented alongside financial ones. The overarching strategy and the sustainability goal that underpins it are clearly laid out, with the business model identifying the Sustainable Living Plan as the company's differentiator and driver of success.

   Antofagasta plc, Aviva plc, and Johnson Matthey plc were short-listed. Access their annual reports. Compare their disclosures with that of another listed company of your choice. How do the reports compare?

2. Research the work on worker (or employee) directors. The UK Bullock Report on worker directors (1977) might provide a useful starting point. What are the arguments for and against the concept?

3. You have been retained by the chairman/chief executive of a company, which is about to be floated on the stock market through an IPO. He is opposed to the advice he has received from his financial advisers that the roles of the chairman and chief executive should be separated. Prepare a report or PowerPoint presentation for him.

Self-test questions

1. What determines shareholder rights?
2. Can shareholders get involved in the day-to-day management of the company or inspect the company financial records?

3. In public companies in the European Union, can members raise questions at the AGM? Do shareholders have a right to put an item on the agenda of the AGM?

4. Under the UK Financial Reporting Council (FRC) Stewardship Code, should institutional investors have a clear policy on voting and disclose their voting activity? Should they vote all of the shares they hold?

5. What distinguishes an independent non-executive director from an affiliated or connected non-executive director?

6. What is an outside director? What is a shadow director?

7. Can people be given the title 'director' without being formally members of a board?

8. Is the chairman legally 'chairman of the company' or 'chairman of the board of directors'?

9. Is it a good idea to appoint a retiring CEO as chairman?

10. Does company law in most jurisdictions distinguish the roles of executive and non-executive directors?

5 The Regulatory Framework

 Learning Outcomes

In which we consider:

- Legislation, regulation, and corporate governance codes
- Corporate regulation in the United States
- Corporate regulation in the United Kingdom
- Corporate regulation in other countries
- Codes from international agencies
- Codes from institutional investors
- Company codes
- Codes for the public and voluntary sectors
- The importance of compliance: corporate governance reports
- Principles or prescription: the governance debate

Legislation, regulation, and corporate governance codes

Being a creation of the law, limited-liability companies depend on company law for their existence, continuity, and winding-up. Company law defines the way in which they are incorporated, how their directors are appointed, and how shareholder relations should be handled, as well as laying down disclosure and filing requirements. Companies must follow the company law of the jurisdiction in which they are incorporated and the laws of other places where they do business. Penalties for failure to obey company law can be heavy on the company, its directors, and its officers, including in many cases both fines and/or prison: in China, the penalty for corruption or other major corporate infractions can be death.

Company laws vary from the highly specific and demanding, as in many US states, the United Kingdom, and most other advanced economies, to the quite undemanding, as in some offshore tax havens. In the United States, as we have seen, companies are incorporated within a state, not federally, and states' company laws vary, which is why many public companies are incorporated in Delaware with its companies legislation, Court of Chancery, and large body of company-friendly case law.

Companies, their directors, and their officers can also find themselves exposed to other legislation, such as health and safety, consumer protection, and environmental standards. In the United Kingdom, a recent development, where lives have been lost, is a potential liability for companies to be charged with manslaughter. Clearly, directors need to ensure that they have the necessary systems and advice to minimize the risk of breaking the law. The company secretary, typically, takes the lead in such matters.

Legislation affecting companies, their directors and managers tends to evolve and expand rapidly: the UK Bribery Act (2010), introduced draconian penalties for acts of bribery, the 2014 Companies Ordinance in Hong Kong brought many new features into company law, the UK Enterprise and Regulatory Reform Act of 2013 produced new legislation on intellectual property, EU directives and regulations covered human rights and environmental sustainability, and in many jurisdictions new corporate reporting was required. Boards need to ensure that such legal requirements are integrated effectively into the internal workings of the company. Companies are, of course, also subject to corporate regulations, which extend and amplify the law; for example, taxation regulations, import/export regulations, and requirements on employee working conditions. Directors and their companies can be liable if found guilty of disobeying or not following the regulations, and again boards should ensure that the necessary safeguards are in place.

Accounting standards, another type of company regulation, apply to the specific jurisdiction in which the company is reporting. Generally accepted accounting principles (GAAP) apply in the United States and some other countries, but there is a trend for countries to converge with the International Financial Reporting Standards (IFRS).

For public companies listed on a stock exchange, there are also the stock exchange's rules that must be followed by listed companies. For example, the New York Stock Exchange (NYSE) Euronext market requires companies to follow an extensive rule book,[1] which was harmonized in 2013. Failure to follow the rules can result in sanctions such as being suspended or ultimately delisted from the exchange.

Company and other relevant law, regulations, accounting standards, and stock exchange listing rules are mandatory: they must be followed if penalties are to be avoided. But in many parts of the world there are also discretionary corporate governance codes, as we will see.

Corporate regulation in the United States

Each state in the United States has its own companies law, each state jealously guarding its own rights. In addition, federal oversight of companies is provided by the Securities and Exchange Commission (SEC), which was set up in 1932–1933, after the stock market crash of 1929 and the Great Depression that followed. The SEC's mission is to protect investors, to maintain fair, orderly, and efficient markets, and to facilitate capital formation. To achieve this protection for investors, the SEC requires public companies to disclose financial and other information that is then publicly available. The SEC oversees the key participants in the securities world, including securities exchanges, securities brokers and dealers, investment advisers, and mutual funds.

Over the years, the SEC developed an extensive corporate governance regime for US listed companies. It was widely believed that US financial regulation would provide a model for the rest of the world. The system seemed to work: companies were well regulated and control was exercised without excessive bureaucracy. The expectation was that the rest of

---

[1] www.euronext.com/regulation/harmonised-rules

the world would gradually converge with this approach to corporate governance. Indeed, some American institutional investors proposed changes to corporate governance practices in Germany, Japan, and other countries to encourage this convergence.

Then came the collapse in 2001 of massive companies such as Enron, WorldCom, Tyco, Waste Management, and the 'big five' auditor Arthur Andersen. The response from the US government was the Sarbanes-Oxley Act of 2002, which added the names of Senator Paul Sarbanes and Representative Michael G. Oxley to the lexicon of global corporate governance.

Known colloquially as SOX or Sarbox, this is probably the most influential piece of companies legislation in the world to date, not least because it emphasized the US belief that the regulation of corporate governance should be under the law, not through discretionary codes.

The Sarbanes-Oxley Act (SOX) required certification of internal auditing, increased financial disclosure, and imposed criminal and civil penalties on directors for non-compliance. It applied to all companies listed in the United States, whether resident in the United States or abroad. All public-traded companies were now required to submit an annual report about their internal accounting controls to the SEC.

Section 302 of the Act mandated a set of internal procedures designed to ensure accurate financial disclosure. Signing officers must certify that they are 'responsible for establishing and maintaining internal controls' and 'have designed such internal controls to ensure that material information relating to the company and its consolidated subsidiaries is made known to such officers by others within those entities, particularly during the period in which the periodic reports are being prepared'. The officers must 'have evaluated the effectiveness of the company's internal controls as of a date within 90 days prior to the report' and 'have presented in the report their conclusions about the effectiveness of their internal controls based on their evaluation as of that date'.

Section 404 required management to produce a report on the company's internal controls as part of the annual report, affirming 'the responsibility of management for establishing and maintaining an adequate internal control structure and procedures for financial reporting'. The report must also 'contain an assessment of the effectiveness of the internal control structure and procedures . . . for financial reporting'. Independent external auditors must also attest to management's internal control assessment, pursuant to the new SEC rules. The section has attracted much criticism, particularly on the unexpectedly high cost of compliance to companies listed in the United States and to companies associated with them (see Case study 5.1).

SOX also established:

- new standards for boards and their audit committees;
- new independence standards for external auditors;
- a new Public Company Accounting Oversight Board (PCAOB), to oversee public accounting firms and to issue accounting standards overseen by the SEC.

The SOX legislation was incorporated into the NYSE's corporate governance rules in 2003 and 2004. SOX undoubtedly focused attention on corporate governance in the United States. In addition to the costs of compliance, SOX brought significant fees to legal and accounting firms, and spawned a new corporate governance advisory and training industry.

Some companies based overseas delisted; others dropped plans to list. More positively, many US companies reported benefits from SOX compliance, including better accountability of individuals, reduced risk of financial fraud, and improved accuracy in financial reports.

Of course, SOX did not prevent the global financial crisis, starting in 2008, in which US companies such as Lehman Brothers failed and American International Group (AIG), Fannie Mae, Freddie Mac and others were bailed out by the US government. The result was further federal legislation. The Dodd-Frank Wall Street Reform and Consumer Protection Act of 2010, called by some SOX 2, was enacted to improve American financial regulation and the governance of the US financial services industry. In the words of Mary L. Schapiro, chairman of the SEC: 'This law creates a new, more effective regulatory structure, fills a host of regulatory gaps, brings greater public transparency and market accountability to the financial system, and gives investors important protections and greater input into corporate governance.'

Some significant non-governmental organizations also contribute to corporate governance practices in the United States, including the Treadway Commission and COSO, the Business Roundtable, the National Association of Corporate Directors, the American Law Institute, and the Council of Institutional Investors.

The Treadway Commission was created in 1985 to consider fraudulent corporate financial reporting. Its first report[2] (1987) led to the creation of the Committee of Sponsoring Organizations (COSO) of the Treadway Commission,[3] a private-sector initiative aiming to encourage executive management and boards towards more effective business activities. COSO is dedicated to guiding executive management and governance entities toward the establishment of more effective, efficient, and ethical business operations on a global basis. It offers frameworks and guidance based on in-depth research, analysis, and best practices, which include:

- *Enterprise Risk Management: Integrated Framework* (2004);
- *Guidance on Monitoring Internal Control Systems* (2009).

The Business Roundtable is an association of chief executive officers of leading US companies comprising nearly a third of the total value of the US stock markets. In 1997, the Roundtable published a statement on corporate governance, followed by Principles of Corporate Governance in 2002, updated in 2005 and 2010. Other publications include:

- *Executive Compensation: Principles and Commentary* (2003 and 2007);
- *The Nominating Process and Corporate Governance Committees: Principles and Commentary* (2004);
- *Guidelines for Shareholder–Director Communications* (2005).

According to its website, the Business Roundtable believes that the United States has the best corporate governance, financial reporting, and securities markets systems in the world.

[2] Report of the National Commission on Fraudulent Financial Reporting (1987).

[3] COSO is supported by: the American Accounting Association; the Institute of Management Accountants; the American Institute of Certified Public Accountants; the Institute of Internal Auditors; the Financial Executives International. See www.coso.org

These systems work because of the adoption of best practices by public companies within a framework of laws and regulations that establish minimum requirements while affording companies the ability to develop individualized practices that are appropriate for them. However, the Business Roundtable also accepts that no one approach is right for all corporations. Each corporation should look to these principles as a guide in developing structures, practices, and processes that are appropriate for it in light of its needs and circumstances.

The Business Roundtable principles[4] are intended to assist corporate boards of directors and management in their individual efforts to implement best practices of corporate governance. However, the Roundtable recommends that should a company's governance practices diverge from common practice, it should consider disclosing the reasons for this and why its practices are appropriate, consistent with its size, industry, culture, and other relevant factors.

First, the paramount duty of the board of directors of a public corporation is to select a chief executive officer and to oversee the CEO and senior management in the competent and ethical operation of the corporation on a day-to-day basis.

Second, it is the responsibility of management, under the oversight of the board, to operate the corporation in an effective and ethical manner to produce long-term value for shareholders. The board of directors, the CEO and senior management should set a 'tone at the top' that establishes a culture of legal compliance and integrity. Directors and management should never put personal interests ahead of or in conflict with the interests of the corporation.

Third, it is the responsibility of management, under the oversight of the board, to develop and implement the corporation's strategic plans, and to identify, evaluate and manage the risks inherent in the corporation's strategy. The board of directors should understand the corporation's strategic plans, the associated risks, and the steps that management is taking to monitor and manage those risks. The board and senior management should agree on the appropriate risk profile for the corporation, and they should be comfortable that the strategic plans are consistent with that risk profile.

Fourth, it is the responsibility of management, under the oversight of the audit committee and the board, to produce financial statements that fairly present the financial condition and results of operations of the corporation and to make the timely disclosures investors need to assess the financial and business soundness and risks of the corporation.

Fifth, it is the responsibility of the board, through its audit committee, to engage an independent accounting firm to audit the financial statements prepared by management and issue an opinion that those statements are fairly stated in accordance with Generally Accepted Accounting Principles, as well as to oversee the corporation's relationship with the outside auditor.

Sixth, it is the responsibility of the board, through its corporate governance committee, to play a leadership role in shaping the corporate governance of the corporation and the composition and leadership of the board. The corporate governance committee should regularly assess the backgrounds, skills and experience of the board and its members and engage in succession planning for the board.

Seventh, it is the responsibility of the board, through its compensation committee, to adopt and oversee the implementation of compensation policies, establish goals for

---

[4] www.businessroundtable.org/resources/business-roundtable-principles-of-corporate-governance-2012

performance-based compensation, and determine the compensation of the CEO and senior management. Compensation policies and goals should be aligned with the corporation's long-term strategy, and they should create incentives to innovate and produce long-term value for shareholders without excessive risk. These policies and the resulting compensation should be communicated clearly to shareholders.

Eighth, it is the responsibility of the corporation to engage with long-term shareholders in a meaningful way on issues and concerns that are of widespread interest to long-term shareholders, with appropriate involvement from the board of directors and management.

Ninth, it is the responsibility of the corporation to deal with its employees, customers, suppliers and other constituencies in a fair and equitable manner and to exemplify the highest standards of corporate citizenship.

These responsibilities and others are critical to the functioning of the modern public corporation and the integrity of the public markets. No law or regulation can be a substitute for the voluntary adherence to these principles by corporate directors and management in a manner that fits the needs of their individual corporations.

Business Roundtable continues to believe that corporate governance should be enhanced through conscientious and forward-looking action by a business community that focuses on generating long-term shareholder value with the highest degree of integrity.

The National Association of Corporate Directors (NACD), founded in 1977, is a national organization for directors. More than 10,000 directors and key executives from public, private, and non-profit companies form a network for director development, strengthening board practices, and influencing opinion on corporate governance issues.

In 2001, a NACD Blue Ribbon Commission published *Director Professionalism*. The report challenged what it believed was the accepted corporate governance paradigm: management is accountable to the board, and the board is accountable to shareholders. In the view of the Commission, 'the board does more than mechanically link those who manage the corporation and those who own it. Rather, as a surrogate for dispersed ownership, the board is at the very centre of corporate governance itself.'

The Commission emphasized the need for director professionalism and believed that such a culture was evolving in boardrooms not only in the United States, but also gradually elsewhere: 'Professionalism places principal reliance on the actions and attitudes of individual board members. Only if each member of the board understands—and all members agree upon—their joint responsibilities as directors, can the entire board truly fulfil its role.'

The American Law Institute (ALI), established in 1923, seeks to clarify American common law. In 2002, the ALI published a set of general principles on corporate governance. This was the Institute's first comprehensive review of company law, and examined the duties and responsibilities of directors and officers of corporations.

Topics covered include the objective and conduct of the business corporation, the structure of the corporation, the duty of care, the duty of fair dealing, the role of directors and shareholders in transactions in control and tender offers, the business judgement rule, and corporate remedies. The business judgement rule is that courts will not intervene even though a board decision is shown to have been wrong, provided that it was made in good faith. Recommendations were also made on sound corporate practices, which are not intended to be legally binding, concerning the composition of the board, the creation, functions, and powers of audit committees, nominating committees, and compensation committees in publicly held corporations.

The review's seven volumes articulate directors' and officers' duty-of-care obligations, and the extent to which directors and officers may rely on other persons in formulating decisions on behalf of the corporation. They also cover the duty imposed upon directors, senior executives, and controlling shareholders to deal fairly with the corporation, particularly when their own interests are involved, such as compensation, connected transactions, and competition with the corporation.

The Council of Institutional Investors (CII) is a non-profit association representing a diverse array of public, pension union, and corporate employees with combined assets that exceed US$3 trillion. In 2002, the CII published a set of corporate governance policies, which suggested goals and guidelines for the effective governance of publicly traded corporations. These policies, which are frequently reviewed and updated, include fundamental core policies that the Council believes should be implemented by all companies, general principles of shareholder rights and board accountability, and other more general position statements on various corporate governance issues.

The Council believes that all publicly traded companies and their shareholders and other constituencies benefit from written, disclosed governance procedures and policies. Although the Council believes that the meaningful oversight a board provides may owe most, on a routine basis, to the quality and commitment of the individuals on that board, policies also play an important governance role. Policies can help an effective board to perform optimally in both routine and difficult times, and policies can help individual directors and shareholders to address problems when they arise.

The Council supports corporate governance initiatives that promote responsible business practices and good corporate citizenship. The Council believes that the promotion, adoption, and effective implementation of guidelines for the responsible conduct of business and business relationships are consistent with the fiduciary responsibility of protecting long-term investment interests.

The following CII corporate governance principles are not binding on either members or companies, but are designed to provide guidelines.

1. All directors should be elected annually by confidential ballots counted by independent tabulators. Rules and practices concerning the casting, counting, and verifying of shareholder votes should be clearly disclosed.

2. At least two-thirds of a corporation's directors should be independent. A director is deemed independent if his or her only non-trivial professional, familial, or financial connection to the corporation, its chairman, CEO, or any other executive officer is his or her directorship.

3. A corporation should disclose information necessary for shareholders to determine whether each director qualifies as independent, whether or not the disclosure is required by state or federal law. Corporations should disclose all financial or business relationships with and payments to directors and their families, and all significant payments to companies, non-profits, foundations, and other organizations where company directors serve as employees, officers, or directors.

4. Companies should have audit, nominating, and compensation committees. All members of these committees should be independent. The board (rather than the CEO) should appoint committee chairs and members. Committees should have the opportunity to select their own service providers. Some regularly scheduled committee meetings should be held with only the committee members (and, if appropriate, the committee's independent consultants) present. The process by which committee members and chairs are selected should be disclosed to shareholders.

5. A majority vote of shareholders should be required to approve major corporate decisions concerning the sale or pledge of corporate assets that would have a material effect on shareholder value.

New York Stock Exchange corporate governance listing standards

NYSE Euronext (NYX) sponsored an independent commission on corporate governance chaired by Larry W. Sonsini, which published its report in 2010. The report outlines some core principles, as follows.

- The board's fundamental objective should be to build long-term sustainable growth in shareholder value for the corporation.

- Successful corporate governance depends upon successful management of the company, because management has the primary responsibility for creating a culture of performance with integrity and ethical behaviour.

- Good corporate governance should be integrated with the company's business strategy and not viewed as simply a compliance obligation.

- Shareholders have a responsibility and long-term economic interest to vote their shares in a reasoned and responsible manner, and should engage in a dialogue with companies in a thoughtful manner.

- While legislation and agency rule-making are important to establish the basic tenets of corporate governance, corporate governance issues are generally best solved through collaboration and market-based reforms.

- A critical component of good governance is transparency, because well-governed companies should ensure that they have appropriate disclosure policies and practices, and investors should also be held to appropriate levels of transparency, including disclosure of derivative or other security ownership on a timely basis.

- The Commission supports the NYSE's listing requirements generally providing for a majority of independent directors, but also believes that companies can have additional non-independent directors so that there is an appropriate range and mix of expertise, diversity, and knowledge on the board.

- The Commission recognizes the influence that proxy advisory firms have on the markets, and believes that it is important that such firms be held to appropriate standards of transparency and accountability.

- The SEC should work with exchanges to ease the burden of proxy voting while encouraging greater participation by individual investors in the proxy-voting process.

The NYSE listed company manual lays down the requirements that listed companies must fulfil to be listed. Section 303A includes a set of corporate governance demands, together with some useful explanatory commentary. The specific requirements are that:

- listed companies must have a majority of independent directors;
- to empower non-management directors to serve as a more effective check on management, the non-management directors of each listed company must meet at regularly scheduled executive sessions without management;
- listed companies must have a nominating/corporate governance committee composed entirely of independent directors;
- the nominating/corporate governance committee must have a written charter;
- listed companies must have a compensation committee composed entirely of independent directors;
- the compensation committee must have a written charter;
- listed companies must have an audit committee that satisfies the requirements of rule 10A-3 under the US Exchange Act of 1934, which defines the rules for audit committees and director independence;
- the audit committee must have a minimum of three members who satisfy the requirements for independence;
- the audit committee must have a written charter;
- shareholders must be given the opportunity to vote on all equity-compensation plans;
- listed companies must adopt and disclose corporate governance guidelines;
- listed companies must adopt and disclose a code of business conduct and ethics for directors, officers, and employees;
- listed companies must have and maintain a publicly accessible website.

Corporate Regulation in the United Kingdom

In the United Kingdom, companies are incorporated at the national level and have to abide by the UK Companies Acts, principally the Companies Act 2006. In 1992, the United Kingdom produced the world's first corporate governance report, which contained a formal corporate governance code. Subsequently, the United Kingdom has published more corporate governance reports than any other country. A more detailed description of each report appears in Appendix 1, but in essence the various UK reports have been as follows.

- The *Cadbury Report* (1992) was produced by a committee chaired by Sir Adrian Cadbury in response to a series of corporate failures in the United Kingdom. It was entitled *The Financial Aspects of Corporate Governance*, and was not intended to be a comprehensive review of the subject, as Sir Adrian subsequently emphasized. The code was discretionary: UK listed companies being required to report that they had complied with the code or, if they had not, explain the reasons. The Report called for:

- the wider use of independent non-executive directors;
- the introduction of an audit committee of the board with a minimum of three non-executive directors, a majority of whom were to be independent;
- the division of responsibilities between the chairman of the board and the chief executive (if the roles were combined in a single person, the board should have a strong independent element);
- the use of a remuneration committee of the board to oversee executive rewards;
- the introduction of a nomination committee with independent directors to propose new board members; and
- adherence to a detailed code of best practice.

It is interesting to note that, despite being written over twenty years ago, this report contained many proposals that remain at the heart of today's corporate governance thinking.

- The *Greenbury Report* (1995) addressed issues of directors' remuneration; then, as now, a matter of concern to directors, the media, and society at large.

The report recommended that:

- the remuneration committees of companies should consist solely of independent non-executive directors;
- the chairman of the remuneration committee should respond to shareholders' questions at the AGM;
- annual reports should include details of all director rewards—naming each director;
- directors' contracts should run for no more than a year to avoid excessive golden handshakes;
- share option schemes for directors should be linked to long-term corporate performance;

- The *Hampel Report* (1998) was a response to a suggestion in the Cadbury and Greenbury reports that a review should be undertaken after a few years' experience. The report argued that:

- good corporate governance needs broad principles not prescriptive rules;
- compliance with sound governance practices, such as the separation of board chairmanship from chief executive, should be flexible and relevant to each company's individual circumstances;
- governance should not be reduced to what the report called a 'box-ticking' exercise;
- the unitary board is totally accepted in the United Kingdom—there is no interest in alternative governance structures or processes such as two-tier boards;

- the board is accountable to the company's shareholders—there is no case for redefining directors' responsibilities to other stakeholder groups;
- self-regulation is the preferred approach to corporate governance—there is no need for more company legislation.

The Hampel Committee consisted mainly of directors of major public companies and their professional advisers. Predictably, it did not criticize contemporary corporate governance practices, nor did it advocate any measures that would further limit directors' power to make unfettered decisions, nor widen the scope of their accountability. In fact, it reduced the force of the original Cadbury proposals by suggesting greater 'flexibility'. It was also strident in its insistence that British companies did not want two-tier boards, and rejected calls for broader accountability to stakeholder groups beyond the shareholders. Taking a shareholder value perspective, the report said that: 'The single overriding objective shared by all listed companies, whatever their size or type of business, is the preservation and the greatest practical enhancement over time of their shareholders' investment.'

The report was also adamant that UK companies did not need any more legislation. Shortly after the report was published, the British government announced a new fundamental review of UK company law.

The Cadbury, Greenbury, and Hampel committees were set up by City of London institutions—that is, by the United Kingdom's financial sector. The codes were essentially voluntary and applied principally to listed companies, although it was suggested that many of the recommendations could be applied to private companies.

- In 1998, the *UK Combined Code* consolidated the Cadbury, Greenbury, and Hampel proposals, and was incorporated into the London Stock Exchange's listing rules. This Combined Code set out standards of good practice on matters such as board composition, director remuneration, accountability, and audit in relation to shareholders. All companies incorporated in the United Kingdom and listed on the main market of the London Stock Exchange were now required to report on how they had applied the principles in the Combined Code in their annual reports to shareholders. In these reports, companies had to confirm that they had complied with the Code's provisions or, if they had not, provide explanations of why not. Although the Code had no legislative basis and enforcement, failure to meet its requirements could lead to delisting from the Exchange. Formal delisting, however, would tend to disadvantage the very shareholders whom the corporate governance codes were designed to protect, so delisting was a last resort (and in fact not used). The Stock Exchange rather tends to rely on informal guidance to companies.

- The *Turnbull Report* (1999 revised 2005) elaborated a call in the Hampel Report for companies to have appropriate internal controls. It set out how directors of UK listed companies should comply with the Combined Code requirements about internal controls, including financial, operational, compliance, and risk management. The report recognized that risk assessment was vital and recommended that reporting on internal controls became an integral part of the corporate governance process. Thus two new dimensions, enterprise risk management and internal management controls, were added to the field of corporate governance.

- The *Myners Report* (2001) addressed the responsibilities of institutional investors. The report suggested that:

  Good corporate governance is essential to all forms of business. It provides checks and balances that ensure that firms are run efficiently and meet the objectives of their owners, whether shareholders or the members of a life mutual. It also has limitations . . . risk is inherent in the conduct of business . . . The recommendations aim to achieve greater accountability by life mutuals to their members . . . This includes measures . . . promoting better internal scrutiny of management by firms' boards as well as the role of the Financial Services Authority (FSA), the UK's financial regulatory body.

- The *Higgs Report* (January 2003) into the role and effectiveness of non-executive directors, unlike previous reports from the City, was commissioned by the UK Chancellor of the Exchequer and Secretary of State for Trade and Industry, and published by the Department of Trade and Industry. The Higgs proposals sharpened the requirements in the previous codes, in particular recommending that in listed companies:

  - at least half the board should comprise independent non-executive directors;
  - all members of the audit and remuneration committees and a majority of the members of the nomination committee should be independent non-executive directors;
  - the role of chief executive should always be completely separate from that of chairman;
  - director recruitment should be rigorous, formal, and transparent;
  - executive directors should not hold more than one non-executive directorship of a FTSE 100 (Financial Times Stock Exchange) company;
  - boards should evaluate the performance of directors and board committees annually, and have a comprehensive induction programme;
  - boards should have a senior independent director to liaise with shareholders.

Some of Higgs' initial proposals were contentious. Among the proposals that were *not* accepted were:

  - a ban on chief executives moving into the chair of their own company;
  - a ban on chairmen heading the nomination committee of their own board;
  - a ban on anyone being chairman of more than one FTSE 100 company;
  - a call for regular meetings between the senior independent director and shareholders.

- The *Smith Report* (2003) looked at the work of the audit committees, a key element in corporate governance concepts. The report called for:

  - a strengthening of the role of the audit committee;
  - all members of the audit committee to be independent;
  - at least one member of the committee to have significant, recent, and relevant financial experience;

- the audit committee should recommend the selection of the external auditor;

- an audit committee report should be included in the annual report to shareholders; and

- the chairman of the audit committee should attend the AGM to answer shareholders' questions.

- The *Tyson Report* (June 2003), commissioned by the UK Department of Trade and Industry, was concerned with the recruitment and development of non-executive directors. Laura Tyson, a US White House adviser and then Dean of the London Business School (LBS), wrote a report, published by LBS, which considered how companies might recruit non-executives from a wider pool of talent following the directive from the Higgs Review for the group to 'describe the profile of relevant skills and experience that make an effective non-executive director with a non-commercial background'. The report called for:

  - more professionalism and transparency in the recruitment of directors;

  - the introduction of director induction and training;

  - the use of a wider catchment area for outside directors, who could be recruited from what the report called the 'marzipan layer' of senior executives—that is, those just below board level—in unlisted companies, as well as consultancies and organizations in the non-commercial sector.

The UK Combined Code was revised in 2003 and again in 2006. In this later edition, the corporate governance requirements were grouped under four headings:

- independence;
- diligence;
- professional development;
- board performance evaluation.

These editions of the Combined Code were published by the Financial Reporting Council (FRC). The FRC is the United Kingdom's independent regulator responsible for promoting high-quality corporate governance and reporting. The FRC, which took over regulatory responsibility from the London Stock Exchange, also oversees the regulatory activities of the actuarial profession and the professional accountancy bodies and operates independent disciplinary arrangements for cases involving accountants and actuaries.

Following the global financial crisis, beginning in 2008, the FRC reviewed the UK Combined Code, and renamed it the *UK Corporate Governance Code* (2010), a name that some commentators felt would have been more appropriate from the start. This Code set out standards of good practice in relation to board leadership and effectiveness, remuneration, accountability, and relations with shareholders. All companies with a listing of shares in the United Kingdom were now required under the Stock Exchange Listing Rules to report on how they have applied the Code in their annual report and accounts.[5] Again, the Code was discretionary,

---

[5] The relevant section of the Listing Rules can be found at: http://fsahandbook.info/FSA/html/handbook/LR/9/8

with companies required to confirm that they have complied with the Code's main principles or, where they had not, to provide an explanation. The Corporate Governance Code was updated in 2012. The Code contains broad principles, plus some more specific provisions. The main principles are as follows.

Section A: Leadership

- Every company should be headed by an effective board [that] is collectively responsible for the long-term success of the company.
- There should be a clear division of responsibilities at the head of the company between the running of the board and the executive responsibility for the running of the company's business. No one individual should have unfettered powers of decision.
- The chairman is responsible for leadership of the board and ensuring its effectiveness on all aspects of its role.
- As part of their role as members of a unitary board, non-executive directors should constructively challenge and help [to] develop proposals on strategy.

Section B: Effectiveness

- The board and its committees should have the appropriate balance of skills, experience, independence and knowledge of the company to enable them to discharge their respective duties and responsibilities effectively.
- There should be a formal, rigorous, and transparent procedure for the appointment of new directors to the board.
- All directors should be able to allocate sufficient time to the company to discharge their responsibilities effectively.
- All directors should receive induction on joining the board and should regularly update and refresh their skills and knowledge.
- The board should be supplied in a timely manner with information in a form and of a quality appropriate to enable it to discharge its duties.
- The board should undertake a formal and rigorous annual evaluation of its own performance and that of its committees and individual directors.
- All directors should be submitted for re-election at regular intervals, subject to continued satisfactory performance.

Section C: Accountability

- The board should present a balanced and understandable assessment of the company's position and prospects.
- The board is responsible for determining the nature and extent of the significant risks it is willing to take in achieving its strategic objectives. The board should maintain sound risk management and internal control systems.

- The board should establish formal and transparent arrangements for considering how [it] should apply the corporate reporting and risk management and internal control principles, and for maintaining an appropriate relationship with the company's auditor.

Section D: Remuneration

- Levels of remuneration should be sufficient to attract, retain and motivate directors of the quality required to run the company successfully, but a company should avoid paying more than is necessary for this purpose. A significant proportion of executive directors' remuneration should be structured so as to link rewards to corporate and individual performance.

- There should be a formal and transparent procedure for developing policy on executive remuneration and for fixing the remuneration packages of individual directors. No director should be involved in deciding his or her own remuneration.

Section E: Relations with shareholders

- There should be a dialogue with shareholders based on the mutual understanding of objectives. The board as a whole has responsibility for ensuring that a satisfactory dialogue with shareholders takes place.

- The board should use the AGM to communicate with investors and to encourage their participation.

The Stewardship Code (2010 revised 2012)

Traditionally, institutional investors have not been closely involved with the companies in which they invested. However, the Financial Reporting Council[6] felt that this passive attitude was inappropriate; institutional investors could improve long-term performance and encourage efficient corporate governance if they were more involved. The Stewardship Code provides a set of principles for the performance of such stewardship responsibilities.

The UK Companies Act 2006

The United Kingdom introduced a revised Companies Act in 2006. This was the largest UK Act ever, with over 1,300 sections. About a third of this was a straightforward restatement of the previous law in clearer and simpler language. However, some new measures were introduced.

- The Act clarified directors' duties for the first time in statute law. Previously, the role and responsibilities of a director had been determined by case law evolving over the years. The new law made clear that directors have to act in the interests of shareholders.

[6] www.frc.org.uk/Our-Work/Codes-Standards/Corporate-governance/UK-Stewardship-Code/UK-Stewardship-Code-statements.aspx

However, significantly, the law also added that, in acting in the shareholders' interests, they must pay regard to the longer-term interests of employees, suppliers, consumers, and the environment.

- The Act encouraged narrative reporting by companies, calling for them to be forward-looking, identifying risks as well as opportunities. Quoted companies have to provide information on environmental matters, employees, and social and community issues, including information on any policies relating to these matters and their effectiveness, plus contractual and other relationships essential to the business, as part of their business review and to the extent necessary for an understanding of the business.

- The Act promoted shareholder involvement in governance by enhancing the powers of proxies and making it easier for indirect investors to be informed and to exercise governance rights in the company. Shareholders were also able to limit the auditors' liability to the company to what is fair and reasonable. The Act also provided powers to require institutional investors to disclose how they used their votes.

- The Act included a new offence for recklessly or knowingly including misleading, false, or deceptive matters in an audit report.

- It enabled auditors to agree a limit on their liability with their audit clients, subject to shareholder approval.

The Act also introduced some measures for private companies, including:

- new model articles of association;
- dropping the need for a company secretary unless the members want one;
- dropping the need for an annual general meeting of shareholders if the shareholders agreed.

The UK Financial Conduct Authority (FCA)

The FCA is a new independent entity that regulates the financial services industry in the United Kingdom, protecting consumers, ensuring the industry is financially secure, and promoting sound competition between providers of financial services. The FCA has rule-making, investigative and enforcement powers, and seeks to reduce financial crime. It is funded by the financial institutions it regulates and governed by a board appointed by the UK Treasury, although it receives no government funding.

British standard for delivering effective governance

Perceived abuses of authority and societal demands for better organizational governance led to the creation of a British Standard, BS13500[7] (2013), which clarified the basic requirements for effective governance in organizations and suggests the fundamentals of good governance.

[7] For details see http://shop.bsigroup.com/ProductDetail/?pid=000000000030228066

Corporate regulation in other countries

The 1992 UK Cadbury Report on corporate governance was first, but other countries at that time were also facing company collapses and inadequate corporate governance, and followed with their own versions of corporate governance codes. Subsequently, almost all economically significant countries published some form of corporate governance code of principles, recommendations, or good practice.

Appendix 1 summarizes the current state of corporate governance codes around the world. The texts of many of these reports are available on the Internet, the majority with an English version. In some countries, ideas on corporate governance can be seen to be evolving. Also notice how the originators of the reports vary, being set up by governments, securities regulating authorities, stock exchanges, or sometimes by an independent business federation, or the local institute of directors.

In this chapter, we will consider examples of codes from three countries, Australia, France, and South Africa, before reviewing worldwide corporate governance codes from the Organisation of Economic Co-operation and Development (OECD) and the Commonwealth, as well as codes from institutional investors and companies themselves. In the next chapter, we will contrast the underlying corporate governance models used in different parts of the world, and in Chapter 12 we will review approaches to corporate governance in Japan, Brazil, Russia, India, mainland China, Hong Kong, and other South East Asian countries, as well as the Middle East and North Africa, where Islamic requirements play a part.

Australia

Australia has been a pioneer in corporate governance developments. The first Australian report on corporate governance was written by Fred Hilmer in 1992. He called it *Strictly Boardroom*, after the film about competitive ballroom dancing *Strictly Ballroom*, in which compliance with the rules had stifled initiative and creativity. This, Hilmer argued, would happen to companies if corporate governance focused only on compliance. 'The Board's key role is to ensure that the board is continuously and effectively striving for above-average performance, taking account of risk,' he wrote, adding that 'this is not to deny the board's additional role with respect to shareholder protection.'

Following the Hilmer work, Henry Bosch wrote a study in 1995 and a corporate governance report for the public sector was produced in 1997. Then, in March 2003, the Australian Stock Exchange (ASX) published *Principles of Good Corporate Governance and Best Practice Recommendations*, which provided a non-prescriptive and principles-based framework for corporate governance for listed companies. As the ASX explained: 'Where a listed company considers that a particular recommendation(s) is not appropriate for its circumstances, it has the flexibility under the "if not, why not?" approach not to adopt the recommendation, provided an explanation is given in their annual reports.' The Principles suggested that a company should take the following actions.

1. Lay solid foundations for management and oversight

Recognize and publish the respective roles and responsibilities of board and management.

2. Structure the board to add value

Have a board of an effective composition, size and commitment to adequately discharge its responsibilities and duties.

3. Promote ethical and responsible decision-making
4. Safeguard integrity in financial reporting
5. Make timely and balanced disclosure of all material matters concerning the company.
6. Respect the rights of shareholders
7. Recognise and manage risk
8. Encourage enhanced board and management performance
9. Remunerate fairly and responsibly: define its relationship to corporate and individual performance
10. Recognise the legitimate interests of all legitimate stakeholders

The ASX Council recognized the evolving nature of corporate governance thinking. Accordingly, the Council is committed to reviewing emerging corporate governance issues to ensure that the principles remain relevant and appropriate to the Australian business community. During 2010, three significant independent reviews were undertaken at the request of the Australian government, leading to further proposed changes to the *Principles and Recommendations* including: the need to promote board diversity with a gender diversity policy and measurable objectives; new policies on blackout periods during which directors with insider information are not allowed to deal in company shares they own; arranging for widely accessible shareholder briefings with electronic communications, including web casting and Internet and conference calls; and highlighting the potential for conflict of interest if executive directors serve on the remuneration committee.

The Australian Securities and Investments Commission updated its policies in 2014, reflecting legislative changes since 1999, including a policy requiring holders of more than 20% of a listed company to indicate any takeover intentions. (Corporate governance in action 5.1 contains the definition of director independence from the Australian Stock Exchange Principles.)

Canada

The Canadian Saucier Report took a performance-orientated view of the nature of corporate governance, arguing that:

> The objective of good governance is to promote strong, viable, and competitive corporations. A committed, cohesive and effective board adds value, first and foremost, by selecting the right CEO for the company. Beyond this, the board contributes to value by
>
> ● setting the broad parameters within which the management team operates, including in particular, strategic planning and risk management, and communication policy;

Corporate governance in action 5.1   Australian Stock Exchange Principles
Definition of director independence

The 2003 ASX Principles usefully defined director independence in ways that are more detailed than the original notion of 'having no interests that could affect objective judgement'.

An independent director is a non-executive director (i.e. is not a member of management) and:

1. is not a substantial shareholder of the company or an officer of, or otherwise associated directly with, a substantial shareholder of the company

2. within the last three years has not been employed in an executive capacity by the company or another group member, or been a director after ceasing to hold any such employment

3. within the last three years has not been a principal of a material professional adviser or a material consultant to the company or another group member, or an employee materially associated with the service provided

4. is not a material supplier or customer of the company or other group member, or an officer of or otherwise associated directly or indirectly with a material supplier or customer

5. has no material contractual relationship with the company or another group member other than as a director of the company

6. has not served on the board for a period which could, or could reasonably be perceived to, materially interfere with the director's ability to act in the best interests of the company

7. is free from any interest and any business or other relationship which could, or could reasonably be perceived to, materially interfere with the director's ability to act in the best interests of the company.

- coaching the CEO and the management team;
- monitoring and assessing performance, setting the CEO's compensation, taking remedial action where warranted, including replacing the CEO; and
- providing assurance to shareholders and stakeholders about the integrity of the corporation 's reported financial performance.

France

Employers' organizations in France have published three discretionary corporate governance codes. The Viénot I Report (1995) called for the wider use of independent directors and board committees, a reduction in cross-directorships, and a limitation to the number of directorships a person could hold. The Viénot II Report (1999) called for the separation of the chairmanship from the CEO, emphasized the notion of director independence, and suggested more information on director remuneration. The Bouton Report (2002) was written following Enron (see Appendix 2) and financial problems facing the French Vivendi company. The report called for more director independence, formal audit, remuneration, and nomination committees, board evaluation, and better financial information. The three codes are addressed to French listed companies and are recognized by France's Financial

Markets Authority as best practice. Although non-mandatory, listed companies are encouraged to declare whether they have complied with the codes on a 'comply or explain why not' basis.

In the opinion of Gérard Charreaux and Peter Wirtz:[8]

> . . . during the last twenty years, the governance of French listed companies has undergone profound transformations, and its formal characteristics appear henceforth close to those of the Anglo-Saxon counterpart. However, even if foreign institutional investors have become its major actors, French capitalism still has a strong family character, and transactions on the market for corporate control are rarely hostile. One may add that minority shareholder activism is modest, even though their rights have been strengthened. The overall evolution of French corporate governance towards Anglo-Saxon standards encounters some resistance, especially due to the characteristics of the market for executives of the main companies, which favour certain elite circles.

Many CEOs of French listed companies graduated from the same top schools (*grandes écoles*). However, the legal context of corporate governance in France is unlike that of the Anglo-Saxon countries. Being based on civil law, with the judiciary strictly administering statutes enacted by the legislature, there is no room for the evolution of practice through the application of successive cases, as in Anglo-Saxon case law jurisdictions. Consequently, the letter of the law is important in France. The basic company law (1966) was supplemented by new laws on economic regulation (2001), financial market security (2003), and laws to bring confidence and modernization to the economy (2005). Reflecting the French voluntary codes of best corporate governance practice and recognizing European directives, the new laws regulate the financial system including companies, and call for strengthening the power of the board, with more transparency on director remuneration, the separation of chairman and CEO, and better protection for minority shareholders.

The legal basis of French corporate governance is composed of three basic laws: the law on new economic regulations (2001—*loi sur les nouvelles régulations économiques*); the law on financial security (2003—*loi de sécurité financière*); and the law on trust and modernization of the economy (2005—*loi pour la confiance et la modernisation de l'économie*).

South Africa

Like Australia, South Africa has also been a pioneer in corporate governance. The first report on corporate governance in South Africa was published in 1994. Sponsored by the Institute of Directors in South Africa and written by a committee chaired by Senior Counsel Mervyn King, the report became known as King I, to be followed by two further reports.

King I (1994) took a more integrated approach to corporate governance than other governance reports at that time, looking at social, ethical, and environmental implications, as well as regulatory and financial. This was the first report to adopt this participative and inclusive stakeholder approach to corporate governance, recognizing that, in the modern world, companies are part of the society and environment in which they exist, but emphasizing that the company was, nevertheless, accountable to its shareholders. In other words, the report

---

[8] Charreaux, Gérard and Peter Wirtz (2006) *Gouvernance des Entreprises: Nouvelles Perspectives*. Recherche d'enterprise series, Economica Press, Paris.

took a stakeholder responsible, rather than shareholder accountable, view of corporate governance. In the words of the report:

> Boards have to consider not only the regulatory aspect, but also industry and market standards, industry reputation, the investigative media, and the attitudes of customers, suppliers, consumers, employees, investors, and communities (local, national, and international), ethical pressure groups, public opinion, public confidence, political opinion, etc. In governance terms, (directors are) *accountable* at common law and by statute to the company, but *responsible* to the stakeholders identified as relevant to the business of the company. The stakeholder concept of being accountable to all legitimate stakeholders must be rejected for the simple reason that to ask boards to be accountable to everyone would result in their being accountable to no one. The modern approach is for a board to identify the company's stakeholders, including its shareowners, and to agree policies as to how the relationship with those stakeholders should be advanced and managed in the interests of the company.

King II (2002), the second King report,[9] extended the view that companies need to take an inclusive view of their relationships, not only with shareholders, but also other groups in society affected by their activities. The need was to move, the report said, from the single bottom line, emphasizing economic success, to the triple bottom line, recognizing the economic,

Corporate governance in action 5.2   King's seven characteristics of good corporate governance

1. Discipline

Corporate discipline is a commitment by a company's senior management to adhere to behaviour that is universally recognized and accepted to be correct and proper.

2. Transparency

Transparency is the ease with which an outsider is able to make meaningful analysis of a company's actions, its economic fundamentals, and the non-financial aspects pertinent to that business.

3. Independence

Independence is the extent to which mechanisms have been put in place to minimize or avoid potential conflicts of interest that may exist, such as dominance by a strong chief executive or large shareowner.

4. Accountability

Individuals or groups in a company, who make decisions and take actions on specific issues, need to be accountable for their decisions and actions. Mechanisms must exist and be effective to allow for accountability.

5. Responsibility

With regard to management, responsibility pertains to behaviour that allows for corrective action and for penalizing mismanagement.

[9] See www.ecgi.org/codes/documents/executive_summary.pdf

6. Fairness

The systems that exist within the company must be balanced in taking into account all those that have an interest in the company and its future. The rights of various groups have to be acknowledged and respected. For example, minority shareowner interests must receive equal consideration to those of the dominant shareowner(s).

7. Social responsibility

A well-managed company will be aware of, and respond to, social issues, placing a high priority on ethical standards. A good corporate citizen is increasingly seen as one that is non-discriminatory, non-exploitative, and responsible with regard to environmental and human rights issues.

environmental, and social aspects of a company's activities simultaneously. The King reports developed seven characteristics of good governance (see Corporate governance in action 5.2) and introduced the concept of corporate citizenship:

> Emerging economies have been driven by entrepreneurs, who take business risks and initiatives. With successful companies come successful economies. Without satisfactory levels of profitability in a company, not only will investors who cannot earn an acceptable return on their investment look to alternative opportunities, but it is unlikely that the other stakeholders will have an enduring interest in the company. The key challenge for good corporate citizenship is to seek an appropriate balance between enterprise (performance) and constraints (conformance), so taking into account the expectations of shareowners for reasonable capital growth and the responsibility concerning the interests of other stakeholders in the company.

KING III (2008) provided a code for responsible investing by institutional investors in South Africa, guidelines for corporate governance in the public sector, and useful governance guidelines and pro forma reports for companies.

Codes from international agencies

In addition to the codes developed by specific countries, some international agencies have published principles and guidelines for the guidance of countries. In particular, the Principles from the Organisation for Economic Co-operation and Development (OECD), the Guidelines from the Commonwealth of Nations, and the Statements on Global Corporate Governance Principles from the International Corporate Governance Network (ICGN) have been influential.

The OECD[10] *Principles of Corporate Governance* provided the basis for the development of good corporate governance in countries. Against the backdrop of major corporate scandals

---

[10] The original member countries of the OECD were Austria, Belgium, Canada, Denmark, France, Germany, Greece, Iceland, Ireland, Italy, Luxembourg, the Netherlands, Norway, Portugal, Spain, Sweden, Switzerland, Turkey, the United Kingdom, and the United States. The following countries became members subsequently in the years shown: Japan (1964), Finland (1969), Australia (1971), New Zealand (1973), Mexico (1994), the Czech Republic (1995), Hungary (1996), Poland (1996), Korea (1996), and the Slovak Republic (2000). The Commission of the European Communities also takes part in the work of the OECD.

around the world, the OECD Council of Ministers recognized the need to update the principles regularly.

The original OECD principles applied to companies with a large and diverse shareholder base. But most companies around the world are dominated by controlling shareholders—individuals, financial institutions, or other companies. Subsequently the Principles were revised to apply to such situations and have become the most widely used benchmark for corporate governance around the world, assisting governments in their efforts to evaluate and improve the legal, international, and regulatory framework for corporate governance in their own countries, and providing guidance to stock exchanges, investors, and corporations.

A summary of the OECD Principles follows.

I. Ensuring the basis for an effective corporate governance framework

The corporate governance framework should promote transparent and efficient markets, be consistent with the rule of law and clearly articulate the division of responsibilities among different supervisory, regulatory, and enforcement authorities.

II. The rights of shareholders and key ownership functions

The corporate governance framework should protect and facilitate the exercise of shareholders' rights.

III. The equitable treatment of shareholders

The corporate governance framework should ensure the equitable treatment of shareholders, including minority and foreign shareholders. All shareholders should have the opportunity to obtain redress for violation of their rights.

IV. The role of stakeholders in corporate governance

The corporate governance framework should recognize the rights of stakeholders established by law or through mutual agreements and encourage active co-operation between the corporations and stakeholders in creating wealth, jobs, and sustainability of financially sound enterprises.

V. Disclosure and transparency

The corporate governance framework should ensure that timely and accurate disclosure is made on all material matters regarding the corporation, including the financial situation, performance, ownership, and governance of the company.

VI. The responsibilities of the board

The corporate governance framework should ensure the strategic guidance of the company, the effective monitoring of management by the board, and the board's accountability to the company and the shareholders.

The *World Bank and the International Monetary Fund (IMF)*, with the support of the United Nations, are charged with assessing the application of the OECD Principles of Corporate Governance in specific countries and have a programme that *Reports on the Observance of Standards and Codes (ROSC)*. The goal of the ROSC initiative is to identify weaknesses that may contribute to a country's economic and financial vulnerability. Each ROSC corporate governance assessment of a country reviews that country's legal and regulatory framework, as well as the practices and compliance of its listed firms, and assesses the framework relative to internationally accepted benchmarks. The OECD produced Guidelines on the Corporate Governance of State-owned Enterprises later in 2004.

Following the global financial crisis of 2007 onwards, the OECD concluded that:

> Corporate governance weaknesses in remuneration, risk management, board practices, and the exercise of shareholder rights had played an important role in the development of the financial crisis and that such weaknesses extended to companies more generally. Nevertheless, the Group found that the OECD Principles of Corporate Governance provided a good basis on which adequately to address the key concerns that have been raised and that there was no urgent need for them to be revised. A more urgent challenge for the Steering Group was to encourage and support the implementation of already agreed international and national standards, including the OECD Principles of Corporate Governance.

The OECD report recognized that executive remuneration was an important public policy issue and concluded that it was important for boards first to set the strategic goals of the company and its associated risk appetite, establishing and overseeing enterprise-wide risk management systems. They would then be in a position to establish a compensation structure that reflected its strategy and risk profile. The report also argued that tests of the technical and professional competence of board members, including general governance and risk management skills, could be subject to a 'fit and proper person test' by a supervisor.

The Commonwealth[11] *Association for Corporate Governance* (CACG) Guidelines—Principles for Corporate Governance in the Commonwealth (1999)—are aimed at the level of individual companies. The executive summary of fifteen Principles of Corporate Governance in the Commonwealth Code suggests that a board should:

Principle 1—exercise leadership, enterprise, integrity and judgment in directing the corporation so as to achieve continuing prosperity for the corporation and to act in the best interests of the business enterprise in a manner based on transparency, accountability and responsibility;

Principle 2—ensure that through a managed and effective process, board appointments are made that provide a mix of proficient directors, each of whom is able to add value and to bring independent judgment to bear on the decision-making process;

Principle 3—determine the corporation's purpose and values, determine the strategy to achieve its purpose and to implement its values in order to ensure that it survives and thrives, and ensure that procedures and practices are in place that protect the corporation's assets and reputation;

Principle 4—monitor and evaluate the implementation of strategies, policies, management performance criteria and business plans;

Principle 5—ensure that the corporation complies with all relevant laws, regulations and codes of best business practice;

[11] The Commonwealth, sometimes referred to as the Commonwealth of Nations and formerly as the British Commonwealth, is a network of 54 independent countries, most of which were formerly members of the British Empire.

Principle 6—ensure that the corporation communicates with shareholders and other stakeholders effectively;

Principle 7—serve the legitimate interest of the shareholders of the corporation and account to them fully;

Principle 8—identify the corporation's internal and external stakeholders and agree a policy, or policies, determining how the corporation should relate to them;

Principle 9—ensure that no person or a block of persons has unfettered power and that there is an appropriate balance of power and authority on the board which is, *inter alia*, usually reflected by separating the roles of the chief executive officer and Chairman, and by having a balance between executive and non-executive directors;

Principle 10—regularly review processes and procedures to ensure the effectiveness of its internal systems of control, so that its decision-making capability and the accuracy of its reporting and financial results are maintained at a high level at all times;

Principle 11—regularly assess its performance and effectiveness as a whole, and that of the individual directors, including the chief executive officer;

Principle 12—appoint the chief executive officer and at least participate in the appointment of senior management, ensure the motivation and protection of intellectual capital intrinsic to the corporation, ensure that there is adequate training in the corporation for management and employees, and a succession plan for senior management;

Principle 13—ensure that all technology and systems used in the corporation are adequate to properly run the business and for it to remain a meaningful competitor;

Principle 14—identify key risk areas and key performance indicators of the business enterprise and monitor these factors;

Principle 15—ensure annually that the corporation will continue as a going concern for its next fiscal year.

The *International Corporate Governance Network* was founded in 1995 at the instigation of major institutional investors, major companies, financial intermediaries, academics, and other parties interested in the development of global corporate governance practices. One of its objectives is to facilitate international dialogue on issues of concern to investors. The ICGN welcomed the OECD Principles. Statements from the ICGN have included those on Global Corporate Governance Principles (1999 and 2005), on Enhancing Corporate Governance for Banking Organizations (1999), Principles for Institutional Investor Responsibilities (2013), and a statement and guidance on Gender Diversity on Boards (2013).

Codes from institutional investors

Some major institutional investors and organizations representing them have also produced corporate governance guidance or codes. The California Public Employees' Retirement System (CalPers), the largest US public pension fund with assets over US$200 billion and members numbering 1.6 million, was a pioneer. CalPers published Global Corporate

Governance Principles in 1997, and also wrote guidance notes on improvements that it felt were needed in corporate governance in France, Germany, and Japan. In 2010, CalPers published an important corporate governance code, *The Global Principles of Accountable Corporate Governance*,[12] which forms the basis for its involvement with companies and on which it bases its proxy voting decisions. The CalPers Global Principles of Accountable Corporate Governance also provide all listed companies with a detailed and professional corporate governance code. Interestingly, throughout the code, CalPers refers to 'shareowner' rather than 'shareholder', reflecting its belief that equity ownership carries with it active responsibilities and is not merely the passive 'holding' of shares. CalPers' evolving experience of corporate governance is striking:

> CalPERS' Corporate Governance 1 Program is a product of the evolution that only experience and maturity can bring. In its infancy in 1984–1987, corporate governance at CalPERS was solely reactionary: reacting to the anti-takeover actions of corporate managers that struck a dissonant chord with one's sense—as owners of the corporate entity—of accountability and fair play. The late 1980s and early 1990s represented a period in which CalPERS learned a great deal about the 'rules of the game'—how to influence corporate managers, what issues were likely to elicit fellow shareowner support, and where the traditional modes of shareowner/corporation communication were at odds with current reality.
>
> Beginning in 1993, CalPERS turned its focus towards companies considered by virtually every measure to be 'poor' financial performers. By centring its attention and resources in this way, CalPERS could demonstrate very specific and tangible results to those who questioned the value of corporate governance. What have we learned over the years?
>
> - That company managers want to perform well, in both an absolute sense and as compared to their peers
> - That company managers want to adopt long-term strategies and visions, but often do not feel that their shareowners are patient enough
> - All companies—whether governed under a structure of full accountability or not—will inevitably experience both ascents and descents along the path of profitability
>
> We have also learned, and firmly embrace the belief that good corporate governance—that is, accountable corporate governance—means the difference between wallowing for long periods in the depths of the performance cycle, and responding quickly to correct the corporate course.

Notice how much this perspective focuses on the performance aspects of corporate governance rather than on conformance and compliance.

Hermes Fund Managers, a UK multi-specialist asset manager, has also produced a set of corporate governance principles,[13] originally in 2002, updated in 2008 (see Corporate governance in action 5.3 for the principles). While the principles are not well written, they capture the essence of the Hermes approach to the companies in which it invests. Hermes is owned by the BT (British Telecom) Pension Scheme, the United Kingdom's largest funded occupational pension scheme, and manages more than £20 billion on behalf of long-term investors, including pension funds, endowments, and charities.

---

[12] www.calpers-governance.org/docs-sof/principles/2010-5-2-global-principles-of-accountable-corp-gov.pdf

[13] www.acga-asia.org/public/files/(2008)%20Hermes_Principles.pdf

Corporate governance in action 5.3   The Hermes Corporate Governance Principles

Hermes' overriding requirement is that companies be run in the long term interest of shareholders. Companies adhering to this principle will not only benefit their shareholders, but also we would argue, the wider economy in which the company and its shareholders participate. We believe a company run in the long-term interest of its shareholders will need to manage effectively relationships with its employees, suppliers and customers, to behave ethically, and have regard for the environment and society as a whole.

Communication

Principle 1: 'Companies should seek an honest, open and ongoing dialogue with shareholders. They should clearly communicate the plans they are pursuing and the likely financial and wider consequences of those plans. Ideally goals, plans and progress should be discussed in the annual report and accounts.'

Financial

Principle 2: 'Companies should have appropriate measures and systems in place to ensure that they know which activities and competencies contribute most to maximising shareholder value.'
Principle 3: 'Companies should ensure all investment plans have been honestly and critically tested in terms of their ability to deliver long-term shareholder value.'
Principle 4: 'Companies should allocate capital for investment by seeking fully and creatively to exploit opportunities for growth within their core businesses rather than seeking unrelated diversification. 'This is particularly true when considering acquisitive growth.'
Principle 5: 'Companies should have performance evaluation and incentive systems designed cost-effectively to incentivise management to deliver long-term shareholder value.'
Principle 6: 'Companies should have an efficient capital structure which will maximise the long-term cost of capital.'

Strategic

Principle 7: 'Companies should have and continue to develop coherent strategies for each business unit. These should ideally be expressed in terms of market prospects and of the competitive advantage the business has in exploiting these prospects. The company should understand the factors which drive market growth, and the particular strengths which underpin the competitive position.'
Principle 8: 'Companies should be able to explain why they are the "best parent" of the businesses they run. Where they are not best parent they should be developing plans to resolve the issue.'

Social, ethical and environmental

Principle 9: 'Companies should manage effectively relationships with their employees, suppliers, and customers and with others who have a legitimate interest in the company's activities. Companies should behave ethically and have regard for the environment and society as a whole.'
Principle 10: 'Companies should support voluntary and statutory measures which minimise the externalisation of costs to the detriment of society at large.'

Teachers Insurance and Annuity Association-College Retirement Equities Fund (TIAA-CREF) was one of the first institutional investors to produce a policy on corporate governance for companies in which it invested. TIAA-CREF took a leadership role in opposing abusive anti-takeover provisions during the 1970s and 1980s, when the governance movement focused primarily on the protection of shareholder interests in the context of takeovers and contests for control. During the 1990s, the focus moved towards director independence, board diversity, board committee structure, shareholder rights, accounting for options, and executive compensation. Most recently, TIAA-CREF has led the movement to establish majority voting in director elections. In the fifth edition of the TIAA-CREF Policy Statement, the Fund comments that:

> Corporate governance standards and best practices are now recognized as an essential means to protect shareholder rights, ensure management and board accountability and promote maximum performance. Although many of the specific policies in this Statement relate primarily to companies incorporated in the United States, the underlying principles apply to all public companies in which TIAA-CREF invests throughout the world.

A limitation to codes produced by institutional investment funds is that they are necessarily investor-orientated, providing corporate governance decision-makers with valuable indications on shareholder expectations, but not necessarily providing them with the guidance they need to improve board-level effectiveness and to produce better long-term corporate performance. A further limitation is that institutional investor codes to date have been Anglo-Saxon, whereas corporate governance is increasingly culturally dependent. Some companies have complained that the proliferation of corporate governance codes and strategic advice from institutional investors has become counter-productive.

Company codes

We have considered corporate governance codes published at the national level, at the international level by international organizations, and from institutional investors. In 2002, the NYSE required all listed companies to adopt corporate governance guidelines and to post them on their websites, so there are now thousands of examples in the public domain.

Among the first of these companies was General Motors in 1994, following a disastrous performance and board restructuring. Today, the company continues this tradition. On its website, General Motors provides investors with details of its corporate governance policies, provides access to various corporate governance documents, and publishes its corporate governance guidelines (see Corporate governance in action 5.4).

Corporate governance in action 5.4   General Motors
Corporate Governance Guidelines

(Adopted July 10, 2009 Revised November 19, 2013)

The Board of Directors of General Motors Company acting on the recommendation of its Directors and Corporate Governance Committee, has adopted the following Corporate Governance Guidelines to promote the effective functioning of the Board and its committees and to set forth a common set of expectations as to how the Board should perform its functions. These Guidelines are in addition to, and should be interpreted in accordance with, any requirements imposed by federal or Delaware law, the New York Stock Exchange (NYSE), and the Certificate of Incorporation and Bylaws of the Company, each as amended. The Governance Committee periodically reviews these Guidelines in light of evolving circumstances and recommends changes to the Board as appropriate.

Introduction

1) Board Mission and Responsibilities

Selection and Composition of the Board

2) Board Designation Rights under Stockholders Agreement

3) Board Membership Criteria

4) Board Membership Selection

5) Extending the Invitation to a Potential Director to Join the Board

6) Majority Voting in Board Elections

7) Director Orientation and Continuing Education

Board Functioning

8) Selection of the Chairman of the Board and Role of Lead Director

9) Size of the Board

10) Mix of Management and Independent Directors

11) Board Definition of What Constitutes Independence for Directors

12) Former Chief Executive Officer Board Membership

13) Directors Who Change Their Present Job Responsibility

14) Limits on Outside Board Memberships

15) Meeting Attendance

16) Retirement Age and Term Limits

17) Board Compensation

18) Loans to Directors and Executive Officers

19) Stock Ownership by Non-Employee

20) Executive Sessions of Non-Management Directors

21) Access to Outside Advisors

22) Assessing the Board's Performance

23) Ethics and Conflicts of Interest

24) Confidentiality

25) Board Interaction with Stockholders and Other Interested Parties

Board Relationship to Senior Management

26) Regular Attendance of Non-Directors at Board Meetings

27) Board Access to Senior Management

Meeting Procedures

28) Selection of Agenda Items for Board Meetings

29) Board Materials Distributed in Advance

30) Board Presentations

Committee Matters

31) Board Committees

32) Committee Performance Evaluation

33) Assignment and Rotation of Committee Members

34) Frequency and Length of Committee Meetings

35) Committee Agenda

Leadership Development

36) Formal Evaluation of the Chief Executive Officer

37) Succession Planning

38) Management Development

To read the detailed provisions go to: www.gm.com/content/dam/gmcom/COMPANY/Investors/ Corporate_Governance/PDFs/Corporate_Governance_Guidelines.pdf

CalPers,[14] the US institutional investor, circulated the GM code to major public companies and, in the next decade, thousands of US companies adopted corporate governance policies or guidelines.

Finally, it should be noted that codes have also been drawn up for individual directors, particularly non-executive directors.

Codes for the public and voluntary sectors

It is now widely recognized that all corporate entities need to be governed, as well as managed. This applies as much to not-for-profit as to profit-orientated entities. Charities, trusts, mutual societies, sports associations, cultural organizations, public authorities, non-government organizations, and other entities in the public and voluntary sectors all need sound governance. Moreover, many of the governance concepts developed in the commercial, profit-orientated world are equally applicable to the public and voluntary sectors.

Three differences are often found between the not-for-profit and the profit-orientated sectors—their objectives and their governance structures. First, their governing bodies have a variety of names—council, committee, board of governors, for example, and occasionally the board of directors.

Second, organizations in the not-for-profit sector usually have many constituencies to satisfy and, consequently, many objectives and multiple measures of performance, rather than a single bottom line. In a hospital, for example, the governing body needs to satisfy the needs and expectations of patients and their families, the medical staff, administrators, the local community, government, and the health authorities. But, as we have already seen, profit-orientated entities also face an increasing call to move beyond the single profit bottom line

[14] For more information, see www.calpers-governance.org/principles/home

to recognize many stakeholder groups with the triple bottom line, with economic, social, and environmental goals.

The governance of voluntary and community organizations in the United Kingdom is addressed in the report *Good Governance: A Code for the Voluntary and Community Sector.*[15] It was launched in 2005 and updated in 2010. Often referred to as 'The Good Governance Code', it is based on the belief that effective boards in the sector provide good governance and leadership by:

- understanding their role;
- ensuring delivery of organizational purpose;
- working effectively both as individuals and as a team;
- exercising effective control;
- behaving with integrity;
- being open and accountable.

The Code recognizes that such principles do not feature separately, but are an integral part of good practice throughout any community or voluntary sector organization.

Third, in many not-for-profit organizations, the governing body is entirely non-executive.

In small voluntary organizations, the members of the governing body may also provide the management and run the operations. But in larger voluntary organizations, the governing body is often made up of non-paid volunteer members who oversee the work of the paid employees. Frequently, the chief executive attends meetings of the governing body, but is not a voting member.

In 2007, the United Kingdom's Chartered Institute of Public Finance and Accounting (CIPFA) published a framework—Delivering Good Governance in Local Government—updating its 1995 framework of principles and standards of corporate governance for the public services. This framework is intended to be a guide to best practice for public sector authorities in developing their own codes of governance, and for discharging accountability through the publication of an annual governance statement. CIPFA sought to capture the spirit of good governance in such a way that it would enable any public service body to operate in a more open, effective, and publicly acceptable way. Where codes already existed, it was envisaged that the framework would be used as a benchmark against which such codes could be compared and developed further. Where such codes did not exist, it was intended that the framework should encourage their development.

The UK Independent Commission for Good Governance in Public Services, chaired by Sir Alan Langlands, published a Good Governance Standard for Public Services in 2005. The Standard had six primary components. 'Good governance', it said, means:

1. Focusing on the organization's purpose and outcomes for citizens
2. Performing effectively in clearly defined functions and roles
3. Promoting values for the whole organization and demonstrating the values of good governance through behaviour

[15] www.goodgovernancecode.org.uk

4. Taking informed, transparent decisions and managing risk

5. Developing the capacity and capability of the governing body to be effective

6. Engaging stakeholders and making accountability real

In 2005, the UK Institute of Chartered Secretaries and Administrators (ICSA) published a code of governance for the voluntary and community sector, which it updated in October 2010.[16] The latest edition recognizes that: 'Governance is high on the agenda in all sectors—public, private and voluntary. As voluntary and community organisations driven by altruistic values and working for public benefit, we are increasingly expected to demonstrate how well we are governed. Good governance is a vital part of how voluntary and community organisations operate and are held accountable.'

The report develops six basic principles based on the belief that:

An effective board will provide good governance and leadership by

1. understanding their role

2. ensuring delivery of organisational purpose

3. working effectively both as individuals and a team

4. exercising effective control

5. behaving with integrity

6. being open and accountable

In the report, the term 'board' means an organization's governing body, whatever it may be called.

The importance of compliance: corporate governance reports

In the early days, compliance with corporate governance codes was voluntary. Exhortation to follow the spirit of the codes came from financial institutions, the media, directors' professional bodies, and academic commentators. Some institutional investors applied specific pressure. But it was in the boardrooms that decisions were taken on the extent that the relevant code was followed. Then, in many countries, the relevant code was incorporated into the stock exchange listing rules. Conformity with the code became a condition of listing.

In 2002, Jaap Winter, Chairman of the High Level Group of Company Law Experts, presented a report on a modern regulatory framework for company law in the European Union.[17] The report recommended that the European Union should:

- improve the EU framework for corporate governance, specifically through:
  - enhanced corporate governance disclosure requirements;

---

[16] www.icsa.org.uk/assets/files/pdfs/guidance/NFP.Charities/Code%20of%20governance%20full%20version.pdf

[17] http://ec.europa.eu/internal_market/company/docs/modern/report_en.pdf

- a strong and effective role for independent non-executive or supervisory directors, particularly in three areas in which executive directors have conflicts of interests—that is, nomination and remuneration of directors and supervision of the audit of the company's accounts;

- provide an appropriate regime for directors' remuneration, requiring disclosure of the company's remuneration policy and individual directors' remuneration, as well as prior shareholder approval of share and share option schemes in which directors participate, and accounting for the costs of those schemes to the company;

- confirm as a matter of EU law the collective responsibility of directors for financial and key non-financial statements of the company;

- produce an integrated legal framework to facilitate efficient shareholder information, communication, and decision-making on a cross-border basis, using where possible modern technology, in particular the company's website;

- set up a structure to coordinate the corporate governance efforts of member states in the European Union.

In most countries, compliance remained voluntary, with the company required to explain why, if it chose not to follow the code. In other words, companies conformed to the code either by following its requirements or by explaining why they had not. In a growing number of jurisdictions, companies were now required to make a corporate governance report to their members, confirming that they had complied with the corporate governance requirements.

A few companies produce their corporate governance reports as a chore necessary to maintain their stock market listing, and consequently provide the minimum information necessary to confirm compliance with the code. But increasingly companies are seizing the opportunity to build a reputation for professional and good corporate governance standards with their shareholders and the market, providing far more information than is necessary merely to confirm compliance. Companies have seen that the corporate governance report provides an opportunity to elaborate on the way in which the board and its committees work, how the board approaches the business strategy and handles strategic risk. Some companies also promote the company's ethical standards, and its concern for corporate social responsibility and environmental sustainability to all of the stakeholders, including the shareholders.

The responsibility in listed companies for ensuring compliance with these new listing requirements and laws often fell to the company secretary, but in some companies a new management function appeared—the compliance officer. Moreover, given the importance that was now being placed on the new rules, many boards entrusted the new responsibility to their audit committee. Others created a new board compliance or corporate governance committee.

Principles or prescription: the governance debate

Many commentators refer to the 'Anglo-American' approach to corporate governance. They contrast the unitary board, which has both executive and non-executive directors in the Anglo-American common law jurisdictions, with the two-tier, supervisory, and executive boards of the continental European and other civil law countries.

But, in recent years, a schism has emerged within the Anglo-Saxon approach. In the United States, corporate governance has increasingly become enforced by regulation and the rule of law. The US Sarbanes-Oxley Act, which was a response to the collapses of Enron and World-Com, as we have seen, reinforced federal and state demands for corporate governance conformance by law: obey the law or risk prosecution, subject to significant penalties, including imprisonment. China also has adopted legally enforceable corporate governance, as we will see later.

However, in many other countries, self-regulation and voluntary compliance with corporate governance codes is preferred: comply or explain. In the United Kingdom and many other jurisdictions, particularly Commonwealth countries the company law of which has been influenced over the years by UK common law, including Australia, Canada, New Zealand, South Africa, India, Singapore, and Hong Kong, compliance is discretionary. In other words, listed companies conform to voluntary codes of principle and best practice, reporting that they have complied or explaining why they have not. The clear preference in business communities around the world, other than in the United States, is still for voluntary compliance and the avoidance of legislation, as the UK Hampel Report had indicated.

However, recent revisions of companies law in some jurisdictions, including Australia (2006) and the United Kingdom (2006), have clarified directors' duties and thus sharpened legal expectations of corporate governance practices. The 'rule versus principle' dilemma has been amplified by the global financial crisis, which has increased calls for more legally enforceable corporate governance, US-style. The intentions of the European Union are not clear, but voices have been heard calling for less discretion and more legislation.

This fundamental dichotomy—between the rules-based approach and the principles-based approach—goes to the heart of corporate governance philosophy. Some years ago, there was a widespread belief that corporate governance around the world would gradually converge on the American model, not least because the world needed access to American capital. That is no longer the case. The 'principles versus prescription' paradox remains unresolved.

Case studies

 Case study 5.1 China Unicom and SOX

China Unicom is involved in the cellular telephone business in thirty provinces, municipalities, and autonomous regions in China, providing nationwide international and domestic long-distance calls, data and Internet services, and other related telecommunication value-added businesses. It is one of the two major mobile telecommunications operators in the People's Republic of China. In 2007, the company had over 140 million subscribers and was the third largest mobile telecommunication operator in the world, and also operated telecommunications businesses in Hong Kong and the United States.

The company is listed in New York and Hong Kong. The board of directors has fourteen members: the chairman/CEO, seven executive directors, and six non-executive directors (four of whom are identified as independent).

The company's 2005 corporate governance report notes the following about SOX:

Internal Control Systems

(1) Requirements under Section 404 of the Sarbanes-Oxley Act (the 'SOX Act') have been strongly emphasized by the company to comply with the requirements under Section 404 of the SOX Act. The relevant section of the Act requires the management of the issuers in other countries with equity securities listing in the U.S. securities market to issue reports and representations as to the internal control system that may affect its financial statements.

The relevant internal control report shall stress the management's responsibility for establishing and maintaining an adequate and effective internal control structure and procedures. The management shall also assess, as of the year end of the financial statements, the effectiveness of the Company's internal control structure and procedures for financial reporting. The Company's auditor shall also conduct testing and assessment to, and report on, the relevant internal control systems.

In order to enhance its corporate governance standards, as well as fulfilling the requirements under the SOX Act, many initiatives were taken in 2004 with respect to the establishment of an internal control system. A steering committee led by the Company's management was established, and formulated the proposals for the establishment of the internal control system. Through endeavours in practical work, such as perfecting the internal control over the business processes, identifying risk management checkpoints, finalizing on the accountability system for risk management and building up a complete and accurate filing system, a comprehensive risk management mechanism was established, which served effectively to manage the risks arising from all economic activities of the Company. The accomplishment of the Company's business strategies and improvement in efficiency is thus assured . . .

Discussion questions

China Unicom has expressed its commitment to fulfilling the demands of Section 404 to report on internal control systems. The details provided above by China Unicom are impressive. But are you satisfied that all companies reporting under Section 404 are competent? Should these statements be independently audited?

(For more information, see www.chinaunicom.com.hk)

 Case Study 5.2   Marconi

The UK group Marconi plc grew out of GEC, a company built by Lord Weinstock, who bequeathed a set of solid, if unadventurous, manufacturing businesses, with large reserves of cash. On his retirement, Marconi adopted a different strategy—to invest in high-tech enterprises. Within a few years, all of the cash had been spent and the company was over £4 billion in debt. Worse, many of its investments were disasters. In July 2001, the company suspended trading in its shares, warning that profits were likely to halve to around £350 million. The company's share price fell and the chief executive, Lord Simpson, met strong opposition to his proposal that executive share options should be repriced to reflect the fall.

Throughout August 2001, the company refused to comment on rumours that things were much worse. No advice was given to investors, the stock exchange, or the Financial Services Authority.

Then, in September 2001, the scale of the disaster became clear, when a loss of £327 million for the three months to June was announced. Various operating explanations were forthcoming: the downturn in the high-tech market was global; the internal control systems had failed to identify financial problems fast enough; the corporate centre was out of touch with its struggling divisions. The opinion that this was a case of poor business judgement, not of corporate governance, smacked of complacency.

Where was the board during this developing debacle? The case raises questions far beyond strategic and operational mismanagement. The issues go to the heart of the board structure and director competence. The case for non-executive directors argues that their independence allows them to question top management and to make tough-minded calls for change if necessary. Subsequently, some Marconi non-executive directors claimed that they had questioned both the strategic direction and the financial situation of the company, but had not received the necessary information. Nevertheless, all directors have the duty to insist that they have the information necessary to understand and make decisions.

But were the Marconi outside directors truly independent? Lord Simpson of Dunkeld was Marconi's chief executive; he was also a non-executive director of ICI and of the Royal Bank of Scotland, one of Marconi's bankers. Sir Roger Hurn, the chairman of the Marconi board, was also chairman of Prudential Assurance, a major shareholder in Marconi, a non-executive director of ICI, and a non-executive of GlaxoSmithKline (as was fellow director, Derek Botham). The non-executive directors included: Sir Bill Castell, chief executive of Nycam, formerly finance director at ICI; John Mayo, previously finance director of ICI and its associate Zeneca; and Derek Bonham, chairman of Cadbury Schweppes and Imperial Tobacco, who had only recently been appointed to the board.

A board meeting was called to face the situation, which one director described as 'Britain's greatest industrial disaster for decades'. Decisive action was needed. Bonham, as senior non-executive director, took charge. By the end of the meeting, both the chief executive Simpson and the chairman Hurn had been replaced.

Discussion questions

1. Did the personal connections between some of the directors make this a cosy club, its members too close to ask awkward questions, to demand satisfactory answers, and to insist on decisive action?

2. Some non-executive directors claimed that they had questioned both the strategic direction and the financial situation of the company, but had not received the necessary information. What should they have done then?

3. Subsequently, commentators on the Marconi debacle commented that the case pinpointed the dangers of cronyism and cross-directorships. But benefits can come from directors who know each other well and serve on a number of other boards. What do you think?

 Case study 5.3   Southern Cross Healthcare

Philip Scott, who trained as a psychiatric nurse, took over Southern Cross, a small provider of care homes in 2000. Within four years, he had built it, largely through acquisition, into the largest provider of care for the elderly in the United Kingdom. His business model relied on sale and leaseback of the homes to generate funds for expansion. In other words, properties were sold and then leased back to Southern Cross for an agreed rent.

In 2004, Blackstone, a US-based private equity firm, bought Southern Cross for £162 million. Its business model recognized that the UK population was ageing, and that vulnerable old people would need housing and care. Moreover, much of the fee income for such protected accommodation would come from the taxpayer, through state support for the elderly provided by local authorities. This fee income was expected to be guaranteed and to rise with inflation, while economies of scale would reduce running costs. This was a relatively risky model, assuming growing demand and state-supported income that would reflect cost rises.

In 2005, Blackstone acquired NHP, a large nursing home group, merged its operations with Southern Cross, and sold most of its homes, leasing them back to Southern Cross.

In 2006, Blackstone floated Southern Cross on the London Stock Exchange into a bull market. Some 60% of its voting shares are held by institutional investors. Financial institutions and advisers took substantial fees from the flotation. Four of the Blackstone nominee directors cashed in their shares, allegedly making over £35 million. The Blackstone holding was gradually sold producing around £1 billion. Philip Scott, who resigned from the board in 2008, made over £10 million.

In 2010, Southern Cross operated over 750 care homes, with more than 38,000 beds and 44,000 staff, offering residential care homes for the elderly who could no longer care for themselves at home, and nursing care homes with additional levels of medical care for those needing it.

Southern Cross runs into trouble

However, by 2010, Southern Cross was struggling with its cash flow, facing rising rents, rapidly increasing energy and food costs, and reducing fee income as councils reacted to lower government grants and cut their expenditure on care for the aged. With less revenue, the quality of some homes declined, and occupancy levels fell.

In December 2010, the possibility of a takeover was rumoured (*Investors Chronicle*).

The UK government became involved when seven age-concerned organizations complained publicly that increasing pressure on public finances was pushing an already overburdened care system to breaking point. An uncertain future and potential hardship facing 31,000 vulnerable, elderly residents of Southern Cross homes would not be well received by voters.

As can be seen from the summary results below, the company was facing real challenges as it entered 2011.

Year to 30 Sept	Turnover (£m)	Pre-tax profit(£m)	Earnings per share (p)	Dividend per share (p)
2006	611	–17.4	–9.35	1.10
2007	732	3.0	0.96	7.50
2008	889	–22.9	–9.57	3.75
2009	937	–19.8	–11.70	nil
2010	959	–47.4	–19.50	nil

(For more information about the company, see www.schealthcare.co.uk)
(For comments on 2010 financial results, see http://investors.schealthcare.co.uk/uploads/resultspresentation2010.pdf)

Stephen Schwarzman, chairman of Blackstone, defended Blackstone's original financial strategy, claiming that the crisis at Southern Cross was a reflection of the global financial crisis and not his business model. Philip Scott accused the current directors of scaremongering and said they were partly responsible for the decline.

The board in 2011

The board had six members, four men and two women, whose profiles follow.

Ray Miles, 66, non-executive director and chairman, who has spent most of his career in the shipping industry, became a non-executive director of the company in June 2006 and served as the senior independent director until he was appointed chairman on 1 January 2008.

Jamie Buchan, 51, chief executive, was appointed as an executive director of the company on 1 January 2009. Between 2002 and May 2008, Mr Buchan, backed by a Malaysian private fund, led the successful turnaround and subsequent sale of the ExCeL Exhibition and Conference Centre in London.

David Smith, director of finance and support services, joined Southern Cross as group finance manager in 2006, was appointed group financial controller in 2008 and director of finance and support services in September 2010 (replacing Richard Midmer). A chartered accountant, he previously spent ten years with accountants PricewaterhouseCoopers.

Christopher Fisher, 57, senior independent non-executive director, who spent most of his career at Lazard, the investment bank, joined the board in June 2006 and became the senior independent non-executive director in January 2008. He is a partner in Penfida, a firm providing independent financial advice to pension fund trustees, and is also president of the Council of Reading University and a trustee of the Imperial War Museum.

Baroness Morgan of Huyton, 51, became a non-executive director of the company in June 2006. A former teacher, Baroness Morgan worked as a senior aide to the British Prime Minister from 1997 to 2005. In 2001, she was made a peer and served as a Minister in the Cabinet Office. From 2001 to 2005, she was Director of Government Relations, Downing Street, working closely with the Prime Minister.

Nancy Hollendoner, 54, joined the board as non-executive director in January 2008 and is a senior adviser on the healthcare market to Hawkpoint Partners Ltd. She previously worked as an equities analyst specializing in the healthcare market and was employed by UBS Investment Bank between 1996 and 2002.

By mid-2011, Southern Cross had run out of cash and the residents of its homes seemed vulnerable. In May of that year, Southern Cross was locked in negotiations with its landlords, demanding a cut of 30% in current rents and looking for longer-term solutions. In June 2011, it announced 3,000 staff redundancies. By July, failure seemed inevitable, the stock market suspended its shares, and the company tried to return the care homes to their landlords. It was then faced with the prospect of having to pay over half a million pounds to its top executives under contractual 'golden parachute' terms, unless they voluntarily waived those rights.

(See the 2010 annual report online at http://investors.schealthcare.co.uk/uploads/schannualreport2010.pdf—Read and study in particular the chairman and chief executive's statement, the corporate social responsibility report, and the corporate governance report, which includes the reports of the board committees.)

Discussion questions

1. Given the situation that faced the company, do you think the board had an appropriate structure and membership? What changes, if any, would you have recommended?

2. What is your opinion of the corporate governance report? How might it be improved?

3. What is your opinion of the formal evaluation of the board, its committees, and individual directors? (See p. 32 of the report.)

References and further reading

Charreaux, Gérard and Peter Wirtz (2006) *Gouvernance des Entreprises: Nouvelles Perspectives*. Recherche d'enterprise series, Economica Press, Paris.

Chartered Institute of Public Finance and Accountancy (1995) *Corporate Governance: A Framework for Public Service Bodies*. CIPFA, London.

Cornforth, C. J. (2001) 'What makes boards effective? An examination of the relationships between board inputs, structures, processes and effectiveness in non-profit organizations', *Corporate Governance: An International Review*, Vol. 9, No. 3, pp. 217–227.

Cornforth, C. J. and Edwards, C. (1999) 'Board Roles in the Strategic Management of Public Service of Non-profit Organizations: Theory and Practice', *Corporate Governance*, Vol. 7, No. 4, pp. 346–362.

Gordon, Jeffrey N. and Mark J. Roe (2004) *Convergence and Persistence in Corporate Governance*. Cambridge University Press, New York.

Jones, Ian and Michael Pollitt (2004) 'Understanding how Issues in Corporate Governance Develop: Cadbury Report to Higgs Review', *Corporate Governance: An International Review*. Vol. 12, Issue 2.

Lee, Thomas A. (2004) *Financial Reporting and Corporate Governance*. Wiley, Chichester.

Various leading corporate governance lawyers (2013) *The International Comparative Legal Guide to Corporate Governance*. Global Legal Group, London.

Projects and exercises

1. Use the Internet to explore some of the corporate governance codes around the world in Appendix 1. Compare and contrast the codes in countries that you find interesting.

2. Prepare an essay/report/presentation on the 'principles or prescription' corporate governance debate. Do you believe that corporate governance codes will converge on one or the other underlying paradigm?

3. Search for the corporate governance reports of some companies with which you are familiar. How do they compare? Do they go beyond the strict requirements of company law and the corporate governance code?

Self-test questions

1. What were the key recommendations of the first ever code of corporate governance—the Cadbury Code (1992)?

2. What are the requirements of the UK Corporate Governance Code (2010) on professional development and performance evaluation?

3. What is the role of the OECD Principles of Corporate Governance?

4. What do the Hermes Principles have to say about a company's relationships with stakeholders?

5. What does Section 404 of the US Sarbanes-Oxley Act require?

6. What do the Hermes Principles have to say about a company's strategy formulation?

7. How does the SOX Act define an INED?

8. What is the minimum number of members of an audit committee under SOX? What qualifications should they have?

9. Is it necessary for companies covered by the SOX Act to adopt and disclose a code of business conduct and ethics for directors, officers, and employees?

10. What are the responsibilities of the board according to the OECD Principles?

6

Models of Corporate Governance

 Learning Outcomes

In which we consider:

- How context and culture affect corporate governance
- The US rules-based model
- The UK/Commonwealth principles-based model
- The continental European two-tier model
- The Japanese business network model
- The Asian family-based model
- Corporate governance: convergence or differentiation?
- Institutions necessary for successful corporate governance

How context and culture affect corporate governance

We compared unitary boards and two-tier boards in Chapter 2, and in the last chapter we saw conceptually different approaches to corporate governance between the legalistic, rules-based, and the discretionary, principles-based approaches. In this chapter, we widen our search for the basic underlying models of corporate governance around the world. Five broad classifications are identified: the American rules-based model; the UK/Commonwealth principles-based model; the continental European two-tier model; the Japanese stakeholder-orientated network model; and the Asian family-based model. We consider why such differences have occurred, and consider whether corporate governance systems around the world are converging, as some suggest. We will explore corporate governance in the Islamic countries, the *chaebol* in South Korea, and the BRIC nations—Brazil, Russia, India, and China—in a later chapter.

Two primary influences can be suggested for the basic differences in corporate governance around the world: context and culture. Looking first at the context in which corporate governance is practised, we review the implications of different patterns of ownership, alternative markets for corporate control, and different ways of financing corporate entities. Then we consider the cultural influences on corporate governance.

Patterns of ownership

Ownership in listed companies around the world varies, from the highly dispersed to the singularly concentrated. Table 6.1 shows, country by country, the proportion of voting shares held by individuals, institutional investors, banks and government, holding companies, and overseas investors.

Table 6.1 Balance of listed company ownership

Country	Individuals	Institutional investors	Banks and government	Holding company	Foreign
Australia	20%	34%	4%	11%	31%
Canada	15%	38%	8%	14%	25%
France	23%	12%	14%	14%	37%
Germany	17%	15%	17%	39%	12%
Italy	18%	14%	40%	18%	10%
Japan	20%	21%	23%	28%	8%
Sweden	23%	30%	8%	9%	30%
Netherlands	14%	21%	1%	23%	41%
UK	19%	58%	5%	2%	16%
USA	51%	41%	3%	0%	5%

Notice how, in the United States, individuals and institutional investors together account for 92% of the shareholdings and in the United Kingdom 77%, whereas in France it is only 35%. In fact, the dispersed ownership found in UK and US companies is the exception rather than the norm around the world. In Germany, Japan, and the Netherlands, many listed companies are held within corporate groups and their boards find themselves responsible to a holding company. The foreign investors in countries such as the Netherlands (41%) or France (37%) may be an overseas parent company, or the holdings may be dispersed among overseas shareholders.

In a company in which the voting shareholders are highly differentiated—that is, where the shares are held by many dispersed external shareholders as in the United States and the United Kingdom—the directors need to respond to their varied expectations, while recognizing that shareholders can, occasionally, act together. On the other hand, where there is a dominant owner, with the other shareholders being in a minority, the directors need to respond to the expectations of that dominant shareholder, while protecting the rights of the minority. Examples include a listed company that is nevertheless part of a corporate group, a company with a dominant shareholder such as a government or financial institution, or cases in which there is a block of connected shareholders.

Obviously, in the longer term, the pattern of ownership fundamentally affects the ability of a board to exercise power over a company. In a company that has a wide spread of shareholders, a board will have more freedom to act on its own initiative than in one the shares of which are dominated by a single or block of investors. Boards need to be acutely aware of which parties have the potential to influence their decisions. Unfortunately, some commentators on corporate governance fail to make this distinction.

Markets for corporate control

In countries with a high proportion of external investors, as in the United States and the United Kingdom, a board can be faced with a hostile takeover bid and a consequential loss of control. In other words, the market for corporate control is strong. Merger and acquisition activity is likely to be widespread. In countries with a relatively low proportion of external investors, the market for corporate control will be weaker, and merger and acquisition activity less. Hostile takeover bids in British companies have been commonplace for generations: the first contested takeover bid for a German company occurred in the 1990s.

Financing corporate entities

In countries where equity markets are relatively large, with high liquidity and significant turn-over, shareholdings are often widely spread. So boards can wield significant power over their companies, even though ultimate power lies with the voting shareholders. In other countries, however, where stock markets are relatively small, listed companies may rely on non-equity loan capital. In companies that have leveraged their equity capital, with a high loan to equity gearing, ultimate power over the company may be in the hands of the lender through the terms of the loan agreement.

Cultural influences on corporate governance

Intuitively, board-level behaviour differs from culture to culture. Later in this chapter we will see how, around the world, board relationships and activities vary, directors' expectations differ, and individual directors behave differently. So, apparently, corporate governance has a cultural component. Not everyone agrees. David Webb, a Western commentator based in Hong Kong, has written:

> People who defend bad corporate governance on the grounds of Asian values or some cultural difference are talking nonsense. Yes, there is a different structure of ownership; it's somewhat Victorian in that most companies (in Asia) are family-controlled, but had I been around in Victorian times in England I think I would have seen similar bad corporate governance.

The position taken in this book is that cultural differences do exist and that, while they should not be used to defend poor governance practices, failure to appreciate their significance is short-sighted. We will now review the context and culture of corporate governance using the five basic models—US rule-based, UK and Commonwealth principles-based, continental European two-tier based, Japanese stakeholder-orientated networks, and the Asian family-based model

The US rules-based model

In the early days of corporate governance thinking experts tended to write about the Anglo-American (or Anglo-Saxon) unitary board model of corporate governance contrasted with the continental two-tier board model. Indeed, many expected a convergence of corporate governance practices towards the Anglo-American model, but, as we saw, some fundamental differences have appeared between the US rules-based and the UK/Commonwealth principles-based models. So we need to explore each model separately.

The American model reflects corporate governance practices throughout the United States and in other countries influenced by the United States. Companies in the United States are incorporated in individual states and are subject to those states' company law and corporate regulation. Investor protection, auditing requirements, and financial disclosure of public companies, however, are federal responsibilities, predominantly overseen by the US Securities and Exchange Commission (SEC). Company law is based on common law, which is rooted in legislation that evolves with a continually growing body of case law at both the federal and the state levels.

The basic governance model for public companies in the United States is the unitary board, with a predominance of independent outside directors. The SEC and stock exchange listing requirements also call for mandatory audit, nomination, and remuneration committees of the board. In the United States, shareholders have little influence on board membership, other than expressing dissatisfaction by not voting, selling their shares, or resorting to litigation.

In the United States, governance is regulated by legal statute and mandatory rules, which are inherently inflexible. Litigation levels are high. Directors face legal penalties for non-compliance. The 2002 Sarbanes-Oxley Act strengthened this emphasis on governance under penalty of law, with disclosure requirements that proved more expensive and burdensome than expected. The role of the regulators is to ensure that the rules are being obeyed. The American financial markets are the largest and most liquid in the world, but their lead, particularly in initial public offering (IPOs), has been eroded.

Generally accepted accounting principles (GAAP) in America call for compliance with the rules. There are signs that the United States is moving towards international standards.

The UK/Commonwealth principles-based model

The law that recognized the incorporation of the joint-stock, shareholder limited-liability company originated in the United Kingdom in the mid-19th century. Purists might argue that France can claim a slightly earlier form of legal incorporation, but that only granted limited liability to investors who were not involved in managing the company. Membership of the old British Empire, in the later 19th and early 20th centuries, meant that UK company law influenced the development of company law in Australia, Canada, Hong Kong, India, New Zealand, South Africa, Singapore, and indeed throughout what is now known as the Commonwealth.

As in the American model, company law in the UK/Commonwealth model is based on common law, rooted in legislation extended by case law. But, by contrast with the American model, in the United Kingdom and in Commonwealth countries, corporate governance is 'principles-based'. Codes of corporate governance principle or good practice determine board responsibilities, not the rule of law. Companies are required to report that they have followed the governance principles laid down in the codes or to explain why they have not. Consequently, this model is often referred to as the 'comply or explain' approach to corporate governance. Self-regulation is the underlying theme. Compliance is voluntary, with the sanctions being the exposure of corporate governance failings to the market and, ultimately, delisting from the stock exchange. The role of the regulators is to ensure that investors and potential investors have accurate information on which to base their judgements.

Throughout the Commonwealth, corporate governance codes for listed companies, although differing slightly in detail, all call for independent non-executive or outside directors, audit, remuneration, and nomination committees of the board, and high levels of transparency and accountability. The codes also call for a separation between chairman and CEO.

The principles-based versus the rules-based view of governance is also reflected in accounting standards. The UK/Commonwealth countries apply standards that are predominantly based on international accounting standards, which emphasize compliance with principles.

In the United Kingdom, unlike the United States, shareholders with 10% of the voting rights in a public company can force an extraordinary meeting and vote on strategic decisions or the removal of a director. Even though that seldom occurs, the possibility can affect board actions.

In a consultation paper[1] in 2014, the UK Financial Reporting Council proposed some changes to the UK corporate governance code, including:

- greater emphasis to be placed on ensuring that remuneration policies are designed with the long-term success of the company in mind;
- companies to explain when publishing the AGM results how they intend to engage with shareholders when a significant percentage of them have voted against a resolution;
- companies should robustly assess their principle risks and explain how they are being managed and mitigated.

The continental European two-tier model

Company law in continental European countries is typically rules-based. In France, for example, it is based on Napoleonic law, in which required corporate behaviour is determined by legally binding rules and evolves by further legislation, not by the precedents of case-based common law. Judges not juries play the dominant role. In these European countries, finance markets tend to be smaller and less liquid. The market for corporate control is weak. Bank and loan finance is widely used to fund companies, and banks wield more influence on corporate affairs, particularly in Germany. Investors tend to be more concentrated, often with dominant family shareholdings, particularly in France and Italy. As we will explore later, gearing chains of companies are sometimes used to leverage controlling shareholders' investment.

Two-tier boards are required in Germany and Holland and are found in France and Italy. Moreover, in line with the social contract found in many European societies, corporate governance practices frequently have a social component. For example, the co-determination rules in Germany require one half of the supervisory board to represent labour, with employee representative directors elected through the trades unions; the other half, representing capital, elected by the shareholders. Many countries in the European Union also require works councils in which representatives of the employees wield power.

The European company (the *Societas Europaea*), enacted under the rules of the European Union, provides for either Anglo-American or continental European approaches. But, despite

[1] https://www.frc.org.uk/News-and-Events/FRC-Press/Press/2014/April/Consultation-on-the-UK-Corporate-Governance-Code-p.aspx

the political orientation of many European countries towards social democracy and the traditional stakeholder orientation in companies, in recent years some continental European firms have nevertheless lent towards strategies based on the maximization of shareholder value.

Critics of the continental European model of corporate governance argue that the management board is often dominated by top management and lacks the information inputs, advice, and wise counsel that can be provided by outside independent non-executive directors on unitary boards. Other critics question the effectiveness of supervisory boards, their lack of real power, and their ability effectively to control the management board. Some argue that the representative character of the supervisory board produces conflicts of interest.

There was a time when countries that employed the two-tier board believed that this was a superior model to the unitary board. Indeed, at one time, the European Union tried to impose the two-tier model on all companies in member states—a proposal strongly resisted in the unitary board countries. Today, the benefits and limitations of each model are more widely recognized.

The Japanese business network model

Keiretsu are networks of companies in Japan connected through cross-holdings and interlocking directorships. Member companies tend to inter-trade extensively. Frequently, the network includes a financial institution. The classical model of the *keiretsu* reflects the social cohesion within Japanese society, emphasizing unity throughout the organization, non-adversarial relationships, lifetime employment, enterprise unions, personnel policies encouraging commitment, initiation into the corporate family, decision-making by consensus, cross-functional training, and promotion based on loyalty and social compatibility as well as performance. This model is currently under pressure, as we will see, but first let us review this traditional approach to corporate governance in Japan.

In the classical *keiretsu* model, boards of directors tend to be large and are, in effect, the top layers of the management pyramid. People speak of being 'promoted to the board'. The tendency for managers to progress through an organization on tenure rather than performance means that the mediocre can reach board level. A few of the directors might have served with other companies in the *keiretsu* network, and in that sense might be able to represent the interests of suppliers or down-stream agents; others might have been appointed to the company's ranks on retirement from the *keiretsu's* bankers, or even from among the industry's government regulators (known as a *amakaduri*, or 'descent from heaven').

But independent non-executive directors, in the Western sense, would be unusual, although the proportion is increasing. Many Japanese do not see the need for such intervention 'from the outside'. Indeed, they have difficulty in understanding how outside directors operate. How can outsiders possibly know enough about the company to make a contribution, they question, when the other directors have spent their lives working for the company? How can an outsider be sensitive to the corporate culture? He might even damage the harmony of the group. A study by the Japanese Independent Directors Network, in November 2010, showed that of all the companies on the Nikkei 500 index, outside directors made up 13.5% of the board, women 0.9%, and non-Japanese 0.17%.

The Japanese *ringi* approach to communication encourages dialogue up and down the management hierarchy, leading, over time, to an agreed position. This means that boards tend to be decision-ratifying bodies rather than strategic decision-initiating and decision-taking forums, as in the West. Indeed, in some companies, meetings of the entire board tend to be ceremonial, with honourable titles used on social occasions, although that aspect of society is in transition.

Chairmen and senior directors of companies in the *keiretsu* meet regularly and have close, informal relationships. Meetings of the managing directors with the directors in their teams are also crucial, as are the informal relationships between the top echelons of the board. Ultimate power lies with the top managers, particularly the president and the chairman.

The Japanese Commercial Code calls for 'representative directors' to be elected by the board. Whereas, from a Western viewpoint, these might be expected to represent the interests of various stakeholders in the firm, their actual role is to represent the company in its dealings with outside parties such as the government, banks, and other companies in the industry. Typically, the representative directors include the chairman and president and other top directors. The Code also calls for the appointment of individuals as full-time statutory auditors. They report to the board on any financial problems or infringements of the company code or the company articles. They can call for information from other directors and company employees, and can convene special meetings of the board. These internal board-level auditors, of course, liaise with the external professional auditors.

Japanese company law does provide for independent outside directors, where they exist, to form a separate committee outside the board. Although the basic governance model is of a unitary board, this committee could be seen as a form of supervisory board. Recently, some independent outside directors have been appointed, usually under pressure from international investors.

Traditionally, investors have played a relatively small part in corporate affairs. The classical model of Japanese corporate governance had a stakeholder, not a shareholder, orientation. Power lay within the *keiretsu* network. There was no market for corporate control since hostile takeover bids were virtually unknown.

However, in recent years, the extent of cross-holdings of shares between companies has fallen and the first apparently hostile takeover in the Tokyo Stock Exchange was reported in 2007.

With the Japanese economy facing stagnation from the 1990s, traditional approaches to corporate governance were questioned. A corporate governance debate developed and the bank-based, stakeholder-orientated, rather than shareholder, corporate governance model came under scrutiny. The poorly performing economy had weakened many of the banks at the heart of *keiretsu*. Globalization of markets and finance put further pressure on companies. The paternalistic relationship between company and lifetime 'salary-man' slowly began to crumble. Some companies came under pressure from institutional investors abroad. Company laws were then redrafted to permit a more US style of corporate governance. But few firms embraced them. More emphasis has, however, been placed on shareholders, with board restructuring and directors receiving performance incentives. Some companies experimented with alternative, hybrid forms of governance structure. Consequently, there is now more diversity in the approaches to corporate governance in Japan, although changes tend to be gradual and incremental. But some have predicted moves towards the US or UK/

Commonwealth models, as Japan responds to the pressures of the globalization of business and finance.

Signs of movement included calls in 2008 by eight international investment funds for greater shareholder democracy, and a report from the Japanese Council for Economic and Fiscal Policy to the Japanese Prime Minister proposing that anti-takeover defences be discouraged and the takeover of Japanese firms be made easier.

Recognizing the importance of corporate governance to the long-term development of Asian economies and capital markets, the Asian Corporate Governance Association (ACGA) was founded in 1999 as an independent, non-profit membership organization dedicated to working with investors, companies, and regulators in the implementation of effective corporate governance practices throughout Asia. An ACGA report provided a critique of corporate governance in Japan:

> We believe that sound corporate governance is essential to the creation of a more internationally competitive corporate sector in Japan and to the longer-term growth of the Japanese economy and its capital markets. While a number of leading companies in Japan have made strides in corporate governance in recent years, we submit that the system of governance in most listed companies is not meeting the needs of stakeholders or the nation at large in three ways:
>
> ● By not providing for adequate supervision of corporate strategy
> ● By protecting management from the discipline of the market, thus rendering the development of a healthy and efficient market in corporate control all but impossible
> ● By failing to provide the returns that are vitally necessary to protect Japan's social safety net—its pension system

In 2013, the ruling Liberal Democratic Party introduced a bill to enhance corporate governance. The bill called for audit committees, controlled by independent outside directors, to give opinions on personnel and other important issues; and for measures to ensure the independence of external auditors from boards of directors. Outside directors would not be made mandatory because of business resistance. But listed companies that lacked such outside directors would be required to explain why at annual shareholder meetings.

Professor Hideaki Miyajima of Waseda University suggests that Japanese corporate governance is evolving into 'a hybrid-type', in which market-based structures are merged together. His research suggests that 'the performance of some Japanese companies that have evolved through incorporating these hybrid-type structures is significantly higher. However, such hybridization involves new costs, as conflicts between differing modes cannot be avoided.' Corporate governance in Japan remains work in progress.

The Asian family-based model

'Overseas Chinese' is the term used to describe Chinese business people who, over the years, as a result of the Chinese diaspora from the mainland, now play a fundamental part in the business life of South East Asia. Many companies in the significant Asian economies—Singapore, Taiwan, Malaysia, Thailand, Indonesia, Hong Kong, and the Philippines—are in the hands of Chinese families. For example, nearly half of the share capital invested in Malaysian companies is owned by Chinese residents and a quarter by foreign-controlled companies. Fewer than twenty families control the companies that dominate the local stock market for Hong Kong Chinese companies (not mainland Chinese companies).

In the governance of overseas Chinese companies, the board tends to play a supportive role to the real exercise of power, which is exercised through relationships between the key players, particularly between the dominant head of the family and other family members in key top management positions. Some of these companies are quite diverse groups with considerable delegation of power to the subsidiary unit, but with the owner-manager, or a family-orientated small group, still holding a strategic hand on the tiller.

Research into the management of overseas Chinese companies has suggested some distinguishing characteristics, which may help to interpret the evidence on governance practices. These studies suggest that overseas Chinese firms are:

- family-centric with close family control;
- controlled through an equity stake kept within the family;
- entrepreneurial, often with a dominant entrepreneur, so that decision-making is centralized, with close personal links emphasizing trust and control;
- paternalistic in management style, in a social fabric dependent on relationships and social harmony, avoiding confrontation and the risk of the loss of 'face';
- strategically intuitive, with the business seen as more of a succession of contracts or ventures, relying on intuition, superstition, and tough-minded bargaining rather than strategic plans, brand-creation, and quantitative analysis.

With outside shareholders in the minority, the regulatory authorities tend to emphasize the importance of disclosure and the control of related-party transactions. Although many corporate governance codes require independent non-executive directors, the independence of outside directors is less important to the owner than their character, trustworthiness, and overall business ability. Of course, corporate governance problems exist in Chinese and overseas Chinese companies: corruption, insider trading, unfair treatment of minority shareholders, and domination by company leaders, to name a few. But these are unfortunate attributes of corporate governance that reflect human behaviour everywhere.

Corporate governance: convergence or differentiation?

Are corporate governance practices around the world converging? This is a question that is often posed by corporate governance practitioners and frequently answered in the affirmative. Certainly, there are many forces that could lead towards convergence, as the following factors show.

Forces for convergence

Corporate governance codes of good practice around the world have a striking similarity, which is not surprising given the way in which they have been influenced by each other.

Although different in detail, all emphasize the importance of independence, transparency, and accountability. The codes published by international bodies, such as the World Bank, the Commonwealth of Nations, and the Organisation for Economic Co-operation and Development (OECD), clearly encourage convergence. The corporate governance policies and practices of major corporations operating around the world can also be global influences.

Securities regulations for the world's listed companies are certainly converging. The International Organization of Securities Commissions (IOSCO), which now has the bulk of the world's securities regulatory bodies in membership, encourages convergence. For example, its members have agreed to exchange information on unusual trades, thus making the activities of global insider trading more hazardous.

International accounting standards are also leading towards convergence. The International Accounting Standards Committee (IASC) and the International Auditing Practices Committee (IPAC) have close links with IOSCO, and are further forces working towards international harmonization and standardization of financial reporting and auditing standards. US GAAP, although some way from harmonization, are clearly moving in that direction.

In 2007, the US SEC announced that US companies could adopt international accounting standards in lieu of US GAAP. However, American accountants and regulators are accustomed to a rules-based regime and international standards are principles-based, requiring judgement rather than adherence to prescriptive regulations.

Global concentration of audit practices into just four firms, since the demise of Arthur Andersen, encourages convergence. Major corporations in most countries, wanting to have the name of one of the four principal firms on their audit reports, are then inevitably locked into that firm's worldwide audit, risk analysis, and other governance practices.

Globalization of companies is also, obviously, a force for convergence. Firms that are truly global in strategic outlook, with production, service provision, added-value chain, markets and customers worldwide, calling on international sources of finance, and the shares of which are held around the world, are moving towards common effective, transparent, and accountable governance practices. Unfortunately, the composition of the boards of the parent companies of such groups seldom reflects such globalization, because they are still dominated by nationals of the country of incorporation. However, the proportion of 'foreign' directors—that is those not nationals of the home country—although small, has been increasing. Companies such as Arcelor incorporated in Belgium, Novartis in Switzerland, Cable and Wireless in the United Kingdom, and ABN Amro in the Netherlands do have a significant proportion of directors who are not from the 'home country'. Significantly, no companies incorporated in the United States figure in this list.

Raising capital on overseas stock exchanges, clearly, encourages convergence as listing companies are required to conform to the listing rules of that market. Although the governance requirements of stock exchanges around the world differ in detail, they are moving towards internationally accepted norms through IOSCO.

International institutional investors, such as CalPers, explicitly demand various corporate governance practices if they are to invest in a specific country or company. Institutional investors with an international portfolio have been an important force for convergence. Of course, as developing and transitional countries grow, generate and plough back their own funds, the call for inward investment will decline, along with the influence of the overseas institutions.

Private equity funding is changing the investment scene. Owners of significant private companies may decide not to list in the first place. Major investors in public companies may find an incentive to privatize. Overall, the existence of private equity funds challenges boards of listed companies by sharpening the market for corporate control. As the power of private equity grows, expect calls for more transparency, accountability, and control.

Cross-border mergers of stock markets could also have an impact on country-centric investment dealing and could influence corporate governance expectations, as could the development of electronic trading in stocks by promoting international securities trading.

Research publications, international conferences, and professional journals can also be significant contributors to the convergence of corporate governance thinking and practice.

Forces for differentiation

However, despite all of these forces pushing towards convergence, there are others that, if not direct factors for divergence, at least cause differentiation between countries, jurisdictions, and markets.

Legal differences in company law, contract law, and bankruptcy law between jurisdictions affect corporate governance practices. Differences between the case law traditions of the United States, United Kingdom, and Commonwealth countries, and the codified law of continental Europe, Japan, and China distinguish corporate governance outcomes,.

Standards in the legal process, too, can differ. Some countries have weak judicial systems. Their courts may have limited powers and be unreliable. Not all judiciaries are separate from the legislature. The state or political activities can be involved in jurisprudence. In some countries, bringing a company law case can be difficult and, even with a favourable judgment, obtaining satisfaction is not always possible.

Stock market differences in market capitalization, liquidity, and markets for corporate control affect governance practices. Obviously, financial markets vary significantly in their scale and sophistication, affecting their governance influence.

Ownership structures also vary between countries. Some countries have predominantly family-based firms; others have external investors, but the proportion of individual investors compared with institutional investors differs; while some adopt complex networked, chained, or pyramid structures.

History, culture, and ethnic groupings have produced different board structures and governance practices. For example, contrast the governance in Japan *keiretsu*, continental European two-tier boards with worker co-determination, and family domination in overseas Chinese companies. Moreover, opinions differ on ownership rights and the basis of shareholder power between countries.

The concept of the company was Western, rooted in the notion of shareholder democracy, the stewardship of directors, and trust—the belief that directors recognize a fiduciary duty to their companies. But today's corporate structures have outgrown that simple notion. The corporate concept is now rooted in law, and the legitimacy of the corporate entity rests on regulation and litigation. The Western world has created the most expensive and litigious corporate regulatory regime the world has yet seen. This is not the only approach—and certainly not necessarily the best. The Asian reliance on relationships and trust in governing the enterprise may be closer to the original concept. There is a need to rethink the underlying idea of the corporation, contingent with the reality of power that can (or could) be wielded. Such a concept would need to be built on a pluralistic, rather than an ethnocentric, foundation if it is to be applicable to the corporate groups and strategic alliance networks that are now emerging as the basis of the business world of the future.

Institutions necessary for successful corporate governance

Having seen some of the different ways in which countries and cultures apply corporate governance, we can now identify the institutional arrangements that are needed to support successful governance. These include:

- a reliable legal system including an independent judiciary, courts that are free of bias and corruption, with judgments that are enforceable, free of state and other political pressures;
- a stock market with liquidity, international standing, and institutional investors;
- financial institutions, including brokers, sponsors for new issues, and financial advisers;
- regulatory authorities, covering corporations, stock markets and futures markets.
- a companies registry that facilitates comprehensive disclosure, with high levels of transparency;
- accounting and legal professions that are internationally respected, and able to discipline their members, and to ensure compliance with accounting standards and legal requirements;
- auditing firms that are professional, reliable, and independent of their clients;
- professional organizations, such as director and company secretary qualifying and disciplining bodies;
- educational institutions able to educate and train for relevant qualifications;
- consulting organizations able to advise companies and directors;
- financial and corporate governance training, plus continuous professional development;
- corporate governance research reported in academic and professional publications.

Obviously, in many countries, particularly those with emergent economies, not all of these institutions yet exist and, where they do, they are still in the process of being developed. Moreover, even in those countries recognized as having relatively high standards of corporate governance, there are opportunities for further development and improvement. However, taking a longitudinal view, it is interesting to see just how far many countries have come in developing their corporate governance infrastructure in a relatively few years.

Case studies

 Case study 6.1 Lehman Brothers Inc.—a corporate governance classic

Before the global financial crisis, which began in 2007, Lehman Brothers was a fabled New York-based brokerage firm and investment bank. Founded 157 years earlier, it had survived the American civil war, the major economic depressions of the 19th and 20th centuries, and two world wars. By 2007, it was the fourth largest investment bank in the United States: only Goldman Sachs, Morgan Stanley, and Merrill Lynch were bigger. But that was not to last much longer.

The Lehman Brothers' board was dominated by Richard S. Fuld Jr, who served as chairman of the board, chairman of the company's executive committee and chief executive officer. Early in 2008, the company's stock was trading at US$65. By October 2008, it had sunk to US$3.65, following the company's filing for bankruptcy in September 2008. Faced with the growing international financial crisis, the US Federal Reserve refused to provide funds, as it did with other banks.

Lehman Brothers' problems had begun to appear earlier in the year: dramatic losses on sub-prime mortgages, devaluation of the company's credit rating by the rating agencies, and the loss of clients. In June 2008, the company announced a US$2.8 billion loss for the second quarter, and the stock dropped to its lowest level for eight years. Yet the board seemed unable to grasp the depth of the problems facing the company: there was no investigation by the independent directors, no special study by the board's finance and risk committee, no call for a capital infusion, although it was apparent that one was needed.

The board of Lehman Brothers Inc. had ten independent directors, half aged over 70, with two in their 80s. The executive committee consisted of Fuld, the chief operating officer (COO), the chief finance officer (CFO), and 80-year-old independent director, John D. Macomber. The board's finance and risk committee was chaired by 80-year-old Henry Kaufman, although this committee met only twice in the financial year 2007–2008, despite the growing global financial crisis.

Why were the directors apparently blind to the reality of risk that the bank was facing? Where were the auditors? Why was the investigative media ignored? Could the culture of the board have encouraged delusions of invincibility? Was this hubris after 158 successful years?

Fuld did change his top management team: president and COO, Joseph Gregory, and CFO, Erin Callan, were 'let go'. In June 2008, Fuld announced that he would decline his bonus for that year. He made no offer to return any of the previous five years' compensation, which in total had been more than a billion dollars.

After the collapse of the company, Fuld was summoned before the Committee on Oversight and Government Reform of the US House of Representatives (Congress). His air of invincibility had gone. Although he accepted personal responsibility, he blamed the circumstances, not himself, saying that:

> In the end, despite all our efforts, we were overwhelmed . . . the destabilizing factors, rumours, widening credit default swap spreads, naked short-selling, attacks, credit agency downgrades, a loss of confidence by clients and counterparties, and strategic buyers sitting on the sidelines waiting for an assisted deal—these were all part of Lehman's story.

He added that this had been a familiar tale for many other financial institutions at the time, but they had been bailed out by the government.

The company had not been immune from regulatory challenge previously. In 2003, the US SEC settled charges against Lehman Brothers that had arisen when Lehman's research analysts gave supposedly independent investment advice on companies in which Lehman had an interest. Along with nine other brokerage firms, Lehman reached a settlement with the SEC, the New York Stock

Exchange, the New York Attorney General, and other state regulators; Lehman agreed to pay US$50 million to settle the conflicts of interest case: one half to state regulators; the other half into a fund for the benefit of customers. In addition, Lehman paid US$25 million over five years to provide the firm's clients with independent research, and US$5 million for investor education.

In March 2010, an examiner appointed by the Bankruptcy Court reported questionable activities in 2007–08, claiming that Lehman had used period-end repurchase agreements, which temporarily removed securities from the balance sheet, showing them as sales to improve its financial standing.

Following the collapse, the British Barclays Bank attempted to buy the company, but was prevented by UK and US regulatory concerns. Eventually, the interests of Lehman Brothers in Japan, Hong Kong, Australia, Asia-Pacific, Europe, and the Middle East were acquired by Nomura Holdings.

Discussion questions

1. The case claims that Lehman Brothers was dominated by Richard S. Fuld Jr. Was this desirable? What steps could have been taken to avoid it? Who could have initiated these steps?

2. The case highlights Lehman's elderly directors. Does the age of directors matter?

3. Is it possible for the research analysts of a financial institution to give independent investment advice to clients about a company in which the financial institution has an interest?

 Case study 6.2 Siemens AG

Siemens is Europe's largest engineering group, manufacturing a diverse range of products from power plants to home appliances, computers to railway engines. Headquartered in Germany, the company has a two-tier board.

In 2007, the chief executive, Klaus Kleinfeld, challenged the supervisory board to renew his contract or accept his resignation. The proposal failed to get the necessary votes in the supervisory board and he resigned.

Previously, Kleinfeld had successfully run Siemens' American operations, listing the company on the New York Stock Exchange in the process. He had served as an outside director on the boards of the major bank Citigroup and the American aluminium company Alcoa. He was recognized as a capable leader. Under his guidance, the Siemens Group had recently reported a 10% increase in revenue and a 36% increase in profits.

But both the union and the shareholder representatives on the supervisory board disliked his aggressive management style. Rumours about him circulated among board members. Heinrich von Pierer, the head of the supervisory board, resigned and was replaced by Gerhard Cromme, a pioneer of corporate governance reform in Germany.

Kleinfeld's problems, according to *The Economist*, were the lack of allies in Germany's chummy corporate elite and 'his American management methods, which seemed brash to industrialists and union representatives who were more used to Germany's consensual style of corporate leadership'.

Discussion question

1. What does this case show about the importance of culture in corporate governance?

2. Was there anything Kleinfeld could have done to avoid resignation?

Source: *The Economist*, 28 April 2007, and www.siemens.com

Case study 6.3 Tokyo Electric Power and the disaster at Fukushima Daiichi

In an unlikely outburst, Naoto Kan, Japanese Prime Minister, shouted 'What the hell is going on?' to executives of the Tokyo Electric Power Company (TEPCO) following Japan's worst nuclear crisis at the Fukushima Daiichi nuclear power plant, after the tsunami and earthquake on 11 March 2011. Were the directors or the corporate governance systems and procedures at fault?

The company appeared to have a commitment to sound corporate governance. As it stated on its website:

At TEPCO, we have developed corporate governance policies and practices as one of the primary management issues for ensuring sustainable growth in our business and long-term shareholder value. We believe in strengthening mutual trust through interactive communication with our valued stakeholders, including shareholders and investors, customers, local communities, suppliers, employees and the public, so we can move forward toward solid future growth and development. Therefore, TEPCO considers enhancing corporate governance a critical task for management and is working to develop organizational structures and policies for legal and ethical compliance, appropriate and prompt decision-making, effective and efficient business practices, and auditing and supervisory functions.

The TEPCO website explains the company's corporate governance processes:

The Board of Directors currently comprises 20 directors, including 2 outside directors. Also, TEPCO has 7 auditors, including 4 outside auditors. The Board of Directors generally meets once a month and holds additional special meetings as necessary. Based on interactive discussion with objective outside directors, the Board establishes and promotes TEPCO's business and oversees its directors' performance. TEPCO has also established the Board of Managing Directors, which meets once a week, and other formal bodies to implement efficient corporate management through appropriate and rapid decision-making on key management issues. In particular, we have established internal committees to deliberate, adjust, and plan the direction of the whole Company across a range of key management concerns, including internal control, CSR, and system security, as well as stable electricity supply.

For more appropriate and quicker decision-making, TEPCO also has the Managing Directors Meeting generally held once a week and other formal bodies to implement key corporate management issues efficiently, including those to be discussed by the Board of Directors. In particular, the Board has inter-organizational committees such as the Internal Control Committee, CSR Committee, System Security Measures Committee, and Supply and Demand Measures Conference to discuss directions of key management issues intensively across the entire company.

But behind the reassuring corporate governance explanations on the TEPCO website lay a different reality. The company's opaque handling of the situation at the stricken plant was widely criticized. The extent of the danger was minimized and the full extent of the damage only gradually became apparent, as the risk severity level was gradually increased to rank alongside Chernobyl as a most severe nuclear accident.

The company's handling of the incident exposed failings in its risk management systems. The company had a history of safety violations: in 2002, it had falsified safety test records, and in 2007, following an earthquake, its Niigata nuclear plant had a fire and a leak of radioactive water, which were concealed.

In fact, the board was dominated by inside directors, qualified by their seniority within the company. Out of the 20 directors, 18 were insiders, while of the two nominally outside directors, one of them, Tomijirou Morita, was chairman of Dai-Ichi Life Insurance, which was connected financially with TEPCO. In 2008, Tsunehisa Katsumata, the company president at the time of the 2007 problem, was elevated to chairman, being replaced by Masataka Shimizu, another career-long TEPCO employee. TEPCO had never appointed a head from outside the company.

The company held its AGM on 23 June 2011 and faced withering criticism from shareholders. The president Masataka Shimizu apologized for the 1.25 trillion yen (US$15 billion) loss. But a motion to cease generating nuclear power was defeated with the support of institutional investors.

Also in June 2011, the Japanese government appointed a five-man team to look into the company's finances. This committee was forced on the TEPCO board as a condition of financial support from the government to compensate those affected by the crisis at the Fukushima plant.

Three years after the earthquake and tsunami damage to the TEPCO atomic plant the situation had worsened. The company was accused of being slow to respond to the radiation crisis. Fuel rods from the damaged reactor were cooled in water held in make-shift metal tanks that were bolted rather than welded together. Leaks were sealed with tape. In September 2013, water from the tanks leaked into the sea. Radiation levels 18 times above the safe level were detected, levels that would kill anyone exposed within hours. Neighbouring countries complained at the contamination of their seas.

The Japanese economy was also affected. Following the Fukushima disaster, most other nuclear reactors in Japan were shut down under public pressure. But rising oil prices and the falling value of the yen meant that the alternative energy sources were becoming unsustainable. The government wanted to restart the other reactors, but the public were hostile. Japan is prone to earthquakes and many of these generators were built close to fault lines. But business interests pressed hard for the nuclear plants to reopen and energy costs to be stabilized.

In November 2013, the most hazardous part of the Fukushima shut-down began. The fuel rods had to be moved from their unstable storage tanks to safety. Normally removing spent rods is a routine process. But these rods were not spent. The storage pool could boil dry and without coolant fuel rods would ignite or even explode. Mistrust in TEPCO reached an all time high.

See www.facebook.com/OfficialTEPCOen, www.google.co.uk/finance?cid=669782

Discussion questions

1. Did the structure of the board contribute to the failures?

2. How do you account for the discrepancies between the company's alleged concern for corporate governance on its website and the catastrophic failure?

3. What advice would you give to the chairman of TEPCO?

References and further reading

Accounting Standards Steering Committee (1975) *The Corporate Report: A Discussion Paper Published for Comment*. Institute of Chartered Accountants in England and Wales, Moorgate Place, London.

Aoki, Masahiko, Gregory Jackson and Hideaki Miyajima (2007) *Corporate Governance in Japan: Institutional Change and Organizational Diversity*. Oxford University Press, New York.

Batra, Sumant, Kesar Dass and Associates (2008) *India: National Experience with Managing Related-party Transactions*. The 2008 Asian Round Table on Corporate Governance, OECD, Hong Kong.

Filatotchev, I. and M. Wright (eds) (2005), *Corporate Governance Life Cycle*. Elgar, London.

Hesterly, William S., Julia Liebeskind, and Todd R. Zenger (1990) 'Organizational Economics: An Impending Revolution in Organization Theory?' *The Academy of Management Review*, Vol. 15, No. 3, July.

Ho Kai Leong (ed.) (2005) *Reforming Corporate Governance in South East Asia*. Institute of South East Asia Studies, Singapore (pubsunit@iseas.edu.sg).

ISI Publications (2004) *The Practitioners' Guide to Corporate Governance in Asia*. www.BooksonBiz.com

McCarthy, Daniel, Sheila Puffer, and Stanislav
Vladimirovich (2004) *Corporate Governance in Russia*.
Edward Elgar Publishing, Cheltenham.

Nader, Ralph and Mark Green (1980) *The Case for a
Corporate Democracy Act of 1980*. Public Citizens
Congress Watch, et al., Washington, DC.

Nottage, Luke, LeonWolff, and KentAnderson (eds)
(2008) *Corporate Governance In The 21st Century—
Japan's Gradual Transformation*. Edward Elgar
Publishing, Cheltenham.

Ohmae, Kenichi (1986) *The Mind of the Strategist*.
Penguin, London.

Pfeffer, Jeffrey (1992) *Managing with Power: Politics and
Influence in Organizations*. Harvard Business School
Press, Boston, MA.

Spencer, Anne (1983) *On the Edge of the Organization:
The Role of the Outside Director*. Wiley, London.

Steger, Ulrich (2004) *Mastering Global Corporate
Governance*. Wiley, Hoboken, NJ.

Watanabee, Shigeru and Isao Yamamoto (1993)
'Corporate Governance in Japan: Ways to Improve
Low Profitability', *Corporate Governance: An
International Review*, Vol. 1, No. 4, October.

Whittaker, D. Hugh and Simon Deakin (2010) *Corporate
Governance and Managerial Reform in Japan*. Oxford
Scholarship Online.

World Bank and IFC (2002) *Corporate Governance in
China*. Washington, DC.

Yu Guang Hua (2007) *Comparative Corporate
Governance in China*. Routledge, Hong Kong.

Zhang, Weidong (2008) *Related Transactions: Analysis of
China's Listed Companies*. The 2008 Asian Round Table
on Corporate Governance, Shanghai Stock Exchange
Research Centre, China, OECD, Hong Kong SAR.

Projects and exercises

1. A distinction is drawn in the text between the US rules-based model and the UK and Commonwealth principles-based model of corporate governance. Which, if either, is likely to prevail in the long term?

2. Research the approaches that were adopted in the privatization of state enterprises in Russia and in China. What were the strengths and weaknesses of each approach? Which has been the more successful?

3. Prepare a report/presentation distinguishing the characteristics of corporate governance around the world.

Self-test questions

1. Distinguish the Anglo-American model of corporate governance from that of the continental European.

2. Does the United Kingdom or the United States have the greater proportion of individual, as against institutional, investors?

3. Describe the Japanese business network, *keiretsu*, model.

4. Name some characteristics of the overseas Chinese family business.

5. Explain 'listing through the back door'.

6. Describe the development of strategy in a Japanese *keiretsu* company.

7. What institutions are necessary for successful corporate governance?

8. Identify some forces for convergence in corporate governance around the world.

9. Identify some forces for differentiation in corporate governance around the world.

10. What value links the original Western concept of the corporation with the contemporary Asian attitude?

Part Two

Policies

7   Functions of the Board

 Learning Outcomes

In which we consider:

- What the board does
- Balancing the board's performance and conformance roles
- Board committees: functions and authority
- Delegating board functions to management
- Corporate transparency

What the board does

A simple framework was introduced in Chapter 2 to provide an overview of the functions of the board, showing its responsibility to be looking inwards at the enterprise and outwards to the organization's external situation, focusing on the past, the present, and the strategic future (see Figure 7.1)

This model involves a dynamic process: the board's involvement in the formulation of strategy leads to the making of policies and plans, with the board then monitoring and supervising executive performance, before subsequently providing accountability, which forms the basis for reviewing strategy for the future.

Note that the terminology used here—of corporate strategy leading to corporate policymaking—is the usage adopted in the business world. In government circles, at both national and local levels, the terminology tends to be reversed, with policy statements leading to strategic initiatives. Here, we will adopt the business usage.

In fact, some boards delegate part of these activities to management. In many large companies in the United States, for example, the predominant role of the board is seen as appointing and monitoring the chief executive officer (CEO), who works with the top executives to develop corporate strategies which are presented to the board for comment and approval. This is depicted in Figure 7.2. In some smaller companies and many subsidiary companies in corporate groups, directors may be executives, so the distinction between the work of the board and that of top management can become blurred. However, every board of directors has a governance responsibility to ensure that its corporate strategy, risk assessment, and ethical profile are in place and appropriate.

Later in this chapter, we will discuss how a balance is achieved between board and management activities. We can now explore each of the four functions of the board's governance role—strategy formulation, policymaking, executive supervision, and accountability—in more detail to see what they involve.

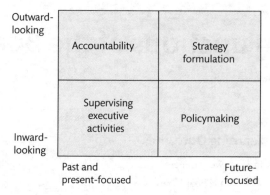

Figure 7.1 The basic board functions

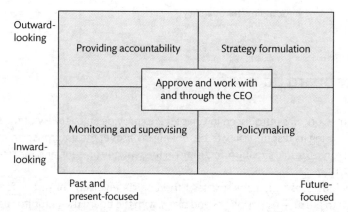

Figure 7.2 Board functions working through management

Strategy formulation

Behind every sound corporate strategy is an idea or vision of what those leading the company want it to be and to be seen to be. In formulating corporate strategy the principal purpose of the organization is identified, its core values established, its risk profile determined, and its longer-term direction set. Directors are so-called because they establish the company's direction. Many companies attempt to encapsulate this sense of purpose and direction in a statement of corporate vision and a mission statement. Some combine the two. Others incorporate a view of the company's values.

Such statements proclaim what the company is trying to achieve and how it intends to achieve it. They provide a mechanism for steering and controlling strategic choices.

They also tend to reflect a company's inherent culture: that collection of assumptions, attitudes, and beliefs that all organizations acquire over time. McDonald's has published both its mission and values (see Corporate governance in action 7.1):

Corporate governance in action 7.1 McDonald's mission

McDonald's brand mission is to be our customers' favourite place and way to eat and drink. Our worldwide operations are aligned around a global strategy, which center on an exceptional customer experience—People, Products, Place, Price and Promotion. We are committed to continuously improving our operations and enhancing our customers' experience.

McDonald's values

- We place the customer experience at the core of all we do.
- We are committed to our people
- We believe in the McDonald's System—a business model, depicted by our 'three-legged stool' of owner/operators, suppliers, and company employees
- We operate our business ethically
- We give back to our communities
- We grow our business profitably
- We strive continually to improve

Sainsbury's, a UK retailer, also has a published vision and sense of mission (see Corporate governance in action 7.2)

Corporate governance in action 7.2 Sainsbury's vision and values statement

We have a clear vision—to be the most trusted retailer, where people love to work and shop. Our goal is to make all our customers' lives easier every day by offering great quality and service at fair prices. Our values are critical to achieving this. Our customers trust Sainsbury's to do the right thing, and expect us to maintain high social, ethical and environmental standards. Our values are—being best for food and health, sourcing with integrity, respect for our environment, making a difference to our community, and being a great place to work.

Microsoft's published statement of mission and values is in Corporate governance in action 7.3:

Corporate governance in action 7.3 Microsoft mission and values

At Microsoft, our mission and values are to help people and businesses throughout the world realize their full potential. We consider our mission statement a commitment to our customers. We deliver on that commitment by striving to create technology that is accessible to everyone—of all ages and abilities. Microsoft is one of the industry leaders in accessibility innovation and in building products that are safer and easier to use.

As a company, and as individuals, we value integrity, honesty, openness, personal excellence, constructive self-criticism, continual self-improvement, and mutual respect. We are committed to our customers and partners and have a passion for technology. We take on big challenges, and pride ourselves on seeing them through. We hold ourselves accountable to our customers,

> shareholders, partners, and employees by honoring our commitments, providing results, and striving for the highest quality.

The company has also made a specific social commitment to promoting accessibility through its technology:

> Accessible technology enables individuals to personalize their technology to make it easier to see, hear, and use. Accessibility and accessible technology are helpful for individuals who experience visual difficulties, pain in the hands or arms, hearing loss, speech or cognitive challenges; and individuals seeking to customize their computing experience to meet their situational needs and preferences.

The Microsoft Company was originated by Bill Gates when he was 19, and Paul Allen, who was then 22. The Microsoft name was first used in 1976 and the company incorporated in 1981. Today the company has revenues over $70 billion and net assets of over $100 billion.

Some say that Microsoft's mission statement is too bland, and fails to provide a clear vision for its strategy. But others commend the clear statement of corporate values and the company's social emphasis on accessibility through technology.

Some directors feel that their mission (or vision) statement provides a concrete description of their company's purpose, values, and direction, which guides strategic decisions, inspires employees, and informs customers and other stakeholders. Such mission statements need to be a clear, but succinct, indication of the core purpose and core values of the enterprise.

Other directors, however, feel that written mission statements can be at best a bland public relations exercise and at worst an exercise in futility. Certainly, unless directors believe in and link their mission with their strategic decisions, a public mission statement becomes little more than a marketing slogan or a sign on the wall for employees.

What does strategy formulation involve? One of the primary duties of every board is to ensure that its enterprise is heading in the right direction. The board that lacks a shared view of the company's purpose and future direction cannot develop an effective corporate strategy. Strategy formulation is the process of generating and reviewing alternative longer-term directions for the firm that lead towards the achievement of its purposes, consistent with the risk profile acceptable to the board.

Who is responsible for formulating strategy? Boards vary in their involvement in the strategy formulation process. In a board with a majority of executive directors, as in many small and family firms, and in some subsidiary companies, the board is likely to be much involved in the strategy formulation process because many of the directors are 'wearing two hats' as both manager and director. Consequently, they can contribute to the strategic discussions directly from their own knowledge and experience of the business. The challenge to boards dominated by executive directors is that they are 'marking their own examination papers', lacking a critical perspective. On such boards, non-executive directors can play a vital role offering alternative insights, raising important questions, for example about risks involved, and by challenging conclusions. Advice from senior managers who are not on the board, external consultants, and other experts can also add important dimensions to strategic reviews.

By contrast, in a board with a majority of independent outside directors, as in most large US and UK companies these days, strategy is inevitably driven by top management—the CEO and the management team. What then *is* the role of the board? Can non-executive directors, who are independent of the company and its business, really know enough about the company and its industry to make a realistic contribution to strategic thinking? Some also question whether they can find sufficient time to make a worthwhile input to strategy, particularly since some of them may be CEOs of companies in their own right. Typically, in such situations, the CEO with the top management team undertakes a strategic review and produces a set of strategic proposals for the board's approval. The independent directors then question, challenge, and maybe refer the strategies back for further work, before giving their approval.

How is strategy formulated? A formal approach to strategic planning, still adopted by a few companies, is the creation of a long-range plan. Essentially, such long-range planning extends the annual budgeting process over a longer strategic time horizon, perhaps three to five years. At least this approach forces boards to focus on the longer term. But the drawbacks are apparent. The planner is, conceptually, inside the organization looking out. The approach fails to take a strategic perspective, perpetuating the existing business, rather than recognizing strategic changes in customer demands, markets, competition, technology, and financing. It also ignores the economic, political, and social context.

A more penetrating approach to strategic analysis is the widely used SWOT analysis (strengths, weaknesses, opportunities, and threats), which seeks to relate the internal situation in the firm with its external strategic context.

An example of a SWOT analysis will explain (see Corporate governance in action 7.4). In the analysis that follows, drawn from the experiences of a realtor (estate agent), the ideas were generated during a half-day strategy seminar attended by the directors and top management from the firm's regional offices. The chart represents a synthesis of the ideas produced by small working groups. The strategic situation facing the firm, both internally and externally, is certainly highlighted by this analysis. What emerges is a picture of a long-established, successful, but over-bureaucratic, firm in the real-estate business facing vulnerability with an increasingly competitive market, which is being driven by franchised high street chains and a shift towards the Internet for property sales. The self-confidence rooted in past success, the difficulty of adapting to change, and the need to develop a sense of urgency for strategic change are apparent.

Corporate governance in action 7.4   SWOT analysis for a long-established realtor (estate agent)

Strengths

- A well-known and respected brand name
- A good market share where we are represented
- We have been successful for thirty-five years
- Both sellers and buyers respect our business methods
- Our leaflets and adverts for promoting properties are successful
- A large and experienced staff
- A reputation as a good employer
- Effective financial and management control systems

Weaknesses

- High overheads, particularly rents and salaries
- Overheads rising
- Cash flow erratic
- Slow to respond to new clients—pressure of work
- Insufficient time with clients
- Higher management authority required for decisions—slows the contract process and stifles staff initiative
- Our website is still being developed
- Telephone inquiries not well handled
- Staff turnover—experienced staff being poached
- Organizational inertia—slow to change direction—overconfidence

Opportunities

- Our business sector is expanding—growth in sales of new house builds and existing properties
- Commercial property sector sales not yet in portfolio
- Many opportunities for development of new client services
- Our competitors may be slow to adopt new technologies

Threats

- Competition rife—high street offices, national franchised chains, private sales
- Vulnerable to Internet—developments unpredictable
- New ways to buy and sell houses erodes our position
- Developments in technology changes the basics of the business
- A new strategy by a large competitor ruins our market position
- More government controls and charges on property transfers

The SWOT methodology offers the prospect of building on corporate strengths, while working to eliminate or at least mitigate internal weaknesses, exploiting external opportunities faster and better than other firms and moving to minimize the effect of external threats. A SWOT analysis can provide a penetrating experience for those involved and produce valuable information for board deliberations. But it tends to focus attention on the existing business, looking for threats that it might face and opportunities it could pursue. It does little to identify causes and effects of strategic change and suggest alternatives. Limitations of the methodology can include a failure to identify what is driving change in the market, the technology, or the economic situation and thus limit the adequate responses. It can also overlook the firm's changing exposure to risk.

In the real-estate case (Corporate governance in action 7.4), the SWOT analysis does not generate strategic possibilities such as growth through acquisition, perhaps by franchising the firm's brand, merger (collaborating with, rather than fighting the opposition), buying into another franchise, and/or investing in buying/selling operations through the Internet.

To formulate strategy effectively, the strategist needs to be, conceptually, above the enterprise looking down, able to see the enterprise in its strategic context, including the industry, the market, customers and competitors, products and services, wherever the company operates, and to identify the wider political, economic, social, and technological context. Figure 2.1 in Chapter 2, which shows the scope of corporate governance, can be expanded to depict the scope of strategy formulation. But, as well as understanding the external situation likely to face the company, directors need to be conversant with the internal situation, including the company's finances, labour, markets, products, and processes.

A well-known metaphor, 'helicopter vision', refers to the ability to *perceive* the enterprise in the context of ever-widening circles of influence: when on the ground, the helicopter pilot can see the ground in great detail, but not very far horizontally. As the helicopter rises, his horizons widen, but the detail lessens. In fact, thinking with helicopter vision is not difficult: the challenge is to determine the appropriate level at which to view the territory.

Surprisingly, many boards fail to devote enough time and attention to strategy formulation. Directors in a professionally led board will have a strategic focus, with relevant, up-to-date knowledge of the internal situation in the company and appropriate information about the firm's external context, covering both the immediate operating situation, including its industry, competitors, customers, products, operations, and financial situation, and the overall political, economic, social, and technological contexts.

Moreover, directors on professionally led boards have to have the ability to think strategically. What is meant by the ability to think strategically? General Sun Tzu, a Chinese leader in the Chou/Zhou dynasty in the first millennium bc, was one of the finest strategic minds the world has ever known. He called for the strategist to 'think with the mind of the enemy'. In business terms, that means identifying existing and potential competitors, understanding their strategic situation, and thinking through the strategies that they might be pursuing. What would directors hear if they were flies on the wall of a competitor's boardroom?

To understand the strategic situation affecting a company, we need to appreciate the forces that determine its competitiveness within that company's industry. These pressures may be harsh because of massive competition; a company in a mature industry, for example, might be facing competition from more advanced or cheaper products, produced in environmentally better circumstances. Alternatively, the pressure to change may be benign because the growth of market leaves all of the players in that sector with unsatisfied demand.

Professor Michael Porter[1] of the Harvard Business School has provided a number of analytical frameworks that provide an understanding of strategic situations. In one, he focuses on the value added by a company to its products and services. In another, often referred to as the 'five forces' model, he challenges the assumptions that a company has about its immediate strategic environment.

1. Who is currently competing in our market?

How are they currently competing—price, service, quality, etc.?
How do their costs compare with the value added by this business?

---

[1] Porter, Michael E. (1980) *Competitive Strategy: Techniques for Analyzing Industries and Competitors*, The Free Press, New York; and (1985) *Competitive Advantage: Creating and Sustaining Superior Performance*, The Free Press, New York.

2. What strategic power do our upstream suppliers have over us?

Are they able to exercise strategic influence on us—by pricing, supply, etc.?

3. Who are our customers—by type, location, volume, etc.?

What customer needs do we satisfy?
What strategic powers do our downstream distributors and ultimate customers have?
Are they able to exercise strategic influence on us—by price demands, etc.?

4. Could our customers' needs be met by substitute goods or services?

5. Could other firms enter the market?

What is keeping them out—high entry costs, know-how, low margins, etc.?

This emphasis on the strategic environment of the company, rather than its internal situation, reflects the advice of General Sun Tse, mentioned earlier, to 'think with the mind of the enemy'. Directors who are thinking strategically try to understand the strategic situation of their competitors, and to deduce what strategies they are pursuing. This is very different from reacting operationally. Crucial questions include the following.

- Who are the competitors?
- What is their current strategic situation?
- What is their current strategy—how are they currently competing?
- What are their capabilities—both strengths and weaknesses?
- What assumptions do they hold about themselves and their market?
- What beliefs do their directors and top management have about the strategic situation?
- Are they satisfied with their present market or financial position?
- Where might the competitors be vulnerable?
- What strategies could they pursue in the future?
- What is the likelihood?
- How might they react to strategic changes that we might make?

Professional directors understand the importance of such information, and professional boards ensure that they have access to it. Unless directors agree on their firm's strategic situation, they cannot formulate objective strategy.

Critics of Porter's approach to strategy formulation argue that, by focusing on the company's external competitive environment, the strength's of a company's internal resource may be underutilized and its strategies be over-influenced by market conditions. By contrast, a currently popular alternative, often known as 'resource-based theory', sees a firm as a collection of resources and capabilities that need to be utilized to create a winning strategy. The resources could include access to capital, employee skills, unique products or services, managerial talent and experience, equipment, and buildings or goodwill. This resource-based perspective seeks to find a fit between a firm's internal capabilities and its external market situation that will produce a competitive advantage.

In a global survey in 2011, McKinsey, the international management consultants, reported that although the financial crisis had exposed inadequate governance, boards had not increased the time spent on company strategy since the previous study in 2008. But they were under pressure to take more responsibility for developing strategy and overseeing business risk. Some outside independent directors even reported that they felt ill-equipped to live up to the new expectations on directors because they lacked knowledge of the business and lacked time to commit to their board duties.

Decision modelling has opened up an additional approach to corporate decision making. Using sophisticated algorithms and the massive amounts of relevant data that are now available on many topics, more accurate predictions and better strategic decisions can be made. The output from such models may help overcome distortions that arise from individual prejudice and bias. Of course, though the output from models may influence decision-makers, the information still has to be acted on to be effective.

Policymaking

Strategies remain nothing more than dreams, statements of intent, until they are turned into actions. To make strategies operational, companies need policies, procedures, plans, and, in some cases, projects. The policies, procedures, and plans provide the criteria against which the board can subsequently monitor management's performance and fulfil their duty to supervise executive management.

Policies can be thought of as the rules, systems, and procedures that are laid down by the board to guide and constrain executive management. Obviously, the details of corporate policies depend on the scale, diversity, and type of operation. Top management may play a large part in the development of policies and in their implementation. In other cases, the board may delegate much policymaking to the CEO and top executive team. Such policies might include policies on customers and marketing, product and service, pricing, technology, innovation and research, employees and labour relations, suppliers and purchasing, down-stream distribution and sales, capital projects, accounting and financial controls, risk assessment, and corporate values and ethics, But every board has a duty to ensure that appropriate policies are in place, that they are functioning effectively, and are regularly reviewed in the light of changing circumstances.

The directors may decide that there are some matters that should not be delegated to management, reserving the power to make such decisions to themselves. In such cases, the board creates a policy on reserved powers as in Corporate governance in action 7.5.

Corporate governance in action 7.5   South American Resources Limited

Board policy on reserved powers

- Matters that must be referred to the board and cannot be delegated
- Approval of overall corporate strategy and direction
- Major business acquisitions or disposals
- Approval of investment projects (over US$1 million)
- Board appointments and removals (executive and outside directors)
- Directors' remuneration policy
- Terms and appointment of CEO and top executives

- Appointments to board committees
- Financial policies
  - Remuneration and selection of auditors
  - Approval of interim and final financial statements
  - Fundamental changes to employee pension scheme rules
  - Main treasury policies, e.g. on gearing, borrowing limits
  - Currency exposure and risk
  - Significant changes to corporate control systems
  - Policy on gearing or leverage
  - Policy on accounting standards to be adopted in all countries
- Labour relations and employment policies
  - Staff terms and conditions policy
  - Trades union policy
- IT policies
  - Policy on IT security and confidentiality
  - Staff use of network
- Merger and acquisition policies
- Corporate ethics policies
  - Policies on core corporate values
  - Code of ethics, creation, training, and enforcement policies
  - Whistle-blower policies
- Corporate governance and compliance policies
  - Relations with auditors, auditor independence policies
  - Internal audit policies
  - Internal reporting policies
  - Regulatory compliance policies
  - Corporate reporting policies
- Enterprise risk management policies
  - Business catastrophe recognition and continuity policies
  - Strategic risk assessment policy
  - Financial exposure policy
  - Employment, health and safety risk management policies
  - Product risk management and contingency policies.

Risk management policies are of particular importance at board level. The global financial crisis showed that many boards, not only of financial institutions, had failed to appreciate fully their companies' exposure to risk. Corporate governance codes now expressly recognize directors' responsibility to ensure that risk management policies are in place and that risks are adequately assessed.

Policies need to flow from the company's strategies. Boards have a responsibility to ensure that appropriate policies exist, either by setting them themselves or by approving those proposed by management. Then the board needs to ensure that appropriate management systems are in place to confirm that the policies are working.

Strategy formulation and policymaking together form the board-level performance role. This is a fundamental component of the work of a unitary board. In a two-tier board, the responsibility falls to the executive management board. We now come to the conformance roles—supervising executive activities and accountability. Again, this is a fundamental part of the work of a unitary board. In a two-tier board, the conformance role is the responsibility of the supervisory board.

Supervising executive activities

Almost all corporate entities, large and small, use financial measures and accounting systems as the primary means of monitoring the state of the enterprise and the performance of its managers. At the very least, this is likely to include a balance sheet and profit and loss (or revenue and expenditure) account. To be able to keep a better track of executive activities, many boards also rely on regular reports from a budgetary control system. Budgetary control systems compare actual revenues and expenditures against budgeted revenues and expenditures. The initial development of cost centres and their budgets enables management at all levels to be involved in the budgeting process, with the resultant motivation to achieve the planned performance.

Obviously, budgetary control systems are expressed in terms of costs and revenues. A more sophisticated approach to financially based controls involves the creation of profit centres within a firm. Managers responsible for such profit centres can now be motivated by and held accountable for the profit performance of their unit, possibly including return on investment criteria.

A further refinement is a management control system, which applies multiple performance measures to business units. An example will illustrate (see Corporate governance in action 7.6).

Corporate governance in action 7.6   A multiple-measure management control system

The board of a company with profit-responsible divisions required its divisional managers to perform appropriately on ten criteria:

- profitability—return on investment in that division;
- growth in market share, revenue, and profit;
- customer satisfaction;
- capital expenditure project performance;
- management development and succession planning;
- product and service development;
- employee training, labour turnover, and employee attitudes;
- contributing to the group's corporate social responsibility;
- monitoring and management;
- balancing the short term with the long term.

The company had created management information and control systems that monitored and measured all of these criteria. Responsible executives were expected to perform well on all ten criteria continuously. Failure to maintain planned performance on any one criterion required an explanation at board level.

Management control systems that use criteria beyond financial measures may have problems with quantifying some of the criteria. Judgement may be required in the measurement of difficult concepts such as customer satisfaction or employee attitudes. However, such systems do exist and some boards rely on their output.

To reduce the number of reports presented to the board, some firms use exception reporting in which only where significant variations from planned performance have occurred is board-level attention required. We noted, in Chapter 3, the potential agency problem of suboptimization, where units of an organization are held responsible for the achievement of specific performance measures; in seeking to achieve those goals, each unit takes actions that achieve its own objectives, but which are potentially detrimental to achieving the organization's objectives as a whole. Directors need to be sensitive to such actions when setting and assessing subsidiary company, divisional, or unit performance measures.

Accountability

To whom is a board accountable? Formally, the answer is 'the members of that corporate entity'. In the case of a joint-stock, limited-liability company that is the shareholder members with voting rights. In a co-operative society, the members are those with voting rights under the constitution. In a professional body or a trades union the members are those who are paid up and qualified to vote under the rules of that association.

The level and detail of accountability reporting required will be determined by the constitution of the organization, the laws under which it is incorporated, and the demands of any regulating authority. In the case of the limited-liability company in the United Kingdom, the required accountability is laid down in the Companies Acts; in the United States by the company law of the state of incorporation and by the Securities and Exchange Commission (SEC). Companies may provide more than this legal requirement: they may not disclose less. Companies in which shares are listed on a stock exchange also have to meet that exchange's requirements for disclosure and the regulatory authorities' rules.

A few companies still take a strictly legal view, arguing that, provided that they obey the laws of the countries in which they operate, they owe no wider duty of disclosure or accountability to stakeholder groups. If a society expects wider accountability, it is up to the legislature to enact laws accordingly, they argue.

However, in recent years, a view has been gaining currency that boards, particularly of significant organizations, which have the potential to affect a lot of people by their behaviour, should recognize some accountability towards a wider range of stakeholders. Many companies recognize this wider responsibility and seek to provide relevant information to a range of connected stakeholders, such as employees, suppliers, and customers. Other companies go further and accept a responsibility to be accountable to society at large.

Balancing the board's performance and conformance roles

Every unitary board faces a challenge to strike a reasonable balance between the performance roles of strategy formulation and policymaking, on the one hand, and, the conformance roles of executive supervision and accountability, on the other. Typically, directors' time is under pressure. So the way in which the work of the board and its committees is allocated is crucial. It is also fundamental to the way in which the board approaches corporate governance. The problem is that the more a board concentrates its efforts on the conformance activities—management supervision and accountability—the more that board comes to see its work as ensuring compliance with the corporate governance requirements of respective codes, regulations, and law.

In fact, some directors *do* believe that corporate governance is essentially about compliance. They see their role as the supervision of management and ensuring accountability to legitimate stakeholders. In other words, they emphasize the conformance side of the conformance/performance dichotomy. The formulation of strategy and policymaking is then largely delegated to top management. By focusing on compliance, such boards tend to see corporate governance activities as an expense and wonder whether it is cost-effective.

In a board with a large majority of independent outside directors, the focus on conformance can become inevitable, if directors believe that their ability to contribute to strategy formulation and policymaking is limited.

In a two-tier board, of course, the separation is complete, with the management board running the business, responsible for performance, while the supervisory board oversees that performance and ensures accountability.

An unfortunate effect of the introduction of corporate governance principles and codes, rules and regulations, is the danger that boards, by concentrating on conformance, may overlook their principal mission, which is to direct the enterprise. That means being involved in strategy formulation and policymaking.

Many boards, of course, do recognize that they are responsible for balancing conformance activities with a commitment and contribution to performance. Directors are responsible for directing the company, ensuring that it is heading in the right direction, aware of the risks, and establishing the way ahead. That means sensibly balancing performance with conformance activities.

The responsibility for determining the board's agenda, ensuring that sufficient time is allocated to each of the four functions, and balancing these activities, lies with the board chairman. Sensibly, he or she will seek advice from the company secretary and the chief executive. Moreover, in a professionally led board, every director will have the opportunity to suggest items that the board should discuss and to express concerns about the balance of the board's deliberations. One chairman actually asks each of his directors to write to him every year about ways in which he might improve his performance as chairman and to suggest matters that need more board attention. But not many chairmen are that professional.

Board committees: functions and authority

Essentially, there are two reasons why unitary boards create subcommittees:

- to enable independent directors to meet separately from the board as a whole, in order to fulfil their oversight roles;
- to delegate board activities to reduce the burden on the board as a whole.

Board committees that provide oversight of management

The audit committee, the remuneration committee, and the nomination committee are required by almost all corporate governance codes for listed companies. Many corporate entities that are not listed, NGOs, and government entities have also adopted similar committees. Board policies should create these committees as standing committees of the board, with formal terms of reference that are regularly reviewed and amended when necessary.

The audit committee

Audit committees existed in the 19th century, with members drawn from shareholders to check directors' reports. But the current notion of the audit committee as a standing committee of the board, comprised of independent outside directors, to provide a bridge between the external auditor and the main board, originated in the United States. The New York Stock Exchange endorsed the concept in 1939. Then, in 1972, the SEC recommended that listed companies establish audit committees of non-management directors, which became a listing requirement in 1977. The first corporate governance report (Cadbury, 1992) called for audit committees. Today, the audit committee has become a fundamental component of corporate governance, with a much-enhanced role.

As a standing committee of the board, the audit committee derives its authority from the formal board policy that created it, and is accountable to the board. In listed companies, the committee derives further authority from listing rules, corporate governance codes, and the law, for example in the United States from the Sarbanes-Oxley Act. Typically, the audit committee has widespread authority to work with the external auditor, senior management (particularly the CEO and chief finance officer (CFO)), the finance function, and the internal audit function. Ideally, the committee has its own secretariat and can call on external expertise as necessary.

The UK Financial Reporting Council produced a guide to boards on audit committees in September 2012.

The remuneration committee

The global financial crisis and the continuing economic problems have thrown a spotlight on top executive and director remuneration. Media attention has been directed particularly at allegedly excessive bankers' bonuses, large awards to retiring directors that have been portrayed as rewards for failure, and the growing differential between the rewards of those at the top of organizations and those at the bottom.

At this point, we should note that, like the audit committee, the remuneration committee is a subcommittee of the main board, consisting wholly or mainly of independent outside directors, set up with responsibility for overseeing the remuneration packages of board members, particularly the executive directors and increasingly members of senior management. As with audit committees, the remuneration committee derives its authority from its formal terms of reference, relevant law, and corporate governance codes.

The nomination committee

There was a time in many countries when boards resembled comfortable clubs of like-minded people, well known to each other, sharing similar interests and often from similar backgrounds. The nominating committee was an attempt to prevent the board becoming a cosy club, in which the incumbent members appointed similar people to join their ranks. In effect, nominating committees offer a check-and-balance mechanism designed to reduce the possibility of dominant directors, particularly chairmen or CEOs, pushing through their own favoured candidates. As a subcommittee of the main board, the nominating committee is made up wholly, or mainly, of independent outside directors, to make recommendations on replacement or additional members of the board.

Unfortunately, the creation of a nominating committee does not resolve an underlying dilemma. On the one hand, an independent nominating committee can suggest potential directors with appropriate credentials, while avoiding claims of the old boys' club. On the other hand, to be effective, a board chairman needs to know, respect, and be able to work with the members of his board. To have members imposed on him or her could be divisive. If a board is to work together as a tough-minded, effective team, it is just as well that they know and respect each other. Otherwise board deliberations could become more like a political adversarial parliament.

A further dilemma can arise if supposedly independent outside directors feel a loyalty towards and the need to support the chairman or CEO who nominated them.

Of the three committees recommended in the codes of good practice in corporate governance—the audit committee, the remuneration committee, and the nominating committee—it is the nominating committee that has been most resisted by boards in some jurisdictions; nor is that surprising, given that the right to appoint to the board of directors goes to the very heart of corporate power.

Other board committees for the oversight of management

In many companies, the board-level responsibility for ensuring compliance with legal, regulatory, and corporate governance code requirements is delegated to the audit committee. However, some companies, recognizing the growing complexity of that committee's function, have created a specific board committee to take on the responsibility. Given various names, one company calls its committee the *governance and compliance committee*; a majority of its members are independent directors.

Other companies have board standing committees, with significant independent director membership, to recommend policies and to oversee corporate activities on corporate ethics codes, whistle-blowing procedures, and corporate social responsibility (CSR). A few companies add corporate concerns about the sustainability of company activities to this committee's remit.

Board committees that reduce the burden on the board as a whole

Few boards meet more frequently than once a month, unless the company is facing a crisis. Some meet far less often, because the outside directors have other responsibilities and may be geographically distant. However, the scale and complexity of issues facing many boards continue to grow. Consequently, some boards have created subcommittees to handle components of their work.

Executive committees, finance committees, and *strategic planning committees* are all examples of board subcommittees formed to handle part of the board's overall work. The terms of reference of such board committees need to be clearly identified and bounded to avoid encroaching on issues that should legitimately be the concern of the board as a whole. The minutes of these committees typically form the basis of their reports to the board. A classical danger of such board committees is that directors who are not members abdicate all responsibility for that area of board responsibility, even though in law all directors are equally responsible. The fact that, in the absence of any cause for concern, they may rely on the word of other board colleagues does not absolve them from responsibility. Effective board chairmen provide opportunities for the other directors to question subcommittee members and, if necessary, to reopen for discussion matters that have been decided by the committee.

Another reaction to the global financial crisis has been a greater focus on boards' responsibility for the assessment and acceptance of risk. Some boards have developed risk management policies and formed a board standing committee with specific responsibility for overseeing the company's exposure to and acceptance of risk. The titles of these committees vary—*enterprise risk management, corporate risk assessment and control, strategic risk governance*, for example—but they are to be found in companies of various sizes and industries, not only in financial institutions. As with other board committees for the oversight of management, such risk committees derive their authority from their terms of reference.

Finally, boards sometimes form *ad hoc committees* with delegated responsibilities for specific projects, such as the oversight of a major investment project, the organizational integration of a recent acquisition, or the launch of a new brand or product line. Such committees will usually include executive directors, and may include relevant managers or outside experts as members. But independent directors may be included to provide objective oversight. The terms of reference of ad hoc board committees should include clear objectives, the scope of their powers, and performance measures, so that they are wound up when they have fulfilled their purpose. Committees have a tendency to perpetuate their existence.

Delegating board functions to management

The interplay between the board and management raises a crucial aspect of corporate governance. Subject to the articles and any regulatory demands, boards have considerable freedom to delegate responsibilities to management. In Figure 7.3, the relationship between the work of the board and that of the CEO and his or her management team is at the heart of the four governance functions of the board, as we saw earlier.

The cell in the centre of the quadrant shows management involvement with the board. It may be relatively small and insignificant, with the directors making most of the executive decisions, or it may be large, with the directors expecting top management to make a major contribution to some or all of the four governance functions.

Some examples will illustrate (see Corporate governance in action 7.7).

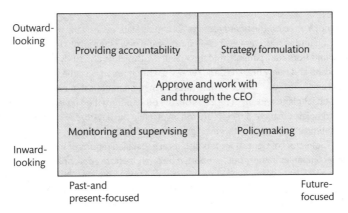

Figure 7.3 Board functions working through management

Corporate governance in action 7.7   Examples of the interplay between the board and top management

Strategy formulation

The Beaumont Executive Press Ltd was a small publisher based in Oxford, England. There were two directors who formulated strategy and made all of the strategic decisions between them. They decided which materials to publish, where to market, and how the business was financed. There was no delegation to others in the company; indeed, many of the other operational functions were outsourced to specialist firms. The two directors, who were also the owners of the company, determined the corporate strategy and identified the business risks they were prepared to take.

By contrast, the board of General Motors delegates most of the responsibility for formulating strategy to its operational divisions. The operating divisions produce strategies and project proposals that are put to the main board for approval and funding. The largely INED (independent non-executive director) board members are not experts in the automotive industry. Their role is to question the strategic proposals, to raise concerns about level of research and development (R&D), product developments, competitor situation, pricing policy, technological developments, and so on, and to probe the exposure to risk. The main board's strategic decisions are largely about the allocation of resources to fund divisional strategies in the light of overall group strategy.

Policymaking

The Vigilance of Brixham Preservation Co. Ltd is a company incorporated to restore and run a heritage sailing trawler in one of England's few remaining fishing ports. All policies are made by the board. Since only cruise skippers are paid and the company is run by volunteers, there is no management to be involved in policymaking.

By contrast, in conglomerate Jardine Matheson Group (for more information, see Case study 10.5 in Chapter 10), only group financial policy, top management staff policies, and a few broad group management policies are made at main board level. Policymaking follows the formulation of strategy at subsidiary company levels.

Executive monitoring and supervision

The Rainbow Hospice Inc. is a charitable foundation involved in the provision of care in terminal illness. The board consists entirely of independent non-executive volunteers. The chief executive attends board meetings, but is not a director. The board receives a monthly statement on the financial and cash/bank position, reports on projects such as new building works and new equipment, drug use reports, and details of complaints from staff, patients, and their relatives. Directors also study the incidents book, which records health and safety breaches, and receive a written report on patient care and an oral report on staff from the chief executive. Directors then question him on matters that concern them, such as variances from budget plans, and anything else from the other information they have been given. The chief executive complains that the directors are too involved in the day-to-day running of the hospice, and from time to time individual directors even give instructions to the nursing staff.

By contrast, the directors of General Motors also receive detailed reports of the performance of each of the subsidiary companies in the group, supported by briefings from appropriate executives. They seek clarification and raise questions about matters that concern them. They discuss apparent problems with executives attending board meetings and, following discussions between themselves, call for more information, or approve the current executive performance. But they do not give instructions to management and seek the approval of the subsidiary company top management before visiting a plant.

Accountability

The board of a leading boarding school in Canada is comprised entirely of independent outside members. The headmaster and the bursar attend board meetings to provide information and advice. The report to the owners of the school comes from the board and it is the board that is held accountable for performance, including the appointment, monitoring, and if necessary removal of the head and senior staff.

By contrast, in General Electric, a large divisionalized company in a number of industries, the chairman and directors accept a primary responsibility for the periodic report and accounts to shareholders, and the chairman of the board and the chairman of the audit committee address and respond to questions at shareholders' meetings. The senior outside director is also available to respond to shareholder issues. But senior financial management, too, is significantly involved in dealings with shareholders, regulators, and the financial media. Much detailed accountability work is delegated to the finance and the shareholder relations functions.

These examples raise an important question: where do boards focus their attention and how do they balance their time between the four basic functions of the board?

Unsurprisingly, research shows that boards vary significantly in the way in which they carry out their functions. In a company with an all-executive board, the directors virtually combine governance with the top management functions and it can be difficult to separate the two. In other cases, particularly in the board of a holding company that has delegated much of the strategy formulation and policymaking in the group to its subsidiary companies, the dominant focus is on setting overall strategies and policies at group level, the internal supervision of the group, and external accountability.

However, research has also shown that there is a basic difference between what experienced directors believe should happen and what does happen in practice. Asked for their opinion on how a board *should* divide its time and effort at board level, directors in the vast majority of cases suggest that the major focus should be on strategy formulation. A typical allocation of time in these studies is shown in Figure 7.4.

Notice that the respondents believe that most of the emphasis of the board's work should be on the right-hand performance aspects of the board's work (63%). They also see the focus of the board's work being predominantly on the company in its outside context (62%). In this idealized world, directors think that the left-hand conformance should be relegated to a

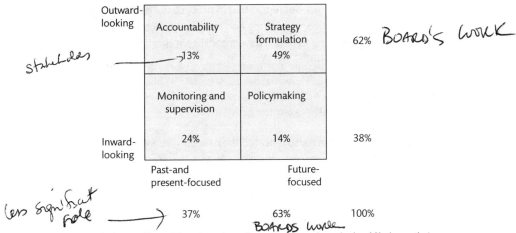

Stakeholders

62% *BOARD'S WORK*

less significant role

37%   63%   100%

BOARDS work

Figure 7.4 Normative balance of board functions: how directors suggest boards *should* balance their activities

less significant role (37%), with executive supervision taking no more than a quarter of their time and accountability to external stakeholders a relatively insignificant 13%.

However, asked to draw on their own experiences of how boards actually *do* focus their time and effort, directors produce data that resembles the results shown in Figure 7.5. In the real world of business experience, the emphasis of the board's work swings to the left-hand conformance aspects of the board's work (63%). They also see the focus of the board's work predominantly focusing inside the company (55%).

This exercise, asking directors to give their normative views on board activity, then their actual experience, has been conducted with hundreds of directors around the world. Although, of course, there is a spread of responses reflecting the different situations that can face boards, broadly the results seldom differ from those shown in Figures 7.4 and 7.5. Directors almost always believe the greater emphasis should be on the performance roles,

	Accountability	Strategy formulation	
Outward-looking	22%	23%	45%
	Monitoring and supervision	Policymaking	
Inward-looking	41%	14%	55% *BOARDS work*
	Past-and present-focused	Future-focused	
	63%	37%	100%

Figure 7.5 Reported balance of board functions: how directors believe boards *do* balance their activities

particularly strategy formulation, but report that in practice the emphasis tends to be on conformance, particularly executive monitoring and reacting to internal short-term problems. Explanations, though varying in detail, have a consistent similarity:

> Events arise that the board could not have foreseen ('a major discrepancy in the stock position', 'the death of the CFO', 'a massive budget deficit', 'the competitor unexpectedly launched a brand new service that was taking away our clients', 'a potential takeover bid'), so we have to spend more time on executive activities.

In recent years, directors have also reported the need to give a greater emphasis to accountability, partly due to greater regulatory demands and partly due to pressure from society ('shareholder expectations', 'stakeholder demands', 'the media', 'CSR needs').

Of course, these results apply to unitary boards, in which directors have to fulfil both the performance and the conformance roles. In the two-tier board, the roles are separated between the management and the supervisory boards. Nevertheless, directors often do see the need to find more time to concentrate on strategy formulation. In some cases, boards achieve this by actively devoting part of each meeting to strategic issues, by deciding to devote the entire board meeting to strategy, or by holding a strategy seminar—a day or two at which the board can be briefed on the strategic situation, can discuss the implications, can think about alternatives, and can evaluate and move towards a shared strategic vision, which will lead to new strategic plans and action in due course. Experience has suggested a number of useful pointers in running a board strategy seminar or workshop; see the guidelines for a board strategy workshop in Corporate governance in action 7.8.

Corporate governance in action 7.8   Guidelines for a board strategy seminar or workshop

- Establish leadership by the board chairman.
- Engage in careful planning, well in advance.
- Ensure a time when all directors can attend.
- Fix a location where all directors can participate.
- Define the objectives clearly, for example:
  - to explore the strategic situation;
  - to discuss the implications;
  - to consider alternative strategies;
  - to determine the next steps to be taken (but not to take strategic decisions immediately).
- All directors must be fully informed about the objectives.
- All directors should be supportive of the event.
- All directors need briefing with relevant data in advance.
- Do not hold the event in the boardroom (boardroom culture tends to be decision-orientated).
- Decide who is going to run the event (this need not be the chairman—consider the senior INED, a past director, a specialist outside consultant).
- Decide whether other people should be invited to participate (senior executives to brief the directors, external experts to provide information, experts to contribute to process).

- At the first session, establish the ground rules:
  - this is not a board meeting to make decisions, but rather a free-ranging exchange of views and insights;
  - strategic decisions will not be made—the place for that is in the normal board meeting after appropriate analysis, reports, and evaluation have taken place.
- During the session:
  - call for imaginative contributions, however unusual, and discourage negative comments ('we tried that—it doesn't work', 'never in a month of Sundays!', 'that will be no good for us').
- The output of the strategy session should be an agreed list of next actions, and who is responsible for taking them and by when.

Corporate transparency

Traditionally, boards used the historical audited financial accounts to tell shareholders the story of their stewardship. Today, listed companies are expected to say far more, not only about how the company has been performing, but also to tell the story behind its current performance and to anticipate its future. Moreover, a whole raft of stakeholders is likely to be interested, and the media of communication include the Internet as well as the printed word. Social media may supersede traditional forms of communication between a company and its stakeholders, including shareholders. The narrative has become as important as the numbers. Some company law jurisdictions and corporate governance codes now call for a statement summarizing the company's mission and main objectives, discussing its performance, its assumptions about the future and its strategies, and its exposures to risk. Indeed, with today's complex financial reporting requirements and standards, the interpretation of accounts and their voluminous footnotes may be well-nigh impossible unless one is a financial expert. Surveys have shown that many readers of annual reports now rely more on the commentary than the accounts.

New UK regulations[2] came into effect in 2014 requiring companies to prepare a strategic report as part of their formal annual company report, with some exemptions for small companies. The need to publish such narrative information can present the chairman, the other board members, and the company secretary with some real challenges. What information should be included and in how much detail? Might any of the information raise false hopes or mislead the stock market and therefore be share-price-sensitive? Could any information be useful to existing or prospective competitors?

The typical narrative report, supporting the financial and audit report, includes at least the chairman's statement, the directors' report, a corporate governance report, a remuneration report, and, increasingly, a corporate social responsibility and sustainability report. The chairman's statement is often the most-read part, because it provides a summary of the company's overall performance, its strategic orientation, and says something about its intentions. The directors' report is likely to contain more detailed management analysis on, for example, products and services, staff, international markets and competition, the corporate mission,

---

[2] The Companies Act (2006) Strategic Reporting and Directors Report Regulations (2013).

values, strategies, and plans. The corporate governance report must contain at least the minimum required by the relevant corporate governance code and listing rules, and may provide a wider discussion on the company's position on governance matters, such as corporate social responsibility and sustainability.

A sound narrative will contain at least:

- a balanced review of the business of the company;
- a comprehensive analysis of key financial and operating performance indicators;
- an explanation of the principal risks facing the company;
- details of any significant events that the company has experienced recently (for example, a major acquisition, a damaging fire, or a change of CEO);
- an indication of any planned future developments;
- a statement about the company's relationships with key stakeholders, including employees, customers, and suppliers;
- a report on the company's policies on corporate social responsibility and sustainability.

Integrated reporting, drawing together the required data from various reports into a connected narrative, is becoming more common. The crucial questions that readers of the report want to have answered are:

- what creates value in the company?
- what makes it profitable?
- what is the risk in the business?
- what is affecting the company's prospects?

The answers show how the directors see the situation and describe the real position facing the company. The directors might see the dominant future issue being in products (for example, a car manufacturer's ideas on future models and pollution controls), customers (for example, the thinking a retailer has on the effect of Internet trading), patents (for example, a pharmaceutical company's hopes for a new drug), rights (for example, an airline's concerns about landing rights), goodwill (for example, the value of a brand name), or human capital (for example, the significance of skilled staff in an IT company). Such intangible resources, although vital to a company, are seldom on the balance sheet, although International Financial Reporting Standard 3 (IFRS3) on business combinations does require the value of intangibles acquired in a takeover to be identified.

Some stock exchanges provide guidelines on what to include in the narrative commentary in a company's report. The International Accounting Standards Board, discussing the basic principles of a good management commentary, calls for 'forward-looking information that focuses on generating value for investors'.

Overall, the aim of the narrative should be to inform the market, both existing and potential shareholders, on the position and trends facing the company. It should be balanced and objective, clear and concise, unbiased and transparent, and should mention all significant possible future changes. The material factors that influence results need to be disclosed. Undue optimism and public relations 'spin' should be avoided. In discussing future expectations, ranges and probabilities can be used instead of absolute predictions. Companies that are seen to have published realistic assessments will become trusted, which in the longer term adds value.

Some stock exchanges have 'safe harbour' provisions in their rules to protect directors from legal actions over statements or omissions in their commentaries, and some Companies Acts limit liability unless statements are untrue, or misleading, in bad faith, reckless or dishonest.

Auditors do not normally report on narrative statements, but are required to ensure that the commentary is not materially inconsistent with the audited figures. Commentaries are not a substitute for the financial accounts; they should be complementary. The trend towards greater corporate transparency is worldwide, and companies that are seen to be open will be recognized and, ultimately, rewarded. Of course, more and better disclosure does not guarantee better corporate governance.

ISS, a provider of voting advice to institutional investors, suggested that for 2014 the four key tenets to be looked for in making shareholder proxy votes in listed companies, were accountability, stewardship, independence, and transparency.

Case studies

 Case study 7.1   Tyco International and Dennis Kozlowski

Tyco International (US) Inc. was incorporated in 1962 in Massachusetts to undertake research on semiconductors, principally for the government. In 1974 Tyco was listed on the New York Stock Exchange and grew, mainly by acquisition. By 1980 Tyco had become a diverse group with sales over $500 million.

The acquisition strategy continued throughout the 1980s and the group organized its many subsidiary companies into four divisions—electronics, healthcare, security and fire protection, and flow control. The electronics and healthcare were subsequently floated as independent companies.

In 1992, Dennis Kozlowski, who had joined the company in 1975, became Tyco's Chairman and CEO. He continued the aggressive acquisition strategy, acquiring many hundreds of other companies in the United States and Europe. By 1996 Tyco had grown sufficiently to join Standard and Poor's top 500 (S&P 500) US listed companies.

In 1997, Tyco merged with ADT, a UK security services company. Under the deal, Tyco International became a wholly owned subsidiary of ADT, which was incorporated in Bermuda. But ADT then changed its name to Tyco International, thus moving the Massachusetts-registered and NYSE listed company to a tax haven.

Kozlowski continued to pursue his acquisition strategy. In 1999, Tyco acquired two other S&P 500 companies—AMP Inc., an electronics manufacturer, and Raychem Corporation, a leading business in materials science. By 2000 group revenues were over $26 billion. The Simplex Time Recorder Company was acquired in 2001, and merged with Grinnell Fire Protection to create the largest fire protection company in the world. Tyco was now valued at over $100 billion, although its long-tern debt had also grown to around $80 billion.

The acquisition strategy continued, with more significant companies joining the group. But managing this vast empire had become complex. Moreover, some of the subsidiary companies began to show significant losses, particularly in fibre-optic cables and electronics. Despite sales for 2002 of nearly $35 billion, Tyco recorded a $9 billion loss. The idea of floating four separate divisions was suggested, but dropped when the group's credit rating was lowered and the share price fell.

Dennis Kozlowski's leadership style

Kozlowski's leadership style was now causing concern. He seemed to treat the company as a private fiefdom, supported by his top management team and a compliant board.

Tyco was then accused by the SEC of failure to disclose significant financial information and artificially inflating its earnings.

Kozlowski resigned.

In July 2002, Edward Breen, an experienced company president, was appointed President, CEO, and Chairman of Tyco. He quickly changed the outside directors on his board, appointing John Krol as lead director with a particular remit to improve Tyco's corporate governance. He also replaced Kozlowski's management team, introducing Eric Pillmore as Senior Vice President—Corporate Governance.

The new board and senior executives then launched an investigation into Kozlowski's past activities, which led to the company filing federal charges against Kozlowski, Mark Swartz, the company's former executive vice-president and corporate counsel, and Frank Walsh, a former director.

Meanwhile in November 2002, the State of New Jersey accused the company and the former top management of violations under the State's Racketeer Influenced and Corrupt Organizations Act. The company was also accused of violations under the Securities Act (1933) and the Securities Exchange Act (1934). The growing scandal led to class actions for damages against Tyco, Kozlowski and other former officers, from many shareholders and members of the retirement pension fund, who faced significant losses.

Kozlowski was accused of the theft of over $100 million through unauthorized bonuses, abused company loan programmes, and selling shares at inflated stock prices. He had apparently siphoned off some hundreds of millions of dollars to support his private lifestyle. He claimed that all the expenditure had been approved by the directors. Moreover he said that his contract, approved by the board, stated that should he be convicted of a felony, he would not be dismissed unless the company had been directly damaged.

Subsequent inquiries identified an infamous gold and burgundy shower curtain, that allegedly cost £6,000 and a lavish US$2 million toga party on a Mediterranean island for his wife's birthday. He had also authorized funding of US$4 million to support a chair in corporate governance at Cambridge University. He claimed that this was jointly funded by the company and himself. Some irate Tyco shareholders, hoping to retrieve some of their squandered funds, tried to recover these funds from the University. But the powers behind the chair of corporate governance insisted that they would hang on to the cash, no matter how tainted by corporate excess it might be, they could put it to good use; although they did have difficulty in finding a suitable incumbent.

The cases rolled on until, in 2005, Kozlowski was fined US$70 million and jailed for up to 25 years. At a parole hearing in 2012, Kozlowski agreed that he 'was living in a CEO-type bubble. I had a strong sense of entitlement at the time...and stole a lot of money.' He was not granted parole.

Eventually in 2014, Kozlowski, now 67, and Swartz were granted parole and left prison.

Under the guidance of John Krol, Tyco's board adopted a new set of board of governance principles and a new policy to control disbursements of cash. A guide to ethical conduct was also published, and all employees were required to take an ethics course and sign an ethics statement periodically.

See http://investors.tyco.com/phoenix.zhtml?c=112348&p=irol-irhome

---

Discussion questions

1. What could a board do to ensure that a CEO does not treat the company as a private fiefdom?

2. Should an outside director resign, or threaten to resign, if dissatisfied with actions being taken by the CEO?

3. Should the CEO be involved in the nomination of directors to the board?

Case study 7.2   Li & Fung Ltd supply chain code of conduct

Li & Fung is incorporated in Bermuda and listed in Hong Kong. Its turnover in 2013 was over US$9 billion, producing a margin of around 15%. The company partners with international brand owners and retailers around the world to optimize its supply chain management. Li and Fung Ltd is the parent of a group of companies which operate an extensive network offering logistics solutions including warehousing, transport, repacking, customs brokerage, freight forwarding, hubbing, and other value added services.

The Group believes that its:

> reputation capital is built on long-established standards of ethics in conducting business. Guidelines of the Group's core business ethical practices as endorsed by the Board are set out in the Company's Code of Conduct and Business Ethics for all Directors and staff. All the newly joined staff are briefed and requested to acknowledge their understanding of the Code.

Supply chain responsibility

Li & Fung has developed a supplier code of conduct to be observed by its approved suppliers around the globe. The code is a set of standards based on local and national laws and regulations, and International Labour Organization core conventions. A copy of the code is available at its corporate website (www.lifung.com).

The Group employs dedicated compliance staff worldwide to conduct supplier evaluations and to monitor compliance to the code among the suppliers that produce its customers' merchandise. The Group's vendor compliance (VC) division is organized independent of its sourcing/merchandising divisions and focuses on improving suppliers' labour, health and safety, environmental, and security standards. The VC division conducts evaluations of approved suppliers on a routine and systematic basis in accordance with industry-defined and customers' specific audit standards, protocols, and methodologies. The scope of an evaluation includes an opening meeting, site inspection, employee and management interview, document review, reporting, and closing meeting.

Li & Fung also provides systematic training both internally to its employees and externally to its suppliers to equip them with awareness, knowledge, and the necessary skills and tools they need to understand and meet compliance requirements. In 2009, the company continued supplier training and education efforts expanding the scope to include additional focus areas of energy efficiency, water pollution prevention, and cleaner production.

Environmental protection

Li & Fung has further enhanced its supplier environmental programmes and initiatives aimed at resource conservation, environmental protection, and product stewardship. Li & Fung enforced its customers' environmental purchasing policies with respect to eco-friendly materials, package waste minimization, and product stewardship. The company also took an active role in supporting its customers in innovating and developing new tools and systems to support their sustainability programmes. By adopting and promoting environmental considerations as an integral part of its business activities, the Group equates the environment to its other critical business considerations such as compliance, quality, and value.

Li & Fung is a component of the Dow Jones Sustainability World Indexes, the world's first global indexes tracking the performance of companies worldwide in the three main dimensions of corporate sustainability: social, economic, and environmental responsibilities. Li & Fung has also been included as a constituent member in the FTSE4Good Index Series from FTSE Group (UK), recognizing Li & Fung's commitment to high corporate social responsibility standards.

Discussion questions

1. Use the company's website to answer the questions:

   What is the structure of the Li & Fung board?

   What board committees does the board have?

   Who are the members and how often did they meet?

   What is the remuneration policy for non-executive directors?

2. What are the key elements of the supplier code of conduct?

3. If you were advising the main directors of Li and Fung, where would you recommend that strategy was formulated and policies made?

References and further reading

Abrahams, Jeffrey (1999) *The Mission Statement Book: 301 Corporate Mission Statements from America's Top Companies.* Ten Speed Press, Berkeley, CA.

Faulkner, David O. (ed.) (2006) *The Oxford Handbook of Strategy.* Oxford University Press, Oxford.

FRC (2012) *Guidance to Audit Committees*, Financial Reporting Council, London.

FRC (2011) *Guidance on Board Effectiveness*, Financial Reporting Council, London.

Hartman, Laura P. and Joseph R. Desjardins (2013) *Business Ethics: Decision-Making for Personal Integrity & Social Responsibility.* 2nd edn, McGraw Hill, New York.

Kakabadse, Andrew and Nada (2007) *Leading the Board.* Palgrave Macmillan, Basingstoke.

Knowdl, Jeremy (2008) *Business Strategy: A Guide to Effective Decision Making.* Economist/Profile Books, London.

McNulty, T. J. and P. Stiles (2003) *Creating Accountability within the Board: The work of the Non-executive Director.* DTI, London.

NACD (2006) *Role of the Board on Corporate Strategy: Report of a NACD Blue Ribbon Commission*, National Association of Corporate Directors, 1133, Suite 700 21 Street, Washington, DC, USA.

Solomon, Jill (2013) *Corporate Governance and Accountability.* 4th edn, Wiley, London.

Steinberg, Richard M. (2000) *Corporate Governance and the Board: What Works Best.* Internal Auditors Research Foundation, Altamonte Springs, FL.

Tarantino, Anthony (2007) *Manager's Guide to Compliance: Sarbanes-Oxley, COSO, ERM, COBIT, IFRS, BASEL II, OMB's A-123, ASX 10, OECD Principles, Turnbull Guidance, Best Practices, and Case Studies.* Wiley, Hoboken, NJ.

Projects and exercises

1. Review the mission statements of leading companies, including those listed earlier in this chapter and others found on company websites.

   - Do you think that they really add anything to the strategy formulation process?
   - Is there a danger that they could become merely part of the public relations effort of an organization?
   - If so, how could this be avoided?
   - Do you think that they contribute to corporate culture and the creation of a common approach to management decision-making?

2. Undertake a strategic assessment of an organization to which you have access. Use both SWOT analysis and a review of the competitive strategic environment of the entity. Prepare a report/presentation for the governing body of that organization.

3. Review the management control systems and the reporting to the board for an organization to which you have access.

4. Identify the strategy formulation, policymaking, executive monitoring, and supervision and accountability activities in other organizations with which you are familiar or from which you can obtain information.

Self-test questions

1. Define 'strategy' formulation.
2. What is a mission statement?
3. Why might long-range planning not be a useful tool for strategy formulation?
4. What are the five forces in the five forces model?
5. What is resource-based strategic theory?
6. What are corporate policies?
7. Name some management control systems that can be used by directors to monitor management performance.
8. What is suboptimization?
9. To whom is a board accountable?
10. What is exception reporting?

8 The Governance of Corporate Risk

 Learning Outcomes

In which we consider:

- The US COSO integrated framework for enterprise risk management (ERM)
- The global financial crisis: a new emphasis on corporate risk
- Levels of risk: the concept of enterprise risk management
- Responsibility for risk profiling, risk strategy, risk policy, and risk supervision
- Identifying types of risk
- Risk analysis
- Risk recognition and assessment
- Risk evaluation
- Risk management information systems
- Risk transfer

Board-level commitment to corporate risk assessment was reinforced by the global financial crisis. For some boards, that was a new experience. The Cadbury Report (1992) mentioned risk only in the context of boards' responsibility for avoiding financial fraud, although, in fairness, that report was only about the financial aspects of corporate governance. A Global Enterprise Risk Management (ERM) Survey,[1] conducted by insurance group Aon, noted the global financial crisis had significantly increased awareness of the need to manage and leverage risk. The report identified some hallmarks of advanced ERM:

- board-level commitment to ERM as a critical framework for successful decision-making and for driving value;
- the engagement of all stakeholders in the development of risk management strategy and policy setting;
- a move from focusing on risk avoidance and mitigation to leveraging risk and risk management options to extract business value.

Another Aon Global Risk Management Survey[2] sought board-level opinions on the top ten business risks recognized in 2013 and projected to 2016. Theses were:

---

[1] Aon (2010) *Global Enterprise Risk Management Survey.* Aon Center, 200 East Randolph Street, Chicago, Ill 60601, USA. www.aon.com
[2] www.aon.com/2013GlobalRisk

Risk description	Risk ranking 2013	Risk ranking Projected 2016
Economic slowdown or slow recovery	1	1
Regulatory and legislative changes	2	2
Increasing competition	3	3
Damage to reputation or brand	4	8
Failure to attract and retain top talent	5	5
Failure to innovate and meet customer needs	6	4
Business interruption	7	11
Commodity price risk	8	7
Cash flow/liquidity risk	9	10
Political risk and uncertainty	10	6

Security of corporate information has emerged as a virulent form of risk. No longer a technical issue at the operational level, boards need to involve information technology expertise in every major decision at the managerial and strategic levels. Hackers can enter corporate systems through employees' personal information devices used to access corporate systems, through malware in external links such as credit card payment systems and video-conferencing equipment, even external access to printers, thermostat controls, and vending machines. Cyber attack is a significant exposure to risk.

In the United States, the Committee of Sponsoring Organizations (COSO) of the Treadway Commission pioneered the development of ERM, emphasizing the significance of the board's involvement, as we saw in Chapter 7.

The US COSO integrated framework for enterprise risk management (ERM)

In 2004, COSO provided an integrated framework for ERM, building on the 2002 Sarbanes-Oxley Act. It explained that:

> Enterprise risk management is a process effected by the entity's board of directors, management, and other personnel, applied in strategy setting and across the enterprise, designed to identify potential events that may affect the entity, and manage risk so that it is within the risk appetite, to provide reasonable assurance regarding the achievement of objectives. The challenge facing Boards is how to oversee the organization's enterprise-wide risk management effectively in a way that balances managing risks while adding value to the organization. An entity's board of directors plays a critical role in overseeing an enterprise-wide approach to risk management.

COSO's Enterprise Risk Management Integrated Framework[3] highlights four areas that contribute to board oversight of ERM:

- understanding the entity's risk philosophy and concurring with the entity's risk appetite;
- knowing the extent to which management has established effective ERM of the organization;
- reviewing the entity's portfolio of risk and considering it against the entity's risk appetite;

[3] An executive summary of COSO's Enterprise Risk Management: Integrated Framework providing an overview of the key principles is available at www.coso.org

- being apprised of the most significant risks and of whether management is responding appropriately.

The New York Stock Exchange's listing rules require the audit committees of listed corporations to explain their risk assessment and management policies.

The global financial crisis: a new emphasis on corporate risk

In the light of the global financial crisis, the Steering Group on Corporate Governance of the OECD re-examined the adequacy of its corporate governance principles. The Group concluded that the board's responsibility for defining strategy and risk appetite needed to be extended, because in some important cases the risk management system was not compatible with a company's strategy and risk appetite. Building on the OECD Principles, the report proposed that it is good practice for:

- the risk management function to report directly to the board;
- the risk management function to consider any risks arising directly from the compensation and incentive systems in place;
- the effectiveness of the risk assessment and management process to be monitored and the results disclosed, noting that experience with such disclosures up until now had not been good.

In the United Kingdom, the 1999 Turnbull Report drew attention to the importance of board-level risk assessment. The UK Corporate Governance Code,[4] previously the UK Combined Code, includes principles on boards' responsibility for risk management, calling for an integrated approach to ERM. The Financial Review Council (FRC) considered the likely effect of the global financial crisis on the governance of companies, but failed to find evidence of serious failings in the governance of British business, outside the banking sector.

In 2008, a Bank of England report on financial stability and risk management called for 'effective firm-wide identification and analysis of risk including information sharing across the organization, particularly between senior management and business lines, and firm-wide plans to reduce exposures or hedge risks'. The report noted that 'one clear shortcoming has been banks' overreliance on credit ratings in determining inherent risk'. Credit rating agencies now include ERM processes in their corporate credit rating analyses.

In 2010, the International Corporate Governance Network (ICGN) enhanced its Global Corporate Governance Principles with a set of Corporate Risk Oversight Guidelines.[5] The Guidelines emphasize that:

- the risk oversight process begins with the board;
- corporate management is responsible for developing and executing an enterprise's strategic and routine operational risk programme;

---

[4] Proposed Reforms to the UK Corporate Governance Code (2009) FRC PN 287, 1 December.
[5] International Corporate Governance Network, ICGN Corporate Risk Oversight Guidelines, ICGN, 16 Park Crescent, London, W1B 1AH, UK, September 2010.

shareholders, directly or through designated agents, have a responsibility to assess and monitor the effectiveness of boards in overseeing risk at the companies in which they invest:

> Strategy, risk tolerance, and risk are inseparable and should be connected in all discussions in the board or supervisory board. Capital allocation and capital structure should be visibly aligned with strategy and risk tolerance. The board should hold management accountable for developing a strategy that correlates with the risk tolerance of the organization.

In 2012, the United Kingdom's Financial Reporting Council (FRC), required listed companies to disclose in their annual report the company's 'principal risks'. In a guidance note the FRC suggested that 'the principal risks should be disclosed and described irrespective of how they are classified or whether they result from strategic decision, operations, organization or behaviour, or from external factors over which the board may have little or no direct control'.

Levels of risk: the concept of enterprise risk management

Corporate risk arises at every level in organizations—strategic, managerial, and operational. Operational risks occur within the enterprise: fire, accident, theft, and so on. Managerial risks reflect hazards that could occur from the organization's activities: product liability, third-party risks, and local pollution, for example. Risks at these levels are typically well handled by ERM policies and systems. They are also readily covered by insurance in many cases. At the operational and managerial levels, the directors' responsibility is to ensure that appropriate policies and control systems are in place and are effective throughout the organization. The board is acting in a supervisory role, overseeing management policies, systems, and performance. Many boards delegate such responsibilities to their audit committee; indeed this is recommended by some stock exchange listing rules.

Critical strategic risk, however, is another matter. Consider the following cases.

- At Enron, the board failed to understand that the company had moved beyond being a supplier of energy to a business trading in financial derivatives (see Case study 4.2). In effect, Enron had become a financial institution with a quite different risk profile. Moreover, the outside directors seemed to be unaware of the high risks that their executive directors were taking.

- The Toyota car company had developed a worldwide reputation for growth based on innovation and quality. The board built up a highly successful company using tight Japan-centred management oversight and control. Unfortunately, the directors failed to foresee the risks when they expanded the company's supply chains and manufacturing locations around the world. The price they paid was massive product recalls of entire ranges of automobiles with problem brakes, steering, and electronics. The financial cost to the company was heavy; the effect on its reputation was worse.

- None of the non-executive directors at the British Northern Rock bank were bankers. The chairman was a zoologist. The executive directors, placing more emphasis on revenue generation than risk management, traded in sub-prime mortgage products. The board failed to appreciate the risks involved and the business was bailed out by the British government and the company nationalized (see Case study 8.1).

- The board of BP plc faced a strategic catastrophe when the collapse of the Deepwater Horizon oil rig led to massive pollution in the Gulf of Mexico. The disaster, which had been treated as operational or managerial risk by the board, had political and economic impacts that more than halved the company's market value and even put its survival at risk (see Case study 8.2).

Responsibility for risk profiling, risk strategy, risk policy, and risk supervision

Running a business, indeed running almost every enterprise, involves risk. Risk can only be avoided by choosing to do nothing—and even then unexpected events can occur. In many business situations, as is well known, the greater the risk, the greater the potential return to the enterprise.

The challenge to boards is to balance risk with acceptable reward. In other words, to understand the exposure of their companies to risk, to determine how those risks are faced, and to ensure that they are handled appropriately. Corporate governance involves creating business value while managing risk. Risk management, not risk minimization, should be the theme. Boards have a specific and vital responsibility to recognize, understand, and accept the risk profile inherent in their corporate strategies, what some people call 'approving the company's risk appetite'.

Every board has a duty to ensure that:

- significant risks facing its company are recognized;
- risk assessment systems exist and are effective throughout the organization;
- risk evaluation procedures are developed and operational;
- risk monitoring systems are robust, efficient, and effective;
- business continuity strategies and risk management policies exist, are regularly updated, and are applied in practice.

We saw earlier that many corporate governance codes and companies law now call for boards to give assurances that systems are in place to handle corporate risk in their regular corporate governance reports to shareholders.

Directors need to understand where value is added within their business, at which points the company is critically exposed to risk, and where the most sensitive areas are in which the very survival of the business could be threatened. Boards need to face up to those risks and to develop relevant risk strategies and policies. Such responsibilities call for a formal system to ensure that risk is properly assessed and considered at board level and then professionally managed throughout the company.

Sophisticated investors around the world focus on the nature and extent of risk in the companies and industries in which they invest. Companies that are recognized as having professional ERM and transparent risk reporting are respected. Their shares can command a premium over those of competitors, and their overall cost of capital is likely to be lower.

Some boards include corporate risk assessment in the mandate of the board audit committee. However, audit committees can be orientated towards the past, involved with audit outcomes and approving accountability information for publication. Whereas risk assessment needs a proactive, forward-looking orientation. Consequently, other boards have decided to create a risk assessment or risk management committee as a distinct standing committee of the board. Such a committee might have four or five members, wholly or mainly independent non-executive directors (INEDs) with appropriate business experience. Initially, when a company is building its risk management systems, the committee might meet quite frequently, but then two or three times a year, reporting to the board as a whole. Members of senior management and external experts in risk are likely to be invited to attend to advise the committee.

An alternative approach is for the board to form a management-based risk management group, perhaps including the chief executive officer (CEO), the chief finance officer (CFO), profit-responsible division or unit heads, and the responsible risk management executive(s). External experts could also be invited to advise the group. A management-based risk management group needs to take a strategic view of corporate risk and to avoid adopting a purely financial view. In other words, the group needs to see the enterprise in the context of its overall risk profile, not only from a financial perspective. A management-based risk group might typically report to the CEO or CFO, but it is essential that its work is reviewed and approved at board level. Of course, it is possible that a company might decide to have both a board-level risk management committee *and* a management-based group reporting to it.

The issue of risk management is particularly significant in the case of financial institutions. Indeed in essence, their entire business involves the management of risk. This was confirmed in a report[6] by the Basel Committee on Banking Supervision, widely known as Basel II: 'The bank's board of directors has a responsibility for setting the board's tolerance for risks.' Favourable capital adequacy decisions need to demonstrate that the bank's 'board of directors and senior management, as appropriate, are actively involved in the oversight of the operational risk management framework'. According to the report, a risk policy committee to fulfil this requirement should have its own written charter, board representation with at least three independent directors with the requisite skills and knowledge to oversee risk management, and a chairman appointed by the whole board.

Many major companies have specialist risk managers to oversee the company-wide risk assessment systems and procedures, who can advise the board on risk issues. The chief risk officer (CRO) is an increasingly important figure in many companies, just as the global head of risk is in international banks. The risk management committee will typically agree the job description, appoint, and monitor the CRO, who is then secretary to that committee.

The global financial crisis, which resulted in the collapse of financial institutions and the need for government support in a number of countries, also led to the re-evaluation of the governance of risk. In some banks, the power of financial risk-takers was rebalanced in favour of the CRO and the risk assessment function. Goldman Sachs achieves a balance between risk-taking traders and potentially risk-averse risk officers by moving traders into risk management functions as part of their career progression, although in other institutions the CRO remains little more than a compliance officer.

Unfortunately, in some companies, risk management issues seldom reach board level. The management of risk is piecemeal and undertaken at the business unit level—sometimes known as a 'silo' or 'bucket' approach, with each part of the organization standing on its own base. Responsibility for risk management is then located in middle management, with managers insuring the business against the classical risks of fire, theft, and accident. This

---

[6] Basel Committee on Banking Supervision (2007) *International Convergence of Capital Measurement and Capital Standards: A Revised Framework* (Basel II).

orientation is likely to be operational rather than strategic, and to have more to do with cost reduction, searching for the cheapest cover available, than with conscientious risk assessment. Moreover, the middle manager can become a bottleneck, even a block, between the board and its responsibility for overall strategic risk assessment and management.

Identifying types of risk

As we have already seen, in every organization, risk arises at various levels:

- *corporate strategic risks*—exposure to threats from outside the organization;
- *management-level risks*—exposure to risks arising from the firm's activities;
- *operational risks*—exposure to hazards within the enterprise.

Corporate governance in action 8.1 gives an example of how one company approaches these risks.

Corporate governance in action 8.1   An approach to corporate risk—the Sage Group plc

Sage is a leading supplier of business management software and services to 6.3 million customers worldwide. Its annual report contains a detailed corporate risk report, with an analysis of each risk, the potential impact, and the factors considered by the company to mitigate that risk.

Principal risks and uncertainties

Risks can materialize and impact on both the achievement of business objectives and the successful running of Sage's business. A key element in achieving business objectives and maintaining services to customers is the management of risks. Sage's risk management strategy is therefore to support the successful running of the business by identifying and managing risks to an acceptable level, and delivering assurances on this.

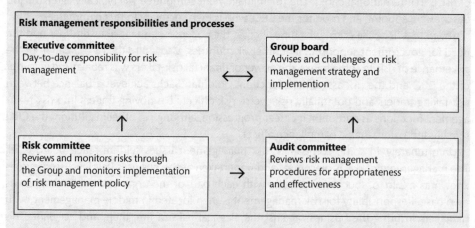

Risk management responsibilities and processes

Executive committee
Day-to-day responsibility for risk management

Group board
Advises and challenges on risk management strategy and implemention

Risk committee
Reviews and monitors risks through the Group and monitors implementation of risk management policy

Audit committee
Reviews risk management procedures for appropriateness and effectiveness

(For the full corporate risk report of the Sage Group, go to http://ar2010.sage.com/Principal-risks.asp for more on the company, see www.sage.com)

One approach to identifying significant risk is to consider what circumstances or events could affect the key drivers of business value and cause planned performance to fail to meet expected outcomes. A board, having recognized potential catastrophic events that could put the very survival of the firm at risk, needs to have a business continuity strategy to respond to such exposure.

Corporate governance in action 8.2 is an extract from the risk management policy handbook of a financial institution, showing the risks recognized at strategic, managerial, and operational levels.

Corporate governance in action 8.2 Levels of risk management policy in a London finance house

The main board of a significant financial institution has developed risk management strategies and policies that cover all levels of the organization, from externally generated risks to in-house hazards. The board regularly discusses its risk management policies at each level. The following contents page from the risk management manual lists the areas of responsibility recognized by the risk assessment programme:

External strategic threats

- Competitors' activities
- Customers' activities
- Stock and finance markets hazards
- Government and regulator activities
- Criminal activity
- Loss of electronic communication and hacking data bases
- Terrorism or politically activated actions
- Economic, political, or social events
- Suppliers' activities
- Other external events, hazards, or risks

Internal strategic and management-level risks

- Board level strategic failings
- Lack of board level security
- Management weaknesses, inability
- Shortages of skilled, experienced staff
- Management-level fraud or corruption

Operational risks and hazards (for each risk management department or unit)

- Fire, explosion, flood
- Loss of power (e.g. inability to carry out trades)
- IT systems malfunction, loss or theft of vital data
- Poor cyber-security

- Shortages of staff (e.g. staff turnover, illness, strike, poaching)
- Errors in trades (unintentional mistakes)
- Deals made by staff beyond their limits, contrary to trading policies
- Fraud and misfeasance (i.e. deliberate actions by traders)
- Theft
- Misuse of company information, equipment, systems, or software
- Other events, risks, or hazards

The extracts from the risk assessment system of a global pharmaceutical company in Corporate governance in action 8.3 give an insight into the types of strategic risk that could have catastrophic outcomes. Much of the literature on risk management focuses on risk at the operational level, for example on health and safety hazards to employees, disease risks in hospitals, and waste management hazards in public health. But contemporary thinking about risk recognizes that risk management policies at the operational level are not enough. An enterprise is more likely to fail disastrously from risks at management or strategic levels. Reputational risk, the damage to corporate reputation arising from a strategic event such as a product failure that leads to the loss of life, a disastrous environmental disaster, or the exposure of a bribery scandal, can be more damaging to profitability and shareholder value in the long term than the immediate direct costs. Yet a 2013 study, conducted in association with the New York Stock Exchange, found that 25% of board-level respondents felt that risk was given insufficient focus in their board meetings and 26% felt that risk information was received too late for thorough review.

Corporate governance in action 8.3   Strategic-level risk assessment policies in an international pharmaceutical company

The main board of this group has agreed a set of risk assessment policies, based on information from a comprehensive and continuous risk management system. The detail runs to many pages, but the following extract indicates the type of risk reviewed at the strategic level.

Strategic-level risks

Marketing area

Competitors

- New entrants into significant products or markets
- Change of ownership of competitors (e.g. mergers)
- Change of competitors' distribution strategy
- New research breakthroughs
- Change of pricing/distribution strategies
- Expansion into new markets (country or type)
- Competitors change manufacturing technology

Customers

- Cost of product recall (financial and reputational)
- Adopting substitute products (e.g. generics)
- Collapse or bankruptcy of major customer
- Change of ownership of main distributor
- Catastrophic failure of our product in use
- Legal actions for damages
- Alleged patent or copyright infringement

Governmental

- New pharmacological control laws
- New environmental or hazard limitation laws
- Constraints on manufacturing or delivery processes
- Monopoly, anti-trust or pricing inquiries
- Cost-cutting by government (e.g. UK NHS)
- Political threats to operations in overseas countries

Finance area

Predators

- Hostile takeover approaches
- Acquisition strategies of private equity firms

Sources of finance

- Recall of debt capital (e.g. bankruptcy of lender)
- Change of ownership resulting in new policies

Shareholders

- Share price collapse following media revelations
- Reputational loss following an adverse law case

Information technology area

e-links with customers, suppliers and shareholders

- Hacking of systems for fraud, spying or mischief

  Management and operational-level risks are also covered by this risk assessment system.

When one board chairman suggested that each director should identify five critical risks that would prove fatal to the achievement of the business plan if they occurred, many of the directors were surprised at the nature and the extent of risks they had not even considered. Such an exercise, of course, leads to the development of strategies and policies to handle the risks. The possibility of the business failing seldom occurs to directors, but business continuity can become a vital issue if a catastrophe occurs.

The WikiLeaks disclosures and subsequent phone hacking scandals heightened awareness in some boardrooms of the importance of IT controls, internal procedures, and a corporate culture that sets strict standards on the use of e-mail, the world-wide-web, and social media to reduce the risk of the loss of trade secrets, the exposure of secret financial negotiations, or the disclosure of confidential market data. The speed of modern media can turn an exposed issue into massive reputational loss unless boards have appropriate policies and plans ready to meet such eventualities.

Environmental challenges arising from climate change, rising sea levels, energy shortages, and other global issues are increasingly seen by some companies as being a significant threat and potential risk.

Risk analysis

The analysis of risk in an organization involves a number of iterative phases:

- Risk recognition
- Risk assessment
- Risk evaluation
- Risk management policies
- Risk monitoring

The basic elements of the risk analysis process are shown in Figure 8.1.

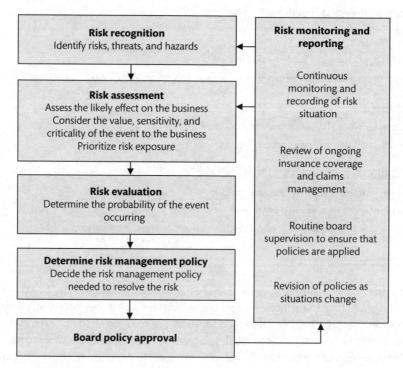

Figure 8.1 The risk analysis and management process

Some countries, including Australia, the United States, and the United Kingdom, have created standards for risk management under the auspices of the International Organization for Standardization (ISO).[7] The Business Continuity Institute also offers benchmarks and evaluation criteria (see www.thebci.org).

The Institute of Chartered Accountants in England and Wales (ICAEW) compiled a list of benefits from the introduction of sound governance and risk management that included:

- greater likelihood of achieving objectives;
- higher share price in the long term;
- greater likelihood of successful change initiatives;
- lower cost of capital;
- early movement into new business areas;
- improved use of insurance;
- reduction in the cost of remedial work and 'firefighting';
- achievement of competitive advantage;
- less business interruption;
- achievement of compliance/regulatory targets.

Some commentators suggest that good corporate governance with professional risk management can reduce insurance costs. This is not necessarily true, but good corporate governance can protect against excessive penalties and improve the ability to get cover, even against substantial risks.

In Chapter 2, we introduced the basic quadrant of board performance and conformance activities (see Figure 8.2).

The components of the risk analysis process depicted, can be mapped onto this quadrant (as in Figure 8.3).

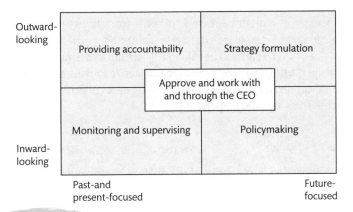

Figure 8.2 Framework for analysing board activities

[7] ISO31000 (1999) AS/NZS 4360.

Figure 8.3 Framework showing board risk analysis and management responsibilities

Risk recognition and assessment

Although some threats that could significantly harm a business may be obvious and easily guarded against, other risks can be hard to recognize. Unless they have occurred before, there will be no previous experience in the organization. Moreover, other companies tend to hide bad news, thus increasing the underestimation of potential risks.

Threats, such as those caused by critical changes in competitors' strategies, serious loss of business through criminal activity, disgruntled employees' actions or terrorist threats, kidnap or other loss of top executives, or the effects of natural disaster, for example, may be difficult to imagine, yet could prove to be catastrophic. Major business interruption—even challenges to business continuity—can come from unexpected occurrences.

How do firms go about the task of identifying risk at every level? The vital element in corporate risk recognition is the creation of a corporate culture that places risk at the centre of thinking throughout the organization. This can be achieved only with motivation from the top: from the chairman and his or her board. In-house workshops and seminars are used by some to generate insights. External experts may be able to offer experience and an independent view. The advice of INEDs can also be valuable. There are also a number of risk assessment and risk management tools available. Many are qualitative in nature; others seek to add an element of quantification; some involve computerized data collection and analysis. The following approaches show the range of options.

A simple tabular approach

The organization is divided into a series of risk analysis centres, which may well reflect the structure of the organization and its management control systems. Executives in each risk analysis centre identify and chart the following:

Nature of risk or hazard	Likely effects and outcome	Likelihood of event occurring	Risk management policy response

The procedures documentation for the risk analysis programme should contain guidance to staff on the range of risks to be covered, including likely effects or outcomes of each occurrence. It is important that the risk analysis is conducted in each part of the organization and at every level. Experience shows that the initial risk assessment report will trigger further ideas and insights, which improve the subsequent risk assessment. The simple narrative table can be turned into a matrix by including estimated costs and an estimated probability of the uncertain risk or hazard occurring. A potential drawback of this approach is that a managerial focus might fail to identify strategic risks.

A questionnaire designed to identify risks and hazards

If this approach is used throughout the organization, insights into risk can be generated in every part of an organization and at every level. A benefit of this approach is standardization of responses throughout the organization. This format can also be used to document compliance and non-compliance with risk management policies. An elaboration of the questionnaire approach is to include multiple-choice responses, as well as to invite a narrative description.

Mind mapping

This involves a visual approach to recognizing risk factors, plotting their interrelationships, and then deriving the possible implications. Users of this method require some training and skill in the methodology. Benefits can include an appreciation of the relationships between risks and the identification of different risk elements from those generated by tabulation or questionnaire.

Risk benchmarking by industry, country, or against other companies

This methodology starts with a list of possible risks or hazards as the basis for developing the risk profile of the subject company. The list can identify risks related to the type of company, its industry, and locations of operation.

Software programs and systems

IT-based solutions to risk analysis and management are used by many organizations. These can provide online access to the identification and reporting of risks. Proprietary programs and systems are available from software houses, consulting firms, and companies in the insurance industry. Some of these programs provide a risk management information system, which link risk recognition and assessment, risk evaluation, and ERM policies, and can also be linked to claims management systems.

Information on strategic-level risks can be generated as part of an ongoing strategic review, as discussed in Chapter 7. The firm's strategy formulation process, using tools such as SWOT analysis, Porter 'five forces' analysis, or some other analytical methodology, can also generate information about potential risk. This can be used to evaluate possible effects, should they happen, estimate the likelihood that they would occur, and decide the suitable policy response. This information can then be incorporated into the strategic-level risk management policies approved by the board.

Experience has shown that a successful risk recognition and assessment programme has a number of critical success factors, including:

- sponsorship and oversight at board level;
- top management commitment;
- involvement throughout all levels of management and in all parts of the enterprise;
- company-wide definition of procedures, documentation, and reporting;
- identification of risk management centres throughout the organization;
- definition of responsibilities for identifying and recommending risk responses;
- risk management centres are given appropriate responsibility;
- areas of risk are carefully defined and bounded, each one limited in scope;
- involvement of business and technical experts with relevant risk assessment experience;
- document at all stages, regularly updated and building on experience;
- define authentication and approval, confidentiality levels, access control, availability, audit, and overall administration responsibilities;
- the creation of a risk awareness, not risk avoidance, attitude throughout the organization;
- ensuring participation by identifying the 'ownership' of risks throughout the organization;
- board-level leadership and approval of risk management policies is vital.

A risk assessment programme not only enables firms to identify risks and to develop appropriate risk management policies, but it also supports ongoing business activities by causing staff to recognize risks and thus avoid them, by enabling directors to appreciate the nature and extent of their risk profiles and to make appropriate judgements, and finally by enabling the firm to report confidently to shareholders and other stakeholders that corporate risks are being well managed.

Risk evaluation

The extent of any risk (R) is a function of the magnitude of the potential cost or loss (L) and the probability (p) that the uncertain future event will occur.

Expressed mathematically:

A specific risk $R_i = L_i\, p(L)i$ and the firm's total risk exposure $R\,(total) = \sum L_i\, p(L_i)$

Unfortunately, both the cost and the probability of some events can often be difficult to assess. Some costs, such as the loss of customer confidence should a product fail, the loss of reputation following a financial or executive scandal, or the effect on the cost of capital following the lowering of a credit rating, can be difficult to estimate. Reliable and current data often preclude an exact estimate, but broad estimates, within ranges, do need to be made.

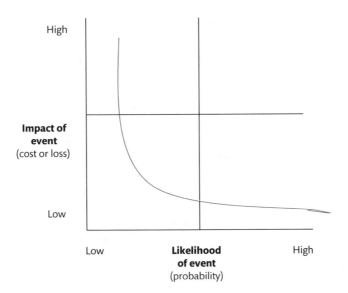

Figure 8.4 Risk mapping

Similarly, the probability of a risk occurring can be problematical. But a view needs to be taken. The judgement of knowledgeable individuals, including INEDs, can be useful. Careful documentation is important and the resultant policy needs to be well written, so that subsequent action can be taken to ensure that the policy is being followed and reviewed when necessary.

A risk that would result in a high loss, but with a low chance of occurring, may well be treated differently in a firm's risk management policies from one with a lower cost, but greater probability. There is all the more reason, therefore, to identify the existence of a risk or hazard in the first place, and for management and, ultimately, the board to face up to the reality of the situation. The risk map in Figure 8.4 illustrates the situation, which highlights the importance of board-level involvement in ERM policies.

- In the high impact/high likelihood quadrant, the board will want to give a lot of consideration to appropriate policies. For example, the directors may decide to incur considerable expenditure on system redundancy or standby systems, on staff training, on reserves of materials, stock, or finance, or on simulation exercises to test response time and quality. This is the quadrant in which sharing risk through financial instruments or external insurance cover can be of fundamental importance. The board will also want to ensure that it has information systems that monitor such situations and that the company is able to respond quickly to the event.

- In the high impact/low likelihood quadrant, the board has the option of taking action to mitigate the impact, assume the risk, or insure.

- In the low impact/high probability quadrant, the board can take defensive action to limit the impact, but may well decide to carry any further costs itself. Of course, insurance remains an option, but the high probability will produce higher premiums.

- In the low impact/low likelihood quadrant, the need for board policies varies from low to insignificant. Control systems to reflect the situation, procedures to respond to it, and some staff training to mitigate adverse effects might be all that are needed.

Risk management information systems

Currently, in some companies, risk management systems are piecemeal and scattered with duplications and errors. Directors in such companies all too often learn of risks once they have become problems. Boards should ensure that they are fully apprised of significant risks so that appropriate business continuity strategies and risk management policies can be put in place ahead of time.

Internationally, the trend is towards centralization of information and risk management responsibility. Such enterprise risk management systems (ERMS) provide information routinely and regularly for management to take executive decisions, and for the board to carry out its monitoring and supervisory function. The ERMS should also generate information to enable the company to communicate externally to auditors, regulators, shareholders, and other legitimate stakeholders, as to well as to its insurers and brokers. However, because such systems hold masses of vital information, data protection, confidentiality, and cyber-security are vital. There are a number of so-called enterprise governance, risk and compliance platforms that provide technology-based under-pinning for ERMS.

A successful ERMS will provide an information interchange, with links throughout the company to the centre, and also link to brokers and insurers. However, online risk management information systems may contain confidential data on strategic issues. Wrongful access could lead to the loss of valuable corporate information. Security and confidentiality are vital. Rights of access need to be controlled. The right to update information also needs to be secure. Such systems are sometimes built in-house, but increasingly packages are available from specialist firms, for example the RiskConsole system from AON Insurance.

Risk transfer

Identifying corporate risk strategies and establishing risk policies are, essentially, board decisions. Board-level strategies that recognize strategic threats to the enterprise are vital, with policies agreed by the board to determine which risk management decisions are reserved to the board. Every board develops a unique risk profile and establishes that board's risk tolerance—that is, the directors' appetite for risks. Detailed work may be delegated to management, but the oversight of risk is a basic element in corporate governance and thus the responsibility of the board. In developing risk policies, a board has to trade off short-term costs against long-term benefits.

In establishing the company's risk policies, every board faces four possible responses to risk.

1. Avoid the risk. Do not commit to the planned action. Abandon the proposed project.
2. Mitigate the risk by making capital investments or incurring ongoing expenditure, for example by investing in standby equipment, duplicate/triplicate critical components,

staff training, risk policies such as requiring top executives to travel in different cars and planes, or never building on flood plains or in typhoon/hurricane locations.

3. Transfer the risk. Spread the exposure with other parties. Insure against the risk, thereby transferring elements of risk to the insurance company, while recognizing that some risks may be uninsurable. Create derivative instruments—that is, agreements with financial institutions that transfer risk to third parties. Negotiate forward contracts for the supply of goods and services.

4. Retain the risk. In other words, accept the risk. Self-insuring is an approach adopted by many governmental organizations. This risk strategy—what some commentators call the firm's 'risk appetite'—needs to be made at board level.

Risk management policies typically involve costs: both capital costs and ongoing expenditure, such as the cost of building hardware and software systems into a company's customer ordering system to reduce opportunities for a sophisticated hacker to steal information, damage system operations, or perpetrate fraud. Continuing expenditure can include staff and operating expenditure for providing security, ongoing training, and updating routines. In determining the overall risk management policy, the board will need to compare the costs of control with the discounted value of the outcome [Li p(L)i] and determine the cost–benefit relationship.

Not only should directors ensure that the firm's risk management policies are in place, but they should also assure themselves that the framework or system for risk management is effective. Induction training and regular updating of directors and senior staff should form part of the firm's risk management programme.

Enterprise risk profiling, risk strategy formulation, and policymaking and risk supervision have now become integral parts of the corporate governance portfolio. Every board has a duty to ensure that risk assessment and management systems are functioning at each level and that appropriate risk management policies are in place.

Moreover, regulators increasingly require firms to report on the quality of their risk management.

Overall, boards that handle risk professionally, as part of their normal corporate governance activities, are able to face increasing risk without making their enterprises riskier.

Case studies

 Case study 8.1   The collapse of Northern Rock bank

A run on a British bank is very rare, but in September 2007 it happened to Northern Rock, the United Kingdom's fifth biggest mortgage lender. Northern Rock had around 1.5 million depositors with savings of £28 billion, and some 800,000 homeowner borrowers. The company, formerly a British building society (savings and loan association), was incorporated as a public company in 1997 and floated on the London Stock Exchange. By 2000, it had grown dramatically to join the FTSE 100 index.

The auditors of the 2006 accounts, the 'big four' firm PricewaterhouseCoopers, expressed no concerns about the financial state of affairs; the company was profitable and had access to funds.

Yet a select committee of the House of Lords was subsequently to 'find this complacency disturbing', recognizing that Northern Rock's business model was 'dangerously risky'.

In July 2007, Adam J. Applegarth, the chief executive, wrote:

> Operationally Northern Rock had a good first half in 2007. Mortgage lending has been particularly strong with a gross market share of 9.7% and a net market share of 18.9%, helped by improvements in retention of home moving customers, keeping customers coming to the end of their product deals, and a strong mortgage market. Credit quality remains robust.
>
> The outlook for the full year is being impacted by sharp increases in money market and swap rates seen in the first half. This has resulted in a negative impact on net interest income as mortgage pricing in the market generally has lagged behind increases in funding costs in the year to date. Action has been taken with changes in our swap transaction policies to minimise exposures in the future to significant changes in interest rates.
>
> The medium term outlook for the Company is very positive.

A warning might have been seen in the second paragraph. Northern Rock was hit by the financial world's reluctance to lend short-term, as other institutions hoarded cash to cope with the fallout from defaulting sub-prime mortgage loans in the United States. By mid-September, Northern Rock could not raise enough money to meet its financial obligations.

On Friday 14 September 2007, the Bank of England, acting as 'lender of last resort', provided an emergency facility to prop up Northern Rock. The company urged its savers not to panic, insisting that it was solvent. But they did. Beleaguered savers, many elderly, queued for hours to withdraw all of their savings. Northern Rock's Internet access crashed as online customers tried to log on to access their funds.

The panic had some justification. The compensation scheme run by the Financial Services Authority, the UK financial market watchdog, guaranteed repayments on only £2,000 in full and 90% on the next £33,000. After that, depositors had no recourse to insurance funds. No wonder people queued and withdrew some £3 billion on that day. The British Secretary to the Treasury said that it was not the duty of government to save institutions from the consequences of making risky investments. Northern Rock shares fell by 40%.

On the next day, the queues lengthened. The government feared that financial panic could spread to other banks. So, on Monday 17 September, the government took an unprecedented step and gave a cast-iron guarantee to all Northern Rock savers that their savings, £22 billion of personal deposits and £6 billion of business deposits in total, would be underwritten by the government and met in full.

The classical model of mortgage lending is to borrow short from personal savers, who can call on their funds with little or no notice, and lend long to home owners against mortgages on their properties. The strategy is based on the assumption that the savers trust the bank.

However, the business model of Northern Rock leveraged this classical model by relying on savers' funds for only part of its mortgage financing. It borrowed additional funds from the money market. Some of its loans were securitized and traded on the swap market. This worked well when interest rates were low and funds readily available. As a result, Northern Rock's business grew and its market share far surpassed its competitors with more traditional and cautious strategies. Then came the funds famine and Northern Rock's crisis.

Corporate governance at Northern Rock

The board had twelve members: the chairman, the chief executive, four executive directors, and six non-executive directors. The board had four committees—audit, nominations, remuneration, and risk.

The chief executive was Adam Applegarth, who joined the company in 1980 as a graduate trainee. The company had a reputation for making internal appointments.

The chairman was Dr the Honourable Matthew White Ridley, son of Viscount Ridley. Educated at Eton College and Oxford, with a doctorate in zoology, he was not a financier. He joined the board as an INED in 1994 and became chairman in 2004. He also chaired the nominations committee. His Northern Rock annual fee was £300,000.

The other INEDs were:

> Adam Fenwick, 46, the group managing director of Fenwick Ltd and an INED of John Swire and Sons Ltd—Northern Rock fee £54,000;
>
> Sir Ian Gibson, 60, the senior INED, who had industrial experience in running Ford Motors and Nissan, and was currently chairman of the publishers of the *Daily Mirror* and an INED of GKN plc and Greggs plc, and previously a member of the Court of the Bank of England—Northern Rock fee £80,000;
>
> Nichola Pease, 46, chief executive of JO Hambros Capital Management, previously with Barings, famous for its collapse after a Singapore trader was allowed to run excessive risks—Northern Rock fee £65,000;
>
> Michael Queen, 45, a director of 3i Group plc—Northern Rock fee £54,000;
>
> Rosemary Radcliffe, 62, a leading chartered accountant and a complaints commissioner for the Financial Services Authority—Northern Rock fee £56,000;
>
> Sir Derek Wanless, 59, former CEO of NatWest Bank, who steered it through an acquisition strategy that proved disastrous and left in 1999 with a £3 million pay-off, who was well respected in the City of London and a member of the actuarial committee of the Financial Reporting Council; he carried out a long-term review of the British National Health Service for the government in 2007—Northern Rock fee £86,000 and he was chairman of Northern Rock's audit committee and risk committee.

In February 2008, Northern Rock was nationalized. The bank came under government control. A new chief executive was appointed. Shareholders were to be recompensed at a level set by an independent panel. The British Chancellor of the Exchequer insisted that the public ownership was temporary, before 'ultimately trying to return it to the private sector'. In late 2011, the sound assets were acquired by Virgin Finance, leaving the toxic debt under government ownership.

In the annual report and accounts for the year ended 31 December 2012, the new directors explained that:

> Northern Rock Asset Management plc (NRAM) and its subsidiary undertakings primarily operate as servicer of mortgage loans secured on residential properties and of associated services. No new lending is carried out.
>
> On 1 October 2010, UK Asset Resolution Limited (UKAR) was established as the holding company for NRAM & Bradford & Bingley plc (another company taken over by the Government), bringing together the two brands under shared management and a common Board of Directors.
>
> NRAM, formerly Northern Rock plc ('NR'), was taken into public ownership on 22 February 2008. During 2007 and 2008 loan facilities to the Company were put in place by the Bank of England all of which were novated to HM Treasury on 28 August 2008. On 28 October 2009, the European Commission approved State aid to the Company confirming the facilities provided by HM Treasury, thereby removing the material uncertainty over the Company's ability to continue as a going concern which previously existed.
>
> Following the completion of a legal and capital restructuring on 1 January 2010, the Company no longer operates as a deposit taking institution under the supervision of the Financial Services Authority ('FSA'). It is now regulated by the FSA as a mortgage administration company and the Directors believe it has appropriate and adequate levels of capital to support these activities. Further, HM Treasury has confirmed that it is its intention to continue to fund the Company so as to

maintain the Company as a going concern and enable the Company to meet its debts as and when they fall due for a period up to at least 1 November 2014. It has also committed to convert up to £1.6bn of the Government loan to meet regulatory capital requirements if so required.

The overall aim of UKAR is to maximise value for the taxpayer. This will be achieved by focusing on key activities and themes based on each of the following three objectives:

- reduce, protect and optimise the balance sheet;
- maximise cost effectiveness via continuous improvement; and
- to be excellent in customer and debt management.

These objectives are underpinned by the need to treat customers and creditors fairly.

The focus of the Group is now on servicing the mortgage book and on the collection of arrears in an effective and efficient manner.

Discussion questions

1. What role did the original board play in this saga?

2. Did the directors understand the underlying business model and how it differed from the classical banking approach to lending? Did they appreciate their company's exposure if the financial markets changed? Did they know the extent of their business risk?

 Case study 8.2   The BP Deepwater Horizon disaster

On 20 April 2010, the Macondo oil well in the Gulf of Mexico blew out, causing an explosion on its oil rig, Deepwater Horizon. The rig caught fire and sank, killing eleven people and creating the biggest oil spill in American history, threatening environmental catastrophe. A few days later, while the oil polluted beaches on America's southern coast, destroying fishermen's livelihoods and killing wildlife, BP's CEO was pictured in cap and sunglasses sailing his yacht off Britain's south coast.

About BP

BP plc is the UK-based holding company of a group that includes BP Holdings North American Ltd, which has a subsidiary BP North America Inc., the parent company of BP Exploration and Production Inc., which owned the Macondo well.

The Deepwater Horizon oil rig was owned by the Transocean Company, which leased it to BP. The rig had drilled through 18,000 feet of rock below 5,000 feet of water to reach oil. Transocean owned the rig, ran it, and maintained the oil well's blowout preventer, a stack of valves at the well head.

At the time, the board[8] of BP plc had six British and six American directors, including:

Sir Bill Castell, 63, the senior INED, who was vice chairman of the GE Group;

George David, 68, a tycoon who built up United Technologies Corporation;

Paul Anderson, 65, former chief executive of BHP Billiton;

DeAnne Julius, 61, previously chief economist of Shell and British Airways;

Cynthia Carroll, 53, CEO of the Anglo-American Group.

[8] For details of the current board members, go to: www.bp.com/en/global/corporate/investors/governance/the-board.html

The disaster and its aftermath

With thousands of barrels of oil pouring uncontrolled out of the well, BP attempted to drill relief wells and put a coffer dam over the well head to pass oil to the surface. Oil washed ashore, where a massive operation was mounted to limit the damage to the shoreline, its industries, and wildlife.

BP blamed Transocean for the failure of the sea-floor blowout preventer, which it alleged was defective. Transocean passed the blame to Halliburton Inc., claiming that it was in charge of cement work that was being used to cap the well, sealing it with plugs of cement and drilling mud.

By mid-June, BP plc's share price had dropped from 655p just before the crisis to 300p. Fitch, a credit-rating agency, downgraded the company to BBB, close to junk bonds. At these prices, commentators raised the spectre of a takeover bid from a foreign competitor.

Anti-BP rage in the United States

A third of America's oil came from offshore sources, and BP is the biggest operator, with licences to drill auctioned by the US Minerals Management Service (MMS). MMS is not only the licensor, but also the regulator of the industry.

By mid-June, with the well still spewing oil, the crisis took on a political dimension.

US President Barack Obama condemned BP, calling it *British* Petroleum, even though the company had changed its name to BP a decade earlier to reflect its global, rather than British, ownership and operations. Obama was facing difficult times politically with his healthcare reforms and forthcoming elections, and used angry rhetoric, saying that he was 'looking for ass to kick . . .' and that he would have sacked BP's CEO. UK Prime Minister David Cameron spoke with him, calling for less anti-British rhetoric.

President Obama visited the Gulf four times in six weeks to show his support. Forty-four US senators published a letter demanding that BP suspend its dividend, using the funds to support disaster relief in the Gulf. That would have adversely affected many British pension funds, because the BP dividend contributes £1 in every £7 that pension funds receive from the top 100 British companies. Lord Oakeshott, chairman of the Economic Policy Unit in the UK Department of Business said it was 'contemptible and illegal to try to bully British savers out of their savings income'. In fact, 40% of BP shareholders were in the United States, and of BP's 83,000 employees, 22,000 of them were in America, twice as many as British employees.

On 11 June 2010, BP decided to defer payment of its planned dividend to shareholders. The US government further demanded that BP divert funds to pay for the clean-up operation and provide compensation to those whose livelihoods had been affected. BP agreed to set up such a fund. Furious senators questioned the company's executives about the oil well explosion. There were suggestions that BP's American operations should be put into receivership by the US government so that the government could run the relief operations.

Reputational loss: the second disaster

Immediately after the disaster, the BP board decided that a single person was needed to head the disaster relief efforts, and that would be the Group Chief Executive, Tony Hayward (53). The board felt that having both the chairman and the CEO involved might confuse Americans, who were used to having major companies led by a single chairman/CEO.

After earning a PhD in geology, Hayward had worked for BP all his life. He took over as Group CEO from Lord Browne in 2007, whose tenure had been dominated by a strategic widening though acquisition, a financial approach to management control, and some safety lapses. At an early stage, Hayward introduced a new system to evaluate corporate risk.

Hayward's handling of the Gulf disaster was strewn with public relations gaffes. His initial reaction was: 'I think the environmental impact of this disaster is likely to be very, very modest.' During a visit to the oil-strewn Gulf coast, he moaned: 'I want my life back.' After the event, he commented: 'I became the public face (of the disaster) and was demonised and vilified. BP cannot move on in the US with me as its leader . . . life isn't fair. Sometimes you step off the pavement and get hit by a bus.'

Where was the chairman?

The board chairman, Carl-Henric Svanberg, Swedish, 58, had only joined BP in January 2010. Just after the Gulf disaster, he went yachting in Thailand with his new partner, Louise Julian. He visited the BP disaster centre in Houston on the way back from his holiday. Faced by TV reporters on his return, he ignored their questions. Shareholders and critics within the company complained at his lack of public profile. They suggested that Svanberg should have camped out in Washington to deal with the political flak, leaving Hayward to handle the practical issues of stopping the leak. Some felt that he should resign. He stated firmly: 'I have no intention of resigning.'

The outcome

On 28 July 2010, Hayward stepped down as CEO, with a golden parachute of his annual £1 million salary and a £10 million pension pot built up during his 28 years with BP. Bob Dudley, born in Mississippi, took over as CEO. One of his early projects was the creation of a new safety division for the group with sweeping powers. Staff bonuses would also reflect compliance with safety rules.

On 25 September 2010, BP claimed officially that the well was sealed. Nearly 5 million barrels of oil had been released. BP had incurred huge costs, with more impending from court actions and the possibility of corporate manslaughter charges. But the reputational loss had probably been greater.

In November 2010, a US Presidential Commission cleared BP of cutting corners to boost profits. It found no evidence, its report said, that BP had made conscious decisions to put dollars above safety at the Macondo well. However, it did suggest that there were 'systemic problems in the industry'. Moreover, it identified a failure of management: 'With better management by BP, Haliburton and Transocean would almost certainly have prevented the blowout.'

Transocean, which owned the rig, was charged with negligence. Halliburton, which provided support services, was fined $200,000, the maximum penalty under the law, for destroying evidence about the spill. But Halliburton did offer $55 million to the National Fish and Wildlife Foundation as a contribution to the damage the spill had caused.

BP's legal battles continued throughout 2013 and 2014. The company's initial response to the catastrophe had been conciliatory, setting up a $20 billion fund for damages, penalties, and legal costs. But the company seemed unfamiliar with America's litigious culture. Facing mounting court battles, and a deluge of claims, many of which it thought fictitious, the company toughened its response.

At BP's suggestion, the court in Louisiana appointed an independent investigator to arbitrate the claims. But when he appeared to see BP as a cash cow, BP called for his claims to be frozen until new controls were imposed. Many of the claims are 'absurd and fictitious', BP told the court, citing a $357,000 award to a shrimp farmer whose tax returns showed he was unemployed at the time of the oil spill. The court agreed.

BP also sought the court's rejection of a $7.8 billion deal it had made to compensate individuals and businesses, who claimed to have been harmed by the spill, calling for 'proper interpretation of the settlement agreement'. But the court rejected that request. By 2014, BP estimated that the $7.8 billion had grown to $9.2 billion. BP's profits for 2013 were 22% down.

BP also filed a fraud suit against a Texan lawyer, representing 40,000 fishermen who claimed to have suffered losses. Many of these claims were 'phantom', BP said, and included people with social security numbers belonging to dead people and others with no involvement in fishing.

Following the disaster, the US government banned BP from winning federal contracts in the United States, including the supply of fuel to the military. BP took court action to overturn the ban, a decision that was supported officially by the British government.

In April 2014, BP refused to pay the US government £88 million ($130 million) for studies into the effects of the oil spill on dolphins, oysters, and shrimp. The company complained that they had not been given access to the data and that these studies apparently duplicated earlier work. Facing legal challenges, BP needed information on the revival of wildlife to support their case for lower penalties for environmental damage.

In April 2014, BP took out a full page advert in the *New York Times*[9] stating that they had reached an agreement with the federal government that allowed the company once again to bid on new deepwater exploration leases; and that within days they had bid on and won twenty-four new leases in the Gulf of Mexico. The advert claimed that BP was the largest investor in the Gulf; that they operated four of the largest production hubs in the Gulf—more than any other company—and that BP employs more than 2,300 people in the Gulf as well as supporting tens of thousands of other jobs in the region.

In June 2014, Pomerantz, a leading US class-action specialist law firm, announced that it had lodged court filings on behalf of thirty-two European shareholders, including several British county councils, London boroughs, and pension funds, claiming damages for losses they had suffered from the dramatic fall in the BP share price following the Deepwater disaster. Previously not allowed, a 2013 ruling in the US courts allowed foreign claims to be joined with US class actions. Damages awarded by US courts are typically substantially more than those of the British High Court. BP maintained that 'all of the plaintiffs' security claims relating to the Deepwater Horizon accident are meritless'.

See www.laed.uscourts.gov/OilSpill/OilSpill.htm, http://louisianarecord.com/news/federal-district-court

---

Discussion questions

1. BP had a group-wide corporate system to evaluate risk, introduced by Hayward. Why did this not predict the Deepwater Horizon disaster?

2. How might BP have managed the Deepwater Horizon disaster differently to reduce its loss of reputation in the United States?

3. Would the outcome have been different if the roles of board chairman and CEO in BP had been combined, as in many large American public companies?

[9] www.theStateoftheGulf.com

References and further reading

Barton, Thomas L., William G. Shenkir, and Paul L. Walker (2002) *Making Enterprise Risk Management Pay Off: How Leading Companies Implement Risk Management.* Financial Times and Prentice Hall, New York.

Conference Board (2005) *From Risk Management to Risk Strategy*, Report 1363, 845 3rd Avenue, New York, NY 10022.

Conference Board (2007) *Emerging Governance Practices in Enterprise Risk Management.* Report 1398, 845 3rd Avenue, New York, NY 10022, USA.

Cornelius, Peter K. and Bruce Kogan (eds) (2007) *Global Issues in Corporate Governance: Risk and International Investment.* Oxford University Press, New York.

Lam, James (2003) *Enterprise Risk Management: From Incentives to Controls.* Wiley, New York.

Moeller, Robert (2007) *COSO Enterprise Risk Management: Understanding the New Integrated ERM Framework.* Wiley, Hoboken, NJ.

National Association of Corporate Directors (2005) *Myths, Realities and Prevention: A Report of the NACD Blue Ribbon Commission on Director Liability.* 1133, Suite 700 21 Street, Washington, DC, USA.

National Association of Corporate Directors (2005) *Risk Oversight: Board Lessons for Turbulent Times—A Report of a NACD Blue Ribbon Commission.* 1133, Suite 700 21 Street, Washington, DC, USA.

National Association of Corporate Directors (2005) *Risk Governance: Balancing Risk and Reward—A Report of a NACD Blue Ribbon Commission.* 1133, Suite 700 21 Street, Washington, DC, USA.

Tonello, Matteo (2006) *Emerging Governance Practices in Enterprise Risk Management: The Conference Board Research Report R-1398-07.* 845 3rd Avenue, New York, NY 10022, USA.

Treadway Commission (2004) *Enterprise Risk Management: An Integrated Approach.* Committee of Sponsoring Organizations of the Treadway Commission, USA.

Van Daelen, Marijn and Christoph Van Der Elst (eds) (2011) *Risk Management and Corporate Governance: Interconnections in Law, Accounting and Tax.* Lexis Nexis, London.

Whitley, Sherry (2004) 'Leadership through Progressive Enterprise Risk Management', *Institute of Internal Auditors, FSA Times,* 4th quarter, Vol. 3.

Projects and exercises

1. Focus on an organization with which you are familiar (perhaps a company, a university, or a sports club). Identify areas of possible risks. Consider strategic, managerial, and operational levels.

2. What consequences might arise should these risks occur?

3. In each situation, make a recommendation to management on what the organization's risk response should be.

Self-test questions

1. Name three regulatory instruments that call for risk management responsibility at board level.

2. Some boards include corporate risk assessment in the mandate of the board audit committee. Why might this have limitations?

3. What alternatives do other companies adopt to bring risk issues to the board?

4. Who might be involved in such a risk management subcommittee, and how does it operate?

5. Where else might responsibility for risk assessment and management be placed in a company?

6. Identify the levels of risk in a business.

7. What should an enterprise risk management systems provide and to whom?

8. Name the iterative phases involved in the analysis of risk in an organization.

9. Identify some risk assessment and risk management tools that are available.

10. What policy options does a board have when deciding its approach to enterprise risk management?

9 Corporate Social Responsibility and Sustainability

Learning Outcomes

In which we consider:

- The concept of corporate social responsibility (CSR)
- Changing expectations in the governance of organizations
- Enlightened shareholder value (ESV)
- CSR strategies and policies
- The CSR competency framework
- Balancing corporate responsibilities
- Sustainability and the triple bottom line
- Communication with stakeholders: integrated reporting
- The United Nations Global Reporting Initiative

The concept of corporate social responsibility (CSR)

Broadly, corporate social responsibility (CSR) is about corporate entities acting as good corporate citizens. But although intuitively obvious, CSR has acquired a range of meanings, which overlap yet focus on different aspects of the topic, as can be seen in the following alternative points of view:

The societal perspective

This view holds that companies have responsibilities beyond just obeying the law and paying their taxes, because their activities have an overall impact on society. A commitment to CSR recognizes that companies should be accountable not only for their financial performance, but also for their impact on society. The definition used by Business for Social Responsibility, a non-profit organization based in San Francisco, is: 'CSR involves operating a business in a manner that meets or exceeds the ethical, legal, commercial, and public expectations that society has of business.' The Chairman/CEO of AT&T, C. Michael Armstrong, summarized his company's view: 'AT&T understands the need for a global alliance of business, society and the environment. In the 21st century, the world won't tolerate businesses that don't take that partnership seriously, but it will eventually reward companies that do.'

But such thinking is not universally accepted. Reich,[1] who was previously a CSR advocate, argued that consumers today have a world of choice and businesses face more competition than ever before. In pursuit of corporate performance, he believes, CEO's incentives become aligned with shareholders' interests so they 'slash payrolls, outsource abroad, and drain our main streets of shops'. Reich concluded that if states want to avoid adverse social consequences, they need to pass laws.

The strategy-driven perspective

This perspective starts from the proposition that business social responsibility is an integral part of the wealth creation process. A company runs in a socially responsible way because its CSR strategies and policies are business-driven, in both the short and long terms. Such companies make a solid business case for their CSR policies based on cost-effective criteria. All corporate strategies—research, exploration, product development, production, marketing, human resources, and financial—are contingent with the CSR objectives. The business case for taking a stakeholder approach to corporate governance is that it enhances competitiveness, increases customer satisfaction, improves employee relations, reduces the cost of capital, and enhances shareholder value, while also investing in communities and increasing wealth creation in society. CSR that is strategy-driven and rooted in a solid business case also produces a more sustainable result long-term. This approach to CSR is now found in many European boardrooms and, increasingly, in the United States. Critics have argued that CSR distracts from the fundamental economic role of business, although studies have actually shown a positive correlation with improved shareholder returns, albeit small.

The stakeholder perspective

Companies with this perception see CSR as the alignment of corporate values and actions with the expectations and needs of their stakeholders—shareholders, customers, employees, suppliers, communities, regulators, other interest groups, and society as a whole. Their CSR policies describe the company's commitment and responsibility to its stakeholders. Adopting this perspective, the European Commission has defined CSR as 'a concept whereby companies integrate social and environmental concerns in their business operations and in their interaction with their stakeholders on a voluntary basis'.

If companies fail to achieve acceptable CSR standards, costs can be incurred such as legal damages, restitution costs, legal fees, or product recalls. The loss of reputation can be even higher, affecting sales, costs, and employee turnover. Investigative media increasingly report cases of firms transgressing accepted CSR behaviour, for example, in the employment of children in developing countries in manufacturing and other industries, the alleged ill-treatment of animals in pharmaceutical product testing, and pollution in the oil drilling and transport industries, even though such practices may be perfectly legal in the places where they occur.

[1] Reich (2006).

The ethical perspective

The ethical viewpoint sees that corporate entities, like individuals, have an obligation to act for the benefit of society as a whole, contributing to society while doing no harm to others. A wide range of laws and guidelines that steer and control corporate behaviour already exist at state, national, and global levels on health and safety, human rights, environmental issues, and sustainability. But ethical CSR activity needs to go well beyond what is required by such basic standards. The board needs to be the conscience of the company—responsible for establishing its corporate values. Ethical codes, understood throughout the organization, reflect the directors' own behaviour. An ethical standpoint is likely to produce voluntary CSR policies that go well beyond the requirements of laws and guidelines.

The political perspective

Interest groups, some with an anti-business agenda, argue that CSR is no more than vested self-interest at best and a public relations window-dressing exercise at worst. Some have called for legislation to impose standards of CSR on companies, particularly multinationals. The response from the Confederation of British Industry (CBI) was that CSR should remain market-driven and voluntary. Attempts to raise standards, the CBI believes, would remove the competitive incentive that drives CSR activity and would place an unmanageable burden on companies, particularly small and medium firms. CSR policies should reflect companies' activities and the context in which they operate, while legislation in this area would constrain business activity and reduce CSR to a lowest common denominator, the CBI said. Other political commentators have argued that companies which pursue broader, social goals have no legitimacy. Such roles should be pursued by governments acting for their citizens. Some business leaders concur with this opinion, feeling that their companies do not have a mandate, nor are they equipped, to pursue broader social goals.

The philanthropic perspective

For many years, some companies have sought to 'put something back' into the society that provided them with customers, employees, and success. Such corporate philanthropy may involve charitable giving to support communities, charities, or other causes, in money or corporate services, such as employees' time. Donating to charitable causes without anticipating any reward, save perhaps a reputational benefit, has long been practised in the United States, some European countries, and by Chinese entrepreneurs in places such as Hong Kong. The European Commission has defined such an approach to CSR as 'a concept whereby companies decide voluntarily to contribute to a better society and a cleaner environment'. But a philanthropic approach to CSR is essentially peripheral to the main business. When times get hard, it is also one of the easiest expenditures to cut.

Discussions about these alternative perspectives continue. Many companies in the economically advanced world now accept that their responsibilities go beyond the generation of wealth, while staying within the laws of the states in which they operate. CSR is widely recognized as part of companies' corporate governance responsibilities. But CSR practices vary between countries and cultures. Different value systems, different economic conditions, and different social priorities mean that no 'one size can fit all'.

Changing expectations in the governance of organizations

The original corporate governance codes, dating from the early 1990s, were voluntary. At the time, they were derided by some company chairmen as being no more than expensive, mindless exercises. But since then three significant changes have taken place:

- First, corporate governance compliance has increasingly become mandatory, enshrined in regulation, law, and stock exchange listing requirements. Complaints from companies now tend to be about the cost of compliance rather than the need for corporate governance principles.
- Second, risk governance and enterprise risk management have become an integral part of the corporate governance process.
- Third, and of relevance to this chapter, CSR and sustainability have been added to the corporate governance portfolio.

Questioning the societal legitimacy of corporate entities has a long history. In the original mid-19th century concept of the company, if the liability of the owners for the debts of the company was to be limited, society demanded that the company's activities should be strictly prescribed. Companies could only carry out those functions described in their memorandum of association. In effect, society gave the corporate entity a licence to operate with limited liability provided that it restricted its specified activities and in some cases for a limited time.

Subsequently, lawyers began to draft the memorandum of association and other constitutional documents so widely that the activities of companies were no longer bounded. So the behaviour of corporate entities has had to be constrained by law. Around the world, laws to control monopolies and markets, to protect customers, to regulate employee relations, to safeguard health and safety, to preserve the environment, and much more are now used to regulate and restrain corporate activities.

This raises the vital question, neatly posed by Milton Freidman: 'What responsibilities does a business have?' His view was that the only legitimate purpose for a company was to create wealth, pursuing its business effectively for the benefit of its customers, while providing a profitable reward to its investors. It was the role of the state, he believed, to provide the legal framework that regulated companies' behaviour in relation to the rest of the community.

As we saw in the discussion of stakeholder philosophies in Chapter 3, the debate continues about companies' responsibilities to their shareholders and other stakeholders. On one side are those who argue, like Friedman, that a company has one and only one objective: to make long-term sustainable profits by satisfying customers for the benefit of its owners, while acting within the law. If society wishes to limit a company's single-minded pursuit of this goal, for example by constraining monopolies, regulating employment, or preventing pollution, it must pass appropriate laws.

On the other side are those who believe that, because a company can and does affect the interests and even the lives of people, it should take account of societal interests over and above those of the owners and beyond the specific requirements of the law. Moreover, some commentators added that companies should be accountable or even responsible to those affected by their actions. Carroll (1979) attempted to answer Friedman's question by suggesting that corporate responsibility had four levels:

- *economic responsibility*—first and foremost, the social responsibility to be profit-orientated and market-driven;
- *legal responsibility*—to adhere to society's laws and regulations as the price for society's licence to operate;
- *ethical responsibilities*—to honour society's wider social norms and expectations of behaviour over and above the law in line with the local culture;
- *discretionary (or philanthropic) responsibilities*—to undertake voluntary activities and expenditures that exceed society's minimum expectations.

As we saw in Chapter 5, the King Report (King I) on corporate governance in South Africa was the first code to recognize the interests of corporate stakeholders as well as shareholders, In the words of its author, Mervyn King:[2]

> That report revolutionised approaches to corporate governance around the world because it said that in the decision-making process you should take account of the legitimate needs, interests, and expectations of stakeholders linked to the company. That did not mean that directors should be accountable to stakeholders, but that they should take account of stakeholder needs and expectations in their decision-making. [Companies should] still act in the best interests of the company through the maximization of the total economic value.

King I has been translated into many languages. But although the King perspective has been widely promoted, the concept has its detractors. Bernstein (2010), head of a South African think tank, pointed out that developing nations need more companies that generate wealth not demands to pursue social responsibilities. In South Africa, where many are jobless and live in poverty, people need work, Bernstein said, not rules designed to protect those already in work, which can reduce the number of available jobs, and environmental demands, which have delayed projects to replace existing shacks with new houses.

In China, the importance of CSR has also been recognized. The Tenth National Congress of the Chinese People's Political Consultative Conference in 2005[3] claimed that business enterprises were the foundation for building a harmonious society. Enterprises should be required to do three things, it argued: to take a scientific and rational attitude towards development; to protect and respect employee rights and benefits; and to undertake more social responsibilities.

As Kofi Annan said, when Secretary-General of the United Nations:

> We have to choose between a global market driven only by calculation of short-term profit, and one which has a human face; between a world which condemns a quarter of the human race to starvation and squalor, and one which offers everyone at least a chance of prosperity, in a healthy environment; between a selfish free-for-all in which we ignore the fate of the

---

[2] Interview in *CSJ* (2010) Hong Kong Institute of Chartered Secretaries, December.

[3] See Chapter 12 for more on Chinese state and corporate governance.

losers, and a future in which the strong and successful accept their responsibilities, showing global vision and leadership.

Enlightened shareholder value (ESV)

Boards adopting an investor-driven ESV approach believe that the satisfaction of the needs of all stakeholders is crucial to corporate success, that it is essential to creating value for shareholders. The ESV concept of corporate governance attempts to overcome apparent conflicts between a shareholder-focused and a stakeholder-focused approach that we saw earlier in corporate governance theory. An ESV perspective suggests that profits are generated, shareholder value created, and society's wealth increased by satisfying stake-holder interests, rather than through the classical attempts of shareholder theory to maxi-mize shareholder wealth. Emphasizing the needs and interests of all corporate stakeholders obviously swings a spotlight onto CSR, argues the World Business Council for Sustainable Development:[4]

> For many companies, managing corporate social responsibility well is no longer seen as an extra cost or burden on hard-pressed management. Rather, CSR is increasingly viewed, not only as making good business sense but also contributing to the long-term prosperity of companies and ultimately its survival. Being a good neighbour and showing that you care on the one hand and being a successful business on the other, are flip sides of the same coin.

Prior to 2006, company law in the United Kingdom required directors to act in the best interests of the company, which effectively meant in the long-term interest of the sharehold-ers—in other words, by attempting to maximize shareholder value. But the Companies Act 2006 specifically spelled out a statutory duty to recognize the effect of board decisions on a wider public. For the first time in UK company law, CSR responsibilities were included among the formal duties of company directors:

> A director of a company must act in the way he considers, in good faith, would be most like-ly to promote the success of the company for the benefit of its members as a whole, and in doing so have regard to:
>
> (a) The likely consequences of any decision in the long term
> (b) The interests of the company's employees
> (c) The need to foster the company's business relations with suppliers, customers and others
> (d) The impact of the company's operations on the community and the environment
> (e) The desirability of the company maintaining a reputation for high standards of business conduct, and
> (f) The need to act fairly as between members of the company

Thus UK company law now requires companies to consider employees, suppliers, customers, and other business partners, as well as the community and the environment, in their decisions.

[4] Holme and Watts (2000).

The UN Principles for Responsible Investment[5] also call for companies to consider environmental, social, and governance (ESG) issues and risks in their strategic decision-making and to report their participation on a 'comply or explain' basis. These Principles were developed by an international group of institutional investors from twelve countries convened by the UN Secretary-General and reflect the increasing relevance of environmental, social, and corporate governance issues to investment practices.

Other examples of calls for companies to adopt CSR policies include the European Union's demand for statements of CSR policies when companies tender for contracts (2005), the UK Department for Environment, Food and Rural Affairs (DEFRA) requirement for occupational pension funds to 'report whether environmental, social, and ethical criteria are taken into account in their investment strategy' (2001), and the Australian Stock Exchange listing rule that requires companies to report their performance under environmental legislation (1998). Some institutional investors have also mounted initiatives for companies to take a broader stakeholder perspective, including CalPers and other US state pension funds.

CSR strategies and policies

A primary duty of the board is to identify the aims of the company, to establish its mission, and to set its values. If the directors are not clear about the firm's purpose and what it stands for, the rest of the organization will be like a boat without a rudder.

To be effective, a company's CSR efforts need to be led by the directors and embedded in its corporate strategy. This will lead to CSR policies, for approval by the board. Basically, a CSR policy determines how the company engages with its shareholders and the other stakeholders, including its employees, customers, and suppliers, the communities in which it operates, and the world generally. A clear CSR policy can also influence potential investors looking for socially responsible, ethical, or environmentally friendly enterprises in which to invest. Successful CSR policies influence management decisions at all levels, and penetrate all aspects and every level of the firm's activities.

Obviously, every company is different and must develop its CSR policies in the context of its corporate strategies, policies, and procedures, including its systems of management supervision and accountability. If they are to be effective, CSR policies should be understood, accepted, and applied throughout the organization. They also need to be reviewed regularly to reflect changing business, economic, and social situations.

A CSR consultant, who was retained by a manufacturing company to advise on its CSR policies, proposed the policy statement in Corporate governance in action 9.1.

The CSR competency framework

To encourage commitment to CSR practices, the British government created a CSR competency framework—a flexible tool, which is offered as a 'way of thinking' for companies

---

[5] The Principles can be found online at http://unpri.org/about/

Corporate governance in action 9.1   Extract from the CSR policy of a manufacturing company

For continuing economic success, all company strategies, policies and management decisions should take account of their long-term effects and impact on the following.

1. *All stakeholders including:*
   - original suppliers and others in the upstream supply chain;
   - agents, distributors, and others in the downstream supply chain;
   - customers of the end product or service;
   - creditors;
   - bankers and non-equity sources of finance;
   - employees including part-time employees and managers;
   - self-employed contractors to the company.

2. *All of the communities in which the company operates including:*
   - local communities;
   - regional communities;
   - national communities;
   - international communities.

Consider the economic implications, socially responsible activities that the company undertakes, and our philanthropic efforts.

3. *The environment*

Consider all of the relevant communities, regions, and countries affected by the company's manufacturing and distribution chain, including possible effects of:

   - our production activities, such as:
     - energy use;
     - depletion of resources;
     - exploitation of labour;
     - pollution;

   - our products and services, including:
     - the effect of the product in use;
     - energy use;
     - health or other risks;
     - pollution;

   - the final disposal of the product, including:
     - energy use;
     - pollution.

Each of these broad policy statements is further amplified in the CSR handbook.

CSR Competency Framework

of all sizes. The framework offers six core characteristics, with five levels of attainment for each:

- Understanding society

  - A knowledge of how the business operates in the broader societal context and a knowledge of the impact that the business has on society, plus a recognition that the business is an important player in society, seeking to make that impact as positive as possible

- Building capacity

  - Working with others to build the capability to manage the business effectively, helping suppliers and employees to understand your environment and to apply social and environmental concerns in their day-to-day roles

- Questioning 'business as usual'

  - Constantly questioning your business in relation to a more sustainable future and being open to improving people's quality of life and the environment, acting as an advocate, engaging with bodies outside the business who share this concern for the future

- Stakeholder relations

  - Recognizing that stakeholders include all those who have an impact on, or are impacted by, your business, understanding the opportunities and risks they present, and working with them through consultation, taking their views into account

- Strategic view

  - Ensuring that social and environmental concerns are included in the overall business strategy so that CSR becomes 'business as usual', with leadership coming from the top and resulting in everyone in the business having an awareness of the social and environmental impacts in their day-to-day roles

- Harnessing diversity

  - Recognizing that people differ and harnessing this diversity, reflected in fair and transparent employment practices, promoting the health, well-being, and views of staff with everyone in the business feeling valued.

The five levels of attainment are.

- Awareness

  - The broad application of the core CSR characteristics and how they might impinge on business decisions

- Understanding

  - A basic knowledge of some of the issues, with the competence to apply them to specific activities.

- Application

  - The ability to supplement this basic knowledge of the issues, with the competence to apply it to specific activities

- Integration
  - An in-depth understanding of the issues and an expertise in embedding CSR into the business decision-making process
- Leadership
  - The ability to help managers across the organization in a way that fully integrates CSR in the decision-making process

Overall, the intention of the CSR framework is to change employees' mindsets and to promote an appropriate CSR strategy throughout the organization and between the company and its stakeholders. Creating a strong CSR culture throughout an organization needs to be part of an ongoing performance assessment of both organizational units and individuals, and should not be allowed to become a form-filling exercise.

An organization's response to its social and environmental impacts, recognized through CSR awareness, can provide a cost-effective, yet comprehensive, way of managing social and environmental risk across an organization. However, corporate groups operating in different parts of the world may find it difficult to achieve homogeneous CSR policies throughout the group. The experience of Exxon in the United States and Exxon in Europe, described in Corporate governance in action 9.2 and 9.3 are cases in point.

Balancing corporate responsibilities

A company does not have morals; directors do. The board has to be the conscience of the company. Directors need to provide the company with its moral compass. In fulfilling its role, the board is responsible for considering the potential effect of the strategies it formulates, for identifying the likely impact of policies it approves (both short- and long-term), for recognizing possible outcomes on people, and for accepting its duty to be accountable.

Every board has a duty to formulate the company's strategy, recognizing the risks involved, and part of that process involves determining how the company will behave—in other words, establishing how social responsibility will be exercised throughout the organization. Balancing competing claims of different stakeholders, while meeting shareholders' expectations, can be quite a challenge. In non-profit entities, broader societal responsibilities also have to be balanced, while meeting the primary duty to its members. Boards need to make choices. Inertia inevitably leads to unresolved dilemmas.

The World Business Council for Sustainable Development (WBCSD) concluded in its first report on CSR, *Meeting Changing Expectations* (1999), that:

- CSR priorities today are human rights, employee rights, environmental protection, community involvement, and supplier relations;
- a coherent CSR strategy, based on integrity, sound values, and a long-term approach, offers clear business benefits;
- companies should articulate their own core values and codes of conduct, or failing that, endorse and implement codes produced by others;

Corporate governance in action 9.2   CSR resisted in Exxon Mobil, US

John D. Rockefeller founded the Standard Oil Corporation, which became Exxon Mobil, the world's largest publicly owned energy company. At the 2008 AGM, some of his descendants brought shareholder motions calling for the company to curb greenhouse gas emissions, to increase renewable energy research, and to develop sources of alternative fuel.

Three resolutions asked Exxon to study the impact of global warming on poor countries, to reduce company emissions of greenhouse gases, and to do more research on renewable energy sources such as wind turbines and solar panels. Neva Rockefeller Goodwin, an economist and great-granddaughter of Rockefeller, told shareholders:

> These increased concentrations of CO_2 in the atmosphere will cause weather disasters that will work against everyone's best hope for robust development in emerging countries, while also increasing the vulnerability of the poor in the rich countries. It will also impact the global economy.

The proposals were opposed by Exxon Mobil's board.

The family also supported resolutions calling for the company to establish an independent chairman, separating the role from that of the current chairman and chief executive Rex Tillerson. Shell and BP, they noted, had already separated the positions. The motion to split the roles, which had been raised for the last seven years of shareholder meetings, was supported by a significant number of shareholders. But the final poll showed only 39.5% of the shares were voted in favour.

Commentators suggested that the US$40 billion profit reported by the company in 2007 may have influenced the rest. 'The past year was an outstanding year and a record for our corporation by nearly every measure,' Tillerson said. 'Millions of people have benefited financially by holding Exxon Mobil shares either directly or indirectly through their pension, insurance, and mutual funds,' he added.

Mr Tillerson said that he thought Exxon had to keep focused on its mission of developing more oil and gas reserves, and that oil and gas would remain the primary fuel source for decades to come. Some shareholders disagreed, arguing that the company's emphasis on developing oil and gas as energy sources threatened the global environment and ultimately the company's financial health. One shareholder suggested that the company was 'acting like a dinosaur by not adapting to a changing environment'. Another shareholder, a Dominican nun, said: 'We're faced with a profound moral and business challenge.' These shareholders were countered by others who defended the management, saying it had been 'a great engine for profit'.

Corporate governance in action 9.3   The CSR policy of Exxon Europe

We take very seriously our responsibilities to our employees, shareholders, customers, communities, the environment, and society at large.

We strongly believe that the way we achieve results is as important as the results themselves. Therefore, we are working hard to embed CSR into the way we do business.

We have integrated CSR policies and practices into our business, which help us ensure that we meet standards of integrity, safety, health, environment and social responsibility day in and day out and across our worldwide operations. We believe that this approach is essential to achieving superior business results.

Our focus is on helping Europe meet energy demand in an economically, socially and environmentally responsible manner. But we cannot be all things to all people. We must balance the needs of a wide variety of stakeholders. To do so sustainably is what the policies, actions and performance improvements behind CSR are all about.

- it is important to be responsive to local and cultural differences when implementing global policies.

The report added that:

- a coherent CSR strategy, based on integrity, sound values and a long-term approach, offers clear business benefits to companies and a positive contribution to the well-being of society;
- a CSR strategy provides the opportunity to demonstrate the human face of business;
- such a strategy requires engagement in open dialogue and constructive partnerships with government at various levels, intergovernmental organizations (IGOs), non-governmental organizations (NGOs), other elements of civil society, and, in particular, local communities;
- in implementing their CSR strategies, companies should recognize and respect local and cultural differences, while maintaining high and consistent global standards and policies; and
- being responsive to local differences means taking specific initiatives.

A report[6] from the WBCSD, *Vision 2050*, called for 'a new agenda for business laying out a pathway to a world in which nine billion people can live well, and within the planet's resources, by mid-century'. The report was compiled following an eighteen month long combined effort between CEOs and experts, and dialogues with more than 200 companies and external stakeholders in some twenty countries. The report featured a set of agreed 'must haves', representing vital developments that the WBCSD hopes organizations will consider putting in place within the next decade, to help ensure a steady course towards global sustainability. These 'must haves' include:

- incorporating the costs of externalities, starting with carbon, ecosystem services and water, into the structure of the marketplace;
- doubling agricultural output without increasing the amount of land or water used;
- halting deforestation and increasing yields from planted forests;
- halving carbon emissions worldwide (based on 2005 levels) by 2050 through a shift to low-carbon energy systems;
- improved demand-side energy efficiency, and providing universal access to low-carbon mobility.

A crucial question is whether there is a link between CSR and economic performance. Although research studies have been conducted, a basic problem has been how to measure CSR. Some studies have also been marred by an ideological bias or limited methodology. Although a few studies have shown some correlation between firms' CSR and their financial performance, current research does not point to a decisive link. However, the longer-term effects of a sound CSR reputation in both the consumer market and the stock market may well persuade boards of the importance of CSR efforts.

[6] www.wbcsd.org/vision2050.aspx

Some firms have claimed that their CSR policies and reports have:

- improved brand recognition and reputation;
- made the firm more attractive to existing and potential employees;
- improved top management and board-level strategic thinking and decisions;
- produced innovations in the way in which the firm operates;
- responded to customers' demands;
- met stakeholders' and society's changing expectations.

For such reasons, many firms approach CSR as enlightened self-interest. But few claim a demonstrable positive correlation between good CSR practices and corporate financial performance. The growing number of investment funds now focusing on 'socially responsible investing' also suggests that there may be a share price premium in due course. In addition, CSR reports can build new links between companies and their stakeholders as relationships between companies and their contractual partners, such as suppliers, distributors, and customers, are enhanced. Employees and their trades unions are also provided with an additional focus in their relations with the employer.

A 2011 ISO standard on social responsibility marked a significant development in the international recognition of the importance of CSR and sustainable development. ISO26000 calls on companies to govern and manage their affairs with equity, honesty, and integrity, respecting the interests of all stakeholders affected by the company's activities. The standard seeks to promote ethical behaviour by requiring the:

- development of governance structures that promote ethical conduct;
- identification, adoption, and application of these standards of ethical behaviour;
- encouragement and promotion of such standards throughout the organization and in its activities;
- establishment of appropriate oversight and control systems;
- identification and reporting of deviations from such company policies with appropriate action.

Sustainability and the triple bottom line

The notion of sustainability has become an important part of the study of corporate governance and business ethics. Recognizing that their activities can have a lasting impact on society and the environment, many companies now accept that the essential generation of profits, although vital to reward the providers of capital and provide for future investment, is not enough.

The World Commission on Environment and Development was convened by the United Nations in 1983 and called the Brundtland Commission, after its chairman Gro Harlem Brundtland. The Commission was created to address growing concern 'about the accelerating deterioration of the human environment and natural resources and the consequences of that deterioration for economic and social development'. The Commission defined sustainable development as 'development that meets the needs of the present without compromising the ability of future generations to meet their own needs'.

Some companies, which support sustainability, talk about their *triple bottom line,* striving for sound performance in three areas—economic, social, and environmental. Some add 'in the long term', recognizing that it is possible to achieve acceptable short-term results, but to leave business successors and future generations with inherited problems. Others have called this a 'profits, people, and planet' approach to corporate performance. Some public sector organizations have also adopted this view of their goals.

The Institute for Research and Innovation in Sustainability in Canada has defined sustainability:

> as being about living and working in ways that meet and integrate existing environmental, economic, and social needs without compromising the wellbeing of future generations. The transition to sustainable development benefits today's society and builds a more secure future for our children.

Some examples of states' recognition of the need for sustainable development include:

- the European Union's fishing quotas and other fishing limits to sustain fish stocks;
- China's Guangdong Province's requirement that companies that pollute the groundwater table in that region clear up or close down;
- South American and EU control of forestry products to protect the rain forest and to ensure that woodland is sustained by replanting;
- the Australian government's climate change strategy, the 'three pillars' of mitigation, to reduce gas emissions, to adapt to unavoidable climate change, and global solutions to help to shape an international response;
- attempts to reduce the world's greenhouse gases below 1990 levels to reduce global warming, which produced the Kyoto Protocol to the United Nations Framework Convention on Climate Change (1997), and continuing rounds of negotiations.

Communication with stakeholders: integrated reporting

Calls for companies to report on their non-financial performance are growing. This includes their CSR and sustainability activities, and the effects they have on the societies in which they operate. Such ESG reporting, as it is sometimes known (environmental, social and governance) has become a significant issue in the business world. The Australian Securities Exchange, and the stock exchanges of Malaysia, Shanghai, and Shenzen, among others, require ESG reports. According to the UK Ethical Corporation,[7] CSR and sustainability reporting is becoming more strategic for innovative, large corporations, while a gap is appearing between them and compliance-driven others, who struggle to compete.

[7] www.ethicalcorp.com

The South African corporate governance code, King III (2008), mentioned earlier, introduced the phrase 'integrated reporting' in its call for companies to report results of their non-financial performance, in addition to traditional information on financial performance. In South Africa, the listing rules of the Johannesburg Stock Exchange now require listed companies to publish such integrated reports. Denmark also requires major companies to report on non-financial aspects of their performance in their annual reports. Other countries, including the United Kingdom, have encouraged the publication of a business commentary to support the published financial results. In 2014, Hong Kong required a statutory business review, including an analysis of the company's environmental policies and performance, an account of its key relationships with its employees, customers and suppliers, and 'others that have a significant impact on the company and on which the company's success depends'.

The International Corporate Governance Network (ICGN) published a statement, and guidance on non-financial business reporting followed, in 2009:

> The ICGN believes that reporting of relevant and material non-financial information is an essential part of the disclosure required to enable shareowners and investors to make informed investment decisions. We use the term 'non-financial' to refer to information relevant to the assessment of economic value, but which does not fit easily into the traditional accounting framework. In a fast-changing, globalizing world, information material to investor decision-making is becoming increasingly diverse and dynamic. Long-term success in managing a business in today's complex economic, environmental, and social landscape is increasingly dependent on factors not reflected in financial statements and in some instances thought to be outside the corporation's sphere of concern.

In considering an integrated report, a number of issues need to be considered:

- who is the report intended for—shareholders and the stock markets (almost certainly), employees, customers, and other contractual stakeholders (very likely), other interest groups including the media, and the general public (possibly),
- why are we publishing this report, what story do we want to tell,
- what material should be included—business strategic achievements, capacity, and issues, key policies, plans and prospects (almost certainly); governance reporting—board and board committee membership and activities, shareholder matters (almost certainly); remuneration reporting (at least to the mandatory level), human resource information including employee standards, turnover, working conditions and welfare, policies on diversity and youth recruitment, health and safety records, training improvements (very likely); product, sales and market information, customer relations (very likely); environmental information such as carbon footprint and other emissions, energy usage, resource scarcity, improvements in waste management, possible effects of climate change, sustainability issues, and corporate social contributions including community involvement and charitable projects (probably); supply chain matters, government or regulatory issues, ethical and anti-corruption policies, media and other societal concerns (possibly),

- does the information provided meet the minimum requirements for reporting under the law, by the regulatory authorities, and other mandatory demands such as the stock exchange listing rules,
- does the report avoid the criticism of being merely a compliance and 'box-ticking' response to demands for information from various sources,
- is the level of detail and writing style appropriate for the intended readership,
- is the information provided coherent, is it interesting, does it flow as an integrated dialogue, or is it a disparate set of unconnected commentaries, is it too long,
- does the final integrated report really inform the intended readership; will they read it,
- how and where should the report be published—as a hard-copy report (almost certainly): on the company's website (very probably), through the social media (quite likely); other forms of publication (possibly). Should it be advertised and made readily available to interested parties?

Predictably, around the world some companies reject the need to tell people any more than is strictly and statutorily required. But such antediluvian thinking is increasingly out of touch with modern governance, CSR, and sustainability beliefs and practice. Companies demonstrating such attitudes are likely to be suspect by the market, attacked by the media, and face reduced investment opportunities.

The United Nations Global Reporting Initiative

The UN Global Compact[8] is a strategic initiative for businesses that commit to aligning their strategies and operations with ten universally accepted principles (the Ten Principles) in the areas of human rights, labour, environment, and anti-corruption. The Compact calls for participating companies to accept a set of core values in the areas of human rights, labour standards, the environment, and anti-corruption. These values were derived from the Universal Declaration of Human Rights, the International Labour Organization's Declaration of Fundamental Principles and Rights at Work, and the UN Convention against Corruption.

Human Rights

Principle 1: Businesses should support and respect the protection of internationally proclaimed human rights
Principle 2: make sure that they are not complicit in human rights abuses.

Labour

Principle 3: Businesses should uphold the freedom of association and the effective recognition of the right to collective bargaining;
Principle 4: the elimination of all forms of forced and compulsory labour;
Principle 5: the effective abolition of child labour
Principle 6: the elimination of discrimination in respect of employment and occupation.

---

[8] www.unglobalcompact.org/

Environment

Principle 7: Businesses should support a precautionary approach to environmental challenges;

Principle 8: undertake initiatives to promote greater environmental responsibility;

Principle 9: encourage the development and diffusion of environmentally friendly technologies.

Anti-corruption

Principle 10: Businesses should work against corruption in all its forms, including extortion and bribery.

The United Nations Environment Programme Finance Initiative[9] (UNEP FI) is a unique global partnership between the United Nations and the financial sectors around the world. Nearly 200 financial institutions work with UNEP to understand the impacts of environmental and social considerations on financial performance. The programme has developed a set of statements, covering the environment and sustainable development, that participating organizations accept. By signing up to these statements, the financial institutions recognize the role of the financial sector in making economies and lifestyles sustainable, and commit to the integration of environmental considerations into their operations.

The Global Reporting Initiative (GRI), which was sparked by the UN Global Compact, is a worldwide, multi-stakeholder network aimed to create and develop a sustainability reporting framework, in which business, civil society, labour, investors, accountants, and others collaborate. The GRI is based on the underlying belief that reporting on economic, environmental, and social performance by all organizations should be as routine and comparable as financial reporting. The GRI facilitates transparency and accountability by organizations of all sizes and sectors across the world—companies, governmental and other public agencies, and non-profit entities.

The Sustainability Reporting Guidelines provide the cornerstone for the sustainability reporting framework, which provides organizations with the basis for disclosure about sustainability performance, and stakeholders with a universally recognized comparable framework within which to assess such information. The Guidelines (Figure 9.1) consist of reporting principles and guidance, with standard disclosures and performance indicators.

The principles and guidance section of the framework defines the sustainability report's content, which helps to determine where its boundaries should be drawn. The content principles cover materiality, stakeholder inclusiveness, sustainability context, and completeness, along with a brief set of tests for each principle. The quality principles cover balance, comparability, accuracy, timeliness, reliability, and clarity, along with tests that can be used to help to achieve the appropriate quality of the reported information.

The standard disclosures section of the framework has guidelines that identify the information that is relevant and material to most organizations and of interest to most stakeholders.

[9] www.unepfi.org

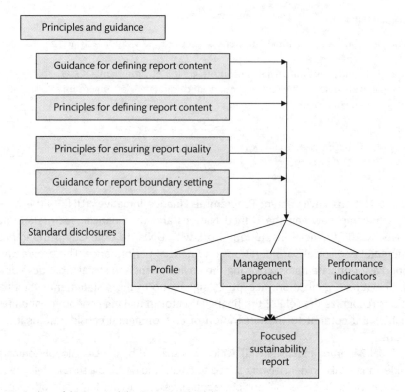

Figure 9.1 Outline of the Sustainability Reporting Guidelines

Three types of standard disclosure are included:

- *the organization's profile*—information that sets the overall context for understanding the organization's performance, including its strategy, profile, and governance;
- *the organization's management approach*—information about the organization that provides the context for understanding its performance;
- *performance indicators*—which provide information on the economic, environmental, and social performance of the organization.

The fourth GRI reporting guidelines were published in 2013. These emphasized the importance for companies to report the things that mattered, not everything they measured; that reports needed to be aligned with and shown to be part of companies' strategies; and that assurance was needed on the reliance that could be placed on the data provided. Such reporting needs to be seen by companies as enhancing their performance and their value, not as yet another business expense.

The GRI has been adopted by organizations around the world: hundreds of companies based in many countries now produce sustainability reports using the GRI framework. In addition, many other companies, particularly those operating globally, have developed their own approaches to environmental and sustainability reporting.

Global
Reporting
Initiat~

Case studies

 Case study 9.1 Foxconn and Apple

When Steve Jobs, the billionaire head of Apple[10] computers, was shown round the facilities of their supplier Foxconn in Shenzen, China he was impressed by the movie theatres, swimming pools and other facilities he saw in this booming city of 17 million people. Thirty years earlier, Shenzen was agricultural with rice paddies, water buffalo, and duck, fish, and shrimp farms, and a small fishing harbour.

When subsequently Jobs learned that workers at the huge Foxconn factory were attempting suicide—fourteen had taken their own lives in 2010—he said that he found the situation 'troubling' and that he was 'all over it'.

Foxconn International Holdings Ltd, which is part of the Hon Hai group, is one of China's largest exporters, and has around 800,000 employees, half of them in Shenzen, just across the border from Hong Kong. The Apple iPhone, iPad, and iPod all have Foxconn components.

The Hon Hai Precision Industry Company Ltd was founded by Terry Gou in 1974. He is alleged to be Taiwan's richest man. A strict disciplinarian and an apparent workaholic, Gou's mantra is 'time is money and efficiency is life'. With over forty production and R&D centres in Asia, Europe, and the Americas, the group is now the world's largest manufacturer of parts for the computer, communications, and consumer electronics industries, sold under contract to customers such as Apple, Dell, and Sony.

Foxconn's Longhua plant was built as a factory town in the countryside north of Shenzen when land in China's Pearl River delta was cheap. It attracted tens of thousands of young people (mostly in their late teens or early twenties) looking to leave the poverty of the provinces and believing that a factory job would offer them a 'city life' with friends and plenty of money. Instead they became cheerless human machines who were too exhausted to enjoy what little free time they had. They were hired to work eight hour shifts but the majority increased their earnings with substantial overtime.

At the start of each shift, thousands of workers in identical uniforms sang the company song. The public address system broadcast music and propaganda. Posters urged the workers to: 'let the company get stronger and stronger,' and 'achieve goals unless the sun no longer rises.' They worked standing in one place under constant camera supervision. Pay was docked under a discipline scheme, which handed out points for being late, yawning, talking, or having long finger nails. Although the plant had modern dormitories, workers slept in three tier bunks with no air-conditioning in summer temperatures that could reach thirty degrees. Eating facilities were considered good, but the quasi-military atmosphere was dispiriting.

Following the spate of suicides, the company took action. Wire fences were put on roofs and nets were erected below the buildings where suicides might occur to catch any who jumped. Social workers were recruited. A suicide prevention hot line was installed and averaged two calls a day. Spotter teams were created to detect employees with possible problems. The Shenzen Mental Health Centre offered support and monks were brought in to ward off evil spirits. Basic pay was increased significantly but overtime was restricted, so this meant that some employees were no better off financially.

Under Shenzen law, employers are required to pay a minimum compensation for death at work: as a good employer Foxconn had paid significantly more. It was feared that some employees might have killed themselves to get this generous compensation for their families. Consequently, all employees were required to sign a declaration that their dependents would not sue the company if they killed themselves. There was also a threat to stop paying medical bills following any attempted suicide.

[10] For more information on Apple's policies supplier responsibility, see: www.apple.com/supplierresponsibility

Although the suicide rate was alarming, a visiting psychology professor from Tsinghau University pointed out that the suicide rate was actually lower than the average for the young people in the rest of China.

Foxconn had been lauded by the Chinese press for creating jobs in modern surroundings. Now the firm became an object of criticism and undercover investigations. On an impromptu visit to Shenzen, Terry Gou insisted that he was not running a 'sweatshop'. Clients, including Apple, Dell, and HP, announced their own inquiries to ward off bad press. Tim Cook, who took over Apple following Steve Jobs' death, went on a highly publicized tour in August 2012. There seemed to be room for improvement.

See http://www.foxconn.com

Discussion questions

1. Does Apple have any responsibility for activities taken on its behalf at Foxconn?

2. Did Apple do enough in response to the problems it found at Foxconn?

3. Were the problems at Foxconn failures of governance, executive supervision, or management?

4. Foxconn had raised its basic wages four times in the past three years and in some areas doubled the starting level pay. Since labour is no longer cheap, should Foxconn invest in automated production lines to keep its competitive edge?

 Case study 9.2   The CLP Group on governance and ethics

CLP is a major generator and supplier of electricity in Australia, China, Hong Kong, India, and Taiwan. CLP has summarized its approach to governance and ethics in the following framework:

Vision	What we must do to uphold our values
Mission	What we want to be
Values	What benefits we will bring to our stakeholders
Commitments	What ideals guide us in our mission
Policies and Codes	What we must do to meet our commitments.

A set of business principles and ethics define the company's vision, mission, and values, creating its identity and guiding its actions. The concept of sustainable development defines corporate actions, balancing the social, environmental, and economic dimensions of the business, while considering the needs of both current and future generations.

CLP believes that good corporate governance enhances credibility and improves shareholders' and other stakeholders' interests. Maintaining a good, solid, and sensible framework of corporate governance is a top priority. The company is committed to a set of ethics and principles covering every aspect of the business. The code on corporate governance creates the framework and principles for defining company policies and procedures. The code covers every aspect of the business to keep actions consistent with the vision, mission, and values. The company also recognizes that corporate governance is an evolving process, and reviews the principles and practices in light of experience, regulatory changes, and international developments.

CLP recognizes its shareholders as key stakeholders and is committed to creating shareholder value with a sustainable rate of return to shareholders. To earn and maintain shareholder support, the company has adopted the following principles:

- deliver value to them through capital appreciation (expressed in the form of the performance of share price over time) and payment of dividends;
- operate the business in a way that corresponds to their values and expectations;
- communicate honestly, effectively, and frequently with shareholders about the stewardship of their assets by the board and management of CLP;
- manage its investments and business risks in accordance with its principles and code of conduct;
- invest in expanding and preserving the value of its assets, capabilities, and relationships.

(For more information, see www.clpgroup.com)

Discussion questions

1. What is your opinion of CLP's corporate governance framework?

2. Would it be suitable for other companies?

3. Could the CLP code on corporate governance be a pro forma code for other companies?

As corporate sustainability becomes increasingly important, systems are being developed to manage the masses of data involved in producing regular CSR and sustainability reports. Software has been developed to use companies' existing intranet facilities to collect and collate the necessary information.

References and further reading

Amao, Olufemi (2013) *Corporate Social Responsibility, Human Rights and the Law: Multinational Corporations in Developing Countries*. Routledge, London.

Andreas, Fred M. et al. (2011) *A Simple Path to Sustainability: Green Business Strategies for Small and Medium-sized Businesses*. ABC-CLIO, Santa Barbara, CA.

Banks, Erik (2004) *Corporate Governance: Financial Responsibility, Controls and Ethics*. Palgrave Macmillan, New York.

Beal, Brent D. (2013) *Corporate Social Responsibility: Definition, Core Issues, and Recent Developments*. Sage, Los Angeles, CA.

Bell, Jeanne, Jan Maaoka, and Steve Zimmerman (2010) *Nonprofit Sustainability: Making Strategic Decisions for Financial Viability*. Jossey-Bass, San Francisco, CA.

Bernstein, Anne (2010) *The Case for Business in Developing Economies*. Penguin Books, Johannesburg.

Blowfield, Mick and Alan Murray (2011) *Corporate Responsibility*. 2nd edn, Oxford University Press, Oxford.

Bolton, Dianne and Suzanne Benn (2012) *Key Concepts in Corporate Social Responsibility*. Sage Key Concepts, Los Angeles, CA.

Carroll, A. B. (1979) 'A Three-dimensional Conceptual Model of Corporate Performance', *Academy of Management Review*, Vol. 4, pp. 497–505.

Chandler, David and William B. Werther Jr (2005) *Corporate Social Responsibility: Stakeholders in a Global Environment*. Sage Publications Inc., London/ Los Angeles, CA.

Cramer, Jacqueline (2006) *Corporate Social Responsibility and Globalisation: An Action Plan for Business*. Greenleaf Publishing, Sheffield, UK.

Crane, Andrew et al. (eds) (2009) *The Oxford Handbook of Corporate Social Responsibility*. Oxford University Press, Oxford.

Crane, Andrew, Dirk Matten and Laura Spence (2013) *Corporate Social Responsibility: Readings and cases in a global context*. 2nd edn, Routledge, Abingdon.

Crowther, David and Lez Rayman-Bacchus (eds) (2004) *Perspectives on Corporate Social Responsibility*. Ashgate Publishing, London.

Eccles, Robert, G. and Michael P. Krzus (2010) *One Report: Integrated Reporting for a Sustainable Strategy*. Wiley, Hoboken, NJ.

Epstein, Marc J., John Elkington and Herman B. Leonard (2008) *Making Sustainability Work: Best Practices in Managing and Measuring Corporate Social, Environmental and Economic Impacts*. Greenleaf Publishing, Sheffield, UK.

Fleming, Peter and Marc V. Jones (2013) *The End of Corporate Social Responsibility: Crisis and Critique*, Kindle edition.

Habisch, André et al. (eds) (2005) *Corporate Social Responsibility across Europe*. Springer, Berlin.

Hamschmidt, Jost (2007) *Cases in Sustainability Management and Strategy: The Oikos Collection*. Greenleaf Publishing, Sheffield, UK.

Hancock, John (2004) *Investing in Corporate Social Responsibility: A Guide to Best Practice, Business Planning and the UK's Leading Companies*. FTSE, London.

Hitchcock, Darcy and Marsha Willard (2009) *The Business Guide to Sustainability: Practical Strategies and Tools for Organizations*. Earthscan, London.

Holme, Richard and Phil Watts (2000) *Corporate Social Responsibility: Making Good Business Sense*. World Council for Sustainable Development, 160 Route de Florissant, CH-1231 Conches-Geneva, Switzerland.

Hopkins, Michael (2012) *Corporate Social Responsibility and International Development: Is Business the Solution?* Kindle edition.

Hopwood, A., J. Unerman and J. Fries (2010) *Accounting for Sustainability: Practical Insights*. Earthscan, London.

ICGN (2009) *Statement and Guidance on Non-financial Business Reporting*. International Corporate Governance Network, 16 Park Crescent, London W1B 1AH.

Kotler, Philip and Nancy Lee (2004) *Corporate Social Responsibility: Doing the Most Good for Your Company and Your Cause*. Wiley, Hoboken, NJ.

Laszlo, Chris and Nadya Zhexembayeva (2011) *Embedded Sustainability: The Next Big Competitive Advantage*. Greenleaf Publishing, Sheffield, UK.

Orsato, Renato, J. (2009) *Sustainability Strategies: When Does It Pay To Be Green?* Insead Business Press, Fontainebleau.

Raynard, Peter (ed.) (2006) *Tomorrow's History: An Anthology of Simon Zadek's Work*. (Academy of Management's 2006 SIM book prize) Greenleaf Publishing, Sheffield, UK.

Reich, Robert B. (2007) *Super-capitalism: The Transformation of Business, Democracy and Everyday Life*. Alfred A. Knopf, New York.

Rezaee, Zabihollah, Lynn Turner, and Diane L. Swanson (2008) *Corporate Governance and Ethics*. Wiley, Chichester, UK.

Schaltegger, Stephan and Marcus Wagner (eds) (2006) *Managing the Business Case for Sustainability: The Integration of Social, Environmental and Economic Performance*. Greenleaf Publishing, Sheffield, UK.

UK Government (2006) *How to Use the CSR Competency Framework: A Resource Pack for Using the CSR Competency Framework*. HMSO, London.

Vogel, David (2006) *The Market for Virtue: The Potential and Limits of CSR*. Brookings Institution Press, Washington, DC.

Waddock, Sandra and Charles Bodwell (2007) *Total Responsibility Management: The Manual*. Greenleaf Publishing, Sheffield, UK.

Werther, William B. and David B. Chandler (2010) *Strategic CSR: Stakeholders in a Global Environment*. Sage, Los Angeles, CA.

Zerk, Jennifer A. (2006) *Multinationals and Corporate Social Responsibility: Limitations and Opportunities in International Law*. Cambridge University Press, Cambridge.

Projects and exercises

1. Develop a CSR policy statement for any organization with which you are familiar. It could, for example, be for a profit-orientated company, an academic institution, or some other not-for-profit enterprise. Develop a set of performance indicators to monitor and measure the organization's achievements.

2. Develop a sustainability report for an organization with which you are familiar.

Self-test questions

1. Name six types of stakeholder that a company might have.
2. What different perspectives on CSR are discussed in the chapter?
3. What might a firm's socially responsible activities include?
4. What is enlightened shareholder value?
5. Who should lead a company's CSR efforts?
6. What is a CSR policy?
7. When might a clear CSR policy influence potential investors?
8. How does the Brundtland Report define sustainable development?
9. What is the Global Reporting Initiative and who is involved?
10. What is the basic belief behind the Global Reporting Initiative?

10 The Governance of Listed Companies

 Learning Outcomes

In which we consider:

- Ownership of listed companies
- Shareholder rights
- Shareholder activism and the role of institutional investors
- Shareholder relations
- Disclosure of substantial shareholdings and directors' interests
- The governance of complex corporate structures
- Block-holders and universal ownership
- Dual-listed companies
- Dual-class shares
- Listings on alternative stock markets

Ownership of listed companies

The reality of corporate governance and the way in which power can be wielded over a company reflects the ownership structure. Although some texts treat the owners of listed companies as though they were homogeneous, the actual pattern of ownership can have a major influence on corporate governance.

Contrast the potential differences of shareholder power in the following cases.

- A listed company in which the shares are widely spread between many individual and institutional shareholders with no one in a dominant position, giving a balanced and mixed ownership; no single investor or group of them acting together can exercise undue influence over company affairs.

- A listed company in which institutional shareholders dominate, particularly one listed in the liquid markets of the United States or the United Kingdom, where a significant proportion of shareholders are institutional investors—banks, insurance companies, pension funds, hedge funds, and sovereign funds. In the United States, institutional investors now account for around two-thirds of the investment in large listed companies. Only three of the world's most valuable listed companies are now American—Exxon Mobil, Walmart, and Microsoft. In the United Kingdom in 1963, individuals held 54%

of British listed companies with less than a tenth of the market being in the hands of overseas investors: today less than 12% of British shares are held by individuals, while 53% are held by overseas interests.

- A state-run enterprise, such as Gazprom, run by the Kremlin in Russia, which is really a state bureaucracy masquerading as a company.

- A listed company in which a single shareholder owns a major shareholding. Such a controlling shareholder may not need a majority holding to exercise considerable influence, given that no other shareholder has significant voting powers. Such ownership structures are common in Europe and many other countries outside the United States and the United Kingdom.

- A listed company in which some large shareholders form a block and are thus able to influence events, even though none hold a majority of the voting rights. Such block holdings are prevalent in Sweden and some other countries. In Italy, legal agreements can be created that enable shareholders to work and vote together through a voting trust.

- A family company which is listed with outside shareholders, but in which a significant proportion of the voting shares are still in family hands. Many family companies are in this category. The family shareholders do not need to hold as much as 50% to exercise considerable influence; 20 or 30% is often sufficient, if the holders of the other shares are widely spread. Most of the family companies listed in Hong Kong maintain control, with outside investors holding significantly less than 50% of the voting rights. Some stock exchanges, including Hong Kong, require listed companies to offer a minimum percentage of their shares in a public offering.

- A company that has been floated on the stock market may still be in the hands of the founder, who dominates because of his status and position, even though he now holds less than a controlling share.

- A listed company could be the subsidiary of another major company, if less than 50% of its shares are available to the public. We shall see examples of such companies in group chains and networks later in this chapter.

It is also worth noting at this stage that, although we tend to think of a direct relationship between shareholder and company, in reality there can be a complex chain of intermediaries acting as agents, as we noted earlier. For example: the ultimate owner of a share could be an individual who invests in a private pension fund:

- which invests some of its funds in a hedge fund,
- which in turn invests in a fund of funds to hedge its risk,
- which invests in a commercial property fund,
- which places some of its funds in the hands of a financial institution,
- which invests ultimately in the listed company,
- but lends the shares as collateral for a deal it has made.

In such a complex chain, how does the listed company demonstrate its accountability to its ultimate owners? Who is responsible for exercising corporate governance influence on the listed company? These are issues that lie behind some of the challenging questions in contemporary corporate governance.

Public companies, those listed on the stock market, face significantly more demanding governance standards than those of private companies, through legislation and regulation, corporate governance codes, and the listing rules of the stock market. Companies planning a stock market listing, probably through an IPO (initial public offering) need to position themselves carefully beforehand. Among the things that need to be considered include:

- Position the company beforehand to meet the requirements of the relevant corporate governance codes and listing rules.
- Ensure the chairman of the board is confident and competent in the role. Chairing a board with outside directors, with divergent experiences and views, can be quite different from the close-knit consensus of a private company board.
- Seek advice from corporate auditors and lawyers, particularly from compliance and governance specialists, and from the financial institution leading the IPO.
- Consider the board structure, ensuring a sufficient number and quality of independent outside directors. Consider board diversity. Acquiring appropriate independent directors and briefing them takes time.
- Ensure that existing directors have the appropriate knowledge, time, and enthusiasm to serve on the board of a quoted company. The time commitment for directors of a listed company is often significantly more demanding than for a private company and the number of board papers much greater.
- Create the required board committees, including the audit committee, the remuneration committee and the nominating committee; and train the members, operating the committees to gain experience.
- Agree board-level remuneration and review policies.
- Consider board succession, director training and development, and director and board evaluation methods.
- Develop the required reporting routines and shareholder interaction processes well ahead of time.
- Develop the board reporting systems to ensure they are comprehensive, timely, and accurate for the governance of a listed company.

Shareholder rights

The rights that shareholders acquire with their shares are determined by the Companies Acts or ordinances of the jurisdiction in which it was incorporated and by the company's articles of association. Although the details obviously vary between countries, ownership of a share broadly provides the right to:

- have your name, address, and shareholding entered onto the shareholder members' register;
- receive notice of all shareholder meetings within a specific time;

- receive the formal company accounts, directors' and auditors' reports, and other statutory notices;
- attend shareholders' meetings;
- vote, either in person or by proxy, at all shareholder meetings;
- view the company's statutory records, including the register of members, the register of loans charged against the company's assets, the register of directors, officers, and company secretary, and the register of their share interests;
- and to receive dividends that have been duly declared for that class of share.

Shareholders do not have a right to attend internal meetings of the company, to access management accounts and other corporate information, or get involved in management. However, shareholder activism is growing and many listed companies now recognize that investor relations are a basic part of sound corporate governance, as we will see.

In shareholders' annual general meetings (AGM), ordinary resolutions require a simple majority with over 50% of the members voting in person or by proxy at the meeting. Decisions made by ordinary resolution include the:

- approval of the accounts presented to shareholders by the directors;
- approval of the reappointment of auditors;
- payment of dividends proposed by the directors;
- approval of transactions between the company and connected persons;
- appointment and reappointment of directors.

Longer notice may be required for resolutions to:

- remove a director;
- remove an auditor during his or her term of office;
- appoint an auditor other than the retiring auditor.

In 2007, the European Union published a Shareholder Rights Directive, which sought to improve shareholders' rights and solve problems in the exercising of such rights across borders in the member states. The Directive applied only to companies in which shares are traded on stock markets within the European Economic Area (EEA), which encompasses the EU countries plus Iceland, Liechtenstein, and Norway. Switzerland is not a member.

In the United Kingdom, the Companies (Shareholder Rights) Regulations were published in 2009 to implement the EU Directive. Shareholders acquired the right to ask questions at shareholder meetings, which companies must answer unless they can show that such disclosure would not be in the company's interest or would be likely to disrupt the meeting. Companies must provide a website, with information relevant to shareholders' interests, including their right to ask questions and how to vote. Holders of at least 5% of the voting shares can now requisition a shareholders' general meeting (previously 10% were required). Also, holders of 5% of the voting shares, or 100 members, can require a company to include an item on the agenda of their company's AGM.

The 2009 Regulations also clarified the way in which companies count proxies when using a 'show of hands' rather than in a formal ballot. The minimum notice for shareholder meetings was increased from 14 to 21 days. An electronic address must be provided for the receipt of proxies and electronic voting by shareholders was facilitated. The Regulations also required listed companies to publish information about AGM ballots: the number of votes cast, the percentage of voting shares represented by those votes, and the number of abstentions.

Shareholder activism and the role of institutional investors

In the 19th-century model of the company, shareholders were individuals and met together periodically to receive the report and accounts of their directors, to re-elect them or to propose new ones, and to approve significant changes, such as an alteration in the share capital, as required by company law or the company's articles. Shareholder democracy, with each share having voting rights, was feasible. Ownership was the basis of governance power.

But today, in most listed companies, the shareholders include corporate institutional investors as well as individuals. The shareholders are numerous, geographically spread, and have different expectations of the company. Shareholder democracy, 'one share, one vote', no longer provides shareholder power.

In many jurisdictions, it has become difficult for shareholders to ask questions if the chairman has no wish to allow them. To get motions onto the agenda of shareholder meetings or to nominate new directors is often near impossible. As Berle and Means showed in the 1930s, in large companies, power has moved from shareholders to management.

Dissatisfaction with boards has increased in recent years, with concerns over poor corporate performance, allegedly excessive directors' rewards, loss of investor confidence following downturn in markets, and company collapses. There have been many calls for greater involvement by shareholders in the governance of companies. But the potential for shareholder activism by individual shareholders is low, given their large numbers, small individual holdings, and diverse interests, although the Internet has provided some small individual shareholders with a platform from which to advance their opinions on corporate issues.

However, institutional investors can wield more power. Even though their shareholding is relatively small, they can have a more significant influence, particularly if they act in concert with their activities coordinated. Many institutional investors now receive voting guidelines from their representative organizations, such as the Council of Institutional Investors or Institutional Shareholders Services in the United States, or the Association of British Insurers, through the Institutional Voting Information Service, and the National Association of Pension Funds in the United Kingdom.

In the United States the incidence of activist shareholders threatening or initiating proposals for the nomination and election of directors has increased significantly.[1] Moreover, many have been successful. Activist calls for shareholder-sponsored directors to public company boards are also receiving support from financial institutions. Activist shareholders can now be a potential risk for incumbent boards by proposing their own nominees (what some commentators refer to as 'short-slate' elections) and need to consider their policies in response to such activism. However, a distinction needs to be drawn between investors that seem more like short-term speculators than share-holders who are interested in the long-term prospects and performance of their company.

[1] Activism Monthly (2013), Vol. 2, Issue 4 and Activist Annual Review 2012.

Private equity investors in listed companies, such as Blackstone, and Wall Street investors such as Carl Icahn, Daniel Loeb, and Nelson Petz caused alarm in some American boardrooms, when they acquired significant equity stakes that led to them becoming predators, sometimes called corporate raiders or greenmailers. Some commentators, however, claim that these activist investors research their targets thoroughly, make sound business recommendations, and can be a force for good. In recent years, there have been signs that these aggressive American investors are casting their nets wider towards the United Kingdom, Europe and elsewhere.

A classical example of shareholder activism occurred in 2014, when the Trian Fund Management company, led by Nelson Peitz, published a report it had sent to PepsiCo Inc., the beverages and snacks business. Trian owned $1.2 billion of Pepsi stock, and in a fifty-seven page report[2] critiqued the board's marketing, manufacturing, and organizational strategies, exposing corporate blunders, and called for a re-organization that would make some brands more independent corporate entities (and, of course, more open to be floated separately for the benefit of investors).

In the United Kingdom, shareholders do have the right to have resolutions put on the ballot and, if successful, they are usually binding on the directors. Research from the Harvard Business School[3] has shown how directors' careers can be affected by shareholder activist campaigns. It was found that directors are almost twice as likely to leave over a two-year period if their company had been the subject of a shareholder activist campaign. Directors are also more likely to leave in the year following activism if they receive lower shareholder support on re-election. However, although directors may leave boards following activism, it does not affect their standing on other boards on which they serve.

Shareholder activism can take a number of forms. Usually it involves communication and negotiation directly with management. But activism can involve media campaigns or blogging to change corporate practices, proxy battles advancing shareholder resolutions to force change, calling shareholder meetings, or litigation against companies or their directors. Some shareholder activists use their shareholding to advance their own social, environmental, or other agenda to influence corporate behaviour.

Hedge fund managers can also become active shareholders, acquiring sufficient voting power to nominate a director to the board. They may also be able to afford financial, accounting, and legal advice to protect and promote their interests. In some countries, controlling block-holders of shares, such as founders and their families, are also able to influence decisions in the boardroom over and above the power of the shareholder vote, although the deepening of stock markets in countries such as Sweden, Italy, and Spain is beginning to reduce the significance of such block-holders.

Some have suggested that increasing shareholder activism is irresistible, leading to an inevitable struggle between shareholders and top management. Predictably, not all directors are enthusiastic about shareholder involvement. They would prefer a return to their earlier experiences when shareholders were relatively passive, seldom raised questions, and readily confirmed board recommendations.

---

[2] www.trianwhitepapers.com

[3] Gow, Ian D., Sa-Pyung Sean Shin and Suraj Srinivasan (2014) *Consequences to Directors of Shareholder Activism*. Harvard Business Scool Working Paper 14-071.

Shareholder activism can be controversial. The view is advanced that shareholders, having elected their directors, should allow them freedom to act without having their business decisions second-guessed. Separation between shareholders and top management, it is argued, lies at the heart of the governance system. Boards need freedom to take business decisions in good faith without interference from interventionist institutions. Otherwise, boards may respond to investor pressure by focusing on the short term, failing to make crucial long-term strategic decisions. Moreover, some add, institutional investors are in effect intermediaries in the chain between ultimate individual owners and companies. Such institutions have governance problems of their own in recognizing and responding to the different aims of their own investors. But most listed companies now recognize the importance of close, positive involvement with their investors.

Shareholder relations

Proactive shareholder relation activities can provide a two-way channel of information, informing both existing and potential shareholders, securities analysts and the financial community, and the company. Shareholder relation activities take many forms, including interactive websites, newsletters, shareholder meetings, press conferences, and road-shows, as well as meetings with individual shareholders, to resolve questions and explore issues about the company's strategies, policies, and financial standing. The digital delivery of shareholder services, electronic many-way communication, and social media are tending to accelerate the interaction between companies, their shareholders and market commentators. Indeed, moves towards paperless relationships between companies and their shareholders, what some call 'dematerialization', is progressing, although some shareholders remain to be convinced.

In the United States, the Sarbanes-Oxley Act of 2002 increased the emphasis on investor relations by demanding greater corporate transparency, compliance, and enhanced financial disclosure, with board-level responsibility for financial reports.

From October 2014, the UK Financial Reporting Council amended the corporate governance code to require companies to explain to their AGM how they intend to engage with shareholders when a significant percentage of them have voted against any resolution.

Many publicly traded companies have set up investor or shareholder relations departments. Typically, these departments report to the finance director or chief finance officer (CFO), with the company secretary or corporate attorney closely involved if legal issues arise. However, some companies link their investor relations activities with their public and media activities. Professional investor relations can improve a company's standing and ultimately its share price, although companies need to be careful to avoid disclosing sensitive information about the share price to only one or a few shareholders.

Investor relations practitioners have achieved a professional status in some countries and have their own professional bodies, for example the National Investor Relations Institute in the United States, the Investor Relations Society in the United Kingdom, and the Australian Investor Relations Association. Some professionals in the field now see investor relations as part of broader stakeholder relations and corporate social responsibility, with the need for a coordinated communications programme.

Disclosure of substantial shareholdings and directors' interests

Many jurisdictions, through their company law, and many stock exchanges, through their listing rules, require the disclosure of shareholders with substantial interests in a listed company. Such transparent and timely disclosure of information about the ownership structure allows existing shareholders and potential investors to make informed decisions. In effect, it enables those dealing with the company to appreciate where the balance of power over its governance really lies.

Corporate governance in action 10.1 Total Oil Company: individual shareholder relations

Total is a leading multinational energy company, based in Paris, France, with over 97,000 employees and operations in more than 130 countries. Together with its subsidiaries and affiliates, Total is the fifth largest publicly traded integrated international oil and gas company in the world; 87% of its shares are held by institutional investors. Total engages in all aspects of the petroleum industry, including upstream operations (oil and gas exploration, development, and production) and downstream operations (refining, marketing, and the trading and shipping of crude oil and petroleum products), as well as being a major player in chemicals. Total also has interests in coal mining and power generation, and is developing solar, biomass, and nuclear energy sources.

Transparency, listening, and dialogue are key to the company's relationship with its shareholders. To strengthen this relationship, the company's individual shareholder relations department provides opportunities to exchange, discuss, and inform, through shareholders' meetings, an annual trade show, meetings with shareholders in a number of cities in France, and the shareholders' newsletter.

In Singapore, the Companies Act requires a substantial shareholder of a listed company holding 5% or more of the total shareholder votes, whether resident in Singapore or not, to disclose their interests in the voting shares. The shareholder must give written notice to the listed company within two business days of becoming or ceasing to be a substantial shareholder. The company must then inform the Singapore Stock Exchange. In Singapore, failure to obey the Companies Act can incur civil penalties and failure to follow the listing rules could lead to the ultimate sanction of delisting.

In 2013, the United Kingdom introduced proposals to enhance the transparency of UK company ownership and increase trust in UK business. These proposals required companies to maintain a registry of companies' beneficial owners, showing who owns and controls them. The proposals also stopped the issue of bearer shares, which do not provide details of the owners. Corporate directors were also prohibited, so that directors would be real people, not other corporations.

Public disclosure is also often required of directors' dealings in their company's shares. Such information is intended to deter directors from benefiting from their confidential inside knowledge of the company's affairs. In Australia, the Corporations Act and the Australian Stock Exchange Listing Rules oblige directors of public companies to notify the exchange of changes to directors' interests in shares.

Insider dealing (or insider trading) is the buying or selling of shares on the basis of information that is not yet available to the stock market. It is now illegal in almost all jurisdictions, although some countries were slow to criminalize the activity. In 2013, SAC Capital, an American hedge fund company, and some of its officers pleaded guilty to federal insider trading charges, and were fined $1.8 billion, the largest penalty for the offence to date.

The governance of complex corporate structures

Thus far we have looked at governance issues in simple corporate structures in which there is one corporate entity, one governing body, and one set of shareholder members. Certainly, this was the situation in the mid-19th century when joint-stock, limited-liability companies were first developed. Although a few companies did merge during this period, this was achieved by creating a new company, which acquired the assets and liabilities of the merging companies, and then winding up the original companies. Not until towards the end of the 19th century did entrepreneurs realize that a company could legitimately own shares in other companies. But these days most listed companies operate through groups of companies, not a single corporate entity. These groups can be quite complex and may include other listed companies. So let us now consider the governance of such companies.

Complex corporate structures can be grouped into three broad categories:

- pyramids, in which the holding company sits on top of a pyramid of subsidiary and associate companies;
- chains, in which one company or shareholder group holds an interest in a string of companies;
- networks, in which a set of companies owns shares in each other. To be clear on definitions:
  - a *holding company* is a company that holds all or a dominant share of the voting rights in another company;
  - a *subsidiary company* is a company in which another company (its holding company) holds all of its voting shares (a *wholly owned subsidiary*) or a majority of its voting shares (a *partially owned subsidiary*);
  - an *associate company* is a company over which another company exercises dominant power, even though it does not hold a majority of the voting rights in that company, for example where the other shareholdings are widely spread.

The governance of pyramid structures

The corporate pyramid is the most straightforward organizational form for a group of companies. It is the structure found most frequently in practice, and is widely used by both private companies and public listed companies. It is also the structure widely used by international groups that own companies incorporated in a number of countries. Figure 10.1 depicts an elementary form of pyramid, showing a holding company with four subsidiaries held at two levels.

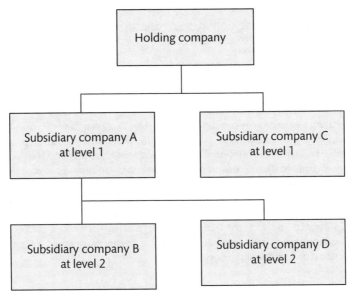

Figure 10.1 A simple group pyramid structure

Research published over thirty years ago[4] showed that twenty companies at the top of the UK Times 1000 list had 4,600 subsidiaries between them: an average 230 subsidiaries each. The smallest group had twelve subsidiaries, the largest a surprising 800. But more surprising was the number of levels (subsidiaries of subsidiaries of subsidiaries, etc.) at which the subsidiaries were held. Most held subsidiaries at two or three levels, but many had subsidiary companies at levels five or six, and one even at level eleven! This had arisen because a company at level five had acquired a company that itself had subsidiaries at five levels. With the growth of globalization and cross-border holdings of companies, the situation today can be even more complex.

Why should a holding company adopt a pyramid structure, rather than operate through a single entity? There are a number of possibilities.

First is strategic positioning: a group structure can be used to bind identifiable parts of the enterprise in line with the group's corporate strategy (see Case study 10.1, the Jardine Matheson Group).

The second reason to adopt a pyramid structure could be legal: operating through a company incorporated in the country of operation often simplifies legal and regulatory aspects, including business regulation, contracting, employment, taxation, health and safety regulation, and so on. However, incorporating a company in an offshore tax haven can also provide significant financial and legal benefits to the group. As an indication of the importance of offshore companies, a majority of the companies listed on the Hong Kong stock market are incorporated in the British Virgin Islands (BVI), Bermuda, Panama, or other tax havens around the world (see Corporate governance in action 10.2).

The third reason to adopt a pyramid structure could be taxation: there can be significant tax benefits in operating through companies registered in countries where the taxation regime is lower than elsewhere. Although the tax laws of most countries seek to ensure that profits are taxed where they are earned, with tough oversight of transfer prices for goods and services

---

[4] Tricker R. I. (1984) *Corporate Governance: Practices, Procedures, and Powers in British Companies and their Boards of Directors.* Corporate Policy Group and Gower, Aldershot, UK.

Corporate governance in action 10.2   Incorporation in a tax haven: the example of BVI

The BVI are situated sixty miles east of Puerto Rico in the Eastern Caribbean. Only about twenty islands have permanent residents. BVI is a British Overseas Territory, which uses the US dollar as its legal currency. The capital is Tortola. The BVI Constitution gives executive and legislative power to the Governor, the Executive Council, and the Legislative Council.

BVI is a world leader in offshore company incorporations. These companies are used for a wide range of purposes, including acting as a holding company for multinational and global corporations, as trusts for asset protection, for collective investment, and to hold intellectual property. Such incorporations can offer tax benefits, limited disclosure of financial and ownership information, secrecy of inter-company dealings, and other benefits.

BVI has good communications, political and economic stability, no exchange controls, low taxation with certain classes of business exempt, no capital gains tax, and no wealth tax. Incorporation in BVI offers flexibility, corporate privacy and confidentiality, a pool of professional service providers, sound company law based on British law, and regulation that is reasonable, but not bureaucratic. BVI is also committed to assist the international fight against money laundering.

passed between group companies in different countries, there are still major benefits to be gained through separate subsidiaries in differently taxed countries.

The fourth reason for a pyramid structure, creating separate limited-liability companies, is an attempt to reduce the group's exposure to the debts of any member company. As we have already seen, the shareholders of a company are not liable for its debts. That applies where the owner is itself a limited company. Consequently, where a group has businesses that could hazard the well-being of the group as a whole if they were to fail, each business can be incorporated as a separate legal entity. For example, some shipping companies operate each of their vessels as a separate limited company. In many jurisdictions, company law protects the owners from liability for the debts of subsidiary companies. Each separate company is shrouded with a veil that that cannot be pierced. However, in some other company law jurisdictions, such as Germany, corporate groups are not allowed to protect themselves in this way from the failure of one member of the group. In these countries, creditors of subsidiary companies in a group can pursue their debts with the parent companies up the ownership structure, right to the top.

The fifth reason for creating a pyramid structure could be to provide a legal home for a non-trading activity or to preserve a name. Such companies are sometimes called 'letter box' companies. Some companies in a group could be dormant—that is, they are not trading—but are not wound up in case they are needed in the future.

Finally, many corporate groups have arrived at their complex pyramid structure through mergers and acquisitions. Rather than rationalize their organization structure following acquisitions and mergers into product or regional divisions, these groups continue with a conglomeration of separate companies reporting through the ownership structure to the holding company.

So, what are the corporate governance implications of a group operating with a pyramid structure?

Every company in a group must obey the legal requirements of the jurisdiction in which it is incorporated. Moreover, if it is a listed company, it must fulfil the listing requirements of the stock exchanges on which its shares are listed. In most cases, that means each subsidiary and associate company must have its own officers and board of directors, keep its own financial records, file the required company reports, and in some cases have an audit (see Corporate governance in action 10.2).

The corporate governance implications for directors of subsidiary or associate companies operating in a pyramid structure are significant. Every director owes a duty to the company on the board of which he or she serves. That board must obey the corporate governance requirements of the relevant company law jurisdiction, the rules of the regulatory regime, and, if a listed company, the listing requirements of the stock exchange. But if the company is controlled through the group management control system, an executive director also has to accept the duties and responsibilities as a member of the group management structure, recognizing that performance appraisal and reward will be determined within that structure. This is particularly important if the subsidiary company on the board of which the director serves has external minority shareholders, in which case the director must ensure that the rights of all shareholders (the external minority shareholders and the group) are recognized. This can be difficult should their interests differ, remembering that the career prospects of a director, who is also a manager in the group, depend on decisions taken in the group. If an independent non-executive director is appointed as a director of a subsidiary company, in order to ensure that the interests of minority shareholders are protected, he or she is a nominee director, with the implications already discussed.

The governance of chain structures

The corporate chain is, as the name suggests, a group of companies in an ownership chain. What distinguishes this structure from a simplified form of pyramid is that the companies in the chain have other outside shareholders, as shown in Figure 10.2.

The head of the chain may be another company, a group of investors such as a private equity fund, or an individual. Companies in the chain may be public and listed companies or private companies.

Why is the chain structure adopted? The answer is simple: those controlling the head of a chain can influence management decisions in the other companies in the chain. With the leveraged power gained from gearing, the head of the chain is able to exercise more influence over the companies in the chain than by investing in each individual company. Figure 10.3 is an example of gearing in a chain of companies.

A successful businessman and his family are the dominant owners in the chain, owning 34% of company A, which owned 40% of company B, which owned 36% of company C. Companies A, B, and C were all public companies listed on a stock exchange. The rest of the shareholdings in each company were held by the public (as in Figure 10.2), with no other dominant holding. In this chain, the financial investment of the head of the chain in company C is actually only 5% (34% of 40% of 36%), yet the head of the chain is able to exercise management control over all of the companies in the chain, by being the dominant holder in each company.

A chain of companies may also offer a defence against predators, because the companies in the chain have some protection from the gearing.

What are the governance implications for the directors serving on the boards of companies in a chain? Primarily, of course, directors of such companies must fulfil their duties to

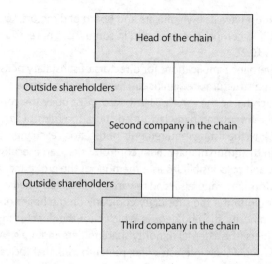

Figure 10.2 A simple chain structure

their company under the company law, the regulatory regime, and, where listed, the stock exchange. But, inevitably, with a dominant shareholder at the head of the chain, the companies in the chain have to respond to the requirements of that shareholder. Indeed, some of the directors may well be their nominees. But, as we have already seen when discussing nominee directors, such directors must also respect the interests of the other shareholders in their company, including any minority shareholders.

Chain structures are found in many countries in Asia, particularly where entrepreneurs and their families leverage their investment with other outside investors through a chain. They are also popular in Europe and other countries where family interests dominate corporate groups. In Italy, for example, the Agnelli family, through family interests held in a limited partnership, were able to exercise considerable influence over Fiat, the automobile firm.

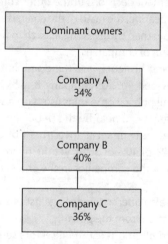

Figure 10.3 Example of gearing in a chain of companies

The governance of network structures

The terminology is obvious: a network structure is one in which the member companies form a network of cross-holdings, each company being a node in the network. One or more companies may be dominant or there may be no dominant member.

Why do groups of companies operate in networks? In some cultures, Japan and South Korea for example, the network is the traditional way in which corporate groups operate, working together with mutual operations and cross-holdings of shares. In the rest of the world, there are a number of reasons why groups operate in networks.

First, strategic links can be created between companies that co-operate operationally. For example, a group of companies may agree to work together, with various companies offering research and technological know-how, manufacturing capability, marketing and distribution services, or managerial capability to the others. Consequently, they may agree to exchange shares and accept cross-directorships between their boards. Such linkages can be reinforced by financial relationships, in addition to the cross-holding of shares. We will discuss the governance of joint venture companies later.

Second, companies may network to provide mutual protection, minimizing the chance of hostile predators. With a cross-holding of shares, a potential hostile bidder has a built-in disadvantage in acquiring enough shares to pursue a bid. Case study 10.1 provides an interesting example. Jardine Strategic Holdings is incorporated in Bermuda and listed in London, Singapore, and Bermuda. A private family-based company, Jardine Matheson Holdings, owns a controlling 82.5% interest in the public company Jardine Strategic Holdings. But Jardine Strategic Holdings in turn holds 55.5% of its parent. The public company is sheltered from predators through the cross-holding that it owns in its parent company. In some jurisdictions, company law prohibits such an arrangement.

Third, networks may be formed to raise funds through equity or loan financing. Pyramids and chains of companies may be buried within the network. In some cases, the apparent complexity of such financing networks can result from the deals made to obtain access to funds. In other cases, however, it can reflect attempts by potential predators to disguise their tracks, where the takeover rules restrict the building of a stake in a target company without notifying the market. Complex ownership networks may conceal the acquisition of dominant positions, at least for a while. Fourth, networks can be used for taxation avoidance, putting profits in tax havens within the law of their home country, rather than as a means of illegal tax evasion. Networks can also be used to provide anonymity for the ultimate owners of companies.

Fifth, networks can be formed to share risks between companies, part of a strategy to reduce exposure to business risk. For example, Companies A, B, and C exchange shares to reinforce an agreement to share risks, profits, and losses from a large construction contract in which they are all involved.

An extreme example is shown in the Sincere Group case (see Figure 10.4), in which the companies virtually owned each other. These cross-holdings would also serve to deter a hostile takeover bid for the listed holding company. As mentioned above, such an ownership scheme would not be permitted in some jurisdictions.

Sixth, networks can arise as the unintentional effect of corporate acquisition activity. Companies accept the network structure rather than incurring the costs and organizational stress of redefining the group structure and organizational systems. This can occur particularly if

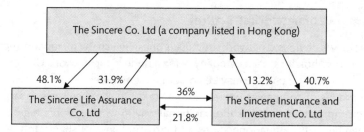

Figure 10.4 The Sincere Co. Ltd

there are outside minority interests in some of the network companies, which interests would have to be valued and redefined in restructuring.

Finally, complex networks can arise as the result of deliberate obfuscation, to reduce a group's visibility, perhaps to confuse competitors, to deter predators, or to avoid the unwanted interest of the authorities. Such network designs may push at the boundaries of legality, for example in taxation, exchange controls, corporate reporting, or money laundering.

Block-holders and universal ownership

Where institutional investors own a significant proportion of the voting shares in a company, and could act together, they form a block of shareholders. If they do act as a block, they may be able to influence corporate decisions, for example on corporate strategy, including acquisition policy, on the appointment or dismissal of directors, and on financial strategy, including dividend policy or capital restructuring.

In Sweden, corporate control became concentrated in block holdings in the second half of the 20th century. The Wallenberg Group and Industriväden typify the Swedish model (see Corporate governance in action 10.4). But controlling ownership is being diluted with the growth of firms and the stock market.

Italian voting trusts or voting syndicates (*patti di sindacato*) are groups of large shareholders who sign an explicit legal agreement to vote together. About a third of large Italian companies are dominated by such coalitions of large shareholders. In Italy, information on all such trusts has to be registered and this knowledge is publicly available. Such voting trusts ensure continuity and stability in management strategies and policies, and prevent conflicts of interest between large shareholders. Some proponents of voting trusts argue that concentrated, rather than diverse, ownership produces more monitoring of executive management, better management discipline, and higher returns. The trust agreement typically provides for a management committee to run the trust, arranges its operating procedures and finances, and confirms that no one shareholder can dominate.

Block-holders are also significant in South Korea, Russia, and China (where state-related organizations provide the block) and, following privatization, from state-ownership in Spain and Poland. Indeed, listed companies in most economies are not widely held, as they are in the United States and the United Kingdom, but are owned and controlled by families or states.

Although there are no apparent block-holders in listed companies with widely dispersed shareholders, it has been suggested that institutional investors could form such power blocks if they were to act together on governance matters. The recently developed terminology of 'fiduciary capitalism' recognizes the potential power of financial institutions to take collective action reflecting the interests of the 'universal owners'. For example, some of the largest pension funds are those of employees in local and state government, teachers, universities, and other public sector organizations. So employee retirement assets might be used as a power basis for action over companies.

Advocates of 'universal ownership' recognize the potential for pension and other funds to improve governance and long-term returns by working together, although each holds only a relatively small percentage of the total shareholding. The idea of universal ownership is most significant where equity holdings are highly diversified and lack a dominant investor. The notion also sees the agency chain of intermediaries that can exist between listed company and ultimate investor/owner. Agents have agents, each acting as the agent for the next principal in the chain, with highly diversified roles, but all bound in law by the fiduciary duty of loyalty and care. But their actions are neither transparent nor accountable. If the idea is to make a contribution, however, a universal holder mindset will be needed to provide the classical governance relationship between corporate body and its owners.

Dual-listed companies

In a traditional takeover situation, one company acquires the shares of the other, which then becomes a subsidiary or associate company of its parent holding company. In a dual-listed company, by contrast, a group structure is created in which two listed companies merge, but both continue to exist and share the ownership of a single operational business. The group maintains its two separate stock exchange listings, with different shareholders typically in different countries. A complex set of contracts defines their relationship with an integrated top management structure and the same directors or some cross-directorships.

The case of the Carnival Corporation (US) and the Carnival Corporation plc (see Corporate governance in action 10.3) is typical. Other examples include BHP Billiton (Australia and UK), Investec Bank (South Africa and UK), and Unilever (Holland and UK).

The benefits for dual-listing include:

- continuing existing successful businesses;
- protecting brand names;
- taxation benefits;
- sustaining national pride, avoiding claims that one country is losing 'its' company to another.

The disadvantages can be:

- conflict between the two managements, for example on resource allocation;
- disagreements between the boards, unless all directors are common to both;
- legal difficulties in applying the inter-company contracts;
- challenges from shareholders about unfair benefits to the other company;

- taxation difficulties, including transfer prices for inter-group trading;
- problems if the group wants to unravel the dual-listing agreements.

Dual-listed companies need to be distinguished from cases in which a single company is listed on more than one stock exchange, sometimes referred to as 'cross-listed companies'. Many international companies raise funds in this way, usually with a primary listing in their home country and one or more secondary listings elsewhere. For example, many Canadian companies are listed in both Toronto and New York.

Corporate governance in action 10.3   Carnival Corporation—a dual-listed group

Carnival Corporation & plc is a dual-listed company with listings in New York and London. Carnival Corporation Inc., incorporated in Panama, is listed on the New York Stock Exchange. It is the larger of the two holding companies. Carnival plc is listed on the London Stock Exchange and was formed from the P&O (Peninsular and Orient Steam Navigation Company's) cruise business. This British-American corporation is the only group in the world to be included in both the S&P 500 and the FTSE 100 indices.

The combined group is the world's largest cruise operator, including: Carnival Cruise Lines, Princess Cruises, Holland America Line, Windstar Cruises, and Seabourn Yachts in North America; P&O Cruises and Cunard Line in the United Kingdom; AIDA in Germany; Costa Cruises in Southern Europe; and P&O Cruises in Australia.

Dual-class shares

Dual-listed corporate groups need to be distinguished from dual-class shares. The corporate constitution (typically the articles of association) of some companies provides for two or more classes of voting shares in which one class enjoys greater voting rights than the other class, or all of the voting rights. For example, a company might issue 'A' class shares, in which each share has one vote, and 'B' class shares, in which each share has 100 votes.

Dual-class shares are often issued to protect the ownership power of a dominant shareholding class, often a family, when a company is floated on the stock market. The founders of Google, Larry Page and Sergey Brin, exercise power through dual-class shares. Although holding only around 20% of the equity, they control around 60% of the votes. The Ford Motor Company has dual-class shares, giving greater power to the Ford family. The Porsche and Piïch families, though owning less than half of the shares in the Porsche company, enjoyed all of the voting rights. In the international media company News Corporation, the Murdoch family held around 13% of the shares, but could exercise over 40% of the voting rights, allowing chairman Rupert Murdoch and his son James effectively to control the company's US$60 billion of global assets. Another classical example is the Wallenberg Group in Sweden (see Corporate governance in action 10.4).

Some stock exchanges will not list companies with dual-class shares, demanding shareholder democracy in which every voting share carries an equal voting right. Other stock exchanges, however, do list companies with dual-class shares. Predictably, the limited or no-voting class shares typically trade at a discount.

Corporate governance in action 10.4   The Wallenberg Sphere—dual-class shares

Corporate governance in Sweden has a number of distinctive characteristics—mandatory co-determination, high private share ownership, dual-class shares, shareholders' board nominating committee, and 'spheres' of private owners. The Wallenberg family forms such a sphere, owning a business empire that is more of a dynasty than a company. Now in its fifth generation of family control, and planning for the sixth, this huge empire dominates Swedish business.

The Wallenbergs own some 40% of the value of the Swedish Stock Exchange, but through dual-class shares, which give greater voting rights to their shares than to others, exercise control over many companies. At one time their interests included around 19% by value, but 38% by votes, of carmaker Saab; 5% by value, but 20% by votes, of Ericsson, a leading telecommunications company; around 11% by value, but 28% by votes, of Electrolux, a white goods manufacturer. They also have major interests in: Atlas Copco; ABB, a global engineering group; SEB, one of Scandinavia's largest banks; and many other companies.

Wallenberg ownership is exercised through the Wallenberg foundations (assets around US$6 billion), which exercise just under 50% of the votes in Investor, a public company, with over 100,000 other investors sharing in the family fortunes. Companies dominated by Investor are run by professional managers with their own boards of directors. However, the Wallenberg family insist that they are 'not just kingmakers', as some claim, but are closely involved in the companies' corporate strategies. The governance style adopted by the Wallenbergs is based on a network of carefully fostered contacts, a policy to shift investment strategies from the past to the future as industries and technologies change, but then to stick with their companies through thick and thin. The family claim that they deserve their special rights in the multiple-voting, dual-class shares because of the family's role in successfully founding and developing Swedish companies over the years, and their tradition of strong and involved ownership.

Listings on alternative stock markets

Some stock exchanges create a second market, often called a second board, to enable smaller, perhaps riskier, companies to raise capital. The London Stock Exchange established the Alternative Investment Market (AIM) in 1995 to raise capital and to provide a market for companies from all industrial sectors and any country. Some of these companies have subsequently progressed to a listing on the main board. Although many AIM companies are businesses at an early stage of development and may operate in high-risk sectors, the failure rate on AIM has been relatively low.

Unlike the main board, AIM does not stipulate a minimum size or market capitalization—the number of shares in public hands—nor does it require a track record of quality profits and financial history. The regulatory regime for AIM companies is a succinct rule book, which is also less stringent than that of the main board, although regulated under EU and British law.

A crucial element in the corporate governance of AIM companies is the nominated adviser (usually referred to as the Nomad), authorized by AIM, which all AIM companies are required to appoint. The Nomad's experience provides a quality control mechanism by checking the company's plans and certifying to the Exchange that the company is suitable and ready for listing. The Nomad assists the company during the flotation, subsequently ensures that it meets its governance obligations, and handles any ongoing market issues. The company deals with AIM through its Nomad, who advises AIM on all regulatory matters. The company's broker, lawyers, auditors, and financial institution also provide support services.

The Stock Exchange of Hong Kong also offers a second board—the Growth Enterprise Market (GEM). GEM advertises itself as a 'buyers beware' market for informed investors, emphasizing that emerging companies carry a high investment risk, with potential market volatility and no assurance that there will be a liquid market. Companies listing on GEM are not required to show a track record of profits, or to forecast future profitability. The initial listing document must show the business objectives and activities. Quarterly operating and financial reports are required, with the directors being responsible for disclosure. The GEM is often used by Hong Kong family-based companies to enable family members to capitalize on the wealth in the family business, as well as to provide additional funds for corporate growth.

Singapore Exchange's secondary market, named Catalist, opened in 2008, replacing the previous Sesdaq board. Catalist attracts fast-growing companies from the region, competing with London's AIM for Asian listings. Approved sponsors are responsible for vetting new listings and supervising them thereafter. To be listed, companies should have a healthy financial position and prospects of profitability, but no operating or profit track record is required.

In the United States, NYSE Euronext was formed in 2007 by the merger of the New York Stock Exchange, itself a public listed company, and Euronext N.V. Then, in 2008, NYSE Euronext acquired the American Stock Exchange, which added a US platform for small-cap companies. The Company's exchanges in Europe and the United States trade equities, futures, options, fixed-income, and exchange-traded products. With approximately 8,000 listed companies from more than 55 countries, NYSE Euronext's equities markets—the New York Stock Exchange, NYSE Euronext, NYSE MKT, NYSE Alternext, and NYSE Arca—represent one-third of the world's equities trading and the highest liquidity of any global exchange group.

Case studies

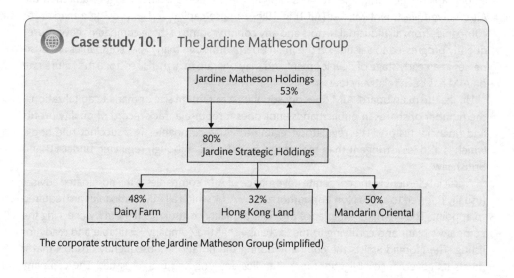

Case study 10.1   The Jardine Matheson Group

The corporate structure of the Jardine Matheson Group (simplified)

Jardine Matheson Holdings (JMH) is a private family company, owned by the Keswick family, descendants from the 19th century founder of the firm. JMH owns 82.5% of Jardine Strategic Holdings Ltd (JSH), while JSH owns 55.5% of JMH, making them subsidiaries of each other. This ownership structure was adopted to prevent hostile takeovers. In 2013 the ownership of JMH included:

Jardine family members and trusts	14.57%
JSH	55.53%
Other (non-family) directors	0.43%
Balance with other shareholders	29.47%

JSH then owns 77.6% of Dairy Farm International Holdings Ltd (DFL), 73.5% of Mandarin Oriental International Ltd (MOL), and 50.01% of Hongkong Land Holdings Ltd (HKL). All of the companies are incorporated in Bermuda, which has company-favourable law, and is a tax haven. JSH is a publicly listed holding company, with a primary (or 'premium') share listing on the London Stock Exchange, and secondary listings on the Bermuda and Singapore stock exchanges. Its shares form part of the Singapore Straits Times share index.

Dairy Farm is a leading pan-Asian retailer, with over 5,300 outlets including supermarkets, hypermarkets, health and beauty stores, convenience stores, home furnishings stores, and restaurants, employing over 80,000 people with sales of over US$9 billion. Dairy Farm International Holdings Ltd has its primary share listing on the London Stock Exchange, and secondary listings on the Bermuda and Singapore stock exchanges.

Hongkong Land Holdings is a leading property investment, management, and development group with a major portfolio in Hong Kong, where it owns and manages some five million square feet of prime office and retail space in the heart of the Central business district. In Singapore, it has interests in a number of major commercial and residential developments. The company has its primary share listing on the London Stock Exchange, and secondary listings on the Bermuda and Singapore stock exchanges.

Mandarin Oriental Hotel Group is a hotel investment and management group operating with over 10,000 rooms in luxury hotels and resorts in twenty-seven countries. The Group has equity interests in many of its properties and net assets of over US$2.3 billion. Like Dairy Farm and Hongkong Land, Mandarin Oriental International Ltd has its primary listing in London, with further listings in Bermuda and Singapore.

At one time, all five companies were listed in Hong Kong and were members of the local Hang Seng Index. However, prior to the 1997 change of Hong Kong's sovereignty from Britain to China, in 1994 they de-listed from Hong Kong and transferred their primary listing to London.

Under Bermudan company law, subsidiaries can vote shares in their parents. Many other jurisdictions, including the United Kingdom and Hong Kong, prohibit companies holding shares in each other in this way. The Bermudan cross-holding allows the boards of JSH and JMH to lock themselves in by voting the cross-shareholdings to pass motions at an AGM. As David Webb, a Hong Kong-based corporate governance commentator, explained:[5]

Under Bermudan law, subsidiaries can vote shares in their parents. The Bermudan cross-shareholding allows the boards of both companies to lock themselves in by voting the cross-shareholdings to re-elect the directors at any AGM. The cross-shareholding was established in late 1986 at lower levels, and since then, the Jardine group has been gradually swallowing its own tail, each of JSM and JSH increasing its stake in the other, partly by accepting scrip dividends, and JSH increasing its stake in DFL, MOL and HKL.

[5] http://webb-site.com/articles/jardown.asp

The Group proposes a down-grade of their London listing

In November 2013, the UK Financial Conduct Authority launched a consultation document proposing changes to the UK Listing Rules 'to significantly enhance the protections for minority shareholders in premium listed companies'. In March 2014, the Jardine Group proposed downgrading their UK listing status from the primary (or premium) listing, to a standard listing. This would reduce the rights of minority shareholders and lower governance standards. Minority shareholders would have very little say in this change, because the controlling shareholders could dominate any vote.

Discussion questions

1. Is the ownership structure depicted in this case a network, a pyramid, or a chain?

2. What is your opinion of this ownership structure?

3. Why do you think the Jardine Group really proposed the down-grading of their London listing?

4. If you were advising Jardines, how would you suggest they justify their proposal to downgrade their London listing?

 Case study 10.2   Alleged vote-rigging at PCCW, Hong Kong

Sir Li Ka Shing is the twentieth richest person in the world[6] and the richest of Asian descent,[7] with a net worth of nearly US$30 billion. Born in China in 1928, his success is a Hong Kong legend. Forced to leave school at 14 by the death of his father, he laboured for 16 hours a day in a plastics factory. At the age of 22, he created his own firm, Cheung Kong Industries, making plastic flowers. Typical of successful Hong Kong entrepreneurs his company broadened into real estate. Then he acquired the large trading house Hutchison Whampoa and the utility company Hong Kong Electric. The parent company of the group, Cheung Kong (Holdings), is now the leading Hong Kong based multi-national conglomerate, quoted on the Hong Kong Stock Exchange, and includes the world's largest operator of container terminals and the world's largest health and beauty retailer.

Richard Li Tzar-kai is Li Ka Shing's younger son. Born in Hong Kong in 1966, educated in Hong Kong and California, he studied computer engineering at Stanford University. He has dual citizenship of the Hong Kong SAR and Canada. In 2009, the Hong Kong English newspaper, the *South China Morning Post*, commented that:

> Since Richard Li Tzar-kai, the younger son of Li Ka-shing, became involved in the Hong Kong stock market 10 years ago, he has hardly been out of the spotlight, capturing the imagination and the indignation of investors as well as the regulators.

Richard Li believed that communication systems, including fixed-line telephones, mobile telephones, broadband internet, and cable television would converge. In May 1999, he acquired a 70% stake in Tricom Holdings, a company listed on the Hong-Kong Stock Exchange. The name Tricom was then changed to Pacific Century Cyber Works (PCCW).

In January 2000, PCCW acquired Cable & Wireless-HKT Telephone Ltd (HKT), Hong Kong's public telephone service and renamed it PCCW-HKT Telephone Ltd, which was later reduced to PCCW. Investors were impressed, and the PCCW share price rose dramatically, turning the company into

---

[6] Forbes list of billionaires 2013.   [7] Bloomberg billionaires index 2013.

the fourth largest on the Hong Kong Stock Exchange by market capitalization. However, some critics wondered about PCCW's underlying business model.

The acquisition of HKT provided Li with a fixed-line telephone company that he felt he could link with his internet interests. But HKT was a capitally-intensive, slow-moving giant, under heavy competition from mobile phone operators. It had a different culture from the fast-moving information-technology firms in the rest of the PCCW group. Moreover, HKT was losing thousands of customers a month to its mobile phone competitors.

Then the internet bubble burst and 'dotcom' companies around the world failed. PCCW's share price fell dramatically. Worse, PCCW had become heavily geared, with significant debt and high interest charges. Shareholders had received no dividends since the HKT take-over. In January 2003, PCCW announced a five-to-one consolidation of its shares in an attempt to stabilize the market. Some small shareholders criticized Richard Li because they had invested their savings in the original, solid HKT, and had to accept shares in PCCW in lieu.

In 2004, PCCW acquired a small Hong Kong mobile operator, Now-TV. With the development of this company PCCW could claim to be a full-service provider. In 2005, Li negotiated a deal with the China Netcom Group, a mainland China fixed-line telephone company, in which China Netcom acquired 20% of PCCW and became a strategic partner.

In June 2006, a foreign private equity firm offered PCCW up to HK$60 billion (US$7.7 billion) for its telecommunications and multi-media business. China Netcom and the central Chinese Government raised strategic objections to the deal. Small shareholders feared they would suffer, although Li said that when the sale went through they would receive a compensatory special dividend.

In October 2008, outside shareholders received a buy-out proposal from Pacific Century Regional Developments Ltd, a company controlled by Richard Li, and China Unicom, which had merged with China Netcom. The offer was HK$4.50 (US$0.58) a share. The company would then be privatized. In other words, it would have no outside shareholders and no listing on the Hong Kong Stock Exchange.

Allegations of vote-rigging

Some shareholders complained at the relatively low price. The company responded that the offer price had been proposed by their financial advisers and was considered fair in the current market conditions.

In Hong Kong there are two ways to buy out shareholders in a listed company. The normal method is with a mandatory offer, which needs the approval by 90% of the minority shareholders by share value. The second method, and the one used by PCCW, is a scheme of arrangement, which requires the approval of the court, plus 25% voting minority shareholders by share value, and 50% in number of minority shareholders not party to the acquisition, voting in person at a shareholders' meeting. This so-called 'headcount rule' is contained in s166 of the Hong Kong Companies' Ordinance. The result is achieved by counting hands raised in favour of the motion. In other words, on the basis of a head count rather than on the number of voting shares held.

A meeting of PCCW shareholders was called to approve the buy-out deal. But an allegation was made that the vote had been rigged. The deal was blocked. As the UK *Economist* newspaper explained the problem (21 February 2009):

Just before the vote took place, insurance agents attached to a former sister company of PCCW appear to have received small blocks of PCCW shares. No one knows how the agents got the shares or how they voted. But the regulator, the Hong Kong Securities and Futures Commission (SFC) received several complaints about it all.

The SFC launched an investigation, and discovered that Lam Han-wah, a regional director of Fortis Insurance Asia, had bought 50,000 PCCW shares and spread them over 400 agents of the company as bonuses. However, the SFC suggested that this occurred after phone calls between Lam Han-wah and Francis Yuen Tin-fan, the deputy chairman of Pacific Century Regional Developments, a company controlled by Richard Li and a major shareholder in PCCW. Yuen had previously been chief executive of the Hong Kong Stock Exchange. The SFC suggested that these shares had been used to increase the hands raised in favour of the buy-out. The Hong Kong Stock Exchange also mounted an inquiry, but concluded that no blame could be attached to anyone.

The matter was brought before the Hong Kong High Court, which decided that Lam Han-wah had not split shares to give a voting advantage to PCCW, that there was no evidence that Francis Yuen had anything to do with the vote-splitting, and that there was nothing wrong with share splitting anyway.

But in April 2009, the SFC appealed to the higher Hong Kong Court of Appeal. Their conclusions were very different. In a written judgment handed down on 11 May, an appellate panel, Mr Justice Rogers, Mr Justice Johnson Lam Man-hon and Mr Justice Arif Barma, ruled that the many phone calls between Yuen and Lam cast doubt over whether Yuen had influenced Lam in distributing the board lots of PCCW shares. They further noted that the 500 or so proxy forms needed to vote these shares had been collected by Lam's secretary from the secretary of Yuen. Mr Justice Rogers wrote in the judgment that vote manipulation is nothing less than a form of dishonesty which the court cannot sanction.

In May 2009, Pacific Century Regional Developments sought leave to appeal against the decision to block the buy-out deal, seeking clarification on whether share-splitting as had occurred in this case was legal and questioning the High Court's right to comment on the pricing of the bid. Outside minority shareholders in PCCW expressed concern about the costs of such actions, should they fall on their company and thus potentially on the value of their shares. The PCCW share price had now dropped to just over HK$2 (US$0.26).

An alliance of PCCW minority shareholders then called on one of the company's independent non-executive directors, David Li Kwok-po, to express their concern about the proposed appeal by the controlling shareholders, as it could be a further drain on shareholders' funds. David Li met with representatives of the PCCW shareholders and passed their views on to Richard Li. In mid-June four non-executive directors, excluding David Li, wrote a joint letter to the PCCW shareholders, saying that the original appeal had already taken shareholder interests into account and that the costs of further legal proceedings would be carefully controlled.

In August 2009 the Court of Appeal declined the PCCW application to appeal their ruling. In their written judgment, the court explained that the Hong Kong government intended to review the voting rules for corporate buyouts.

PCCW today

PCCW Ltd (PCCW) is still a Hong Kong-based company quoted on the Hong Kong Stock Exchange. It has interests in telecommunications (voice, data, broadband, and mobile), media, IT solutions, property development and investment, and other businesses; and operates in Hong Kong and Macau, Beijing, Shanghai, Guangzhou and other cities in China, Japan, Korea, and Singapore. A new service, Smart Living, uses a customized home broadband network and automation systems to control multiple home settings such as entertainment systems, lighting, curtains, air-conditioning, and security surveillance, through a customized remote control, a smart phone, or a tablet computer.

In 2014, PCCW's share price moved between HK$3–4 (US$0.40–0.50)) and the market capitalization was HK$28 billion (US$2.8 billion) with a price/earnings ratio of 14.

Questions

1. Why is it necessary to protect the rights of minority shareholders; surely investors with the majority of voting rights ought to be able to determine the strategic future of their company?

2. The Hong Kong Court of Appeal said that vote manipulation was a form of dishonesty. Why do you think that is?

3. Do you consider the facts in this case amounted to vote manipulation?

References and further reading

Berle, Adolf A. and Gardiner C.Means (1932) *The Modern Corporation and Private Property*. Harcourt, Brace & World, New York.

Colpan, Asli M., Takashi Hikino, and James R. S. Lincoln (eds) (2010) *The Oxford Handbook of Business Groups*. Oxford University Press, Oxford.

Kaen, Fred R. (2003) *A Blueprint for Corporate Governance: Strategy Accountability and the Preservation of Shareholder Value*, American Management Association, New York.

Kane, Yukari Iwatani (2014) *Haunted Empire—Apple after Steve Jobs*. Harper Collins Business, New York.

Lufkin, Joseph C. F. and David Gallagher (1990) *International Corporate Governance*. Euromoney Books, London.

NACD ([2005] 2008) *Board: Shareholder Communications—A report of a NACD Blue Ribbon Commission*. National Association of Corporate Directors, 1133, Suite 700 21 Street, Washington, DC, USA.

Wright, Robert E. (2004) *History of Corporate Governance: The Importance of Shareholder Activism*. Pickering and Chatto, London.

Projects and exercises

General Electric (GE)

General Electric (GE) is a vast, US-based company with an international reputation for excellence in operations, performance, and corporate governance. The GE board of directors focuses on areas important to shareowners and other stakeholders: namely, strategy, risk management, and people. The GE Group is organized into business units, each of which includes a number of companies and other units aligned for growth. Explore the material on the GE's website (at www.ge.com). Read the GE governance principles at www.ge.com/investor-relations/governance/principles

1. What impression have you formed of corporate governance in this company?

2. If you were to serve on the board of a GE subsidiary company, how much freedom would you expect to have over your corporate strategy? What would be the role of the holding company board?

3. Explore the corporate structure of some listed companies operating in your country. Most listed companies provide a wealth of information about their businesses, organization structures, and corporate governance arrangements, as well as financial information, on their websites. In particular discover the following.

   - Where are the companies in the group incorporated? Where are their shares listed?
   - Are these cases of networks, pyramids, or chained structures?

- What is your opinion on the quality of disclosure on the group structure and corporate governance arrangements?

Self-test questions

1. Distinguish a holding company, a wholly owned, a partly owned subsidiary company, and an associated company.
2. Why might a company incorporate in an offshore jurisdiction?
3. Can shareholders attend internal meetings of the company or access management accounts and other corporate information?
4. Why do groups adopt a chain structure?
5. What are dual-class shares?
6. What is a Nomad?
7. What is a dual-listed company?
8. Why might companies consider entering into a joint venture agreement?
9. What activities might shareholder activism include?
10. Can companies hold shares in themselves? Give examples from the chapter.

The Governance of Private Companies and Other Corporate Entities

 Learning Outcomes

In which we consider:

- The governance of private companies
- The governance of family-owned companies
- The governance of subsidiary and associated companies
- The governance of employee-owned companies
- The governance of joint ventures
- The governance of mutuals, social enterprises and non-profit entities
- The governance of partnerships and limited-liability partnerships
- The governance of hedge funds, private equity, and sovereign funds
- The state as shareholder

In this chapter we first focus on the governance of private rather than public companies, including those owned by individuals, families, or their employees. We also review the governance of subsidiary companies and joint-venture companies.

But there are other forms of corporate entity in modern society that are hugely important to economic, social, and environmental well-being, which are not limited-liability companies, Examples are legion: organizations created to benefit the community, such as the British Broadcasting Corporation (BBC), the UK National Health Service, or the US Smithsonian Institute, enterprises trading with a social purpose such as co-operative societies, educational trusts and universities, charities, sports and cultural clubs, trades unions, non-government organizations (NGOs), to identify just a few.

This governance of entities in this sector has been largely overlooked. But there is now a growing recognition that such enterprises and organizations face significant governance issues and, although many of the tenets of corporate governance applicable to companies are relevant to them, they have unique governance concerns of their own.

Once the members of an organization are separate from its managers, the way power is exercised over its resources and activities becomes important; consider the need to govern co-operative societies, trades unions, and other clubs and societies.

Similarly, the governance of large partnerships and limited-liability partnerships raises issues, as does the governance of hedge funds, private equity funds, and sovereign funds. This is a relatively new field for corporate governance study.

The governance of private companies

The emphasis in corporate governance principles, policy, and practice to date has been on public, listed companies. The Sarbanes-Oxley Act in the United States, the corporate governance codes in other countries, and most corporate governance research have focused on companies in which shares are available to the general public. Of course, much more information is available about such public, listed companies. Transparency, accountability, and the protection of shareholders' interests, particularly minority shareholders, are major concerns.

Yet the number of unlisted, private companies far exceeds those that are listed. These unlisted companies include firms owned by individuals and families, subsidiary and associated companies owned by holding companies, and joint ventures. Many unlisted companies are small or medium-sized enterprises, although some are large and complex. Together, these companies make an essential contribution to economic growth, employment, and the creation of wealth around the world. Unlisted companies present some unique corporate governance challenges. Although many of the basic governance concepts that apply to public companies are also relevant.

The governance of family-owned companies

In the early days of the joint-stock limited-liability company, all companies were public companies, incorporated to raise capital from outside investors. Today, most companies around the world are private companies, providing taxation benefits to the proprietors (because corporation tax is often preferable to personal income tax) and giving them the benefit of limited liability. A large proportion of these private companies are owned and controlled by their founders or families. In Asia, India, and Latin America, some 95% of companies are family-owned. The importance of the small and medium-sized enterprise is seen in the *Mittlestand*—medium-sized companies in Germany. Of course, not all family-owned companies are small: some large companies in Asia, Latin America, and Europe are family-owned. Nor are these family companies always private: in France, one in four of the listed companies on the CAC40 stock market index is family-controlled.

The governance of family-controlled private companies raises some interesting issues. Tracing the evolution of ownership and control in a typical family firm will highlight some of them. Initially, a small company may be incorporated for a business start-up or to take over the existing business of a sole trader, a family firm, or a partnership. The shareholders will be the entrepreneur starting the business, the family members involved in the firm, or the partners in the existing partnership. At this stage, the shareholders are also likely to be directors. In the early years of the family company, management and governance tend to be intertwined, because both are being done by the same people. Distinctions between the two are seldom identified until there is some separation between the owners, the directors, and top management.

Many companies fail within the first two or three years. Thereafter the focus shifts to maintaining success and seeking further growth. The running of the business and its internal management, as well as the governance tasks of strategy formulation, policymaking, periodic supervision, and accountability are all in the heads and hands of the owner/managers. Formal board meetings and meetings of shareholders are likely to be minimal. At this stage, it is important for dominant shareholder-directors to understand that the company is a separate entity and its assets are not their own.

The next stage of governance comes as the company thrives. A need for additional expertise is recognized. Perhaps the existing directors lack the marketing, financial, or international experience, which the company now needs. But the company cannot yet afford to employ a full-time executive in this field. So it invites an outside director with these skills, knowledge, or network contacts to join the board. This is cheaper in the short term than hiring a consultant, although a consultant is much easier to be let go when his or her usefulness has ended. Inviting external directors to join the board is likely to change the board culture, not because they fulfil the independent compliance role of the independent non-executive director (INED) in the listed company, but because they are not members of the family and inevitably add a non-family dimension to discussions. The United Kingdom's Institute of Directors (IoD) suggests the creation of an advisory board (see the IoD corporate governance principles for unlisted companies in Corporate governance in action 11.1).

Corporate governance in action 11.1   The UK Institute of Directors Corporate Governance Principles for Unlisted Companies

Phase 1 Principles: Corporate governance principles applicable to *all* unlisted companies.

Principle 1: Shareholders should establish an appropriate constitutional and governance framework for the company.

Principle 2: Every company should strive to establish an effective board, which is collectively responsible for the long-term success of the company, including the definition of the corporate strategy. However, an interim step on the road to an effective (and independent) board may be the creation of an advisory board.

Principle 3: The size and composition of the board should reflect the scale and complexity of the company's activities.

Principle 4: The board should meet sufficiently regularly to discharge its duties, and be supplied in a timely manner with appropriate information.

Principle 5: Levels of remuneration should be sufficient to attract, retain, and motivate executives and non-executives of the quality required to run the company successfully.

Principle 6: The board is responsible for risk oversight and should maintain a sound system of internal control to safeguard shareholders' investment and the company's assets.

Principle 7: There should be a dialogue between the board and the shareholders based on a mutual understanding of objectives. The board as a whole has responsibility for ensuring that a satisfactory dialogue with shareholders takes place. The board should not forget that all shareholders have to be treated equally.

Principle 8: All directors should receive induction on joining the board and should regularly update and refresh their skills and knowledge.

Principle 9: Family-controlled companies should establish family governance mechanisms that promote coordination and mutual understanding among family members, as well as organise the relationship between family governance and corporate governance.

Phase 2 principles: Corporate governance principles applicable to *large and/or more complex* unlisted companies

Principle 10: There should be a clear division of responsibilities at the head of the company between the running of the board and the running of the company's business. No one individual should have unfettered powers of decision.

Principle 11: All boards should contain directors with a sufficient mix of competencies and experiences. No single person (or small group of individuals) should dominate the board's decision-making.

Principle 12: The board should establish appropriate board committees in order to allow a more effective discharge of its duties.

Principle 13: The board should undertake a periodic appraisal of its own performance and that of each individual director.

Principle 14: The board should present a balanced and understandable assessment of the company's position and prospects for external stakeholders, and establish a suitable programme of stakeholder engagement.

Long-serving executives may also be appointed to the board as executive directors, reflecting their contribution to the success of the firm, and tying them more securely to the company. Such appointments can provide reward, recognition, and prestige.

Successful companies often need additional capital, since the plough-back of profits is no longer sufficient to fund growth opportunities. Sometimes the financial institutions providing such facilities call for a nominee director on the board to oversee their interests.

The progression of family members through management to a place on the board can be a reward for success, but can also trigger resentment within the family. Ultimately, a successful family company has to face the challenge of passing governance and management onto the second generation. One solution is for the founder/father figure to assume the role of chairman of the board, while a family member from the second generation becomes chief executive. But experience has shown that such a switch can be difficult to achieve successfully. The new chairman often finds it difficult to let go of the executive reins and adopt an advisory role, delegating the executive decision-making to a younger family member.

Throughout the life cycle of the family company, from start-up to the passing of governance power to the next generation, it is vital that the corporate governance framework is appropriate to the stage of development. The corporate governance policies and board-level practices need to reflect the scale and complexity of the company's activities, determining the relationships between shareholders, directors, and management. The structure and composition of the board should reflect the stage of maturity of the company and its business. Similarly, board-level information, board appraisal, and director development need to be appropriate. The UK IoD corporate governance principles for unlisted companies (see Corporate governance in action 11.1) emphasize that corporate governance 'is about establishing a framework of company processes and attitudes that add value to the business, help build its reputation, and ensure its long-term continuity and success'.

The family council

As ownership of the company passes through the generations of a family company, an inevitable split occurs between shareholders who are involved in management and those who are not. Frequently, one branch of the family runs the company, while another branch is only interested as shareholders. This situation can produce a major headache for families. Those involved in management want to conserve cash, limit dividends, and plough any surplus into the business while maximizing their own remuneration and benefits (cars, class of travel, pensions, benefits in kind, and so on). But the non-management members of the family want to increase dividends so that they can benefit from their stake in the company or even to sell their shares. If the company wants to change strategy, the interests of the family members in management may well differ from those of the non-management members.

Directors' meetings and shareholders' meetings are not appropriate forums for the discussion of family affairs, because they need to focus on issues affecting the company and its business.

How might this dilemma be overcome? Many experts in the governance of family companies recommend setting up a family council. This consists of all of the family members who own shares, both those who are in management and those who are not, or their representatives. The council enables family members to identify and discuss matters of inheritance, management succession, remuneration, dividend policy, and corporate strategy prior to board or shareholder meetings. In this way, potentially acrimonious issues can be resolved, in the interest of the family as a whole, before formal meetings of directors or shareholders. This becomes particularly important if there are non-family shareholders whose minority interests need to be protected. A family council can also discuss the employment, development, and career planning of younger family members in the company.

In the family-controlled company, the challenge is to incorporate sound corporate governance practices that, on the one hand, ensure continuing professional management while, on the other hand, preserving family unity. Of course, some successful family-controlled companies never reach this stage: the company is sold and the capital distributed within the family before the succession issue arises.

As private companies grow, mature, and become more complex, some of the principles adopted in the corporate governance codes for public companies may become applicable. For example, separation between the roles of the chairman of the board and the chief executive or managing director may be desirable to avoid domination by one person. The addition of independent directors may also be useful, to protect the interest of any non-family shareholders, to provide additional maturity and experience to board deliberations, and to add some discipline to board-level thinking.

The creation of an audit committee and a remuneration committee may also benefit the board as a whole.

The governance of subsidiary and associated companies

The governance of subsidiary and associated companies raises some interesting issues. Essentially, the holding company determines the governance policies and practices of the companies in its group. As we saw in the previous chapter, there are broadly two distinct options in governing and managing a group of companies.

1. *Subsidiary company self-governance* allows each company in the group to govern itself and to manage its own affairs, subject to overall group-wide policies and resource

allocation. Control is exercised through the group's shareholdings, emphasizing the decision-making autonomy of the board of each subsidiary company. Profitability and return on investment in each subsidiary are likely to be the measures of performance. This structure will often be adopted in a conglomerate group in which the subsidiary companies run diverse businesses.

2. *Group-wide governance* treats the group companies as divisions or departments of the holding company with control exercised through the group's management control system—in other words, emphasizing management through the group management organization structure and management control systems, not governance through the boards of each subsidiary.

The performance measures set for each subsidiary company will depend on the group control systems.

Subsidiary company self-governance

The first approach, delegating decision-making power to the group's subsidiary company boards, requires each subsidiary in the group to act as an autonomous company, subject to policy requirements and resource allocations determined by its shareholder, the holding company. In other words, the directors of each subsidiary company are expected to run their company as an autonomous entity, within group policies, to meet the performance criteria required by the group.

With subsidiary company self-governance, the structure and membership of the subsidiary and associate company boards becomes important. The holding company has the option of drawing the directors of subsidiary companies from:

- the staff of the group holding company, who might or might not be on the main board;
- the management of the subsidiary company;
- the management in other group companies;
- outside the group.

The benefits of drawing subsidiary company directors from other companies in the group include the opportunity for cross-group coordination, the sharing of expertise, training, and development of future main board directors, management development, and the building of group norms and culture. In associate companies and in subsidiaries with outside minority interests, it would be normal to find nominee directors representing the interests of the outside shareholders.

Group-wide governance

In the second approach, the group holding company imposes management control systems and organization structures on the entire group operations, which transcend the operations of the individual subsidiary companies. The control system divides the group into appropriate operating units, which may or may not map onto the subsidiary company structure. Group resources are allocated to these performance units through the management control system,

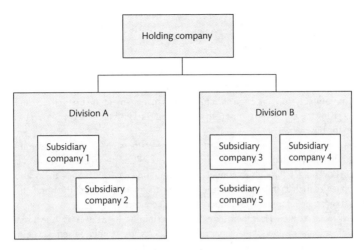

Figure 11.1 Control through a group management control system

performance criteria are laid down for management of each unit, and outputs are monitored. The power to make decisions throughout the group is delegated along the lines of the management control system, not the legal structure of the subsidiaries.

With group-wide governance, the members of subsidiary company boards are typically drawn from the management of group head office and the subsidiary company, because power lies in the management organization structure throughout the group, not in the boardrooms of the subsidiary companies.

For example, in Figure 11.1, the holding company manages its group through a group organization structure with two divisions, A and B. Its management control system, consequently, will monitor the management of the divisions. Managers have their responsibilities delegated down through the levels of management in the organization structure and are accountable back up that structure. Managers owe their primary allegiance to their line manager, not the directors of the subsidiary company of which their business unit may be part.

You might ask why such holding companies controlling through the group management system have subsidiary companies at all. The reasons could be legal (the ability to contract under the laws of the state in which the subsidiary is incorporated and operates), taxation (the opportunity to reduce taxation in high tax regimes), strategic positioning (to protect a brand name or other strategic benefit), or risk reduction (to obtain the benefit of limited liability). Because such subsidiaries are legal entities, they must, of course, fulfil their legal reporting and taxation requirements. But power lies in the management organization structure throughout the group, not in the boardrooms of the subsidiary companies.

The governance of employee-owned companies

Some public, listed companies offer shares to their employees, either free as part of their remuneration, or for purchase on favourable terms. Such schemes are intended as a reward for service and to motivate and commit employees to the long-term interests of the company.

Corporate governance in action 11.2   The John Lewis Partnership—an employee-owned company

The founder of the company, John Spedan Lewis, signed away his personal ownership rights in favour of his employees, whom he called 'partners', in pursuit of what he called 'an experiment in industrial democracy'. The company's organization structure allows management the freedom to run the business, while giving the employee partners the rights and responsibilities of ownership through active involvement in the business.

The company has over 90,000 employee-partners, and a Partnership Council, representing all the partners, meets quarterly with management representatives. All partners receive a share of profits. They also take part in governance through an annual partnership survey, which enables them, anonymously, to comment on issues such as the running of the business, the management of their branch, their job satisfaction and career development, and other issues that concern them.

Employees say that the system gives them a sense of ownership, having a say in how the business is run.

For more information, see: www.johnlewispartnership.co.uk/csr/our-employees/employee-ownership.html

To watch a video of partners' reactions to the ownership system go to: www.johnlewispartnership.co.uk/media/webcasts-and-videos/being-a-partner.html

However there are some companies that are substantially or wholly owned by their employees. The largest employee-owned company in the United Kingdom is the John Lewis Partnership, a country-wide chain of retail stores, including the Waitrose food supermarkets. Corporate governance in action 11.2 summarizes the John Lewis approach to corporate governance. In the United States, most employee-owned companies are relatively small,[1] the largest being Publix supermarkets with around 160,000 employees.

A frequently cited example of employee-ownership is the Mondragon Corporation, which is a federation of worker co-operatives in the Basque region of Spain. It was founded in 1956, on the instigation of a Catholic priest, Father José Arizmendiarrera, who encouraged humanistic attitudes leading to inter-personal harmony, participation, and technical skills. The Mondragon group is now the seventh largest Spanish company with some 80,000 employees, working in manufacturing, retailing, construction, and insurance. Initially a federation of employee co-operatives, the Mondragon Co-operative Group was established in 1984, which coordinated activities and developed the underlying corporate values—participation, social responsibility, solidarity, and innovation. At Mondragon a Co-operative Congress formulates policies and develops four-year strategy and annual business plans for the component parts of the organization. Ratios of wages between managers and levels of other workers are agreed.

Mondragon survived the European economic malaise, which followed the global financial crisis of 2008 and the problems of the Euro, but in 2013 one of its major entities, having lost money for five years, became bankrupt. The remaining members of the co-operative, themselves facing the slump in Spain and cost competition from the East, were not able to bail it out. Nevertheless, some scholars have portrayed the Mondragon experience as a bastion of workplace democracy and an alternative to capitalism.

Employee-owned businesses take many forms, but all emphasize the importance of employee commitment and participation in decision-making.[2]

---

[1] www.nceo.org/articles/employee-ownership-100
[2] For more information go to www.employeeownership.co.uk

The governance of joint ventures

Joint ventures between companies, or strategic alliances as some call them, have been the preferred way for many companies to enter markets, transfer technology, procure supplies, obtain finance, share management skills, manufacture products around the world, or share risk on an international scale. Sometimes, the partners in a joint venture are competitors in other fields.

Many joint ventures involve the incorporation of a joint venture company owned by the two or more partners in the joint venture. Top management of such joint venture companies are often drawn from among the senior management of the partners.

Governing joint venture companies can present special challenges. As in Case study 11.1, disagreements can arise between the partners that were not envisaged in the initial joint venture agreement. Directors then face conflicts of interest between their responsibilities to the joint venture company and to the partner company that employs them. Moreover, joint venture companies may be incorporated in foreign jurisdictions, with diverse and different company laws and regulatory regimes, and have overseas partners with different cultural expectations.

A crucial aspect of the governance of joint venture companies is to realize that only matters concerning the joint venture can properly be handled by the joint venture company board. Issues affecting the relationship between the joint venture partners, such as those in Case study 11.1, cannot be resolved at the joint venture company level. They need to be handled at the level of the joint venture partners, if necessary revising the joint venture agreement.

The composition of the board of joint venture companies needs to be considered carefully and written into the joint venture agreement, including how many representative directors there will be from each side and whether INEDs are desirable. Although many joint venture companies do appoint the managing director or CEO of the joint venture to the board, to avoid Bill Torrington's dilemma in Case study 11.1, others now appoint representative directors from the partner companies, plus INEDs in some cases, with the joint venture project manager attending meetings in a non-voting, non-partisan way.

The governance of mutuals, social enterprises, and non-profit entities

It is now recognized that all corporate entities, not just limited companies, need sound corporate governance, This includes organizations in the voluntary and community sectors, including charities, education authorities, co-operatives, trades unions, savings and loan associations (building societies), hospital trusts, sports organizations, and other not-for-profit entities. Non-governmental organizations, such as public sector corporations, also need sound governance as well as good management. They all need to be well organized and managed, and they all need to be appropriately governed.

The typical distinguishing features of such organizations are as follows.

- They are working for the public good (rather than the benefit of shareholders).
- Their aims reflect community objectives (not long-term profit and growth).

- Their legal status may be rooted in the law of trusts, charities, co-operatives, or other legal acts or ordinances (not company law).
- Their form can have various legal structures (other than a limited company).
- Their underpinning constitution determines their form and purpose (not a corporate memorandum and articles of association).
- Governance is provided by a governing body, which can be known variously as a council, board of trustees, management committee, and so on (not necessarily as a board of directors).
- They have a 'multiple bottom line' to satisfy a range of objectives and stakeholders (rather than a single financial profitability measure).
- Their performance is measured by the achievement of multiple goals and is often difficult to measure
- Their governing bodies are often large and drawn entirely from outside, non-executive members (unlike the size and structure of corporate boards with both executive and non-executive directors).
- Their objectives can conflict: for example, a hospital may find that it cannot simultaneously deliver the highest performance on patient care and medical standards, financial effectiveness, administrative efficiency, staff welfare, and community approval.
- Nomination to the governing body may come from members, funding bodies including the state, representative bodies (staff, beneficiaries, funding bodies, the local community etc.), subject to the constitution. Difficult conflicts of interest can arise where governing body members are 'representative' of interest groups associated with the organization.
- The top executive and the top management team are typically invited to attend meetings of the governing body, to make reports, and to answer questions, but are seldom voting members of it (unlike the corporate sector in which the CEO and other senior executive directors are usually board members).
- Membership of the governing body is usually voluntary and unpaid, with no fees, remuneration, or capital gains, subject perhaps to reasonable expenses (again unlike the corporate sector).
- Trustees are the guardians of a voluntary organization, watching over its activities, and need to be competent, informed, but personally disinterested.

The significance of the constitution

The foundation of governance in such organizations is the constitution. This determines its name and purpose, the way those associated with it (often its members) elect the governing body, the rights and meetings of those members, the way the governing body operates, the officers of the organization, the keeping of records, financial reporting and audit, and other matters relevant to sound governance.

Constitutions can take many forms and have many names. Oxford colleges are often created under a Royal charter granted by the United Kingdom's Privy Council. Some NGOs, such as the Port of London Authority and the New Jersey Turnpike Authority, are formed under their own legislative acts. However, the governance of many organizations is based on just a rule book. Nevertheless, the constitution is basic to governance.

In earlier days, charities and other public-interest organizations relied on values in society to ensure that their trustees behaved appropriately. Today, given the greater diversity of voluntary and community organizations, their many aims, and changing social norms, in some parts of the world more use is being made of codes and legal sanctions.

UK Code for the voluntary and community sectors

In 2005, the UK Charity Commission published a non-mandatory code for good governance for the voluntary and community sector. Working with the National Council for Voluntary Organizations (www.ncvo.org.uk), the following 'hallmarks' of good charity trusteeship were suggested.:

1. Board leadership

Organizations should be led and controlled by an effective board of trustees, which collectively ensures delivery of its aims, sets its strategic direction, and upholds its values. The board has ultimate responsibility for ensuring that the organization is well run, solvent, and delivers the desired outcomes. Further, the board should focus on strategic direction and avoid becoming involved in day-to-day operations, unless strategic and operational roles of individuals are separated.

2. Board control

The board is responsible and accountable for monitoring and ensuring that the organization is performing well, including compliance with its constitution, the law, and regulatory requirements. The board should maintain and regularly review the organization's internal controls, policies, and procedures for reporting performance, and organization risk management. Principles of equality and diversity should be upheld and the organization should be fair and open to all sections of the community in its activities.

3. The high performance board

The board should have and achieve clear responsibilities and functions, with a statement of trustees' duties and responsibilities, which the trustees understand. The board should have a diverse range of skills, experience, and knowledge, and make the most effective use of trustees' time and abilities. Induction, training, and ongoing support should be available to trustees, along with appropriate information and advice. The board is responsible for the supervision, support, appraisal, and remuneration of its chief executive.

4. Board review and renewal

The board should periodically review its own effectiveness, and that of its committees and the organization as a whole.

5. Board delegation

The board should set out the functions of its subcommittees, the chief executive, and other staff in clear, delegated authorities. The terms of reference and roles should be clear and the delegation effective.

6. Board and trustee integrity

Individual trustees and the board as a whole should act according to the highest ethical standards and ensure that any conflicts of interest are properly disclosed and handled. Trustees must not benefit from their position beyond that allowed by the constitution and the law.

7. Board openness

The board should be open, responsive, and accountable to the organizations' members, beneficiaries, other users, partners, and all those with an interest in its work. Stakeholder communication should be effective, and key stakeholders should be involved in the organization's planning and decision-making.

In the UK public sector, an independent commission for good governance in public services, chaired by Sir Alan Langlands, produced a good governance standard for public services in 2005. The standard argued that good governance means:

1. focusing on the organization's purpose and on outcomes for citizens and service users;
2. performing effectively in clearly defined functions and roles;
3. promoting values for the whole organization and demonstrating values of good governance through behaviour;
4. taking informed, transparent decisions and managing risk;
5. developing the capacity and capability of the governing body to be effective;
6. engaging stakeholders and making accountability real.

In the United States, even though the Sarbanes-Oxley Act (SOX) does not formally apply to non-profits, SOX standards are being applied to not-for-profit entities. In California, SOX-like standards have been imposed on all large non-profit organizations.

Problems frequently found in governance of voluntary/community organizations include:

- founders of the organization who become permanent members of the governing body;
- stagnant board membership and poor chairmanship;
- lack of succession planning for the governing body;
- board members elected by representative groups who have conflicts of interest either as individuals or as representatives of the stakeholder group they represent;
- boards packed with representative members who are well-meaning, but who contribute little;

- lack of board members with necessary skills, knowledge, or experience;
- executive management failing to keep board members informed;
- board members not well briefed on the organization's activities;
- inadequate control systems, performance measures, and monitoring of executive actions;
- failure to meet reporting obligations;
- lack of a strategic focus and failure to rethink strategies as circumstances change;
- interpersonal politics among members of the governing body.

Some community and voluntary sector organizations include limited companies within their organization structure, for example running a profit-making mail order catalogue company to raise funds. Such companies, of course, must abide by company law, regulations, and governance codes as appropriate.

The United Kingdom has created two legal forms for such companies—the community interest company (CIC) and the incorporated charitable company (ICC). CICs are regulated by a government appointed regulator, who determines whether organizations meet the necessary criteria of community interest and ensures compliance with the CIC regulations.

In the United States such entities are called mutual-benefit non-profit corporations. Such corporations are required to file tax returns and are different from public-benefit non-profit corporations, whose objectives are for the common good.

The key criteria for board membership of a voluntary or community organization should be merit and contribution, not representation and status. In many communities, the importance of the voluntary sector is growing. In some countries, more governmental funds are being made available to such organizations, with related calls for wider accountability and transparency. Inevitably, there is a growing need to recognize the vital significance of sound corporate governance.

The governance of partnerships and limited-liability partnerships

A partnership is a legal organizational form in which two or more people agree to join together to achieve common goals under a partnership agreement that determines the contribution that each partner is required to make to the partnership, the way in which the partnership will be governed and managed, and the way in which profits and losses will be shared. Typically, partners are personally liable for the debts of the partnership. A partnership is not a company and in most jurisdictions operates under specific partnership law. The partnership model has a long tradition and has shown itself to be robust and flexible. Around the world, professional practices, in accountancy and medicine for example, have adopted the partnership form for many years.

A partnership has fewer constraints and lower requirements for reporting than a limited-liability company. As a result, partners are free to decide how they want to govern their partnership. In a small partnership with relatively few partners, the normal form of governance is through a meeting of all the partners. In larger practices, with many partners and particularly if they are geographically spread, the partnership may decide to appoint a managing partner and a governing body, perhaps called an executive or management committee or board, which meets regularly to manage partnership affairs, with a periodic, perhaps annual meeting of the entire partnership to accept the accounts, to transact business reserved to that meeting and to appoint members to the governing body. In the past, some partnership law put a limit on the maximum number of partners allowed in a partnership. But this law has been relaxed in some jurisdictions, and partnerships in those places can now be large and international. As a result, partners could find themselves personally exposed to the partnership risks of a widely spread and diverse partnership practice, without being personally able to influence partnership decisions, except though periodic voting for members of the governing body. This was the case when the international accountancy partnership Arthur Andersen found itself financially exposed in the collapse of Enron (see Corporate governance in action 11.3).

Following the Enron and Andersen debacle, a call to limit the exposure of audit firms to unlimited actions for damages in such cases was widely heard. It was further suggested that many claimants sued the auditors, even though they might have had only a relatively small part in the overall collapse, because they had 'deep pockets'—the result of insurance cover— whereas the directors of the company, who might have been far more culpable, had only their private resources.

Some countries have now provided for a form of *limited-liability partnership (LLP)*. This governance vehicle gives the benefits of limited liability to the members, but allows the flexibility of organizing as a traditional partnership. The governance of an LLP is similar to that of a partnership: members provide the capital, contribute personally, and share profits and losses. To give some protection to those dealing with a limited partnership, however, the disclosure requirements tend to be more stringent than for a traditional partnership, and similar to those of a company. For example, in the United Kingdom, LLPs are required to have a registered office, to file an annual return with financial accounts, and to notify changes to their membership.

Corporate governance in action 11.3 The collapse of the Arthur Andersen partnership

Arthur Andersen was one of the big five global accounting practices. Operating in many countries in the world, the firm provided audit, accountancy, and consultancy services to its client companies. The firm had developed many pioneering accounting practices and systems. Its reputation, and certainly the partnership's self-image, was as the international leader of the profession.

Then, in the early years of the 21st century, things went badly wrong. Some of Andersen's major US clients—Waste Management, Worldcom, and Enron—became spectacularly insolvent and the auditor was claimed to be less than blameless. The claims for damages from disgruntled creditors and shareholders of the failed companies threatened the financial viability of the Andersen firm. The American firm was also found guilty of destroying evidence, although that verdict was quashed on appeal.

The question was whether the Andersen partnership was based in America, or were the partners in the Andersen practices around the world also exposed? Some claimed that the partnerships were legally distinct; in the event, the rapid loss of clients in countries around the world and partners leaving for other firms resulted in the failure of the global practice and the end of the Arthur Andersen partnership.

In the United States, the *master limited partnership (MLP)* has become a significant means of raising capital. A MLP combines the advantages of limited liability for the owners, the tax advantages of a partnership, and the more limited governance of a private business. Commentators have suggested that the growing interest in the MLP, as a means of raising capital and governing entities, has been a response to the regulatory burden on companies under the Sarbanes-Oxley Act and other rules designed to make business safer, but at a cost. Others comment that if the MLP becomes a significant means of raising funds and limiting tax payments, it will change the face of American capitalism.

The governance of hedge funds, private equity, and sovereign funds

Hedge funds

As the name suggests, the essential element of a hedge fund is to provide its investors with a hedge against future uncertainty. For example, the managers of a normal fund might invest in shares in, say, the commercial property sector because they believe that there will be significant growth there. Hedge fund managers might also buy such shares, but will complement the purchase by selling short an equivalent value of other stocks (that is, they sell shares they have borrowed for a fee, buying them back later). If the price rises, the purchase of the commercial property shares will show a profit; if the market falls, the shorted shares will compensate for the loss. So whichever way the market moves, the fund is hedged. Of course, the fund is still at risk of losing money if its managers misjudged the prices at which they bought and sold. Moreover, in reality, hedge funds are involved in much more complex trades than these and are typically highly geared, increasing their exposure.

Large sums of money are provided to hedge fund managers by sophisticated rich individuals who have been attracted by the fund's prospectus, the fund managers, and their track record. Institutional investors, including some public and corporate pension funds, also invest in hedge funds to improve their overall performance, subject to the aims of the fund.

Hedge funds may take positions in commodities, buy equity shares, trade in debt, invest in futures, such as energy futures, sugar prices, carbon emission prices, even the weather, or make other exotic contracts, while using all of the tools in the contemporary financial management tool box, such as economic forecasting, statistical analysis, mathematical modelling, gearing, short-selling, securitization, and more. The massive sums often involved in hedge fund investments can result in spectacular profits and, of course, correspondingly devastating losses. But the aim of most hedge funds is to produce consistent returns, recognizing that providing a hedge will tend to damp down major rises or falls in the market. Sensible investors further spread their exposure by investing in a basket of hedge funds.

It is estimated that there are now more than 10,000 hedge funds around the world. The most successful funds are often closed to new investors. The majority trade trying to provide sustained returns and raising new investment as necessary. The least successful fail and lose their investors' money.

Hedge funds typically make heavy use of gearing, thus increasing their potential return and their exposure to risk. If investments are successful, the firm reaches break-even between revenues and costs earlier, and thereafter contributes more rapidly to investors' profit. Conversely, if investments are unsuccessful, the fund reaches break-even more slowly, because it still has to meet the interest costs, and the investors are saddled with a loss.

Some politicians around the world have expressed suspicion of hedge funds. Germany's Deputy Chancellor called hedge funds 'locusts', when blaming them for the hostile takeover of German companies. Others claimed that hedge funds forced Britain out of the European Exchange Rate Mechanism in 1992. Malaysia's Prime Minister blamed hedge funds for the East Asian financial crisis in the late 1990s. In each case, there were other forces at work as well. There is little doubt that most hedge funds take a short-term view of their investments, rather than assuming the role of stewards working with management long term. Warren Buffet's highly successful Hathaway Fund, however, proved to be a classic exception to this generalization.

Other criticisms of the governance of hedge funds include their concern for privacy, the lack of disclosure on matters such as their investment strategies and profitability, the extraordinary earnings of successful fund managers both from fees and percentages on gains, and that share traders are not responsible shareholders, but interested only in the short term. At the societal level, there is also the fear that, as we saw with banks around the world during the sub-prime mortgage crisis in 2007–2008, things can spiral downwards. The collapse of one fund could affect the others by driving down prices on the market, triggering margin calls, forcing more selling, driving prices still lower, with more margin calls and more losses, until funds collapse and the pension funds providing the capital and the banks providing the gearing funds would be hit.

Compared with the heavy regulation of listed companies, the hedge fund industry is relatively unregulated, except for controls on the financial viability and available wealth of those allowed to invest. Of course hedge fund managers have to abide by insider-dealing laws and stock exchange regulations when they trade in equities. There have been calls for regulation or voluntary codes. The International Corporate Governance Network supports the creation of a code of best practice for hedge funds, based on the 'comply or explain' principle. Others call for information on hedge funds' indebtedness and society's exposure to risk, rather than requiring them to disclose their business models, their complex statistical programmes, or their investment strategies.

Private equity firms

Private equity firms operate funds that can invest massively in the acquisition of limited liability companies. These can include listed companies, which are taken private, thus avoiding the public company disclosure requirements of the stock market and corporate regulators. These funds may also provide venture capital to grow existing businesses or new start-up ventures, and some also seek special investment opportunities, such as buying a failing company from which value can be realized.

Private equity firms seek capital for their funds mainly from institutional investors, including state and corporate pension funds, banks and other financial institutions, and from rich individuals. Some states restrict investment in such funds to accredited investors who are able to shoulder the risk. Usually, investors subscribe to a specific fund managed by a firm, becoming a limited partner in the fund rather than becoming an investor in the firm itself. Investors in such limited partnerships recognize that their funds can be locked in for a long period and that the risk is high with the potential to lose their entire investment, and they therefore expect high returns. Some private equity funds spread their risk by investing in a range of other private equity funds, sometimes called a fund of funds. The managers of private equity firms may also invest in their own funds, typically providing up to 5% of the overall capital.

Mergers and acquisition activity in the United States and the United Kingdom reached an all-time high prior to the sub-prime lending crisis in 2007–2008. Much of this growth in acquisition activity was due to private equity institutions acquiring control of previously listed companies. In the United States, many well-known companies have been helped by private equity investment, including Apple Computers, Avis, FedEx, and Microsoft.

In the United Kingdom, some well known companies have come into private equity ownership, including Boots the Chemist, Hilton Hotels, and the EMI music business. Britain has probably gone further than any country in allowing its core companies to be sold to overseas interests: Thames Water is now owned by a German company; London Electricity by a French company; and the ownership of the British Airports Authority, which runs major UK airports, is Spanish.

Typically, private equity funds generate returns on their investments by the sale of acquired business to other interests, or by floating the acquired company through an initial public offering.

Private equity is a notoriously secretive sector. Firms do not often publish information on their history, their ownership, the senior members of their management and advisory teams, or their investment strategy. Private equity funds also provide little indication of the partners in the fund, or of their capacity to invest. Nor do they disclose the portfolio of companies in the fund, other than to their investors. However, a few private equity firms have been floated as public companies and are listed on stock markets. In these cases, more information is available on the overall funding, but not of individual funds, nor of their investors. The vignette case of Blackstone provides a good example (see Corporate governance in action 11.4).

Corporate governance in action 11.4   The private equity Blackstone Group

Peter G. Peterson and Stephen A. Schwarzman founded the Blackstone Group with a shared secretary and a balance sheet of US$400,000 in 1985. Today, Blackstone is a leading global alternative asset manager and provider of financial advisory services listed on the New York Stock Exchange, with total assets under management of US$110 billion in 2010. The asset management businesses include the management of:

- corporate private equity funds;
- real estate opportunity funds;
- marketable alternative asset management funds, including:

    - funds of hedge funds;
    - mezzanine funds;
    - senior debt vehicles;
    - proprietary hedge funds;
    - closed-end mutual funds.

The corporate private equity operation, established in 1987, is a global business with offices in New York, London, Mumbai, and Hong Kong, and is a world leader in private equity investing, having managed five general private equity funds as well as one specialized fund focusing on communications-related investments.

From an operation focused in the early years on consummating leveraged buyout acquisitions of US-based companies, the company has grown into a business pursuing transactions throughout the world and executing not only typical leveraged buyout acquisitions of seasoned companies, but also transactions involving start-up businesses in established industries, turnarounds, minority investments, corporate partnerships, and industry consolidations—in all cases, in friendly transactions supported by the subject company's board of directors.

Income for 2010 was US$1.4 billion, and distributable earning was US$702 million. Blackstone acquired, floated, and sold Southern Cross Healthcare (as described in Case study 5.3).

Source: www.blackstone.com

Some commentators have felt that the acquisition of listed companies by private equity interests would dilute stock markets through 'privatization'. In fact, such developments could be seen as a return to the earlier 19th-century model of joint-stock companies, when a handful of external shareholders invested in a public company, elected the directors, and held them to account for their stewardship.

Typically, private equity firms are unregulated, other than within the company and banking regulations and laws of the relevant jurisdiction. Calls for more transparency and greater disclosure are sometimes heard on the grounds of potential conflicts of interest, finance market stability, or public interest, particularly when a well-known listed company disappears under the veil of private equity. The response of private equity interests is, predictably, that their responsibility is to the owners of their firm and the investors in their funds. Greater exposure of their funding, strategies, or portfolios would inhibit the private deals that enable private equity to generate impressive returns on the back of significant risk.

The strengths of private equity investment also reflect its potential weaknesses. In essence these can be summarized as:

- high gearing, which increases volatility and risk (private equity firms are typically highly leveraged, using interest-bearing debt rather than equity capital for growth);
- a strategic orientation towards financial rather than business strategies—in other words, private equity investors are more interested in realizing value from underperforming companies and undervalued assets, than in acting in the best long-term interests of the companies in their portfolio;
- cost reduction policies, seen by some as stripping out costs without regard for other stakeholders, particularly staff and customers;
- the disposal of unnecessary assets, sometimes described by others as asset-stripping or 'selling the family silver';
- the use of tax advantages on the sale of entities in some tax jurisdictions; and
- the charging of high fees and top management remuneration.

Corporate governance in action 11.5   Sir David Walker's voluntary code for UK private equity firms

An equity firm should publish, either as an annual review or as a regular update on its website, information including:

- a description of the way in which an entity authorized by the Financial Services Authority fits into the firm of which it is a part, with an indication of the firm's history and investment approach;

- a commitment to conform to the guidelines on a 'comply or explain' basis and to promote conformity on the part of the portfolio companies owned by its fund(s);

- an indication of the leadership of the UK element of the firm, identifying the most senior members of the management or advisory team, and confirmation that arrangements are in place to deal appropriately with conflicts of interest;

- a description of the UK companies in the firm's portfolio;

- a categorization of the limited partners in the fund(s) that invest or have a designated capability to invest in companies that would be UK portfolio companies.

Sir David Walker's voluntary code for private equity firms (summarized in Corporate governance in action 11.5) applies only to the United Kingdom, although many private equity deals involve cross-border deals.

Sovereign-wealth funds

Surging Asian exports and high oil prices in the Middle East generated massive surpluses. In some developing Arab and Asian countries, state-owned funds have been used to recycle some of these surpluses by investing in companies in developed countries. These sovereign-wealth funds have invested in telecoms, technology, real estate, ports and transport operations, and significantly in the financial sectors, particularly in the United States and Europe.

The Sovereign Wealth Fund Institute is an organization designed to study sovereign wealth funds and their impact on global economics, politics, financial markets, trade, and public policy. Table 11.1 lists the larger sovereign funds and gives an indication of the scale involved. According to the Institute, sovereign wealth funds have now surpassed US$6 trillion.

Sovereign wealth funds raise two basic corporate governance issues:

- the shortcomings of the funds' governance;
- the strategic potential of the sovereign nation to exert power over its investments.

The Linaburg-Maduell transparency index, shown in Table 11.1, is a method of rating transparency in sovereign wealth funds, developed by the Sovereign Wealth Fund Institute. The index is based on ten essential principles that depict sovereign wealth fund transparency to the public, with 10 as the top score.

Criticisms of the corporate governance of sovereign funds include complaints that they lack transparency and are secretive, neither stating their objectives nor disclosing their portfolios, that they lack accountability except to their government paymasters, and that they

Table 11.1 Top ten sovereign funds

Country	Fund name	Assets ($bn)	Inception	Origin	Linaburg-Maduell transparency index
UAE—Abu Dhabi	Abu Dhabi Investment Authority	$773.0	1976	Oil	5
Norway	Government Pension Fund—Global	$838.0	1990	Oil	10
Saudi Arabia	SAMA Foreign Holdings	$675.9	n/a	Oil	4
China	SAFE Investment Company	$567.9	1997	Non-commodity	4
China	China Investment Corporation	$575.9	2007	Non-commodity	7
Kuwait	Kuwait Investment Authority	$410.0	1953	Oil	6
China—Hong Kong	Hong Kong Monetary Authority Investment Portfolio	$326.7	1993	Non-commodity	8
Singapore	Government of Singapore Investment Corporation	$320.0	1981	Non-commodity	6
China	National Social Security Fund	$160.6	2000	Non-commodity	6
Singapore	Temasek Holdings	$173.0	1974	Non-commodity	10

Source: The Sovereign Wealth Fund Institute 2014 www.swfinstitute.org/about

are inadequately regulated. Unlike most other corporate entities, they are not accountable to their members, shareholders, or regulators; neither are they accountable directly to the citizens or voters in their sovereign nation.

Concerns about the strategic intent of sovereign nations include the worries that they may not be driven solely by a financial motive and that financial markets could be manipulated, because with their enormous wealth a fund could detrimentally affect financial markets. Others see a potential abuse of power if sovereign wealth funds use their investments to exercise strategic, possibly political, power around the world, for example, promoting or protecting their own national champions, restricting competition, or using the investment as a pawn in a diplomatic wrangle. For example, they fear that a sovereign wealth fund with a controlling stake in a European or American bank might threaten to withhold funds unless the country accedes to its demands, or, having acquired an oil or mineral producer, close it down to protect the fund's own industries, although running a company for political rather than economic reasons could well prove expensive.

An international working group of sovereign wealth funds (SWFs) produced what have become known as the 'Santiago principles and practices' in 2008. Among the 24 principles are the statements that the policy purpose of the SWF should be clearly defined and publicly disclosed, and that where the SWF's activities have significant direct domestic macroeconomic implications, those activities should be closely coordinated with the domestic fiscal and monetary authorities, so as to ensure consistency with the overall macroeconomic policies.

A predictable nationalistic and protectionist backlash, expressing concerns about 'national treasures' such as energy, airlines, ports, and utilities being owned by foreigners, has been heard in developed nations. The US Congress objected to the proposed Kuwait ownership of US port management and to China owning a US oil firm. However, it would be somewhat hypocritical to erect national barriers to inward investment from developing countries when expecting access to their developing markets. On the positive side, Singapore, Kuwait, and South Korea provided a multibillion-dollar lifeline to Citigroup and Merrill Lynch, two banks that had lost massively in America's sub-prime credit crisis in 2008, which helped to stabilize the financial markets.

In 2013, one of the largest sovereign wealth funds, Norway's oil fund, did appoint a board to advise it on corporate governance matters. Some took this as a sign that it intended to take a more active role in managing it portfolio, for example in the appointment of directors, and calling for corporate governance changes. However, investment managers of other sovereign wealth funds say that their strategy limits them to minority stakes, so that they do not get locked into a massive investment, which could involve them in governance responsibilities and which they might have difficulty selling.

The governance of sovereign-wealth funds is likely to remain in focus for some time. As Bob Monks has commented, 'sovereign wealth investors raise all the questions of ownership power and responsibilities'. In the longer term, some international agreement may be reached, with a code of conduct for sovereign funds, perhaps regulated by an international body such as the International Monetary Fund.

The state as shareholder

During the 20th century, around the world, the nationalization by governments of enterprises in the private sector was a political feature. Typically, these operations were then run under strong government supervision. In state-owned public enterprises, sometimes called 'political' companies, political processes can affect corporate decisions. On nationalization, the government established the governing body, nominating and appointing its members. Government determined corporate objectives, provided funding, and decided performance criteria. Government intervened in management, influencing operations, appointing managers, and in some cases fixed market prices. Incentives for managers to meet corporate objectives came to be determined politically. Concerns about security of managerial employment arose. Companies were used to pursue political objectives. Managers of the company might then find themselves following different strategies from those of the controlling governmental body. In democratic countries, a change of political party could also mean a change of corporate objectives, sometimes causing confusion. In nationalized companies, longer-term corporate strategic objectives could be sacrificed to shorter-term political expediency.

Towards the end of the 20th century and into the 21st century, the privatization of nationalized firms became politically desirable in some countries—electricity in New Zealand; energy, water supply, communications, and rail transport in the United Kingdom (see Network Rail in Case study 3.2); and many state-owned enterprises (SOEs) in Russia and China.

In China, the SOEs were first corporatized, creating an ownership balance sheet and an equity structure, and then privatized by offering their shares on the stock markets in China and sometimes abroad. However, in many cases the state still maintained the dominant voting shareholding.

In response to the global financial crisis, which started in 2007, the governments of the United States, the United Kingdom, and some other countries became the unwilling shareholders of some of their countries' financial institutions, being forced to bail them out to protect the rest of their economies. The UK government, for example, acquired all the shares of the Northern Rock Bank (Case study 8.1) and a substantial portion of the much larger Lloyds Bank, creating a special organization, United Kingdom Financial Investments, for the purpose. In the United States, it was Bear Stearns, Fannie Mae, and Freddie Mac, which provided funds for American homeowners, and AIG, which provided hedging cover for the US insurance industry. Special governance arrangements had to be made to handle the governments' new corporate responsibilities.

The governance of state-owned companies, whether they are wholly owned as nationalized entities, or partially owned with outside minority shareholders, needs to have clear and independent lines of responsibility. The relationship between the company and the government, through the overseeing state department or regulatory body, needs to be crystal clear. The company's constitution, whether that is a parliamentary Act or ordinance creating the entity, or a more typical memorandum and articles of association, needs to determine how the governing body is to be nominated and elected, the directors' terms of service, and their role. The responsibility for establishing strategies, laying down policies, and setting prices, particularly in monopoly markets, needs to be predetermined. Appropriate financial incentives for top management also need to be agreed—sufficient to secure, hold, and motivate key personnel, while being justifiable politically. Precise criteria of corporate transparency and accountability are essential. There needs to be an appropriate balance between freedom of corporate decision and state bureaucratic control.

Case studies

 Case study 11.1   Teletronic Riches Ltd—governance of a joint venture

Teletronic Riches Ltd was a joint venture company set up between Lichfield Teletronics Ltd [Lichfield], a UK company, and Great Riches Ltd [Riches], a company based in Hong Kong, although incorporated in Bermuda. Riches was quoted on the Hong Kong Stock Exchange, although 66% of the voting stock was owned by Albert Li Cheuk Yan and his family. Lichfield was the wholly owned subsidiary of a US-based public company, listed on the NASDAQ stock exchange.

The joint venture had been set up to manufacture the Teletronic range of integrated i-phones and recording machines in Shenzen, China. In the joint venture agreement, Lichfield would provide technological know-how, specialist manufacturing equipment, and the top management; Riches would introduce the manufacturing site, labour, and local management. Both sides put up an equal amount of working capital and would share equally in profits. The entire output was to be supplied to

Lichfield for distribution through its worldwide marketing organization, except for sales to the market in China, for which Riches were given the rights.

Lichfield and Riches had equal shareholdings and voting rights, and each appointed three members to the board. Teletronic's managing director, Bill Torrington, was also made a member of the board. He had run a very successful division of Lichfield in the United Kingdom and in 1997 was seconded to Teletronics on a five-year contract. He expected, when the joint venture was successful, to become a director of the Lichfield main board on his return to England.

Initially, all went well, but after three years tensions emerged. Relations between the two sets of directors on the Teletronic board were frosty. The Riches-nominated directors complained that the venture was not being given the latest products or technology. The Lichfield directors claimed that their company's products, made in Schenzen, were being sold throughout Asia, in contravention of the joint venture agreement.

Bill Torrington found himself in an impossible position. He wanted what was good for Teletronics, but his Lichfield colleagues expected him to side with them. His career prospects were on the line.

Discussion question

1. What should Bill Torrington do?

 Case study 11.2 The governance of the Co-op

The first co-operative society in England was formed in 1844 in Rochdale, a northern mill town. The Co-op, as it was soon called, sold food and other goods to its members and the profits were shared between them according to their purchases. Similar co-operative societies soon sprang up in other towns and cities around the country, reflecting the self-help attitudes of newly industrializing mid-Victorian society.

But the Co-op was more than a business: it was a movement based on ethical trading, a belief in democracy among its members, and a mission to improve the local community. Anyone over sixteen could join, as long as they shared the values of the society, working together for everyone's benefit.

The co-op movement in Britain thrived and is now one of the main food retailers, with over 4,000 outlets, runs a country-wide funeral service, and offers insurance, legal, and travel services, with around 90,000 employees. It also has a bank.

Nevertheless, the underlying principles to build a better society still influence its community-led programmes, social goals, and political ambitions. The Co-op regularly funds charities and local community groups. The movement spread around the world, with the International Co-operative Alliance[3] describing a co-operative as 'an autonomous association of persons united voluntarily to meet their common economic, social and cultural needs and aspirations through a jointly-owned and democratically controlled enterprise'.

The original governance of the Co-op

Despite the size of the modern movement in Britain, the Co-op tried to maintain its local orientation by linking local co-op societies, initially through an association, and then forming a group, which

---

[3] Statement on the Co-operative Identity, Manchester 1995.

now represents the interests of the 80 independent local co-operative societies and over six million individual members.[4]

The Co-operative Group had three levels of governance:

- *Area Committees*

  Any member could stand for election to their local area committee. All members in each area had one vote, irrespective of how much money they had in their share account, reflecting a democratic principle developed by the co-op movement. Area committees represented their members' interests—from how the businesses might be improved, to how to help their local communities.

- *Regional Boards*

  The seven regional boards were made up or representatives nominated by the area committees. Each regional board helped manage the businesses in their region, for example, by approving spending on new and improved stores, and supervising the strategy for assisting that region's local communities.

- *The Co-operative Group Board of Directors*

  The Group Board was entirely non-executive, consisting of twenty-one directors: five nominated by the independent co-operative societies, and fifteen nominated by the Regional Boards, plus one independent non-executive director. Each year one-third of Group Board members retired and could seek re-election.

The Group Board was responsible for the long-term success of the Co-op Group by:

- ensuring that the Group's affairs are conducted and managed in accordance with its objectives, in the best interests of the independent co-operative societies and the individual members

- determining the vision and strategy of the Group in consultation with the Group Chief Executive and executive management

- monitoring performance against key financial and non-financial indicators

- supervising the Group's risk management systems

- overseeing the Group Chief Executive and executive management in the day to day management of the Group

- setting standards in governance matters

A chairman of the Group Board was chosen by the Board's members. The Group Board Group also appointed the Chief Executive to implement the agreed strategic objectives, who was accountable to the Board for the financial and operational performance of the Group.

Recent troubles

The return on capital employed of the Trading Group for 2013 was 6.9%—down from 8.6% in 2012. The fall in profitability was largely due to the decline in the food business' profits from £383 million in 2010 to £247 million in 2013 and the rise in central overheads from £98 million in 2010 to £192 million in 2013. As newly appointed Group Chair, Ursula Lidbetter, wrote in her 2013 annual report:[5]

This report will make painful reading for our members, customers, colleagues and other stakeholders. 2013 was the worst year in our history, and the report that follows lays bare some fundamental failings of management and governance . . . During a most difficult period, our (over) 87,000 colleagues stuck resolutely to the task of serving our members and customers

---

[4] Extracted from www.co-operative.coop/corporate/Investors/Governance/
[5] www.co-operative.coop/corporate/Investors/Annual-Results-2013/

throughout our diverse businesses. I am hugely grateful to them for their loyalty and for sticking with us in adversity. We owe it to all of them to recover the fortunes of this great organisation, an obligation that I and the executive team are determined to fulfil.

She continued:

We entered 2013 focused on the future development of the organisation. Our food business was developing a new strategy and underlying performance from our trading businesses was encouraging. In May 2013, we welcomed our new Chief Executive, Euan Sutherland, recruited from outside the organisation, to revitalise the Group for the next generation.

Within days of his joining, an unfolding crisis in our Bank emerged that risked not only its future but that of the entire Group. There followed a six notch downgrade by Moody's in the credit rating of the Bank, as the extent of a significant capital shortfall became apparent. In order to meet regulatory capital requirements as laid-down by the Prudential Regulation Authority (PRA) the Bank was required to raise a further £1.5 bn. of new capital. Although this reduced the Group's ownership in the Bank to a 30% stake, this action was essential in order to safeguard the Bank for customers, colleagues and members. The battle to save the Bank dominated our activity for the remainder of the year, only concluding in December 2013.

The near-collapse of the Bank led to a wholesale change of leadership at both the Group and Bank. Euan moved decisively to recruit a new team well equipped to deal with the crisis. We were particularly fortunate that Richard Pym agreed to take the role of Chair at the Bank during such a crucial period.

His experience and authoritative leadership have helped steer the Bank through this difficult phase.

Additionally, we could not have succeeded without the support of our syndicate banks and the considered response of our pension trustees, and I thank them too for their contribution. Finally, I would like to acknowledge the contribution of Andrew Bailey and his team at the PRA for their calm guidance through a difficult time.

It was at this point that I was appointed by the Board as Chair of the Group, with a determination to resolve the weaknesses of our governance structure which had been made plain by the events of the year.

The unprecedented nature of our crisis inevitably led to the establishment of a number of inquiries by official bodies, including the Financial Conduct Authority, the Treasury, the Prudential Regulation Authority, a Treasury Select Committee, and the police. We co-operated fully with each of these. We also commissioned our own reviews. The first, by Sir Christopher Kelly, examined the circumstances that led to the Bank crisis.

Later in the year, Lord Myners[6] agreed to undertake an independent governance review on behalf of the Board, whilst also agreeing to join the Group Board as Senior Independent Non-Executive Director. His recommendations are covered later. Lord Myners stood down from our Board at the AGM in May 2014. We are indebted to him for being so generous with his time and expertise.

The near-failure of our Bank also highlighted wider financial weaknesses across the Group. In particular, our overall indebtedness is too high for an organisation of our nature. When the recent problems arose, we had limited resources with which to cover losses. Consequently, and regrettably, we have had to take some difficult decisions to sell some of our businesses. This will change the shape of our Group significantly as we adapt our strategy and cost base accordingly.

[6] Lord Myners, an experienced City of London financier, whose corporate governance report was mentioned in Chapter 5.

It is a matter of great regret that Euan Sutherland felt compelled to resign subsequent to the year-end.[7] Without question his leadership saved our Bank, and he built a top-flight team capable of redefining the purpose and relevance of our Co-op.

As Group Chair, I recognise the scale of the change required to our governance. This essential and urgent work is critical to our future and will enable us to build a more effective organisation which can deliver for all our members, customers and colleagues.

What went wrong?

Facing enormous competition

In recent years, the Co-op retail stores have faced massive and increasing competition. In addition to national competitors, Tesco, Sainsbury, Asda and Morrisons, two German firms, Aldi and Lidl, recently entered the British market, taking market share with lower prices for high quality goods. The Co-op stores no longer rate highly in customers' opinion.

A dubious super-market acquisition

In 2009 following an expansionist strategy, the Co-op acquired the Summerfield chain of small to medium-sized food stores in a £1.6 billion deal. Other supermarket chains were not interested. The Summerfield name was replaced and supply chains changed. But a rolling programme of refurbishment meant that in many towns there are now two co-ops within a few hundred yards of each other, each duplicating a stock of similar goods.

A poor banking merger

Also in 2009, the Co-op Bank took over the ailing Britannia Building Society (savings and loans association) in a merger that put considerable debt on the bank's balance sheet, significantly increasing its risk profile. Due diligence studies were 'extremely cursory,' it was reported. Claims were made of a cover-up of the extent of dubious loans.

The Co-op Bank is in trouble

In April 2013, following a protracted period of due diligence, the Co-op Bank withdrew from the acquisition of branches and accounts from Lloyds Banking Group, which had been hit by a disastrous bail-out during the global financial crisis.

In May 2013, the Co-op Bank reported losses of £600 million. Moody's downgraded its credit rating by six notches to junk level (Ba3). A bail-out by other financial institutions and hedge funds reduced the Co-op Bank's holding to around 30%. The bank's chief executive, Barry Tootell, resigned.

The bank's dubious chairman

For three years, from April 2010 to June 2013, the chairman of the Co-op Bank was the Rev. Paul Flowers, a minister in the Methodist church and a former Labour party councillor. Under his chairmanship the bank reported substantial losses and had its credit rating downgraded. Flower's lack of knowledge about the bank's balance sheet was highlighted by a Parliamentary Select Committee. Apparently, he had been appointed to the chairmanship after an hour and a half interview without references.

In November 2013, Flowers was exposed by a Sunday newspaper buying crack cocaine and methamphetamine. He was suspended by the Labour Party, the Methodist Church, and the Co-op. In November 2013, the Co-op Group Chairman, Len Wardle, who had led the board that appointed Flowers, resigned.

[7] Sutherland is reported to have said that 'the co-op is ungovernable.'

Labyrinthine voting structure and board domination

Despite the Co-op's oft repeated claim to be a democratic organization, the grass-roots members had little opportunity to influence significant decisions. Governance power lay with the 100, or so, regional board members, who controlled the majority of votes in members' meetings, and each of whom received between £30,000 and £80,000 a year in fees. As the press pointed out, the future of the Co-op lay with a handful of members, most without business experience, including an engineer, a retired deputy head teacher, a computer technician, and a plasterer. In March 2014, private investigators were hired to discover which director had leaked information about executive salaries. In April 2014, it was reported that another director had been suspended for claiming that he was a chartered accountant when he had been struck off by the professional body for being bankrupt.

Lord Myners' governance recommendations

Following a comprehensive review of the Group's governance, Lord Myners, the Co-operative Group's Senior Independent Non-Executive Director, published his detailed report[8] in May 2014. The report described 'deplorable governance failures' that had been exposed over the past year which had led to the 'near-collapse of the Group'. He warned that without change, the Group's level of debt will see its 'autonomy and independence being strictly curtailed'. He described the present governance architecture and allocation of responsibilities as 'not fit for purpose' and called for radical change.

Despite the repeated claims that the Co-op was democratic, the Myners' report identified a 'significant democratic deficit,' in which the vast bulk of ordinary members had limited ability to influence the Group. Lord Myners urged the current members of the group board and regional boards to 'put their self-interest to one side for the greater good', and vote through far-reaching reforms.

In his report Lord Myners says:

> The co-operative ownership model can—and often does—deliver powerful economic advantages. But its superiority over other forms of ownership is not inevitable and guaranteed. For a consumer co-operative, such as the Group, its advantages have to be earned, day by day, through delivering outstanding service and value for money to customers who, especially in food retailing, have plenty of choice where to spend their money...There is no short cut to recovery from the present weakened state. It will require retrenchment and some painful choices. Financial health can only be restored through steady, step by step, re-building of the Group's profitability and repayment of its excessive debt.

> Because of the losses exposed last year and their severe impact on the Group's balance sheet, the high level of debt now being carried by the Group has made it inevitable that the bank syndicates providing this funding will, for quite obvious reasons, continue to take the closest interest in the Group making rapid progress to strengthen its governance. Elected members need to understand that while autonomy and independence are cherished principles of co-operation, the harsh truth is that bad governance results directly in such autonomy being strictly curtailed.

> The reforms I have set out are fully compatible with the core values and principles of co-operative ownership. I have no interest in advocating the adoption of a PLC model, as some of my critics have claimed. But I do want to see a governance structure that works; the present one has lamentably failed.

---

[8] www.co-operative.coop/MynersReview

The Myners' report contained three specific reform objectives:

- To produce a highly competent and qualified Group Board with independent non-executive directors who possess the skills and experience needed to exercise leadership and effective oversight of executive management running a business of massive scale and complexity, quite unlike any other co-operative business in the UK.

- To ensure that, without compromising the effectiveness of the Group Board, genuine co-operative values and principles are protected and securely embedded in the future governance architecture.

- To ensure that as a customer-owned organisation, the tangible benefits of membership are not deliberately restricted to a tiny and potentially quite unrepresentative body of elected members, but are extended so that the interests of the entire membership are properly understood and promoted and their fundamental rights are respected.

The report then set out four key reforms to the governance structure.

Reform the Group Board

- Create a new Group Board with six to seven independent non-executive directors and two executive directors and an independent chair with no previous association or involvement with the Group. The non-executive directors will have the skills and experience of the non-executive directors that sit on the boards of the Co-operative Group's primary competitors.

Establish an influential National Membership Council

- Establish an elected National Membership Council ('NMC') of around 50 individuals, including provision for representation of around 10 employees. The NMC will elect from its membership a Steering Committee of 12 which will also include corporate representation from independent co-op societies.

Create a Nominations Committee

- Create a Nominations Committee to screen and propose candidates for Group Board approval and for election/re-election by members at each AGM. The Committee would comprise five non-executive members, including up to two representatives designated by the NMC and the balance from the Group Board.

Extend constitutional rights

- Extend constitutional rights to the entire membership of the Group, consistent with the fundamental co-operative principle of 'one member one vote'.

The Co-op Group's response to Myners

Lord Myners faced bitter in-fighting against his turnaround plans. Indeed, his was a case of the messenger being shot at before he even delivered his message. The principal complaint was the potential loss of 'co-operative values,' but for some the Co-op's original support for working people in their local communities had been replaced by a central support for socialism and the Labour Party. Others pointed out that the existing regional and group board members would lose their power over the organization and the privileges that went with it. Faced with such opposition, Myners resigned his independent non-executive directorship after four months.

Some of the current leaders of the Co-op, calling themselves 'the apex body for the co-operatives', proposed[9] some amendments to the Myners' proposals, addressing what they saw as potential risks to the co-operative ideals.

A strong alignment with co-operative values is essential for every board director, as the Myners' Review recognizes. There can also be a form of expertise that may be needed, alongside professional business and retail strategy, financial and innovation skills, which is the ability to re-represent the interests of everyday members.

The Apex Group accepted the real need for change, and appointing professional non-executive directors to the main board, but added that they should be 'member-representative,' rather than independent. To achieve this they proposed that the appointment of these directors would be made by members of the NMC, rather than the new nominations committee of the main board, as Myners proposed.

In addressing what they meant by 'member representatives', the authors said that:

it is a misunderstanding of governance practice to say how many expert or lay members should be on a board, since ultimately all directors are accountable to the members . . . When people say [we] want to ensure that 'co-operators' are on the board, it is easy then for skeptics to read this as saying that they want to keep existing representatives in place rather than to disband. In truth, they ought to be saying something very different.

The Apex Group called for a single chairperson for both the Group Board and NMC. Two chairs would lead to cost and potential conflict, they suggested. They also called for the social goals programme to be overseen by the Group Board, rather than being a separate activity run by the NMC. 'Activity on social goals needs to be embedded in core operations, and become a source of commercial innovation,' said the authors, 'rather than sitting as a separate exercise, as if it was a semi-detached corporate charitable trust.'

At a meeting of the members on 17 May 2014, dominated by the regional members, a watered down version of the Myners' Report was accepted.

Discussion questions

1. Are Lord Myners' recommendations on the future governance of the Co-op consistent with the culture of Britain's largest mutual company?

2. If you were advising the board of the Co-op what would you propose?

3. Is the concept of a business enterprise 'owned' by its customers a viable alternative to one owned by its shareholders (including individual investors, institutional investors, such as pension funds and insurance companies, and hedge funds)?

[9] www.thenews.coop/85555/news/democracy/sector-body-proposes-additional-changes-co-operative-group-governance/#.U3XaQiIOUdU

References and further reading

Burrough, Bryan and John Helyar (1990) *Barbarians at the Gate: The Fall of RJR Nabisco*. (The story of two private equity firms—Forstmann Little and Kohlberg Kravis Roberts—and their aggressive $25 billion takeover of RJR Nabisco.) Random House/Jonathan Cape, London.

Cogan, Philip (2009) *Guide to Hedge Funds*. The Economist/Profile Books, London.

Cornforth, C. (2003) *The Governance of Public and Non-profit Organisations: What Do Boards Do?* Routledge, New York/London.

McCahery, Joseph A. and Erik P. M. Vermeulen (2010) *Corporate Governance of Non-Listed Companies*. Oxford University Press, Oxford.

Solomon, Jill ([2004] 2007) *Corporate Governance and Accountability*. Wiley, Chichester, UK.

Wright, Robert E. (2014) *Corporate Nation*. University of Pennsylvania Press, Philadelphia, PA.

Projects and exercises

1. Explore the Internet for information on voluntary and community organizations and NGOs in your country. Draft a report to the government on the extent to which they appear to conform to international norms on corporate governance.

2. Draft an explanatory paper and presentation for the chairman of a voluntary or community organization in your country explaining what is needed for successful corporate governance in his or her organization.

3. Draft an explanatory paper and presentation for the head of a family–based company on the pros and cons of a family council.

Self-test questions

1. Should the managing director/CEO of a joint venture company, who is also employed by one of the joint venture partners, be a member of the joint venture company board?

2. How are partnerships governed?

3. What is a limited-liability partnership?

4. Explain the differences between a holding, a subsidiary, and an associated company.

5. Explain the two distinct options in governing and managing a group of companies.

6. What are the benefits of drawing subsidiary company directors from other companies in the group?

7. Explain what a family council is and does in a family company.

8. Explain what a sovereign wealth fund is and which countries have been particularly involved.

9. What are some of the sectors in which sovereign funds have invested?

10. List some of the distinguishing characteristics of a not-for-profit corporate entity.

12

Corporate Governance around the World

 Learning Outcomes

In which we consider:

- Corporate governance in China
- Corporate governance in India
- Corporate governance in Russia
- Corporate governance in Brazil
- Corporate governance in Hong Kong and Singapore
- Corporate governance in South Korea: the *chaebol*
- Corporate governance in Japan
- Corporate governance in the Middle East and North Africa

We saw how context and culture affected corporate governance around the world in Chapters 5 and 6, when we studied some of the regulatory frameworks and basic corporate governance models, in particular the American rules-based model, the UK/Commonwealth principle-based model, the continental European two-tier model, the Japanese business network model, and the Asian family-based model. We turn now to the details of corporate governance in specific countries, starting with China, India, Russia and Brazil.

Corporate governance in China

In a country with strong central control, in which the National People's Congress, the State Council, and the Communist Party play significant roles in the governance of enterprises, share ownership is not the obvious basis for governance power. Yet the People's Republic of China (PRC) has developed an innovative corporate governance regime, while becoming one of the world's leading economies.

The evolution of corporate governance in China

The Communist Revolution began in 1927, with the state subsequently proclaiming ownership of the means of production, with private property and incorporated companies forbidden. In 1958, Chairman Mao Tse Tung initiated the Great Leap Forward, when millions of farmers, peasants, and city workers were relocated. Massive economic dislocation and famine resulted. The Cultural Revolution began in 1966 and lasted a decade. Communes were reorganized and many state-owned enterprises (SOEs) were created, most needing state subsidy.

In the 1970s, a new leader, Deng Xiao Ping, introduced a form of market economy, but with a centralized, Communist-state orientation. The industrial SOEs, which were large bureaucracies, continued to receive their production and distribution orders from state planners. SOE employees benefited from housing, medical care, and schooling for their children.

Between 1984 and 1993, a transitional model of governance for SOEs was introduced to increase productivity and profitability throughout China, which gave them more autonomy. In 1994, a new corporate law provided for the restructuring of traditional large and medium-sized SOEs as legal entities.

In 1988, the State Council of the PRC, advised by Organisation for Economic Co-operation and Development (OECD), experts, produced a set of corporate governance directives for SOE reform. In September 1999, the Fourth Plenary Session of the 15th Chinese Communist Party's Central Committee took a vital decision on enterprise reform, in what was termed a 'strategic adjustment' of the state sector, agreeing that the state should be 'withdrawing from what should be withdrawn'. Interestingly, corporate governance was recognized as being at the core of the modern enterprise system. The 16th Congress of the Party called for a joint-stock system with the state controlling critical enterprises, while other SOEs continued their corporate reforms. Many small and medium-sized firms were transformed into non-state owned enterprises, and some SOEs were restructured prior to stock market listing.

Some of the reformed corporate entities were floated on the two China stock markets in Shanghai and Shenzen (a city across the border from Hong Kong), which had been set up in 1991 and 1992 respectively.

The corporate governance of listed Chinese SOEs

In the early days, many listed companies were dominated by their majority internal shareholders, who often represented state, provincial, or local governments. They nominated the directors for confirmation by the other shareholders. Board membership overlapped management, control by insiders was a widespread problem, and the major shareholders controlled shareholders' meetings.

The roles and responsibilities of key players were often unclear and internal management control measures were not well established. Since the duties of the board and top management were often vague, the chairman sometimes usurped the chief executive's role, and the chief executive encroached on the work of the chief operations officer and divisional heads. In some cases, information was manipulated, delayed, even falsified. Performance assessment of individual directors was immature and not necessarily linked to incentives. Reviews of the performance of the board and its committees were seldom undertaken. Worse, the supposedly independent audit firms were not experienced and not always independent, sometimes hiding, rather than disclosing, financial problems.

In 2001, the China Securities Regulatory Commission (CSRC) formulated some basic norms of corporate governance, promoting the separation of listed companies from controlling shareholders. At least one third of the board should consist of independent directors, and include at least one accounting professional, although initially there was a lack of suitable people. Independent directors could be nominated by the board of directors, the board of

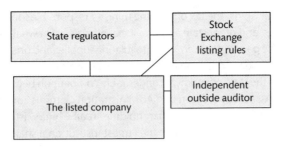

Figure 12.1 The overall regulatory structure

supervisors, or any shareholders holding 5% of the shares. China became a member of the World Trade Organization (WTO) in 2001.

In 2002, a Code of Corporate Governance for listed companies was formulated which included basic principles for the protection of investors' rights, basic behaviour rules, and standards for directors, supervisors, and senior management.

In 2006, a fundamental review of Chinese company law was enacted, creating two types of limited company—the limited-liability company (LLC private companies) and the joint-stock company (JSC public companies)—bringing the legal context much in line with the company law of other countries.

The state's control of listed Chinese SOEs

The state at the national or provincial level has maintained ownership control of many of China's listed companies. In other words, the overall regulatory structure can be depicted as shown in Figure 12.1.

The lines of control from various state and provincial authorities can be numerous, as reflected in Figure 12.2.

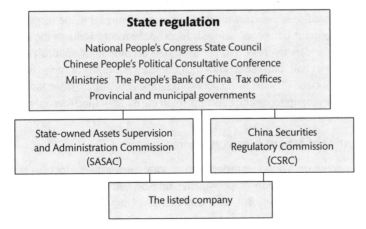

Figure 12.2 The overall regulatory structure

The People's Bank of China, the tax offices, the ministry responsible for the industry in which the company operates, and other state and provincial officials act in what they see as the interests of the state and the people, for example by regulating supplies and prices, by taking action to avoid unacceptable economic or social stress including unemployment, bankruptcy, corruption, financial pressures on the state economy, or undesirable competition between state enterprises.

The State-owned Assets Supervision and Administration Commission of the State Council (SASAC) holds the China government's shareholding in all China's listed companies (other than those in the finance sector). SASAC is the largest institutional shareholder in the world, with eight in the Fortune list of the world's top 500 companies. SASAC ensures that the state's interests are represented in the activities of China's listed companies, including the appointment of directors and top executives to state majority-owned companies. In 2013, the head of SASAC, Jiang Jiemin, was investigated for 'serious disciplinary violations', which usually refers to corruption related issues.

The CSRC is the Chinese government's corporate regulator. The CSRC issues the Corporate Governance Code and other corporate governance regulations, and publishes regular reports on corporate governance reform and performance in China. The CSRC also liaises closely with the management of the stock exchanges in Shanghai and Shenzen, and with those exchanges overseas that list Chinese stock.

Comparing China's corporate governance with other models

China has created a unique form of corporate governance structure—a management board of directors, with some independent outside directors, and a board of supervisors, with both employee and other members—thus combining elements of both the German-style two-tier board model and the unitary board use of independent outside directors, as well as recognizing China's traditional concept of employees being masters of enterprises.

Some commentators have suggested that China's model is more closely aligned to the Japanese model, which, although essentially a unitary board system, provides for the independent outside directors on the board to form a separate committee outside the board.

Figure 12.3 attempts to differentiate the models.

Officially, the board of supervisors oversees finances, ensures the due diligence of directors and senior management personnel, safeguards company assets, reduces the company's risks, and protects shareholders' interests. In practice, leaders of companies' political party committees have often taken the chair and vice chair of their companies' boards of supervisors. Some commentators have criticized the effectiveness of some supervisory boards, because their members have less professional experience and education than the directors and managers they supervise.

The governance of other China companies

Much of the writing on China's approach to corporate governance focuses on the corporatization and part-privatization of previously state-owned enterprises: what the Chinese call 'ownership-diversification'. But, in a useful study, Leng Jing[1] considered the range of

---

[1] Leng Jing (2009) *Corporate Governance and Financial Reform in China's Transition Economy.* Hong Kong University Press, Hong Kong.

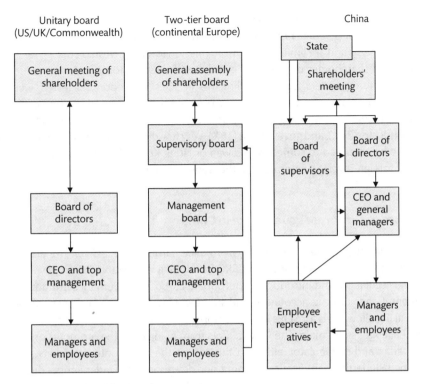

Figure 12.3 Differentiation of models of corporate governance

enterprises that have contributed to the growth of the Chinese economy. She classifies Chinese business entities into five categories:

- *state-owned enterprises (SOEs)*, which may be large, medium, or small, with state ownership at the national, provincial, or local level, many now corporatized, and partly privatized through listings on China's two stock exchanges, Hong Kong and overseas, as we have seen;

- *collectively owned enterprises*, including urban collectives and rural township and village entities (TVEs), which she describes as transitional, but efficient, organizations;

- *privately owned organizations*, defined as firms with more than seven employees, created from the privatization of state small or medium enterprises, or through the 'dual-track' provisions that allow new enterprises to run alongside state enterprises;

- *small, individually owned enterprises* with no more than seven employees;

- *foreign-invested firms*, although she does not cover these because, to date, they have had only a moderate impact on China's corporate governance regime.

The dawning of the market economy in China produced many private enterprises and foreign-invested enterprises (many of them joint ventures with Chinese partners). On private enterprise boards, the study found that 'like Chinese society, patriarchy prevails, similar to the cultural context of the Asian family-based model' (as discussed in Chapter 6). 'The tendency of a weak board and strong chairman is common, and boards tend to be tight-knit groups built on business or personal networks. Independent directors tend to be brought in to fulfil legal requirements and are limited to advisory roles.' In foreign-invested enterprises, the high proportion of shareholder directors reflected the interests of local and overseas investors and joint venture partners. Employee directors in SOEs, the report suggested, were often opposed to corporate reform, resulting in protracted negotiations on the board. The independent directors were drawn principally from universities (35%), the professions (25%), the relevant industry (21%), and government (15%). Very few directors were foreign nationals and those who were tended to come from Taiwan or Hong Kong. The average board size of the SOEs and foreign-invested enterprises in the study was nine.

The future of corporate governance in China

Three decades ago, Chinese corporate governance hardly existed. Given the dramatic and sustained economic growth since, the CSRC has done a remarkable job in developing law, rules, and regulation, and introducing appropriate corporate governance attitudes. China is also attempting to bring its accounting and auditing rules in line with international standards, while making allowances for SOEs in a transitional economy.

But challenges still remain. The CSRC suffers from being both the promoter of the investment market and its regulator, although this can be the case in other markets, too. Other problems include: the identification, training, and development of independent directors; the potential influence of members of the Communist Party, particularly where directors are also members of a company's Party Committee; and changing attitudes from the previous centralized state-directed decision-making to a market-orientated perspective.

The legal system, although it has ancient traditions, is somewhat lacking in transparency and predictability. The training of judges is still evolving. Bringing private legal action against companies is difficult, although a new contract arbitration law was enacted in 2008, which set up a framework for resolving disputes. The Supreme People's Court and the people's courts around the country act primarily in what is seen as the interests of the people, in other words of the state. The recognition of contractual and corporate relationships tends to be limited, and enforcing legal judgments can be problematical.

Although corruption and rigorous penalties (including the death penalty) for wrongdoers are widely reported in the Chinese press, the law against commercial corruption is not well enforced.

Recent developments in China affecting corporate governance

After more than two decades of dramatic economic growth that changed the face of China, this inevitably slowed. A substantial middle class developed with growing middle class aspirations—property and cars, children's education, overseas holidays. Despite controls, a more aggressive news media illuminates political concerns of this increasingly educated, informed, and vocal population: a potential challenge to the centralist control of the state. People are more aware of the wealth and privileges enjoyed by those at the centre of the Party. Such concerns have generated a large number of non-governmental organizations, which although registered are difficult to regulate and whose governance is important.

The Communist Party Plenum in 2013 called for the market to play a decisive role in the economy, while confirming that the state sector should remain the main body of the economy, despite the large number of private enterprises that now generate a significant proportion of China's GDP.

The Plenum emphasized that major industries and their corporations—energy, transport, heavy industry, for example—should remain SOEs with external investment. Other outstanding issues that the Plenum recognized included the need for land reforms, pension problems raised by an ageing population living longer, and the challenge of the floating population of over 200 million, moving from rural areas to the towns, denied rights because they are not registered under the *houkou* system.

Some deregulatory reforms had encouraged freer movement of capital, less involvement by the central bank, and wider use of the small and medium enterprise and over-the-counter stock markets. Rules on insider trading had been tightened and the crack-down on corruption continued. In Shanghai, the creation of a Free Trade Zone provided some tax incentives, the freer conversion of currencies, and allowed foreign companies to invest in industries previously out of bounds.

Commentators on corporate governance in China saw a need to improve board effectiveness, for example, noting the low attendance of independent directors at board meetings. The call was for boards to be more tough-minded business-oversight teams, rather than meetings of collaborators linked to the state and regional authorities.

Corporate governance in India

As with China, history has played a part in the development of corporate governance in India. Originally a member of the British Empire ('the jewel in the Crown'), India benefited from the early creation of government administrative processes, with the rule of law, including a body of company law backed by a reliable judiciary, as did Hong Kong and Singapore. A drawback was the accompanying bureaucracy.

Following independence, the country took a socialist road, with large state-owned enterprises and the public sector dominating the economy. Bureaucracy grew and inefficiency, corruption, and nepotism flourished. By the 1990s, the need for India to develop its business infrastructure and attract capital was recognized. Better corporate governance of companies and improved regulation of its stock markets was needed. In 1992, Parliament created the Securities and Exchange Board of India (SEBI).

The first corporate governance code was published in 1998, by the Confederation of Indian Industry entitled 'Desirable Corporate Governance'. Unlike codes in some other countries, the Confederation's code did not make statements of principle, but addressed specific business issues in India. Focused on the governance of listed companies, the code called for 'professionally competent, independent non-executive directors' to constitute at least 30% of the board if the chairman is a non-executive director and at least 50% where the chairman and the managing director were the same person. Non-executive directors should 'play a material role in corporate decision-making and maximizing long-term shareholder value (becoming) active participants in boards, not passive advisers'. No one should hold directorships in more than ten listed companies. The code also called for audit committees, but it was exhortatory and not endorsed by the regulatory body, nor incorporated into the listing rules.

A year later in 1999, a government committee, chaired by Shri Kumar Manalam Biria, a businessman, released India's National Code on Corporate Governance. Reflecting international standards, the Code was approved by the SEBI and incorporated into stock exchange listing rules.

Corporate governance standards in India's top-tier listed companies, such as Infosys and the major banks, are high. But such commitment is not general. Small and medium capital companies are largely unconvinced of the value of corporate governance activities and expenditures.

As in other parts of the world, interest in corporate governance in India was a reaction to corporate scandals, often involving stock price manipulation, for example the Harshad Mehta scam, the UTI case, and the so-called 'vanishing company scam'. As the Central Vigilance Commissioner, N. Vittal, said in the Tata Memorial Lecture in 2002:

> I find that the legal and administrative environment in India provides excellent scope for corrupt practices in business. As a result, unless a management is committed to be honest and observe the principles of propriety, the atmosphere is too tempting to observe good corporate governance in practice.
>
> Many feel that the situation is no better more than a decade later. In 2002, reflecting international concern at the fallout from the US Enron debacle, the government set up a high-level committee chaired by Shri Naresh Chandra to examine corporate auditing and independent directors. The report called for independent directors to represent at least 50% of the board of listed companies, strengthened the definition of independence, and called for the rotation of audit partners (but not audit firms).

A further committee, chaired by Shri Narayana Murthy, chairman of Infosys, was set up in 2003 by SEBI to 'evaluate the adequacy of existing corporate governance practices'. Audit committees, risk management, director remuneration, codes of conduct, and the role of independent directors were all addressed.

The Indian Companies Act of 1956 was amended in 1999 to improve shareholder rights, and in 2000 to require audit committees. In 2002, a committee reported on a revision of the 1956 Act. In 2005, an expert committee on company law, chaired by Dr J. J. Irani of Tata Industries, reported, leading to the 2013 Companies Act.[2]

In 2007, the government issued guidelines on corporate governance in central public sector enterprises covering the composition of boards, audit committees, management of group companies, accounting standards, and risk management.

In many companies in India, both those in the public sector, multinationals, and private sector companies, boards find themselves dominated by majority shareholders. Pre-emption rights for minority shareholders are frequently ignored. Competent regulators and capital market action are needed to protect minority investors.

In 2013, India introduced a revised Companies Act, sharpening controls, and SEBI improved the corporate governance disclosure norms required of listed companies. Stock exchanges were required to ensure compliance with these disclosure norms.

But corruption remained entrenched, not least in government administration. India ranked 94th out of 177 countries in the 2014 Index of Corruption Perceptions. Distrust of government is high, with bureaucracy and red tape sometimes stifling entrepreneurial flair. The Indian

[2] http://indiacode.nic.in/acts-in-pdf/182013.pdf

Ministry of Company Affairs and SEBI need more competent staff experienced in corporate governance matters.

The chairman of SEBI, U. K. Sinha, commented in 2013 that 'nearly one-fifth of listed companies in India do not comply with basic shareholding reporting norms set by the regulator'. He expressed concern at the quality of filings companies make, and stressed the need for stock exchanges to hire more people to monitor whether companies were complying with the letter and spirit of listing agreements. Poor corporate governance remains a concern for both Indian and international investors, particularly the stock exchanges' failure to take action against companies that fail to meet SEBI standards.

Corporate governance in Russia

Some of the Eastern European transitional economies, including Hungary, Poland, and the former East Germany, took a similar approach to China in privatizing their state enterprises, creating companies in which shares were sold to external strategic investors, often foreign investment institutions.

Russia, however, along with Bulgaria and the Czech Republic, took a different approach. Many Russian citizens were dubious about privatization, holding old Soviet beliefs that industry should be run by the state, that everyone should be guaranteed a job, and that incomes should be controlled. Recognizing the need to overcome such resistance and to make changes irreversible, during the 1990s, the state attempted to transfer ownership to the people through three forms of voucher privatization.

1. The free distribution of vouchers to all Russian citizens, which could be exchanged for company shares or invested in voucher investment funds. Although all citizens were supposed to have equal shares, insiders often benefited, particularly incumbent management, who were given bonus shares to overcome resistance.

2. Investment tenders, in which investors had to make substantial investments to redevelop companies. There was little or no state monitoring or control, which led to deception, with investment proposals that were not undertaken or else were fictitious.

3. Loan-for-shares auctions—the government provided finance from the federal budget for the purchase of shares in public companies that were put up for auction, such as Yukos, Sibneft, and Lukoil. Fraudulent practices, violence, and social injustice were rife, and many of the major businesses that emerged were dominated by relatively few people, many of them now very rich. Small banks evolved into major financial institutions and industrial groups.

Ownership concentration was high, typically involving the previous managers. The minority shareholders, who typically included members of the public and foreign investment institutions, saw their rights violated by these dominant interests.

Some Russian companies were floated on foreign stock exchanges, mainly London and New York. Of course, these companies had to comply with the listing agreements reflecting the corporate governance requirements of the countries concerned, including independent directors, board committees, and corporate governance compliance reports.

The first federal law on joint-stock companies in Russia was enacted in 1995, followed by securities laws in 1996, and laws on the protection of rights and legal interests of investors in the securities market three years later in 1999. Shareholders with at least 2% of the voting rights gained the right to introduce items to the agenda of shareholders' meetings and to nominate candidates for the board. Shareholders with 1% could file a complaint against the board or specific directors for damages to the company caused by their actions. In 1998, a new bankruptcy law was enacted.

But there were problems with implementation, not least because many directors felt that they owed their allegiance not to the shareholders as a whole, but to the controlling share-holders who had nominated and, in effect, appointed them. Although the law called for directors to act reasonably and in good faith towards the company, neither directors nor the courts had relevant experience. Moreover, state interests could take precedence. The need for director training and board development was apparent.

In the early stages of privatization, the state was inevitably involved in the process, but companies tended to adopt the unitary board structure with some independent outside directors, reflecting the US and UK/Commonwealth models based on the rule of law and regulation by the stock market. Unfortunately, the company and securities law that was enacted did not reflect the way in which companies were typically run.

But, in 1998, Russia faced a major financial crisis: the state defaulted on government bonds, the currency was devalued, and rising oil prices provided the opportunity for the existing owners to consolidate their control.

Faced with the domination of many boards by insider and controlling shareholder interests and widespread corruption, there was a call for better understanding of corporate governance. In 2000, a Centre for Business Ethics and Corporate Governance was founded to encourage corporate governance reform in Russia. The OECD, through its Centre for Co-operation with Non-members, offered advice and created the Russian Corporate Governance Roundtable, which brought together an influential network of Russian and international policymakers. The Roundtable produced a White Paper for reform in corporate governance in Russia in 2002 and a report on improving the transparency of related party transactions in 2005. The International Finance Corporation, working with the World Bank, also produced a corporate governance manual for Russia, including drafts for a corporate charter, director contracts, and by-laws on shareholder meetings, the corporate secretary, proxy voting, and the board of directors. Russia also formed an Independent Directors Association.

Under the company law and corporate governance code recommendations, companies are governed by the general shareholders' meeting, which elects the members of the board through cumulative voting, a board of directors (sometimes confusingly called the supervisory board) with both independent directors and management directors, and an executive (or management) committee. The audit committee reports to the board, the chairman of which is not allowed to be the head of the executive committee.

The need for sound corporate governance is recognized in Russia. There is more transparency, standards for corporate governance are more widely understood, and losses through unfair practices have been reduced. A new Russian Code of Corporate Conduct[3] was published in 2013.

[3] www.ecgi.org/codes/documents/final_code_english.pdf

But, under Vladimir Putin, who has been both president and prime minister twice since 1999, the role of the state has expanded, the substance of democracy has disappeared, the press muzzled, and opponents imprisoned. Government influence over companies has increased. In some cases ownership has been transferred back to the state by expropriation or by acquisition in the market.

The current corporate governance situation in Russia is well summarized by KPMG:[4]

> Corporate governance in Russia is characterized by a high degree of concentration of ownership and the leading role of majority shareholders, frequently including the state, in company management. The existence of attributes such as the low level of protection of shareholder rights, the nominal nature of the board of directors, and also the lack of bodies responsible for internal control and audit that are independent from executive management, is cited in numerous studies and expert comments.

Corporate governance in Brazil

Brazil's economy boomed until around 2012. Then it faltered disastrously. Rising costs, lack of improvement in business efficiency, and failure to re-invest the profits of the boom years were cited. So were a Byzantine tax system, endemic poverty, and corruption. With tax rates and state pension costs dramatically high, economic growth in Brazil stalled.

In Brazil, many companies are either state-owned or family-dominated. The Brazilian Institute of Corporate Governance was founded in 1995. The Brazilian Code of Best Practice of Corporate Governance was published by the Institute in 1999. Now in its fourth edition (2009), it serves as the primary reference for corporate governance in Brazil. Brazilian company law and the Brazilian Code have three unusual corporate governance features—the fiscal council, the family council, and the advisory board.

A *fiscal council* can be provided by the company's constitution or established at the request of shareholders. The role of the fiscal council is to inspect the work of the board, to review the activities of the company, to ensure compliance with legal and statutory duties, and to provide an opinion on the annual management report and on board proposals for investment projects, changes to capital, and dividend payouts. The fiscal council is required, at least quarterly, to analyse and comment on the balance sheet and other financial statements, and to provide an opinion to the shareholders' general meeting on board proposals. Fiscal councils have the right to consult with outside professionals, and are typically recognized as adding value to the company's owners by providing independent control.

The Brazilian Code encourages the creation of a *family council* in family-dominated companies. Its role is to discuss family issues and the alignment of its members' expectations with those of the other shareholders. Family councils enable boundaries to be set between family and company interests, preserve longer-term family values, and formalize succession planning for family members in both management and on the board. Family councils can also consider issues of inheritance and the transfer of property, which are inappropriate in shareholders' meetings.

[4] www.kpmg.com/CH/en/auditcommittee/newsletter/Documents/pub-20130916-ac-news-43-article-09-en.pdf

The constitutions of some Brazilian companies also provide for an *advisory board*. The Code suggests that:

> The existence of an advisory board, preferably made up of independent members, is good practice, particularly for organizations taking the first steps in the adoption of good practices of corporate governance. It allows independent members to contribute to the organization and gradually improve its corporate governance.

The Code calls for the advisory board's performance to be guided by the same principles that govern the board of directors. The ideas of the fiscal board, the family council, and the advisory board might provide approaches to corporate governance for other developing countries.

Corporate governance in Hong Kong and Singapore

In Hong Kong and Singapore, corporate governance is a fascinating melange of Anglo-American and Asian ideas. We briefly reviewed the essence in Chapter 6. The corporate governance systems in both territories are an outgrowth of British company law and are among the more advanced in Asia.

Hong Kong

When Hong Kong became a Special Administrative Region (SAR) of China in 1997, it kept its currency (tied to the US dollar), legal system, and institutions including the Securities and Exchange Commission, the Institute of Certified Public Accountants, and the Law Society. On the Hong Kong stock market most listed companies are either family firms with control kept firmly within the family, or mainland China-based corporations, plus a handful of large trading companies. Although the Hong Kong regulatory authorities require a minimum of three independent non-executive directors, the heads of some family companies see little value in them. Their secretive, authoritarian, and family-centric approach to business does not lend itself to outside directors who might disagree with their decisions. Furthermore, evidence of abnormal dealing prior to acquisition or merger activity has suggested insider dealing. Incidentally, most Hong Kong-listed Chinese family companies are incorporated in Bermuda or the Cayman Islands, so that, while Hong Kong's listing rules and takeover code apply, Hong Kong companies' ordinances do not (other than those applying to overseas companies). As the Far Eastern Economic Review commented:

> Instead of strategy, the successful Hong Kong businessman has a *modus operandi* that is orientated towards the short term: endless opportunism is backed by a determination to narrow the odds. Their empires grow amoebae-like, feeding on whatever comes to hand. The only predictable direction of growth is outwards.

In 2014, after many years of deliberation, Hong Kong (SAR) introduced a new Companies' Ordinance designed to simplify and rationalize company law. Among many other provisions, the new law extended the exposure of directors and 'other responsible persons' to prosecution for failing to exercise 'due care, skill, and diligence'. The law also introduced a new solvency test that companies needed to meet.

Singapore

The Singapore corporate governance code, like those of Hong Kong and most Asian countries, is based on a 'comply or explain' approach, and calls for independent directors, audit committees, director training, and so on. Compliance is high, although companies listed on the SESDAQ market (Stock Exchange of Singapore Dealing and Automated Quotation System)—now called the Catalyst market—tend to meet only the minimum requirements, unlike companies listed on the Singapore main board. In Singapore, the government is a significant player in the market, using government funds and those of the state pension fund to own and control significant companies incorporated there.

Corporate governance in South Korea: the *chaebol*

Chaebol groups in South Korea developed following the Second World War, when the government advanced loans on attractive terms to family-based firms to stimulate economic revival. Over time, some of these family firms prospered and became large groupings of associated companies. Even *chaebol* companies that are listed are often still controlled by the dominant owner-family interests. Even though companies attracted outside capital, family domination was maintained predominantly through insider boards and cross-ownership with subsidiary companies.

Attempts to introduce independent outside directors into South Korean boards have had only limited effect against the entrenched power of the existing block owners. At times, this has led to protests from employees and social unrest. In recent years, the South Korean government sought to reduce the power of the *chaebol* by requiring them to divest some of their interests. But before the financial and economic crisis of 1997, success was limited. Subsequently, the *chaebol* found it increasingly difficult to compete with other Asian producers, because of their tradition of lifetime employment and militant trade unions, and governance changes were forced on them.

Corporate governance in Japan

In the 1970/80s, Japanese business methods were applauded by Western business schools; with 'just-in-time' manufacturing procurement systems, worker participation methods, and *ringi* decision-making throughout organizations. Then Japan hit more than two decades of deflation, poor economic growth, and poor corporate performance.

Corporate governance in Japanese companies had not evolved from the hierarchical, insider culture of the networked *keiretsu* groups, already described in Chapter 6. The result was highlighted by the case of Olympus, the optical-equipment maker, in 2012 (Case study 17.1), in which the British President/CEO was unceremoniously dumped by his Japanese board for exposing fraud, without any comment from Japanese shareholders.

But, at last, Japanese companies are coming under more outside governance scrutiny. Among a number of reforms designed to restart the sluggish economy, the government of Prime Minister Shinzo Abe launched a new corporate governance code calling for independent, outside directors on company boards. Like corporate governance codes in the West, adherence to the code would be voluntary, but companies would report whether they had complied with the code or explain why if they had not. The government also introduced a new stewardship code giving shareholders more powers to monitor the boards of companies in which they invest.

Together, the new corporate governance code and the stewardship code promise to change corporate governance in Japan. Previous attempts to bring about change had been thwarted by the Japanese employers' federation, the *keidanren;* but facing falling influence with government, the federation seems more likely to comply. Moreover, with around a third of investment in major firms now coming from abroad, companies are under more pressure to conform to international norms. A number of major companies, including Canon, Toyota, and Nippon Steel, have now brought in outsider directors.

However, corporate governance cultures take time to evolve. The existence of outside directors does not, of itself, guarantee that the dominating power of executives at the top of companies will be broken. Independent directors could be little more than token members of ceremonial boards, while the real power, for example over succession, remains with the chairman and his henchmen.

Corporate governance in the Middle East and North Africa

The states that are typically grouped together as the Middle East and North Africa (MENA) are:

Algeria	Jordan	Morocco	Tunisia
Bahrein	Kuwait	Oman	United Arab Emirates (UAE)
			(Abu Dhabi, Dubai, and five other states)
Egypt	Lebanon	Qatar	Saudi Arabia

Some of these countries are, of course, oil-rich, while others have relatively low GDPs with slow industrial growth. In recent years, the oil-producing countries, benefiting from rising oil prices, have generated large surpluses, which have been deposited abroad. Banking reforms have attempted to channel some of these savings into local growth, but domestic financial markets are emergent. States also appreciate the need to attract inward investment and therefore recognize the importance of sound corporate governance. The capital markets are small and illiquid, but slowly evolving. Consequently, the market for corporate control is poor. Of course, there are exceptions to such general observations: for example, Dubai made massive investments in tourism and property, while attempting to become an international financial centre, although subsequently running into financial difficulty.

Businesses in the region can be typified as having:

- concentrated ownership, with strong family ownership of both private and listed companies or state ownership;
- dominant family oversight and control, with leadership from the head of the family, entrepreneurial decision-making, opaque communications, and relationship-based trading;

- debt financing in which bank financing is often more than shareholders' equity;
- banking sector equity investment, with banks holding significant shares in companies.

The legal underpinnings around the region vary interestingly. In the Gulf states, Egypt, and Jordan, jurisdictions are orientated towards common law, reflecting earlier UK/Commonwealth influences. Elsewhere, jurisdictions have adopted European-style civil law. Throughout the region, company and securities laws exist, but are evolving to meet changing circumstances.

However, the most significant legal influence is the overarching Islamic *shariah* law introducing religious rules and interpretations, which can affect attitudes towards contracts, property rights, and borrowing. Essentially, finance is based on the principle that charging interest is forbidden and that both sides of a deal must share risks.

The framework for corporate governance is broadly in place, although development is at an early stage and implementation and enforcement varied. Government securities commissions have also created different sets of rules. The OECD, through the MENA/OECD Investment Programme, has sponsored an important study of corporate governance in the region, analysing the position in each country and recommending developments. Essentially, the OECD has recommended the adoption of rules-based corporate governance because of the state of financial markets, the lack of experience, and poor corporate discipline. In other words, it calls for legal and regulatory control, not self-control by management, shareholders, and creditors.

As the OECD has concluded:

> For the countries of the Middle East and North Africa (MENA), private investment, both domestic and foreign, is needed to provide new engines of growth and dynamism. The biggest challenge for MENA countries lies in strengthening the process of change, maintaining, supporting and tracking the progress of policy implementation as well as providing capacity building assistance.

So, in retrospect, we see around the world how corporate governance is conditioned by local cultures: heritage and expectations about the way business should be done; the legal system and the reliability of the judiciary; the standing of the governance infrastructure; and the economic, social, and, in some cases, religious circumstances.

Case studies

 Case study 12.1 China Sinopec

China Petroleum & Chemical Corporation (Sinopec) is a China-based integrated energy and chemical company. Sinopec was set up in 2000, under the Company Law of the People's Republic of China, and that year issued 16.78 billion shares in Hong Kong, New York, and London, raising close to US$3.4 billion. In 2001, the company floated a further 2.8 billion 'A' shares on Shanghai Stock Exchange. In 2007, Sinopec's total number of shares was 86.7 billion, of which 75.84% were held by the state, 19.35% by international shareholders, and 4.81% by investors in China.

The business covers oil and gas exploration, development, production and marketing, oil refining, production and sales of petrochemicals, chemical fibres, chemical fertilizers, and other chemical products. It is China's largest producer of oil products and major petrochemical products and the second largest producer of crude oil. Sinopec is a dominant brand in China, and its gas stations, which are modern with courteous staff, are found all around the country. Sinopec was ranked 17th in the Global Top 500, by its core assets and operating revenue, in the Fortune magazine list of 2006.

Similar to its international peers, Sinopec has set up a standardized structure of corporate governance and adopted a management system of centralized decision-making, delegated authorities in management, and business operations handled by specialized business units. It has more than eighty subsidiaries and branches, including wholly owned equity holding and equity participating companies, engaging in oil and gas exploration and production, refining, chemicals, marketing, R&D, and foreign trade.

Sinopec bases its corporate governance on the Code of Corporate Governance for Listed Companies issued by the CSRC, the Company Law of the People's Republic of China, the Mandatory Provisions for the Articles of Association of Companies to be Listed Overseas, the Guidelines for the Articles of Association of Listed Companies, Standards of Corporate Governance of Listed Companies, Sinopec's articles of association, and other governing regulations in the countries where Sinopec is listed. In China, the regulation and enforcement of a company's corporate governance is primarily the responsibility of the board of directors and the supervisory committee.

Prior to its listing, Sinopec restructured its board to satisfy both overseas regulators and the state government. It installed a two-tier system, with a board of directors and a supervisory board (which Sinopec translates in English as the 'supervisory committee').

The board of directors has eleven members, with a chairman, a vice-chairman, a president, three senior vice-presidents, two executive directors, and three independent non-executive directors.

There is an audit committee, which reports to the management board, not to the supervisory committee. The supervisory committee has nine members, with a chairman, four employee representative supervisors, and four other members.

....

Discussion question

1. What is your opinion of the corporate governance structure at Sinopec? Consider the role of the supervisory committee, its relationship with the board of directors, and (unlike the continental European model of the two-tier board) the inclusion of three independent non-executive members.

(For more information on Sinopec, see its informative website http://english.sinopec.com)

 Case study 12.2   Yukos and Mikhail Khodorkovsky

The Yukos Oil Company, founded by Mikhail B. Khodorkovsky in 1993, acquired vast assets from the privatization of Russia's state enterprises. Yukos owned and operated oil and gas fields, oil refineries, and pipelines across Russia and Central Europe, and was the largest non-state oil company in Russia, producing around 20% of Russian oil. At its peak in mid-2003, Yukos was worth more than US$40 billion.

Khodorkovsky was keen to introduce Western style corporate governance to his vast Yukos group. In 2000, he had the *Economist Pocket Director*, an ABC of corporate governance and effective board-level direction, translated into Russian, adding a personal foreword and a discussion of governance in Yukos.

At its peak in mid-2003, Yukos was vastly rich. But within two years the company had been seized by the state, with the company claiming 'an unprecedented campaign of illegal, discriminatory, and disproportionate tax claims escalating into raids and confiscation, culminating in intimidation and arrests . . .', and Mikhail Khodorkovsky was in jail in Siberia. The Yukos story is long, complex, and still controversial. In this vignette case, we see the need for the state's approval in Russia for the exercise of corporate governance power.

The Yeltsin years

Following the dissolution of the Soviet Union, Boris Yeltsin became President of Russia in 1991, with a mission to turn a Communist centrally planned economy into a capitalist market economy. The 1990s proved to be a turbulent period in Russian history. The economic reforms came too slowly and the living standards of many people were devastated, especially those dependent on Soviet-era state subsidies.

In 1998, Russia's economy collapsed, bringing economic chaos, humiliation, and suffering. The state was unable to pay its workers. With their personal savings destroyed, millions of Russians were plunged into poverty. The currency fell 70%, Russia defaulted on its foreign debt, and the International Monetary Fund (IMF) bailed the country out with loans of US$40 billion, but with demanding conditions.

However, a few people were able to enrich themselves during the decade. Called oligarchs, or the 'novi Russki', they benefited from the privatization of Russian state assets. They became super-rich, lived extravagantly, imported expensive cars, and travelled the world. The era also saw the rise of a middle class, unthinkable in Soviet days. Unexpectedly, Yeltsin resigned at the end of 1999, passing the presidency to Vladimir Putin, a former secret service chief.

The Putin era

Putin's first term of office was a significant success. He was able to end the chaotic excesses of the Yeltsin years and brought millions out of poverty. Under the watchful eye of the IMF, Russia repaid her international loans. The people developed a new confidence and, in 2004, Putin was re-elected with a huge majority.

As the journal *Prospect* said in 2005:

> Putin agrees that the Soviet system did not work, but still calls its collapse a tragedy. He is probably closer to the thoughts and feelings of ordinary people than any other Russian leader in history. Putin has never disguised his intention to build a modified version of the authoritarian, centralized Russian state under which the Russians have been governed, mostly badly, for six centuries . . .

Actions in the Crimea and the Ukraine backed by Putin in 2014 support this thesis.

Inevitably, Putin saw the privatized entities as a problem and thought that the oligarchs were a potential threat to his plans. Khodorkovsky was arrested at gun-point in October 2003 on charges of fraud and tax evasion. Commentators suggested, however, that the real reason was Khodorkovsky's support for political opposition parties and championing an anti-corruption campaign. He was held in a gulag, where Russia's once richest man worked in the prison sewing shop. Tried and found guilty on further charges at the end of his first sentence, he was finally released in December 2013. Now outside Russia, he wrote a short book[5] on his prison experiences. He concluded that Russia is 'a society where goodness and empathy are seen as synonymous with madness'.

Discussion question

1. What lessons might be learned from the Yukos case about corporate governance in Russia?

[5] Khodorkovsky, Mikhail (2014) *My Fellow Prisoners*. Penguin Books, London.

References and further reading

Chen, Jian (2005) *Corporate Governance in China*. RoutledgeCurzon, New York/Abingdon, UK.

Clarke, Thomas and Jean-François Chanlat (eds) (2009) *European Corporate Governance*. Routledge, New York/Abingdon, UK.

Clarke, Thomas (2007) *International Corporate Governance: A Comparative Approach*. Routledge, New York/Abingdon, UK.

De Groot, Cornelis (2009) *Corporate Governance as a Limited Legal Concept (European Company Law)*. Kluwer Law, Netherlands.

Gul, F. A. and J. S. L. Tsui (2004) *The Governance of East Asian Corporations: Post Asian Financial Crisis*. Palgrave Macmillan, London.

Hadjiemmanuil, Christos and Joseph Jude Norton (eds) (2009) *Corporate Governance Post-Enron: Comparative and International Perspectives (Studies in International Financial, Economic and Technology Law)*. British Institute of International and Comparative Law, London.

Morris, Ian (2011) *Why the West Rules—For Now: Patterns of History and What They Reveal About the Future*, Profile Books, London.

Projects and exercises

1. Use the Internet to research the governance practices in one of the countries in this chapter. Draft a report on the development and present state of corporate governance in that country for a potential major investor.

2. Research the Internet to draft a note for the owner-manager of a large family company owned by two generations of the family, on the benefits and costs of a family council.

3. Identify some major companies listed in South Korea. Choose one and research its approach to corporate governance using the Internet.

Self-test questions

1. In the market for Chinese listed companies, what are the differences between A shares, B shares, N shares, L shares, and H shares?

2. Distinguish the roles in China of the SASAC and the CSRC.

3. What are the five types of corporate enterprise identified in the text?

4. What is a major problem facing boards in many Indian companies? How does the Asian Corporate Governance Association rate Indian corporate governance?

5. In Russia, what have been the significant changes in corporate governance under the presidency of Vladimir Putin?

6. What are the unusual corporate governance features in Brazilian company law and corporate governance codes?

7. Hong Kong is a Special Administrative Region (SAR) of China. Do Hong Kong listed companies have to follow the Chinese corporate governance rules laid down by the CSRC?

8. Who often controls listed *chaebol* companies in South Korea? How is that control maintained?

9. What typifies the governance of businesses in the MENA region?

10. What is the most significant legal influence on corporate governance in the MENA countries?

Part Three

Practices

13 Board Membership: Directors' appointment, roles, and remuneration

 Learning Outcomes

In which we review:

- The appointment of directors
- Desirable attributes in a director
- Core competencies of a director
- Roles that directors play
- Directors' duties, rights, and powers
- Directors' disclosures, service contracts, and agreements
- Directors' remuneration

The appointment of directors

Director appointments arise:

- on the initial incorporation of a company;
- on reappointment at the expiry of a director's term of office;
- to fill a vacancy; and
- on the creation of an additional directorship.

The rotation of directors

Companies' articles of association typically lay down the terms of service for directors, including how long they will act before coming up for re-election and when that should occur. In the past, many companies' articles called for a fixed proportion of the directors to retire each year. For example, if directors' appointments were for three years, a third would stand down each year, offering themselves for re-election if eligible. It was felt that this practice provided stability, since there would always be a proportion of directors on the board with experience of the company's business, enabling a longer-term strategic perspective to be taken. Critics of these so-called 'staggered' or 'classified' boards complain that, in a poorly performing company, underper-forming directors become entrenched. Because the entire board cannot be replaced at a single election, staggered boards effectively block hostile takeover bids, and can be used as a takeover defence. Annual election of all directors allows a change of control through a single successful proxy contest. Resolutions opposing staggered boards and calling for declassification have been high on shareholder activists' calls for change in the United States in recent years.

The size of boards

Many articles of association put upper and lower limits on board size. Some company law jurisdictions also have rules on board size, particularly the minimum number of directors; some prohibiting single director boards. Others do not allow corporate directors, insisting that directors are real persons. Where corporate directors are allowed, the directors of the corporate director take on the responsibilities of the directorship.

In practice, the case is often made for additional directors to join a board to remedy perceived weaknesses, to add necessary skills and experience, or to bring new knowledge or contacts. The case is seldom heard for a reduction in numbers. The ideal number, obviously, depends on the circumstances in each case, but boards can become too large. Beyond a certain number, psychologists say between eight and ten, a board ceases to be a cohesive, decision-making body. The time each director has to contribute to discussion is limited. Directors are more likely to form cliques or cabals. Chairmanship becomes difficult, so that leading the board to a consensus is more problematic.

Retirement, disqualification, and removal of directors

Company law in some jurisdictions puts an age limit on directors, often seventy. Elsewhere, the view is taken that this is ageist and that many older people have the wisdom, experience, and abilities to make significant contributions to companies. The important factor is to ensure that older directors are making that contribution and not being re-elected out of a misplaced sense of respect or loyalty. Many articles of association also have rules on directors' ages, calling for shareholder approval. Company law often imposes a minimum age on appointments to the board, frequently sixteen or eighteen.

Company law can also disqualify certain people from serving as directors, including becoming bankrupt, mentally ill, or being disqualified by the courts from being a director. Disqualification by the courts usually follows a guilty verdict of an offence in running a company or persistently defaulting in the filing of official returns.

In principle, the shareholders of a company have the right to appoint and to remove their directors. In practice, this can prove to be difficult. Subject to company law and the company's articles, members can propose a resolution calling for the removal of directors, and seek a shareholders' meeting to consider this resolution. Much depends on the voting power of the recalcitrant shareholders. The incumbent board may resist, adopt delaying tactics, and circulate contrary information at the company's expense, while requiring the challenging shareholders to cover the costs of their campaign.

How are directors appointed?

In the original 19th-century model of the limited-liability company, the founder of the business, the existing directors, and perhaps the shareholders suggested possible directors. The shareholders then met, and a decision was reached. This is still the case in most private companies: decisions are taken by dominant shareholders, such as family members in a family firm, or the directors of the holding company in a corporate group.

But as listed companies became larger, more diverse and geographically spread, so did their shareholders. With a large number of shareholders located around the world, with varying interests in the company, it was no longer feasible for them to influence decisions on the choice of directors. Power had shifted from shareholders to directors, as Berle and Means had shown in 1932. Directors of major listed companies were now nominated by the chairman and existing directors, and then routinely approved by shareholders in their annual general meeting. Critics complained that boards became self-perpetuating clubs of like-minded people, routinely chosen from small networks of influence, typically those who came from similar backgrounds to themselves. In the United States, recommendations from business contacts, fellow members of the country club, or business school fraternity held sway. In England, director appointments were influenced by 'the old school tie' and social standing such as a knighthood. In France, those educated in the elite *grandes écoles* dominated both boardroom and government.

The board-level nomination committee is an attempt to overcome this dilemma. This is a standing subcommittee of the main board, made up wholly, or mainly, of independent non-executive directors, called on to recommend new directors. Relying on independent directors is intended to avoid a dominant director, such as the chairman or chief executive officer (CEO), pushing through his or her own preferred candidates.

Unfortunately, the supposed independence of outside directors on the nomination committee can be illusory. If the committee's members have themselves been selected by the chairman, and have worked with him or her for years, they are likely to feel an allegiance towards him or her and support his or her candidates. On the other hand, it can be argued that newly appointed directors need to be acceptable to the chairman if they are to work in harmony as part of an effective board team.

In the United Kingdom, Hong Kong, and some other countries, although listed companies have adopted most of the requirements of the corporate governance codes, the requirement to have a nominating committee has been resisted by some. This is not surprising, since the right to influence appointments to the board goes to the very heart of corporate power.

Shareholders in public listed companies still have little opportunity to influence the nomination of new directors, unless they hold a significant proportion of the voting shares. Various proposals have been put forward to enable shareholders to nominate directors. Some would have the institutional investors play a larger role; others would allow shareholders to create and vote on a 'slate' of directors, including those they had proposed. Another idea, from Shann Turnbull, is for shareholders to form a shareholders' committee, which would represent all of the shareholders in dealings with the company, including the nomination of new directors.

Desirable attributes in a director

In the first part of this book, we focused on corporate governance principles; in the second, on corporate governance policies. But behind the corporate constitutions, board structures, and corporate governance codes are people—people who bring a wide range of prejudices, political behaviours, and power plays to board affairs. So what personal attributes are needed to be a successful, professional director?

The primary prerequisite for every director is *integrity*. Directors are stewards of the interests of the company (that is, of the entire body of shareholders). The enterprise does not belong to the directors. They hold it in trust for the owners to whom they owe a fiduciary duty to act openly and honestly in their interests. This applies whether the company is a family business, with a few shareholders, or a vast, listed company.

What does integrity mean? It means being ethically aware, able to distinguish right from wrong, and able to judge corporate behaviour accordingly. It implies honesty, fairness, and sound moral principles. It means acting in the company interest, not self-interest, resisting the temptation to make a personal gain to the detriment of the company. Integrity also means being able to recognize and declare a conflict of interest. Essentially, integrity means acting honestly for the benefit of the company. A director with integrity is trusted, which is basic because the very concept of the company is based on trust.

In law, a company is a legal entity and enjoys many of the rights of an individual person. But, unlike a real person, a company does not have a conscience. The board has to act as the corporate conscience. Clearly, that means ensuring that the company obeys the laws of the jurisdictions in which it operates. Further, the board creates the company's value system, its corporate character establishing the way the whole organization operates, over and above just staying within the law.

In practice, as we have seen, many boards produce a formal statement of their corporate mission and the core values to which they aspire. In some cases, these statements are no more than pious aspirations, which do little to affect the way in which the company is run. In other cases, however, such mission statements can lead to rigorous policies, approved and monitored by the board on, for example, how the company treats its customers, its relations with employees, and its commitment to corporate social responsibility. The Microsoft statement of its corporate mission and values (see Corporate governance in action 13.1) provides an example.

In addition to integrity, high-calibre directors demonstrate other personal qualities. These can be summarized as intellect, character, and personality.

Intellect is what, in Oxford colleges, they call having 'a good mind'. It combines an appropriate level of intelligence, the ability to think at different levels of abstraction, and the imagination to see situations from different perspectives, rather than always seeing things from a fixed viewpoint. A sound intellect is able to exercise independent judgement, to think originally, and to act creatively.

Character traits, what some call 'strength of character', include being independently minded, objective, and impartial. A director needs to be capable of moving towards consensus. Yet, from time to time, a director needs to be tough-minded, tenacious, and resilient, with the courage to make a stand. Further, a director needs to be results-orientated, with a balanced approach to risk—neither risk-averse nor rash. Finally, some might add wisdom or just plain common sense to useful director character traits (even though common sense is not all that common).

Desirable *personality* traits in a director include the ability to interact positively with others, which from time to time may call for openness, flexibility, sensitivity, diplomacy,

Corporate governance in action 13.1   Microsoft corporate mission and values

Our Mission

At Microsoft, we work to help people and businesses throughout the world realize their full potential. This is our mission. Everything we do reflects this mission and the values that make it possible.

Our Values

As a company, and as individuals, we value:

- Integrity and honesty.
- Passion for customers, for our partners, and for technology.
- Openness and respectfulness.
- Taking on big challenges and seeing them through.
- Constructive self-criticism, self-improvement, and personal excellence.
- Accountability to customers, shareholders, partners, and employees for commitments, results, and quality

persuasiveness, the ability to motivate, and a sense of humour. Such interpersonal abilities are particularly important in interactions with the chairman and boardroom peers. Other desirable personality traits include being a sound listener and a good communicator, as well as being politically sensitive.

A successful director looks ahead, anticipates problems, and can articulate possible solutions. He or she is open, welcomes questioning, and seeks feedback. But he or she also listens, tries to understand others' points of view, and seeks consensus. Overall, he or she is reliable and trusted by his or her chairman and peers. On the other hand, poor directors tend to adopt a negative attitude, offering platitudes, and fail to face up to serious issues. Strategic thinking is replaced by reliance on past successes and rigorous risk analysis by hope. Obviously, an independent outside director needs to be genuinely independent. As the Cadbury Report put it, 'independent of management and free from any business or other relationships which could materially interfere with the exercise of their independent judgement'.

These attributes tend to be inherent in people by the time they are nominated for a board appointment, having been culturally determined and acquired over a lifetime. By contrast, there are certain core competencies that a director needs, which can be developed or acquired through director induction programmes, director training, and director development and updating.

A committee, chaired by Lord Nolan in the United Kingdom, produced a set of principles to guide the holders of public office in the United Kingdom. These principles can be readily applied to company directors in fulfilling their fiduciary duty. See Corporate Governance in Action 13.2.

Corporate governance in action 13.2   Lord Nolan's Seven Principles of Public Life

1. Selflessness—Holders of public office should serve the public interest, and not seek gains for their friends.
2. Integrity—They should not place themselves under financial obligation to outsiders who might influence their duties.
3. Objectivity—They should award public appointments and contracts on merit.
4. Accountability—They should submit themselves to the appropriate scrutiny.
5. Openness—They should give reasons for their decisions.
6. Honesty—They should declare conflicts of interest.
7. Leadership—They should support these principles by personal example.

Core competencies of a director

Every corporate entity and every governing body is different, and each director brings a different set of experience, skills, and knowledge to the board. But, in the aggregate, every board needs to have a mix of capabilities that provide a balanced and well-qualified team relevant to that board and that company. So every director needs to have some basic core competencies appropriate to the type, location, and scale of the enterprise. What experience, skills, and knowledge should a director have?

The *experience* of outside directors should be used to supplement the knowledge available to the board, not to second-guess the executives in the company. For example, a director could bring experience about corporate governance, board procedures, or strategy formulation and policymaking from other (non-competing) companies. Or a director might have experience of overseas markets, frontier technologies, international finance, or other areas that supplement the experience of the existing board.

The essential director-level *skills* include:

- strategic reasoning, perception, and vision;
- a critical faculty capable of quantitative and qualitative analysis and financial interpretation;
- planning and decision-making capabilities;
- communication and interpersonal skills;
- network and political abilities.

Directors also need appropriate *knowledge* of the enterprise, its business and board-level activities, as well as relevant information about the company's political, economic, social, and technological contexts. If directors are to make sense of board information and contribute meaningfully to board discussions, they must have basic knowledge about the company itself, its business and the company's financials.

Knowledge of the company includes:

- a clear understanding of the basis of power (who the shareholders are and where the power lies to change membership of the governing body);
- the basis of law under which the company operates and what the governance rules and regulations are (for a limited company, these are company law and the company's memorandum and articles of association, plus the listing regulations for a listed company);
- the board structure, membership and directors' personalities;
- the board processes, including the use of board committees, the focus of board and committee activities, and the nature of board information.

An awareness of the history of the entity can also be helpful in understanding the board culture, interpreting the current situation, and appreciating the perspectives of the chairman and other board members.

Knowledge of the business embraces an understanding of the basic business activities and processes: its purpose and aims; its strengths and weaknesses, and how it measures success; the field of its operations (including markets, competitors, and its current operating context); the strategies being pursued; the structure of the organization; its culture, management, and people; and the form of management control and management control systems. Risk assessment is an important aspect of the board's role and all directors need to know where the enterprise is exposed to risk and its nature. Increasingly, knowledge of the company's stakeholders and its approach to corporate social responsibility and sustainability should form part of directors' knowledge base.

Knowledge of the financials includes knowing how the company is financed, a sound appreciation of its annual accounts and directors' reports, knowledge of emerging trends in key financial ratios, the criteria used in investment appraisals, the calibre of financial controls, and who the auditors are. Many board-level reports are presented in financial terms and the ability both to interpret them and to appreciate their strengths and weaknesses is important. It is not necessary to be an accountant to be a good director; indeed, some might argue the reverse! But an ability to appreciate the financial aspects of the company is vital.

Roles that directors play

Given their various personal attributes and different competencies, directors inevitably make a variety of contributions to their boards and can play a number of roles. Some of these roles contribute to the performance aspects of the board's work (strategy formulation and policymaking); others contribute to the conformance aspects (executive supervision and accountability).

The following are examples of some performance-orientated roles that directors play.

- *Bringing wider business and board experience* to the identification, discussion and decision-making. Identifying issues that the board, not management, should be handling. Directors tend to respect the wisdom of the director who brings to bear accumulated knowledge and experience in business and elsewhere on issues facing the board. As the Cadbury Report put it, 'the board should include non-executive directors of sufficient calibre and number for their views to carry significant weight in the board's decisions'. Long-serving directors may well find themselves cast in this role by newer board colleagues. Accumulated wisdom can, of course, have limitations in rapidly changing situations.

- *Adding specialist knowledge, skills, and know-how* to board deliberations. Here, a director relies on his or her particular professional training, skills, and knowledge to make a contribution. For example, the specialism might be in the realm of accountancy, banking, engineering, finance, or law, or it could stem from specialist knowledge of a particular market, technology, or functional area, such as marketing, manufacturing, or personnel. In some newer, growing companies, outside directors are appointed to the board specifically to provide such specialist inputs until such time as the company can afford to acquire such skills in-house at the executive level. When a board is relying on such expertise, it is important to ensure that the director remains up to date in the subject, which can sometimes prove difficult for those operating at board level.

- *Being the source of external information* for board discussions—a window on the world for other directors. The director is used as a source of information on issues relevant to board discussions. Usually, this will be on matters external to the company, such as insights into market opportunities, new technologies, industry developments, financial and economic concerns, or international matters. Obviously, it is essential that the information is relevant, accurate, and current. This is often a role specifically sought from outside directors, who are in a position to obtain such information through their other day-to-day activities. A danger is that directors, chosen because of their access to specific information, lose touch with it.

- *Being a figurehead or an ambassador for the company*, being able to represent the company in the outside world. The director represents the company in the external arena: for example, in meetings with fund managers and financial analysts, or in trade and industry gatherings. The chairman of the board often takes on this responsibility, perhaps being invited to join public committees, commissions, and the governing bodies of important public institutions, as well as joining the boards of other, non-competing companies. These days, this role can be taken by the director identified as the senior independent non-executive director. For many companies, a figurehead is increasingly important in dealing with the media.

- *Connecting the board to networks of useful people* not otherwise available to the board. This can be an important role for outside directors, who are able through their personal contacts to connect the board and top management to networks of potentially useful people and organizations. For example, the director might be well placed to forge contacts in the world of politics and government, to link the company with relevant banking, finance, or stock exchange connections, or to make introductions within industry or international trade. Retiring politicians are sometimes offered directorships on the assumption that they have useful contacts and influence in the corridors of power. Such a role may also provide advice on succession in the board and in top management.

- *Providing status to the board and the company, adding capability, reputation, and position.* This role is not as significant today as it was a few years ago. In the past, eminent public figures were often invited to join boards just to add status, rather than any specific contribution they could make to board deliberations. Previous service as a US Senator or a knighthood in the United Kingdom almost guaranteed an invitation to join the board of a public company in the past. But these days boards need professionalism ahead of prestige. However, the status role can be useful at times; for example when a particular listed company faced a financial crisis, the market was reassured when a well-known financier joined the board. Exposure to litigation may now deter some public figures from accepting directorships. However, even today, if a company has been experiencing problems, confidence may be restored if a high-profile, well-respected figure joins the board.

The following are examples of some conformance-orientated roles that directors play.

- *Providing independent judgement,* the ability to see issues in their totality and from various perspectives, leading to objective judgement—in other words, 'helicopter vision'. This can be a vital contribution of the outside director, who, obviously, has the opportunity to see board matters from an external and independent point of view. As the Cadbury Report suggested, 'non-executive directors should bring an independent judgement to bear on issues of strategy, performance, resources, including key appointments and standards of conduct'. Such an objective evaluation of top management performance can overcome the tunnel vision sometimes found in those too closely involved with the situation, or the myopia brought on by being personally affected by the outcome. Overall, providing independent judgement brings wise counsel that leads to better decisions.

- *Being a catalyst for change,* questioning existing assumptions, introducing new ideas and approaches, and stimulating developments. This role can be played by a director who questions the board's assumptions, and makes others rethink situations. Catalysts point out that what appears to be an incontrovertible truth to some board members is, in fact, rooted in some questionable beliefs about the company, its markets, or its competitors. They highlight inferences that are masquerading as facts. They show when value judgements, rather than rigorous analysis, are being used in board deliberations. Most valuably, catalysts stimulate the board discussions with new, alternative insights and ideas.

- *Being a monitor of executive activities,* offering objective criticism and comments on management performance and issues such as the hiring and firing of top management. The entire board is responsible for the monitoring and supervision of executive management, but independent non-executive directors can bring a particular focus to this role.

- *Playing the role of watchdog,* able to provide an independent voice and protect the interests of minority shareholders or lending bankers. Directors cast in this role are seen as protectors of the interests of other parties, such as the shareholders or, more often, a specific interest group. As we commented in Chapter 3, nominee directors inevitably find themselves in this position, as they look out for the interests of the party who nominated them to the board. This might be a representative of a major investor in the case of a director on the board of an American or British listed company, a representative of the employees for a director on a German supervisory board, or a representative of the *keiretsu* group interests for a director on the board of a major Japanese company. Every director has a duty to be concerned with the interests of the company as a whole (that is, with the interests of *all* of the shareholders without discrimination), so the watchdog role has to be applied with care.

- *Being a confidante or sounding board for the chairman*, the chief executive or other directors; a trusted and respected counsellor in times of uncertainty and stress; someone to share concerns about issues (often interpersonal problems) outside the boardroom. Political processes at board level inevitably involve the use, and sometimes abuse, of power, and the confidante can sometimes make a valuable contribution. But it is vital that he or she commands the trust of all of the directors, otherwise the problem can be reinforced rather than resolved.

- *Acting as a safety valve*, able to act in a crisis in order to release the pressure, prevent further damage, and save the situation. A classical example would be when a company has run into financial problems, management performance has deteriorated, or the chief executive has to be replaced. Another example might be if the company faces an unexpected catastrophe. The sensible and steadying counsel of a wise member of the board could overcome an otherwise disastrous situation.

Directors' duties, rights, and powers

Duties

As we saw in Chapter 4, directors around the world have two fundamental duties: a duty of trust and a duty of care—a duty of trust to exercise a fiduciary responsibility to the shareholders, and a duty of care to exercise reasonable care, diligence, and skill. Beyond those two broad duties, directors' responsibilities are often enshrined in laws designed to protect consumers, employees, the environment, and so on. Directors' duties in case law countries have not been specifically laid down by statute, but developed through cases. In Australia, for example, directors' duties are designed to promote good governance and to ensure that directors act in the interests of the company, which means putting the interests of the shareholders ahead of their own. In particular, a director in Australia has a statutory duty:

- to act bona fide (in good faith) in the interests of the company as a whole;
- not to act for an improper purpose;
- to avoid conflicts of interest;
- not to make improper use of position;
- not to make improper use of information;
- not to trade while insolvent;
- as well as duties of care and diligence.

The US Sarbanes-Oxley Act of 2002 added some directors' duties to statute, including the need to confirm the effectiveness of the company's reporting and management control systems, and the handling of strategic risk.

The United Kingdom is an exception to the general rule that directors' duties are not specifically defined by statute law. The UK Companies Act 2006 attempted to consolidate the common law duties of directors in a definitive statement. In the United Kingdom, directors must act in the way they consider, in good faith, would be most likely to promote the success of the company for the benefit of its members as a whole, and in doing so have regard to:

- the likely consequences of any decision in the long term;
- the interests of the company's employees;
- the need to foster the company's business relationships with suppliers, customers, and others;
- the impact of the company's operations on the community and the environment;
- the desirability of the company to maintain a reputation for high standards of business conduct;
- the need to act fairly, as between members of the company.

Notice that, for the first time, statute law explicitly required directors to recognize their corporate social responsibility to employees, other stakeholders, the community, and the environment. The Act links responsible business behaviour with business success.

In civil law countries such as Germany, the managing director is given the responsibility for managing the company and acts as its legal representative. He or she must employ the diligence of an orderly businessman, specifically to:

- pursue the business purpose;
- manage the company properly;
- be loyal to the company;
- not disclose confidential information or company secrets;
- not take advantage of his or her position.

Rights

Companies' articles of association determine the power of the directors. They typically grant a wide degree of freedom, but could, for example, restrict corporate activities by defining the purpose for which the business was created, or limit borrowing powers. The website of the UK Companies Registry has a model set of articles (go to www.companieshouse.gov.uk and use the search facility).

All directors have the right to knowledge about the company, its business, and its situation. This right to information goes beyond routine board papers and reports, to receiving answers to any question a director wants to ask about the company's affairs. All directors have a right to attend and take part in board meetings and meetings of the shareholders.

Powers

In general, boards have a wide discretion to take business decisions, provided that they act within the company's constitution and respect their duties of trust and care. The directors run the company for the benefit of its shareholders—to contract, invest, pledge its assets, buy and sell, hire and fire, set its strategies and corporate policies, and supervise management. Directors must act within powers granted by the company's articles and only exercise powers for the purposes for which they were conferred. It is the board's role to take risks in pursuit of business. Should the company run into trouble as a result, the courts will not usually question decisions taken by the directors in the normal pursuit of business. Provided that the directors have acted within the company's constitution and not failed in their duties of trust and care, they will not normally be held liable for any resulting loss suffered by the company.

The detail of the law surrounding directors' duties, rights, and powers varies between jurisdictions and can be complicated. Obviously only a general indication of basic practice can be given here. If a director is in any doubt, he or she should raise the matter with the company secretary, who might well be in a position to explain the situation, discuss the matter with the board chairman, and if necessary seek legal advice.

Directors' disclosures, service contracts, and agreements

Conflict of interest and conflict of role

A *conflict of interest* arises if a director could benefit personally from a situation involving the company or from a decision taken by the board. A conflict can arise directly from a director's own interests or indirectly if a family member or close associate is involved. For example, a conflict of interest would arise if a director:

- owned a business that supplied the company or was a major customer, sometimes called 'connected transactions';
- served on the board of another company that had business dealings with the company;
- had a significant personal shareholding in another company that the board was considering as an acquisition target;
- interviewed a relative or close friend in a recruitment exercise;
- had the personal use of property belonging to the company;
- used company information for his personal benefit.

Every director has a fiduciary duty to recognize and disclose any conflict of interest they perceive. As commentators have pointed out—if someone perceives a conflict of interest, they have one. Recognizing potential conflicts is sometimes glaringly obvious to everyone involved, but in other cases the conflict may only be known to the person involved, so making the decision to declare the conflict and lose the personal benefit is an ethical choice based on that person's own moral compass; although the risk to personal finances and reputation can be significant if a failure to disclose is found out.

In some jurisdictions reporting conflicts of interest is required by company law. Many companies have policies on the handling of conflicts of interest and include rules on their identification and disclosure in their code of conduct. Conflicts can also exist with other employees and professional advisers to the company, such as lawyers and accountants. Of course, the obligation to disclose conflicts of interest also applies to those involved in other non-commercial public sector organizations.

Having disclosed the interest to the chairman of the board, typically before the board meeting through the company secretary, the director with the conflict should not take part in any board decision-making on the matter, until the chairman and fellow directors have decided on the appropriate action. The director might be asked to leave the meeting while that matter is discussed; or to listen but not participate in the discussion and abstain from voting; or having noted the declaration of a personal interest decide that it is not material and allow the director to participate in the decision-making. Should the chairman of the board be the one declaring the conflict of interest, someone else should chair the meeting for the discussion of that agenda item.

Directors should ensure that any conflict of interest they have declared is clearly recorded in the minutes with the board's ruling in response. This provides written evidence should there be a subsequent challenge.

In some cases shareholder approval may be needed on a board decision involving a conflict of interest. For example, in a listed company with dominant shareholders, such as the founding family, the approval of the minority public shareholders might be required. The company's articles, the listing rules of the stock exchange, and company law would be relevant.

A conflict of roles can arise if an executive director holds more than one position in the company: for example, as chief executive and chairman of the board. As chief executive, the role is that of the head of the management team; as chairman the role involves ensuring a full discussion of issues including dissenting views, and leading the board towards consensus. Most corporate governance codes, of course, consequently call for these two posts to be held by separate people.

In fact, a similar challenge faces all executive directors during board deliberations, if the responsibilities and interests of the executive post conflict with what appears to be best for the company as a whole. Role conflict can then arise, particularly if the individual concerned is a dominant personality—as such people often are. Members of the management team report to the chief executive; but as directors their responsibility is to the company, which may mean disagreeing with the chief executive. In some smaller companies the role of company secretary may be held by the finance director, again introducing potential conflicts of interest. In larger companies the work of the company secretary is usually sufficiently demanding to require a separate person.

Insider dealing

Directors of listed companies have to be particularly careful not to trade in their company's shares when they are in possession of inside or privileged information, such as the company results just prior to publication and before the stock market has that information. The company secretary will often inform directors when the window of opportunity for trading in the company's shares is open and, more importantly, when it is closed. The listing rules of many stock exchanges lay down a 'blackout' period, just prior to the announcement of a company's results, during which time directors may not trade in shares in that company.

Insider dealing, sometimes called insider trading, involves the buying or selling of shares in a listed company on the basis of privileged, share-price-sensitive insider information. Insider dealing may involve making a secret profit by buying shares in the privileged knowledge of events that would drive the price up, or avoiding a loss by selling shares on the basis of privileged intelligence that would cause the price to fall. Insider dealing laws do not apply only to directors, officers, and senior executives of companies. Anyone with access to privileged information, however obtained, can be held liable.

The argument against the practice is not so much that it is morally wrong or unfair, or that it involves a misuse of information, but that insider dealing destroys the credibility and the integrity of the stock market. Insider dealing is a breach of a director's fiduciary duty: it is also illegal in almost all countries. Japan, Hong Kong, and Germany were among the last jurisdictions to make insider trading a criminal offence.

It can be difficult to obtain convincing information to support a prosecution, which is why some jurisdictions waited so long to introduce anti-insider legislation. The United States has the most severe penalties for insider dealing. China has added more quite recently. Listed companies often include statements about insider dealing in their corporate ethics or values codes, using compliance officers to ensure that directors and employees do not trade on privileged, insider information.

The requirement to treat all shareholders equally can place nominee directors in a potentially difficult position, as we saw in the first part of this book. In board deliberations, a director must consider the interests of all shareholders equally and should not just represent the interests of the party who nominated him or her to the board. Moreover, a director should not divulge sensitive board information to the party who nominated him or her.

Related-party transactions

A related-party transaction is one between a company and a party closely related to it, such as a director or a major shareholder. For example, the purchase by a company of a property from one of its directors would be a related-party transaction and would need to be disclosed by that director to the board. The listing rules of most stock exchanges and the rules of securities regulators require related-party transactions to be disclosed and, in some cases, to be approved by the shareholders. Related-party transactions are frequently found in family firms where there are close links between family members and companies connected with the family. Related-party transactions proved to be a significant problem in the early days of privatization of state companies in both China and Russia, as existing senior managers arranged transfers of assets for their own benefit.

Directors' service contracts and agreements

An executive director is both an employee and a director of the company, as we discussed in Part One of this book. The employment is regulated by employment law; the directorship by company law. An executive director's employment agreement is a contract between the director and the company, which regulates the employment relationship, and will include terms required by employment law, such as remuneration, holidays, and pension arrangements. It may also include entitlements to a company car, the right to acquire shares, and the need for confidentiality.

However, all directors, executive and non-executive alike, may have a service contract as a director, which lays down the terms of the directorship. In some jurisdictions, shareholder approval is required before a company enters into long-term service contract with its directors. In the United Kingdom, a long-term service contract is defined as a contract for a guaranteed term of more than two years, which cannot be terminated by notice within that period. Without shareholder approval, the company may terminate the contract at any time having given reasonable notice. UK law also gives shareholders a right to inspect such service contracts and to request copies.

Directors' remuneration

In many countries, directors' remuneration has become contentious. Investors, particularly in the United States and the United Kingdom, encouraged by investigative media, have been challenging allegedly excessive levels of directors' remuneration, suggesting that they are out of line with the market, unrelated to performance, and sometimes even a 'reward for failure'.

The remuneration committee

In 1995, a group of City of London institutions commissioned Sir Richard Greenbury, then chairman of Marks and Spencer plc, to look into board-level pay. The Greenbury Report provided a code of conduct, which has now been incorporated in the UK Combined Code, as we saw in Chapter 5. This report recommended that companies should have remuneration committees consisting solely of independent non-executive directors. Most corporate governance codes now call for remuneration committees. The remuneration committee's remit is sometimes broadened to include other highly paid senior executives.

The remuneration committee needs to establish a formal and transparent procedure for developing policy on executive director remuneration. The challenge is to provide sufficient incentive to attract and retain top management in a competitive market for talent, rewarding success, while avoiding excesses and apparently rewarding failure.

Independent directors form the committee because the principle is that directors should not be involved in fixing their own remuneration. However, a committee comprised entirely of independent directors may not be completely independent in its judgement. Members may feel a loyalty towards the top executives because they were nominated by them to the board. Further, they may be executive directors of other companies themselves, so recommending high rewards may tend to inflate their own market rates. Of course, there remains an unanswered question: who should fix the remuneration of the members of the remuneration committee? For an example of the terms of reference for a remuneration committee see Corporate Governance in Action 13.3.

Corporate governance in action 13.3   J Sainsbury plc

Terms of Reference for the Remuneration Committee

The Remuneration Committee shall have the following terms of reference.

1. Constitution

1.1 The Board has established a committee of the Board known as the Remuneration Committee.

1.2 The Terms of Reference for the Committee outlined below are defined by the Board and may be amended by the Board at any time.

2. Membership

2.1 The Board is responsible for the appointment of members to the Remuneration Committee, for setting the term of members' appointments and for the revocation of any such appointments.

2.2 The Remuneration Committee shall comprise not less than three members, all of whom shall be independent Non-Executive Directors. The quorum shall be two Committee members one of whom should be the Committee Chairman unless he/she is unable to attend. All members of the Committee shall be advised of the business to be transacted at any meeting even if they are unable to be present.

2.3 The Chairman of the Committee shall be a Non-Executive Director. No one other than members of the Committee is entitled to be present at Committee meetings. The Company Chairman, Chief Executive Officer and HR Director shall normally be in attendance except when issues regarding their own remuneration are discussed. The Committee's remuneration consultants shall attend meetings as requested by the Committee Chairman.

2.4 The Committee should consult the Chairman and/or the Chief Executive Officer about their proposals relating to the remuneration of other Executive Directors. The Committee shall be supported by the HR Director. The Company Secretary shall act as secretary to the Committee and shall produce such papers and minutes of the Committee's meetings as are appropriate, in a timely manner.

2.5 The Remuneration Committee is authorised by the Board to obtain legal, remuneration or other professional advice from both inside and outside the Group as and when required, at the Company's expense, and to appoint and secure the attendance of external consultants and advisors if it considers this beneficial.

3. Frequency of meetings

3.1 Meetings of the Remuneration Committee shall be held as necessary but not less than three times a year and at such other times as the Chairman of the Committee shall require.

3.2 The Chairman of the Committee shall report to the Board after each meeting. The minutes of the meetings shall be circulated to all members of the Committee, the Company Chairman and Chief Executive Officer and HR Director and, if not members of the Committee, the other Non-Executive Directors of the Company.

4. Duties

4.1 The Committee shall:

i. determine and agree with the Board the broad policy for the remuneration of the Board Executive Directors, the Chairman and other members of the executive management referred to below;

ii. have delegated authority to set individual remuneration arrangements for the Company Chairman, the Chief Executive Officer and other Board Executive Directors;

iii. recommend and monitor and note the level and structure of remuneration for senior management. The Committee shall determine which colleagues are 'senior management' for this purpose—as at the date of adoption of these terms this covers members of the Operating Board, the Company Secretary and any other executive whose salary exceeds that of any Operating Board Director;

iv. in determining remuneration for those referred to above, the Committee shall review and agree
   - overall market positioning of the remuneration package;
   - individual base salaries and increases;
   - annual and long-term incentive/bonus arrangements, and set the relevant targets for performance related schemes;
   - pension arrangements.

4.2 The Committee is also responsible for authorising all remuneration arrangements for those referred to above that involve the use of shares, including all employee share schemes.

4.3 The Committee shall consider the achievement of the performance conditions under annual and long terms incentive/bonus arrangements.

4.4 The Committee shall note any major change to the terms of the Company's all employee share plans.

4.5 The Committee shall approve the service contracts of each Executive Director, including termination arrangements.

4.6 In determining remuneration policy and packages, the Committee shall have regard to the Combined Code on Corporate Governance, the UKLA Listing Rules and all other relevant codes, laws and regulations.

4.7 The Committee shall ratify the appointment of the HR Director.

4.8 The fees and other payment arrangements for Non-Executive Directors are matters for consideration by a sub-committee of the Board, consisting of the Chairman and one or more Executive Directors, which shall make recommendations to the Board as a whole.

5. Other Matters

5.1 The Committee will consider and recommend to the Board the content of the Directors' Remuneration Report, having regard to the Directors' Remuneration Report Regulations 2002, the Combined Code and the UKLA Listing Rules.

5.2 The Chairman of the Committee shall be available to answer questions at the Annual General Meeting on remuneration issues with regard to the Board and senior management and generally on remuneration principles and practice.

5.3 The Committee shall undertake any other duties as directed by the Board.

Determining directors' remuneration

So, how are the appropriate rewards for executive directors to be determined? Clearly, they need to be sufficient to attract the necessary top executives, to provide an incentive for better than average performance, to reward success, and to retain the vital executives' commitment to the company. The challenge is to balance the interests of the directors with those of the shareholders both in the short and the long term.

The focus on board-level remuneration has created a market for remuneration consultants to advise remuneration committees. Comparative information about similar companies can clearly be useful, but consultants' recommendations can mislead. One problem has been called 'remuneration ratcheting'. Various arguments are sometimes advanced to justify high board-level rewards, including the following:

- International comparison is essential 'to ensure that our company attracts and holds executive directors of the calibre we need against international competition, it is essential that we give our directors rewards that are broadly comparable to those they could obtain in our industry anywhere in the world'. Such an argument may be advanced even if the directors concerned have no prospects of being headhunted and whether or not they have any possibility of working anywhere else in the world.

- The head-hunter argument: 'We have just recruited a new executive director and the headhunters assured us that he had to receive a package that is 30% more than that of the highest paid director. Of course, we all had to have an increase to maintain differentials.' This argument conveniently overlooks the fact that the fee of the head-hunter may be based on 30–35% of the first year's salary of the new appointee.

- The better than average argument: 'We cannot pay our directors below the median for firms our size in this industry'—an argument that has a built-in escalation effect.

- The 'top of the industry' claim: 'Our firm prides itself on being one of the leaders in the industry, even though at the moment we are not among the most profitable. We expect to pay our directors in the upper quartile of the industry range as shown by the comparator pay research.' This argument totally ignores the performance of the firm or its directors.

- The transparency effect: 'Greater transparency in directors' pay leads to higher remuneration as companies play "catch-up".'

- The fear of loss of people: 'The best people receive offers from elsewhere. We could lose our directors and top management to the competition unless we pay competitive rates.' This argument is sometimes advanced even though the directors concerned are within a year or two of retirement and would be of absolutely no interest to competitors.

- Doubling up the bonus: 'We believe that it is important for directors' rewards to be performance-related. Moreover, we expect excellent performance in both the short and the long term. So we calculate bonuses on the annual profits, then we have a parallel three-year scheme that rewards directors if earnings per share grow by 30% over that period.' This way, directors get rewarded twice for the same performance, inflation is ignored, and there is no upside cap should there be exceptional circumstances. Moreover, directors do not get penalized for poor performance.

As an indication of the escalation in top executive pay, in 1980 executives at the top of US organizations earned around twenty times more than those at the bottom of their organizations; today, those at the top were receiving nearly 200 times more than those at the bottom. Interestingly, the remuneration of senior executives in the John Lewis Partnership, a retail group in the United Kingdom owned by its employees, is actually determined as a ratio of the pay of the lowest-paid workers, thus removing any pressure on pay from external comparisons.

What are appropriate fees for non-executive directors? In the past, these have often been relatively low. But it is now widely recognized that sufficient rewards are necessary to persuade people of the required calibre to afford the time and, increasingly important, to shoulder the risk of being an independent director. In the United States, share options are often issued to outside directors. Hermes, one of the United Kingdom's largest fund managers, has suggested that non-executive directors should receive some of their remuneration in shares. But the counter-argument is that share options should be linked to outstanding performance and given only to those top executives whose actions directly determine the results.

Share options

Ideally, the component parts of executive directors' remuneration should be structured to link rewards with both corporate and individual performance. The hope is that incentives rewarding exceptional performance will align managers' interests with those of the shareholders. But rather than encouraging exceptional performance, such schemes can encourage exceptional deception, as directors manipulate share prices, revenues, or profits to meet the target criteria of the incentive scheme.

Share options have been used as a way of rewarding and motivating top executives for many years. Options give the right to buy shares at a predetermined price at some time in the future, thus enabling the recipient to benefit by exercising the right once the share price has risen. The exercise price is typically that at the time the option is given. Obviously, the belief is that options provide a strong incentive to directors to raise the share price by improving corporate performance.

Following the global financial crisis, the European Union called for bankers' remuneration to be linked to risks taken. Reflecting this policy, the Financial Services Authority (FSA) in the United Kingdom required financial institutions to apply 'remuneration policies, practices, and procedures that are consistent with and promote effective risk management'. The FSA Remuneration Code calls for at least 50% of variable remuneration (bonuses) to be in shares that must be retained for a given period.

Some argue that such incentives reward exceptional performance and align directors' interests with those of the shareholders. Unfortunately, that is not always the case. In fact, the interests of shareholders are not the same as those of the holders of share options. Shareholders have to invest their funds and run the risk of loss; option holders have no downside, having invested nothing, and are not at risk.

Moreover, on a rising stock market, all prices rise, so option holders reap a reward that is not linked to performance. Some schemes attempt to overcome this problem by building in a market index, so that only performance better than the market is rewarded. Such indexation can work on a falling market as well, benefiting executives if their company outperforms the market.

Other disadvantages of options include the possibility of unscrupulous directors attempting to bolster the firm's share price with short-term manoeuvres that do not really reflect improved performance—a classical agency dilemma. If a company gives new options, whenever they are exercised (reloading), executives may be able to play the market, irrespective of their performance. Share options are obviously unattractive on a falling market, so some companies lower the bid price of their directors' options (resetting). This clearly fails to reward outstanding performance.

In the past, firms were not required to account for share options, merely issuing more shares. Boards tended to act as though they were free of cost to the company. But, obviously, although not a cash charge on the company, when an option is exercised, there is a cost, because the interests of the other shareholders are diluted. Today, accounting standards require options to be valued, at their net present values using appropriate valuation models, and a charge to be shown.

The use of share options tends to be falling and attention has turned to bonuses and other incentive schemes to reward performance. But, unfortunately, unless carefully handled, such schemes can also encourage sub-optimization as directors manipulate the target criteria of the incentive scheme.

Reporting and voting on director remuneration

In many jurisdictions, a company's annual report needs to contain a statement of remuneration policy and details of the remuneration of each director. Transparency is vital in corporate governance. Legislation enacted in the United Kingdom in 2003 required quoted companies to publish a directors' remuneration report and put them to shareholder vote at the annual general meeting (AGM). The report had to contain details of the members of the remuneration committee and anyone who advised that committee, a statement of the company's policy on directors' remuneration for the future, details of individual directors' remuneration, giving details of the performance criteria in incentive schemes, pensions, and retirement benefits, their service contracts, and a line graph for the past five years showing how the company's performance has compared with that of competitors.

In the United States, Securities and Exchange Commission rules since 2007 have required full disclosure of pay packages of top management. The US Corporate and Financial Institution Compensation Fairness Act, passed in 2009 in response to perceived excessive rewards in financial institutions following the global financial crisis, did not impose pay limits, but passed the responsibility to shareholders. In the United Kingdom, shareholders have had the opportunity to vote on directors' pay since 2002. Admittedly, the result is then only advisory: the board does not have to take any notice, but in practice shareholders' opinions, plus private conversations with institutional investors, resolve most issues and avoid confrontation. An interesting initiative by the UK Institute of Management Accountants, Pricewaterhouse-Coopers, and Radley Yaldar has produced a model remuneration report, which shows the principles of a company's remuneration policy, the link between performance and reward, and the alignment with shareholder interests.[1]

The Commission of the European Union announced a cap on bankers' bonuses, which came into force in January 2014, limiting them to 100% of annual salaries, or 200% with shareholder approval. The EU ruling was opposed by many banks and the UK government. In their annual reports, both Barclays Bank and Lloyds Banking Group said they would pay their chief executives in shares, on top of their salaries and bonuses, thus sidestepping the EU rules. It

---

[1] www.reportleadership.com

was reported that the EU Commission was also considering whether shareholders should be given power to veto directors' compensation packages. An attempt by the British Government to resist the EU cap failed.

In 2013, the US Securities and Exchange Commission decided to implement the section of the Dodds-Frank Wall Street Reform and Consumer Protection Act that called for public companies to disclose the median of the total annual compensation of the employees and the ratio of that median to the CEO's annual remuneration. In other words how many times more the CEO was paid compared with the average worker. In the United Kingdom, a typical FTSE 100 chief executive now receives around £4.5 million a year, which is 170 times average earnings. In the United States, an analysis[2] of Standard and Poor's top 500 companies headed by the same CEO for the past two years showed median pay—salary, bonus, perks plus realized stock and options—jumped 13% to $10.5 million with 15 CEOs receiving over $100 million.

The UK government introduced legislation, which came into force in 2013, requiring reporting and shareholder voting on directors' pay. The Financial Reporting Council commented on arrangements to claw-back bonuses if performance failed to meet expectations, and on what action companies should take if a significant percentage of shareholders voted against director remuneration. The FRC also considered whether independent directors, who were executives of other companies, should be members of remuneration committees because, having a vested interest, they might lack independent judgement.

Shareholder votes on remuneration reports seldom bind a board, but can indicate shareholder dissatisfaction, which can lead to the movement of top executives. At a stormy meeting of BP shareholders in 2014, 32% voted against or abstained on the 2013 remuneration report, with several shareholders criticizing the remuneration committee. Institutional investors voted with the board. At the AGM of Barclays Bank, shareholders, including some institutional investors, voted against the reappointment of the chairman of the remuneration committee, Sir John Sunderland, criticizing the bonus awarding regime at the bank. He was replaced as an independent director. The chairman of the Association of British Insurers, commenting on the backlash against the pay of Barclays' 'star investment bankers', said that such levels of remuneration were dependent on the United States. 'We may be creating an environment in Europe,' he said, 'which will not allow for the presence of a global investment bank headquartered here.'

Executive director remuneration remains a provocative corporate governance issue.

Case studies

 Case study 13.1   News Corporation

News Corporation (NewsCorp) is a media conglomerate, founded by Rupert Murdoch in Australia in 1979. In 2010, the company, now headquartered in New York, had worldwide revenues of over US$30 billion, profits of over US$2.5 billion, and over 50,000 employees. The company's main revenues come from cable networks, with the Fox News channel, and filmed entertainment. Publishing,

[2] *USA Today* 4 April 2014.

including newspapers, accounted for less than 20%. NewsCorp shares are listed on NASDAQ and the Australian Securities Exchange.

Rupert Murdoch, born in 1931, has enjoyed unrivalled political influence around the world, being described by *The Economist* (23 July 2011) as 'a press baron, a manipulator of politicians, and a king maker'. The Murdoch family dominates the control of NewsCorp using dual-class shares. The A shares, which account for 70% of the equity, have no voting rights, and consequently the holders of these shares have no say in board-level appointments. The B shares, which account for 30% of the equity, carry all of the votes. The Murdoch family control about 39% of these voting shares, giving them unassailable control.

News International Ltd is the wholly owned British subsidiary of NewsCorp, publishing *The Times* newspaper, among others. The chairman of News International is James Murdoch, born in 1972, Rupert Murdoch's son.

The seventeen directors of NewsCorp in 2010 included nine who were nominally independent, but whose length of service and connections would make that definition doubtful in some corporate governance codes.

Rupert Murdoch, Chairman and Chief Executive Officer, NewsCorp

José María Aznar, independent director; former President of Spain; president, Foundation for Social Studies and Analysis

Natalie Bancroft, 34, independent director; member of the family that controlled Dow Jones and Wall Street Journal prior to their disputed takeover by NewsCorp

Peter Barnes, independent director; chairman of Ansell Limited, a US-based and Australian-registered maker of industrial gloves

Chase Carey, Deputy Chairman, President and Chief Operating Officer, NewsCorp

Kenneth E. Cowley, independent director; chairman, R.M. Williams Holdings Pty Ltd

David F. DeVoe, Chief Financial Officer, NewsCorp

Viet Dinh, 43, independent director and chairman, NewsCorp Nominating and Corporate Governance Committee; Professor of Law, Georgetown University (Having fled war-torn Vietnam, he served as Assistant Attorney General under President George Bush.)

Rod Eddington, independent director appointed in 1999; chairman for Australia and New Zealand, J.P. Morgan; former chief executive of British Airways and of Australia's Ansett Airlines (Said to have been mentor to Rupert.)

Murdoch's son Lachlan, also a NewsCorp director

Joel Klein, Executive Vice President, CEO, Education Division, NewsCorp

Andrew S. B. Knight, independent director; chairman, J. Rothschild Capital Management Ltd

James Murdoch, Deputy Chief Operating Officer, NewsCorp; chairman and CEO, International News Corporation

Lachlan Murdoch, executive chairman, Illyria Pty Ltd

Thomas J. Perkins, independent director; partner, Kleiner, Perkins, Caufield & Byers

Arthur M. Siskind, senior advisor to the chairman, NewsCorp

John L. Thornton, independent director appointed in 2004; Professor and director of Global Leadership, Tsinghua University of Beijing; formerly chief operating officer of Goldman Sachs and an independent director of HSBC involved in power struggles at board level

Stanley S. Shuman Director Emeritus; managing director, Allen & Company LLC.

The matter of succession has been raised by some analysts. The possibility of a dynasty passing from father to son was questioned, and the suggestion made that Rupert Murdoch move to non-executive chairman and a new appointment be made as CEO. The name of Chase Carey, COO NewsCorp, was often mentioned.

The concern for ethical conduct is reflected in a letter in 2012 from Rupert Murdoch , chairman and chief executive officer:

Dear Colleagues:

For more than a half century, News Corporation has shaped global media by ensuring the public's needs are met and that our offerings are of the highest calibre. Today, hundreds of millions of people around the world trust us for the best quality and choice in news, sports and entertainment.

This public trust is our Company's most valuable asset: one earned every day through our scrupulous adherence to the principles of integrity and fair dealing.

We have revised this Standards of Business Conduct to make it easier to read and use, and to clearly outline what we should all expect of ourselves as colleagues. Each of us has the power to influence the way our Company is viewed, simply through the judgments and decisions we each make in the course of an ordinary day.

It's an important responsibility and I'm honored to share it with you.

Rupert Murdoch

Disaster strikes NewsCorp and its subsidiary News International

In July 2011, the best-selling British Sunday newspaper, the *News of the World*, was closed after 168 successful years. For some years, the company had faced damaging allegations of telephone hacking to obtain stories, but had claimed that this was the work of a single rogue, freelance investigator, who went to jail. But subsequently it emerged that the practice was widespread and known to senior executives. The public were not too concerned when they believed that the hacked telephones belonged to entertainment and sports stars, and other celebrities. But when it emerged that the journalists had intercepted voice messages of a missing 13-year-old schoolgirl, Milly Dowler, who was subsequently found murdered, the public mood changed. Worse, it was alleged that journalists had deleted messages from her mobile phone to make more space for subsequent material, leading her parents to believe she was still alive—although this was subsequently denied. Evidence emerged that telephone hacking to obtain stories was widespread and ran to thousands, including families of soldiers killed in Iraq and Afghanistan and people killed in the terrorist bombings in London. It was then alleged that large sums had been paid to celebrities, who had discovered that their voicemails had been listened to by the *News of the World*, to settle actions for breach of privacy. On 19 July 2011, Rupert and James Murdoch were summoned before a committee of the British House of Commons to answer questions. Rupert Murdoch said that 'this is the most humble day of my career'.

Worse was to come when it appeared that payments had been made to police for information. This raised the possibility of prosecution for bribery under the US Foreign Corrupt Practices Act of 1977. Some senior police officers resigned.

The BSkyB deal fails

News International owned 39% of the company BSkyB, which ran the successful British satellite Sky TV station. James Murdoch was chairman of BSkyB. In early 2011, News International bid for the remaining shares. Expectations were high that the bid would be approved by the broadcasting and competition authorities, and accepted by the shareholders. However, the saga over telephone hacking and payments to police caused the government to block the bid, which was abandoned on 14 July 2011. News Corp shares plunged 7%, wiping US$3 billion off its market value. Nevertheless, on 29 July 2011, the BSkyB board of directors unanimously voted for James Murdoch to remain as chairman.

In 2012 two divisions were formed—21st Century Fox, the owner of Hollywood film and TV studios, and NewsCorp, publisher and owner of the UK *Times*, the *Sun* and other newspapers.

In 2014, Rupert Murdoch promoted his elder son, Lachlan Murdoch, 42, to become co-chairman of the two divisions of his global media empire, suggesting that he was planning for his succession. Lachlan Murdoch stood down from the chairmanship of Australia's Ten TV network and assumed his new role in both 21st Century Fox and NewsCorp. Commentators said that this suggested Murdoch intended to keep control of his empire firmly in family hands.

Details of the board committees can be found online at http://newscorp.com/corporate-governance/board-committees which also provides access to the charters of those committees, including the nomination and corporate governance committee. The News Corporation Statement of Corporate Governance is available online at http://newscorp.com/corporate-governance/statement-of-corporate-governance

NewsCorp publishes the group's standards of business conduct online at http://newscorp.com/corporate-governance/standards-of-business-conduct

Discussion questions

1. What is your opinion of the governance of NewsCorp, at the time of the case study?

2. As the top executives of the subsidiary and the holding companies respectively, should either James or Rupert Murdoch be held responsible for the bad behaviour in a small and not very significant part of the group?

3. What is your opinion of Murdoch's intention to keep control of the NewsCorp empire in the family?

 Case study 13.2   RBS and Fred the Shred

The Royal Bank of Scotland (RBS) was founded in 1727 by royal charter from King George I. This case describes its incredible growth and acquisition strategy under entrepreneurial chief executive, Sir Fred Goodwin, until its collapse in 2008 and nationalization by the British government.

The RBS Group, which is headquartered in Edinburgh, has branches throughout Scotland, the rest of the British Isles, and the Republic of Ireland, with banking operations elsewhere in the world. Its subsidiaries include the Royal Bank of Scotland, the London-based Westminster Bank, the Citizens Financial Group, the eighth largest bank in the United States, Ulster Bank, and Her Majesty the Queen's bankers Coutts and Co. It also owns insurance companies including Churchill Insurance, Direct Line, and Privilege. RBS is listed on the London Stock Exchange and the New York Stock Exchange. Before its collapse in 2008, RBS was briefly the largest bank in the world by both assets (£1.9 trillion) and liabilities (£1.8 trillion).

Growth and death by acquisition

Chief Executive Sir Fred Goodwin's strategy was to grow by acquisition. In 2000, in a campaign to reduce costs and improve efficiency, Sir Fred cut around 18,000 jobs from the RBS group, earning himself the moniker 'Fred the Shred,' a nickname that was to stick.

Sir Fred was conscious of risk: in his 2006 annual corporate review, he had written that 'sound control of risk is fundamental to business . . . central to this is our longstanding aversion to sub-prime lending, wherever we do business'. But the acquisition of the Dutch bank ABN Amro, in 2007, was to prove his undoing, because it was full of toxic sub-prime debt.

In February 2009, RBS reported a loss of £24 billion, the highest loss ever recorded for a UK company. In October 2008, the British government arranged a £37 billion bail-out and guaranteed £325 billion against the toxic sub-prime loans. In return it took a 58% stake in RBS voting shares, which was to increase to 82%. Sir Fred Goodwin resigned in November 2008, and was subsequently stripped of his knighthood.

Concerns over Goodwin's compensation package

Despite being credited with destroying the bank, Sir Fred left with a pension of £703,000 a year for life, estimated to be worth £17 million (US$25 million) including an initial tax-free lump-sum of £3 million (US$4.5 million). Even though Sir Fred was only 50, his pension became payable immediately.

The UK Chancellor of the Exchequer challenged him to return all, or at least some, of his gains; but he replied that he did not intend to return a penny.

A leader in *The Times* newspaper (18 March 2009) wrote:

> it is a public scandal that, while his business decisions have incurred immense social costs, his compensation packages confer huge personal benefits . . . The behaviour of the RBS board was beyond generous and worse than ludicrous. It was craven. It deemed that Sir Fred had joined the pension scheme at the age of 20, although he was in fact 40. It allowed him to choose his 12-month earnings figure from the best year in the previous decade. It even gave him the choice of taking his full pension at the age of 60 or at 50.

Lord Myners, a financial expert, had approved Sir Fred's remuneration package on behalf of the government. Many asked how such a huge figure had been negotiated. Myners replied that the deal had been done while trying to avoid the collapse of RBS, and he had relied on Sir Tom McKillop, then RBS chairman, Bob Scott, the senior non-executive director, and the RBS board's remuneration committee.

The UK financial regulator, the FSA, was criticized for its failure during the 2008 financial crisis and for its apparent inability to withstand pressure from the financial industry.

A UK Treasury Select Committee concluded in 2012 that the ABN Amro acquisition should have been subjected to regulatory control in what amounted to 'a serious indictment' of the FSA's senior management. A 'failed culture of box-ticking' at the FSA had contributed to the collapse of RBS and the huge costs to the taxpayer. The FSA should have stopped this toxic takeover.

RBS subsequently

Even though RBS reported losses of £1.1 billion in 2010, staff bonuses amounted to nearly £1 billion. More than 100 senior bank executives received at least £1 million, causing some criticism. Fred Goodwin's chief executive successor, Stephen Hester, renounced a £1 million bonus after complaints about the bank's subsequent performance. Sir Philip Hampton, chairman of the board, admitted that the level at which the bonus scheme would pay out, based on a rise in the share price, was too low and pledged to start stricter criteria for the chief executive's bonus.

In 2012, Hester wrote:

> RBS has completed the first three years of its recovery plan. Over that period the Bank's results across our key goals—customers, risk and value—have exceeded the plan targets we put together in 2009. This is pleasing and puts the bank in a vastly better position than before to serve our different constituencies.

The RBS board chairman, Sir Philip Hampton, added:

> When I became chairman in 2009, our urgent task was to stabilise RBS and then to begin the job of rebuilding the company. We have made good progress in three years. The balance sheet has been reduced by over £700 billion from its peak. Our reliance on short-term wholesale funding, which stood at £297 billion at the end of 2008 has been cut to £102 billion. We repaid more than £20 billion of government guaranteed debt in 2011.

But in November 2012, Hester faced an uncomfortable two hours in front of the UK Banking Commission. Justin Welby, the future Archbishop of Canterbury, head of the Anglican Church, and a member of the Commission, asked 'what is the duty of an enormous bank like yours, approaching 100% of GDP, well into the hundreds of billions of pounds, what is your duty to society, and why didn't you mention it (in earlier comments)?' Hester responded by suggesting that RBS fulfilled a role in society by providing saving accounts, paying taxes, and employing people responsibly. The Archbishop replied: 'That is motherhood and apple pie. I am really looking for a bit more penetrating analysis of what your duty is to society—other than just saying obeying the law and paying taxes.'

In 2013, an RBS Shareholder Action Group launched a £4 billion (US$6 billion) law suit against RBS, its former chief executive Fred Goodwin, and former chairman Sir Tom McKillop. The action group claimed that investors had thought RBS was a solid, well-funded business when they responded to a £12 billion (US$18 billion) rights issue in 2008, although financial collapse loomed. Goodwin claimed that he was being 'unfairly and wrongly' chased for compensation. 'I did no wrong', he said, 'you're wasting your time and money.'

Repercussions from involvement in toxic sub-prime loans continued. The RBS Group was fined £26 million (US$39 million) by the state of Nevada in 2012 for selling such loans, potentially triggering claims from other states. With the UK government still owning 84% of RBS, such charges effectively hit the UK taxpayer. The US Federal Housing Finance Agency, which controls government-sponsored lenders Freddie Mac and Fannie Mae, also threatened action on US$32 billion of securities they had bought from RBS Group companies.

In February 2013, RBS chief executive, Stephen Hester, launched an impassioned plea to keep his bonus of £780,000 (US$1,250,000) in shares. RBS chairman, Sir Philip Hamilton, backed his plea, describing Hester's basic pay of more than £1.6 million (US$2.5 million) as 'modest'. Sir Philip's comment was described by campaigners as an insult to ordinary British taxpayers who had bailed out RBS during the financial crisis.

Stephen Hester had joined RBS as CEO in 2008, after it had been bailed out by the British government. His annual salary was £1.1 million (US$1.7 million), plus an annual bonus and pension fund contributions. The bonus was £1.5 million in 2010. For 2011 Hester was offered a bonus of £963,000 in shares, but under pressure from politicians and the media he declined it for both that year and the next. For 2013, Hester, along with seventy-six other senior staff expected bonuses of more than £1 million, in many cases doubling their salaries, despite the bank posting an £8million loss. But the British Chancellor of the Exchequer intervened[3] to stop the payments, because RBS was still 81% owned by the government.

In June 2013, RBS announced that Hester would stand down as CEO in December 2013 after five years with the bank. He received a pay-off of £1.65 million plus £23,000 to cover legal costs negotiating his termination agreement. His successor, Ross McEwan, was alleged to have been offered annual remuneration of £2.75 million rising to £4.75 million.

In May 2014, the bank revealed a profit for the first three months of the year of £1.2 billion and immediately planned to give senior staff the maximum bonus allowed under the European Union's

---

[3] *Daily Mail*, 26 April 2014.

bonus cap of the equivalent of one year's salary. McEwan, the new CEO, said that less than half a percent of staff were involved and that he would 'do whatever it takes to hold on to higher paid bankers'. But the annual report also stated that executive directors will no longer receive bonuses related to performance but will be given an allowance, paid in RBS shares, which is not part of basic pay and not tied to performance.

Discussion questions

1. What do the comments of interviewers on the Select Committee, appointed by the UK Treasury, tell you about the culture at the top of RBS?

2. In your opinion, how should Goodwin's compensation have been calculated following his resignation? Who should have been involved in the decision?

3. Was the remuneration paid to Hester appropriate?

References and further reading

Berle, Adolf A. and Gardiner C. Means (1932) *The Modern Corporation and Private Property*. Harcourt, Brace & World, New York.

Bower, Tom (2006) *Conrad and Lady Black—dancing on the edge*. Harper Press, London.

Dorff, Michael (2014) Indispensable and other Myths: why the CEO pay experiment failed and how to fix it. University of California Press, Oakland, CA.

ICSA (2013), *The Non-executive Directors; Handbook*. 3rd edn, ICSA for the Non-executive Directors Association, London.

ICSA (2013) *Corporate Governance Handbook*. 3rd edn, ICSA, London.

McNish, Jacquie and Sinclair Stewart (2004) *The Fall of Conrad Black*. Allen Lane, London.

NACD (2010) *Audit Committees—a practical guide*. Report of a NACD Blue Ribbon Commission, National Association of Corporate Directors, 1133, Suite 700 21 Street, Washington, DC, USA.

NACD (2006) *Director communications—purpose, principles and best practice*. Report of a NACD Blue Ribbon Commission, National Association of Corporate Directors, 1133, Suite 700 21 Street, Washington, DC, USA.

Spira, Laura F. (2002) *The Audit Committee—performing corporate governance*. Kluwer, Boston, MA.

Turnbull, Shann (1975) *Democratising the Wealth of Nations*. Company Directors' Association, Sydney, Australia.

Wearing, Robert T. (2005) *Cases in Corporate Governance*. Sage, London.

Projects and exercises

1. Design a pro forma checklist for the appointment of a director, identifying the core competencies needed and outlining personal attributes that would be desirable for the appointment.

2. Lord Nolan produced a set of principles (see Corporate governance in action 12.2) to guide the holders of public office in the United Kingdom. Do you believe that these are equally appropriate for directors of a listed public company? If not, why not? Would your answer be different if the company were a private, family firm?

3. Draft a briefing paper for a newly appointed director of a listed company explaining the legal duties as a director. Do you think that most directors know this information?

4. Major companies in some European countries adopt the two-tier board structure, with supervisory and executive boards. Advise the directors of a company incorporated in

Delaware, USA, which is considering the acquisition of a German subsidiary, on two-tier boards.

Self-test questions

1. What is a remuneration committee?
2. What does integrity mean?
3. Name some of the corporate values declared by Microsoft.
4. In addition to integrity, what other personal qualities are found in high-calibre directors?
5. Name some essential director-level skills.
6. What character traits are desirable in a director?
7. What are the essential legal duties of a director?
8. How does a related-party transaction affect a director?

14

Board Leadership: The reality of the boardroom

 Learning Outcomes

In which we consider:

- How people, power, and politics affect practice
- The chairman's leadership role
- Sources of governance power
- Games that directors play
- Board styles and the culture of the board
- Business ethics begin in the boardroom
- Corporate codes of ethics and their enforcement
- Implementing corporate governance below board level

How people, power, and politics affect practice

Unless they have served on a board, people may imagine that directors behave rationally, that board-level discussions are analytical, and that decisions are reached after a careful consideration of alternatives. Not often. Experience of board meetings, or the activities of any governing body for that matter, shows that reality can be quite different. Directors' behaviour is influenced by interpersonal relationships, by perceptions of position and prestige, and by the processes of power. In fact, corporate governance is more about human behaviour than about structures and strictures, rules and regulations. Corporate governance involves the use of power. It is a political process.

The experience and prestige of board members does not guarantee a successful board. Members of Enron's audit committee had some eminent and experienced people, including one of America's best-known accounting academics, and a member of the British House of Lords who was chairman of the UK Press Complaints Council. In board activities, so much depends on board leadership and the way in which the directors work together. Good leaders create successful teams. Sound boards have sound leaders.

It has been said that 'outside directors never know enough about the business to be useful and inside directors always know too much to be independent'. Successful boards avoid this claim, because all of the directors, executive and non-executive alike, form a cohesive team in which independent, tough-minded individuals work together with trust and mutual understanding towards a common goal. To achieve that needs leadership.

By contrast, poorly performing boards probably have weak leadership and members with little commitment, focus, or time. Some directors may lack interest or, worse, be motivated by self-interest; others may be complacent, arrogant, or dominating; some may be easily led or weak-willed, failing to speak out when in disagreement; and a few may be just incompetent.

The chairman's leadership role

Many people speak broadly of the chairman of the company, whereas the role is strictly chairman of the company's board of directors. Shareholders do not vote to elect someone chairman, although the chairman will usually chair meetings of the shareholders. Unless there is anything to the contrary in the company's articles, the directors elect one of themselves to be chairman. There are few statutory requirements for the role, so chairmen vary considerably in the way they carry out the responsibilities. At one extreme is the powerful chairman, who acts as a leader of the company, influences its strategic direction, interacts strongly with the chief executive, and provides wide-ranging leadership of the board. At the other extreme, the weak chairman just runs board meetings.

Before proceeding, there are some other issues of nomenclature to settle. Although the chairmen of most major companies are men, many women occupy the position in quangos and not-for-profit organizations. To avoid the use of the inelegant terms 'chairperson' or 'chairwoman', some boards refer to their board leader as 'Lady Chairman' or 'Madam Chairman'. Others have adopted the genderless title of 'chair', as in 'the chair announced the results'. Here, we will avoid confusion and controversy by treating the word 'chairman' as genderless.

Another confusion can arise with the term 'executive chairman', which is typically used to indicate either that the holder has a full-time commitment to the office of chairman, rather than being part-time as is frequently the case, or that the chairmanship and chief executive roles are combined, as in the boards of many US companies. Some companies use the title vice-chairman to spread the work of the chairman; others use the title to indicate a chairman-elect; and it is used by a few boards to confer prestige without necessarily giving additional responsibilities or powers.

An effective board operates as a team, not just a legal necessity or an occasional meeting. A successful board depends on the personality, commitment, and leadership qualities of the chairman. The chairman is the keystone of every board. Even a board composed of brilliant and highly experienced individuals is unlikely to be effective unless it is well led. The chairman of the board does not lead by being at the top of a power hierarchy; he or she is 'first among equals', exercising leadership through the trust and respect of fellow directors.

So what should a chairman do? In the opinion of the Cadbury Report:

> The chairman's role in securing good corporate governance is crucial. Chairmen are primarily responsible for the working of the board, for its balance of membership subject to board and shareholders' approval, for ensuring that all relevant issues are on the agenda, and for ensuring that all directors, executive and non-executive alike, are enabled and encouraged to play their full part in its activities. (It is important for chairmen to ensure that executive directors look beyond their executive duties and accept their full share of their

responsibilities of governance.) Chairmen should be able to stand sufficiently well back from the day-to-day running of the business to ensure that their boards are in full control of the company's affairs and alert to their obligations to shareholders.

The following six functions for a board chairman elaborate the above perspective.

1. Leadership of the board

Leadership of the board team is the chairman's primary duty. This provides the foundations of the board's culture and style of operation. The chairman sets the tone for board activities.

The chairman should play a pivotal role in determining the size, structure, and membership of the board, along with the nominating committee and subject to the articles. This involves determining the balance between executive, independent, and connected non-executive directors. The chairman will normally want to be involved with the nominating committee, in the identification, selection, and nomination of directors. He or she will want to ensure that they have the necessary qualifications and experience, that they will fit into the existing board culture, that they have the time to devote to board activities, and that they have no conflicting interests. After all, these will be members of the team that he or she is responsible for leading. Succession issues can call for the guiding hand of the chairman, sometimes with the support of the independent directors, particularly the senior independent director.

Following appointment, the chairman will often brief a new director on the corporate situation and board practices and will want to ensure that the director's induction programme is adequate. The chairman also has a vital role in reviewing the performance of each director: a responsibility that in the past was often informal and casual, but is now formally expected under some of the corporate governance codes. Similarly, the chairman needs to ensure that director training, updating, and development, both for individuals and the board as a whole, are appropriate: again, an expectation of some governance codes. The duties, membership, and chairmanship of board committees also need to be managed by the chairman. Finally, he or she needs to initiate the project that evaluates the effectiveness of the board and board committees, and to follow through on necessary changes within the board and its policies, procedures, and practices.

2. Management of meetings

This is the conventional view of the role of chairman and, for most directors, the most visible. In the management of board meetings, the board's culture and the chairman's style become apparent. A sound chairman:

- encourages independence of thought in the boardroom;
- ensures that the views of all present are heard, controlling the garrulous, while encouraging others;
- handles in an adult way discussions that can be tough and testing;
- encourages an atmosphere in which all directors feel able to ask questions and to probe issues;
- ensures that discussions stay focused;

- keeps the climate of discussion open, with challenges to the point, rather than aggressive;
- avoids boardroom cosiness;
- does not make a stand on issues, forcing them through, but leads the board towards a consensus;
- is not a cheerleader for management, discouraging mutual self-congratulation;
- ensures that directors are not playing games (a section on games that directors play follows).

Some chairmen cannot handle challenges, discouraging disagreements and branding directors who ask too many questions as members of the awkward squad. Others interpret their leadership role as an opportunity to impose their own will on the meeting, instead of ensuring that all points of view are considered and leading towards agreement.

Meetings need planning as well as running. Prior to the meeting, the chairman needs to consider the time, location, duration of the meeting, and who should attend, both as statutory members, but also to provide information or to observe. The chairman has to agree the topics on the agenda, not only the conventional ones, but any issue that he or she feels the board should be aware of and discuss. The chairman should ensure that each director is adequately and appropriately informed, not only through routine board reports, but also with individual material and briefings if necessary. In conducting the meeting, the chairman needs to ensure that each director has the opportunity to contribute, that different points of view are succinctly summarized, and that the board, as far as possible, is led to a consensus on the outcome. Getting directors involved, restraining the dominant, while focusing attention where needed and balancing the available time appropriately between topics, is the essence of good meeting management. The diffident director may seldom speak, but when he or she does that insight can be worth more than many tedious moments from the garrulous. The chairman should beware of the pitfalls of 'group-think', political game-playing, and anchoring discussions in past experiences. We will explore some of these matters further in Chapter 16 on board effectiveness.

Most of the above comments about sound chairmanship and the running of meetings apply to the chairmanship of board subcommittees. Although many board committees are made up wholly of independent directors, the chief executive officer (CEO), other executives, or indeed anyone who can provide information and contribute to deliberations could be invited to attend. But they will be non-voting members and could be asked to leave committee deliberations at some stage.

3. Strategic leadership

Although some boards delegate a lot of the responsibility for developing the corporate strategy to the CEO and top executive team, the directors still have overall responsibility for setting the company's strategic direction. So the chairman needs to ensure that the board pays appropriate attention to strategy formulation and policymaking. All of the directors should understand the company's mission and its strategic context, and share a common view of the strategic direction being followed.

4. Linking the board with management

Where the chairmanship is separate from the CEO, the chairman provides the link between the board and management, working through the CEO and any other executive directors on the board. Where the CEO and the executive team are strong, the chairman and independent directors need to be able to interact. Likewise, the CEO and the top management team must engage with the board.

The relationship between the chairman and the CEO is one of the most crucial, most sensitive, and most subtle relationships in the organization. The relationship is crucial because these are the two most important roles in the entire organization. It is sensitive because these are often people of significance with high public profiles, and big stakes can be involved. And it is subtle because it involves close liaison between two people who each have the power to affect the other. At its best, the CEO perceives the chairman as a wise counsellor, someone with wide and relevant experience, and a person to be trusted implicitly; the chairman sees the CEO as the most successful appointment the board has made.

At times, of course, the relationship can prove difficult. Typical problems arise through a clash of personalities, interference by the chairman in the executive running of the business, or when disciplining or ultimately replacing the CEO. The 'promotion' of a retiring CEO to the chairmanship (discouraged or prohibited in some governance codes) is also a potential disaster, unless the new chairman can adapt to the duties of chairman and leave the running of the business to the new CEO.

5. Arbitration between board members and others

Occasionally, some chairmen find themselves playing the role of safety valve, arbitrating between feuding members of the board, responding to aggrieved shareholders, or negotiating with other parties in disagreement with management. In some cases, the best advice may be for the parties to see their lawyers. But a respected chairman can, at times, provide wise counsel and conciliation to the benefit of the parties, the board, and the company.

6. Being the public face of the company

Finally, we come to a role that chairman of major corporations are increasingly expected to fulfil: being a representative for the board and the company. Where the chairman takes on this role, the CEO can focus more specifically on running the business, which can be useful given a climate of corporate complexity and change. As the public face for the company, the chairman might be called on to interact with shareholders, particularly institutional investors, financial institutions, and analysts, to meet with customers or clients for the company's products, and to represent the company in the external world of public inquiries, media investigations, and public relations exercises.

Although some corporate governance codes now give the role of interacting with institutional investors and financial analysts to the independent director nominated under the code as the senior independent non-executive director, in other cases this can fall to the chairman. Occasionally, the chairman will represent the company, providing a shareholder perspective to the workforce and management. But treading on the chief executive's legitimate territory needs to be avoided. As the public face of the company, the chairman could be called on to make public statements, to appear at inquiries, and to represent the company. The UK Corporate Governance Code now includes an emphasis on the leadership role of the chairman, and a suggestion for the annual re-election of the chairman or the whole board.

Sir Adrian Cadbury[1] identified three principles that, he believes, chairmen should apply:

Openness is one of them—the need to be open to ideas and open in explaining the company's actions and intentions. Openness is particularly important in dealing with people. *Balance* is another of them—the duty to weigh up the consequences of decisions on all those who will be affected by them, and to hold the scales between the demands of today and the needs of tomorrow. A third principle is the well-established one that *rights and responsibilities* go together. Chairmen, therefore, have responsibilities to their boards, as do boards to their chairmen.

Dean Jay Light[2] of the Harvard Business School wrote in 2009 about leadership:

The need for leaders who know how to make a difference in the world has never been greater than it is today . . . qualities that are fundamental to good leadership (include) judgment that leads to sound decision-making, an entrepreneurial point of view, the ability to listen and communicate effectively, a deep sense of one's values and ethics, and the courage to act, based on those values and ethics. The need extends beyond business to the social, government, and non-profit sectors as well.

Obviously, each chairman brings a different style to the leadership of the board. Some have a light touch full of humour and charm, others bring a decisive, no-nonsense approach, and a few are downright Napoleonic. Chairmanship of a board or board committee can be challenging. Successful chairmen often claim that the success is due to their team. But that team needs good leadership.

The UK Financial Reporting Council (FRC) provides useful guidance on the role of chairman based on good practice suggestions from the Higgs Report (2003). The Council points out that good boards are created by good chairmen. The chairman creates the conditions for overall board and individual director effectiveness. Moreover, the chairman should demonstrate the highest standards of integrity and probity, and set clear expectations concerning the company's culture, values, and behaviours, and the style and tone of board discussions.

The FRC suggests that the chairman's role includes:

- demonstrating ethical leadership;
- setting a board agenda that is primarily focused on strategy, performance, value creation, and accountability, and ensuring that issues relevant to these areas are reserved for board decision;
- ensuring a timely flow of high-quality supporting information;

[1] Sir Adrian Cadbury (2002) *Corporate Governance and Chairmanship: A Personal View.* Oxford University Press, Oxford, p. 242.
[2] Dean Jay Light (2009) *Harvard Business School Annual Report.* Available online at www.hbs.edu/about/annualreport/2009

- making certain that the board determines the nature, and extent, of the significant risks that the company is willing to embrace in the implementation of its strategy, and that there are no 'no go' areas, which prevent directors from operating effective oversight in this area;
- regularly considering succession planning and the composition of the board;
- making certain that the board has effective decision-making processes and applies sufficient challenge to major proposals;
- ensuring the board's committees are properly structured with appropriate terms of reference;
- encouraging all board members to engage in board and committee meetings by drawing on their skills, experience, knowledge, and, where appropriate, independence;
- fostering relationships founded on mutual respect and open communication—both in and outside the boardroom—between the non-executive directors and the executive team;
- developing productive working relationships with all executive directors, and the CEO in particular, providing support and advice, while respecting executive responsibility;
- consulting the senior independent director on board matters in accordance with the Code;
- taking the lead on issues of director development, including through induction programmes for new directors and regular reviews with all directors;
- acting on the results of board evaluation;
- being aware of, and responding to, his or her own development needs, including people and other skills, especially when taking on the role for the first time;
- ensuring effective communication with shareholders and other stakeholders and, in particular, ensuring that all directors are made aware of the views of those who provide the company's capital.

Sources of governance power

As we have seen, corporate governance can be thought of as the way in which power is exercised over corporate entities. The issue now is how that power is derived, who wields it, and how it is used. What is power? Mary Parker Follet's definition will serve us well: 'Power is the ability to make things happen.'

The fundamental legal power of the board derives from the shareholder members who have delegated the running of the company to their directors. This power is reinforced by authority derived from the company's constitution, backed up by company law. However, a board can also find itself influenced in a number of ways, for example:

- by a dominant shareholder or group of shareholders putting pressure on the board— for example, the board of a wholly owned subsidiary company must conform to the business policies, plans, and investment decisions made by the group holding company;
- from the threat of a potential takeover—in a public company quoted on a liquid financial market, the ambitions of predators through the market for corporate control can be a constant source of power over a board's behaviour;

- by the prospect of litigation—in a litigious climate, the threat of significant lawsuits from customers (e.g. claiming damages for a faulty product or service), from employees (e.g. suing for damages from heath hazards), or competitors (e.g. alleging infringement of patents or copyright) can concentrate a board's collective mind;

- through the influence of the auditors—an independent external auditor's threat to qualify the audit report, unless significant changes are made to the declared profit, perhaps because of disputed asset valuations, backdated share options, or unrecorded exposure to risk, is likely to affect a board's deliberations;

- from the effects of legislation and regulation—the prospect of new rules regulating the way the company does its business (immigration controls on employees, tariff barriers, corporation tax changes, for example) are bound to influence a board's deliberations;

- from media pressure and other external exhortation—recent years have seen a significant increase in the interest an investigative media has in companies, and external lobbyists, interest groups, and institutional investors may all seek to exert power over a board's thinking;

- from the risk of damage to personal reputations—directors' decisions can be affected by individual directors' concerns about their exposure to risk, both financial and reputational;

- by a dominant or charismatic leader—as we will see later, the effect of the chairman, chief executive, or other board member exerting leadership can have dramatic effects on other members and on the way the board acts; and

- through changing business circumstances.

How a board handles these potential influences is a mark of its professionalism. But in addition to external sources of power over a company and the decisions of its board, individual directors can also wield personal power over board matters.

The power of individual directors also derives from a variety of sources, for example:

- *personality power*—in other words, the power wielded by a charismatic or a dominant individual over other members of the board;

- *knowledge power*—that is, the power derived from access to information, skills, or experiences not available to the other directors, such as the influence that an independent director, who is also a director of an international bank, has when the board is discussing the effect changes in currency rates might have on the company's finances;

- *sanction power*, which is the power that exists if a director can apply some sanction to the company or to other directors, such as, in a joint venture company, the possibility of one partner removing access to an essential source of supply, or in a family company the threat of the father to cut his son out of his will;

- *political power*—that is, the ability of directors to play boardroom games, which we will briefly consider in the next section;

- *interpersonal power* that one person might have over another because of their relationship, such as where a father and son serve on the same board, or where one director has private knowledge about another;

- *organizational power* derived from position in the organizational hierarchy—for example, a CEO inevitably has potential power over other executive directors because managerially they work for him and their prospects depend on that relationship;

- *networking power* derived from contacts and acquaintances of value to the company and useful in board decisions, as captured in the well-known phrase 'it's not what you know but who you know that matters in this world';

- *societal power* derived from a position of influence in society—a well-respected and connected member of society may be able to influence decisions to the company's benefit and public opinion about company activities, which is why retiring politicians are offered board positions, and why 'cooling-off' periods are written into their contracts;

- *ownership power* and the ability to determine board membership—a director who is also either the majority shareholder in a company or his or her nominee has undoubted influence on board deliberations, even though the right to hire or fire other directors may seldom be mentioned;

- *representative power* delegated from an external power source such as an institutional investor, a joint venture partner, or, in a not-for-profit entity, the members.

Games that directors play

Board-level processes, the conduct of meetings and interactions between directors, above all involve communication. Deconstructing directors' comments—mainly spoken, but sometimes written—can identify many layers of underlying meaning. What a director says, and even more significantly what he or she chooses not to say, can demonstrate their understanding of and involvement in a topic under discussion. At a higher level of abstraction, it can illustrate their views on that subject. But it may also illuminate their personal beliefs and values, their opinions of other members of the board, and their sensitivity to what other people are feeling.

In board-level dialogue, the manner and form of communication are significant. Many board members are powerful people, with high self-esteem and big egos. Some are arrogant, self-opinionated, or boastful; a few may be bullies. But others can be diffident, insecure, and shy. Being a good listener is a hallmark of an effective director. Sensitivity to the views of colleagues, hearing not only what they say, but also deducing why they are saying it, creates a climate of mutual trust.

Of course, being a good advocate for an issue under discussion, being able to advance a case clearly, concisely, and with conviction, is also an important attribute. So is the ability to debate contentious issues, in which others hold contrary views. The effective director is aware that if a person's proposals are rudely attacked, he or she is more likely to counter-attack than change his or her mind. Politeness has its place in the boardroom.

In badly led boards, personalities and political manoeuvring can prevail and directors will play games. An awareness of some of these games can help to create a board culture in which they become apparent and are stopped. In a light-hearted review, the following are a few of the games that directors play.

Alliances

Two or more members of the board conspire together to influence a board decision. For example, two executive directors, each responsible for an operating division in a group, work together to prevent the introduction of a proposed management control system that would result in greater transparency of their divisional activities; however, they both agree to argue their case on the grounds that the system would prove expensive and that cost would outweigh any benefit.

Coalitions and cabals

Groups of directors work together, inside and outside the boardroom, to bring about a specific outcome to a board decision. Coalition building involves the canvassing of support for an issue informally outside the boardroom so that there is a sufficient consensus when the matter is discussed formally in the boardroom. For example, a group of directors in a not-for-profit company incorporated to run a sports facility opposed plans to build a new swimming pool. The members of this clique were tennis players not swimmers, and refused to sanction other expenditure unless the swimming pool plan was dropped.

Conspiracy of silence

In some boardrooms, there are issues that everyone recognizes are not discussed: the classical 'elephant in the room', seen but never mentioned. For some, this is a coping strategy, to avoid facing up to an unpleasant reality. Other directors can feign a selective deafness, by refusing to accept a situation. In such circumstances, the chairman needs to make the board face the truth.

Cronyism

Relationships between directors can influence decisions on the basis of personal relationships rather than the rational merits of the case. Cronyism can produce decisions that are not in the best interests of the company. For example, three directors on the board of a listed company were all members of the same country club. They tended to support each other in board discussions, all favouring the same outcome, and opposing the same alternatives. Cronyism can affect an entire board. For example, a director declared a personal interest in a tender for a project being discussed by the board. He was asked to leave the room during the discussion of that contract. But the board decided to support this bid because of their personal relationships with that director, even though the bid was not the most worthy.

Deal-making

Agreements made outside the boardroom between two or more directors to achieve a specific outcome on a board issue. Deal-making is a classic game, usually involving compromise. The medical members of a hospital board agreed, during a private dinner, to put pressure on the board to acquire some new sophisticated medical equipment that they wanted. They were successful, even though there were more pressing needs for the available funds, including cleaning equipment for the wards.

Dereliction of duty

On a board, all directors have equal responsibility. But some directors fail to accept that responsibility. They concur with the thinking of the chairman or CEO, and thereby are transferring their power and forgoing their duty as directors.

Divide and rule

When a contentious issue is being discussed, the outcome wanted by one faction is more likely to be achieved if the other directors can be divided into a number of disagreeing factions. This is a ploy adopted from the chair in some boards. Divide and rule can be a dirty game, in which the player sees the chance to set one director against another, or groups of directors against each other. An issue in the financial accounts might be used, for example, to divide the executive directors, the non-executive directors, and the auditors from each other, in order to achieve an entirely different personal aim. For example, a senior outside director serving on the board of a Canadian cooperative advanced arguments that divided the board into three groups reflecting the views of the various representative groups—suppliers, customers, and the administration; thus he could push through the strategy he wanted.

Empire building

Usually adopted by executive directors, empire building involves the misuse of privileged access to information, people, or other resources to acquire power over organizational territory. The process can involve intrigue, battles, and conquests. Consider the example of a company in the IT consulting business, which acquired a marketing company to promote its business. The operations director of the IT company moved his staff to the more palatial offices of the marketing company, took over its fleet of cars, and argued in the board meeting that his deputy should also become a board member because of his enlarged portfolio of responsibilities.

Group-think

Some boards, particularly if the members have served together for a long time, can tend to think the same way, interpreting situations and reaching conclusions without debate or dissension. Group-think is not so much a game as a board-wide attitude of mind. Sound chairmanship will avoid the danger, prompting constructive challenge. The probability of group-think is reduced with a diverse board of directors holding different perspectives and able to speak their minds.

Half-truths

By presenting only part of the information on an issue before the board, an unscrupulous director can bias the discussion in favour of his or her own preferred result. While the director does not actually lie, the half-truth obscures the full story. For example, an executive director argued strongly in favour of his own project, presenting impressive cost–benefit information in support, but failing totally to mention that the risk of stoppage to the firm's entire operation would be significantly increased.

Hidden agendas

An individual director offers a convincing argument in support of a particular line in a board discussion without adding that additional outcomes to their advantage would then arise—this is the hidden agenda. Hidden agendas usually involve the pursuit of secret goals that benefit a director's own interests or further their own career against the interest of the organization as a whole. In other words, the ploy is another example of the agency dilemma. For example, in advocating a contract to acquire services for a joint venture, a director on the joint venture company board failed to mention that this contract would bring significant sales discounts on products bought by one of the joint venture partners—his employer.

Lobbying

Lobbying involves attempts to influence directors, or those in a position to influence directors, usually outside the boardroom. Consider the implications when a director of a consulting practice sought out the wife of the CEO of a client company during a cocktail party and encouraged her to persuade her husband to accept a quotation.

Log rolling

Two or more directors colluding, to their mutual benefit, is a classic board-level game. For example, two executive directors in a manufacturing company came to an agreement before the board meeting: the first would enthusiastically support an investment proposal benefiting the second; while the other would offer mitigating arguments during the review of the poor budgetary performance of the first.

Personal agendas

Without strong chairmanship, a lot of board time and effort can be wasted on directors who hijack board meetings by promoting matters in which they have a personal interest.

Propaganda

Propaganda is the dissemination of information to support a cause, without attempting to show the complete picture. The chief executive of a finance institution made a PowerPoint presentation to his board, advocating the introduction of a new derivative-based product, without once mentioning the word 'risk'. Unfortunately, none of the non-executive directors raised the question, the board approved the proposal, and a year later the company had to issue a profit warning following losses on the new product.

Rival camps

Rival camps occur where there are opposing factions on a board in an extreme case of coalitions and cabals. Hostilities, spies, and double agents can be involved. The board of a

'Fortune 500' company were totally split on a proposal led by the chairman/CEO to bid for a rival company. Leaders of each faction emerged and the two groups began to hold separate meetings, to brief the press independently, and to talk with institutional investors about their own perspectives on the bid.

Scaremongering

Scaremongering is used by some directors to emphasize the downside risks in a board decision, casting doubts on the situation without presenting a balanced perspective, thus attempting to have the proposal turned down. As a director in a multinational manufacturing group argued convincingly, when the board was considering building a new manufacturing facility in another country: 'We shall have nothing but labour troubles and high taxes, if we locate there, and possibly government interference . . . and who knows what might happen if the present government falls? We could find all our assets nationalized without recompense.' A risk assessment would have shown the probability of those uncertain future events to be low.

Snowing

Snowing involves deluging any director who asks for more information on a topic with masses of data, thus confusing the situation and hiding any cracks. This game is usually played by executive directors on unsuspecting outside directors.

Spinning

Spinning, a form of gaming developed at governmental level, intentionally presents a distorted view of a person or a situation, in a way that favours the spinner's interests. In corporate governance, spinning can be carried out at the level of board committees, the board as a whole, the shareholders, or the media.

Sponsorship

Sponsorship is support by a powerful director for another director, often a newly elected director, usually for their joint benefit. For example, the long-serving director of the Australian subsidiary of an American global group commented during a board meeting: 'Mr Chairman, I'll have a word with Robert (a new director) after the meeting to explain how we handle these things. As you know I've a lot of experience of this type of situation and what we've done in the past.' In the ensuing discussion, the experienced director relayed a lot of gossip about the ways of the board and its chairman to his own future benefit.

Sub-optimization

Sub-optimization occurs when a director supports a part of the organization to the detriment of the company as a whole. We have explored this situation already, both when considering the agency dilemma and in group management control systems.

Some executive directors suffer from tunnel vision, because they are too closely involved with a functional department, division, or subsidiary company. Others may have a myopic view of the situation because they would be personally affected by the outcome. An independent evaluation of the overall strategic situation and top management performance by outside directors can help to overcome such problems.

Window dressing

Window dressing includes making a fine external show of sound corporate governance principles and practice, while minimizing failures. Some companies' mission statements, social responsibility, and sustainable reports, as well as core principles, suffer from window dressing. Window dressing can also involve showing financial results in the best possible light, while hiding weaknesses, although this runs the risk of an adverse audit report or worse.

One of the problems facing companies publishing non-financial statements to shareholders, such as those increasingly required in operating reviews, can give rise to concerns about window dressing. Information about strategic intentions is open to optimistic presentation and is not amenable to conventional financial audit. On the other hand, few boards are likely to expose their shareholders to information about potential risks facing the company from competitors, predators, or other uncertain future events.

Notice that most of the 'games' described involve the subtleties of communication and interpersonal relations. Most of the tactics are not illegal, do not amount to fraud, nor are they inherently dishonest. They are a means to achieving directors' personal preferences. Notice, too, that many of these 'games' are commonplace in the world of government, where they are considered legitimate. Indeed, in some boards, too, game playing becomes an art form and board meetings more like the deliberations of an adversarial parliament. Strong chairmanship can reduce the disadvantages of game playing, unless of course the chairman is also playing games! The ideal is a well-led professional board team working together with integrity, in which directors understand and trust each other, and do not need to resort to game playing. In such situations, directors can take tough-minded positions and defend their point of view strongly, but are also flexible enough to see other points of view and seek consensus.

Before leaving the topic of board-level politics, here are a few more light-hearted thoughts on the board-level game of manipulating meetings.

Meeting manipulation

There are a number of devices that directors have been known to use to achieve the results they want in meetings.

- *Management of the agenda* determines what is and is not discussed. Influencing the agenda is a powerful weapon and experienced chairmen will ensure that they remain in control.
- *Challenging the minutes* of the last meeting at the start of the next meeting can be used to re-open discussion of an item that was resolved, against the manipulator's interests, previously. Strong chairmanship prevents such activities.

- *Hijacking the chair*—in other words, taking over the running of the meeting—can only work if the chairman is new or ineffective.

- *Refocusing the debate* when the tenor of the meeting is running against the manipulator's interests can involve a number of devices. Talking around the subject, while shifting the discussion onto favourable ground, is a particular skill of the meeting manipulator. Profound irrelevance is their stock-in-trade. But filibustering to run the discussion out of time will seldom work in the boardroom.

- *The 'put-down'* involves the skilful introduction of doubt when responding to a proposal before the board, as in 'the bank would never agree with anything like that'. Good put-downs often adopt an air of superiority, as in 'we discussed this matter before you joined the board and decided against it'.

- *Presenting ideas in the context of other people's* can be powerful: 'I was inclined to believe ... until I heard X, now I am sure we should ...' The fact that X was advocating something quite different is not the point.

- *Summarizing* the discussion thus far can be used to emphasize favourable points and to downplay others: 'What the meeting seems to be saying is ...'

- *Predetermining the outcome* is an extension of the summarizing device used to foreclose discussion by stating the outcome of a decision, preferably in Latin, as in 'Chairman, we seem to have reached the decision *nem con*' (*nemine contradicente*: 'no one against or without objection'), whether anyone is against or not.

- *A challenge*, when a discussion seems to be flowing against the manipulator's interests, can be persuasive. 'On a point of order, chairman' is a call that, if offered with sufficient challenge and conviction, will stop an orator in full flight. Strictly, points of order are only relevant if there are standing orders covering the running of the meeting—but that will not deter a skilful meeting manipulator.

- *A call to the chair* that the discussion has strayed from the point of the agenda item, that irrelevant issues are being raised, or that the discussion would be more appropriate under another item can be used to deflect an ongoing discussion that is moving against the manipulator's interests.

- *'Any other business'* on the agenda can also be used to re-open debate or introduce new items. However, the chairman may insist that only items previously notified can be discussed and that no papers can be tabled. No matter: the manipulator will use the agendum 'date of the next meeting' to introduce a new topic, to explain the issue, to hand out the papers, to express an opinion, to suggest further discussion or the formation of a subcommittee with him or her in the chair. 'We need to look into this issue with the care and attention it deserves', ensuring that the subcommittee has a majority of those who favour the idea.

- *Calling for a postponement of discussion* until the next meeting, on the grounds of the lack of information, the need for more reflection, or until an absent member is present,

- can also be used to postpone a decision that seems likely to be decided against the manipulator's interests.

- *Calling for an adjournment of the meeting* is a heavier version of the postponement device.

- *Lack of a quorum* can be used to stymie a decision if the articles of association or the rulebook specify a quorum, so that the lack of a quorum will prevent further decision-making. The chances are that few present will know if there is a quorum in the rules or what it is.

- Finally, the *management of the minutes* can provide a crucial opportunity to manipulate a meeting.

Some will say that this section on game playing and meeting manipulation takes a cynical view of board-level interaction. Others will believe that it more closely mirrors their own experience of boardroom life than explorations of board structures and codes of good governance practice. What is undoubtedly true is that the reality of boardroom life involves people, power, and politics as much as rigorous analysis and rational debate.

Board styles and the culture of the board

It is apparent that the dynamics of the boardroom vary considerably. Boards differ in their cultures and their styles. Some boards are highly professional in their operations, with experienced, well-informed, and collaborative directors, often holding strong views and engaging in tough-minded, but amicable, debate. Outside directors are closely involved in decision-making and share a common view of the corporate strategy. Deliberations in such boards tend to seek consensus and votes are rarely taken. The boards of many listed companies in Western cultures fall into this group.

However, even in Western cultures, the behaviour of boards is not always professional. For example, board culture can evolve into a comfortable, convivial relationship between the directors. Outside directors may ask questions and offer suggestions, but not probe in depth. Some never challenge the executive directors. In board deliberations, such directors tend to support each other and do not have tough-minded exchanges. In such companies, the climate in the boardroom is cosy—in fact, more like that of a privileged old-boys club.

Then there is a category of company in which the board provides little more than a legalizing rubber stamp for decisions taken elsewhere. As we shall see, there are some situations in which this can be legitimate.

Finally, there is a fourth category of board, which has members representing different interests. A hospital board, with members representing the hospital administration, the medical team, the patients, and funding bodies, would be an example. In such boards, members tend to take positions that reflect the interests of the groups they represent. Debates can be lively and votes are often called for on issues. The governance style, in fact, is more like that of opposing political parties in a national government.

What determines board style? Board style is a function of a number of variables. First and foremost is the board leadership and the role played by the board chairman. The size of the board also affects its style: too many members and the opportunity for individuals to contribute become limited and the board may divide into factions; too few and there may be insufficient diversity of view. The balance of the board between executive directors, both independent and connected, will clearly affect the tenor of board deliberations, as will the balance of experience and background among the board members as well. The actual set of attributes among all the directors—their combined experience, knowledge, and skills—is also a major causal factor in determining board style.

The culture of the board, including its history, its past leadership, and previous events affecting the business, will also influence its style. The following set of criteria lists various attributes affecting board style and shows some of the likely effects. Notice the range of differences that can exist between boards.

Board traditions

In some boards, rituals and customs mean a lot. Corporate stories and traditions are frequently mentioned. Board procedures and precedents are well established. Many members of the board are likely to be long-serving. There is probably a formal boardroom and there may be pictures of past chairmen on the wall. At the other extreme are boards with no time for tradition, in which board practices change readily. The average length of directors' service is short. Informality is the keynote of their meetings, which are held wherever and whenever it is convenient.

Corporate vision

This attribute of style indicates the extent to which directors share the same strategic vision about the company's present position and its future direction and prospects. In some companies, all of the directors can readily articulate the company's mission and strategic situation; in others, directors either do not understand the company's strategic context or, worse, disagree on what it is.

Innovation

Here, the issue is the extent to which each director is expected to contribute new ideas. In some boards, all ideas are welcomed, even if controversial. In others, new thinking is discouraged, developments are expected to fit established norms, change is resisted, and past successes influence views on the future.

Control

This reflects the way in which the board accepts responsibility for exerting overall control over the enterprise, if necessary becoming involved in responding to business problems, or delegating that responsibility down to management through the chief executive. In some companies the top executives wield more power over more possessions than medieval monarchs.

Decision taking

Decision taking may be strongly influenced by one person or a small group of directors, in which case there may be little analysis and many dogmatic statements; alternatively, decisions may be reached after much talking, leading to an eventual consensus among all directors.

Leadership

In some boards, authority is jealously guarded by one or a few of the directors, with other board members expected to give advice only when called on. In other boards, the leadership style encourages all directors to contribute to board deliberations, with people respected for their experience, knowledge, and wisdom.

Commitment

At one extreme are those boards the members of which show a low commitment to the board, with high levels of self-interest; at the other extreme, all directors are highly committed to the company, the board, and their fellow directors.

Adaptability

Some boards are slow to adapt to changing circumstances. Consequently, board meetings tend to be predictable. Other boards are highly adaptive, with flexible responses to changing situations, even though their meetings can sometimes be turbulent.

Collaboration

In some boards, the directors support each other, ensuring that everyone is informed, involved, and committed. At the other extreme are boards the members of which tend to compete with each other, showing distrust, poor interpersonal relationships, and even hostility towards one another.

Conflict

Board-level conflict can be either desirable or destructive. Conflict that is creative, with tough-minded, but courteous, interactions between people who say what they believe, but try to understand conflicting points of view, is found in some boards. In others, overt conflict may be discouraged, but then there may be behind-the-scenes political activity.

Relationships

In some boards, directors see themselves as part of the board team, and treat each other with frankness, respect, and trust. In others, directors act as individuals, rather than as part of the board team. In such cases, image building, posturing, and boardroom games may be prevalent.

Communication

Access to information, as we have seen earlier, is a source of potential board-level power. Consequently, in some boards, directors guard the information they have, protecting their sources, and encouraging secrecy. Gossip and grapevine communication are likely to be prevalent. Other boards, however, seem to encourage open communication, with a ready exchange of data, information, and knowledge.

Status

Directors' perceptions of their status can be important, with visible signs of the directors' prestige being of value, with formal even ritual meetings, and probably ornate boardrooms and elaborate meals. Conversely, in other boards, status is relatively unimportant, with directors seeing each other as equals, and not needing ego-reinforcing signals to be sent to the rest of the organization or the outside world.

Conformity

Some board chairmen, believing that a board has to be united, expect their directors to conform to group norms. Non-conformists are not tolerated; indeed they are unlikely to be appointed in the first place. By contrast, other chairmen welcome non-conformists, recognizing that they can bring fresh insights and enliven board thinking.

Trust

As we have seen, trust is the underpinning of the concept of the corporation. Typically, this refers to the fiduciary duty owed by directors to their shareholders. But the relationship *between* directors also plays an important part. In some boards, directors trust each other implicitly. But it has to be noted that in others trust can be low and directors suspicious of each other. As we will see later, much hinges on the ability and leadership style of the board chairman.

Some of these characteristics of board style reflect relationships at board level and the way in which the board members work together. Others affect how well the board does its work and achieves its goals. The challenge is to balance concern for relationships with concern for achieving board success. The simple matrix in Figure 14.1 contrasts a board's concern for the relationships between its members with its concern for getting the job done.

Boards that show a high concern for board relationships and have a high regard for the achievement of the board's task can be considered to have a professional style. Concentrating on the board task, but less on relationships, is a feature of the representative board. The board of the hospital discussed earlier, in which board members represented various stakeholder groups, provided a good example. Whereas a board that focuses more on personal relationships than on the task in hand is the hallmark of the country club board style. Those scoring low on each count are effectively acting as rubber stamps to decisions taken elsewhere. This can be appropriate in subsidiary companies that are managed through a group management structure, or in 'letter box' companies incorporated to protect a name, to limit liability on an exposed risk, or for tax planning purposes.

The characteristics listed above can be used as the basis for a board-level exercise to plot a board's style. Obviously, the results reflect the perceptions of those making assessment on the range between the extremes for each criterion. The exercise can be used both in director development and the assessment of board performance.

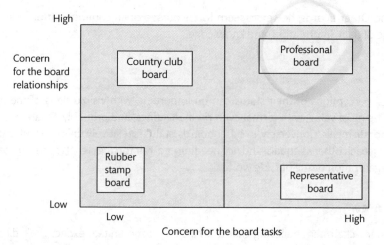

Figure 14.1 Different board styles

Business ethics begin in the boardroom

Whether at the level of a country, a society, or a company, every culture incorporates a value system, which reflects the attitudes, beliefs, and expected behaviour in that culture. Corporate values influence the way the people in the organization behave towards each other and towards those with whom they come into contact outside the organization. Corporate values are involved in every activity, from board-level decisions of strategic significance, such as switching production to a developing country, to everyday interactions between managers and employees, staff and customers.[3]

Corporate values reflect the values of the corporate leaders. Ruthless leaders produce ruthless followers. Weak leaders create weak organizations. Leaders who display a short-term, bottom-line orientation will produce organizations in which these characteristics dominate: some Wall Street institutions prior to the global financial crisis provide perfect examples. Leaders who are tough-minded yet fair create organizations that encourage these attributes. The respected leader has to earn that respect both in personal actions and behaviour towards others.

Corporate values are often implicit, part of people's perceptions about what sort of behaviour is expected, how people relate to each other, 'what you do and don't do around here'. However, increasingly companies are trying to make corporate values explicit, articulating what the board aspires to and wants to encourage.

Recent years have seen a spate of business crises and corporate collapses around the world. The actions of key executives and the attitudes of their directors have come under the public spotlight. Fraudulent management in Australia's HIH Insurance, corruption in Italy's Parmalat, allegations of bribery against BAE Systems and Rolls Royce, the world-wide collapse of auditors Arthur Andersen, the rigging of interest rates by bankers provide ready examples.

---

[3] Extracted from Tricker, Bob and Gretchen (2014) 'Business ethics begin in the boardroom'. European Financial Review, 23 April.

Such cases have raised concerns about business ethics. The media focus on companies' social responsibilities, relations with their stakeholders, and call more ethical business. Regulators, commentators, and business school professors push for better corporate citizenship. Recently, green credentials and sustainability have been added to the agenda.

But business ethics are not an optional exercise in corporate citizenship, they are fundamental to the governance and management of every organization. Decisions at every level in a company have ethical implications—strategically in the board room, managerially throughout the organization, and operationally in each of its activities. Ethics reflect behaviour *in* business and the behaviour *of* business. In business, ethics involve the recognition and management of risk.

With risks that arise from moral hazards, that is ethical risks, mitigation—for example by duplicating systems, or transferring the risk, such as through insurance—is seldom a viable option. Recognizing and accepting a risk may be the only alternative to abandoning that opportunity. Consequently, the consideration of exposure to ethical risk needs to be part of every board's strategy formulation, and enshrined in corporate policy and enterprise risk management. With moral dilemmas in business it is seldom a matter that actions are good or bad, right or wrong, but what's the best choice, the most appropriate decision, for the company and those affected by its actions.

Most boards insist that their company should not break the laws of any jurisdiction in which they operate. Unfortunately such an attitude does not address ethical questions that can arise in other countries. Major companies, including Google, Amazon, and Microsoft, have been criticized for 'aggressive tax avoidance' when they manoeuvred funds through tax havens to reduce global taxation, even though their actions were perfectly legal (Case study 15.2). Alleged excessive top management remuneration has also been a source of concern, particularly to increasingly vocal shareholder activists.

Business ethics have not traditionally been thought of as part of corporate governance. They have been seen (and researched and taught) as separate subjects. Corporate governance is concerned with the way companies use their power and the way power is exercised over them. The use, and sometimes the abuse, of that power can raise ethical issues.

Enron, the giant American energy business (case study 4.2), failed dramatically. Some of its directors went to jail. Yet that company appeared to meet the tenets of good corporate governance: the board had distinguished independent directors; there were audit, nomination, and remuneration committees; and the role of board chairman was separate from that of the chief executive, unusual for large American corporations at the time. What the board failed to realize was that the company's risk profile had changed dramatically when it moved from generating energy to trading in energy futures. It had moved from being a producer of energy to a financial institution. Moreover, the directors failed to see the moral hazard in some of the accounting methods that management had adopted.

Despite written policies on corporate social responsibility and sustainability, the oil company BP faced a disaster in the Gulf of Mexico (Case study 8.2) when its Deepwater Horizon oil-rig exploded and sank. The board had failed to recognize or had accepted this exposure to risk in their operations. Further, following the disaster top management were slow to respond to public and political concerns, failing to realize the company's exposure to reputational damage. The company lost over half its share value.

Critics of business behaviour point to fraud, bribery and corruption. They allege price-rigging, pollution, and counterfeiting. They claim arrogance, greed, and abuse of power by those at the top of companies. Trust in business has been eroded. For some, business ethics has become an oxymoron, as they cite corporate avarice, disparity of wealth, and director rewards that are not reflected in corporate performance.

Yet business exists by satisfying customers, creating employment, and generating wealth. Business provides the taxes that society needs to function. Many companies accept a social responsibility to be sound corporate citizens. They recognize that they have a duty to respect the interest of all the stakeholders who might be affected by their actions. Many also seek a sustainable, environmentally friendly approach to their operations. To those who doubt whether modern business can be trusted, they point out that business dealings and the very concept of the limited-liability company are based on trust. Trust in business will not be rebuilt by more rules, regulations, or corporate governance codes, but as directors create cultures that recognize and handle ethical risk.

Ultimately, the board of directors and top management are responsible for the ethical behaviour of their enterprise. Directors set the standards for their organization, provide the corporate conscience, fashion its culture, determine the risks to be taken, and set the ethical climate. They generate the value system for the organization. Business ethics begin in the board room.

However, some boards delegate responsibility for developing policies by creating and enforcing codes of conduct or ethics to their audit committee. Others form a corporate governance or compliance committee that includes such duties, although the use of the word 'compliance' could suggest a conformist approach to corporate governance, overlooking the performance aspects. Yet other boards believe that the corporate culture, corporate values, and ethical issues are properly the responsibility of the board as a whole.

Corporate codes of ethics and their enforcement

Corporate values can be influenced from within an organization, but predominantly corporate values are derived from the top. A successful ethics policy reflects a company's core values, stems from its corporate mission, and is consistent with its corporate strategies. Without board and top management involvement and commitment, ethics policies are unlikely to succeed.

Some companies develop ethics policies that set standards for employee behaviour and require employee compliance with those norms. The codes of ethics that flow from such policies set standards of expected behaviour, seek to enforce discipline, and are inevitably employee-centred. Other companies set ethical policies to encourage commitment to good relations with all stakeholders. A successful ethics policy probably embraces both of these perspectives: describing the expected relationships between the organization and each of its stakeholders, while outlining the behaviour expected from employees.

A sound ethics policy is likely to:

- be orientated towards corporate values, rather than organizational discipline;
- seek genuine commitment rather than being a cosmetic exercise;
- recognize the cultural context;
- avoid credibility gaps between ethical codes and actual behaviour;

- link with corporate governance policies and practices;
- have associated ethics management systems, including information and control systems, regular audit, policy review procedures, and social accounting systems;
- demonstrate accountability with regular reports.

Corporate codes of ethics

A corporate ethics policy is usually supported by a corporate code of ethics or code of conduct. This is an explicit statement setting out the ethical standards expected of everyone in that organization. Typically, it will be approved and issued by the board of directors. Ethical codes can be found at various organizational levels:

- corporate codes that relate to a single corporate entity;
- professional codes that apply to the members of a particular profession;
- industry codes that are developed for use throughout a specific industry;
- group codes that are used within a given set of members, for example companies that are part of a marketing standards programme.

Codes of ethics can be used to:

- define and create the value system required for the organization;
- define and set standards of expected behaviour;
- improve individuals' ethical awareness and judgement;
- promote high standards of practice;
- set benchmarks for self-evaluation and monitoring by peers and others;
- inform external stakeholders of the values of the organization.

In some cases, companies require every employee formally to accept the code and to confirm that he or she has followed it. Companies with a global supply chain sometimes also create supply chain codes of conduct, typically a set of standards based on local and national laws and regulations, which reflect the International Labour Organization core conventions, including, for example, standards on underage labour, forced/prison labour, wages and compensation, working hours, discrimination, disciplinary practices, freedom of association, health and safety, and the environment. For an example, see the supplier code of Li & Fung Ltd (at www.lifung.com).

Since sound business ethics involve being seen to be 'doing the right thing' by all those likely to be affected by a company's activities, involving stakeholders in the ethical management process can be important. This may be little more than occasional dialogue to obtain feedback on past performance and future plans. Or it could take the form of more formal consultations on specific issues, for example noise-reduction plans with local communities affected by corporate activities. It might even involve a more formal partnership relationship, in which representatives of stakeholder groups, such as suppliers, customers, or local interest groups, become involved in an ongoing relationship that directly influences corporate behaviour.

Information is fundamental to successful ethics management. Information about ethical codes, policies, and procedures needs to be promulgated to all those concerned. Standards, goals, and performance criteria need to be set and accepted. Achievement of these criteria needs to be monitored and relevant, timely information reported so that managers can monitor situations within their area of responsibility and take appropriate action when necessary. Some organizations create reporting channels for all employees, including ethics hotlines that can be used to report ethical concerns, sometimes anonymously, sometimes providing feedback advice.

On whistle-blowing and whistle-blowers

'Blowing the whistle' means informing on a person or an organization believed to be acting improperly. The whistle-blower provides the information to someone with the authority to take appropriate action. The alleged wrong-doer could be a colleague, a manager, or an entire organization. The issue might be the breaking of laws or regulations, contravention of an ethical code, or offending in some other way.

Whistle-blowing can have many implications and should not be undertaken lightly. What action should a potential whistle-blower take? The first, most obvious step is to convey the concern to a person in authority. Should that resolve the problem, there is no call for whistle-blowing. But if the person in authority assumes responsibility for the issue yet takes no action to put it right, the whistle-blower has to decide whether to take the next step: to go to a higher authority, perhaps the chairman of the audit committee, the chairman of the board, or the auditors.

Clearly, whistle-blowing can have serious ramifications for informers. They may be seen as trouble-makers and victimized. Their career prospects could be damaged. They might be fired. They could be 'black-listed,' unable to get a reference for another job.

An Enron accountant had sent an email to her boss saying that the company's financial policies were suspect and could lead to a collapse. She was fired. The boss knew that the company was in financial trouble, but he publicly encouraged other employees to invest in the company's shares, while he sold his own.

The Ethics Resource Center reported in 2011 that retaliation against whistle-blowers had risen dramatically, including acts of physical violence. More than one in five of employees who reported workplace misconduct also experienced some form of retaliation, nearly twice the number reported in 2009.

How far should a whistle-blower go? Of course, if a whistle-blower leaves the organization, a number of channels may be open to pursue the problem further: contact the company's auditors, the company regulator, or the media, for example, although the laws of libel, slander, and defamation need to be considered. These days, whistle-blowers might use the internet or write a blog; although again they need to be aware of laws designed to protect privacy and wrongful allegation. Sometimes, companies offer whistle-blowers an acceptable bonus if they resign from the company, provided that they sign an agreement not to disclose the issue to anyone else. Obviously, such an action creates a further ethical dilemma.

In recent years, some governments have recognized the value of whistle-blowers in drawing attention to wrongs in society, and realized that whistle-blowers need some protection from the potential reaction to their whistle-blowing. Following the Enron case, the

Sarbanes-Oxley Act of 2002 specifically required US-listed companies to provide systems for reporting unethical behaviour and other wrongdoing anonymously to an audit committee made up of independent outside directors.

The US Securities and Exchange Commission (SEC) introduced new rules in 2011 to encourage corporate whistle-blowing. Whistle-blowers can receive between 10–30% of fines levied by the regulator over $1 million. The US Chamber of Commerce deprecated such payments, calling them 'a bounty program that will reward amateur sleuths in search of a big pay-day' Keith Edwards, a junior vice-president in JPMorgan Chase, was sacked in 2008 for whistle-blowing on alleged false payments made under government contracts. The bank was fined $614 million under the US False Claims Act and Edwards received $63 million for blowing the whistle. The US Internal Revenue Service paid a whistle-blower $104 million in 2012 for information about the Swiss Bank UBS, which had encouraged over 4,000 wealthy Americans to place funds with them in Switzerland to avoid US tax. UBS was fined $780 million. There have been calls for similar cash payments to whistleblowers in the United Kingdom, noting that many companies are now multi-nationals and rules on whistle-blowing should converge.

In the United Kingdom, the Public Interest Disclosures at Work Act 1998 provided some protection for potential whistle-blowers. In 2013, a whistle-blowing commission, formed by the charity 'Public Concern at Work,' published a report on the Act and concluded that it was not fit for purpose. It called for a whistle-blowers code. In 2014, it emerged that UK public sector bodies, including the National Health Service, had paid large sums to staff who had drawn attention to failings, provided they signed 'gagging clauses' not to publicize the issues.

Both the European Union and the Organization for Economic Co-operation and Development (OECD), an international organization formed to help governments tackle economic, social and governance problems, have indicated the importance of member states having legislation to protect whistle-blowers.

Changing expectations against corruption and bribery

Integrity in business life and anti-corruption policies have been long-standing traditions in the United States, enshrined in the laws of the various states and federally in the act that set up the SEC in 1934. The anti-bribery provisions of the Foreign Corrupt Practices Act of 1977 prohibit companies incorporated in the United States or having their principal place of business in the United States, any individual who is a citizen, national, or resident of the United States, from offering anything of value to a foreign party to obtain business. The Act also has provisions that require companies to keep records that reflect the transactions of the corporation, to maintain an adequate system of internal accounting controls, and to report to the SEC. The Act does allow so-called 'grease payments' to facilitate the operation of a contract once the agreement has been made.

More recently, the United States and over thirty other countries agreed to work together to reduce corruption and money laundering throughout the global financial system, acting together against bribery of government officials.

The UK Bribery Act 2010 made it a criminal offence to offer, ask for, or accept an inducement for acting improperly. Moreover, companies commit an offence if they fail to prevent bribery by an employee. The Act applies to UK organizations, whether the alleged offence was committed in the United Kingdom or abroad.

Hong Kong has extensive and tight regulations against bribery and other forms of business corruption. An organization separate from government, the Independent Commission against Corruption, has police-like powers of investigation, arrest, and prosecution. Similarly, Singapore has the Corrupt Practices Investigation Bureau. Consequently, these two places rank highly on indices of sound places in which to do business.

Around the world, many business people still protest that, in some countries and cultures, the only way to do business is by accepting local attitudes to 'commissions', 'discounts', and other personal favours, which are expected, indeed demanded, by those able to influence the outcome of business negotiations. They complain that the restrictions imposed on them by their own country's anti-bribery legislation puts them at a negotiating disadvantage. Such attitudes emphasize the importance of board-level policies on corporate values, the creation of corporate codes of ethics, and their enforcement.

Implementing corporate governance below board level

Although the need for sound corporate governance is widely accepted in boardrooms around the world, and despite the basics of corporate governance being clearly articulated in principles and codes, many directors and particularly board chairmen still question how it applies in their own case. They ask, for example:

- what is the *real* role of the board?
- how should a board relate to top management?
- how should the board balance collaboration with control?
- what should a board delegate to management?
- how much freedom of action should the CEO have in practice?
- how can a unitary board contribute to performance while ensuring conformance?

In an earlier chapter, the recommendation was made that boards should establish a policy on decisions that are retained to the board—that is, those that cannot be delegated to management. But the concerns listed above go far beyond the establishment of a formal checklist of retained decisions. They go to the heart of the board's role, the directors' work, and the way in which corporate governance links with management. In particular, the leadership role of the chairman comes under the spotlight.

Surprisingly perhaps, answers to the questions posed above vary significantly between companies and between cultures. Much depends on how corporate governance is perceived and, particularly, on the attitudes and competence of the chairman.

In the UK/Commonwealth model, the principles-based 'comply or explain' approach to corporate governance gives boards freedom to interpret the relevant corporate governance code and allows directors considerable freedom to determine their relationship with management. In these circumstances, boards face a range of options. These are reinforced by the separation of board chairmanship from the chief executive. At one extreme, the directors can delegate power over the business of the company to CEOs and their management teams, in effect discussing and eventually approving strategies, policies, and plans proposed by management, then ensuring that the proposals are followed and the expected results achieved. At the other extreme, the directors can retain power over much of the strategic direction and planning of the business, requiring the CEO and his or her management to carry out those plans and be accountable for results. In between the extremes, the delegation of power from the board to management can vary considerably and may change as chairmen, directors, senior managers, or business circumstances change.

In the American model, the rules-based approach to corporate governance gives boards fewer degrees of freedom. Combining the roles of board chairman and CEO concentrates power in that person. The top management team, which reports to the chairman/CEO, runs the business operations whatever and wherever they are. The chairman/CEO is then accountable to the board, and in effect becomes the linchpin between the board and the management. The presence of one or two other executive directors on the board—say the chief operating officer (COO) and the chief finance officer (CFO)—typically serves only to reinforce the chairman/CEO's position. In these circumstances, a board consisting predominantly of independent outside directors is likely to perceive its role as advising the chairman/CEO—perhaps questioning the strategies, risks, and resources, ensuring conformance to plans, and confirming compliance with legal requirements.

Although the board is responsible for the CEO's remuneration and contract, disciplining a successful and strong-minded CEO can be difficult. Some critics have suggested that, given the abundance of independent directors, this form of board is closer to the European two-tier supervisory board model than the UK/Commonwealth model. The primary differences are, of course, that the American board *does* have some executive directors, probably the CEO and perhaps the COO and CFO, whereas in the European board no common membership is allowed between the supervisory board members and the executive management board.

The powerful chairman/CEO is at the apex of the American model of corporate governance. This fundamentally differentiates the perception of the board's role and its relationship with management from the UK/Commonwealth model. The American model tends to see the board as a group of independent outside directors, whose experience and knowledge provide advice and oversight. Primarily, the power lies in their duty to appoint, to assess, and ultimately, if necessary, to sack the chairman/CEO. But overall responsibility for the company then lies with that powerful CEO/chairman. Indeed, this has caused shareholder activist Bob Monks to question whether boards of some American corporations have ever really understood corporate governance.

In the continental European model, the two-tier board structure, as we have seen, attempts to overcome the fundamental problem of the unitary board by separating the performance role of the management board from the conformance responsibility of the supervisory board. Thus, unlike the unitary board, no single body is responsible for both performance and conformance. Consequently, the relationship between the board and management has quite different dimensions from the unitary board model. In the two-tier model, the relationships between the members of the supervisory board and the top executives on the management board is basic. Experience shows that, although the separation of performance and conformance functions between the two boards is conceptually appealing, in practice significant problems can arise between the supervisory board and top management.

In the family-centric model of Asian corporate governance, the head of the family is typically the head of management as well as the leader of the board. In the *keiretsu* and *chaebol* models of Japanese and South Korean corporate governance, power to determine what decisions are delegated from board to management is often heavily centralized. In the state-owned or state-dominated models of Asian corporate governance, the state often retains the power to appoint directors and influence the work of the board, which in turn determines what is decided at board level and what is delegated to management.

The implementation of corporate governance below board level goes to the heart of corporate governance: it is about the reality of power. Who wields what power over the corporate entity and in what way? The ultimate challenge is to achieve compliance with competence. Such dilemmas are still unresolved in some companies, and grow particularly apparent if the company's activities become international and the directors have to face alternative perspectives.

Case studies

 Case study 14.1   Should Terry blow the whistle?

Many companies listed on the Hong Kong Stock Exchange are family firms with a minority of the voting shares available to the public. Under the Listing Rules of the Stock Exchange, public companies must have a minimum of three independent non-executive directors on the board, at least one of whom must have professional qualifications in accounting or financial management expertise.

LTN Manufacturing was a typical case. Founded by K. L. Lee in the 1970s, the company started as a furniture maker in the Wanchai District of Hong Kong, but over the years had developed into a significant shop fitting business and supplier of stands for exhibitions. Mr Lee, who was the major shareholder and chairman/managing director, had a paternalistic management style and continued to play a hands-on role in the day-to-day management. 59% of the voting shares were held by the Lee family, the balance by international and local institutional investors and Hong Kong people.

Terry, Tam Tat Sing joined the company in 2002 as internal auditor, reporting to Mr Lee. Terry had trained with one of the big five accounting firms and was a member of the Hong Kong Institute of Certified Public Accountants (HKICPA).

To his surprise, Terry received an anonymous letter, alleging that the head of the purchasing department had incorporated a company, which was invoicing LTN with goods that were not being supplied. The head of the purchasing department, Poon K.K., was an executive director of the company. He was also married to Mr Lee's sister. However, Terry knew that if these allegations were true, this was a serious situation, and as internal auditor he needed to investigate.

With the help of his staff, Terry began checking the goods inwards records with invoices. After a while it became clear a company was being paid for goods that had not been delivered. All the invoices from this company had been approved by Mr Poon but entries in the goods inwards records were missing. Terry traced the fraudulent payments for the past two years and had a colleague double-check his figures. Now what should he do?

He wrote a confidential report to Mr Lee, the Managing Director and head of the family, explaining the situation, suggesting that it was serious, and should be referred to the board of directors, including the independent non-executive directors, for a decision on the appropriate action to be taken. Alternatively, he proposed that the independent external auditors, or the firm's lawyers should be notified.

Terry was surprised at Lee's reaction. He defended Poon, accused Terry of acting without proper authority, and said he had been over-zealous. Lee said:

> You should have referred the anonymous letter to me immediately. I would then have decided how to react. Remember this is a family business. My family and I own most of the shares and we decide how to treat issues like this. Personally, I ignore people who write anonymously. Clearly they lack the courage of their convictions. It must have been somebody in the company. I want you to find out who it is, tell me, and I'll make sure they don't cause any more trouble.

Lee went on to say that he did not want the matter taken any further and certainly not referred to the board. He said:

> Mr Poon has worked for this company for many years and is a respected member of staff, and of my family. I have studied your report in detail and, in fact, the amounts involved are not significant. There is no need to involve the board at all in any of this.

As a trusted employee, Terry did as he was told: he did not involve the board, he did not inform the auditors or the lawyers, neither did he seek the advice of his professional organization, the HKICPA. Instead. as instructed, he began an inquiry into all the employees who could possibly have known about the alleged fraud. And he found the whistle-blower. Under cross-examination she admitted writing the letter. Now what should Terry do?

He gave the details to Mr Lee, who said that the company wanted to keep the matter private and that the whistle-blower should be offered a substantial payment if she resigned from the company, having signed an agreement not to disclose the matter to anyone.

Questions

1. Why did the whistle-blower make the original claim?

2. Did Terry do the right thing in just informing Mr Lee?

3. What should Terry do, if anything, about Mr Lee's decision to pay off the whistle-blower?

 Case study 14.2 Libor rate rigging scandal

'Dude, I owe you big time. Come over one day after work and I'm opening a bottle of Bollinger,' wrote a bank trader in an email to his opposite number at Barclays Bank in London who had manipulated the Libor inter-bank interest rate, making a lot of money for him and his bank. The Barclays trader replied 'please keep all this to yourself, otherwise it won't work'. In another email, he wrote, 'this is the way you pull off deals like this chicken, don't talk about it too much'. In June 2012, Barclays Bank was fined £291 million ($440 million) for its part in manipulating the interest rates.

What is Libor? How is it set? Who benefits if it is rigged?

The London Interbank Offer Rate (Libor) is the interest rate, set daily, that all participating banks charge on short-term loans between each other. Libor rates provide the benchmark for trillions of pounds and dollars in complex financial derivative transactions. They also influence the rates that banks charge their own customers. A small increase in Libor could add hundreds of pounds to the repayments on a private mortgage or thousands on a business loan. The rate is set by a panel of bankers from participating banks, who submit details of the interest rates their own bank is paying on the international money market for overnight money and on loans for up to twelve months. There are Libor rates for different currencies, and for loans over various time periods. In principle, the bank officials submitting the daily rates to Libor should have no connection with the traders in their bank who are making the deals. The system was overseen by the British Bankers' Association[4] (BBA).

If the Libor rates were manipulated, bankers in the know could make dramatic profits for their banks and significantly improve their own bonuses.

A further incentive to rig the rates was provided by the international financial crisis which began in 2007, with the failure of the Northern Rock Bank.[5] The supply of funds in financial markets dried up[6] and interest rates rose. If a bank reported a high rate to Libor, it would suggest that the money market thought that the liquidity and credit quality of that bank was doubtful. If it reported a relatively low rate, it would imply that the market thought that bank was sound.

In June 2008, Timothy Geithner, then President of the New York Federal Reserve (who is now the US Treasury Secretary), sent a note to the Governor of the Bank of England warning him of the 'incentive to misreport' interest rates to Libor. He proposed a raft of reforms,[7] including increasing the number of reporting banks, a plan to overhaul the Libor process, and better governance. The report was not pursued.

The Barclays Bank story

Evidence emerged that Barclays Bank had tried to manipulate the Libor interest rates at the suggestion of its own derivatives traders in London, New York, and Tokyo, as well as at the request of traders in other banks. The UK Financial Securities Authority (FSA) reported that the rate had been manipulated on 257 occasions between 2005 and mid-2009.

During the 2007–2009 financial crisis Barclays was one of the few major British banks that did not have to appeal to the government for financial support. This was partly due to its ability to raise funds in a very tight money market. It was also due to contentious fund-raising in Abu Dhabi and Qatar, and a financing scheme that shifted billions of pounds of toxic debt from Barclays' balance sheet to a company in the Cayman Islands called Protium. The scheme had been developed by Bob Diamond, CEO of Barclay Capital, the investment banking arm of Barclays, an American-trained investment banker.

On 28 October 2008, the Deputy Governor of the Bank of England, Paul Tucker, telephoned Diamond. The financial crisis was at its height. Fear, distrust, and confusion reigned in the money markets. Bank shares were collapsing. Barclays did not want to fail as RBS had done (see Case study 13.2). The Deputy Governor said that 'some senior figures in the government' were fearful that Barclays' high Libor rates suggested that Barclays was under financial pressure, and would possibly have to be bailed out or nationalized. Diamond wrote to Barclays' CEO, John Varley:

> Mr. Tucker stated that the level of the calls he was receiving from Whitehall [i.e. the UK government] were 'senior' and that, while he was certain that we did not need advice, it did not always need to be the case that (our Libor rates) appeared to be as high as (they) have been recently.

Diamond believed that the Bank of England was complicit in manipulating Barclays' Libor rates. The Bank of England subsequently denied that it had intervened in an attempt to lower rates during the financial crisis. Not everyone believed them.

---

[4] www.bba.org.uk   [5] See Case study 8.1.   [6] See Case studies 13.2 and 17.2.
[7] In a report 'Recommendations for enhancing the credibility of Libor'.

In December 2007, the US Commodity Futures Trading Commission[8] (CFTC) was contacted by a Barclays employee in New York responsible for submitting that bank's dollar Libor rates. He said that the rates the bank had been reporting were not honest, but patently false. By early 2008, the suspicion that Libor was being fixed grew, and the US CFTC, the US Department of Justice, the UK FSA, the BBA, and the Bank of England co-operated in investigating.

Barclays did not have a impenetrable firewall (a so-called 'Chinese Wall') between its derivatives traders and the officers reporting the bank's rates to Libor until December 2009. In June 2010, new rules at Barclays prohibited any communication with traders that could 'be seen as an attempt to agree on or impact Libor levels'. The rules required Libor rate submitters to report to the company's compliance department if any attempts were made to influence them.

On 1 January 2011, Bob Diamond took over as chief executive officer of Barclays Bank. The FSA, concerned that a major bank was now led by a risk-taking investment banker, questioned his lack of experience in retail banking.

In the United Kingdom investigations by the regulators into rate fixing continued at Lloyds Bank, HSBC, and Royal Bank of Scotland. In late 2011, four bankers were dismissed by the Royal Bank of Scotland for their part in Libor rate manipulation.

Barclays admits wrong-doing, is fined—and subsequent developments

It took until 2012 for the investigations into Barclays' part in the Libor scandal to come to a head. In April 2012, the FSA raised concerns about the culture of the bank, questioning 'the tone from the top'. In June 2012, the bank admitted wrong-doing and was fined £291 million ($440 million) by the CFTC, the US Department of Justice, and the FSA for manipulating the Libor rate.

Shares in Barclays fell from £1.96 to £1.65. Shareholders threatened legal action. On 28 June 2012, the British Chancellor of the Exchequer, George Osborne, called for fines levied on banks to go to the national treasury, not to the other banks as had been the practice previously. He also planned to give new power to the regulators. In July 2012, the British Prime Minister, David Cameron, set up a parliamentary review of the banking sector led by Andrew Tyrie, Chairman of the House of Commons Treasury Select Committee.

At Barclays Bank, Marcus Agius the Chairman; Bob Diamond, the CEO; and Jerry del Missier, the COO of Barclays Capital, all resigned in July. Alison Carnwath, a Barclays independent director and chair of the board remuneration committee, also resigned. She had only been a Barclays director since August 2010, and was untainted by the Libor scandal. Allegedly she had been overruled by Agius when she called for Diamond's £2.7 million bonus to be cut. It also emerged that del Missier, who resigned as COO of Barclays Capital, had received a cash payout of around £9 million ($13.5 million) even though some commentators said he had 'resigned in disgrace'. Agius also resigned his chairmanship of the BBA, which ran the Libor system.

Also in July, the US Federal Reserve chairman, Ben Bernanke, told a Senate hearing that the Libor system was 'structurally flawed', and the Governor of the Bank of England, Sir Mervyn King, told the parliamentary treasury committee that the UK authorities had had concerns about the culture of Barclays' top management for some time.

The senior independent director on Barclays' board was Sir Michael Rake, a former senior partner of the big-four accountants, KPMG, and also chairman of the board of BT, Britain's largest telephone company, and of Easyjet, an airline. Sir Michael's name was mentioned as a possible replacement for Marcus Agius. But under the UK corporate governance code, a person may only chair the board of one FTSE 100 company. However, the founder of Easyjet, Stelios Haji-Iannou, questioned why Sir Michael, who had been chairman of Barclays' audit committee and a member

---

[8] www.cftc.gov

of its risk committee, failed to detect and expose the wrong-doings. He was 'the dog who didn't bark', said Haji-Iannou.

Sir David Walker (72), a former Deputy Chairman of the Bank of England was appointed chairman of Barclays in August 2012, promising a 'root and branch reform of the bonus culture'.

A UK Independent Commission on Banking, chaired by Sir John Vickers, called for the 'casino' risk-taking investment banking to be ring-fenced from retail banking. The two arms of banking had been legally separated until the mid-1980s, when the then UK Labour government, seeking to enhance the international competitiveness of the City of London, introduced 'light-touch' financial regulation, and allowed banking conglomerates to be built. The Governor of the Bank of England, Sir Mervyn King, launched a scathing attack on 'shoddy' and 'deceitful' bankers. 'We can see what has gone wrong,' he said, 'the idea that the culture of investment banking is the same as the culture of basic banking. I think it is very clear now that those two cultures are completely different, and they need to be separated.' Anthony Jenkins, previously head of Barclaycard, the bank's credit card arm, was appointed chief executive of Barclays on an £8.6 million ($13 million) pay package. He promised that Barclays would become a 'more honourable bank'. But that claim was challenged when the bank then announced a pay-out of £40 million to nine top executives, including Jenkins, while all the media attention was on reporting the details of the British budget.

In August 2012, the Commons Select Treasury Committee reported. Diamond had misled Parliament, it said, failing to 'act with candour and frankness' and giving 'highly selective evidence' about the Libor scandal. The report said that Diamond had presided over a culture at the bank where there was 'something deeply wrong'.

A new financial regulatory regime

In September 2012, the BBA members voted to withdraw from its responsibility to manage the Libor system. The British government accepted that the existing financial regulatory system was discredited: 'failing to sound the alarm as the financial system went wrong', in the words of the British Chancellor of the Exchequer. The FSA, the regulator throughout the financial crisis, was disbanded. Regulatory power was passed to the Bank of England and two new regulatory bodies were created:

- The Prudential Regulation Authority[9] (PRA) became responsible for the regulation and supervision of banks, buildings societies (savings and loan associations), credit unions, insurance and major investment firms—a total of some 1,700 financial firms.

- The Financial Conduct Authority[10] (FCA), a quasi-governmental agency, incorporated as a company limited by guarantee, is not part of the Bank of England. In effect the successor to the FSA, the FCA is responsible for promoting effective competition in the financial markets, ensuring that they function well, and for regulating the conduct of all financial services firms.

The chief executive of the FCA, Martin Wheatley, previously headed the regulator of Hong Kong's financial markets, the Securities and Futures Commission.[11] The chairman of the FCA, John Griffiths-Jones, previously head of 'big-four' accountants KPMG, immediately came under pressure to resign from Pirc,[12] an independent corporate governance and shareholders advisory group.

Subsequent developments in the Barclay's Libor scandal

In January 2013, the former head of the FSA, Sir Hector Sants, joined Barclays as head of compliance. In April 2013, Barclays published a report about deficiencies at the bank, which it had commissioned from well-known lawyer Anthony Salz (at a cost of £14.8 million). Salz commented that although the

---

[9] www.bankofengland.co.uk./pra   [10] www.fca.org.uk
[11] www.sfc.hk/web/EN   [12] www.pirc.co.uk

bank had originally been founded on prudent Quaker religious principles, it had 'become aggressive, too clever by half, and looked to the letter, rather than the spirit of the law'. Increasingly dominated by the investment bank's culture, the report suggested that 'winning at all costs comes at a price: collateral issues of rivalry, arrogance, selfishness, and a lack of humility and generosity'.

Three months after he had said that he expected to stay in his job 'for years to come', Rick Ricci 'retired' on 30 June 2013. This American-born investment banker, known for his flamboyant life style including racehorses and private jets, was reputed to have earned £44 million ($66 million) in 2010.

Court actions against Barclays multiplied from customers alleging that they had lost money from loan products based on the rigged Libor rates. Calls to bring the Libor manipulators to trial, to obtain a judicial view on bankers' morals, also grew. Other banks around the world were hit with even larger fines over Libor rate rigging.

The feelings of many Barclays' shareholders, and the general public, were voiced at Barclays' annual shareholders meeting on 25 April 2013 by Joan Woodward, a 75-year-old widow. She lambasted the board: 'banks have brought us down—brought the entire global economy down. Yet none of you have gone to jail.'

Discussion questions

1. Why did this situation occur?

2. Who failed: Barclays' external auditors, the outside directors, its chairman, its CEO and top executives, its traders, the bank officers who submitted the bank's interest rates to Libor, Barclays' compliance systems, the BBA who operated Libor, the British government who introduced light-touch banking regulation, the Bank of England, the FSA, or anyone else?

3. Should investment banking be ring-fenced from retail banking?

References and further reading

Brountas, Paul P. (2004) *Boardroom Excellence: A Commonsense Perspective on Corporate Governance.* Jossey-Bass, San Francisco, CA.

Cornford, F. M. (1908) *Microcosmographia Academia: A Guide to the Young Academic Politician.* Bowes & Bowes, London.

Conger, Jay A. and Ronal Riggio (2007) *The Practice of Leadership: Developing the Next Generation of Leaders.* John Wiley & Sons, San Francisco, CA.

Lipman, Frederick D. and L. Keith Lipman (2006) *Corporate Governance Best Practices: Strategies for Public, Private and Not-for-Profit Organizations.* John Wiley, Hoboken, NJ.

Low, Chee Keong (ed.) (2002) *Corporate Governance: An Asia-Pacific Critique.* Sweet and Maxwell (Asia), Hong Kong.

NACD ([2004] 2005) *Board Leadership: A Report of a NACD Blue Ribbon Commission.* National Association of Corporate Directors, 1133, Suite 700 21 Street, Washington, DC, USA.

Roe, Mark J. (2003) *Political Determinants of Corporate Governance.* Oxford University Press, Oxford.

Salter, Malcolm (2008) *Innovation Corrupted: The Origins and Legacy of Enron's Collapse.* Harvard University Press, Cambridge, MA.

Projects and exercises

1. Review the section on board-level games and meeting manipulation. Develop other examples in each case that might be used to illustrate the idea.

2. Use recent examples of corporate problems, discussed in the financial press, to identify examples of the effect of power on board-level situations.

3. Prepare a set of guidelines for chairmen of listed companies, outlining their duties.

4. In groups of eight or ten, simulate a board meeting.

Self-test questions

1. What is the fundamental basis of board power?

2. Name some other ways in which a board can find itself influenced.

3. What is the knowledge power that a director might have?

4. Name five other sources of director power.

5. Name four different board styles.

6. What criteria affect board style?

7. What is a chairman's primary duty?

8. Name six functions of a chairman.

9. Explain the chairman's role in strategic leadership.

10. In what ways might a chairman be the public face for the company?

15 Board Activities: Corporate governance in practice

 Learning Outcomes

In which we review:

- Committees of the board
- The influence of the audit committee
- The role of internal audit in corporate governance
- The importance of the external auditor
- The significance of the company secretary

Committees of the board

Thus far, our study of corporate governance practice has focused on the membership and leadership of the board of directors as a whole. We now turn to some other contributors to sound governance practice: committees of the board—in particular the audit committee, independent external auditors, and company secretaries.

An important development in corporate governance was the formalization of board sub-committees. A principal requirement now under almost all corporate governance codes is for at least three board committees—the remuneration committee, the nomination committee, and the audit committee. These standing subcommittees of the main board are established for specific purposes, usually with a charter or formal terms of reference. Being composed entirely (or in some jurisdictions mainly) of outside, non-executive directors, these board subcommittees can provide independent and objective corporate governance supervision, avoiding executive domination of board deliberations.

The remuneration (or compensation) committee is responsible for recommending to the board the remuneration packages of executive directors, and sometimes other top management, as we saw earlier, including their salary, fees, pension arrangements, options to acquire shares in the company, and other benefits. The role of the nomination committee is to suggest names for board membership, in an attempt to introduce different experience, personalities, and diversity to the board, and to avoid domination of the nomination process by the chairman, chief executive officer (CEO), or any other dominant directors. The audit committee plays a fundamental role in corporate governance practice and will be discussed at length later in this chapter.

As we have seen, some boards also create other standing board committees to handle specific areas of board responsibility, such as risk governance (or management) committees, corporate governance and compliance committees, and corporate social responsibility and ethics committees. Microsoft (see Corporate governance in action 15.1) has created five subcommittees: an antitrust compliance committee; an audit committee; a compensation committee; a governance and nominating committee; and a finance committee.

Given the heavy workload facing many boards and the demands on the time of directors, particularly the outside non-executive directors, some chairmen decide to delegate other aspects of the board's work to sub-committees. Some boards appoint a risk committee, to ensure that the company's activities conform to the risk profile accepted by the board in its strategy. For example, as businesses become increasingly dependent on the Internet for their activities, the risk of cyber-crime becomes increasingly important. Other boards have an executive committee or general purposes committee to cover aspects of the board's role in supervising executive activities, a finance committee able to devote more time to financial issues, or a strategic committee to address longer-term strategic matters. Such arrangements can contribute to board effectiveness, provided that the deliberations and decisions of any subcommittee are carefully minuted and reported to the main board, with opportunity for the other directors to be informed, to question, and, if necessary for the board to amend the subcommittee's decisions.

The challenge with such subcommittees can be keeping the other directors informed and involved in their activities and decisions. Since all directors are equally responsible for the governance of the company, delegation to a subcommittee must not result in abdication of the responsibility of the other directors. Certainly, they may rely on the work of subcommittees, unless they have any cause for doubt, in which case their duty is to pursue the issue at main board meetings until the issue is resolved.

Some boards also form ad hoc committees to be responsible for handling specific one-off issues: for example, a committee to provide board-level oversight of a major investment project, to respond to the threat of a hostile takeover bid, or to handle the merger of two organizations. In setting up an ad hoc committee, it is important that the objectives of the committee, the scope of its powers, and the form of its output are carefully described in the board's policy document that creates it. Even more important is establishing how and when an ad hoc committee is to be wound up once its mission has been completed: committees have a tendency to find other matters to pursue and perpetuate their existence.

To be effective, board subcommittees require clear terms of reference, which need to cover:

- a name and a constitution with:
- details of membership—committee size and quorum, qualifications for membership (e.g. independent directors), the nomination process, terms of appointment, rotation and removal of members, remuneration (if any);
- chairman's appointment and responsibilities;
- committee duties—with authority delegated by the main board;
- relations between the committee and top executives;
- frequency of meetings;
- secretary to the committee, notice for meetings, agenda, minutes;
- staff support, access to legal and other professional advice;

- accountability, transparency, reporting requirements, circulation of committee minutes to all directors;
- opportunity for other directors to raise questions and discuss subcommittee issues at main board meetings;
- regular review of committee's performance and purpose;
- amendments to constitution and terms of reference where appropriate.

The influence of the audit committee

Inevitably, questions arise during an audit, such as the valuation of assets, whether certain expenditures should be capitalized or written off to the profit and loss account, or concerns about the financial control systems. Every director should be aware of significant matters that have been raised during the audit by the independent, external auditor. However, since the finance director and, perhaps, the CEO tend to be closely involved with the auditors, such issues are often resolved before the auditor writes a detailed report on the audit. Consequently, other directors could be left ignorant of matters that they might well have wanted to explore. The concept of the audit committee, which originated in the United States in the 1970s, was developed to provide a solution.

The audit committee, a standing committee of the main board, comprised entirely or predominantly of independent, outside directors, provides a bridge between the external auditor and the board. Its charter aims to avoid any domination of the audit process by senior executives. Typically, the audit committee meets three or four times a year to discuss the details of the audit, to consider any contentious points that had arisen on the accounts, and to receive the auditor's recommendations on audit-related matters such as management controls. The audit committee will often negotiate the audit fee and, if appropriate, recommend to the board if a change of auditor is needed.

Today, all codes of good practice in corporate governance and stock exchange listing requirements require listed companies to have audit committees. In most cases, the members must all be independent non-executive directors, at least one of whom should have current financial expertise. Over the years, the role and responsibilities of the audit committee have expanded. In many cases, they now include: advising the board on the company's systems of internal management control; oversight of internal audit; liaising with the external auditors and reporting to the board on the audit process and on any audit issues; reviewing financial information to be provided to shareholders, the stock market, and the media; advising the board on matters of board accountability; the oversight of enterprise risk management; and corporate governance compliance.

The role and responsibilities of the audit committee should be established in writing in a charter agreed by the board, and should be regularly reviewed. The specific duties of an audit committee might include:

- liaising between the board and the independent external auditors, including:
  - making recommendations to the board on their appointment, reappointment, or removal and replacement;

- reviewing and approving their terms of engagement;
- ensuring their objectivity and independence from the company, confirming that no conflicts of interest exist that could affect the auditor's ability to issue an unbiased opinion on the company's financial statements;
- developing and implementing a policy for their engagement on non-audit work;
- approving their remuneration;
- working with them on audit procedures and plans, receiving the auditors' report and management letter about issues that have arisen during the audit, and reviewing and acting on these issues;

- liaising between the external auditor, the internal auditor, and the board as a whole;
- ensuring the independence of the external auditors, reviewing the extent of non-audit work undertaken by the external auditors, and the fees involved (in the United States, since the Sarbanes-Oxley (SOX) Act, and elsewhere given the review of many codes of best practice, ensuring the external auditor's independence has become an important responsibility);
- reviewing the audit fees and advising the board accordingly;
- considering the scope and process of the audit by the external auditors;
- agreeing to the scope of the work and plans of the internal audit;
- supervising the work of the head of the internal audit function, including the setting of policies, procedures, and plans, the budgeting of resources, the remuneration and performance of staff, the regular monitoring of results, and the overall effectiveness of the function;
- ensuring that the activities of the external and internal auditors are co-ordinated, avoiding both duplication or incomplete coverage;
- reviewing the appointment, performance, remuneration, and replacement, or dismissal, of the head of the internal audit function, and ensuring continuing independence of the internal audit function from undue managerial influence;
- reviewing with the external and internal auditors, and advising the board on, the adequacy of the company's internal control systems, security of physical assets, and protection of information;
- reviewing with the external and internal auditors, and advising the board on, the conduct of the external audit, particularly on any important findings or matters raised, usually contained in the auditor's 'management letter', with the management's response, and reporting any significant changes to the reporting of financial results or to procedures and management controls that resulted;
- reviewing with the external and internal auditors, and advising the board on, the company's financial statements (interim and annual) prior to publication, the auditor's report to the shareholders, any changes to accounting policies, material issues arising in or from the financial statements, and compliance with accounting standards, company law, stock exchange reporting requirements, and corporate governance codes of good practice;
- reviewing and approving all financial reports and disclosure to shareholders and the market, ensuring the integrity of any judgements made in them before publication;

- reviewing other published information, such as the directors' report, and operating statement, and ensuring that they are consistent with the audited financial statements;
- reviewing the exposure of the company to risk and any issues that might have a material affect on the company's financial position, including any matters raised by company regulators or stock exchange listing committees;
- reviewing annually the charter of the audit committee itself and advising the chairman of the board if changes are necessary;
- approving the company's internal risk assessment and management policies, and assessing and monitoring related control systems, unless this responsibility has been delegated to another board committee;
- monitoring and reporting to the board on the company's internal audit function—in some organizations, the internal audit function reports directly to the audit committee, rather than to the finance function, to ensure independence and objectivity;
- ensuring compliance with all legal, regulatory, and corporate governance code requirements, unless this responsibility has been delegated to another board committee;
- recommending policies on corporate code of ethics, whistle-blowing, and corporate social responsibility, and ensuring compliance, unless this responsibility has been delegated to another board committee;
- reviewing regularly the committee's terms of reference, membership, and performance, and recommending changes for board approval.

In practice, audit committees frequently have between three and five members, with at least one, often the chairman, experienced in the world of accounting and finance.

Formal audit committee meetings tend to follow the audit cycle, typically at least four times a year. But ad hoc meetings may be more frequent, particularly where the committee's responsibilities have multiplied. The meetings held by the audit committee of Microsoft and their purpose are shown in Corporate governance in action 15.1 and 15.2.

Corporate governance in action 15.1 Microsoft Corporation Audit Committee Charter

Microsoft's board of directors has four committees to assist it in discharging its oversight responsibilities:

- audit committee;
- compensation committee;
- governance and nominating committee;
- regulatory and public policy committee.

The directors who serve on each of the five committees are independent. In determining the independence of a director, the board has adopted director independence guidelines to assist in affirmatively determining that a director has no relationship that would interfere with the exercise of independent judgement in carrying out the responsibilities of a director. The guidelines include, and either meet or are more restrictive than, the independence requirements of NASDAQ listing standards and SEC rules.

Microsoft's board has ten members who serve on the following board committees.

C = Chairperson   M = Member

Director	Audit	Compensation	Governance and Nominating	Regulatory and Public Policy
Independent				
Ms. Dublon	M	C		
Dr. Klawe		M		M
Mr. Marquardt			M	
Mr. Morfit	M			
Mr. Noski	C		M	
Dr. Panke	M	M		C
Mr. Stanton		M		
Mr. Thompson			C	M
Non-Independent				
Mr. Gates				
Mr. Nadella				

Source: www.microsoft.com/investor/CorporateGovernance/BoardOfDirectors/committees/audit.aspx
Charters for other Microsoft board committees can be found online at www.microsoft.com/investor/
    CorporateGovernance/BoardOfDirectors/committees.aspx

Corporate governance in action 15.2   Microsoft Corporation Audit Committee Responsibilities Calendar

	Responsibility	Q1	Q2	Q3	Q4	As needed
1.	The agenda for Committee meetings will be prepared in consultation between the Committee chair (with input from the Committee members), Finance management, the senior internal audit employee designated by the Committee to act as its direct liaison (the 'Internal Audit Executive'), and the independent auditor.	•	•	•	•	•
2.	Review and update the Audit Committee Charter and Responsibilities Calendar annually.				•	
3.	Complete an annual evaluation of the Committee's performance.			•		
4.	Provide a report in the annual proxy that includes the Committee's review and discussion of matters with management and the independent auditor.	•				

	Responsibility	Q1	Q2	Q3	Q4	As needed
5.	Include a copy of the Committee charter as an appendix to the proxy statement at least once every three years, or disclose annually in the proxy statement where the charter can be found on the Company's website.					•
6.	Appoint or replace the independent auditor and approve the terms on which the independent auditor is engaged for the ensuing fiscal year.	•			•	
7.	At least annually, evaluate the independent auditor's qualifications, performance, and independence, including that of the lead partner. The evaluation will include obtaining a written report from the independent auditor describing the firm's internal quality control procedures; any material issues raised by the most recent Public Company Accounting Oversight Board inspection, internal quality control review, or PCAOB review, of the firm or by any inquiry or investigation by governmental or professional authorities within the past five years, concerning an independent audit or audits carried out by the firm, and any steps taken to deal with those issues; and all relationships between the independent auditor and the Company.				•	•
8.	Resolve any disagreements between management and the independent auditor about financial reporting.					•
9.	Establish and oversee a policy designating permissible services that the independent auditor may perform for the Company, providing for preapproval of those services by the Committee subject to the de minimis exceptions permitted under applicable rules, and quarterly review of any services approved by the designated member under the policy and the firm's non-audit services and related fees.	•	•	•	•	•
10.	Review the responsibilities, resources, functions, and performance of the Company's internal audit department.			•		
11.	Review and approve the appointment or change in the Internal Audit Executive.					•
12.	Ensure receipt from the independent auditor of a formal written statement delineating all relationships between the auditor and the Company, consistent with applicable requirements of the Public Company Accounting Oversight Board regarding the independent auditor's communications with the Committee concerning independence, actively engage in a dialogue with the auditor about any disclosed relationships or services that may impact the objectivity and independence of the auditor, and take appropriate action to oversee the independence of the independent auditor.	•				•

	Responsibility	Q1	Q2	Q3	Q4	As needed
13.	Set clear hiring policies for the Company's hiring of employees or former employees of the independent auditor who were engaged in the Company's account, and ensure the policies comply with any regulations applicable to the Company.					•
14.	Advise the Board about the Committee's determination whether the Committee consists of three or more members who are financially literate, including at least one member who has financial sophistication and is a financial expert.					•
15.	Inquire of management, the Internal Audit Executive, and the independent auditor about significant risks or exposures, review the Company's policies for enterprise risk assessment and risk management, and assess the steps management has taken to control such risk to the Company, except as to those risks for which oversight has been assigned to other committees of the Board or retained by the Board.		•		•	
16.	Annually conduct a joint meeting with the Regulatory and Public Policy Committee to review with management cybersecurity and other risks relevant to the Company's computerized information system controls and security.			•		
17.	Review with management the Company's policies and processes for tax planning and compliance.		•			
18.	Review with Finance management, the independent auditor, and the Internal Audit Executive the audit scope and plan, and coordination of audit efforts to ensure completeness of coverage, reduction of redundant efforts, the effective use of audit resources, and the use of independent public accountants other than the appointed auditors of the Company.	•				•
19.	Review with Finance management, the independent auditor, and the Internal Audit Executive:					
	a. The Company's annual assessment of the effectiveness of its internal controls and the independent auditor's attestation.	•				
	b. The adequacy of the Company's internal controls, including computerized information system controls and security.	•	•	•	•	
	c. Any 'material weakness' or 'significant deficiency' in the design or operation of internal control over financial reporting, and any steps taken to resolve the issue.	•	•	•	•	
	d. Any related significant findings and recommendations of the independent auditor and internal audit together with management's responses.					•

	Responsibility	Q1	Q2	Q3	Q4	As needed
20.	Review with Finance management any significant changes to GAAP and/or MAP policies or standards.	·	·	·	·	
21.	Review with Finance management and the independent auditor at the completion of the annual audit:					
	a. The Company's annual financial statements and related footnotes, and recommend that the audited financial statements be included in the Form 10-K.	·				
	b. The independent auditor's audit of the financial statements and its report thereon, including any matters to be communicated by the independent auditor pursuant to Section 10A of the Securities Exchange Act of 1934.	·				·
	c. Any significant changes required in the independent auditor's audit plan.					·
	d. Any serious difficulties or disputes with management encountered during the course of the audit, and management's response.					·
	e. Other matters related to the conduct of the audit, which are to be communicated to the Committee under generally accepted auditing standards.					·
22.	Review with Finance management and the independent auditor at least annually the Company's critical accounting policies and significant judgments and estimates, including any significant changes in the Company's selection or application of accounting principles and the effect of regulatory and accounting initiatives on the financial statements of the Company.				·	·
23.	Review policies and procedures with respect to transactions between the Company and officers and directors, or affiliates of officers or directors, or transactions that are not a normal part of the Company's business, and review and approve those related-party transactions that would be disclosed pursuant to SEC Regulation S-K, Item 404.				·	·
24.	Review with Finance management, the independent auditor, and the Internal Audit Executive:	·	·	·	·	·
	a. Significant findings by the independent auditor or the Internal Audit Executive during the year and management's responses.					
	b. Any difficulties encountered in the course of the audit work of the independent auditor or internal audit, including any restrictions on the scope of their work or access to required information.					
	c. Any changes required in planned scope of the audit plans of the independent auditor or internal audit.					

	Responsibility	Q1	Q2	Q3	Q4	As needed
25.	Participate in a telephonic meeting among Finance management, the Internal Audit Executive, and the independent auditor before each earnings release to review the earnings release, financial information, use of any non-GAAP information, and earnings guidance.	•	•	•	•	
26.	Review with Finance management and the independent auditor the Company's quarterly financial statements and analyses prepared by management setting forth significant financial reporting issues and judgments made in connection with the preparation of the financial statements, including analyses of the effects of alternative GAAP methods on the financial statements.	•	•	•	•	
27.	Review with the independent auditor the following:	•	•	•	•	
	a. Alternative treatments of financial information within generally accepted accounting principles related to material items that have been discussed with management, ramifications of use of the alternative disclosures and treatments, and the treatment preferred by the independent auditor.					
	b. Other material written communications between the independent auditor and management (e.g., schedule of unadjusted differences).					
	c. Any correspondence with regulators or governmental agencies, and any published reports that raise material issues, concerning the Company's financial statements or accounting policies					
28.	Review with Finance management, the Internal Audit Executive, and the independent auditor the periodic reports of the Company (including the disclosures under 'Management's Discussion and Analysis of Financial Condition and Results of Operations') and other financial filings with the SEC prior to filing with the SEC.	•	•	•	•	
29.	After review, recommend to the Board acceptance and inclusion of the annual audited financial statements in the Company's Annual Report on Form 10-K.	•				
30.	In connection with each periodic report of the Company, review:	•	•	•	•	
	a. Management's disclosure to the Committee and the independent auditor under Section 302 of the Sarbanes-Oxley Act, including identified changes in internal control over financial reporting.					
	b. The contents of the Chief Executive Officer and the Chief Financial Officer certificates to be filed under Sections 302 and 906 of the Sarbanes-Oxley Act and the process conducted to support the certifications.					

	Responsibility	Q1	Q2	Q3	Q4	As needed
31.	Review the adequacy of the Company's compliance programs.				•	•
32.	Review with the Compliance Officer legal and regulatory matters that may have a material impact on the financial statements or internal controls over financial reporting, related Company compliance policies and programs, and related reports received from regulators.	•	•	•	•	
33.	Develop, review, and oversee procedures for (i) receipt, retention, and treatment of complaints received by the Company regarding accounting, internal accounting controls, and auditing matters, and (ii) the confidential, anonymous submission of employee concerns regarding accounting or auditing matters.				•	•
34.	Meet with the independent auditor in executive session to discuss any matters the Committee or the independent auditor believes should be discussed privately with the Audit Committee.	•	•	•	•	
35.	Meet with the Internal Audit Executive in executive session to discuss any matters the Committee or the Internal Audit Executive believes should be discussed privately with the Audit Committee.	•	•	•	•	
36.	Meet with Finance management in executive session to discuss any matters the Committee or Finance management believes should be discussed privately with the Audit Committee.					•
37.	Meet with the Compliance Officer in executive session to discuss any matters the Committee or the Compliance Officer believes should be discussed privately with the Committee.					•
38.	Review with management the Company's (i) investment philosophy and policies, (ii) allocation of its investment portfolio, (iii) management of investment risk, and (iv) policies and procedures to comply with laws and regulations pertinent to investment portfolio.	•				•

The audit committee reports to the main board, which has delegated to it a vital part of the financial oversight of the business and financial reporting to the shareholders, the stock market, and the financial media; also the filings required by the Securities and Exchange Commission (SEC) in the United States, the Financial Reporting Council (FRC) in the United Kingdom, and other regulatory bodies. The increasing expectation of detailed narrative discussions of the company's strategy, business model, and prospects also add to the audit committee's work. All directors have fiduciary responsibilities to ensure that the company is financially sound and that the internal and external audit have been satisfactory, so they need to be able to trust the chairman and their fellow directors on the audit committee. Most audit committees now publish a public report of their activities, which has become an increasingly important document.

Role

The Audit Committee assists the Board of Directors in fulfilling its responsibility for oversight of the quality and integrity of the accounting, auditing, and reporting practices of the Company, and such other duties as directed by the Board. The Committee's purpose is to oversee the accounting and financial reporting processes of the Company, the audits of the Company's financial statements, the qualifications of the public accounting firm engaged as the Company's independent auditor to prepare or issue an audit report on the financial statements of the Company and internal control over financial reporting, and the performance of the Company's internal audit function and independent auditor. The Committee reviews and assesses the qualitative aspects of financial reporting to shareholders, the Company's financial risk assessment and management, and the Company's ethics and compliance programs. The Committee is directly responsible for the appointment (subject to shareholder ratification), compensation, retention, and oversight of the independent auditor. The Committee also reviews and assesses the Company's processes to manage and control risk, except for risks assigned to other committees of the Board or retained by the Board.

Membership

The membership of the Committee consists of at least three directors, each of whom shall meet the independence requirements established by the Board and applicable laws, regulations, and listing requirements. Each member shall in the judgment of the Board have the ability to read and understand fundamental financial statements and otherwise meet the financial sophistication standard established by the requirements of the NASDAQ Stock Market, LLC. At least one member of the Committee shall in the judgment of the Board be an 'audit committee financial expert' as defined by the rules and regulations of the Securities and Exchange Commission. The Board appoints the members of the Committee and the chairperson. The Board may remove any member from the Committee at any time with or without cause.

Generally, no member of the Committee may serve on more than three audit committees of publicly traded companies (including the Audit Committee of the Company) at the same time. For this purpose, service on the audit committees of a parent and its substantially owned subsidiaries counts as service on a single audit committee.

Operations

The Committee meets at least eight times a year. Additional meetings may occur as the Committee or its chair deems advisable. The Committee will meet periodically in executive session without Company management present. The Committee will cause to be kept adequate minutes of its proceedings, and will report on its actions and activities at the next quarterly meeting of the Board. Committee members will be furnished with copies of the minutes of each meeting and any action taken by unanimous consent. The Committee is governed by the same rules regarding meetings (including meetings by conference telephone or similar communications equipment), action without meetings, notice, waiver of notice, and quorum and voting requirements as are applicable to the Board. The Committee is authorized and empowered to adopt its own rules of procedure not inconsistent with (a) this Charter, (b) the Bylaws of the Company, or (c) the laws of the state of Washington.

Communications

The independent auditor reports directly to the Committee. The Committee is expected to maintain free and open communication with the independent auditor, the internal auditors, and management. This communication will include periodic private executive sessions with each of these parties.

Education

The Company is responsible for providing new members with appropriate orientation briefings and educational opportunities, and the full Committee with educational resources related to accounting principles and procedures, current accounting topics pertinent to the Company, and other matters as may be requested by the Committee. The Company will assist the Committee in maintaining appropriate financial literacy.

Authority

The Committee will have the resources and authority necessary to discharge its duties and responsibilities. The Committee has complete authority to retain and terminate outside counsel or other experts or consultants, as it deems appropriate, including complete authority to approve their fees and other retention terms. The Company will provide the Committee with appropriate funding, as the Committee determines, for the payment of compensation to the Company's independent auditor, outside counsel, and other advisors as it deems appropriate, and administrative expenses of the Committee that are necessary or appropriate in carrying out its duties. In discharging its oversight role, the Committee is empowered to investigate any matter brought to its attention. The Committee will have access to the Company's books, records, facilities, and personnel. Any communications between the Committee and legal counsel while obtaining legal advice will be privileged communications of the Company, and the Committee will take all necessary steps to preserve the privileged nature of those communications.

The Committee may form and delegate authority to subcommittees and may delegate authority to one or more designated members of the Committee.

Responsibilities

The Committee's specific responsibilities in carrying out its oversight role are delineated in the Audit Committee Responsibilities Calendar. The Responsibilities Calendar will be updated annually as necessary to reflect changes in regulatory requirements, authoritative guidance, and evolving oversight practices. The most recently updated Responsibilities Calendar will be considered to be an addendum to this Charter.

The Committee relies on the expertise and knowledge of management, the internal auditors, and the independent auditor in carrying out its oversight responsibilities. Management of the Company is responsible for determining the Company's financial statements are complete, accurate, and in accordance with generally accepted accounting principles, and establishing satisfactory internal control over financial reporting. The independent auditor is responsible for auditing the Company's financial statements and the effectiveness of the Company's internal control over financial reporting. It is not the duty of the Committee to plan or conduct audits, to determine that the financial statements are complete and accurate and in accordance with generally accepted accounting principles, to conduct investigations, or to assure compliance with laws and regulations or the Company's standards of business conduct, codes of ethics, internal policies, procedures, and controls, or to manage and control risks to which the Company may be exposed.

Audit committees manage their own agenda and produce minutes of the meetings they hold. But they do need to work closely with senior officers, particularly the chief finance officer (CFO), and with the finance function, internal audit, and, obviously, the independent auditors, particularly the audit firm's partner leading the audit. Private meetings with key members of management or the external auditors are often scheduled to obtain information about financial issues, risk, or management control, and to receive feedback about the progress of the audit. The minutes of audit committee meetings are often circulated to all board members, with an opportunity given at board meetings for questions to be raised.

An audit committee should have the power to hold whatever meetings, interviews, or investigations it deems necessary, seeking information directly from any company employee, although normally this should be done with the knowledge of the CEO or finance director. The head of the internal audit function often reports directly to the chairman of the audit committee, thus providing a degree of independence from the finance function. An audit committee may also be able to obtain independent professional advice in pursuit of its responsibilities.

The chairman of the audit committee is typically appointed by the board. Frequently, the CFO or members of the finance function, the internal auditor, and a representative of the external auditors are invited to attend meetings of the audit committee. Other executive directors or members of management may be asked to attend if necessary. The audit committee may meet separately with the external auditor, the internal auditor, other directors, or members of management, should they have matters they wish to raise directly with them. At least once a year, the audit committee should meet with the external auditor without any members of management being present. The external auditors should also meet with the entire board at least once a year and be available to answer questions at meetings of the shareholders.

The chairmanship of an audit committee in any company and particularly a listed company can be an onerous responsibility, as the chairman of Enron's audit committee discovered. Indeed, some directors may be hesitant to take on the duty. Nevertheless, the role of the audit committee and the leadership of its chairman should be a fundamental plank in every company's corporate governance platform.

A board will rely on its audit committee to ensure that a balanced and understandable assessment of the company's position and prospects is presented to shareholders and other legitimate stakeholders, such as the taxation authorities. The board may also expect the audit committee to ensure that the systems of internal control in the organization are sound, to safeguard share-holders' investment and the company's assets. Further, the audit committee may be expected to have formal and transparent arrangements applying financial reporting and internal control principles, and for maintaining an appropriate relationship with the company's auditors.

The audit committee should set itself clear and measurable objectives, and review perfor-mance against them. The reasons for failing to meet their objectives should be diagnosed and remedied, reporting accordingly to the board. Some corporate governance codes now call for a regular evaluation of the performance of the audit committee. Experience of this process varies from a simple discussion among the members about the process and progress of the committee, through an evaluation carried out by an independent director who is not a mem-ber of the committee, often the board chairman, to commissioning a detailed performance evaluation and formal report from an experienced, independent external professional.

In the United States, the SOX Act (2002) introduced new and strict requirements on inde-pendent external auditors and increased audit committees' responsibilities and authority. In the United Kingdom, the Smith Report (2003) focused on the audit committee with requirements that have subsequently been enhanced by the UK Corporate Governance Code (for account-ing periods after June 2010), which is now published by the Financial Reporting Council.

Criticisms of audit committees include the concern that members can get too involved in executive management matters and interfere in management's legitimate responsibili-ties. Others complain that an audit committee can become bureaucratic and process-driven rather than exercising sound commercial judgement. Concerns have also been expressed that the creation of a subset of the board with specific responsibility for ensuring compliance represents a move towards the European-style two-tier supervisory board, which proponents of the unitary board distrust.

Many companies that are not listed have adopted the concept of the audit committee to improve their own governance, as have some not-for-profit entities, NGOs, and government bodies. The Internal Control Standards for the Public Sector[1] published by the International Organization of Supreme Audit Institutions define the audit committee for central and local government corporate entities as:

> A committee of the board of directors whose role typically focuses on aspects of finan-cial reporting and on the entity's processes to manage business and financial risk, and for compliance with significant applicable legal, ethical, and regulatory requirements. The audit committee typically assists the board with the oversight of (a) the integrity of the entity's financial statements, (b) the entity's compliance with legal and regulatory requirements, (c) the independent auditors' qualifications and independence, (d) the performance of the en-tity's internal audit function and that of the independent auditors and (e) compensation of company executives (in the absence of a remuneration committee).

Although the modern concept of the audit committee stems from the later years of the 20th century, in fact the notion of an audit committee, drawn from the shareholders rather than independent directors, dates back to the late 19th century. See Corporate governance in

---

[1] www.issai.org/media/13329/intosai_gov_9100_e.pdf

action 15.3 for the report of the audit committee to the shareholders of the Great Western Railway Company in England in 1872.

> ### Corporate governance in action 15.3   Great Western Railway Company—the report of the original Audit Committee in 1872
>
> The auditors and Mr. Deloitte attended the committee and explained the various matters concerned with the Finances and other departments of the railway, which explanations were highly satisfactory.
>
> The Committee considered the auditors had performed their arduous duties with great care and intelligence and therefore confidently recommends that they be continued in office.
>
> Paddington Station   Benjamin Lancaster
> 22 February 1872   Chairman

The role of internal audit in corporate governance

Recent developments in corporate governance around the world, such as the US Sarbanes-Oxley Act (2002), have highlighted boards' responsibility for the oversight of internal controls and for ensuring the effectiveness of their companies' management control systems. An internal audit function can make a major contribution if it is efficient and effective. Yet, while the potential value of an internal audit function is widely recognized, the US SOX Act makes no mention of internal audit. However, the rules of the New York Stock Exchange state that each listed company must have an internal audit function.

The Institute of Internal Audit[2] explains the role of internal audit:

> The role of internal audit is to provide independent assurance that an organization's risk management, governance, and internal control processes are operating effectively . . . Internal auditors deal with issues that are fundamentally important to the survival and prosperity of any organisation. Unlike external auditors, they look beyond financial risks and statements to consider wider issues such as the organisation's reputation, growth, its impact on the environment, and the way it treats its employees . . . Internal auditors have to be independent people who are willing to stand up and be counted. Their employers value them because they provide an independent, objective, and constructive view. To do this, they need a remarkably varied mix of skills and knowledge.

In many cases, boards, and in particular their audit committees, look to the internal audit function to provide them with:

- an ongoing analysis of business processes and the associated control systems;
- an evaluation of the extent and effectiveness of these control systems;
- regular reviews of operational and financial performance;
- assessments of the achievement corporate mission, policies, and objectives;
- identification of areas for more efficient use of resources;

[2] www.iia.org.uk/about-us/what-is-internal-audit

- confirmation of the existence and value of the company's assets;
- ad hoc inquiries into possible irregularities and frauds;
- reviews of the compliance framework;
- identification of compliance issues and confirmation of compliance;
- reviews of the organization's values and code of conduct or ethics.

The board-level risk committee, where there is one, or otherwise the audit committee, may call on the internal audit function to provide:

- an evaluation of the risk assessment and review systems;
- regular evaluation of risk at all levels in the organization;
- ad hoc reviews of unacceptable levels of risk.

However, there is an ambiguity surrounding the internal audit function in some companies: to whom is it responsible and where does it fit in the organization's structure? Should internal audit be treated as part of the management organization and report to senior management such as the CFO, as is frequently the case, or to the board, probably through the audit committee, as some authorities recommend?

The UK Smith Report (2002), now reflected in the UK Combined Corporate Governance Code (2010), is ambiguous. Its guidance to audit committees suggests that management has the responsibility for 'the identification, assessment, management, and monitoring of risk, for developing, operating, and monitoring the system of internal control, and for providing assurance to the board that it has done so', but then adds 'except where the board is expressly responsible for reviewing the effectiveness of the internal control and risk management systems'.

In Australia, the ASX Principles of Good Corporate Governance also recommend that internal audit 'should report to management and should have all necessary access to management and the right to seek information and explanations'. But then the Principles add that 'companies should consider a second reporting line from the internal audit function to the board or relevant committee'. The Principles also suggest that the audit committee has access to internal audit without the presence of management, and that 'the audit committee should recommend to the board the appointment and dismissal of a chief internal audit executive'.

According to a study by KPMG,[3] the international accounting firm, 'the only satisfactory solution to this problem is for internal audit to report primarily and directly to the board and its audit committee rather than to senior management'.

The report provides an interesting summary of the pros and cons of the reporting relationship. The benefits of the audit function being responsible to and reporting directly to the audit committee, it suggests, are:

- the ability to transcend all departments without fear of limitation of scope by being tied to, for example, the finance department;
- the board and audit committee know that the information they are receiving on the internal controls and risk management systems reflects a true description and has not been 'watered down' or filtered by management beforehand;

[3] www.kpmg.com.cn/en/virtual_library/Risk_advisory_services/Internal_audit_role.pdf

- the independence of the internal audit function is absolute;
- the funding of the internal audit function is outside the normal process of budgeting, thereby allowing resources to be allocated by the assurance needs of the organization as assessed by the board or the audit committee;
- it enables the board/audit committee to directly and critically analyse and evaluate the internal audit function in its contribution to the fulfilment of the board's responsibility for internal control;
- it reinforces the board/audit committee's knowledge of the business and its risk profile when dealing with management and stakeholders.

On the other hand, the downside of the audit function being responsible to and reporting directly to the audit committee, the report suggests, includes the following:

- Internal audit may not be privy to all sources of information throughout the company if seen as 'outside' the management structure.
- The chairman of the audit committee may not have allocated sufficient time, or have adequate resources/capacity, to deal with the oversight of the internal audit function.
- It would be necessary to set up a specific charter outlining the roles and responsibilities of the board in relation to internal audit, as separate from management. For example, who would look after human resources issues, such as personnel evaluations, compensation, and career planning? Could the head of internal audit have a career elsewhere in the organization?
- The audit committee would be assuming more responsibility and therefore, perhaps, more liability in relation to the adequacy of the internal control and risk systems of the organization.
- Potentially, it restricts the ability of the CEO to use internal audit as a tool to reinforce control principles, or in special projects.

The Institute of Internal Auditors suggests that whoever the internal audit function[4] is responsible to, there are some key measures to ensure that the reporting lines enable effectiveness and independence. These key measures are as follows.

- The head of internal audit should meet privately with the board/audit committee without the presence of management, thus reinforcing the independence and direct nature of the reporting relationship.
- The board or audit committee should have the final authority to review and approve the annual audit plan and all major changes to the plan.
- The board or audit committee should review the performance of the head of internal audit and the overall internal audit function at least once a year, as well as approve the compensation levels for the head of internal audit.
- The charter for the internal audit function should clearly articulate both the functional and administrative reporting lines for the function, as well as its principal activities.

[4] Institute of Internal Auditors, 'Practice Advisory 1110–2: Chief Audit Executive Reporting Lines', December 2002.

- The reporting line should be to someone with sufficient authority to provide internal audit with sufficient support to accomplish its day-to-day activities.

- The reporting line should facilitate open and direct communications with the CEO, the senior executive group, and line management.

- The reporting line should enable adequate communications and information flows, so that internal audit receives adequate and timely information concerning the activities, plans, and business initiatives of the organization.

- Budgetary controls and considerations imposed by the administrative reporting line should not impede internal audit in accomplishing its brief.

Given the ever-increasing expectations of directors' knowledge and experience, and demands on their time, it seems likely that the contribution of internal audit to corporate governance can only be enhanced and grow.

The importance of the external auditor

The external, independent auditor is a fundamental component of the corporate governance system. Traditionally, the independent auditor had access to all of the books and records of the company, and reported to the shareholders that the financial statements provided to it by the directors gave a true and fair view of the state of the company's financial affairs. However, the auditor's role has evolved, as the need for professional risk management and the assessment of internal control became apparent, following the collapse of Enron and other companies around the world in the early years of the 21st century, and the effects of the global financial crisis from 2007 onwards.

In the United States, the Public Company Accounting Oversight Board (PCAOB), set up by the SOX Act of 2002, has enhanced the external auditor's role in companies listed in the United States and their subsidiaries around the world. The PCAOB standards require auditors to:

- obtain reasonable assurance that effective internal control over financial reporting has been maintained;

- assess the risk that a material weakness exists, testing and evaluating the design and operating effectiveness of internal control based on the assessed risk;

- perform such other procedures as are considered necessary in the circumstances.

These standards have been incorporated into the traditional approaches to financial audit. The report of the external auditors to General Motors (see Corporate governance in action 15.4) provides some useful insights into the audit standards that are now being followed and the processes involved.

The appointment, remuneration, and removal of auditors

In most jurisdictions, the auditor of publicly listed companies is formally appointed and reappointed by the shareholders in general meeting on the advice of the board, typically

Corporate governance in action 15.4   General Motors Company

Report of Independent Registered Public Accounting Firm

To General Motors Company, its Directors, and Stockholders:

We have audited the internal control over financial reporting of General Motors Company and subsidiaries (the Company) as of December 31, 2012, based on the criteria established in *Internal Control–Integrated Framework* issued by the Committee of Sponsoring Organizations of the Treadway Commission. The Company's management is responsible for maintaining effective internal control over financial reporting and for its assessment of the effectiveness of internal control over financial reporting, included in Management's Report on Internal Control over Financial Reporting. Our responsibility is to express an opinion on the Company's internal control over financial reporting based on our audit.

We conducted our audit in accordance with the standards of the Public Company Accounting Oversight Board (United States).

Those standards require that we plan and perform the audit to obtain reasonable assurance about whether effective internal control over financial reporting was maintained in all material respects. Our audit included obtaining an understanding of internal control over financial reporting, assessing the risk that a material weakness exists, testing and evaluating the design and operating effectiveness of internal control based on the assessed risk, and performing such other procedures as we considered necessary in the circumstances.

We believe that our audit provides a reasonable basis for our opinion.

A company's internal control over financial reporting is a process designed by, or under the supervision of, the company's principal executive and principal financial officers, or persons performing similar functions, and effected by the company's board of directors, management, and other personnel to provide reasonable assurance regarding the reliability of financial reporting and the preparation of financial statements for external purposes in accordance with generally accepted accounting principles. A company's internal control over financial reporting includes those policies and procedures that (1) pertain to the maintenance of records that, in reasonable detail, accurately and fairly reflect the transactions and dispositions of the assets of the company; (2) provide reasonable assurance that transactions are recorded as necessary to permit preparation of financial statements in accordance with generally accepted accounting principles, and that receipts and expenditures of the company are being made only in accordance with authorizations of management and directors of the company; and (3) provide reasonable assurance regarding prevention or timely detection of unauthorized acquisition, use, or disposition of the company's assets that could have a material effect on the financial statements.

Because of the inherent limitations of internal control over financial reporting, including the possibility of collusion or improper management override of controls, material misstatements due to error or fraud may not be prevented or detected on a timely basis. Also, projections of any evaluation of the effectiveness of the internal control over financial reporting to future periods are subject to the risk that the controls may become inadequate because of changes in conditions, or that the degree of compliance with the policies or procedures may deteriorate.

In our opinion, the Company maintained, in all material respects, effective internal control over financial reporting as of December 31, 2012, based on the criteria established in *Internal Control–Integrated Framework* issued by the Committee of Sponsoring Organizations of the Treadway Commission. We have also audited, in accordance with the standards of the Public Company Accounting Oversight Board (United States), the consolidated financial statements of General Motors Company and subsidiaries as of and for the year ended December 31, 2012.

Corporate governance in action 15.5   Auditors' relations with client companies—more on Arthur Andersen

Arthur Andersen, one of the world's top five accounting firms, prided itself on the quality and originality of its work. But it went dramatically out of business following a number of audit failures, including Waste Management, Worldcom, and Enron.

Andersen's audit and consultancy fees from Enron were running at about US$52 million a year, more on consultancy than audit. Enron also employed several former Andersen partners as senior financial executives. Partners of Andersen discussed dropping Enron because of their client's accounting policies, but decided not to give up the audit. Memorably, after Enron collapsed, Andersen was accused of shredding Enron papers sought by an SEC investigation, and appeared before a grand jury on charges of obstructing justice, although it was subsequently exonerated.

Clients quickly distanced themselves and many Andersen partners around the world smartly joined one of the remaining big four global audit firms. The confidence of the accounting profession, which traditionally had relied on professional self-regulation, was threatened when it realized that the market was really in control.

Subsequent concerns have been expressed about the loss of competitiveness in the audit market with a potential oligopoly of just four firms, competing for the business of the major global corporations. In the United States, the SOX Act of 2002 introduced new controls on the audit profession.

working through its audit committee. In private companies, the auditor is typically chosen by the board. Indeed, some jurisdictions, including the United Kingdom, do not require private companies to have a formal audit unless the shareholders so wish.

Auditors' remuneration and their removal, should it become necessary, are also generally agreed by the board on the advice of the audit committee. In most jurisdictions, the external auditor has to be a member of a recognized accounting profession, such as the American Institute of Certified Public Accountants (AICPA) in the United States, or the Institute of Chartered Accountants and various other recognized bodies in the United Kingdom, Canada, and other Commonwealth countries.

But who does the auditor work for and report to: the management, the directors, or the shareholders? Historically, in North America, the external auditor reported to management. That was changed by the SOX Act and the creation of PCAOB. In North America, the external auditor now works for and is accountable to the independent outside directors forming the audit committee, and through them to the board of directors, as the representatives of the shareholders. This is now enshrined in PCAOB and securities regulation in the US and Canadian Instrument 52–110. In other jurisdictions, including the United Kingdom, the external auditors work for and report to the shareholders, although de facto they work with management and report to the directors through the independent directors on the audit committee.

The independence of external auditors

The standing of independent external auditors clearly hinges on the definition and confirmation of independence. In the past, some audit firms developed a close relationship with their audit clients, earning significant fees from consultancy advice, taxation services, and other non-audit work. Questions have been asked about whether this violated their independence as auditors. It has even been suggested that some firms used the audit as a 'loss-leader' to attract consultancy income.

In the United States, communications between external auditors and audit committees concerning independence are covered by PCAOB rule 3526.[5] The rule requires that a registered public accounting firm take the following steps.

Prior to accepting an initial engagement:

- describe, in writing, to the audit committee of the listed company all relationships between the registered public accounting firm or any affiliates of the firm and the potential audit client or persons in financial reporting oversight roles at the potential audit client that, as of the date of the communication, may reasonably be thought to bear on independence;
- discuss with the audit committee of the listed company the potential effects of the relationships should it be appointed the listed company's auditor;
- document the substance of its discussion with the audit committee of the issuer.

At least annually with respect to each of its listed company audit clients:

- describe, in writing, to the audit committee of the issue listed company, all relationships between the registered public accounting firm or any affiliates of the firm and the audit client or persons in financial reporting oversight roles at the audit client that, as of the date of the communication, may reasonably be thought to bear on independence;
- discuss with the audit committee of the listed company the potential effects of the relationships;
- affirm to the audit committee of the listed company, in writing, that, as of the date of the communication, the registered public accounting firm is independent in compliance with Rule 3520; and
- document the substance of its discussion with the audit committee of the listed company.

Independent assessment of audit practitioners

In the past, the accounting profession was self-regulating, relying on peer assessment to maintain standards. More recently, demands have been made for independent assessment of audit quality. In 2008, the European Commission issued a recommendation on external quality assurance for firms auditing public companies. It provided guidance to member states to establish an independent and effective system of inspections on the basis of the Directive on Statutory Audit. In essence, this recommendation gave more responsibilities to the public oversight bodies, strengthened the independence of inspection teams, and enhanced transparency on the results of inspections of individual audit firms. In 2014, after four years of deliberation, the European Parliament introduced changes to prevent the relationship between auditor and company becoming too close. In addition to measures restricting the services that an audit firm could provide, other than the audit, the new rules required companies to put their audit out to tender at least every ten years and to change to a new auditor every twenty years.

---

[5] http://pcaobus.org/Rules/PCAOBRules/Pages/Section_3.aspx#Rule3526

The significance of the company secretary

Many company law jurisdictions require the appointment of a company secretary with statutory duties. Like directors, the company secretary is an officer of the company and, like them, has a duty to act in good faith in the best interest of the company and to avoid conflicts of interest. Some listing rules require that all directors should have access to the advice and services of the company secretary, with a view to ensuring that board procedures, and all applicable rules and regulations, are followed.

The duties of the company secretary might typically include:

- advising the chairman on legal rules and regulations affecting the company;
- convening board, board committee, and company (shareholder) meetings;
- advising on and guiding board and board committee procedures.

In some companies, the company secretary plays a part in shareholder communications; in others that is the responsibility of the finance director or chief financial officer.

In the United States, the role of company secretary, typically known as the corporate secretary, is frequently carried out by the corporate lawyer. The American Society of Corporate Secretaries suggests that the duties and responsibilities include organizing meetings of the board, board committees, and shareholders, maintaining the corporate records and stock (shareholder) records, and liaising with the securities markets. It further states that the corporate secretary should be 'the primary liaison between the corporation's directors and management'. The company secretary need not be an employee of the company; he or she may work for an outside agency or partnership.

In the United Kingdom, until the Companies Act 2006, all companies, however small, had to have a company secretary. That Act required only public companies to have one and gave private companies the option to have a company secretary only if the shareholders wanted one. In some jurisdictions, the company secretary can be a 'legal person'—that is, a limited company—and smaller companies may appoint a firm of accountants, lawyers, or a specialist company registrar firm to act as company secretary. In other jurisdictions, including Australia, the company secretary must be an actual person.

The UK Cadbury Report (1992) felt that:

> The company secretary has a key role to play in ensuring that the board procedures are both followed and regularly reviewed. The chairman and the board should look to the company secretary for guidance on what their responsibilities are under the rules and regulations to which they are subject and on how these responsibilities should be discharged. All directors should have access to the advice and services of the company secretary and should recognize that the chairman is entitled to strong support from the company secretary in ensuring the effective functioning of the board.

The UK Corporate Governance Code requires that 'the company secretary should be responsible for advising the board through the chairman on all governance matters', and under direction of the chairman, the company secretary's responsibilities include ensuring good information flows within the board and its committees and between senior management and non-executive directors, as well as facilitating induction and assisting with professional development as required. The Code adds that the removal of a company secretary should be a matter for the whole board.

The evolution of the company secretary's role highlights its current significance. In Britain in the mid-19th century, when the joint-stock limited-liability company was developed, directors needed someone to keep their records. This was the job of the secretary to the board. The function was largely clerical, with the directors holding the power. The above list of duties, however, shows just how far the function has moved, not least in line with the growing complexity of modern organizations, the globalization of business, and the vast array of modern regulation, legislation, and exhortation about company affairs. For the views on the role of the company secretary from a prominent British businessman see Corporate governance in action 15.6, and on the development of that role by a prominent British judge see Corporate governance in action 15.7.

Corporate governance in action 15.6   Sir Harvey Jones on the role of the company secretary

Sir Harvey Jones, previously the CEO of the British company ICI, wrote:

> a company secretary should have considerable personal integrity and be seen to stand for probity and right within the company. The secretary should be seen to 'side with the angels' and be prepared to state when the occasion demands that 'I fear that while what we are doing is within the letter of the law we are not within the spirit'. They have to be trusted by everyone. It is a bloody tough job.

Corporate governance in action 15.7   Lord Denning on the evolution of the company secretary's role

Changing attitudes to company secretaries can be seen in the contrasting comments of two senior British judges.

In 1887, Lord Esher, Master of the Rolls (the head of the judiciary), said:

> A secretary is a mere servant. His position is that he is to do what he is told and no person can assume that he has the authority to represent anything at all, nor can anyone assume that statements made by him are necessarily accepted as trustworthy without further enquiry.

A century later, things had changed. Corporate life had become complicated. Many companies ran diverse enterprises through complex groups of subsidiary and associated companies. Legislation affecting companies had become substantial. The role of the company secretary called for professional knowledge and skill. In 1971, Lord Denning, Master of the Rolls, said:

> Times have changed. A company secretary is a much more important person nowadays than he was in 1887. He is an officer of the company with extensive duties and responsibilities. This appears not only in modern Companies Acts but also by the role, which he plays in the day-to-day business of companies. He is no longer merely a clerk. He regularly makes representations on behalf of the company and enters into contracts on its behalf . . . so much so that he may be regarded as (doing) such things on behalf of the company. He is certainly entitled to sign contracts connected with the administrative side of the company's affairs, such as employing staff, ordering cars, and so forth. All such matters come within the ostensible authority of a company secretary.

Case studies

 Case study 15.1   Waste Management

In 1992, Arthur Andersen, the auditors of Waste Management, a refuse collection company in the United States, identified some improper accounting practices, which had resulted in an overstatement of reported profits. These misstatements totalled US$93.5 million, which was less than 10% of reported profit. Also, one-off gains of over US$100 million, which should have been shown separately in the accounts, had been netted against other expenses. A 'clean' audit certificate was signed.

In 1993, the auditors identified further misstatements of US$128 million, which represented 12% of reported profit. Andersen again decided that these misstatements were not sufficiently material for the audit report to be qualified. But the auditors did decide to allow the company to write off prior misstatements over a number of years, instead of making immediate disclosure, as required by generally accepted accounting principles. In 1994, the company continued its practice of netting expenses against one-off gains. In fact, the SEC claimed that, between 1992 and 1996, Waste Management restated over US$1 billion.

Waste Management was an important and lucrative client for Andersen. Between 1991 and 1997, audit fees totalled US$7.5 million, while other fees, such as consulting services, contributed US$11.8 million. In the firm's own words, Waste Management was a 'crown jewel' among its clients. Moreover, Waste Management's top finance executives had all previously been Andersen auditors.

In June 2001, the SEC brought settled enforcement actions against Arthur Andersen LLP and four of its partners in connection with Andersen's audits of the annual financial statements of Waste Management Inc. for the years 1992 through 1996. Those financial statements on which Andersen issued unqualified or 'clean' opinions overstated Waste Management's pre-tax income by more than US$1 billion.

The SEC found that Andersen 'knowingly or recklessly issued false and misleading audit reports . . . [which] falsely stated that the financial statements were presented fairly, in all material respects, in conformity with generally accepted accounting principles'. Without admitting or denying the allegations or findings, Andersen agreed to pay a civil penalty of US$7 million, the largest ever SEC enforcement action against a big five accounting firm.

This case raised the vexed issue of auditor independence (now resolved by the SOX Act). Andersen had a close relationship with a valuable client, which led to creeping year-on-year acceptance of less than acceptable auditing standards. The SEC's director of enforcement commented that 'Arthur Andersen and its partners failed to stand up to company management and thereby betrayed their ultimate allegiance to Waste Management's shareholders and the investing public'.

The Arthur Andersen firm collapsed following the Enron saga, reducing the 'big five' international accounting firms to four.

Discussion questions

1. The SEC's director of enforcement said that 'Arthur Andersen and its partners failed to stand up to company management'. Does the potential loss of a client and its audit fee cause a real problem in the conventional relationship between auditor and client?

2. How might it be overcome? Consider regulatory devices such as the PCAOB, introduced by the SOX Act, greater transparency, or state involvement.

Case study 15.2 Aggressive tax avoidance

This case is an edited discussion between experts in the field of corporate taxation in Britain. Their insights and opinions were reported on the understanding of anonymity. The group included the CFO of an international business, an academic economist, a lawyer, an accountant with one of the 'big-four' firms, a business school professor, and a researcher working for a doctorate in corporate governance.

Professor: Welcome. There has recently been a lot of criticism of international companies apparently avoiding tax in the countries where they generated profits, using accounting dodges to move those profits offshore to low tax regimes. Media commentators and politicians have been vocal in condemning such manoeuvres. The plan this afternoon is to share our experiences to see if we can reach any conclusions.

Lawyer: Before we start rehearsing experiences, let's be clear on the law. In almost all jurisdictions, there is nothing illegal in tax avoidance, in other words arranging your affairs so that the tax man takes the minimum possible from you. Indeed, in some countries, the courts have actually confirmed that doctrine.[6] What is illegal, totally unacceptable, and unethical, is breaking the law to evade paying tax that is legitimately due. We need to distinguish tax avoidance from tax evasion[7] at the outset.

Economist: With respect, that's not really the issue here. Everyone accepts that tax evasion is illegal and morally corrupt. The issue is about the ethical boundaries of tax avoidance. What may be within the law may not be morally, socially, or politically acceptable. For some companies paying corporation tax has become a matter of taste. I read a report that Apple[8] paid no UK tax on sales in the UK of £1.7 *billion*! Nissan sells its cars in the UK through a Swiss company, saving it millions of pounds in tax every year.

CFO: That's exactly the problem we face. My company has been criticized in the press, backed-up by considerable heckling on the internet, for doing what every international company does. We try to minimize tax within the boundaries of the law. The board has a duty to maximize the value of the company for the benefit of the shareholders.

Professor: But what exactly do you do to reduce taxation?

CFO: We use transfer pricing to shift profits from high tax regimes to low ones. Since this is to be written up, I will not quote my own company. Let me give you a hypothetical example. An international company in the coffee business has a subsidiary company in Jamaica that grows coffee beans. The coffee is shipped and sold through other group companies in France, Germany, the UK, and elsewhere. But the coffee is not sold directly to those companies. It is all sold to another group company in Jersey, which is an offshore, low-tax regime. The Jamaican group company sells the coffee to its Jersey sister-company at low prices; the Jersey company then sells it on to its European affiliates at high prices. The profits are then left in Jersey where they attract low tax. Totally legal.

Economist: Totally legal. But is it ethical? That coffee has been sold throughout Northern Europe where corporate taxation is high. That's where the revenue is generated and profits really made. And that's where tax on those profits should be paid. But by artificially trading the coffee through Jersey, the profit has ended up there. As a result, Jersey, which doesn't grow a single coffee bean, shows up in the statistics as a major coffee exporter!

[6] 'The legal right of a taxpayer to decrease the amount of what otherwise would be his taxes, or altogether avoid them, by means which the law permits, cannot be doubted.' Chief Justice Charles E. Hughes in *Gregory v Helvering (US Commissioner of Internal Revenue)* 293 U.S. 465 (1935).

[7] For more on the difference between tax avoidance and evasion go to www.bbc.co.uk/news/business-27372841

[8] For more on Apple and Starbuck's tax plans go to www.telegraph.co.uk/finance/newsbysector/mediatechnologyandtelecoms/electronics/10891981/EU-tax-inquiry-into-Apple-Starbucks-and-Fiat.html and for the EU response to tax avoidance go to www.wallstreetdaily.com/2014/06/16/apple-tax-avoidance/

Accountant: The transfer price mechanism you have described we call 'the plain vanilla option'—simple and much liked. In fact, tax authorities try to force companies to use arm's length prices for inter-group transfers. But of course if the transactions go through a third country they can't do that. But companies use far more sophisticated devices to move profits off-shore to low tax regimes. The tax department in my firm has a whole section devoted to advising clients on such schemes. They work with the lawyers. It's a game of keeping a step ahead of the revenue authorities: you find a loophole, and exploit it before it's closed.

Professor: Give us an example of such schemes.

Accountant: Well, you could incorporate a company in a tax haven to hold the group's intellectual property rights—its brand name, its patents, its trade secrets—and charge the group companies making profits in high-tax countries for the use of them. Nothing to stop charging really high fees for what, after all, is the reason for the profits in the first place. Or you could move some head office administration to the tax haven and charge group companies a hefty fee.

Economist: Isn't another way to move profits around to create inter-group loans and charge high rates of interest?

CFO: Yes. Incidentally, my coffee importing example can work in the other direction. A subsidiary in a high-tax country can sell its output to one in a low-tax country at a price way below its true value, thus moving potential profits to the buying company. And it's not only corporation tax: some big companies avoid UK added-value tax by exporting goods to Britain from Luxembourg.

Economist: I think that all this talk about devices used to transfer profits and avoid tax is missing the real point. What the accountants and the lawyers are doing is messing with real economic activity. It's the third world country that should be getting the better prices.

CFO: But that's not how international business works.

Researcher: It seems to me that the high-tax countries need to sharpen up their regulations and their compliance efforts. I read that Microsoft[9] registers its brand name in tax-shelter Bermuda and charges its associated companies to use the name.

Lawyer: For corporate tax dodging to be stopped, all the major economically-advanced countries would need to co-operate. They would all have to introduce the same controls.[10] The matter has been raised at meetings of the G8 and the G20 countries. The British Chancellor told them that the UK wanted a 'fundamental reform of rules that allow companies to move profits to low-tax jurisdictions'. The OECD has also warned that an international crackdown is needed.[11] But as long as we have nation states, everyone wants the taxable profits to be in their own country. International tax treaties have evolved over the years, to avoid double taxation. It is a very complex field that cannot be amended without a lot of unforeseen economic and political consequences.

Accountant: I wonder whether a change in the disclosure laws might help. At the moment companies are required to show how much tax they pay in total, but not where they pay it. If governments, and the public, knew the facts there might be a ground swell for change to the rules.

Accountant: Well I think it's hypocritical of governments and the media to go on about tax dodging being immoral. If a company pays the tax that is legally due, that's it. If a government wants to change things, change the law.

CFO: I agree. Tax planning is legitimate and necessary. I feel sorry for the domestic companies that can't exploit the tax planning opportunities open to the big multi-nationals. It's the small and medium firms that get hit.

[9] To access more on Microsoft's tax policies go to www.taxresearch.org.uk/Blog/2012/12/10/microsofts-tax-avoidance-4-6-billion-worldwide/

[10] For a policy statement by the British government go to www.gov.uk/government/policies/reducing-tax-evasion-and-avoidance

[11] http://economia.icaew.com/opinion/june-2014/the-global-clamp-down-on-tax-evasion

Researcher: You said 'exploit': that's just the right word.

Professor: But we should remember that companies that engage in legitimate tax reducing plans are also providing employment and satisfying market needs. If a company had to pay a lot more tax, the long term effect might be to cut employment, limit corporate expansion, reduce shareholder returns, and the company would probably increase its prices.

Economist: Frankly, I think all this talk about the immorality of tax planning is bunk. Company directors have a legal duty not to pay more tax than is legally necessary. I believe that is their moral obligation too. Minimizing costs and using the factors of production as well as possible creates more wealth. Competition, in an open economy, lowers the cost of production, reduces excess profits, and the benefits are passed on to consumers.

Lawyer: Wait a minute, it's not as simple as that. There are laws involved. In March this year (2013) Britain's largest property company, Land Securities, tried to avoid £61 million (US$90 million) in a tax avoidance scheme run by Morgan Stanley through the Cayman Islands, using loans and the buying back of shares.[12] The London Upper Tier Tax Tribunal found that the material reason for this 'ingenious scheme' was to avoid tax. As a result the company was threatened with a ban on tendering for public contracts.

CFO: Consumers can also react negatively if they get aroused about tax avoidance. Starbucks found that out to their cost, when protests were staged at dozens of their coffee shops, after the British Chancellor of the Exchequer, George Osborne, condemned tax avoidance as 'morally repugnant' even if legal. Starbucks had been recording losses in Britain and paid no British corporation tax for some years. It turned out that the company sent a percentage of their British revenues to their regional headquarters in the Netherlands as royalties for 'intellectual property,' and all their coffee was bought through Switzerland. A parliamentary committee found that even though the British drink gallons of Starbucks coffee, the British taxpayer had been deprived of millions. The company took out full page adverts apologizing and offered a £20 million voluntary payment to calm down the public outcry and avoid the boycott.

Researcher: I like Starbucks coffee and they are not alone in paying no tax. The *Mail* reported that one in four of the UK's top companies paid no tax. They make their profits here, but pay the tax abroad: if they pay any tax at all. Google paid just £7 million in corporation tax last year on UK sales of over £3 billion. Their chairman said that this was alright because 'the people we employ in Britain certainly pay British taxes'.

Professor: I wonder if it's really a matter of fairness. If companies generate revenues in a country, they should pay their fair share of tax in that country. It shouldn't be optional or voluntary.

Accountant: But most countries tax profits not sales, except for sales taxes, which are relatively small, and paid by purchasers anyway.

CFO: Your suggestion that it's not fair has another side. Fair to whom? You are thinking of the taxpayer. But if companies paid higher taxes what about the effects on employees, customers, and, of course, shareholders? Remember the shareholders are not just rich individuals and financial institutions. They include millions of pensioners whose pension funds are invested in those companies.

Lawyer: For me it's not a matter of fairness, or morality. It's a matter of law, full disclosure, and compliance, with proper regulation. Companies don't have morals.

Researcher: But their directors do. The board has to be the conscience of the company.

CFO: We have focused on companies avoiding tax, but they're not the only ones. Many rich individuals avoid millions in income tax through off-shore schemes. Celebrities, film stars, TV personalities, sportsmen and women, they all avoid tax quite legally.

Economist: And the accounting firms keep coming up with schemes to help them.

[12] www.moneymarketing.co.uk/hmrc-wins-60m-morgan-stanley-tax-avoidance-battle/1068577.article

Accountant: Quite legally.

Researcher: Legally, but not morally. I think companies need to follow the spirit of the law, not just its letter. I agree with David Alexander, a cabinet minister, who said: 'multi-millionaires who use tax avoidance schemes are the moral equivalent of benefit cheats.'

Professor: Tax avoidance by individuals opens up a whole new field. But we shall have to leave that for another occasion. Dinner is about to be served. Thank you all very much.

Note: subsequent to the meeting described above, media investigations continued to expose multi-national companies with large revenues generated in high-tax countries on which they paid little or no tax. US drugs giant Pfizer,[13] for example, paid £12 million tax in the United Kingdom in 2013 but because the British subsidiaries had reported losses, it received £118 million in tax credits from the British government. A spokesman for the company explained that the losses were due to restructuring and investment allowances. The group was reported to have over 200 subsidiaries, 40% based in tax havens or low tax countries, including the Cayman Islands, the Netherlands, and Jersey.

Discussion questions

1. In your opinion, which of the speakers made the most convincing case?

2. Is it ethically wrong for companies to avoid tax through legal schemes? Is it moral for accounting firms and financial institutions to advise them how to do it?

3. What would be the best way to require companies with substantial sales in a country to contribute a fair share to that country in tax?

[13] www.ibtimes.co.uk/pfizers-possible-100bn-deal-astrazeneca-sparks-tax-dodging-concerns-us-1446486

References and further reading

Armour, Douglas (2013) *The Company Secretary's Handbook*. 8th edn, ICSA, London.

Ashton, Helen (2008) *The Company Secretary's Handbook: A Guide to Statutory Duties and Responsibilities*. 5th edn, Kogan Page and Sunday Times (Business Development Series), London.

Braiotta, Louis, Jr, et al. (2010) *The Audit Committee Handbook*. 5th edn, Institute of Internal Auditors, Wiley, Hoboken, NJ.

Bromilow, Catherine L. and Barbara L. Berlin (2005) *Audit Committee Effectiveness: What Works Best*. 3rd edn, PricewaterhouseCoopers, The Institute of Internal Auditors Research Foundation, New York.

Carver, John (2002) *Corporate Boards that Create Value—governing company performance from the boardroom*. Jossey-Bass, San Francisco, CA.

Charan, Ra (2005) *Boards that Deliver: Advancing Corporate Governance from Compliance to Competitive Advantage*. Jossey-Bass, San Francisco, CA.

Bowman, Brenda and Alison Dillon Kibirige (2014) *CSIA Corporate Secretaries Toolkit—a modular training programme*. Corporate Secretaries International Association, Hong Kong.

Cosserat, Graham W. and Neil Rodda (2009) *Modern Auditing*. 3rd edn, John Wiley, Chichester, UK.

Cutler, Sally F. (2009) *Audit Committee Reporting: A Guide for Internal Auditing*. The Institute of Internal Auditors, New York.

Gray, Ian and Stuart Manson (2008) *The Audit Process: Principles, Practice, and Cases*. 3rd edn, Thomson Learning, London.

Lai, Gerry P. L. (2010) *Tolley's Company Secretary's Handbook 2010–2011*. LexisNexis, London.

NACD ([2005] 2010) *The Audit Committee: A Report of a NACD Blue Ribbon Commission*. National Association of Corporate Directors, 1133, Suite 700 21 Street, Washington, DC, USA.

Pickett, K. H. Spencer (2010) *The Internal Auditing Handbook*. 3rd edn, John Wiley, Chichester, UK.

Porter, Brenda, Jon Simon and David Hatherly (2008) *Principles of External Auditing*. 3rd edn, John Wiley, Chichester, UK.

Ridley, Jeffrey (2008) *Cutting Edge Internal Auditing*. John Wiley, Chichester, UK.

Swanson, D. (2010) *Swanson on Internal Auditing: Raising the Bar*. IT Governance Publishing, Ely, UK.

Trautmann, Ted and James Hamilton (2005) *Guide for Audit Committees*. 3rd edn, Perfect Paperback CCH Inc., New York.

Verschoor, Curtis C. (2008) *Audit Committee Essentials*. Institute of Internal Auditors, Wiley, Hoboken, NJ.

Weiss, Renee (2009) *Audit Committee Characteristics and Monitoring Effectiveness: An Evaluation of Independence, Financial Expertise, Firm Support, and Oversight Activities*. VDM Verlag, Saarbrücken, Germany.

Projects and exercises

1. The governing body of a not-for-profit organization is comprised entirely of outside members, with the chief executive and other senior officials attending meetings. Write a report to the chairman explaining why an audit committee of the governing body might be a good idea. The organization could be, for example, a hospital, a charity, or an educational body,

2. Use the Internet to compare the annual accounts of a variety of companies in different countries and different industries. Do they all include a report from their independent external auditor, and one from the internal board audit committee? If you find any significant differences, explain why this might be.

3. Draft a briefing note for the chairman of an audit committee of a listed company outlining other questions that should be asked during the meeting with the external auditors on the completion of their audit.

4. What is your opinion of the following ideas offered to preserve the independence of audit firms:
   - Prohibiting audit staff from joining a client company (at least until after a given period of time)
   - Requiring the staff leading the audit of a client company to rotate periodically
   - Requiring the auditors of listed companies to be changed periodically?

Self-test questions

1. What is the principal role of the remuneration committee of the board?
2. What is the principal role of the nomination committee of the board?
3. What is the primary role of the audit committee?
4. What might that primary role include?
5. What other duties might a modern audit committee undertake?
6. What might boards, and in particular their audit committees, look to the internal audit function to provide?
7. Who is responsible for the financial accounts of a listed company—the auditors or the directors?
8. In the United States, what do the PCAOB standards require auditors to do?
9. In the United States, what is the company secretary typically known as, and who carries out that role?
10. What might the duties of a company secretary typically include?

16 Board Effectiveness: Building better boards

 Learning Outcomes

In which we consider:

- Making a board effective
- Director orientation and director induction
- Director development, training, and updating
- Directors' liabilities and indemnity
- Board information
- Managing meetings, agenda, and minutes
- Communications with shareholders and other stakeholders
- Appendix to Chapter 16: Director's induction checklist

Making a board effective

In the past, many board meetings were relatively cosy affairs—but no longer, as economic pressures, competitive forces, and investors' demands for performance have created a tough environment. Decisions that used to be straightforward have become complex and difficult. Comfortable meetings between friends have been replaced by tough-minded discussion and difficult decisions.

The principle attributes of an effective board are sound leadership with an appropriate leadership style, supported by a well-balanced board team, as discussed in Chapter 14. The 'six Cs' of board behaviour provide an insight into the characteristics that an effective board needs:

1. Commitment

    A commitment by every member of the board to the company's mission, values and strategy is essential. Without a shared vision of the company's future, there can be no real commitment to success.

2. Character

    Boards have a character. Effective boards depend on the integrity of each director. Their personal values reflect in the standing of the board and permeate the organization as a whole. Companies have a character too. Strong companies have strong characters.

3. Collaboration

    Boards work as a team, each member playing a part. Effective teamplay calls for communication based on trust, reliance on others, and mutual respect. Balance in deliberations means being prepared to question, to challenge with tough-minded discussion not group-think, but always to be open to others' points of view. Perseverance is sometimes needed. So is enthusiasm, which can be reinforced by lightness of touch and occasional humour to hold the board together.

4. Competence

A well-balanced board has the appropriate experience, skills, and knowledge, which it draws on to ensure confidence, reliability, and excellence.

5. Creativity

Creativity means challenging conventional wisdom, encouraging unconventional ideas rather than resisting them, and facilitating change. Yet creativity is probably the least appreciated hallmark of an effective board.

6. Contribution

An achievement-orientated board strives to achieve the company's full potential.

The UK Financial Reporting Council (FRC) guidance on board effectiveness,[1] written to assist companies to apply the principles of the UK Corporate Governance Code, suggests that:

> The board's role is to provide entrepreneurial leadership of the company within a framework of prudent and effective controls which enables risk to be assessed and managed.
>
> An effective board develops and promotes its collective vision of the company's purpose, its culture, its values, and the behaviours it wishes to promote in conducting its business. In particular it:

- provides direction for management;
- demonstrates ethical leadership, displaying—and promoting throughout the company—behaviours consistent with the culture and values it has defined for the organisation;
- creates a performance culture that drives value creation without exposing the company to excessive risk of value destruction;
- makes well-informed and high-quality decisions based on a clear line of sight into the business;
- creates the right framework for helping directors meet their statutory duties under the Companies Act 2006, and/or other relevant statutory and regulatory regimes,
- is accountable, particularly to those that provide the company's capital, and
- thinks carefully about its governance arrangements and embraces evaluation of their effectiveness.

To be effective, all board members need to bring a tough-minded independence to board deliberations. The range of alternative views needs to be declared, the various positions probed, challenged, and debated, without unnecessary provocation or obstruction. Board relationships are vital, with members respecting and trusting each other. The complacent

---

[1] Guidance on Board Effectiveness (2011) Financial Reporting Council, London, March. Available online at www.frc.org.uk/getattachment/c9ce2814-2806-4bca-a179-e390ecbed841/Guidance-on-Board-Effectiveness.aspx

'group-think' culture needs to be avoided. The chairman is responsible for creating the climate in which this can happen.

Director orientation and director induction

Director orientation

A newly appointed director needs orientation on the company, its business, and the company's financials before joining the board. Some companies use a director mentoring programme, in which an experienced member of the board accepts a responsibility, usually quite informally, to orientate and guide a new member into the ways of the board and the company. This relationship can help a new director to contribute more quickly and effectively.

Corporate governance in action 16.1, an extract from the Board Manual of the Vancouver Coastal Health Authority, provides a useful example of the sort of matters that might be included in a director orientation programme.

Corporate governance in action 16.1   Vancouver Coastal Health Authority Board Manual

Director orientation and professional development

The Vancouver Coastal Health Authority provides public health services, including adult day care, family planning, and alcohol and drug services, in parts of Vancouver. The company has designed a director orientation programme and explains it as follows.

1.0 Purpose

All new members of the Board of Directors of the Vancouver Coastal Health Authority ('the Authority') will be provided with a comprehensive orientation program, which addresses the Authority's mandate, the Board's role and the Authority's governance structure, and the nature and scope of its operations. The purpose of the orientation program is to help new directors assume their responsibilities quickly, maximizing their potential contribution and the capacity of the Board as a whole. The Board aims to foster a culture that encourages new directors to participate fully and effectively in board activities as soon as possible.

In addition, this policy outlines the Board's commitments around the continuing professional development of the directors.

2.0 Overall objectives of orientation

Properly planned and executed, the orientation program should ensure that each new director comes to his/her initial meeting of the Board with an understanding of:

2.1. the regulatory setting, the relationship with the Government and the responsible Minister, the constitution, and the bylaws;

2.2. the formal governance structure, including the role of the Board and its committees and the terms of reference for an individual director;

2.3. the Guidelines and Policies established by the Board to set the standards for personal and organizational conduct;

2.4. the Authority's mission and vision and current strategic planning documents;

2.5. the Authority's operations and working environment, including: the range of services provided;
  – the principal assets, liabilities, significant contracts, and major stakeholders;

  – the organizational structure and key management assignments;

  – the major risks the organization faces and its risk management strategy;

  – the key performance indicators; and

  – the requirements for reporting and public disclosure (e.g. *Budget Transparency and Accountability Act, Financial Information Act*, etc.);

2.6. the financial circumstances of the Authority and its performance against approved budgets and the expectations set out in the Performance Agreement between the Authority and the Government;

2.7. the human resources that support the operations including:
  – the contract and non-contract staff components and distribution;

  – the employee unions and associations;

  – the role of the HEABC;

  – the medical staff working within and in association with the Authority; their relationship with the Government and the British Columbia Medical Association; and the role of the Health Authority Medical Advisory Committee; and

  – The initiatives in place to promote staff recruitment, retention and development.

The orientation should also:

2.8. build a personal link for the new director with fellow directors;

2.9. introduce the new director to key members of the senior management team;

2.10. provide the new director, as quickly as is practical, with an opportunity to gain a more in-depth appreciation of the nature and scope of the Authority's operations by visiting individual sites to view the facilities; observe first-hand the services being provided; and meet members of the local staff; and

2.11. be supported by a library of written educational and reference material.

Where timing permits, the new director will be invited to sit as an observer at the meeting of the Board and its committees prior to the date at which his/her appointment becomes effective, a final step that should encourage the new director to take an active part in the work of the Board from the outset.

Source: www.vch.ca/media/Orientation_Development.pdf

Director induction

Many companies use an induction programme for new directors to provide the necessary orientation. An independent director, because of that independence, is unlikely to have much knowledge of the company, its business, and probably its industry. Consequently, an induction programme can provide vital information and knowledge. Otherwise, new independent directors can learn only from their experiences in the boardroom. Interestingly, however, newly appointed executive directors may also need a suitable induction programme, since they were 'promoted' to the board for their successful performance as executives in a particular function or division. They then need information on their duties as directors, on the company's board-level processes, and probably about the way in which the company as a whole runs. A well-planned induction programme can reduce the learning time before a new director begins to contribute meaningfully to board deliberations.

It is the duty of the board chairman to recognize the needs of new directors for orientation and to ensure that a suitable induction programme is provided. The chairman may undertake the responsibility of providing the induction experience himself or herself, but is more likely to delegate the task to the company secretary or another director, such as the senior independent director. Induction programmes may be built on a standard foundation, but different directors have different needs for briefing. Induction programmes should be tailored to the specific needs of individuals.

The three fundamental areas in which the new director needs to be fully informed are knowledge of the company, its business, and its financial situation. The Institute of Chartered Secretaries and Administrators also offers guidelines on the induction of directors.

Director development, training, and updating

Until quite recently, many directors saw no call for director-level training and development. They felt that the business knowledge and management experience that had led them to a seat in the boardroom demonstrated their capacity to be a director. Few hold that view today. Most corporate governance codes now call for director training. A professional approach is needed. With the rapid acceleration of new regulations, codes, and legal requirements, with the ever-changing aspects of global business life, and given the litigious society that exists in many parts of the world, the need for continuous updating and professional education and training for directors has become vital.

The interest in corporate governance, in general and director training in particular, has increased dramatically in recent years, in many parts of the world. The various alternative approaches to director training and development can be classified as follows:

- *Formal external training courses* on aspects of the director's work. Many organizations around the world—institutes of directors; legal, accounting, and managerial professional bodies; and specialist consulting and research organizations—now run programmes for director training and updating. The NYSE Euronext announced in 2011 a board education programme designed to provide voluntary education for public and private board members. An advantage of such programmes is that they enable directors to be given relevant theoretical frameworks, principles, and practice updates that reflect the latest situation. Such experience can be enhanced by having directors from different types of entity, different industries, and various styles and scales of operation in the programme to exchange experiences.

- *In-house board development programmes* designed specifically for the entire board. It is vital that all directors understand the current and emerging issues of strategic significance to the company and the possible risks involved. Such activities may involve board-level evaluation, with discussions that lead to learning in the context of that board. We will discuss director and board evaluation in the next chapter.

- *Updating and briefing sessions for the board, or individual directors.* Workshops with experts to lead and provide relevant knowledge, for example on recent developments in relevant company law or employee legislation, new developments in financial instruments, or the implication of private-equity-funded acquisitions of previously listed companies, can be valuable learning experiences.

- *Relevant higher degree courses and focused professional courses* in corporate governance, corporate strategy, and other board-related topics are now offered by some business schools around the world.

- *Experiential sponsorship programmes* can provide individual directors with relevant experience and knowledge. An executive director might be encouraged to become an independent director of a non-competing company to gain experience of board, governance, and managerial topics. Another director might be encouraged to chair an in-house inquiry, to join the board of a subsidiary in the group, or to lead an in-house project team. Such activities, however, may lack depth and relevance to the needs of the sponsoring company.

- *Mentoring* provides another learning opportunity with a one-to-one personal trainer. Although it should be mentioned that such relationships are not value-free, particularly if the mentor is a fellow director, when hidden agendas may affect the relationship.

- *Self-directed learning and continuous self-development* is, probably, the most prevalent learning experience adopted by directors. Participating in conferences, networking with peers, following distance learning courses, and reading books, journals, and professional articles can all provide learning experiences. As the old saying goes, 'if you want a helping hand, look at the end of your arm'.

- *Site visits to different company locations* can be a useful source of knowledge. Some chairmen decide to hold an occasional board meeting in the offices of a division or subsidiary company, which can be motivating to the local staff as well as informative to the directors.

- *Board experience* itself can be one of the best learning opportunities, provided that the learning experience is recognized. A professional chairman will sometimes raise the question with his or her board: 'What have we learned from this experience?'

A challenge to every director today is to remain up to date. That means continuous learning. Executive directors may need to delegate some day-to-day managerial work to focus on their director responsibilities. In addition to director evaluation programmes discussed in the next chapter, directors can recognize their own development needs. They can question whether they are sufficiently knowledgeable to contribute fully and responsibly to board-level discussions and decision-making. Professional directors understand their strengths and their weaknesses, and create an informal self-development plan to remedy the gaps in their knowledge and their competencies. By reinforcing their strengths and remedying weaknesses, directors can increase their self-confidence and increase their contributions to their boards.

Listed companies in the United States[2] and the United Kingdom[3] are required to provide information to their shareholders and the public about their induction and continuing education policies. This does not apply in all countries.

Directors' liabilities and indemnity

Many years ago, a member of the British royal family, who was being trained as a potential independent non-executive director, said to the author: 'You speak of the limited-liability company: does that mean the liability of the directors is limited?' He was obviously hopeful; but the answer was a resounding 'no'.

When serving as a company director, exposure to personal liability is real. In some countries, including the United States and the United Kingdom, the threat of litigation is significant. Contingency or conditional fee arrangements, the so-called 'no win, no fee' arrangements, are available in some jurisdictions. Lawyers accept a share of the risk in exchange for larger fees or, in some jurisdictions, a share of any damages awarded on a successful outcome. In some jurisdictions, class actions enable groups of litigants to combine their claims and bring a consolidated action against a company, its board, or a named director. Such hostile litigation, long accepted in the United States, is now growing in other jurisdictions, including the United Kingdom.

Who might bring such actions? Suits against directors can be brought by shareholders, employees, creditors, customers, suppliers, government and regulatory bodies, auditors, and liquidators. For directors of significant listed companies, investor-led proceedings are most likely. Directors of small or medium-sized enterprises are more likely to face proceedings from customers, clients, or, employees. Should the company become insolvent, a liquidator or administrator could bring an action against a board or a director. The extent of the risk will depend on the jurisdiction in which the action is brought. Most significantly, the propensity to sue the company, its auditors, the board, or specific directors is increasing in many countries.

Directors can be held legally accountable in their personal capacity for actions that they are alleged to have taken or failed to take, but also for the actions of other members of the board or top management. Claims may be for unlimited amounts. Even if an action is successfully defended, legal costs can be incurred and directors' personal reputation damaged. Directors' personal assets can be at risk, which is why some people think twice before accepting a directorship. The need for sound legal advice in such circumstances is paramount.

In addition to the duties that directors may owe to third parties under corporate contracts, in many jurisdictions statute laws now impose statutory duties on directors. This legislation may include company law, and laws protecting health and safety, the environment, anti-corruption, consumer protection, employment and creditor protection, as well as legislation designed for specific industries, such as financial services. In many countries, the criminal and regulatory authorities have strong investigative powers, and are able to bring prosecutions or levy penalties themselves. The need for all directors to have access to clear legal advice and for director orientation and induction programmes to cover such matters is vital. Contravening some Acts can lead to a criminal conviction with fines, prison, and in China even death.

[2] NYSE Listed Company Manual 303A.09.   [3] UK Combined Corporate Governance Code Principle A5.

Disqualification from service as a director and personal liability for the company's debts can also occur.

Further, directors are responsible for ensuring that company accounts, reports, and other statutory documents are prepared and filed with the relevant regulatory body under the local companies' legislation. If in doubt, take professional advice. Failure to do so can incur serious penalties.

Directors and officers insurance

Directors might legitimately expect their companies to provide them with some protection from the risks of litigation, but there are no formal standards. In most jurisdictions, directors can take some steps to protect themselves. Most jurisdictions allow a company to take out directors and officers liability (D&O) insurance on behalf of its directors.[4] In the United Kingdom, for example, as a result of legal changes in 2005, companies are now permitted to indemnify their directors in respect of a broad range of liabilities and defaults. It is even possible for a company to fund the cost of the defence of any civil, regulatory, or criminal proceedings, provided that any such loan to a director is repaid immediately if the director is found liable.

However, directors cannot be indemnified by their company or by insurance for acts that are shown to be illegal, contrary to companies' legislation, or for other misfeasance. D&O insurance provides some protection to directors, company officers, such as the company secretary, and senior managers, if they are sued as the result of decisions taken while governing or managing the business. Some investors, such as venture capitalists, insist on D&O insurance before providing funds to a company. D&O insurance should not be confused with E&O (errors and omissions) cover, which is concerned with performance failures with respect to products and services.

D&O insurance policies pay for actual or alleged wrong decisions, what policies call 'wrongful acts'. Each insurer defines coverage in its own way, but typically covers 'any actual or alleged act or omission, error, misstatement, misleading statement, neglect or breach of duty by an insured person in the discharge of his/her duties'. For example, a D&O policy might cover claims of mismanagement of assets, claims by the shareholders of an acquired company that they had been misled by former directors, claims under health and safety legislation (although many D&O policies exclude bodily injury or property damage), actions under employment legislation including harassment, discrimination, and wrongful termination, and environmental legislation (although pollution damage is often excluded in D&O policies).

D&O insurance cover is not available for all who seek it. Successful, long-established companies are more likely to be able to obtain cover than companies in riskier situations, such as start-ups or those with financial problems. Some directors expect lower D&O premiums if their company is recognized as having high corporate governance standards, although this is seldom the case. What is almost certainly true, however, is that a reputation for poor corporate governance will result in higher premiums, a reduction in cover, or even a failure to find insurance.

---

[4] The author acknowledges helpful advice from the Corporate Governance Practice of Aon Asia.

A 2004 report from the Australian Corporations and Markets Advisory Committee noted that:

> there is an increasing trend to impose personal liability on directors and other officers for the shortcomings of companies. In considering the practical consequences of this liability regime, it cannot be assumed that all those exposed to personal liability are able to obtain protection through insurance. The availability of insurance cover reflects the market's appreciation of relevant risks. D&O insurance does not serve as an across-the-board mitigation of the personal financial liabilities to which corporate directors and officers are increasingly exposed. It cannot provide a complete cushion.

Just as all boards need a strategy for assessing and handling risk, they need a related policy on D&O insurance. The hope that misfortune will be avoided is neither a strategy nor a policy.

Board information

As we saw earlier, directors have a right to the information that they feel is necessary to fulfil their responsibilities as directors. Obviously, different directors are likely to have different information needs. Executive directors usually know more about the internal operations of the firm than the independent directors. Conversely, some outside directors are likely to have a wider knowledge of fields such as finance, international markets, or the economy than the executive directors. Each may need additional briefing on specific items on the agenda.

The UK Cadbury Report (2002) suggested that 'it is for chairmen to make certain that their non-executive directors receive timely, relevant information tailored to their needs, that they are properly briefed on the issues arising at board meetings, and that they make an effective contribution as board members in practice'. The same applies to executive directors.

Types of information

The information that directors acquire can come from both formal and informal sources on both a routine and non-routine basis. Table 16.1 illustrates this quadrant, indicating some of the likely sources for such information. Each of the quadrants can highlight different types and sources of information.

Official and regular information

Most boards develop a routine set of board papers, which go to all of the directors with the agenda for each meeting. These papers might include, for example, the latest financial accounts, a cash flow report, a report on business activity levels, the current order situation, a market report, and a routine report from the chief executive officer (CEO). Increasingly these 'papers' are provided electronically.

A good report with high-quality information will be all of the following.

- *Understandable*—at a level of detail, language, and content appropriate to the likely readers. It would be counterproductive to produce a document assuming technological

Table 16.1 How directors get their information: sources and provision of board-level information

	Provision on a regular and routine basis	Provision on an occasional and non-routine basis
Unofficial and informal sources	Briefings to the board Contacts within the company Questioning in meetings Discussions with staff 'Grapevine' gossip	Contacts outside the company 'Off the record' comments Casual reading/TV reports etc. Unofficial probing and inquiry Visits, presentations, conferences
Official and formal sources	Regular board operating reports Regular board financial reports Statutory and regulatory reports Use of the company seal report Minutes of board committees Presentations to the board	Ad hoc reports and presentations –in-house studies –consultants' reports –investment proposals –merger & acquisition proposals –market reports –technology reports –financial studies Details of legal actions

or financial knowledge that the readers lacked. Conversely, an expert might find a lay-person's guide patronizing and irritating.

- *Reliable*—of fundamental importance, the reader must be able to trust that any facts given are accurate and any opinions advanced clearly shown as such.

- *Relevant*—reports need to refer to the matter in hand. However interesting, significant, or worthy the information, unless it refers directly to the issue under consideration, the material is not useful.

- *Comprehensive*—half of a story, like half-truths, can mislead. Reports need to be complete and cover all relevant aspects of the situation.

- *Concise*—directors are inevitably under time constraints. Verbose reports may not be given the attention they deserve, being merely scanned and some of the salient information missed. Good report writing involves a skill that can be learned and developed with practice.

- *Timely*—directors need reports in sufficient time for them to study the contents, but with material that is up to date. The frequency of provision needs to be appropriate to the decisions that are being faced.

- *Cost-effective*—an aspect of report writing that is often overlooked. Report writing involves a cost, sometimes a substantial one. Chairmen need to ensure that unnecessary expense is not incurred producing reports with little value. With formal board reports a periodic review is sound policy: there can be a tendency to go on producing standard reports long after the need for them has disappeared.

The entire board or committee can also be informed by presentations made to them, for example by a senior executive, a consultant, or other expert in a relevant field. Such information may be supplemented by visits made by the board as a whole to various locations.

Occasional and non-routine sources of information

Some agenda items may call for special reports with information that is required by all of the directors. Ad hoc papers can then be developed for these items. For example, a proposal for a major capital investment, a report on an ongoing project such as a re-organization, or an acquisition proposal would all require one or more specific non-routine reports.

A professional chairman will not assume that the information needs of all directors can be met by a standard set of routine board papers, however comprehensive. Some directors need information that others already have. A good chairman, as the Cadbury Report recommended, should ensure that each director is adequately briefed on every item on the agenda to contribute to the board's deliberations. Such briefings might be with the chairman, the CEO, chief finance officer (CFO), or a divisional, regional, or departmental head, the company's auditors, its lawyers, management consultants working with the firm, or other relevant professional advisers. If independent non-executive directors are allowed to approach company staff below board level for information, a clear policy is needed to ensure that managerial authority is not compromised. Courses, tutorials, and mentoring can also provide sources of information for directors.

Director information systems

Many formal board and board committee reports are still provided on paper, particularly in smaller companies. However, in the six years since the first edition of this book, there have been significant developments in the electronic provision of board information. Portable electronic communication devices are changing the way in which directors are informed. The IT industry has produced some useful tools to facilitate board support, including the compilation and distribution of board papers. Board portals, combined with advanced spreadsheets, word-processing, and database software, can now provide directors with online information that replicates hard-copy board papers. The Internet is emerging as the foremost vehicle for handling corporate information.

Devices such as Apple's iPad, other tablet computers, and iPhones are providing the ability to access director-level data anytime, anywhere, at less cost, and often with the facility to annotate the screen with personal notes.

A number of programs have been written that present board papers on the screen. The applications now available include BoardPacks,[5] BoardPad,[6] BoardVantage,[7] Accelus Boardlink,[8] and Diligent Boardbooks.[9]

In considering an electronic solution as an alternative to traditional board papers, a number of issues need to be considered.

[5] www.boardpacks.com [6] www.boardpad.com [7] www.boardvantage.com
[8] http://thomsonreuters.com/accelus-boardlink [9] www.boardbooks.com

- *Confidentiality*—corporate information at board level needs to be sacrosanct, being commercially valuable and share-price sensitive. Organizational, physical, and technological security measures need to be in place, effective, and regularly tested. Directors' passwords need to be seen as extremely valuable keys to strategic data and not noted down on post-it notes on the iPad. Information transmitted as email attachments carries too high a security risk for board-level strategic information.

- *Security*—service providers need to demonstrate that they operate to the highest security standards at all times and in all locations. To be trusted to host sensitive board materials, suppliers' systems need to be designed to meet the stringent security requirements in industries such as banking, defence, and health. Where client databases are hosted on service providers' systems and transmitted over publicly accessible channels, particular reassurance is needed. The WikiLeak and other disclosures show that hackers can breach the most stringent security walls. But even where dedicated corporate intranet systems are used, special care is needed when board-level data is involved. Controls at the corporate level need to be in place against the loss of data, for example from hacking, system failure, error, or theft. Right of access to the information needs to be rigorously defined and policed through access controls such as PINs, passwords, and codes, which should be changed frequently.

- *Integrity*—the accuracy, robustness, and stability of corporate information, at the level of both the Internet server and the local communication devices, needs to be ensured.

- *Availability*—access to all files of data needs to be assured at all times and everywhere in the world that access might be needed. With communication systems reliant on satellite or ocean cable links, this can prove to be quite a challenge.

- *Assurance*—compatibility with the US auditing standards (Statement SAS No. 70) confirms that service providers' control activities, servers, and processes have been audited to meet the standard as this reassurance is disclosed to their customers and their customers' auditors.

- *Cost-effectiveness*—detailed cost–benefit studies need to be undertaken before dropping hard-copy paper delivery of board papers. For example, the costs of mobile communications across international borders can be high.

- *Flexibility, simplicity, and ease of use* of the paperless system should be at least as good as that of the printed page.

The significant advantages of online access to board information are that it is timely, easy to update, and usually costs less. Some older directors, and perhaps a few not so old, will still prefer paper reports. In introducing a paperless system, training, experience, and patience will be required. In the early stages, information could be provided in tandem with both hard copy and electronic access. When the paperless system is operational, companies should seek feedback, review regularly, and update as necessary.

Director-level information systems, which enable individual directors to access company files from remote locations and to seek answers to questions about the business situation, are in the relatively early stages of development. Such facilities go far beyond providing directors with corporate reports online. They provide access to the company databases. At issue, however, is how to provide access to the material that the director needs in order to be appropriately informed, while preventing the tendency to 'drill down' into the data to obtain material that is far too detailed and irrelevant to a director's needs.

Again, ensuring that confidentiality is maintained and that security is protected is vital. Such systems have the potential to change the nature of director information. Routine reports, in which management (the company secretary, the CEO, CFO, etc.) decide what directors need to know and produce reports accordingly, are essentially one-way—company to director. Face-to-face communication and question-and-answer opportunities provide a two-way link. When directors can search for the information they feel they need, the direction becomes director to company.

Board information audit

A board information audit is a useful exercise. The framework that was introduced in Chapter 2, illustrated in Table 16.1, can be used as a checklist for analysing the extent and quality of board information. The audit would review the extent and nature of information made available at board level in each segment of the quadrant. What is the source? Is it adequate? What is its quality? How might it be improved in content, presentation, or availability? Can all directors readily access any information they might need, given the extent of their knowledge of the company, its business, and its strategic context?

In strategy formulation, for example, is each director adequately briefed on the firm's strategic situation—its markets, distribution, customers, competitors, its suppliers and sources of finance, the labour market, the political, economic, social, and technological environment in all of the countries in which the firm operates? Is that knowledge current?

In policymaking, is every director familiar with the firm's policies and able to contribute fully to discussions when they are reviewed? Do directors have the background knowledge, for example, about labour relations, trades unions, product safety, or credit control, to take an informed view of corporate policies?

In most organizations, the management information and control systems, rooted in the ongoing transactions of the business, report on the performance and the state of internal resources. Board-level reporting of recent performance for monitoring and management supervision is most fully developed. As we saw earlier, boards too readily concentrate on management supervision and control, because that highlights issues that need immediate board action. Nevertheless, it is also frequently an area in which reporting systems can be improved.

Accountability, reporting to the outside world, has tended to be the least well-developed segment of board-level information. Of course, companies must satisfy the minimum disclosure requirements of company laws and stock market listing rules. But for many companies, reporting in a narrative beyond financial matters, including detailed strategic plans and projections, corporate social responsibility and sustainability reporting, and risk analysis, is still evolving.

The review of the current director-level information should be documented and discussed with those involved, looking for improvements. Consider the sensitivity of each piece of information and confirm that existing confidentiality controls are adequate. Also review the cost of providing access. The documentation produced by a board information audit can provide the start of an exercise to put board data online. A danger in director-level reporting is that reports produce more data, but not more information. In fact, what is needed is not even more information, but better-informed directors, better able to contribute to the board's activities, and to produce better-quality discussion, and more successful decisions.

Managing meetings, agenda, and minutes

Meetings need planning as well as running. Meetings also need managing and leading. Meetings of the board and its committees should be learning experiences for all involved. The basic considerations in planning a meeting involve the questions: why, what, when, where, and who? The first questions—'why' and 'what?'—are not often asked by chairmen when calling a meeting. Why is it being called? Clarify its purpose and, also, what it is intended to achieve. Sometimes a meeting may not be necessary at all. At other times, consideration of the purpose can avoid repetitious and time-wasting issues being brought up and discussed.

The question 'when?' highlights the need to give adequate notice of the meeting. Some meetings, such as the annual general meeting of shareholders, have the minimum period of notice determined by statute, corporate constitution, or standing orders. Notice may also have to be in writing. Whether notice by email will suffice is a matter for the law of the jurisdiction.

The question 'where?' emphasizes that not all meetings need to be held in the conventional location, typically the boardroom. Holding an occasional company board meeting in one of the other locations of the company—a divisional headquarters, or a regional location—can provide an opportunity for directors to learn from first-hand experience and meet the personnel, for whom the arrival and interest of the directors can be motivating. Meetings are increasingly held by teleconference. Provided that proper attention is given to notice, agenda, and chairmanship, and given that the technical facilities are appropriate, such meetings can bring together members from different locations, saving travel time and expense.

Finally, the question 'who?' makes the point that other people, in addition to the board members, can be invited to attend meetings, either for specific items or for the whole meeting on a non-voting basis. Such people could include those who have relevant information to present to the board and whom directors might question, those who can relay board discussion and decisions to others, and also potential future directors as part of their learning experience and development. In some public organizations, members of the public have the right to attend meetings of the council, governing body, or committee. Of course, subject to the constitution, parts of such meetings may be held in private (in camera).

An agenda is a list of the items of business to be covered in a meeting. The decision regarding what matters get on the agenda can be a crucial issue in boards playing political games. So who should decide each item on the agenda? The final decision should rest with the chairman, but in many cases the company secretary and/or the CEO make suggestions. Professional chairmen give all members of the board the opportunity to ask for matters to be discussed and arrange a periodic review of matters covered. For the comments of experienced chairmen on building an agenda, see Corporate governance in action 16.2 and 16.3.

Corporate governance in action 16.2   Lord Caldecote on building an agenda

Lord Caldecote, when chairman of the Delta Group, wrote to each of his directors periodically to ask whether there were matters they felt that the board should be discussing for the future benefit of the firm. 'In the past year, what have we not discussed that we should have discussed?' he would ask, 'and how could I improve my chairing of our meetings?'

Corporate governance in action 16.3   Another opinion on drafting agenda and minutes

The head of an Oxford college, after a career in the British civil service, believed that good chairmen, among whom he counted himself, should put much effort into designing agenda. Care should be taken in choosing the items to be discussed; attention given to the time allocated to each, and in their positioning on the agenda. Matters likely to be controversial should come towards the end, he recommended, when members were expecting the meeting to end, or had already left, thus increasing the chairman's chances of getting the decision he or she wanted. This chairman also drafted the minutes along with the agenda, because he believed that a good chairman always has a preferred outcome. He knew that those who draft the minutes wield the power. His colleagues had to agree.

Three approaches to agenda design can be distinguished:

- the *routine approach*, in which each meeting follows the pattern of the previous (apologies, approval of the minutes of the last meeting, matters arising from those minutes, the usual substantive items—such as the financial and operating reports—and any other business);

- the *chairman-led approach*, in which the chairman determines the agenda and probably dominates the meeting;

- the *professional approach*, in which the chairman seeks advice from relevant people about the agenda, and takes great care in balancing the items and ensuring that adequate time is available for a competent discussion and sound resolution of each issue.

Another important role for the chairman prior to the meeting is to ensure that all directors have adequate information and are properly briefed, if necessary, on each item on the agenda. Directors cannot opt out of certain items because they lack appropriate knowledge, although they may rely on information received and the opinions of fellow directors, given in good faith, unless they have any reason to doubt—in which case, they must pursue the issue to its root. Similarly, a director may rely on information from a board subcommittee, unless unsure, in which case again the director has a duty to pursue the issue until satisfied.

The minutes are the formal record of a meeting. Although, subject to the articles, there are no specific rules governing the content or format of minutes of board or board subcommittee meetings, they should provide a competent and complete record of what transpired, what was decided, and what actions are to be taken by whom and when. Should there be any future challenge, the minutes, which have been duly approved as a true and fair report at a subsequent meeting, can be used as strong evidence of what was intended.

Companies tend to develop their own style in minute-keeping. Some boards note the names of the key contributors to the discussion; others do not. In some cases, it has to be admitted, the minutes are no more than a staccato record of who attended and what was decided. At the other extreme, there are minutes that are almost a verbatim report of the proceedings, complete with stage directions. The ideal lies between the two. Minutes should contain sufficient information to capture the key threads of the discussion, any disclosures of personal interest, the alternatives considered, the agreement reached, and plans and responsibilities for action. The person responsible for writing the minutes potentially wields considerable power, although typically minutes of the last meeting are approved and can be challenged at the following meeting.

A few boards record their meetings audio-visually. This can help in writing the minutes, but, if used as a record of proceedings, may inhibit discussion. In a few companies, minutes are occasionally created for meetings that did not take place, in order to meet statutory requirements. This is bad practice, as is the backdating of minutes, which could be considered fraudulent.

Communications with shareholders and other stakeholders

Demonstrating accountability is one of the four principal elements of the board's role, the way in which it proves its performance. Corporate transparency is increasingly demanded by investors, other stakeholders, and society generally. But companies' approach to their communications with their shareholders and the wider world vary considerably among:

- the minimum disclosure necessary to satisfy statutory requirements, including companies' legislation, auditing and accounting standards, and, for listed companies, the demands of the stock exchange's rules;

- a directors' report and financial accounts that go beyond the minimum statutory requirements by reporting corporate activities and major developments, but make no attempt to comment on the company's strategic situation, its risk profile, or its prospects;

- a recognition that the annual report and accounts, together with other periodic shareholder communications, provide a way of presenting the company, its products, policies, and processes as part of an ongoing public relations and advertising policy;

- a board-level communications policy, which identifies and differentiates audiences for the company's communications, establishes the purpose and the appropriate content of communications to each, and uses a wide range of different media. (Such a policy enables the success of board-level communications to be assessed and developed where appropriate.)

A survey of board reporting[10] by UK FTSE 100 companies commented that many annual reports are 'predictable, indistinguishable compliance statements'. Few take the opportunity to communicate with shareholders on real governance issues. The report suggests that

[10] Independent Audit Ltd board reporting in 2006: a survey of FTSE 100 annual reports. See www.independentaudit.com/wp-content/uploads/2006/07/Board-reporting-in-2006.pdf

companies need to turn their corporate governance statement into a story that investors want to read, emphasizing performance not compliance. It suggests that companies:

- drop statements of the obvious, such as 'boilerplate' statements that the board supports sound corporate governance;

- separate out the compliance statements, which are necessary, but can be put in boxes, so that the report flows;

- focus on the changes, referring back to the last report to show changes.

However, the study also reported that more audit committees were reporting in detail on the independence and the effectiveness of their external auditor, and on how the committee made that assessment.

Some countries have now included a requirement for major companies to include a commentary on the company's situation, strategies, prospects, and perceived risks. In the United Kingdom, the original intention in the Companies Act 2006 was to require listed companies to publish a detailed operations and financial review with their annual accounts, including a commentary on the company's strategic situation. However, that requirement was dropped because it was felt that such disclosure could put British firms at a disadvantage against their international competitors.

Where a company does have a board-level communications policy, it is likely to identify a range of potential audiences for corporate communications, including:

- existing and potential shareholders, perhaps recognizing that the interests, knowledge, and skills of small retail investors are likely to be different from those of institutional investors, and attempts to produce material that will satisfy both may satisfy neither;

- for listed companies, the stock market, financial analysts, the financial press, and other media; for companies in a group, the interests of the holding company; for other private companies, the expectations and needs of minority shareholders, family members, and potential acquirers;

- regulators, including those appointed under companies' legislation, mergers and acquisition law, competition and monopoly law; for listed companies, the requirements of the listing rules, tax authorities, and national and international financial regulators, including money laundering controls;

- for other stakeholders, the interests of customers and the marketplace for the company's products and services, middle management, employees and their trades unions, suppliers and others in the company's added-value chain, and providers of non-equity funds. (Such a policy projects a coherent corporate image and supports the corporate culture.)

Having identified a wide range of those who might be interested in corporate communications, it is a small step to accepting that different content and means of delivery might be required. Companies with a professional board-level communications policy recognize that a traditional directors' report and financial accounts will not suffice: the inevitable and increasing complexity of financial reporting may satisfy the financially sophisticated, but is too complex for many others.

Consequently, some companies attempt to produce summaries or separate documents to satisfy the needs of different audiences. Where this is done, it is vital, of course, for the various documents to correspond and to conform to regulatory requirements. Other companies adopt a range of communication media including:

- the delivery of statutory information to shareholders electronically, which company law in some jurisdictions now permits. This option has opened a range of new opportunities for communicating with shareholders and, if necessary, receiving responses, such as proxy votes—information available might include the periodic financial statements, stock exchange announcements, newsletters and factsheets, and messages from the chairman, CEO, or other corporate officials;

- corporate websites giving access to a wide range of information about the company;

- CD-ROMs, telecasts, and video distribution of shareholder meetings, briefings, and other presentations;

- use of Twitter, Facebook, and other social media for pages of company information and commentary;

- access to company directors and officers by email and the company's website.

While printed documents distributed through the mail are likely to remain a significant vehicle for board-level communication, companies with a professional communications policy will be continuously looking for new opportunities to improve their communications and to reduce their costs.

Case studies

 Case study 16.1   Directors' right to information—Hong Kong Stock Exchange

After graduating in mathematics from Exeter College, Oxford, David Webb had experience as a merchant banker in London before moving to Hong Kong in 1991 to continue his investment banking career. Subsequently, he became a corporate governance activist, lobbying for greater transparency and accountability of boards of Hong Kong listed companies. His website (www.webb-site.com (note the hyphen)) is a constant source of revelations, insights, and commentary on listed company practices. Having purchased shares in all of the companies in the Hang Seng index, he regularly demands polls on resolutions he feels are not in the interests of minority shareholders.

Webb was elected as an independent non-executive director of the company that owns the Hong Kong Stock Exchange in 2003. Subsequently, he criticized the Hong Kong government, which held over 5% of the shares listed on the Hong Kong Exchange, for voting those shares to influence the appointment of directors, who might share their political orientation, to the boards of influential Hong Kong companies, thus 'interfering in business in a way governments should not'. Webb resigned his directorship before its expiry, complaining that the management of the Exchange was withholding information from him. This was denied by management.

Commenting on the issue, John Brewer, a Hong Kong barrister, noted the international case law that emphasized directors' personal liability to acquire sufficient knowledge and understanding of the company's business to be able to discharge their duties as directors. He cited case law from Australia in which the presiding judge had stated:

> It would be difficult for the court to over-emphasize the importance of the directors' statutory rights of access to corporate information. They are the foundation of the system of corporate governance . . . Directors cannot be expected to carry out any of their substantial responsibilities, including their fiduciary duties and to attend to the solvency of the company and its general management, unless they can be sure of having full and unfettered access to the documents of the company.

Webb is a significant investor in smaller Hong Kong companies and is a member of the Hong Kong Securities and Futures Commission's Takeover and Mergers Panel.

Discussion question

Can you think of any information that the management of the stock exchange might not want to provide to David Webb?

Case study 16.2   The corporate culture at Goldman Sachs

Founded in 1869, the Goldman Sachs Group is headquartered in New York and maintains offices in all major financial centres around the world, including London. The firm provides investment banking, institutional client services, financing and investment management to a substantial client base of companies, financial institutions, and high-net-worth individuals. The Group has over 30,000 employees world-wide and produces around $30 billion in revenue and $2.5 billion in profit. The corporate website[11] describes the firm's activities:

- advising companies on buying and selling businesses, raising capital and managing risks, which enables them to grow
- helping local, state and national governments finance their operations so they can invest in infrastructure, like schools, hospitals and roads
- transacting in all key financial markets for clients, including equities, bonds, currencies and commodities, so that capital flows, jobs are created and economies can grow
- helping markets remain efficient and liquid, so investors and companies can meet their needs, whether to invest, raise money or manage risk
- preserving and growing assets for institutions, including mutual funds, pension funds and foundations, as well as individuals
- investing our capital alongside our clients' capital to help businesses grow
- developing ideas and analysis that drive new perspectives, new products and new paths to growth

The firm was a partnership until 1999, when the partners decided to go public.

Initially, only a small portion of the shares were listed, but after further stock offerings Goldman Sachs is now owned around 70% by institutional investors. The first chairman and CEO of the company was Henry Paulson, who left in 2006 to become US Treasury Secretary. Lloyd C. Blankfein

[11] For more on Goldman Sachs, see www.goldmansachs.com Financial accounts are at www.goldmansachs.com/investor-relations/financials/index.html

replaced him, receiving a bonus of $67.9 million in his first year, some of which he took in cash unlike Paulson who took his bonus entirely in company stock.

Goldman Sachs is one of the most prestigious investment banks in the world, but since the global financial crisis began in 2007, its business practices, ethics, and culture have been questioned.

Goldman Sachs profits from the sub-prime mortgage crisis

In the sub-prime mortgage market, banks provided loans to high-risk customers against their property, sometimes at over 100% of the property's current value, in the belief that it would increase. The banks then bundled their mortgages together and sold them on as bonds to investors. Many believed that they were spreading and thus reducing their exposure to risk. A few commentators, however, warned that rather than reducing risk, derivatives merely spread the risk and made tracing the underlying assets more difficult.

Goldman Sachs created structured products called collateralized debt obligations (CDOs), which it sold to investors around the world. CDOs were pools of bonds backed by bundles of mortgages. CDO volume grew dramatically between 2000 and 2006. As long as global investors had the confidence to buy them, all was well.

Then in 2007 the property market began to collapse. Starting in the United States, property prices fell, and borrowers found themselves in negative equity, their properties now worth less than their loans. Doubts about the worth of sub-prime mortgages grew. Uncertainty about the bonds and CDOs derived from them spread. Global investors were no longer prepared to risk their funds. The source of financial liquidity had dried up. The sub-prime market crisis had arrived and spread quickly around the world as banks were unable to raise funds.

Some Goldman Sachs traders foresaw the potential worsening position in the sub-prime market and began to sell CDOs short, that is they contracted to sell them at a lower price on a future date. The firm claims that this was prudent hedging to protect their position. Others criticized them for 'betting' against their own clients, gambling that the price would fall as the derivative market collapsed. As that happened Goldman Sachs was able to write down its losses from sub-prime securitized loans it held by offsetting gains on its shorted market position.

Goldman Sachs made substantial profits from the sub-prime mortgage crisis, rather than being caught out like many other financial institutions. The *New York Times* lauded its financial prowess. But in 2009 the paper also told the story of how the firm had created CDOs, sold them to investors, and then bet short against them. Goldman Sachs claimed that its investors knew it was betting against the products it was selling to them.

The Goldman Sachs culture

William D. Cohen, who won the 2007 FT/Goldman Sachs Business Book of the year award, subsequently wrote a penetrating book about the Goldman Sachs.[12] In it he quotes a Goldman banker: 'The people who are going to be successful at Goldman are the folks who are prepared to sacrifice all. All. Everything. To the greater glory.' Cohen explained: 'Goldman takes only the brightest and the best . . . academic success is not enough. Each job applicant has to be thoroughly investigated by the reputational risk department. The hours are famously punishing. Cars collect senior executive at 5.30 a.m. Breakfast, lunch, and dinner are taken at desks. Breaks are unheard of. Brokers routinely work past midnight. Bosses expect you to be available nothing less than 24-7. The answer to why so many staff keep going is money . . . huge bonuses that will set them up financially for life.' The success

---

[12] Cohan, William D. (2011) *Money and Power: How Goldman Sachs Came to Rule the World*. Anchor Books, Random House, New York.

of such experience can be seen as former Goldman employees went on to head the New York Stock Exchange, the World Bank, the US Treasury Department, the White House staff, as well as major banks and financial institutions.

But this demanding culture had its downside. In March 2012, the *New York Times* published, as an opinion piece, a resignation letter from Greg Smith,[13] the former head of Goldman Sachs' equity derivatives business in the firm's Europe, Middle East and Africa Division. Smith claimed that the firm was 'morally bankrupt'. 'The decline in the firm's moral fibre', he wrote, 'was due to Chairman/Chief Executive Officer Lloyd Blankfein and President Gary Cohn.' They had changed the company's culture from 'the secret sauce that made this place great and allowed us to earn our clients' trust' to a 'toxic culture' in which 'the interests of the client continue to be sidelined'. Colleagues talked about 'ripping their clients off', and senior management described clients as 'muppets'—a reference to amusingly stupid puppets created for TV's 'The Muppet Show' in the United Kingdom and 'Sesame Street' in the United States. A friend of Smith's said that, by resigning, Smith had thrown away his career for his principles. 'I admire the man and I admire his courage. But there's no way I'd do that myself.'

Goldman Sachs responded to the letter by saying: 'we don't think [the letter] reflects the way we run our business. We will only be successful if our clients are successful.'

Discussion questions

1. What is your opinion of the board-level culture and its effect on the bankers at Goldman Sachs?

2. His friend said that by resigning, Greg Smith had thrown away his career for his principles. 'I admire the man and I admire his courage. But there's no way I'd do that myself.' What would you have done in Smith's position?

[13] Smith, Greg (2012). 'Why I Am Leaving Goldman Sachs'. *New York Times*, 14 March.

References and further reading

Brenkert, George G. and Tom L. Beauchamp (eds) (2009) *The Oxford Handbook of Business Ethics*. Oxford University Press, Oxford.

FRC (2011) *Guidance on Board Effectiveness*. Financial Reporting Council, London.

NACD (2005) *Board Leadership: A Report of a NACD Blue Ribbon Commission*. National Association of Corporate Directors, 1133, Suite 700 21 Street, Washington, DC, USA.

NACD (2005) *Director Liability: Myths, Realities, and Prevention—A Report of a NACD Blue Ribbon Commission*. National Association of Corporate Directors, 1133, Suite 700 21 Street, Washington, DC, USA.

NACD (2005) *Governance Committee: Driving Board Performance—A Report of a NACD Blue Ribbon Commission*. National Association of Corporate Directors, 1133, Suite 700 21 Street, Washington, DC, USA.

Steger, Ulrich and Wilfgang Amann (2008) *Corporate Governance: Cases in Adding Value*. Wiley, Chichester, UK.

Stiles, P. and B. Taylor (2001) *Boards at Work: How Directors View Their Roles and Responsibilities*. Oxford University Press, New York.

Wallace, Peter and John Zinken (2003) *Corporate Governance*. Mastering Business in Asia series, John Wiley, Singapore.

Projects and exercises

1. Use the Internet to study the websites of five companies, the names of which you know. What is your opinion of their communications? Do they seem to have a board-level

communications policy? How do their communications with shareholders and other stakeholders compare?

2. Draft a set of briefing notes for directors on the following topics:
   - director orientation and director induction programmes;
   - director development, training, and updating;
   - directors and officers insurance.

3. Knowing that you have been studying corporate governance, the chairman of an organization has asked your advice on how he might improve the effectiveness of his governing body. Draft a letter giving some advice.

Self-test questions

1. What are the 'six Cs' for an effective board?

2. Name eight matters that new directors should know about if they have followed a properly planned orientation programme.

3. Name some issues that need to be considered before adopting an electronic paperless system for board reports.

4. What are the key questions that should be posed before calling a meeting?

5. If a director lacks appropriate knowledge on a subject before the board, can he or she, legitimately, opt out of discussions on that item?

6. Are there any specific rules governing the content or format of minutes of board or board subcommittee meetings?

7. Name five qualities of a good report with high-quality information.

8. Why should companies have a director induction programme?

9. What is D&O?

10. In a limited-liability company, are the liabilities of the directors limited?

Appendix to Chapter 16

Director's induction checklist

Working through the items on this checklist will improve the quality of a director's contribution and reduce the time taken to contribute fully and effectively to the board. Induction exercises for directors ensure that all board members are fully informed about the company, the business, and its financials, which are the three fundamental areas in which directors need to be conversant and competent. Obviously, directors vary in the extent of their knowledge of the company and its business, but the checklist will provide an aide-memoire for both executive and non-executive directors.

The checklist can be used by chairmen, CEOs, and company secretaries to plan an induction programme for new board members and also by newly appointed directors wanting to brief themselves. It has also proved useful for directors of long standing, by highlighting areas of knowledge and work that they might previously have overlooked.

1. Knowledge of the company

The first broad focus of the induction programme is on the company and its governance situation. The chairman, other long-serving directors, and the company secretary can often be very helpful in this sector. If in any doubt, it is always wise to seek legal opinion.

Ownership power

In the joint-stock, limited-liability company, ownership is the ultimate basis of governance power. What is the actual balance of the equity shareholding and voting power in this company? Has the balance changed in the past and how have the votes been used? How might it change and the voting strength be used in the future? Consider, in a family company for example, what might happen as shares are transferred on succession. Or, in a widely held public company, consider the potential for a merger or hostile bid. What anti-takeover provisions, if any, are in place? How effective might they be?

In a company limited by guarantee, or any other corporate entity governed by its membership, how active is the membership in governance matters? Could this situation change in the future? Explore the way in which the board communicates with the members and whether there have been any attempts by members to influence corporate affairs. Not-for-profit organizations often seem to generate controversial, even adversarial, member activity.

Governance rules, regulations, and company law

Study the constitution of the entity: its articles of association and memorandum; its corporate rulebook; or the relevant statute, ordinance, or charter for an entity created by the state. These are the formal documents created on incorporation and updated subject to the approval of the members. Within the constraints of the company law and the listing rules (for a quoted public company), they determine the way in which the company can be governed. The articles, for example, could limit the size of the board, lay down rules for the selection of the board chairman, or define conditions for the meeting and voting of the members. All too often, directors are not familiar with the contents of the company's memorandum and articles of association and are surprised to find themselves constrained in some way, for example in the percentage of members' votes needed to change the capital structure or to sell off part of the enterprise.

In a listed, public company, familiarity with the listing rules of the stock exchanges on which the company's shares are quoted can be important. Some directors feel that this is a matter that can reasonably be left to the company secretary, share registrar, or corporate legal counsel. It is difficult to ask appropriate questions to ensure compliance if one is not familiar with the basic requirements. There is an important distinction between delegation and abdication of responsibility.

Be familiar with the broad scope of the company laws of the jurisdiction in which the company is incorporated and operates. Obviously, the detailed requirements of company law vary between Delaware and California, Australia and Japan, or the United Kingdom and France—but there can also be fundamental differences, particularly in the handling of private companies. Companies incorporated in the British Virgin Islands, for example, are not required to have an audit, there is virtually no public filing of documents, and the rights of members can be severely limited if they are not also directors, which is why, of course, so many companies are incorporated there.

It is not necessary for a director to be a lawyer or an accountant to fulfil such responsibilities—but company laws around the world typically expect directors to show that degree of knowledge and skill that a reasonable person would associate with company directorship. In the old days, this might not have amounted to very much; today, expectations can run high.

Board structure, membership, and processes

What is the structure of the board—that is, what is the balance between executive and non-executive directors? In your opinion, is this appropriate? Are the outside, non-executive directors genuinely independent, or do they have some connection with the company, such as being a nominee for a major shareholder or lender? Are they members of the family of the chairman or CEO or have they held an executive position in that company in the past? Such matters could affect your assessment of the position they take on board issues.

Is the board chairmanship separated from the role of chief executive? If not, is there a danger that a single individual dominates the board: are you able to operate in such a climate? What is the style of the chairman of the board: can you work well under these conditions?

Who are the other board members? Do you know them? If not, some effort to learn about their backgrounds, experience, and reputations could reinforce your early contributions to board discussions. Meeting individual directors to discuss corporate matters before your first board meeting might help you to discover whether the chemistry of the board is likely to be appropriate for you. Can you work with them? Is there a succession plan for key directors and top management? Is there a strategy for development at board level to ensure that the business does not outgrow the board?

How often does the board meet? Typically how long do the meetings last? What role does the chairman play in board matters? Ask for the agenda and minutes of recent board meetings. Talk to the company secretary about the way the board meetings are run. Does the board operate with committees—an executive committee, audit, remuneration, or nominating committees, for example? Find out what you can about the membership, chairmanship, and style of these committees. Again, study their minutes and discuss with their chairman or the company secretary how they operate.

What information do the directors routinely receive? Ask for all of the documentation provided for recent meetings: study the reports, and consider the scope of the routine performance data provided. Is it adequate? Does the board have briefings and presentations from non-board senior executives or other experts from time to time? Do the directors meet with the auditors periodically?

2. Knowledge of the business

The second focus of this induction checklist is on the business itself. Do you know enough about the business to make an effective contribution? Obviously, this is a reasonable question to ask an outside director who has little or no experience in this particular industry. Interestingly, though, it is also a pertinent question to put to many executive directors. Expertise and success in a particular function (finance and accounting, perhaps), or high managerial performance in running a division or group company, does not necessarily provide a view of the business as a whole. Indeed, it might have created a narrow window of experience through which the entire corporate business is viewed. This part of the checklist is again relevant to *all* directors.

The basic business processes

Can you outline the fundamental steps in the added-value chain or network of the firm? This is as pertinent a question for directors of a bank, a telecommunications company, or an airline, as it is to a manufacturing business (although the basic processes are often more difficult to identify). Where is the business most exposed to risk? What are the core competencies or capabilities of the business? What is the range of products and services provided by the business? Are you familiar with the major sources of the business inputs—where they come from and who provides them?

Which business activities or processes add value and provide competitive advantage? Which business activities or processes drive the costs? Who are the customers? What sectors and markets are served? Pareto's law often applies to products and customers—80% of the value comes from 20% of the list. Which products and customers form this 20%?

Find out all you can from catalogues, trade literature, customer promotions, trade shows, and similar sources of information. Do directors have access to the firm's customer and competitor information systems—capturing and abstracting information, often qualitative, about the activities and plans of customers, competitors, and strategic allies? These systems can be more akin to military or police intelligence systems than typical transaction-based systems.

Corporate strategies

Does the firm have a written mission statement or a set of core values? Is there a shared view of the business direction, clearly articulated in strategies, plans, and projects? Obtain copies; discuss them with the chairman or CEO. If not, what is the broad direction of the business? What strategies are emergent from recent actions, such as strategies of growth through investment in new product development or through acquisition and divestment? Are there any written policies or management manuals? Again, study and discuss them. For example, as far as customers are concerned, are there specific pricing policies, credit policies, and returned goods policies?

Who are the principal competitors? What competitive advantages and disadvantages do they have? What strategies are they pursuing? Are there potential new entrants into the market or new technological developments, products, or services that might provide alternative competition? Is the business involved in strategic alliances: for example, joint ventures to develop new strategic areas, to supply goods or services, or to provide access to distribution channels?

Where is the company exposed to significant strategic risk? What is the company's strategic risk profile? Can you be comfortable with the company's underlying appetite for risk? Are the systems by which the company recognizes, assesses, and manages risk at all levels in the organization reliable?

How is strategic change initiated in the firm? Does the board respond to ideas put up by the CEO and top management, or is the board intimately involved in strategy formulation?

Organization, management, and people

What is the formal organization structure? Discuss with the CEO and other members of top management how the organization works in practice. Form a view of the management culture and style throughout the business: it may differ around the world.

What management control systems are used—budgetary planning and control, profit centres, performance centres, etc.? What management performance measures are used? Are they linked to managerial incentives? Are there employee or top management share option schemes?

How many employees are there in the various parts of the business? What are the characteristics of the workforce? Are trades unions important: is there a policy towards them? What are the remuneration and other employment policies? What are the policies on top management and executive director remuneration? Are you comfortable with this policy and the levels of remuneration involved?

Overall, how would you assess the current position of the business? What needs to be done to maintain and enhance future performance?

What is the company's position on monitoring and reporting corporate social responsibility and sustainability? Does the company have written policies on corporate social responsibility or business ethics? If so, are they in line with what you can accept? If not, are you able to work with this organization and its leadership?

3. Knowledge of the financials

Finally, we turn to a sector that inevitably features large in typical board discussions—the financial aspects.

Study the annual accounts and directors' reports for the past few years. What have been the trends? Consider trends in key financial ratios, for example: overall performance ratios, such as return on equity and return on investment, inventory turnover rates, liquidity ratios, and debt collection rates. Does the company measure shareholder added-value?

Trends are likely to convey more information than the actual data for the business itself, although financial ratios at a point in time can be useful for cross-industry comparisons. What are the future projections for these financial criteria? How does the financial position of the company compare with those of its key competitors?

Review the financial performance of parts of the business, such as product or geographical divisions, or subsidiary companies. Review the criteria used in investment project appraisals.

How is the company financed? What is the financial structure? What implications might the debt/equity ratio have for the future—for example, what might be the effect of a significant change in interest or currency rates, given this gearing or leverage?

Who are the auditors? Ask to see the 'management letter' written after the last audit discussing any issues that arose during the audit.

4. Expectations on appointment

Every director, executive and non-executive, should discuss with the chairman what is expected of the directorship, before accepting nomination. Have you discussed the expectations of your directorship: are you expected to bring particular skills, knowledge, or experience to the board? Some chairmen allow potential directors to sit in on board and board committee meetings before joining the board. A crucial part of any induction briefing should review the expectations of the chairman and the other directors.

Has the director been proposed to fulfil a specific role? Is there a special reason for the nomination to the board? For example, did the nomination reflect particular knowledge in some area, to bring special skills or experience to board discussions, or to provide a channel of communication or networking? Or was the nomination made because of relevant overall experience and potential contribution to all aspects of the board's work? Are you capable of fulfilling these expectations? If not, what other information, knowledge, or skills will you need to obtain?

How much time are you expected to give to the board, its committees, and other aspects of the company's affairs? This should cover not only attendance at regular meetings, but also the time needed for briefings and discussions, visits within the company, and preparation. Outside directors will have to ensure that this is compatible with other demands on their time. Inside executive directors will need to harmonize these expectations and their director responsibilities with the duties required under their contract of employment with the company.

Although all directors have the right to be informed on all board matters, confirm that you will have appropriate access to the information you require. This should cover not only formal board papers, but also the right to seek additional information if necessary. Are you able to talk with the members of management? If so, under what circumstances?

Last, but not least, review the details of the contractual relationship between you and the company. What are the terms of appointment as a director? Is there a written contract or a formal letter of appointment from the chairman? What is the length of appointment? What are the terms and likelihood of reappointment? What is the basis of the remuneration package and the manner of review? Does the package include performance-related rewards or a pension commitment? What are the terms of directors' and officers' indemnity insurance (particularly important in the increasingly litigious climate facing directors in many parts of the world)?

Finally, a word of encouragement: all directors, without exception, face a challenge as they join a new board. Effective board membership involves a learning experience: it should start well before the director attends that first board meeting and should continue during all of the rest. Successful directors are those who say, 'Aha! I hadn't realized that, but now I understand,' not once, but continuously, throughout their service on the board.

17 Board Evaluation: Reviewing directors and boards

 Learning Outcomes

In which we consider:

- Assessing boards and board committees
- Assessing individual directors' performance
- Corporate governance rating systems for companies
- Corporate governance assessment systems for countries
- Appendix to Chapter 17: The Fannie Mae corporate governance guidelines

Assessing boards and board committees

The corporate governance rules of the New York Stock Exchange require boards of listed companies to conduct a self-evaluation at least annually to determine whether the board and its committees are functioning effectively. The US National Association of Corporate Directors has recommended that all boards introduce formal procedures to assess both their own collective performance and that of individual directors.

Two main principles of the UK Corporate Governance Code are that the board:

- should undertake a formal and rigorous annual evaluation of its own performance and that of its committees and individual directors;
- should state in the annual report how the performance evaluation of the board, its committees, and its individual directors has been conducted.

Supporting principles encourage the chairman to act on the results of the performance evaluation by recognizing the strengths and addressing the weaknesses of the board, and, where appropriate, proposing new members be appointed to the board or seeking the resignation of directors. Further, individual evaluation should aim to show whether each director continues to contribute effectively and to demonstrate commitment to the role (including commitment of time for board and committee meetings and any other duties).

Corporate governance codes in many other countries now have similar requirements. An extension to the UK Corporate Governance Code required the evaluation of the board of FTSE 350 companies to be *externally* facilitated at least every three years. A statement is also required explaining whether the external facilitator has any other connection with the company.

Of course, companies in countries with voluntary corporate governance codes can refuse to follow the code principles, explaining why they have not done so in their corporate governance report. A continuing challenge is how to ensure compliance with the spirit, as well as the letter, of corporate governance codes.

The UK Stewardship Code (2010), published by the Financial Reporting Council (FRC) and reviewed in Chapter 4, states that institutional investors should monitor investee companies to determine when it is necessary to enter into an active dialogue with their boards. This monitoring should be regular and the process clearly communicable and checked periodically for its effectiveness. As part of this monitoring, institutional investors should:

- seek to satisfy themselves . . . that the investee company's board and committee structures are effective, and that independent directors provide adequate oversight, including by meeting the chairman and, where appropriate, other board members;
- maintain a clear audit trail, for example, records of private meetings held with companies, of votes cast, and of reasons for voting against the investee company's management, for abstaining, or for voting with management in a contentious situation; and
- attend the General Meetings of companies in which they have a major holding, where appropriate and practicable.

Institutional investors should consider carefully explanations given if companies in which they invest depart from the UK Corporate Governance Code and make reasoned judgements in each case. They should give a timely explanation to the company, in writing where appropriate, and be prepared to enter a dialogue if they do not accept the company's position. In effect, the FRC was calling on institutional investors to support it in applying the stewardship code and to take a pro-active role in their relations with companies.

When board assessment was first introduced, some directors faced the prospect with trepidation. But experience has shown that a board with strong and respected leadership, with directors who trust each other, and which is directing a successful enterprise, finds the exercise worthwhile and the experience rewarding. Unfortunately, on the other hand, experience also suggests that a poorly led board, with directors in disagreement, leading an organization that is failing to meet its goals, finds the process antagonistic and the outcome potentially catastrophic.

Interestingly, research has shown that the typical corporate governance indicators, such as board structure, the independence of directors, and the use of board committees, are not the best predictors of board effectiveness. Rather, less specific indicators, sometimes called 'soft' governance, such as the working relationships between directors, the standard of chairmanship, or directors' knowledge of the company, were found to be more significant.

Why undertake a board review? The worst response is 'because we are required to by the regulations'. A more positive response would be that 'we see the review as a fundamental part of our corporate governance strategy, which forms part of our overall corporate strategy'.

Sir Bryan Nicholson, when he was chairman of the FRC,[1] commented:

> . . . the evaluation process is particularly important. It provides the opportunity for companies to create a virtuous circle of sustained improvement in board effectiveness based on

---

[1] Sir Win Bischoff was appointed Chairman of the FRC in May 2014. He was previously Chairman of Lloyds Banking Group from 2009.

regular objective assessment of past performance and the company's changing needs and circumstances. It introduces a new dynamic which companies can use to improve the quality of their corporate governance and secure competitive advantage.

A competent and regular board performance review can:

- check whether directors' knowledge of the business and its strategic situation is up to date;
- review the board structure, including board diversity and the balance between independent outside directors and executive directors;
- assess the balance of skills, knowledge, and experience on the board and its committees;
- identify director weaknesses to be remedied by director training and development, or by additional or replacement board members;
- review current board and board committee practices, including directors' access to information and opportunities to improve efficiency;
- review the effectiveness of the board's strategic thinking, risk management, and decision-making;
- provide an ongoing challenge to attitudes in boards with long-serving directors;
- confirm the succession plan for the board is current and create the climate for change particularly if a change of chairmanship is needed;
- review the quality of reporting and announcements to the market, for listed companies
- confirm that the company is compliant with all relevant law, regulations and, where appropriate, listing rules, including the disclosure of directors' interests and controls on insider dealing
- provide information for the board's corporate governance report and respond to questions from shareholders and other legitimate stakeholders.

A board review holds up a mirror to the board, its behaviour, and its performance. It is as important for well-performing boards as for those that are not performing well. A board review should take a strategic perspective, considering the directors' ability to handle long-term issues as well as reflecting on recent experience in the short term. Otherwise the board may not be adapting to the company's changing strategic situation. The board review process to be explored later in this chapter takes just such a strategic perspective. The entire review process is set in the context of the overall corporate strategy and leads to a corporate governance strategy. The outcome can lead to changes in corporate governance policies and plans for board-level development.

Who should initiate the board assessment?

The board as a whole is responsible for ensuring that its company is complying with the corporate governance laws, rules, and regulations, and any other related policies that the board has agreed. The board chairman should ensure that appropriate time and attention are given to such matters, which can easily be overshadowed by other claims on the board's time from pressing business issues, as we have already seen. Detailed work on the board review may be delegated to the company secretary or other officer, but the board's overall responsibility and accountability cannot be delegated. A regular corporate governance and board review ensures that all directors periodically pay attention to this area.

Who should carry out the board assessment?

In many companies, the chairman assumes the role. But experience has shown that this approach lacks the independence and objectivity that a serious review really needs. Such chairmen are effectively marking their own examination paper. An experienced independent director, perhaps the senior independent non-executive, could be asked to lead the work. Some boards form a special board committee, typically nominating independent directors, to undertake the review; others give the responsibility to the audit committee supported by the internal audit function. While an executive director such as the chief executive officer (CEO) or chief finance officer (CFO) will have appropriate knowledge of the business and the board, his or her perspective is unlikely to be seen as objective by other board members. Self-evaluation by boards needs initial agreement on goals, and openness and honesty from every director, including the chairman. A thorough board review demands a lot of time and effort, in marshalling written material, interviewing directors and support staff, talking with auditors, institutional investors, and so on. Staff support will be needed if a board member or a committee undertakes the review.

The real concern is whether an internally driven evaluation process (particularly where it is limited to the use of questionnaires) has been objective and rigorous in every case. Adherence to an internally driven process carries with it the danger over time of the evaluation becoming devalued. This is where shareholders should be taking a closer interest.

Externally facilitated independent assessment

An alternative approach is for the board to seek an independent perspective, inviting someone outside the board to lead the review process and report. A past chairman might be a possibility: he or she would have knowledge of the business, but may lack objectivity on board politics. Another possibility might be a respected chairman or director from the board of another, non-competitor company.

The requirement of the UK Corporate Governance Code for the evaluation of the board to be externally facilitated at least every three years has led to the creation of specialist units in consultancy firms, executive search firms, and the formation of board assessment advisers and firms. Some professional bodies and other independent organizations also undertake board assessment projects.[2] Two caveats: executive search firms may not be entirely independent, and management consultancy projects often call for a different mindset from those dealing with board-level interactions and political processes. For an example of an organization's guidelines on board evaluation, see Corporate governance in action 17.1; and, for further advice, see Corporate governance in action 17.2.

---

[2] For a code of practice for independent external board evaluation, see www.abexcellence.com See also National Association of Corporate Directors at www.nacdonline.org

Corporate governance in action 17.1   Fannie Mae Corporate Governance Guidelines (7)

Board Performance Evaluation

The Board conducts an annual self-evaluation to assess its effectiveness and the adequacy of the information flow to the Board, on the basis of criteria developed by the Nominating and Corporate Governance Committee and reviewed by the Board. Each of the Board's committees conducts an annual self-evaluation.

The Nominating and Corporate Governance Committee evaluates the performance of individual directors on an annual basis. The Nominating and Corporate Governance Committee takes into consideration:

(i) a director's contribution to the effective functioning of the corporation;

(ii) any change in the director's principal area of responsibility with his or her company or in his or her employment;

(iii) the director's retirement from his or her principal area of responsibility with his or her company;

(iv) whether the director continues to bring relevant experience to the Board;

(v) whether the director has the ability to attend meetings and fully participate in the activities of the Board;

(vi) whether the director has developed any relationships with Fannie Mae or another organization, or other circumstances have arisen, that might make it inappropriate for the director to continue serving on the Board; and

(vii) the director's age and length of service on the Board.

Source: www.fanniemae.com/portal/about-us/governance/corporate-governance.html

The benefits of an external review include:[3]

- bringing objectivity and a fresh perspective;
- encouraging candour and richer insights through wide-ranging discussions;
- addressing uncomfortable issues;
- diagnosing root causes of board-level problems;
- reviewing board papers independently;
- interviewing key players objectively;
- observing the dynamics of board meetings;
- improving board presentations and facilitation;
- providing comparisons with the performance of other boards
- ensuring that the board is focused on continuous improvement.

[3]A report from Hermes Fund Managers suggested that companies that are recognized for the best boardroom practice also deliver substantially higher returns for shareholders: The Times, 22 January 2014.

Corporate governance in action 17.2   Board evaluation—advice from the ICSA

The UK Institute of Chartered Secretaries and Administrators (ICSA) notes that a well-conducted evaluation helps the board, committees and individual directors perform to their maximum capabilities, and:

- assess the balance of skills within the board;
- identify attributes required for new appointments;
- review practices and procedures to improve efficiency and effectiveness;
- review practices and procedures of the board's decision-making processes;
- recognize the board's outputs and achievements.

See www.icsa.org.uk/products-and-services/icsa-board-evaluation

What does a board assessment involve?

Some boards and their consultants take an external perspective of the corporate governance activities of the company. The review checks whether the accountability reporting demands of company legislation, codes, and stock exchange regulation are being met, and whether the reporting by the company of financial, operational, and corporate social responsibility matters to shareholders and other legitimate stakeholders is appropriate. The opinions of major shareholders, regulators, financial commentators, and others are sought. The resultant report can then be used by the board to confirm that their corporate governance conformance and reporting responsibilities are being met. However, such an approach does not address the company's corporate governance process itself.

The more thorough approach described here, in addition to ensuring that appropriate disclosure and accountability are being provided, analyses the board and committee structures, studies the strengths and weaknesses of the board, and reviews the processes of the board and its committee. The resultant report leads to a new strategy for board development and corporate governance improvement. This might include proposals to increase directors' competencies and to improve board-level performance.

Just as an enterprise may have longer-term strategies for market development, technological development, or management development, so too the board review project should lead towards an agreed strategy for board and corporate governance development. Because the review will affect all of the members of the board, it is vital for all directors to understand fully the project's objectives, the processes, and the intended outputs. Moreover, it is essential that every director is committed to the project. Lack of commitment by a director can easily lead to poor co-operation in the project, unwelcome political manoeuvres, and unhelpful criticism of the proposals.

A real danger in long-serving boards is that members all grow older together and become increasingly out of touch with the dynamics of the organization and the strategic situation of the underlying business. The more successful the company, the more likely the board is to have long-standing retainers whose focus is on the past. A rigorous board review will highlight any such possibility.

The process now to be described establishes the board review in the context of the overall corporate strategy. See the flowchart (Figure 17.1), which we will consider section by section. This schema depicts the elements of a board review and assessment. We can now work through the stages to see what is involved.

The chairman has an important role in establishing an enthusiastic climate for the study and the report's conclusions. The strategic focus of the study should be emphasized: it is not only reviewing existing corporate governance and board activities, but also looking forward to developing strategies and policies for the future. A strategic time horizon should be established, which links the corporate governance and board development strategy with the other elements of the company's overall corporate strategy. In this way, the board development strategy will be consistent with the overall corporate strategy. For example, if the corporate strategy calls for strategic developments in new technologies, new markets, new territories, or new forms of finance during the life of that strategy, the board development strategy will ask whether the board's composition and processes will be adequate to these challenges.

Information for a board review is obtained from an analysis of board and board committee agenda, papers, and minutes, from interviews with each director, company secretary, and staff, top executives, group discussions, and director workshops, and from interviews with investors, auditors, analysts, and internal staff.

Some tools have been developed to facilitate board reviews. For example, 'Thinking Board'[4] is a web tool specifically designed for directors with internal audit to review how well the boards and board committees are working. This tool has question banks, based on corporate governance assessments for major companies to provide relevant insights, providing results that can be viewed and investigated online. The approach can be used by itself for board self-assessment or as part of an independent externally facilitated review.

Review the overall governance structure

The first step in the study is to review the entity's overall governance structure. In essence, this establishes the governance power base of the enterprise and determines where ultimate power lies to change the governance structure. Who controls the voting equity? Is there majority control? Do informal power blocks exist? What changes might occur over the strategic time horizon? Consider, for example, predator bids, shifts in dominant institutional investor holdings, or changes in family ownership.

In a widely held listed company, establish if there are any blocks of voting shares that do or could influence corporate governance, an association of institutional investors, or a hedge fund acquiring shares, for example. What is the possibility of a merger or acquisition approach within the strategic time horizon? What is preventing such a move? In a public company with a dominant shareholder, discover that investor's aims. If the dominant shareholder is the founder, what power does he or she exercise over governance matters? If the dominant shareholder is a parent company, what influence does that shareholder exercise over board membership? Within the strategic time horizon, what influence could be exercised?

[4] www.independentaudit.com/thinking-board

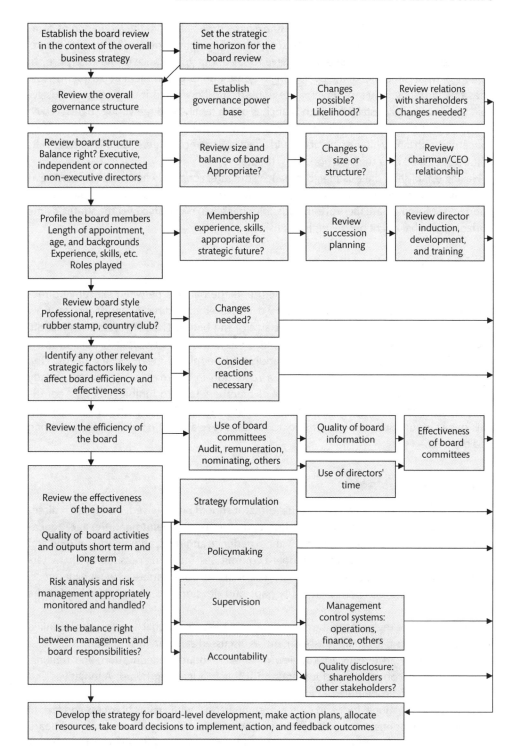

Figure 17.1 Elements of a board review

In a subsidiary or associate company, establish the expectations of the group parent company. Are there any minority shareholders? How are their rights protected? In a joint venture, what does the joint venture agreement have to say about governance of the enterprise? In a quango, what is the role of the overseeing organization or government department? How does that currently influence governance matters and how could it change? In a closely-held family company, establish which branches of the family hold the voting shares. Which members of the family are involved in management? Is there a family council or committee concerned with family interests, which could affect governance matters? Could there be shifts in the power base over the time horizon of the study?

Having established the existing governance structure, consider whether the present relationships with the investors, owners, and shareholders are satisfactory. How could they be improved? Moreover, are there are any possible changes in ownership over the strategic time horizon, and what might be the implications?

Review the board structure

The next step is to review the board structure. Is the balance between executive directors, independent directors, and connected non-executive directors appropriate, now and for the strategic future? Consider the size of the board. The corporate constitution, such as the articles of association, may put limits on board size. Boards tend to grow in size. The case tends to be made for additional people to meet specific needs. One seldom hears the case being argued for a reduction in board size. Yet, as has already been noted, boards with a large number of members tend to inhibit directors' contributions and are in danger of splitting into cliques. Identify any changes necessary. This stage also provides the opportunity to review the relationship between the chairman and the CEO.

Profile board members

Now the contributions of each individual director should be reviewed. Profile each director, noting the length of service on the board, the terms of appointment, the age, education, and professional background, relevant experience and skills, and the roles played and contributions made to the board and board committees, including personality characteristics and interpersonal abilities. In the context of the corporate strategy, what experience, skills, and roles will be needed? Identify gaps and develop succession planning for the board.

The profiling and reviewing of the contributions made by individual directors can be linked with each director's performance assessment, as discussed earlier in this chapter.

This can then lead directly to a review of director induction, education, and training, whether there is continual development and if this is a learning board. Alternatives and improvements can be identified.

Given the international focus on director remuneration, with claims of excess and lack of linkage between bonuses and performance, some boards are using the review of the board to take a strategic view of executive director and top management remuneration. Others continue to rely on their board remuneration committee.

Review board style, efficiency, and effectiveness

The next stage involves a review of board style. Consider how the board and board committees spend their time, the issues on the agenda, the quality of leadership, and how meetings are planned and run. The board style (see Chapter 14) can then be identified and the need for any changes clarified.

Now board efficiency and effectiveness can be considered. It is worthwhile to reflect, at this stage, whether there are any other relevant strategic factors that could affect the governance of the company over the strategic time horizon. For example, are there any changes to company law, corporate regulation, or stock exchange listing requirements likely that would affect corporate governance activities? For companies in a group or network, are there any feasible shifts of power and influence over the strategic time horizon? What might be an appropriate reaction?

Next, the review process turns to the efficiency of the board. Does the board have audit, remuneration, and nominating committees? Are there other board standing committees—such as an executive committee, a strategy committee, or a compliance committee? How effective are each of these committees?

Assess the quality of board information: formal and informal reports, opportunities for directors to obtain information and answers to their questions, access to corporate data, as considered in the previous chapter.

How do directors spend their time: on main board meetings, board committee meetings, and in other board-related activities, including visits and preparation time? Is this efficient? What improvements might be made?

We next turn to the effectiveness of the board and its committees. Essentially, here the concern is with the quality of board processes and outputs, both in the short and the longer terms. The four functions of the board—strategy formulation, policymaking, executive supervision, and accountability—need to be considered separately.

Strategy formulation, as we have seen, is a prime function for the board. This stage of the review considers the time and effort, the depth and quality of analysis that goes into the board's strategic thinking. Could a new competitor unexpectedly intervene in the firm's markets? Could a new technology significantly change the cost structure? Would a different way of delivering the firm's service dramatically affect the market share, or might an alternative product meet customer needs better? This part of the review also considers whether external risks are adequately recognized. As we saw in Chapter 7, the significance of strategy formulation to the board's work might call for a special effort—perhaps a board strategy seminar or workshop to explore the firm's strategic situation and review the overall corporate strategy.

Moving from strategy to policy, the review asks whether the board's policies are still appropriate to the company's situation. This is the place to explore the delegation of board responsibilities to board committees and the work of those committees. Are the terms of reference of the audit committee, the remuneration committee, the nomination committee, and any other board committees still relevant? If not, what changes are needed?

In considering the performance functions—strategy formulation and policymaking—is the balance right between those activities delegated to management and those retained by the board? Will this be appropriate through the changing situations envisaged over the company's strategic time horizon?

Reviewing the third function of the board—executive supervision—provides an opportunity to review management controls and management reporting systems. Can the board monitor management in an active, accurate, and timely manner? Enterprise risk assessment and management systems, which are now seen as fundamental to corporate governance, should be reviewed at this stage.

The fourth function of the board—ensuring adequate accountability—has, in recent years, been under the corporate governance spotlight. Is the company conforming to the requirements of the corporate governance codes, company law requirements, and, where appropriate, stock exchange listing requirements? Are the company's public statements to the shareholders, the media, and other legitimate stakeholders meeting the legal requirements and, ideally, projecting the company as the board expect? In addition to the required audited financial statements, are operating statements and corporate social responsibility and sustainability reports and other narrative reports at the level and in the form that the board want?

Determining a strategy for board development

Finally, after all of the data collection and analysis has been done and the results collated, comes report writing and the determination of a strategy for board development, consistent with and part of the overall corporate strategy.

Directors tend to spend relatively little time together, and board-level assessment should provide information for valuable board discussion. In successful companies, particularly those with long-standing boards, inertia and complacency can be a danger. Once the directors have discussed and accepted the report, they should develop a strategy for board development, and create related policies and plans that lead to action. The chairman's leadership role is vital at this stage.

Unlike the directors mentioned earlier in this chapter, who reported that corporate governance was a matter of complying with corporate governance codes, an informed professional director might reply that:

> . . . in our company we have a set of board-level policies which lay down how the board and its committees operate; then a periodic board-level review enables us to check on whether these policies are being followed, that we are meeting all the accountability criteria the board has set for the organization, and whether our corporate governance strategy is still appropriate.

Experience has shown that board assessments often identify a similar set of issues, including the need to spend more board time and effort on:

- corporate strategy and risk assessment;
- executive succession;
- executive remuneration;
- the tenure of outside directors;
- problems in the link between board and management;
- concern about directors' abilities and the need for more training and briefing;
- corporate social responsibility policies and links with stakeholders.

In summary, the approach to board assessment advocated here analyses the board and committee structures and processes, studies the strengths and weaknesses of the directors, reviews the processes of the board and its committee, and ensures that appropriate disclosure and accountability are being provided. The outcome is a strategy for board development and corporate governance improvement. Just as an enterprise has longer-term strategies for developing its operations, technologies, markets, finances, and people, the board review project leads towards an agreed strategy for board and governance development. In other words, the strategy for board development becomes part of the overall corporate strategy. The assessment of boards and board committees is at the core of professional corporate governance.

Once the assessment exercise has been completed, a review of the results can provide a valuable learning experience and provide some useful insights for the future. The review questions might include the following.

- Is the company's corporate governance compliant with company law, corporate governance codes, and listing rules?
- How does the company's corporate governance performance compare with the industry average and the industry leaders? Are benchmarks available?
- Did the appraisal identify critical issues? Has anything been done about them?
- Did the appraisal deal with 'elephants in the room'—that is, things that everyone knows, but about which no one will speak?
- Have the objectives of the assessment been met?
- Has the assessment led to improved board effectiveness?
- Was the assessment well done, did it conform with best practice, and how might it be improved?

Assessing individual directors' performance

Not many years ago, many directors would have baulked at the idea of having their own performance assessed. Appointment to the board, they would have argued, proved that they had the requisite knowledge, experience, and skills, as we saw earlier. Moreover, how can director-level performance *be* assessed when boardroom activity is a collective team effort? Inevitably, directors make different contributions, they would claim, which have to change as the circumstances facing the company change, so assessment is pointless.

Today, few directors hold these opinions. Attitudes have changed. Corporate governance codes and stock exchange listing rules now recommend, or require, an annual assessment of the performance of individual directors. Further, listed companies in many jurisdictions now have to report on their corporate governance practices. Most directors now recognize the importance of an effective director-level appraisal programme, just as they accept the need for management-level appraisal systems.

Currently, many director appraisals are informal, with the chairman personally assessing each director's performance and commenting privately to the director involved. The UK Corporate Governance Code calls on chairmen to hold regular development meetings with every director. But the pressure is on for director appraisals to be more formalized. A board policy decision, with the full support of all the directors, is needed to set up such a process. Given that directors often have considerable experience, strong personalities, and high self-esteem, the need to obtain everyone's support for the process at the outset is vital. Without that support, an appraisal exercise can become threatening, adversarial, and dysfunctional.

First, the contribution that is expected of each director needs to be known to provide the basis for the assessment. Ideally, when a director is nominated to the board, the chairman will provide a clear explanation of what is expected. A welcome letter from the board chairman can be used to elaborate these expectations. The chairman should explain what time commitment will be needed, what board level skills are required, and why the director has been chosen, including any specific expertise, knowledge, experience, or contacts that the director is expected to bring to the board. As we saw in the previous chapter, an induction briefing can provide an opportunity for the incoming director to explore the way in which the board and its committees work, to have appropriate briefings, visits, and discussions with key people. Once a director's contribution has been agreed, the foundations for director performance appraisal have been laid.

Next, the criteria to be used for the evaluation need to be clarified. The chairman needs to play a key role, outlining the purpose and the process of the assessment, and leading his or her board to recognize the value of a rigorous and regular appraisal system. The director attributes and core competencies, discussed in detail in Chapter 13, can provide a pro forma for the individual appraisal. The experience, skills, and knowledge expected of the director when he or she first joined the board need to be reviewed in the light of subsequent changes in the company's strategic situation. Directors particularly need to be aware of the critical success factors in the business and where it is significantly exposed to risk.

Corporate governance in action 17.3   Fannie Mae Corporate Governance Guidelines (8)

Management Evaluation and Succession

The Compensation Committee conducts an annual review of the performance of the corporation, the CEO, and senior management. Neither the CEO nor senior management is present when the Committee meets to evaluate their individual performance. The Chairman of the Board presents the CEO's annual performance review for the Committee's approval. The CEO's annual performance review is based, in large part, upon an annual performance report prepared by the Chairman of the Board and upon ratings and commentary provided by individual Board members. The senior management performance reviews include the Compensation Committee's own assessment and reflect discussions with other Board members. The Board's independent directors approve the compensation of the CEO, and the full Board approves the compensation of the corporation's executive vice presidents, both approvals subject to the consent of the conservator.

On an annual basis, the Compensation Committee reviews management succession planning with the CEO in preparation for discussion by the entire Board. The Board discussion on management succession occurs during executive session, and focuses on succession planning for the CEO and other key members of senior management.

The next stage in the appraisal is to determine who is to lead the exercise. Typically, the board chairman will take the initiative, instigating the review—but the chairman need not necessarily carry it out personally. The chairman of the board nomination committee could be asked to play a significant role. A past chairman, the senior independent director, an experienced independent consultant, or a firm specializing in board appraisal could also be considered. Some company secretary organizations, institutes of directors, and consultancies offer professional services for the assessment of individual directors and boards.

In a formalized director performance review, the data collection stage follows. Typically, this involves interviewing each director to discuss his or her experience as a member of both board and board committees. Information is also obtained by analysing attendance records, and board and board committee minutes, looking for innovative inputs and contributions to discussions and decisions. Sometimes, peer-review techniques are used in board reviews. So-called '360 degree' inputs seek comments from 'above', such as from auditors, institutional investors, and others outside the company dealing with a director, from the 'same level', including the chairman and other board members, and from 'below', involving staff who come in contact with a director.

Typically, following the data gathering, a confidential report is drafted to the chairman. Given the personal nature of the report, most chairmen will not table it at a board meeting, but will discuss the relevant portion with each director. During that discussion, a strategy for further personal development should be discussed, resulting in an action plan including any training or development activities, such as committee leadership, or service on other boards. The intention, of course, is that each director will be able to make a greater contribution to board effectiveness in the future. Records of the discussion can be used to check progress at the next appraisal.

There could be opportunities for accelerating the contribution of outside directors by asking them to lead various board projects, to chair board committees, and to lead board discussions on specific topics. But even without a formal review, for example in subsidiary companies or family firms, self-evaluation that leads to the recognition of needs and a drive for continuous personal improvement can be valuable.

Finally, in considering individual director performance appraisal, we come to the ultimate question: who evaluates the chairman and against what criteria? As the Roman general Juvenal asked: '*Quis custodes ipsos custodiet?*' (Who will guard the guards?) Although, it has to be admitted, he was worried about the guards on his wife when he went off to battle. Professor Fred Neubauer, when at IMD Business School in Lausanne Switzerland, recommended that the performance of board chairmen should be evaluated. In some cases, an appraisal of the chairman is carried out by a senior independent outside director, or the chairman of the audit or nomination committees. The UK Corporate Governance Code calls on the non-executive directors, led by the senior independent director, to be responsible for performance evaluation of the chairman, taking into account the views of executive directors. But, in the end, a chairman's performance is reflected in the performance of the company as a whole. Continued poor performance will bring calls for a change of chairman from major investors, the media, or occasionally from dissatisfied board colleagues. For an example of director evaluation, see Corporate governance in action 17.3.

Corporate governance rating systems for companies

The financial climate changed significantly after Enron and the US Sarbanes-Oxley Act, not only in the United States, but around the world. The quality of a company's corporate governance is now seen as vital to its longer-term performance. Investors, particularly institutional investors, focus on corporate governance in valuing companies. The standard of corporate governance is an important element in the risk evaluation of a company. A reliable corporate governance rating from an independent and respected organization can reduce a company's cost of capital, reflecting the premium that investors are now prepared to pay for sound governance.

Consequently, there is a need to measure, evaluate, and rate standards of corporate governance. Various systems have been developed: some by rating agencies, some by financial institutions, and others by organizations providing consultancy services. However, it is important to recognize that they use different criteria, that the scores are not necessarily compatible, and that their conclusions sometimes differ. Let us review some of the more popular rating schemes.

Standard and Poor's (S&P), an organization better known for its credit ratings, offers a corporate governance rating service to companies. Unlike some other providers of corporate governance ratings, S&P is independent and does not also offer company advisory or training services. It acts with the co-operation of the company, interviewing senior executives and directors, and reviewing information in both the public domain and confidential data. S&P's GAMMA governance metric reflects the S&P's opinion of the relative strength of a company's corporate governance practices. Designed for equity investors, the score provides some protection against governance-related losses or failure to create value. The GAMMA rating also provides companies with a comparative rating and a means of identifying opportunities for improvement in governance practices. The proprietary methodology produces a score based on a synthesis of best practices and codes around world. The final score is numeric and based on the following four sectors:

- ownership structure and external influences, which considers the transparency of ownership structure, the concentration and the influence of ownership, and other external stakeholders;
- shareholder rights and relations, including shareholder meetings and voting procedures, ownership rights and takeover defences, and other stakeholder relations;
- transparency, disclosure, and audit, such as the content of public disclosure, the timing and access to public disclosure, and the audit process;
- board structure and effectiveness, including director independence, the role and effectiveness of the board, and director and senior executive compensation.

As part of their well-known credit rating service, *Moody's* offers an 'Enhanced Analysis Initiative' which reviews the corporate governance reviews of large debt issuers in North America, including financial institutions. In their experience, corporate governance is a key driver in good credit ratings. *Fitch Ratings* also offers a corporate governance rating service, as do some financial institutions including:

- *Deutsche Bank*, with a corporate governance scoring system based on four 'pillars'—board independence, shareholder treatment, information disclosure, and best practices;
- *Prudential Securities*, a US-based brokerage, based on three key corporate governance categories for banks—board independence, board accountability, and external audit.

Institutional Shareholder Services (ISS) offers a proprietary analytical tool called Governance Risk Indicators™ (GRId) to help listed companies to improve their corporate governance practices, and investors to assess the governance quality of their investments. The GRId indicators rank companies' governance standing (low, medium, high) across five independent dimensions of governance:

- compensation schemes for executive and non-executive directors, including the remuneration structure and schemes that are used to reward directors;
- executive and non-executive director stock ownership, such as the alignment of director equity ownership with shareholder interests;
- equity structure, including the protection of shareholder rights and the existence of any anti-takeover devices;
- structure of the board, independence of directors, processes of the board and board committees, and the independence of directors;
- independence and integrity of the audit process, including the audit process, audit fees, services provided, and members of the audit committee.

Each company is assessed using between sixty and eighty variables depending on its local market, and the GRId indicators are based on that assessment. ISS also offers subscribers a benchmark proxy-voting policy service aligned with the GRId indicators, and access to a range of corporate governance services, including webcasts, White Papers, surveys, and expert analysis and advice. Online discussion forums facilitate dialogue on corporate governance issues between corporate executives, institutional investors, and board directors.

Governance Metrics International (GMI) has over ten years' experience of its rating system monitoring corporate governance. Subscribers to its service receive an independent evaluation of the governance characteristics of each company across a large universe of companies. GMI ratings cover over 4,000 companies, including companies in all significant markets. The GMI rating criteria are based on securities regulations, stock exchange listing requirements, and various corporate governance codes and principles, which produce a set of metrics structured to produce 'yes', 'no', or 'not disclosed' answers, to eliminate a large degree of subjectivity. The GMI research process starts with a review of a company's relevant public data, including regulatory filings, company websites, news services, and other specialized websites. Once the research template answers have been compiled and have been subjected to various quality control checks, data entry reports are sent to each company for an accuracy check. The GMI scoring model calculates ratings for each company on a scale of one (lowest) to ten (highest).

The *Investor Responsibility Research Center (IRRC)* is a leading source of impartial information on corporate governance and social responsibility research and proxy voting services. Founded in 1972, the IRRC also provides corporate benchmarking service on governance issues to more than 500 institutional investors, corporations, law firms, foundations, academics, and other organizations.

The *International Finance Corporation (IFC)* works with countries that have an important potential for growth, but weak corporate governance practices. It engages at various levels:

- the firm—corporate governance assessments, advisory services to improve governance practices;
- the sector—capacity building of local consulting firms, institutes of directors, educational institutions, and stock exchanges;
- the market—alignment of standards and practices, development of corporate governance codes, and listing requirements;
- public policy and awareness—media training, conferences and roundtables, and sharing best practices.

IFC offers a corporate governance methodology and assessment service to client companies. The methodology uses assessment tools tailored to the different governance priorities of publicly listed companies, founder and family-owned firms, financial institutions, newly privatized enterprises, and state-owned enterprises. IFC staff review the client's governance practices and use that review for risk analysis, investment decision-making, and, where necessary, to develop a corporate governance improvement programme with the client.

In the IFC's experience:

> Sound corporate governance helps businesses operate more efficiently, better manage risks, and attract investment on better terms. Good governance makes clients more accountable and transparent to investors, and enables them to respond to legitimate stakeholder concerns, such as sustainable environmental and social development.

CoreRatings is a European-based rating agency, providing independent investment analysis of corporate responsibility risks. CoreRatings takes an investor's view on corporate governance, environmental, and social performance, and provides services to asset managers, pension funds, and companies worldwide. CoreRatings benchmarks the standing of companies' corporate governance and corporate responsibility against comparable companies. The methodology works with the company for answers to detailed questions derived from the international codes, best practice experience, and the writings of corporate governance experts. The resultant rating assesses the company's risk profile in seven areas:

- governance policy and business ethics;
- risk management processes;
- ownership structure and control;
- financial reporting, audit, and verification;
- board structure and management;
- board executive compensation;
- investor rights and relations.

Corporate governance assessment systems for countries

Attempts have also been made to monitor and assess the overall level of corporate governance country by country. This reflects the growing recognition that corporate governance is important to national financial markets and, ultimately, to national economic success.

In the wake of various financial crises, the *World Bank* and the *International Monetary Fund* (IMF) launched a joint initiative to assess corporate governance country by country, recognizing the major role that the observance of international standards and codes of best practices can play in strengthening national and international financial systems. The executive boards of the World Bank and the IMF identified a group of twelve areas that they deemed to be important for the institutional underpinning of macroeconomic stability and central to the operational work of the two institutions. The *Reports on the Observance of Standards and Codes (ROSC)* programme considers each country's legal and regulatory framework, as well as the practices and compliance of listed firms, against the OECD Principles of Corporate Governance. The diagnostic work is intended to strengthen international financial systems. An ROSC study leads to an assessment of the degree to which a country observes internationally recognized standards and codes.

The *European Bank for Reconstruction and Development* (EBRD) is one of the largest lenders and investors in Central and Eastern Europe, and other transitional economies. As an investor, EBRD is interested in promoting better standards of corporate governance, because it is limited to a minority shareholder position in its investments or co-invests with minority shareholders. The bank is, therefore, particularly concerned with how its investee companies treat their shareholders and whether minority shareholders are able to have their legal rights protected. As a law reformer, the EBRD is also actively engaged in promoting better corporate governance rules at the country level. The bank believes that:

> Good corporate governance is essential for companies wishing to access external capital and for countries aiming to stimulate private sector investments. If companies are well run, they will prosper. Poor corporate governance weakens the company's potential and paves the way for financial difficulties and even fraud.

The EBRD tries to encourage, influence, and provide guidance to governments, policy-makers, and all those in charge of promoting new legislation for the development of corporate governance-related legal reform. To study corporate governance in a country, the EBRD devised a checklist with lists of questions covering key corporate governance issues.

The financial institution *Society General Global Equities* also addresses the corporate governance of countries, identifying five key corporate governance categories—shareholder rights, the enforcement of shareholder rights, disclosure, analysts' access to management, and board independence.

The most comprehensive country-level corporate governance rating to date is the FTSE ISS corporate governance index. FTSE and International Shareholder Services (ISS) joined in a global corporate governance ratings and index project in 2004. With over US$2.5 trillion benchmarked against its indices, the FTSE had proven international index experience. The initiative was rooted in the belief that international investors needed a reliable, cost-effective standard to measure governance practice across a range of international companies, with tools to evaluate companies' corporate governance risk. The partners believed that investors would tend to reward companies with sound governance practices and possibly underweight companies with poor governance practices to reduce portfolio risk.

After reviewing a wide range of accepted standards and codes, the project identified a set of common principles—independence, accountability, and transparency. The index was then based on five major areas:

- structure and independence of the board (44%);
- equity structure (21%);
- compensation system, for executive and non-executive directors (17%);
- executive and non-executive stock ownership (9%);
- independence and integrity of the audit process (9%).

The index allows comparisons to be made across countries, across industrial sectors, and across financial markets. For example, it was discovered that Canada and the United Kingdom had the highest average corporate governance scores by country, that the oil and gas industry scores highest by sector, and that the FTSE 100 had the highest score by stock market sector. Research findings from the project showed that 88% of respondents expected interest in corporate governance to increase over the next two years, and 75% expected their consideration of corporate governance factors in their day-to-day operations to increase.

Case studies

 Case study 17.1   Board failings at Olympus Japan

When British-born Michael Woodford[5] (51) was promoted to the top executive position of Olympus, the Japanese camera firm in 2011, he did not expect that within weeks he would be dismissed, stripped of his house and company car, and told to take a bus to the airport. Following a thirty-year career with Olympus, Woodford had become the company President; the first non-Japanese to lead the company in its ninety-three-year history. Olympus, better known for its cameras, actually made more money from medical equipment such as endoscopes.

Soon after his arrival in his new job, Woodford was alerted to an article in a journal called *Facta*, which made some wild allegations that Olympus had massively over-paid nearly US$1 billion to buy three small companies. This led Woodford to uncover accounting irregularities and suspicious deals involving the recent acquisition of UK medical equipment manufacturer Gyrus. He called in the company's auditors, PriceWaterhouseCoopers, to examine payments of £460 million (US$687 million) for financial advice made to an unknown and now defunct firm incorporated in the Cayman Islands with a New York address,. A fraud of £1.1 billion (US$1.7 billion) emerged, including an accounting scandal to disguise losses. Woodford spoke to the chairman, Tsuyoshi Kikukawa, expecting immediate action. But Kikukawa refused to discuss the matter.

So Woodford confronted the board of directors, raising embarrassing questions. The other directors were hostile. Blowing the whistle offended their corporate culture. In October 2011,

[5]For a personal account of the Olympus case, see Woodford, Michael (2012) *Exposure: Inside the Olympus Scandal—How I went from CEO to whistleblower*. Portfolio Penguin, London.

Woodford was summarily sacked and told to leave the company and take a bus to the airport. He disobeyed these orders, went public with the information, informed the Japanese serious fraud office, and sought police protection while he stayed in hotels under pseudonyms.

The board initially claimed that Woodford had left because of 'differences in management styles'. Employees were warned not to support Woodford or 'their careers might be damaged'. But by November 2011, the company admitted a cover-up of losses going back to the 1990s. Chairman Tsuyoshi Kikukawa resigned his chairmanship but stayed on the board. In December, Tokyo prosecutors raided the Olympus offices, and in February 2012 the former chairman and other top officials were arrested.

In March 2012, Olympus declared a loss of £383 million (US$575 million). During this saga the share price fell by 80%. In April 2012, Japanese prosecutors charged Olympus and six of its directors with a £1.1 billion (US$1.7 billion) fraud. The company's ex-chairman and other executives were accused of inflating the company's net worth by hiding huge investment losses in a complex web of acquisitions and buy-backs. Woodford was also questioned by the FBI over the Cayman Island transactions.

Following the prosecution a company spokesman said: 'we take these charges very seriously and will continue to strengthen our corporate governance. We again express our deep apologies to shareholders, investors, business partners, and customers.'

The Japanese business network model

Traditionally, investors play a relatively small part in corporate affairs. There is no significant market for corporate control since hostile takeover bids are virtually unknown. The classical model of Japanese corporate governance has a stakeholder, not a shareholder, orientation. Power lies within a network of companies, the *keiretsu*, which are connected through cross-holdings, interlocking directorships, and inter-trading. Frequently the network includes a financial institution.

The classical model of the *keiretsu* reflects the social cohesion within Japanese society, emphasizing unity throughout the organization, non-adversarial relationships, lifetime employment, enterprise unions, personnel policies encouraging commitment, initiation into the corporate family, decision-making by consensus, cross-functional training, with promotion based on loyalty and social compatibility as well as performance. Boards of directors tend to be large and are, in effect, the top layers of the management pyramid. People speak of being 'promoted to the board'.

Independent non-executive directors, in the Western sense, are unusual in Japan, although the proportion is increasing. Many Japanese do not see the need for such intervention 'from the outside'. Indeed, they have difficulty in understanding how outside directors operate. 'How can outsiders possibly know enough about the company to make a contribution,' they question, 'when the other directors have spent their lives working for the company? How can an outsider be sensitive to the corporate culture? They could even damage the harmony of the group.'

Chairmen and senior directors of companies in a *keiretsu* meet regularly and have close, informal relationships. Meetings of the managing directors with the directors in their teams are also crucial, as are the informal relationships between the top echelons of the board. Ultimate power lies with the top managers, particularly the president and the chairman.

Woodford offer to run the company is rebuffed

At an Olympus shareholders' meeting, Woodford offered to return to run the company. He was supported by international investors. But the largest shareholders, Japanese institutional investors and members of the Olympus *keiretsu*, did not. The chairman of that meeting was asked if 'anti-social forces' had been involved in any of these transactions, a code meaning the Japanese *yakuza* or mafia. 'I am absolutely not aware of such a thing,' the chairman replied.

Woodford claimed damages for unfair dismissal in the London courts, demanding ten years' salary of £35 million (US$52 million), because he said that the debacle had made him unemployable. His claim was settled by the company out of court for an undisclosed sum, widely reported as around £10 million (US$15 million).

Subsequently, under new leadership, Olympus laid off workers, closed twelve of its thirty factories, sold off the three divisions implicated in the fraud case, raising capital and acquiring a strategic partner by selling a 10% stake in the company to Japanese company Sony.

The Japanese authorities proposed some changes to company law to strengthen corporate governance, including a requirement for at least one independent non-executive director. But that proposal was dropped when the employers' lobby, the *Keidanren*, objected.

Discussion questions

1. Having discovered the accounting irregularities and suspicious deals, did Woodford take the most appropriate action? What would you have done?

2. Do those Japanese critics of the concept of the independent non-executive director have a point?

3. What can we learn about Japanese corporate governance and management from this case? Do you think it might change? Why?

 Case study 17.2   The collapse of HBOS bank

The Halifax Mutual Building Society (savings and loan association) was corporatized and floated on the London Stock Exchange. In 2001, Halifax merged with the Bank of Scotland, a long established Scottish bank, to form the HBOS Group. During the 2000 to 2008 bull market, under chief executive James Crosby, HBOS became the world's fifth-largest bank, by pursuing a culture which emphasized sales and profit growth led by salesmen, rather than prudent, risk-orientated banking led by bankers.

As early as 2004, Mike Ellis, the Finance Director, alerted the board to a concern expressed by the Financial Services Authority (FSA) that HBOS was growing too fast. He said subsequently that 'the conclusion being drawn by the FSA and the shift in internal capital ratios were significant warning shots'.[6] Neither the chief executive nor the board acted on this advice.

In the same year, Paul Moore, the Head of Regulatory Risk at HBOS, who had previously been a partner with accounting firm KPMG, warned the board that HBOS was over-exposed to risk. He was also ignored. In December 2004, Moore felt that he should contact the UK regulator, the FSA. The FSA mounted an investigation, but called on the HBOS auditors, KPMG, to undertake the study. Moore said their report merely gave the answer HBOS wanted. In 2005, Moore accepted a six-figure pay-off and left the bank.

HBOS in serious financial trouble is bailed out by Lloyds

In 2008, the global financial crisis and the resultant shortage of funds left HBOS in serious financial trouble. The British government became involved. Chancellor of the Exchequer, Gordon Brown, spoke

[6]In evidence subsequently given to a UK Parliamentary Commission on Banking Standards.

to the chairman of Lloyds TSB Bank, Sir Victor Blank, over dinner. 'If Lloyds would take on the ailing HBOS,' Brown suggested, 'normal competition rules (which would have referred such a merger to the Monopolies Commission) will be waived.'

Intuitively, the idea seemed to make strategic sense to Sir Victor. So Lloyds rode to the rescue of HBOS, taking over its assets and liabilities for £7.7 billion (US$11.5 billion). Sir Victor assured his shareholders that the deal would 'create great value for both sets of shareholders'. What he did not know was that HBOS had around £200 billion (US$300 billion) of toxic assets in doubtful loans.

Traditionally, Lloyds had been a robust and conservative lender, recognized as one of the more cautious British banks. Now it, too, needed support from the government, which offered a £260 billion (US$390 billion) loan guarantee, in exchange for equity capital. With an initial 43% of its equity in government hands and more promised, Lloyds had lost its independence and its conservative reputation, whilst its shareholders' capital had been seriously diluted. The chief executive of Lloyds, Eric Daniels, admitted that they had done much less due diligence on this deal than would be normal because of the urgency of the negotiations. 'We would have liked more time to examine HBOS accounts. If we had not taken HBOS over, we would not have needed government money,' he said. Lloyds' share price plunged.

Lloyds' chairman, Sir Victor Blank, stepped down in 2009, and there was pressure on chief executive, Eric Daniels, to follow suit. US-based shareholders sued both Sir Victor and Daniels, alleging that they had shown 'a reckless disregard to the truth during the HBOS merger'. A group of UK shareholders, 'Lloyds Action Now', also threatened legal action. In 2013 however, Daniels was reported to have said that 'I think we did a very good job in due diligence of HBOS. We understood the nature of loans, but I don't think any one would have called the financial crisis.'[7]

Toxic loans in Bank of Scotland part of HBOS

The commercial lending division of the Bank of Scotland, led by Peter Cummings, who had been with the bank since the age of sixteen, had made huge loans to property companies: a cyclical industry which would be exposed in a market downturn. The commercial lending division accounted for about 40% of the bank's profits. Asked about his approach to risk, Cummings had said that 'I just make sure I don't lend to idiots'.

Cummings was criticized in a FSA report for making increasingly risky loans, even as it became clear the credit bubble was about to burst. Cummings had 'failed to exercise due skill, care and diligence by pursuing an aggressive expansion strategy . . . without suitable controls in place to manage the associated risks', the report said. Denying these failings, Cummings claimed he had done nothing wrong, and had followed the bank's guidelines. Subsequently Cummings was fined £500,000 and barred from the City of London financial sector.

The FSA report also found that the auditors, KPMG, had been unable to see the full extent of the problems, and their attempts to persuade the bank to take a more prudent attitude to provisions for bad debts had been ignored.

In 2006, the chief executive of HBOS, Sir James Crosby, handed over to Andy Hornby, who had been top of his MBA class at the Harvard Business School. The FSA brought no disciplinary proceedings against either Crosby or Hornby, even though insiders allege that Hornby put pressure on Cummings to increase lending and profits to make up the shortfall that had arisen when the bank adopted more prudent policies on home loans.

In 2012, the report of an inquiry into events at HBOS by the FSA found that when Halifax had taken over Bank of Scotland to form HBOS, it had failed to control its affairs responsibly. The report

[7] *Daily Mail*, 15 February 2013.

suggested that staff had been given incentives to build revenue, not monitor risk. The culture was all about getting business. The report said that corporate culture believed that 'risk management was for wimps'.

The findings of the Parliamentary Commission on Banking Standards

In late 2012, the British Parliamentary Commission on Banking Standards cross-examined leading players in the collapse of HBOS.

Moore, the HBOS Head of Regulatory Risk until 2005, when he resigned in disgust, said:

> There was an 'us and them' culture at the bank in which risk officers had told him: 'People hid papers. They wouldn't turn up for meetings. They were rude and would swear at us. The culture was resistant to any sort of challenge.'

Peter Cummings, the former head of the corporate lending division of HBOS, complained[8] that he had been singled out for punishment. 'Sir James Crosby and Andy Hornby were behind disastrous decisions to ratchet up lending targets,' he said, 'putting pressure on me to boost profits.'

Sir James Crosby admitted under hostile questioning that incompetence had brought down the bank, and apologized. He agreed that he had sold two-thirds of his holding in HBOS in advance of the bank's collapse. But he rejected suggestions that he should forgo his knighthood or pay back any of the rewards he had received, including a £572,000 a year pension. Sir James had resigned from HBOS in 2006 just before the bank's collapse, was knighted for his services to the banking industry, and became the deputy chairman of the financial industry's watchdog, the FSA.

Lord Stevenson, the former chairman of HBOS, was shown a letter he had written to the FSA six months before the bank collapsed, saying 'HBOS is 'boringly boring' and a 'highly conservative organization'. That, said the commission chairman, was a travesty of the truth. 'The bank was by then dangerously exposed because of its reliance on wholesale funding and in the wake of a prolonged and reckless lending binge.' Stevenson explained that he had been a non-executive chairman and could not remember details. In his letter to the FSA he had written that he was 'part-time (but not non-executive)'. He had assured the regulator that he was not the type of chairman who took an interest in 'only Olympian matters'. He agreed with Commission members that 'there was a lot of mistaken lending', but added 'I wasn't there in the trenches with the people making the decisions. I was only there at the most part-time.' Stevenson was paid £815,000 (US$1.2 million) a year in fees and benefits. As the *Daily Mail's* financial commentator wrote:

> No one expects a bank chairman to sign off on every loan. But it is inconceivable that Stevenson was not made aware of the multi-billion pound loans, many to the property sector, handed out by the Bank of Scotland.

Members of the commission accused Stevenson of being 'either delusional or dishonest', one commenting that 'you are living in cloud cuckoo land. You were responsible for a strategy of reckless growth and that is what led you into difficulties.' The chairman of the commission concluded that his evidence had been 'evasive, repetitive, and unrealistic'. Despite his role in the collapse of HBOS, Stevenson continued to serve on the boards of Western Union, the *Economist* newspaper, and a number of private equity and venture capital firms.

Sir Charles Dunstone, a former non-executive director of HBOS, said that 'while the bank modelled a variety of threats in its stress tests, it never hypothesized the collapse of the wholesale market.'

[8] In evidence given in December 2012 to a member of the Parliamentary Commission on Banking Standards.

Sir Ronald Garrick, former deputy chairman of HBOS, said in evidence:

> I did not recognize the depiction of the doomed bank set out by the Financial Services
> Authority [report]...that did not chime with what was going on at the time . . . I have no doubt
> that the HBOS board was by far and away the best board I have ever sat on.

Pressed on why HBOS relied so heavily on wholesale funding, and that a senior manager had warned that this was reliance was 'untenable and unsustainable', Sir Ronald admitted that the words were 'quite strong'. But added, 'but I wouldn't be sure they went to the board'.

Parliamentary Banking Commission report a 'manual for bad banking'

In April 2013, the Parliamentary Banking Commission reported on the HBOS collapse. In what it described as 'a manual for bad banking', the report concluded that the collapse was caused by 'a colossal failure of senior management and the board'. The report named the successive chief executives Sir James Crosby and Andy Hornby and the chairman Lord Stevenson as having 'primary responsibility for these failures'. All three men left HBOS to take up lucrative top posts in other companies.

The report also expressed surprise that the FSA had chosen to criticize Peter Cummings, a more junior HBOS employee, instead of the CEOs and chairman. The report concluded: 'The commission was very disappointed by the attempts of those who led HBOS into the abyss to acknowledge even now either the nature of the problems that eventually consumed the bank or the extent to which they flowed from their own decisions rather than unforeseeable events.' The commission rejected the reason for the bank's collapse given by all three that it had been caused by wholesale funds drying up following the international financial crisis.

Following the publication of the commission's report, Sir James Crosby agreed to take a 30% reduction in his inflation-proofed pension, worth £240,000 (US$360,000) a year. He also offered to hand back his knighthood. Lord Stevenson and Andy Hornby came under pressure in the press to react likewise to the Commission's criticism.

Another fall-out from the Commission's report was growing criticism of the HBOS auditors, KPMG, for failing to notice the extent of the toxic loans when they signed clear audit reports between 2001 and 2009. It was suggested that KPMG could now be sued by Lloyds Bank, which had taken over HBOS. KPMG denied any liability. PIRC[9] called for an independent investigation. The chairman of KPMG at the time of the HBOS implosion was John Griffith-Jones.

Regulators in the spotlight

By 2013, the regulators were also coming under the spotlight for not investigating the apparent audit failure by KPMG more fully. The FRC, which is responsible for investigation of alleged audit failures, said it was monitoring the situation. But an insider said that the FRC had not investigated KPMG at the time of the HBOS collapse because 'it lacked the necessary resources. It was reluctant to get into it, as it would be just too disrupting and damaging. It had left the HBOS investigation to the Financial Services Authority (FSA).'

The FSA had been created by the previous Labour government to provide deliberately 'light touch' regulation of the finance industry. There were close links between banks, the 'big four' auditors, the regulators and the Treasury. In 2003, James Crosby, then CEO of HBOS, was appointed to the board

---

[9] PIRC is a leading UK independent research and advisory consultancy providing services to institutional investors on corporate governance and corporate social responsibility. See www.pirc.co.uk

of the FSA. He was knighted in 2006. In 2008, he was promoted to deputy chairman of the FSA at a salary of £63,000 a year (part-time). He resigned in 2009, several months after the HBOS debacle.

The weaknesses of the FSA were recognized by the new Coalition government, and in April 2013 the FSA was replaced by the Financial Conduct Authority (FCA), with John Griffith-Jones of KPMG as its chairman.

Discussion questions

1. Where do you think the blame lies for this debacle?

2. Why did they act as they did?

3. Why do you think the chief executive and the board ignored comments from the Finance Director and the Head of Regulatory Risk as long ago as 2004?

4. What is the role of the chairman of the board?

5. Should the auditors or the regulators take any share of the blame?

References and further reading

Anand, Sanjay (2007) *Essentials of Corporate Governance*. Wiley, Hoboken, NJ.

Garratt, Bob (2003) *Thin on Top—why corporate governance matters and how to measure and improve board performance*. Brealy Publishing, London.

NACD [2005] 2010) *Board Evaluation: Improving Director Effectiveness—A Report of a NACD Blue Ribbon Commission*. National Association of Corporate Directors, 1133, Suite 700 21 Street, Washington, DC, USA.

NACD [2005] 2010), *Performance Metrics: Understanding the Board's Role—A Report of a NACD Blue Ribbon Commission*. National Association of Corporate Directors, 1133, Suite 700 21 Street, Washington, DC, USA.

Solomon, Jill (2004) *Corporate Governance and Accountability*. Wiley, Hoboken, NJ.

Projects and exercises

1. Draft a note in response to a director who has told you that assessing the performance of individual directors is unnecessary and unrealistic, because directors bring different skills, experience, and knowledge to the board table.

2. Study and compare the corporate governance rating systems noted in the text. Which would you recommend?

3. What problems might be encountered in using the board review process described in the schematic in the text?

Self-test questions

1. How does one go about assessing a director's performance?

2. How are many director appraisals done at the moment?

3. Is the pressure on for director appraisals to be more formalized? What is needed to set up such a process?

4. What is the usual output of an individual director performance assessment? How is it used?

5. How is the performance of a chairman assessed?

6. Do many corporate governance codes and stock exchange listing rules now call for an annual assessment of the performance of individual directors, and of the performance of the board and board committees?

7. Who might be asked to undertake a board review?

8. Describe the stages in a board review project.

9. What are the principal elements in the Standard and Poor's GAMMA corporate governance ratings?

10. Name some of the systems for evaluating corporate governance at the country level.

Appendix to Chapter 17

The Fannie Mae corporate governance guidelines

Chapters 13 to 17 have looked at the practical aspects of applying sound corporate governance. Some organizations attempt to codify their corporate governance practices. One of them is Fannie Mae in the United States. Their corporate governance guidelines follow as a summary of many of the points covered in this section of the book.

Fannie Mae

Fannie Mae, formally the Federal National Mortgage Association, provided a large proportion of housing mortgage finance in the US with the support of government funding. During the global financial crisis, it had to be rescued by the US government. In September 2008, the Federal Housing Finance Authority (FHFA) was appointed regulator and conservator of Fannie Mae under the Federal Housing Finance Regulatory Reform Act (2008). The FHFA took over Fannie Mae and reconstituted its board of directors. Subsequent attempts were made to privatize the organization, without success to date. The following corporate governance guidelines were developed by the company's Nominating & Corporate Governance Committee, and updated annually, the most recent being formally adopted by the Board in 2014.

These guidelines (along with the charters of the Board committees as well as the corporation's Bylaws, its Employee Code of Conduct and Directors' Code of Conduct and Conflicts of Interest Policy) are published on Fannie Mae's corporate website: www.fanniemae.com

Fannie Mae Corporate Governance Guidelines

Board Composition, Size, and Membership Criteria

The Fannie Mae Charter Act provides that the Fannie Mae Board will consist of thirteen persons, or such other number that the Director of FHFA determines appropriate. FHFA, in its capacity as conservator, has determined that the appropriate number of directors shall be a minimum of nine and not more than thirteen directors. It is the policy of the Board that a substantial majority of the seated Fannie Mae directors will be independent, in accordance with the standards adopted by the Board. In addition, the Board, as a group, must be knowledgeable in business, finance, capital markets, accounting, risk management, public policy, mortgage lending, real estate, low-income housing, homebuilding, regulation of financial institutions, technology, and any other areas as may be relevant to the safe and sound operation of Fannie Mae.

It is the responsibility of the Nominating and Corporate Governance Committee to identify and evaluate prospective candidates for the Board that have expertise in the areas described above. The Committee will also seek out Board members who possess the highest personal values, judgment, and integrity; who represent diversity in ideas, perspectives, gender, race, and disability; and who have an understanding of the regulatory and policy environment in which the corporation does its business. The Committee is committed to considering minorities, women and individuals with disabilities in the identification and evaluation process of prospective candidates. The Committee also considers whether a prospective candidate for the Board has the ability to attend meetings and fully participate in the activities of the Board, including whether the candidate's service on outside boards and other activities will permit the candidate sufficient time to devote to responsibilities associated with being a Fannie Mae director. Stockholders may submit written recommendations for candidates directly to the Chair of the Nominating and Corporate Governance Committee in care of the Office of the Secretary of the corporation. To assist the Nominating and Corporate Governance Committee in its evaluation, stockholder recommendations as to potential candidates should include the information set forth in Section 4.20 of the corporation's Bylaws. The Chair of the Nominating and Corporate Governance Committee formally invites new director candidates to stand for election to the Board.

Directors are required to inform the Nominating and Corporate Governance Committee of any changes in employment responsibilities in order for the Committee to determine whether it is appropriate to re-nominate the Board member for continuing Board service. A director will not be re-nominated after having served for ten years or after reaching the age of 72, whichever comes first, except with the approval of FHFA. A director may serve his or her full term if he or she has served less than ten years or is 72 years of age on the date of his or her election or appointment to the Board.

Unless otherwise requested by the Board, the CEO will cease to be a member of the Board at the termination of his or her employment as CEO. The CEO must obtain approval from the Nominating and Corporate Governance Committee before accepting a seat on the board of another for-profit organization. Non-management directors must notify the Nominating and Corporate Governance Committee before accepting a seat on the board of another for-profit organization, and the Committee will determine, in its judgment, whether such service will interfere with the director's service on the Fannie Mae Board. Unless the Nominating and Corporate Governance Committee determines otherwise, directors may not serve on the boards of directors of more than six public companies. Unless the Board determines otherwise, Audit Committee members may not serve on the audit committees of more than three public companies.

Director Independence

The Board, with the assistance of the Nominating and Corporate Governance Committee, on an annual basis, reviews the independence of all directors. The Board affirmatively makes a determination as to the independence of each director, and Fannie Mae discloses those determinations. The definition of 'independence' adopted by the Board meets, and in some respects exceeds, the requirements of independence as set forth in FHFA corporate governance regulation 12 C.F.R.§ 1710.10, which requires the standard of independence adopted by the New York Stock Exchange. An 'independent director' must be determined to have no material relationship with Fannie Mae, either directly or through an organization that has a material relationship with Fannie Mae. A relationship is 'material' if, in the judgment of the Board, it would interfere with the director's independent judgment. In addition, FHFA corporate governance regulation 12 C.F.R.§ 1710.12 requires the Audit Committee to be in compliance with the New York Stock Exchange's listing requirements for audit committees, under which Audit Committee members must meet additional, heightened independence criteria. Fannie Mae's own independence guidelines require all independent directors to meet these criteria.

To assist it in determining whether a director is independent, the Board has adopted the guidelines set forth below:

- A director will not be considered independent if, within the preceding five years:
  - i the director was employed by Fannie Mae; or
  - ii an immediate family member of the director was employed by Fannie Mae as an executive officer.

- A director will not be considered independent if:
  - i the director is a current partner or employee of Fannie Mae's external auditor, or within the preceding five years, was (but is no longer) a partner or employee of Fannie Mae's external auditor and personally worked on Fannie Mae's audit within that time; or
  - ii an immediate family member of the director is a current partner of Fannie Mae's external auditor, or is a current employee of Fannie Mae's external auditor and personally works on Fannie Mae's audit, or within the preceding five years, was (but is no longer) a partner or employee of Fannie Mae's external auditor and personally worked on Fannie Mae's audit within that time.

- A director will not be considered independent if, within the preceding five years:
  - i the director was employed by a company at a time when a current Fannie Mae executive officer sat on that company's compensation committee; or
  - ii an immediate family member of the director was employed as an officer by a company at a time when a current Fannie Mae executive officer sat on that company's compensation committee.

- A director will not be considered independent if, within the preceding five years:
  - i the director received any compensation from Fannie Mae, directly or indirectly, other than fees for service as a director; or
  - ii an immediate family member of the director received any compensation from Fannie Mae, directly or indirectly, other than compensation received for service as an employee (other than an executive officer) of Fannie Mae.

- A director will not be considered independent if:

    i   the director is a current executive officer, employee, controlling stockholder, or partner of a company or other entity that does or did business with Fannie Mae and to which Fannie Mae made, or from which Fannie Mae received, payments within the preceding five years that, in any single fiscal year, were in excess of $1 million or 2 percent of the entity's consolidated gross annual revenues, whichever is greater; or

    ii   an immediate family member of the director is a current executive officer of a company or other entity that does or did business with Fannie Mae and to which Fannie Mae made, or from which Fannie Mae received, payments within the preceding five years that, in any single fiscal year, were in excess of $1 million or 2 percent of the entity's consolidated gross annual revenues, whichever is greater.

- A director will not be considered independent if the director or the director's spouse is an executive officer, employee, director, or trustee of a nonprofit organization to which Fannie Mae makes or has made contributions within the preceding three years that, in a single year, were in excess of 5 percent of the organization's consolidated gross annual revenues, or $120,000, whichever is less (amounts matched under the Matching Gifts Program are not included in the contributions calculated for purposes of this standard). The Nominating and Corporate Governance Committee also will receive periodic reports regarding charitable contributions to organizations otherwise associated with a director or any spouse of a director.

Where the guidelines above do not address a particular relationship, the determination of whether the relationship is material, and whether a director is independent, will be made by the Board, based upon the recommendation of the Nominating and Corporate Governance Committee.

The Board may determine in its judgment, and consistent with the New York Stock Exchange definition of independence, that a director that does not meet these guidelines nonetheless, under the relevant facts and circumstances, does not have a relationship with Fannie Mae that would interfere with the director's independent judgment. The Board will disclose the basis for any such determination in the corporation's next annual report or proxy statement.

Board Leadership

The positions of Chairman of the Board and CEO are separate and the Chairman is an independent director.

Board Meetings

The Fannie Mae Board holds regularly scheduled meetings and calls at least eight times per year, and once per quarter. At least one of these meetings includes a session at which the Board reviews strategic matters. In addition to regularly scheduled meetings, unscheduled Board meetings may be called with adequate notice, if needed. Directors are expected to attend in person all regularly scheduled Board and committee meetings and the Annual Meeting of Stockholders, if any. The presence of a majority of the seated directors at the time of any meeting constitutes a quorum for the transaction of business, and the act of a majority of such directors present at a meeting at which a quorum is present constitutes the act of the Board. Directors may not vote or participate by proxy. The Board may act by unanimous written consent of all incumbent directors. The Chairman, in consultation with the Chairs of the Board's committees, determines the agenda for Board meetings. Directors will be asked regularly by the Chairman to evaluate the information being provided to the Board and to submit suggestions for Board agenda items.

Fannie Mae's non-management directors meet in executive session on a regularly scheduled basis. Time for an executive session is placed on the agenda for every regular Board meeting. The Chairman of the Board presides over these sessions. Board dinners are scheduled at least quarterly each year to give Board members an opportunity to informally discuss Fannie Mae issues.

Minutes

At each meeting of the Board and its standing committees, minutes will be taken. The minutes will reflect the deliberative process and actions taken in those meetings. The minutes will also reflect whether an executive session occurred and identify the issues addressed during executive session, as reported to the Corporate Secretary.

Board Materials

Fannie Mae management provides directors with information and materials necessary for the Board to fulfil its oversight functions. Directors are expected to review and devote appropriate time to studying Board and committee materials. Materials for meetings are generally distributed one week in advance of each Board and committee meeting to allow directors to prepare for discussion of the items at the meeting and to request additional information as appropriate. In certain cases, due to the sensitive nature of a matter or rapidly evolving developments, presentations and/or other materials are provided only at the Board or committee meeting.

Committees

The current standing Board committees are the Executive, Audit, Compensation, Nominating and Corporate Governance, Risk Policy and Capital, and Strategic Initiatives Committees. The Bylaws give the Board authority to create additional committees. Each committee, except for the Executive Committee, has a written charter setting forth the responsibilities, duties and authorities of the committee. The responsibilities, duties and authorities of the Executive Committee are set forth in the Bylaws. The full Board reviews and approves committee charters.

The Audit, Compensation, and Nominating and Corporate Governance Committees consist solely of independent directors. Committee assignments, including the designation of committee Chairs, are made annually by Board resolution, based on recommendations from the Nominating and Corporate Governance Committee. Assignments are made based on a combination of factors including each individual Board member's expertise and the needs of the corporation.

Each committee meets as frequently as needed and for an appropriate length of time based on the specific meeting agenda. Committee agendas are developed by the committee Chair in consultation with the appropriate members of management and with the input of other directors. Each committee Chair makes a report on committee matters to the Board, generally at the next scheduled Board meeting.

Director Access to Management and Outside Advisors

The corporation's senior management team attends Board meetings as needed to make special presentations and as a discussion resource, and is available directly to Board members outside of meetings.

The Board and its committees (consistent with the provisions of their respective charters) generally have the authority to retain such outside counsel, experts, and other advisors as they determine necessary to assist them in the performance of their functions. The retention and termination of external auditors and law firms serving as consultants to the Board requires prior consultation and consent of the conservator.

Communications with the Board

To facilitate the ability of interested parties to communicate their concerns or questions, Fannie Mae publishes on its website and in its proxy statement a mailing address and an e-mail address for communications directly with the Board. Communications may be addressed to a specific director or directors, or to independent directors as a group. The office of the Corporate Secretary is responsible for processing all the communications to the relevant director or directors. Communications that are commercial solicitations, ordinary course customer inquiries or complaints, incoherent or obscene, will not be forwarded to the Board. In addition, Fannie Mae publishes on its website and in its proxy statement a procedure for communicating with the Audit Committee regarding accounting, internal accounting controls or auditing matters.

Director Compensation

Compensation for members of the Board will be reasonable, appropriate, and commensurate with the duties and responsibilities of their Board service. The Nominating and Corporate Governance Committee is responsible for recommending compensation for non-management directors on the Board and reviews non-management director compensation as appropriate. A change to director compensation requires prior consultation and consent of the conservator. Management directors do not receive additional cash or equity compensation for Board service.

Director Orientation and Continuing Education

New directors participate in an orientation program to assist in familiarizing them with Fannie Mae's business and their responsibilities as directors. The orientation program addresses at a minimum Fannie Mae's corporate powers and limitations; an overview of Fannie Mae's business; the housing finance industry; strategic goals; risks; the Fannie Mae workforce; and Fannie Mae's corporate governance practices. Orientation sessions are also provided to new members of Board committees. Fannie Mae supports directors' periodic participation in continuing education programs to assist them in performing their Board responsibilities. In addition, on at least an annual basis, the corporation provides, directly or through third parties, in-house director education programs on significant developments applicable to the Board and Fannie Mae's operations.

Board Performance Evaluation

The Board conducts an annual self-evaluation to assess its effectiveness and the adequacy of the information flow to the Board, on the basis of criteria developed by the Nominating and Corporate Governance Committee and reviewed by the Board. Each of the Board's committees conducts an annual self-evaluation.

The Nominating and Corporate Governance Committee evaluates the performance of directors on an annual basis. The Nominating and Corporate Governance Committee takes into consideration: (i) a director's contribution to the effective functioning of the corporation; (ii) any change in the director's principal area of responsibility with his or her company or in his or her employment; (iii) the director's retirement from his or her principal area of responsibility with his or her company; (iv) whether the director continues to bring relevant experience to the Board; (v) whether the director has the ability to attend meetings and fully participate in the activities of the Board; (vi) whether the director has developed any relationships with Fannie Mae or another organization, or other circumstances have arisen, that might make it inappropriate for the director to continue serving on the Board; and (vii) the director's age and length of service on the Board.

Management Evaluation and Succession

The Compensation Committee conducts an annual review of the performance of the corporation, the CEO and senior management. Neither the CEO nor senior management is present when the Committee meets to evaluate their individual performance. The Chairman of the Board presents the CEO's annual performance review for the Committee's approval. The CEO's annual performance review is based, in large part, upon an annual performance report prepared by the Chairman of the Board and upon ratings and commentary provided by individual Board members. The senior management performance reviews include the Compensation Committee's own assessment and reflect discussions with other Board members. The Board's independent directors approve the compensation of the CEO, and the full Board approves the compensation of the corporation's executive officers (as defined by Securities Exchange Commission rules), both approvals subject to the consent of the conservator.

On an annual basis, the Compensation Committee reviews management succession planning with the CEO in preparation for discussion by the entire Board. The Board discussion on management succession occurs during executive session, and focuses on succession planning for the CEO and other key members of senior management.

Compliance; Codes of Conduct

Fannie Mae's Board oversees the corporation's legal and regulatory compliance program. The Board has adopted a Code of Conduct applicable to all Fannie Mae employees, which is posted on the corporation's website. Each employee must annually commit to follow the Code. The Audit Committee has primary responsibility for overseeing implementation of and compliance with the Code.

The Board has adopted a Code of Conduct and Conflict of Interests Policy for Members of the Board (Directors' Code), which is posted on the corporation's website. Each director must annually certify compliance with the Directors' Code. The Nominating and Corporate Governance Committee oversees implementation and compliance with the Directors' Code.

The Board reviews at least once every three years the adequacy of the employee Code of Conduct and the Directors' Code for consistency with best practices and practices appropriate to Fannie Mae, and makes revisions as appropriate.

18

Corporate Governance: The next thirty years

 Learning Outcomes

In which we consider:

- Today's frontiers of corporate governance
    - Shareholder activism
    - Chairman of the board and CEO
    - Director information
    - Controls on director and top executive remuneration
    - Gender diversity
    - Governance of strategic risk
    - Integrated reporting
    - Corporate governance, CSR, and sustainability
    - Core principles of corporate governance
- Beyond today's frontiers of corporate governance
    - Should corporate governance be based on principles or rules?
    - Emphasis on board culture and dynamics, not governance structures
    - New organizational forms and corporate nationality—meta-nationals
    - The independence of external auditors and board-level advisers
    - New theories of corporate governance
    - The need for taxonomy of corporate entities
    - The governance agenda
- Drivers of change
    - Responses to corruption, corporate collapse, and economic catastrophe
    - Efforts by reformers and interest groups
    - Corporate governance research and development
    - Social, political, and economic changes
    - Society's changing expectations

So we come to the final chapter of this textbook, but not to the end of the story of corporate governance. Thirty years ago the phrase 'corporate governance' was not used. Today, Google had 322 million references to the term. What are the frontiers of corporate governance today? What might they look like in another thirty years? What could drive such changes?

The 19th century saw the foundations laid for modern corporations: that was the century of the entrepreneur. The 20th century became the century of management, with new management theories, management gurus, and management consultants. But the 21st century has become the century of corporate governance, when the way in which power is exercised over corporate entities is under the spotlight.

We traced the evolution of the limited-liability company from the elegantly simple concept of the 19th century to the complex, diverse, and often massive groups that typify today's listed companies. The original basis for power over companies was ownership. But over the years that power has swung from owners to directors, to the extent that shareholders, even institutional shareholders, have relatively little power over the companies they own, and they struggle to make their voices heard.

Moreover, other types of corporate enterprise have multiplied: family companies, joint-ventures, public-interest companies, not-for-profit enterprises, non-government organizations, and many more. All need sound governance. Around the world, in large and small enterprises, in the public and the private sectors, governance has become the focus of attention. The effectiveness of governing bodies, their responsibilities, and their accountability are crucial topics. The legitimacy of corporate entities, their transparency, and their role in society are being questioned. Ultimately, nothing less than a re-balancing of the interests of the individual, the enterprise, and the state are involved. The field of corporate governance is expanding and changing dramatically.

Today's frontiers of corporate governance

First, we consider topics on the minds of directors and those who advise them at the moment, issues that feature in professional journals, and the proceedings of director conferences.

Shareholder activism

Over the years, many commentators have called for investors to 'exercise their power' and to vote shares they hold at company meetings. They argue that by focusing on performance they can provide checks on excesses, including executive remuneration, rein in inefficiencies, and challenge strategies and capital investments. There have been pressures for board renewal, less director entrenchment, and limits to tenure: predictably resisted by some boards. Classified boards, in which only a proportion of the directors are elected each year, have also come in for criticism.

But despite these calls, many fund managers show relatively little interest in the governance of companies in which they invest, preferring to 'do the Wall Street walk' by trading their shares, rather than incurring the costs of involvement in governance, and risk getting locked in with a falling share price. Moreover, if institutional investors do become proactive in governance and the stock price falls, might they themselves be held accountable for losses?

In many markets, particularly the highly liquid US and UK markets, high-frequency trading on the basis of computer models has increased. Such traders seek opportunities for short-term advantage, and have little inclination to do detailed analysis of the long-term prospects of the companies in which they invest, let alone become involved in their corporate governance. The pharmaceutical industry offer by Pfizer for AstraZeneca in 2014 highlights the case: some Wall Street hedge funds, having built up stakes, were critical of the AstraZeneca board for refusing to accept an increased offer, which potentially cost them millions. They commented on the potential conflict of interest of the incumbent AstraZeneca board. On the other hand, other institutional investors countered by claiming that AstraZeneca would be strategically stronger alone.

The primary responsibility of institutional investors, including investment trusts, mutual funds, unit trusts, life assurance companies, banks and brokers running portfolios for clients, is to their members or investors. If they do vote their shares, it must be in the interests of those beneficial owners, whose objectives may well differ from each other. Some regulations now require institutional investors to declare whether and how they have voted their shares. Some institutions offer tracker funds, which must invest in all of the companies in the market they track. In such cases, they may get involved in the governance of those companies; meeting with executives, attending meetings, and voting their shares.

Of concern, particularly in the United States, has been the growing practice of the lobbying of companies by interest groups. Institutional Investor Services listed key 2014 corporate governance policy issues as pay for performance, board responses to shareholder proposals supported by a majority, and proposals related to lobbying on issues such as climate change and human rights.[1]

Chairman of the board and CEO

It is now widely accepted around the world that in major companies, the role of chairman of the board should be separated from that of the chief executive officer (CEO) to avoid domination of decision-making and overenthusiastic risk-taking by a single, all-powerful individual. Most codes of good corporate governance principles and practice call for this separation. A few codes do recognize that, in some circumstances, a single leader may be appropriate, but in that case a strong group of independent non-executives is needed, with their own appointed leader.

Nevertheless, in the United States, the roles of CEO and chairman of the board, sometimes with the added title of 'president', are frequently combined in a single, powerful individual, who leads the company in both managerial and governance matters. The independent outside directors provide a check-and-balance mechanism, supported by independent external auditors and the requirements of the law, Securities and Exchange Commission (SEC) regulations, and stock exchange rules. The question is which is preferable: a dominant leader, who can provide single-minded leadership and enhance performance, or shared responsibility, which reduces risk? The duality issue is unresolved.

Where the roles are separated, another issue: should a retiring chief executive step up to become chairman? Retiring CEOs have experience of the company, the business, and the board. Their personal qualities—integrity, leadership, and communication skills—are well known. Moreover, the retiring CEO is known and trusted by investors, customers, employees, and others dealing with the company. So risks associated with introducing a new chairman would be reduced.

However, arguments against allowing a retiring CEO to become chairman are also formidable. Chairmanship of the board, it is argued, is a quite different role from that of CEO: strong performance at one does not guarantee success at the other. Moreover, some retiring CEOs find it hard to pass on the responsibilities of top management to their successors.

[1] www.issgovernance.com/file/files/2014USPolicyUpdates.pdf

Director information

In the first edition of this book (2009), we predicted that technology would allow directors to receive information electronically on personal devices, wherever and whenever needed. That has now happened. Such access enables them to be updated immediately on relevant aspects of the company, to be kept informed about the financial situation, on the competitive market position, and with relevant information about the firm's political, economic, technological, and societal context. But that is still a one-way information process—from company to director.

More sophisticated board-level information systems seek to allow directors to search for the information they feel they need, applying other tools such as simulations to explore possible outcomes, while communicating their ideas to other board colleagues online in a multiple information process.

Predictably, some directors still prefer the old one-way, hard-copy, set of monthly board papers.

Controls on director and top executive remuneration

Institutional investors in both the United States and the United Kingdom have challenged the levels of director rewards. Prompted by an investigative media, the issue has attracted the attention of the general public, 'fat cats' being the media term to describe directors with allegedly excessive remuneration packages. Although, given the work done, and the personal risks involved, it is a legitimate question in some companies whether director remuneration is sufficient. But the real concern is about directors' rewards that appear excessive, or even directors who are apparently rewarded for failure.

Although the justification for most director remuneration schemes is the maximization of long-term shareholder value, the bias of power on many boards in favour of incumbent executive directors can mean that remuneration schemes are structured to benefit top executives at the expense of the shareholders. The practical question is: how should directors' remuneration be determined? The preferred solution in the corporate governance literature, as we saw, is for a board remuneration committee, comprised entirely of independent outside directors, to determine executive director remuneration. The problem with that is whether such directors can be seen to be genuinely independent or whether they are really members of the 'directors' club', themselves in receipt of high rewards in other businesses.

Other proposals for monitoring directors' rewards have included mandatory shareholder voting on director rewards, as now occurs in the United Kingdom, or legislation that would impose statutory duties and rewards. In the United States shareholders can now vote on proposed director remuneration, but their decisions are advisory, potentially able to influence board decisions, but not able to override them. The issue remains on the frontier. The European Union sought a cap on executive bonuses of twice the annual salary, but this invited the raising of basic salaries and other forms of game-playing.

More consistent, multifactor measures of director, board, and company performance are being developed and linked to director remuneration. Emerging reward systems reward long-term success, while avoiding the distortions and short-termism that can arise with complex incentive schemes. Board remuneration committees will have to pay more attention to the wishes of shareholders, particularly institutional investors, who will become ever more vociferous and may be backed by legislation. Remuneration packages need to be sufficiently generous to attract and hold people of high calibre, but end the transfer of shareholder wealth to those directors whose overriding motivation is personal greed.

Gender diversity

Diversity in board membership has become a major interest around the world in recent years, particularly gender diversity, driven by a concern for greater equality between men and women at the top of large corporations. A UK government-commissioned report by Lord Davies, *Women on Boards*, recognized the benefits of different skills and perspectives, called for listed companies to explain their board recruitment policies, and suggested that 25% of FTSE 100 board members should be female by 2015 and 40% by 2020. The European Union has proposed 30% board representation by women by 2015. However, not all member states have accepted the proposal and it remains just that—a proposal.

To redress the gender balance, some countries have adopted quotas for women on boards. Norway introduced a quota in 2005 and the percentage of women has increased significantly. Eleven EU member states have laws to promote gender equality on company boards and the European Union is considering introducing quotas in all member states. India, Malaysia, and South Africa have also adopted quotas. The European Union has also suggested that companies should use clear, gender-neutral criteria when choosing non-executive directors, and that if candidates are found to be equally qualified, preference should be given to women.

Many directors are opposed to quotas, arguing that they do not guarantee that the most appropriate people become directors and, if mandated, the women board members could become 'token directors', with important decisions taken by powerful male elites outside the boardroom. Many believe that quality, not equality, is what is needed for board-level success, and argue that discriminative action has not worked in other situations.

However, a growing body of research[2] has shown improvements in corporate governance and financial performance as gender diversity has grown.

Governance of strategic risk

While there is evidence that boards are taking their company's exposure to risk more seriously, new issues are extending the nature and extent of that exposure. Unfortunately, the risk management systems in some organizations are still immature.

Regulations on the recognition and reporting of risk have increased, for example on data protection. In 2014, the UK Financial Reporting Council published new rules requiring boards to report significant behavioural, organizational, and reputational risks in the annual strategy reports of the companies it regulated.

Modern approaches to business have all increased exposure to strategic, managerial, and operational risk, including cyber-crime, interactive market-based systems which link

---

[2] For example, see Littenfeld, Doreen and Nell Beckman (2014) 'The Imperative for Gender Diversity on Boards'. The Corporate Governance Advisor, May/June.

customers and firms through the internet, data theft through hacking or employees attaching their own portable IT devices to corporate systems, and the use of social communication media. Reports of the loss of customer data have also increased the potential for serious reputational risk, even the possibility of law suits from customers or investors for alleged losses. Risk expertise is needed at board level, from board members as well as external advisers. Some companies have expanded the role of audit committee to include the oversight of risk.

Meanwhile, new approaches to catastrophe cover are emerging; by sharing strategic risk with an investor through bonds that are repaid with interest or drawn on if the catastrophic loss covered occurs, such as the long-term flooding of an underground railway.

Integrated reporting

Already many jurisdictions allow companies to communicate electronically with their shareholders and the market. Some permit electronic proxy voting on shareholder matters. Leading companies link investor relations with their marketing and public relations efforts. More frequent and more informative communication between boards, shareholders (particularly institutional investors), and the public is certainly a critical corporate governance frontier.

The call is for 'integrated reporting', in other words corporate communication that tells a coherent, linked narrative which explains the current situation and directors' expectations, strategies and policies for the future. Strategic reporting, going far beyond classical financial reports, might now include transparency protocols, the disclosure of metrics for long-term product cycles, and comments on exposure to risks. The reporting of remuneration, for example, used to be highly summarized, but modern remuneration reports may now detail remuneration by employee number, level, type, and location around the world, facilitating useful comparisons of corporate policies.

Regulations in some countries now require reporting on, for example, sustainability, pollution indices, carbon emissions, and human rights issues. Demands for access to more information using shareholder proxies have increased significantly, particularly in the United States, meeting resistance from management and their advisers. De-materialization, that is reliance on electronic links rather than paper-based systems, has increased this trend.

Another trend is an expectation from significant shareholders for personal interaction with board members, not just shareholder relations officers or more junior members of the management team. This development can offer a dialogue that is valuable to both parties, provided that the topics to be discussed are identified, the privilege is not abused, and all major investors are offered the same rights.

Corporate governance, corporate social responsibility, and sustainability

Most corporate governance codes require formal reporting that the code has been followed or, if not, explanations given for any divergence. Unfortunately, such reporting can too easily become a recital of the company's conformance to each element of the code: what some authorities refer to as 'boiler plate' reporting. Successive reports begin to look strikingly familiar.

However, a corporate governance report actually provides an opportunity for the board to explain and comment on the way it governs the company, describing how power is exercised over shareholders' funds, how employee, customer, and investor relations are handled, how business ethics, corporate social responsibility (CSR), and sustainability are reflected in corporate policies on, for example, whistle blowing, avoiding human rights abuses, or bribery and corruption.

The growing emphasis on corporate governance, CSR, and sustainability has added another dimension to corporate reporting, acknowledging the rights of stakeholders and society to be informed on corporate issues that could affect them. The disclosure of environmental, social, and governance information, often now called ESG reporting, which was originally voluntary, has increasingly become mandatory.

Moreover, rather than being a self-serving rehearsal of a firm's achievements, mandatory business reviews require companies to quantify non-financial factors using key performance indicators, as well as providing contextual and forward looking information. Expect more such quantitative metrics to be introduced, allowing comparison of companies' changing performance over time and between companies.

ESG reporting is becoming as important to the commercial and community well-being of companies as financial reports have been to investors in the past.

Core principles of corporate governance

In 2013, the Institute of Chartered Accountants in England and Wales published what it felt were the five over-arching principles of corporate governance.[3] These were:

- Leadership: an effective board should lead the company, steering it to meet the business purpose in both the short and long term
- Capability; the board should have an appropriate mix of skills, experience and independence
- Accountability: the board should communicate to the company's shareholders and other stakeholders at regular intervals a fair, balanced and understandable assessment of how the company is achieving its business purpose and meeting its other responsibilities
- Sustainability: the board should guide the business to create value and allocate it fairly and sustainably to reinvestment and distribution to stakeholders including shareholders, directors, employees, and customers
- Integrity: the board should lead the company to conduct its business in a fair and transparent manner that can withstand the scrutiny of stakeholders

In 2010, the New York Stock Exchange (NYSE) published the report[4] of a Commission on Corporate Governance that it had sponsored. Chaired by Larry W. Sonsini, this independent commission represented investors, issuers, broker-dealers, and governance experts, and was established to examine core governance principles that could be widely supported by issuers, investors, directors, and other market participants.

The report affirmed a number of basic beliefs, namely that:

- the board's fundamental objective is to build long-term sustainable growth in shareholder value, and thus corporate policies that encourage excessive risk-taking for the sake of short-term increases in stock price are inconsistent with sound corporate governance;

[3] www.icaew.com/en/technical/corporate-governance
[4] www1.nyse.com/pdfs/CCGReport.pdf

- corporate management has a critical role in corporate governance, because management has the primary responsibility for creating an environment in which a culture of performance with integrity can flourish;

- while independence is an important attribute for board members, the NYSE's Listing Standards do not limit a board to only one non-independent (outside) director, and boards should seek an appropriate balance between independent and non-independent directors to ensure a proper mix of expertise, diversity, and knowledge;

- while legislation and agency rule-making are important to establish the basic tenets of corporate governance, the Commission believes that overreliance on legislation and agency rule-making may not be in the best interests of shareholders, companies, or society, and the Commission therefore has a preference for market-based governance solutions whenever possible.

The Commission predicated ten core principles of corporate governance, which appear in Corporate Governance in action 18.1.

Corporate governance in action 18.1   Ten core principles of corporate governance

1. The Board's fundamental objective should be to build long-term sustainable growth in shareholder value for the corporation.

2. Successful corporate governance depends upon successful management of the company, as management has the primary responsibility for creating a culture of performance with integrity and ethical behavior.

3. Good corporate governance should be integrated with the company's business strategy and not viewed as simply a compliance obligation.

4. Shareholders have a responsibility and long-term economic interest to vote their shares in a reasoned and responsible manner, and should engage in a dialogue with companies in a thoughtful manner.

5. While legislation and agency rule-making are important to establish the basic tenets of corporate governance, corporate governance issues are generally best solved through collaboration and market-based reforms.

6. A critical component of good governance is transparency, as well governed companies should ensure that they have appropriate disclosure policies and practices and investors should also be held to appropriate levels of transparency, including disclosure of derivative or other security ownership on a timely basis.

7. The Commission supports the NYSE's listing requirements generally providing for a majority of independent directors, but also believes that companies can have additional non-independent directors so that there is an appropriate range and mix of expertise, diversity, and knowledge on the board.

8. The Commission recognizes the influence that proxy advisory firms have on the markets, and believes that it is important that such firms be held to appropriate standards of transparency and accountability.

9. The SEC should work with exchanges to ease the burden of proxy voting while encouraging greater participation by individual investors in the proxy voting process.

10. The SEC and/or the NYSE should periodically assess the impact of major governance reforms to determine if these reforms are achieving their goals, and in light of the many reforms adopted over the last decade the SEC should consider the expanded use of 'pilot' programs, including the use of 'sunset provisions' to help identify any implementation problems before a program is fully rolled out.

These beliefs characterize the frontier of today's corporate governance thinking and practice in the United Kingdom and the United States. They also suggest some of the issues that might lie beyond that frontier in the future.

Beyond today's frontiers of corporate governance

Although corporate governance has evolved significantly in recent years, as we have seen, some basic issues remain unresolved. We turn now to concerns that underlie many of today's corporate governance frontiers. These are often more conceptual, can raise some tricky philosophical, political, and economic matters, and their solutions will be longer term.

Should corporate governance be based on principles or rules?

Should the regulation and practice of corporate governance be based on principles or rules? In other words, should companies have discretion in the way in which they run their affairs or should they be constrained by the rule of law? Voluntary or mandatory: this is a fundamental issue that goes to the heart of corporate governance.

Some commentators still refer to the 'Anglo-American' approach to corporate governance, contrasting the unitary board of the Anglo-American common law jurisdictions with the two-tier supervisory and executive boards of the continental European and other civil law countries. But, in reality, a schism has appeared between American and British concepts of corporate governance.

In the United States, corporate governance is increasingly enforced by the rule of law and mandatory regulation. The US Sarbanes-Oxley Act of 2002, which was a response to the collapses of Enron, WorldCom, and the big-five auditor Arthur Andersen, is backed up by federal and state laws, and reinforced by SEC requirements. 'Obey the law and the rules or risk the consequences' has become the norm.

By contrast, the basis of corporate governance in the United Kingdom and other countries[5] whose company law has been influenced over the years by UK common law, as well as countries with codes based on the OECD Principles, involves a discretionary approach. Listed companies need to conform to voluntary codes of principle and best practice then report that they have complied, or explain why they have not.

Some years ago, the belief that corporate governance around the world would converge on the American model was widespread, not least because the world then needed access to American capital. That is no longer the case. So this dilemma remains unresolved. Countries that rely on the 'principles' model stoutly defend the discretion allowed by this approach, arguing that this gives companies the flexibility they need in the business world.

In recent years, financial accounting standards in most economically advanced countries have tended to converge. International Financial Reporting Standards (IFRS), which began as an attempt to harmonize financial reporting in Europe, were originally called International Accounting Standards. The standards are published by the International Accounting

---

[5] Including Australia, Canada, Hong Kong, India, Malaysia, New Zealand, Singapore, and South Africa.

Standards Board (IASB), the standard-setting arm of the IFRS Foundation, an independent, not-for-profit, private sector organization. The objectives of the Foundation are:

- to develop a single set of high quality, understandable, enforceable and globally accepted International Financial Reporting Standards (IFRSs),
- to promote the use and rigorous application of those standards,
- to take account of the financial reporting needs of emerging economies and small and medium-sized entities (SMEs),
- to promote and facilitate the adoption of IFRSs, being the standards and interpretations issued by the IASB, through the convergence of national accounting standards and IFRSs.

In fulfilling its standard-setting duties, the IASB follows a transparent process, with the publication of consultative documents, discussion papers, and exposure drafts for public comment. All meetings of the IASB are held in public and webcast.

In the United States, companies must follow the US generally accepted accounting principles (GAAP). The SEC has stated that it intends to move towards IFRS, although progress is slow.

In the United Kingdom, work on financial reporting policy is carried out by the Accounting Council (AC), including financial standards, often called the UK GAAP. From January 2015, a new set of standards replaced almost all existing accounting standards with three Financial Reporting Standards (FRS 100, 101, and 102). French GAAP are called Plan Comptable Général (PCG), published by the French Committee of Accountancy Regulation, and validated by the French government. All of these financial reporting standards around the world are rule-based.

Trends in corporate governance around the world seem to be towards a law and rules-based approach. To attract investors, countries need to move towards the corporate governance expectations of economically advanced nations. In the European Union, the search for company law harmonization is leading towards some standardization; although such moves meet opposition from those who prefer a country-based, discretionary approach.

The Corporate Secretaries International Association (CSIA) is an international federation of professional bodies promoting good governance and corporate secretary-ship. CSIA asked corporate governance experts from around the world for their opinions on the corporate governance implications of the global financial crisis and subsequent economic hiatus. Their responses were condensed into twenty practical steps to better corporate governance[6] (see Corporate governance in action 18.2):

Emphasis on board culture and dynamics, not governance structures

The laws, regulations, and rules surrounding corporate governance set boundaries, limit and constrain corporate activities, and prevent abuse and excess; but they can also restrict imaginative, original, and entrepreneurial endeavours.

---

[6] www.corporategovernanceoup.wordpress.com/2010/05/31/twenty-steps-to-better-corporate-governance

Corporate governance in action 18.2   Twenty practical steps to better corporate governance

1. Recognize that good corporate governance is about the effectiveness of the governing body—not about compliance with codes
2. Confirm the leadership role of the board chairman
3. Check that the non-executive directors have the necessary skills, experience, and courage
4. Consider the calibre of the non-executive directors
5. Review the role and contribution of non-executive directors
6. Ensure that all directors have a sound understanding of the company
7. Confirm that the board's relationship with executive management is sound
8. Check that directors can access all the information they need
9. Consider whether the board is responsible for formulating strategy
10. Recognize that the governance of risk is a board responsibility
11. Monitor board performance and pursue opportunities for improvement
12. Review relations with shareholders—particularly institutional investors
13. Emphasise that the company does not belong to the directors
14. Ensure that directors' remuneration packages are justifiable and justified
15. Review relations between external auditors and the company
16. Consider relations with the corporate regulators
17. Develop written board-level policies covering relations between the company and the societies it affects
18. Review the company's attitudes to ethical behaviour
19. Ensure that company secretary's function is providing value
20. Consider how corporate secretary's function might be developed

Corporate governance codes, which evolved to reflect accepted best practice, emphasizing board structures, board committees, and corporate governance reporting, seem to have reached a plateau. They have not provided a solution to the search for universal corporate governance principles. Despite complying with their code, many boards still fail to fulfil their potential.

More penetrating insights are now needed. Boards are not just legal entities or compliers with codes. They are human artefacts; living, changing organisms. Each team of directors has its own dynamic. Over time, each board develops its own culture—that set of shared experiences, perceptions, and beliefs which defines how it sees and responds to corporate situations. Directors and potential directors can have their personal abilities honed through experience and training: the Directors' College, run by McMaster University and the Conference Board of Canada, runs courses that use simulation as a learning device.

Boardroom behaviour can differ significantly. Some boards reach agreement easily; others are more like debating societies, even adversarial parliaments. Interpersonal relations between directors can be significant; so can the role of dominant members. Leadership styles of the chairman, the CEO, and perhaps the lead independent director can differ significantly. Relationships between the CEO and other executive directors; and between the executive directors and the outside directors are fundamental to board culture.

Independence in outside directors is rigorously defined in most codes, but only personality and experience can determine the real contribution that an independent director makes. Character, inter-personal skills, and toughness of mind determine independence, not code definitions.

Critical insights into a board's culture can sometimes be found in its approach to corporate strategy, how it responds to crises, and the way it deals with disagreements. Changes in membership of the board can affect its culture as new expectations are introduced and old beliefs challenged. In the future, expect more emphasis on board dynamics, culture, and leadership, than on structure and compliance with codes.

New organizational forms and corporate nationality—meta-nationals

The original corporate concept did not envisage the complexity of today's organizational structures, with inter-woven supply chains, networks of subsidiary and associated companies, companies with off-balance-sheet vehicles, chains of companies giving leveraged power to companies at the top of the chain, limited partnerships controlling listed companies, groups with cross-holdings of shares and cross-directorships, and other networks with joint ventures and strategic alliances. Frequently, these networks of corporate interest operate in multiple jurisdictions, cultures, and currencies. They may have voracious appetites for growth, with the attendant risks. These new organizational forms may have alternative approaches to financing than the stock market.

Such organizational forms raise significant questions for corporate governance and financial reporting. Moreover, such entities can be dynamic and evolve rapidly. Corporate regulation and financial disclosure rules may struggle to keep pace. How such organizations are governed in the future will provide a major challenge.

New forms of networked organizations could emerge that link entities created as classical joint-stock limited-liability companies with government and non-government organizations and community groupings.

The implications of globalization have been well recognized for years. Multi-national groups operate in many countries and in different jurisdictions, sometimes generating more wealth than the GDP of host countries. But multi-national companies have tended to have a specific 'home' country, often defined by the nationality of their directors, where they are incorporated, where the head office is located, where they are listed, and where most of their investors live.

But a new phenomenon is emerging: corporate groups which operate not only *in* many nation states but operate *above* them. Such groups can be defined by the many nationalities of their main board directors, the diversity of their markets and customers, the international spread of their facilities and where their employees are located, where they have headquarters, and probably most significantly, where they have decided to be domiciled for tax purposes. Such entities might be defined as meta-nationals. Nestle, AstraZeneca, and some of the international oil companies fit this model, which may become more prevalent.

The independence of external auditors and board-level advisers

Independent external auditors play a fundamental role in corporate governance systems throughout the world. Their principal role is to reassure investors, tax authorities and others that the financial reports produced by the directors truly and fairly reflect the state of the company's affairs. Clearly, to fulfil this role objectively, they need to be independent of the company and its directors.

But the company appoints the auditors and pays them for their services. Auditors to the world's major companies are major businesses. The formal audit provides a platform to offer non-audit work, such as tax services, management consultancy, information technology, and other services. Partners are judged by fee generation, growth, and profit performance.

Serious questions have to be asked about the auditors' position. Does the auditors' economic dependency infringe their independence? Who are their real clients: the directors or the shareholders? The *de jure* response, that the client is the company, which means the share holders, does not wash. The *de facto* reality is that the client is the board, particularly the board's audit committee.

The dilemma is that, in effect, external auditors serve two masters—the financial market, for whom they provide an independent external check, and the directors with whom they must work closely, who pay their fees, and determine their reappointment. There is a potential conflict of interest.

What are the alternatives? Some have suggested breaking the oligopoly of the four international accounting firms, by breaking them up and opening the market for audit, with second-tier firms to audit major listed companies. But financial markets like the assurance they believe they get from an audit opinion signed by one of the big four. Occasional tendering for audits to reduce over-familiarity has been suggested and introduced in some countries. Periodic mandatory rotation of audit firms has also been suggested. Others have proposed further rules to regulate auditors' activities, like the US Sarbanes-Oxley Act of 2002. But this approach has proved more expensive and less effective than expected, as seen in the subsequent collapse and bailout of financial institutions and some other companies.

The suggestion has been made[7] that auditors be appointed by and report to the regulators, as well as the directors. In this way, close relationships between directors and auditors would be avoided. If auditors reported to the regulator rather than the directors, a new mindset would be needed.

The independence of other board advisers, such as lawyers, recruitment consultants, and compensation consultants, has also been questioned because of apparent conflicts of interest.

New theories of corporate governance

At the moment, there is no universally accepted theory of corporate governance, as we saw in Chapter 3. Relationships between corporate governance practices and the performance of companies, their boards and directors are still unclear, although evidence that sound corporate governance leads to better sustainable performance, higher share prices, and

[7] Tricker, Bob (2011) 'Re-engineering the limited liability company'. *Corporate Governance: An International Review.* Vol. 19, No. 4, July.

lower cost of capital is growing. But, to date, developments in corporate governance policies and practices have often been more responses to corporate collapses and malaise in the
finance markets than from the results of rigorous research.

New insights from such research could lead to future developments in the subject.
Fundamental rethinking may follow the recognition that the statistically significant conclusions from agency theoretical studies are based on a bounded model of reality. New fields
for research could include academic perspectives other than those of financial economics,
including interpersonal, behavioural, or political concepts. New models, frameworks, and
concepts are needed and are likely to emerge. Systems theory offers the potential of a better
understanding of boundaries, levels, and input/output relationships. Corporate governance
could be studied as an information process. Other insights could come from studies of the
socio-politics of boards, studying boards as teams, or as communication networks.

New thinking and better understanding might also emerge from studies of board leadership and the style of the chairman. The concept of power in corporate governance might
repay further exploration. The psychology of boards and the individual motivations of key
players could also offer insights. A real problem with corporate governance research has been
getting access to the boardroom. But that is being overcome and further rigorous studies are
likely to be reported.

The need for taxonomy of corporate entities

However, before such thinking can be developed, a dilemma has to be resolved. The classification of corporate entities has not changed for over 100 years. Around the world, limited
companies are still divided into just two categories: public and private. This simple distinction
between public companies, which permit the raising of outside investment, and private companies, which do not, is naïve, and a totally inadequate categorization of corporations. Nor
is there a comprehensive classification of the myriad other organizational forms that need
governing.

A classification scheme, or taxonomy, is needed that distinguishes different species and
subspecies of corporate entity. Too many different types of corporate entity are currently
treated as though they were homogeneous. One approach might be to differentiate
corporate types by the way in which power is, or could be, exercised over them. Such a
categorization would need to cover all types of corporate entity in every jurisdiction,
including, for example, South Korean *chaebols*, Japanese *keiretsu*, and Italian chained
companies. It would need to include entities in different cultures, with different legal
systems, institutions, and regulatory bodies. There seems little justification for excluding
other corporate types such as non-government organizations (NGOs), charities, professional bodies, and not-for-profit organizations.

Clearly, investment is not the only basis for the exercise of power over corporate entities. Classically, monarchs, dictators, or the church wielded power over valuable resources,
which were subsequently replaced in some places by the federal state. Elsewhere, community
organizations at the state, regional, or local level manage resources, provide local facilities
and run utilities, with power exercised through members of that community. Members of
organizations provide the basis for corporate governance, in membership organizations such
as trades unions, consumer and supplier co-operatives, savings and loan associations (building societies), mutual insurance associations, the accountancy, legal, and medical professions,

universities, and some charities. Governance by employees can be though employee shareholdings as in United Airlines in the United States, through partnership as in the John Lewis Partnership in the United Kingdom, or through worker co-operatives as in the Mondragon worker co-operative in Spain.

Tighter definition is also needed for listed companies to differentiate those with widely held shareholdings, those dominated by one or a block of shareholders, those owned by another listed company, state-chartered companies with a minority of shares listed, and public companies that are not listed on a stock exchange.

Private companies also need to be differentiated between parent companies of groups, wholly owned subsidiaries in a group, partly owned subsidiaries, and associated companies dominated by another company. Other categories could include private equity firms, sovereign funds, hedge funds, and private equity firms, joint venture companies, and private companies dominated by family interests. Partnerships, both with and without limited liability, could form other classes; as could government departments, organizations mandated by government, NGOs, not-for-profit entities with guarantors not shareholders, self-governing social organizations, unincorporated family firms, and sole traders.

Each of these arrangements can provide the base for wielding power over corporate resources—in other words, for corporate governance. So far, a great deal of corporate governance thinking has been focused on the governance of quoted companies. The list above suggests that there is considerable scope for further work. The opportunity exists to create a new paradigm of corporate governance which would rethink the relationship between individual, enterprise, and state in a way appropriate to the 21st century rather than the 19th or 20th.

In all ecosystems, diversity is essential for survival. The rich variety of organizational forms and potential governance mechanisms above suggests that the frontiers of corporate diversity, far from converging, are evolving and multiplying quickly. Indeed, it has been suggested that the era of the listed, public company has reached its zenith.

Taxonomy of different types of corporate entity could lead to new theoretical insights and developments. Corporate entities are at once legal beings, economic artefacts, and social organizations. They can be studied as any of them. As a legal entity, the corporate entity is an artificial being created, bounded, and controlled by the laws of the country in which it was incorporated and operates. As an economic artefact, it strives to respond to market forces and to meet the economic goals of its owners and directors. But instead of legal or economic entities, corporate bodies could be seen as self-governing social institutions. Their boundaries, connections, and functions could be defined by cybernetic communication and control linkages with the nodes defined with requisite variety, rather than legal rules and governance regulations.

Organizations could be defined by the ability of external parties to exercise power over them. Information boundaries and data linkages to stakeholders, rather than ownership boundaries, could be used to define an entity. Dynamic and rapidly evolving groupings of networked or chained entities could be represented as organic systems rather than through the mechanistic, legal model.

Some companies operating globally are now larger than the states in which they operate. Nevertheless, they have to act in the legal, economic, and cultural shadows of these host countries. Not since the days of the East India Company can they operate their own armies. Companies do not acquire power from their global scale. States give corporate entities the licence to operate. What states give, they can take away. Governance power could be redefined by the state.

The governance agenda

Finally, in considering the present frontiers of corporate governance around the world, we need to recognize legitimate differences between developed and developing economies. Countries with advanced economies are likely to have the instruments and institutions necessary for successful corporate governance: well-developed company law and regulation, corporate governance codes, reliable legal systems, liquid stock markets, financial institutions including brokers, sponsors, and financial advisers, comprehensive disclosure with high transparency, respected accounting and legal professions, reliable auditing firms, director-related professional organizations and educational institutions, and reputable corporate governance research.

While many nations with developing and transitional economies properly aspire to such situations, allowances have to be made for the evolution of, for example, company law, the legitimacy of the courts, the prevention of corruption, or state interference in corporate affairs. The frontiers of corporate governance vary and are constantly on the move.

Drivers of change

The forces that have driven changes in corporate governance thinking and practice over the years are likely to continue in the future, but there may be some additional pressures.

Responses to corruption, corporate collapse, and economic catastrophe

The original driving forces in corporate governance thinking and practice came from the United States. Federal protection for investors and the regulation of listed companies dates back to the 1930s, with the creation of the SEC. America's current pre-eminence in corporate governance reflects the vast amounts of capital provided through reliable and liquid markets, the availability of sophisticated legal and accountancy services, and the existence of well-developed investor information systems, with strong and trusted regulation, backed up by a massive and successful economy.

The corporate collapses of Enron, WorldCom, and others in the United States were rooted in management malfeasance and fraud. The Sarbanes-Oxley Act (2002) was the regulatory response and increased the influence of US governance practices on governance thinking worldwide. Most significantly, it reinforced and emphasized the rules-based underpinning of American corporate governance: a mandatory and legal 'obey or face the consequences' regime.

But the focus has changed. In recent years, corporate governance initiatives have originated in other countries, starting with the influential 1992 Cadbury Report on the financial aspects of corporate governance from the United Kingdom. As we have seen, many other countries then produced their own governance codes, followed by international codes from organizations such as the OECD and the World Bank. The underpinning philosophy of these codes has been principles-based, not rules-based, a voluntary 'conform or explain' regime.

International access to US funds has become less important as other economies, including the Middle East and China, generate surpluses on the back of oil prices and economic growth. Emerging economies, such as China, need less inward investment and have become sources of outward investment around the world. Other finance markets are growing in scale, sophistication, and reputation, particularly in Asia. Therefore the pressure to adopt American corporate governance processes is less marked, as corporate governance initiatives from other financial markets and company law jurisdictions become more significant.

Moreover, the expensive regulatory demands and, as some perceive them, challenging attitudes of the Sarbanes-Oxley Act, SEC regulation, and US listing rules could be a disincentive for non-US companies to list in the United States. The lighter regulatory touch of other jurisdictions and financial markets are seen as more attractive, with their call to comply with corporate governance principles (or explain why not), rather than strictly adhere to legally binding rules risking litigation or even prosecution. The costs of compliance in some of these markets may also be lower. Successful capital markets will inevitably be those that are judged effective by their users—both those investing and those raising capital.

Efforts by reformers and interest groups

Over the years, efforts to reform and improve corporate governance have come from many sources. Corporate governance interest groups have been formed to encourage sound corporate governance and contribute to the development and improvement of the subject. The *Organisation for Economic Co-operation and Development* has been prominent, advising government regulators seeking to establish norms, and publishing the OECD Principles of Corporate Governance and the OECD Guidelines on Corporate Governance of State-Owned Enterprises. The *International Corporate Governance Network* links those interested in corporate governance reform and seeks to raise standards of corporate governance worldwide. In the United States, the *Committee of Sponsoring Organizations of the Treadway Commission* (COSO), a private sector organization, is dedicated to improving the quality of financial reporting through business ethics, effective internal controls, and corporate governance. Based in the United States and operating across ten countries, *International Shareholder Services* (ISS) advises institutional investors on corporate governance issues in companies around the world. ISS has an influential proxy advisory service offering analysis and recommendations. The *European Corporate Governance Institute* has become a focal point for academics working on corporate governance. The *Global Corporate Governance Forum* provides assistance to developing transition economies on corporate governance. The *Asian Corporate Governance Association* works with companies and regulators to improve corporate governance practices throughout Asia.

Some professional bodies also contribute to the development of ideas on corporate governance. Prominent among them are *The Conference Board* in the United States and other countries, professional accounting and auditing bodies, including the *Institute of Chartered Accountants in England and Wales*, the *Institute of Chartered Secretaries and Administrators* in London, and various law societies. Some institutional investors as well as organizations developed to support and advise them have also contributed to the development of the subject. The California Public Employees Retirement System (*CalPers*) has influenced corporate governance practices in countries and companies in which it invests, by demanding US levels of governance, and publishing advisory reports. *PIRC*, an independent research and advisory consultancy based in the United Kingdom, which provides services to institutional investors, has also contributed to corporate governance research and development.

It seems likely that corporate governance reformers and interest groups will continue to be drivers of change; in the future, perhaps, introducing ideas from other cultures, regulatory jurisdictions, and market orientations in addition to those based on Western free-market ideology.

Corporate governance research and development

On a theoretical level, more academic research and publications on corporate governance have come from American scholars than the rest of the world combined, although the extent and quality of published research from around the world is developing quickly.

In 2009, Professor Jay Lorsch[8] and colleagues at the Harvard Business School interviewed directors of major US corporations about their reactions to the global financial crisis. Their research paper[9] argued that recent boardroom failures differed from the previous corporate failings. However, recent corporate governance problems, the researchers found, were primarily attributable to the growing complexity of the companies that boards governed.

The Harvard research found a strong consensus among directors that the key to improving boards' performance was not government action, but action by each board. Moreover, the researchers emphasized that companies and boards differ. Each board needs to develop structures, processes, and practices that fit the needs of the company and its business: 'one size fits all' was viewed with scepticism.

The Harvard paper identified six areas for improvement:

- clarifying the board's role;
- acquiring better information and deeper understanding of the company;
- maintaining a sound relationship with management;
- providing oversight of company strategy;
- assuring management development and succession;
- improving risk management.

Unfortunately, much corporate governance research has remained in academe and has not influenced the development of corporate governance law, regulation, or practice. The metamorphosis that will determine the ultimate structure and processes of the subject has yet to occur. Present practice is still rooted in a 19th-century legal concept of the corporation that is totally inadequate in the emerging global business environment. Present theory is even less capable of explaining coherently the way in which modern organizations are governed.

What is needed is a vibrant alternative that explains how power is exercised, over every type and form of corporate entity and strategic alliance around the world, in a way that ensures both effective performance and appropriate social accountability and responsibility. It would be good for such concepts to be rooted in rigorous and replicable research. Unfortunately,

---

[8] Professor Jay Lorsch is Louis Kirstein Professor of Human Relations at Harvard Business School, a member of the editorial board of *Corporate Governance: An International Review* and author (with Colin B. Carter) of *Back to the Drawing Board* (2004) Harvard Business School Press and other books.

[9] www.people.hbs.edu/jlorsch/BoardroomIssues.pdf

the driver of further changes in corporate governance is most likely to be exposure to further board-level excesses, corporate collapses, and economic failure.

Social, political, and economic changes

The growing political importance and wealth-generating capacities of the emerging economies, particularly China, India, and perhaps Brazil, are likely to provide them with the leverage to influence international corporate governance requirements and accounting standards. Some of their companies have the potential to become global through cross-border acquisitions, influencing the economies of the host nations. Calls for new corporate governance standards and controls might arise in response to such acquisitions by overseas companies, where the economic performance and political interests of a host country could be affected. Nationalism and economic patriotism could lead to attempts by nation states to protect domestic employment, wealth creation, and their tax base.

The governance of sovereign wealth funds, particularly their transparency, will have to be addressed at an international level. The outcome could be a code of conduct for sovereign funds requiring disclosure of their strategic aims, and details of their main holdings, perhaps regulated by an international body such as the International Monetary Fund.

Classical audited annual accounts are being replaced by more frequent financial reviews, strategic reports, risk analyses, corporate resource reviews, operating statements, and corporate governance reports, some responding to events as they occur. Statements of directors' expectations of the likelihood of future events are likely to include estimates of probability ranges.

In relation to the qualifications and characteristics of directors: as the complexities, challenges, and risks of taking on a directorship grow, more clarification and better definition of the skills, experience, and knowledge that directors need will be required. Going beyond the structures and strictures of the compliance codes, more attention is likely to be paid to board dynamics and the chairman's leadership role to achieve corporate success. The vital importance of the leadership role of the chairman is likely to be reinforced. Forms of network governance structures, based on responsibility centres and information flows, might emerge to replace the static governing body, as a response to growing complexity, improving performance, and providing easier adaptation to change.

The importance of corporate governance systems that mirror the reality of a country's political, social, and economic situation, and its expectations for the future is apparent. Developing nations may have as much to learn from each other as from Western experience. The future of corporate governance is unlikely to look like its past.

Society's changing expectations

The limited liability company was a child of mid-19th century Victorian England. This was an era of institutional invention. Britain was at the height of Empire-led self-confidence. Other corporate entities—trades unions, building societies (savings and loan associations), cooperative societies, missionary societies, and professional bodies including law societies and accountants' associations—were all formed in the latter half of the 19th century. Religion, individualism, and self-help flourished. This was a society in which the concepts of duty, trust, and self-reliance were basic.

These qualities were reflected in the brilliant idea of the joint-stock company. The state passed legislation that permitted the incorporation of corporate entities separate from those managing and investing in them, while limiting the liability of those shareholders for their companies' debts. In effect, the state licensed corporate entities, and regulated their behaviour, while the directors, appointed by the investors, were trusted to act on their behalf.

As Daniel Bell[10] commented, capitalism developed and drew its strength from an ethic of sobriety, saving, and deferred gratification—although he also noted that free-market capitalism actually worked to undermine these qualities, stimulating hedonism and instant gratification.

Every subsequent development—the formation of millions of private companies; power over companies shifting from shareholders to directors; the creation of regulatory bodies; the formation of complex corporate groups with pyramids, chains, and networks; the growth and concentration of the auditing profession; corporate governance codes; the Sarbanes-Oxley Act; calls for CSR and sustainability; indeed, everything that has happened since—is still rooted in that 19th-century creation: the virtual reality of an autonomous corporate entity.

But a company is a concept. It is a fiction, albeit a legal one. The directors and officers, managers and employees, individual shareholders, customers and suppliers, competitors, government and tax authorities, auditors and regulators are the reality. All corporate governance to date has been based on the old legal-entity paradigm. The corporate governance literature has uncritically embraced this virtual reality. As we have seen throughout this book, the corporate form has its limitations—corporate collapses, environmental hazards, corruption, and abuse of power, with personal greed, rather than a fiduciary concern for members' interests, as the driving force.

But society today is not satisfied with corporate behaviour. Evidence is widespread. Scepticism abounds about business which is seen to lead to greed, excessive remuneration that erodes shareholder wealth, retirement awards and performance bonuses not linked to performance, and growing social wealth disparity. Taxpayers resented having to bail out failing financial and other companies in the 2007–2012 world-wide financial melt-down. Around the world corruption seems rife at every level. Too many cases are reported of top management domination, arrogance, and abuse of power.

Just as economic and political forces around the world are driving change in corporate governance, society's changing expectations, particularly in the developed world, are also prompting change. Society is demanding more of corporate entities operating in its midst. Demands for CSR, sustainability, and business ethics are increasingly commonplace in the advanced world. Eventually, they are likely to be written into regulations and law. Current initiatives in this area by the United Nations are diffuse, but are being taken up at national level. The inevitable differences between cultures, jurisdictions, and stages of economic development need to be recognized more specifically in defining governance requirements, and appropriate risk profiles created, avoiding the process of merely applying advanced country norms where they are inappropriate.

It is apparent that there is no one ideal structure for the governance of all corporate entities. Many alternative structures can work in the appropriate context. In fact, despite

---

[10] Bell, Daniel (1962) *The End of Ideology*. Harvard University Press, Cambridge, MA.

all of the commentary on governance structures—unitary and two-tier boards, the proportion of outside directors with lead independent director, defining director independence, the separation of chairman and CEO, board committees, and the rest—the issue of effective governance is not really about structure, but about process, not about procedures, but about people.

Governance involves a political process. Governing bodies need to ensure that the entity fulfils its mission and meets its aims, whether these are providing goods or services to satisfy markets, offering a social service to meet society's needs, or fulfilling some other purpose. In the process, the entity may create wealth, provide employment, facilitate innovation, and contribute to society, not least by paying taxes, at the local and national levels.

A successful governing body needs a cadre of the competent. Respected leadership is a crucial driving force. Professionalism, with continuous personal development and learning, is fundamental. In future, governing bodies may have to be less rigid, less bounded, and more adaptable. That might mean board styles that are transient, more flexible, and certainly less formal.

Eventually, the place of companies in society will need to be rethought, moving beyond shareholder primacy towards a form of capitalism that embraces and links individuals, enterprises, and states.

The originators of the limited-liability company in the 19th century created a corporate governance system in which society required them to meet specific roles and responsibilities, and bounded their activities. Subsequently, the growing diversity of corporate objectives, confused ownership structures, and complex corporate groups, led to abuse. Society lost the control that it originally demanded for the right to incorporate companies in which shareholders had no liability for corporate debts beyond their equity stake. Companies again need to be held responsible for meeting societies' expectations. Incorporating a company, in which shareholders are not responsible for their company's debts, should require them to meet society's expectations. Limited liability is a privilege, not a right. What society grants, it can take away.

In the 19th century, trust was at the heart of business; it underpinned the original concept of the limited-liability company. Trust was at the heart of the capitalist system. Agreements were sealed with a hand-shake. Directors were recognized as reliable stewards of the interests of others. But, with the passage of time, trust has been replaced by contract and litigation.

The first edition of this book called for governing bodies with people who could be trusted, people who understood their fiduciary responsibilities, people who could put the rights and needs of others ahead of their own. Critics argued that, desirable though this might be, such altruism is not feasible: successful organizations are run by people who are primarily acting in their own best interests. However, the best interests of people need not be solely power, personal aggrandizement, or greed. In the not-for-profit sector, and indeed in the corporate sector too, people do act responsibly in the interests of others, showing integrity, treating employees and other stakeholders fairly, and contributing to their community's and society's needs, being reliable stewards for the interest of others. Trust remains the foundation of corporate governance.

Case studies

 Case study 18.1   Explaining the structure and membership of the board

In 1998, after a successful career as a researcher at the Massachusetts Institute of Technology (MIT), Dr Jeremy Cunniford III[11] decided to branch out on his own to research, develop, and test batteries based on lithium ion technology, in which he had acquired an international reputation. He negotiated funding from a well known manufacturer of electronic equipment for an initial five years, on the understanding that patents derived from his work would belong to the sponsor, while Cunniford would receive funding for his research, a generous salary, a commission on related sales, and the promise of shares if the project succeeded and a business was floated on the stock market or sold.

Cunniford took a lease on a small research facility near Mountain View, in Silicon Valley, and recruited a few staff, including one of his former MIT colleagues, Bruce Lamb. Initially, the research group was funded through a subsidiary of the sponsor based in Switzerland. In 2003, after the initial five years, the project was reviewed. A number of patents had been obtained, at least one thought to have considerable potential. The sponsor seemed content with progress and what it described as 'the rate of burn' of project funding: as far as they were concerned this was research and development expenditure done on their behalf by an independent contractor in whom they had a lot of faith. Looking ahead for the next decade, the sponsor decided that the project should now be launched as a private company, Cunniford Batteries Inc., with 10% of the shares going to Cunniford, 5% to Lamb, and the balance to the sponsoring group.

Around 2008, it became apparent that a range of batteries, based on new technology developed by Cunniford Batteries, had made a breakthrough. Lithium ion batteries had become important in aviation electronics and the Cunniford design was more efficient, lighter, and less of a fire hazard than its competitors. The company now entered a manufacturing cycle, as well as continuing its research and development activities.

In 2013, the parent company decided that the time had come to launch its subsidiary, Cunniford Batteries, on the stock market, through an initial public offering. This generated additional funds to support the continuing growth of the company and provide a reward for over fifteen years of investment support. The sponsoring group would take 45% of the equity, Cunniford 10%, and Lamb 5%, with three significant institutional investors taking the remaining 40%. The sponsor group formalized an agreement to use Cunniford products and to continue to have access to Cunniford research.

The challenge

In 2014, the company received a proxy request from one of the institutional investors calling for 'an explanation of the structure and membership of the board and whether it was representative'. Jeremy Cunniford asked the corporate secretary to draft a paper for discussion at the next board meeting. What follows is that paper.

Cunniford Batteries Inc.
Board meeting 10 December 2014

Agendum 17. To discuss the future structure and membership of the board.

The company has received a formal request from a shareholder for 'an explanation of the structure and membership of the board and whether it was representative.' Jeremy has asked me to draft this paper to provide the basis for a board discussion prior to our response.

[11] The names and some of the details in this case have been disguised.

Reasonably, our major shareholders want to ensure that our governance structure is consistent with the planned growth of the company. Our corporate strategy looks to significant growth over the next five years, followed by accelerating expansion in the next five, despite the inevitable uncertainties and risks in our industry. We are also required by the Securities and Exchange Commission to explain our policies on nominating directors, including our attitudes towards diversity. Currently, we have no formal policy on such matters.

Current structure and membership of the board

Inevitably, our board reflects the evolution of the company, and currently consists of:

Executive directors

Jeremy Cunniford III (1966–) Chairman and CEO, PhD MIT 1996, senior researcher MIT 1996–1998, formed independent research team 1998
> Bruce Lamb (1970–) Chief Research Officer, PhD MIT 1998, joined Cunniford's research team 1998
> Peter Bennett (1964–) CPA, Chief Finance Officer

Independent outside directors

Robert T. Jones (1944–) CPA, retired senior partner from the sponsoring company's audit firm.
> Henry G. George (1950–) lawyer, nominated by the sponsoring company.
> Anthony P. Parker (1945–) financier, prominent in the IPO flotation, nominated by one of the institutional investors.

Size and structure of the board

Role and size of the board

The real challenge we face is deciding what we expect the board to do, and whether we have the appropriate mix of experience and skills. We have the statutory board committees in place—audit, remuneration, and nomination—and they fulfil their compliance and reporting duties. Main board meetings have tended to be opportunities for the chairman/CEO to report progress on research projects, and for the CFO to explain the financial situation. Annually, prior to the AGM we have a longer meeting to receive the auditor's report, to approve the published accounts, and to discuss and agree the budgets for the following year.

There are no legal restrictions on the number of directors on our board. We could add further members if that was felt appropriate, but a larger board would inevitably change the inter-personal dynamics. Large boards, with lots of independent directors, can be difficult to handle, with diverse views and potential domination by strong characters.

The shareholder's request for an explanation of the structure and membership of the board does not, necessarily, mean that they are looking for significant changes at board level. They may be seeking assurance that we have policies in place to review board membership that are consistent with our business strategy.

Executive directors

As our organization grows, it might be appropriate to identify potential main board directors from within top management. The nomination committee could propose a short-list reflecting the structure of the organization planned for the future. We might feel the need for board level representation from our growing product division. We could ensure that those selected are given appropriate responsibilities, experience, and training for directorship. They could be invited to attend board meetings as observers, for example.

Independent outside directors

If we add more executive directors, we would need to increase the number of outside directors to maintain the proportion of independent directors required by the listing rules. The nomination committee could also be asked to produce a short-list of candidates. At the moment, our outside directors are heavy on the financial and legal side. We might consider whether a technical expert in our field of research would be useful: perhaps from one of the universities we have contracted out research. Of course, we could continue to rely on the advice of consultants and other experts, as we do now, this means we can dispense with their services when no longer needed—not so easy with elected directors.

Chairman and CEO

Since the company was first incorporated, we have combined the roles of chairman of the board and chief executive of the company. This has worked well, with a single leader as its figurehead, directing the company's efforts. However, we may need to consider whether this is the best model for the longer term. Companies are coming under some pressure to split the roles, perhaps with a non-executive chairman. This issue may be concerning the shareholder who asked for information on board structure and membership.

On Board Diversity

The challenge to show that the board was 'representative' raises some interesting issues. Board diversity can have a number of meanings.

Diversity of skills, experience and knowledge

If a board is to work well together it needs to have a balance of skills, experience, and knowledge relevant to the company's business. Our leading executive directors are both research orientated, reflecting the company's origins. The nomination committee may want to consider whether this will be appropriate in the future. Similarly, the balance of skills among the outside directors is strongly in the financial and legal fields.

Age diversity

Our present executive directors are aged 44, 48, and 50; and continue to serve the company well. The outside directors are older being 64, 69, and 70. We may want to establish a policy for board renewal over time, bringing in younger people with fresh ideas and experiences, both as executive and no executive directors.

Gender diversity

Gender diversity is a goal being pursued by many governments, institutions, and interest groups to achieve better representation of women at board level. Some board members and investors have been unenthusiastic, calling for the best candidates irrespective of gender. despite the obvious missed talent and benefits of a female perspective. Overall, however, North American companies have appointed women to their boards in recent years: the Federal Reserve, the International Monetary Fund and General Motors are now all led by women.

   Our problem is that although there are women in middle management, we have no one in senior management who might be earmarked for executive directorship. Of course, there are experienced women we could consider as outside directors. We may want to include in our policy a statement about our commitment to appointing suitable women to the board.

Representative diversity

On a higher plane, some commentators suggest that boards should reflect the interests of all stakeholders affected by companies' actions—employees, suppliers, customers, for example—not just the shareholders. Some have even called for corporate boards to mirror the diversity of society. Our company is probably too small to consider such matters. However, we are already committed to being good corporate citizens and might consider creating a corporate social responsibility, sustainability, and environmental committee of representative employees, led by a director, to make recommendations to the board on these matters.

Proposal

That the nomination committee be asked to develop a policy on the structure and characteristics of the board and board members for further discussion.

Discussion questions

1. What are your reactions to the paper presented to the board?

2. Draft a policy statement that the nomination committee might propose to the main board.

References and further reading

Boubaker, Sabri, Bang Dang Nguyen and Duc Khuong Nguyen (eds) (2012) *Corporate Governance—recent developments and new trends*. Springer, Berlin.

Carter, C. B and J. W. Lorsch (2004) *Back to the Drawing Board*. Harvard Business School Press, Boston, MA.

Chew, Donald H. and Stuart L. Gillan (2005) *Corporate Governance at the Crossroads: A Book of Readings*. McGraw Hill, Boston, MA.

Clarke, Thomas and Douglas Branson (eds) (2012) *Handbook of Corporate Governance—The limitations in corporate governance best practice*. Sage, London/Thousand Oaks, CA.

Denis, Diane K and John J. McConnell (2004) 'International corporate governance'. *Journal of Corporate Finance*, Vol. 10, issue 5, November.

Ferguson, Niall (2011) *Civilization: The West and the Rest*. Penguin Press, New York.

Lipton M. (2007) *Some Thoughts for Boards of Directors*. Watchell, Lipton, Rosen & Katz, New York.

La Porte, Rafael and Florencio Lopez-de-Silaries (2003) 'Investor protection and corporate governance'. *Journal of Financial and Quantitative Analysis*, Vol. 38, Issue 1, March.

Lowery Kellan V. (2008) *Corporate Governance in the 21st Century*. Nova Science Publishers Inc., Hauppage, NY.

MacAvoy, P. W. and I. M. Millstein (2003) *The Recurrent Crisis in Corporate Governance*. Palgrave Macmillan, Basingstoke, UK.

Mayer, Colin (2011) *Firm Commitment—why the corporation is failing us and how to restore it*. Oxford University Press, Oxford.

Monks, Robert A. G. (2008) *Corpocracy: How CEOs and the Business Roundtable Hijacked the World's Greatest Wealth Machine—and How to Get it Back*. Wiley, Chichester, UK.

Multi-author (2000) Special issue on international corporate governance, *Journal of Financial Economics*, Vol. 58, Issue 1–2.

Nordberg, Donald (2011) *Corporate Governance: Principles and Issues*. Sage, London.

Semple, Kirsty (2014) *The ICSA Charities Handbook*. ICSA, London.

Sun, William, Jim Stewart, and David Pollard (2011) *Corporate Governance and the Global Financial Crisis*. Cambridge University Press, Cambridge.

Tricker, Bob (2011) 'Reinventing the limited liability company', *Corporate Governance: An International Review*, Vol. 19, No. 4, July.

Zattoni, Alessandro and William Judge (2012) *Corporate Governance and Initial Public Offerings*. Cambridge University Press, Cambridge.

Zinkin, John (2014) *Rebuilding Trust in Banks— the role of leadership and governance*. John Wiley, Singapore.

Projects and exercises

1. Consider a corporate entity with which you are familiar. In the next ten or twenty years, what forces for change could occur that would cause the organization to change its approach to governance?

2. What will corporate governance look like in ten or twenty years' time? Prepare a report/presentation outlining your expectations.

3. In 2008, all public companies in Norway were obliged by law to ensure that at least 40% of their board directors were women. Advance the arguments for and against such legislation in your country.

Self-test questions

1. Explain the paradox of the unitary board developed in the chapter.

2. What did the NYSE-sponsored Commission on Corporate Governance have to say about the NYSE requirements on independent directors?

3. What is the schism that has appeared between American and British concepts of corporate governance?

4. What is the key question in deciding whether the chief executive should also be chairman of the board?

5. What is the first step to better corporate governance according to the CSIA?

6. What evidence suggests that society is no longer satisfied with corporate behaviour?

7. What might be some of the interesting and more important developments in the future that could affect corporate governance?

8. What might board-level information systems offer directors in the future?

Corporate Governance Codes around the World

For access to codes go to: www.ecgi.org/codes/all_codes.php

International

ICGN Global Governance Principles, 2014.

The Practice of Corporate Governance in Microfinance Institutions, 2012.

EFAMA Code for External Governance, April 2011.

EcoDa Corporate Governance Guidance and Principles for Unlisted Companies in Europe, March 2010.

Sovereign Wealth Funds: Generally Accepted Principles and Practices (GAPP)—Santiago Principles, October 2008.

United Nations Guidance on Good Practices in Corporate Governance Disclosure, 2006.

OECD Guidelines on Corporate Governance of State-Owned Enterprises, September 2005.

The Auditor's Procedures in Response to Assessed Risk, International Standard on Auditing (#330), International Federation of Accountants (IFAC), New York, 2005.

Understanding the Entity and its Environment and Assessing the Risks of Material Mis-statement, International Standard on Auditing (#315), International Federation of Accountants (IFAC), New York, 2005.

Communication of Auditing Matters with those charged with Governance, International Standard on Auditing (#260), International Federation of Accountants (IFAC), New York, 2005.

Principles of Corporate Governance, Organisation for Economic Co-operation and Development (OECD), Paris, 1999 and 2004.

Principles of Auditor Independence and the Role of Corporate Governance in Monitoring an Auditor's Independence, International Organization of Securities Commissions (IOSCO), Madrid, 2002.

Corporate Governance: A Framework for Implementation (Iskander and Chamlou), World Bank, Washington, DC, 2000.

Africa

Algeria

Code Algérian de Gouvernance d'Entreprise, 2009.

Egypt

Code of Corporate Governance for Listed Companies, February 2011.

Ghana

Corporate Governance Guidelines on Best Practices, 2010.

Kenya

Draft Code of Corporate Governance Practices for Public Listed Companies in Kenya, May 2014.

Principles for Corporate Governance in Kenya, Private Sector Corporate Governance Trust, 2002.

Sample Code of Best Practice for Corporate Governance, Private Sector Corporate Governance Trust, 2002.

Malawi

The Malawi Code II: Code of Best Practice for Corporate Governance in Malawi, June 2010.

Morocco

Code Marocain de Bonnes Pratiques de Gouvernance des Etablissements et Entreprises Publics (EEP), February 2011.

Code Spécifique de Bonnes Pratiques de Gouvernance des PME et Entreprises Familiales, October 2008.

Moroccan Code of Good Corporate Governance Practices, March 2008.

Nigeria

Code of Corporate Governance for Banks and Discount Houses in Nigeria, and Guidelines for Whistle Blowing in the Nigerian Banking Industry, May 2014.

Code of Corporate Governance, January 2011.

Code of Corporate Governance for Banks in Nigeria Post Consolidation, March 2006.

Code of Corporate Governance in Nigeria, October 2003.

South Africa

Draft Code for Responsible Investing by Institutional Investors in South Africa, September 2010.

King III Code of Governance for South Africa 2009.

King II Report on Corporate Governance for South Africa, Institute of Directors in South Africa, 2002.

King I Report on Corporate Governance in South Africa, Institute of Directors in South Africa, 1994.

Tunisia

Guide de Bonnes Pratiques de Gouvernance des Entreprises Tunisiennes, 2008.

Asia

Armenia

Code of Corporate Governance of the Republic of Armenia, December 2010.

Australia

Corporate Governance Principles and Recommendations (3rd edition), March 2014.
Governance for Good: The ACNC's guide for charity board members, 2013.
Corporate Governance Principles and Recommendations, June 2010.
Revised Corporate Governance Principles and Recommendations, August 2007.
Principles of Good Corporate Governance and Best Practice Recommendations, Australian Stock Market ASX Corporate Governance Council, March 2003.
Corporate Governance, Volume One: In Principle, Audit Office of New South Wales, Sydney, June 1997.
Corporate Governance, Volume Two: In Practice Audit Office of New South Wales, Sydney, June 1997.
Bosch Report, Australian Financial Institutions, Sydney, 1995.
Strictly Boardroom, Fred Hilmer, InfoAustralia, 1992.

Azerbaijan

Azerbaijan Corporate Governance Standards, 2011.

Bangladesh

The Code of Corporate Governance for Bangladesh, Bangladesh Enterprise Institute, March 2004.

China, People's Republic of

Code of Corporate Governance, CSRC, 2004.
The Code of Corporate Guidance for Listed Companies in China, CSRC, 2001.

Hong Kong

Consultation Conclusions on Review of the Corporate Governance Code and Associated Listing Rules, October 2011.
Hong Kong Stock Exchange and Hong Kong Institute of Directors Joint Statement on Explanations Required on a Director's Resignation, May 2007.
Hong Kong Code on Corporate Governance, Stock Exchange of Hong Kong, November 2004.
Model Code for Securities Transactions by Directors of Listed Companies: Basic Principles, Hong Kong Stock Exchange, 2001.
Corporate Governance Disclosure in Annual Reports, Hong Kong Society of Accountants, 2001.
Code of Best Practice, Hong Kong Stock Exchange, 1999.

India

Corporate Governance Voluntary Guidelines, 2009.
Report of the Kumar Mangalam Birla Committee on Corporate Governance, Securities and Exchange Board of India, 2000.
Desirable Corporate Governance in India: A Code, Confederation of Indian Industry, 1998.

Indonesia

Code of Good Corporate Governance, January 2007.
Code for Good Corporate Governance, National Committee on Corporate Governance, 2001.
Code for Good Corporate Governance, National Committee on Corporate Governance, 2000.

Japan

Principles for Responsible Institutional Investors (Japan's Stewardship Code), February 2014.
Principles of Corporate Governance for Listed Companies, December 2009.
Principles of Corporate Governance for Listed Companies, Tokyo Stock Exchange, April 2004.
Revised Corporate Governance Principles, Japan Corporate Governance Forum, October 2001.
Corporate Governance Principles: A Japanese View, Committee of the Corporate Governance Forum of Japan, Tokyo, October 1997.
Urgent Recommendations Concerning Corporate Governance, Japan Federation of Economic Organisations (Keidanen), September 1997.

Malaysia

Malaysian Code for Institutional Investors, June 2014.
Malaysian Code on Corporate Governance, March 2012.
Malaysian Code on Corporate Governance, October 2007.
Malaysian Code on Corporate Governance, Securities Commission Malaysia, March 2000.

Maldives

Corporate Governance Code, February 2012.

Mauritius

Guideline on Corporate Governance, August 2012.
The Report on Corporate Governance for Mauritius, April 2004.

Mongolia

Corporate Governance Code of Mongolia, 2007.

New Zealand

Corporate Governance in New Zealand: Principles and Guidelines, The New Zealand Securities Commission, Wellington, February/March 2004.
Corporate Governance Principles, New Zealand Securities Commission, November 2003.

Pakistan

Code of Corporate Governance, April 2012.
Code of Corporate Governance (Revised), Securities and Exchange Commission of Pakistan, March 2002.
Stock Exchange Code of Corporate Governance, Securities and Exchange Commission of Pakistan, March 2002.

Philippines

Revised Code of Corporate Governance, July 2009.
Code of Corporate Governance, 2002.
Code of Proper Practices for Directors, Institute of Corporate Directors, March 2000.

Singapore

Code of Corporate Governance, May 2012.
Guidelines on Corporate Governance for Banks, Financial Holding Companies and Direct Insurers which are incorporated in Singapore, December 2010.
The Monetary Authority of Singapore and the Singapore Stock Exchange Joint Statement Dissolving the Council of Corporate Disclosure and Governance, and Jointly Assuming Responsibility for Overseeing Corporate Governance of Listed Companies, May 2007.
Code of Corporate Governance, Council on Corporate Disclosure and Governance, July 2005.
Revisions to the Code of Corporate Governance, December 2004.
Code of Corporate Governance, March 2001.

South Korea

Code of Best Practices for Corporate Governance, February 2003.
Code of Best Practice for Corporate Governance, Committee on Corporate Governance, September 1999.

Sri Lanka

Best Practice on Corporate Governance, July 2008.

Taiwan

Corporate Governance Best-Practice Principles for TSE/GTSM Listed Companies, December 2010.
Corporate Governance in Taiwan, May 2007.
Taiwan Corporate Governance Best-Practice Principles, Taiwan Stock Exchange: GreTai Securities Market, 2002.

Thailand

The Principles of Good Corporate Governance for Listed Companies, March 2006.
Code of Best Practice for Directors of Listed Companies, Stock Exchange of Thailand, October 2002.
Best Practice Guidelines for Audit Committee, Stock Exchange of Thailand, June 1999.
The Code of Best Practice for Directors of Listed Companies, Stock Exchange of Thailand, January 1998.

Europe

Albania

Corporate Governance Code for Unlisted Joint-Stock Companies in Albania, April 2008.

Croatia

Corporate Governance Code, 2010.
Code of Corporate Governance, 2009.

Cyprus

Corporate Governance Code (3rd edition) (Amended), September 2012.
Corporate Governance Code (3rd edition), September 2009.
Cyprus Corporate Governance Code, March 2006.

Czech Republic

Corporate Governance Code based on OECD Principles, June 2004.

Denmark

Recommendations on Corporate Governance (Updated), May 2014.
Recommendations on Corporate Governance, May 2013.
Recommendations on Corporate Governance, August 2011.
Recommendations on Corporate Governance, April 2010.

European Union

EFAMA Code for External Governance, April 2011.
ecoDa Corporate Governance Guidance and Principles for Unlisted Companies in Europe, March 2010.
European Corporate Governance Forum Created to Encourage Coordination and Convergence of National Codes, June 2007.
Directive on the Formation of Public Companies and the Maintenance and Alteration of their Capital, September 2006.
Directive on Cross-Border Mergers, October 2005.
Discussion paper on the Financial Reporting and Auditing Aspects of Corporate Governance, Féderation des Experts Comptables Européens, 2003.
Final Report of High Level Group of Company Law Experts, chair Jaap Winter, Corporate Governance and the Modernisation of European Company Law, November 2002.
Euroshareholders Corporate Governance Guidelines, the European Shareholders Group, February 2002.
Recommendations on Auditor Independence, EU, 2002.
Statute for a European Company, October 2001.
Principles and Recommendations, European Association of Securities Dealers (now APCIMS-EADS) Corporate Governance Committee EASD, May 2000.
Corporate Governance Guidelines 2000, European Shareholders Group (Euroshareholders), February 2000.
Sound Business Standards and Corporate Practices: A Set of Guidelines, European Bank for Reconstruction and Development (EBRD), September 1997.
The Role, Position, and Liability of the Statutory Auditor in Europe, EU Commission, 1996.
Report of Centre for European Studies Working Party, CEPS, Brussels, 1995.

Austria

Austrian Code of Corporate Governance, July 2012.
Austrian Code of Corporate Governance, January 2012.

Austrian Code of Corporate Governance, January 2009.

Austrian Code of Corporate Governance, Austrian Working Group on Corporate Governance, January 2006 amended 2007.

Austrian Code of Corporate Governance, Austrian Working Group on Corporate Governance, February 2005.

Austrian Code of Corporate Governance, Austrian Working Group on Corporate Governance, November 2002.

Baltic States

Guidance on the Governance of Government-owned Enterprises, June 2010.

Belgium

The 2009 Code on Corporate Governance, March 2009 (draft 2008).

Code Buysse: Corporate Governance for Non-listed Companies, Commission Corporate Governance pour les Entreprises non Cotées, September 2005.

Belgian Corporate Governance Code, Corporate Governance Committee, December 2004.

Corporate Governance for Belgian Listed Companies (The Cardon Report), Belgian Corporate Governance Commission, February 2004.

Director's Charter, Directors Foundation (Fondation des Administrateurs), January 2000.

Guidelines on Corporate Governance Reporting, La Commission Bancaire et Financière, November 1999.

Commission Bancaire et Financière, December 1998.

Corporate Governance: Recommendations, Federation of Belgian Enterprises, January 1998.

Bosnia Herzegovina

Standards of Corporate Governance, October 2011.

Corporate Governance Code, March 2009.

The Standards of Corporate Governance, January 2006.

Bulgaria

Bulgarian Code for Corporate Governance, February 2012.

Bulgarian National Code for Corporate Governance, October 2007.

Cyprus

Cyprus Corporate Governance Code (2nd edition), Cyprus Stock Exchange, March 2006.

Corporate Governance Code, Cyprus Stock Exchange, September 2002.

Czech Republic

Revised Corporate Governance Code based on the OECD Principles, Czech Securities Commission, June 2004.

Corporate Governance Code based on the OECD Principles, Czech Securities Commission, February 2001.

Denmark

Revised Recommendations for Corporate Governance in Denmark, Copenhagen Stock Exchange Committee on Corporate Governance, August 2005.

Report on Corporate Governance in Denmark, Copenhagen Stock Exchange Committee on Corporate Governance, December 2003.

Nørby Committee's Report on Corporate Governance in Denmark, Copenhagen Stock Exchange, December 2001.

Guidelines on Good Management of a Listed Company (Corporate Governance), Danish Shareholders Association, February 2000.

Estonia

Corporate Governance Recommendations, Financial Supervision Authority and Tallinn Stock Exchange, January 2006.

Finland

Finnish Corporate Governance Code, June 2010.

Proposals for Finnish Corporate Governance Code, October 2008 and 2006.

Improving Corporate Governance of Unlisted Companies, Central Chamber of Commerce of Finland, January 2006.

Corporate Governance Recommendations for Listed Companies, HEX plc, Central Chamber of Commerce of Finland, Confederation of Finnish Industry and Employers. December 2003.

France

AFEP-MEDEF Corporate governance code of listed corporations, June 2013.

Recommendations on Corporate Governance, March 2011 and 2010.

Corporate Governance Code of Listed Companies, April 2010 and 2008.

Code de Gouvernement d'Entreprise pour les Valeurs Moyennes et Petites, December 2009.

Recommandations sur le Gouvernement d'Entreprise, L'Association Française de la Gestion Financière (AFG), March 2004.

The Corporate Governance of Listed Corporations, MEDEF and Association Française des Entreprises Privées (AFEP), October 2003.

Promoting Better Corporate Governance in Listed Companies, AFEP-AGREF/MEDEF September 2002.

Viénot II Report, Mouvement des Entreprises de France (MEDEF) [formerly CNPF] and Association Française des Enterprises Privees (AFEP), July 1999.

Recommendations on Corporate Governance, AFG-ASFFI Commission on Corporate Governance, June 1998.

Viénot I Report, Conseil National du Patronat Français (CNPF) Association Française des Entreprises Privees (AFEP), June 1995.

Georgia

Corporate Governance Code for Commercial Banks, September 2009.

Germany

German Corporate Governance Code (Amended), May 2013.

German Corporate Governance Code (Amended), May 2012.

German Corporate Governance Code, amended May 2010, and 2007/8/9.

Amendment to the German Corporate Governance Code (The Cromme Code), Government Commission German Corporate Governance Code, June 2005.

Corporate Governance Code for Asset Management Companies, The German Working Group on Corporate Governance for Asset Managers, April 2005.

Amendment to the German Corporate Governance Code (The Cromme Code), Government Commission German Corporate Governance Code, May 2003.

The German Corporate Governance Code (The Cromme Code), German Corporate Governance Kodex, February 2002 (Government Commission amendment 2003).

Baums Commission Report, Bericht der Regierungskommission Corporate Governance, July 2001.

German Code of Corporate Governance, Berliner Initiativkreis, June 2000.

Corporate Governance Rules for German Quoted Companies, German Panel on Corporate Governance, January 2000.

DSW Guidelines, Deutsche Schutzvereinigung für Wertpapierbesitz e.V., June 1998.

Gesetz zur Kontrolle und Transparenz im Unternehmensbereich (KonTraG), Deutsche Bundestag, German Ministry of Justice, March 1998.

Greece

Hellenic Corporate Governance Code for Listed Companies, October 2013.

SEV Corporate Governance Code for Listed Companies, March 2011.

Principles of Corporate Governance, 24 July 2001.

Principles on Corporate Governance in Greece: Recommendations for its Competitive Transformation, Committee on Corporate Governance in Greece (under the coordination of the Capital Market Commission), October 1999.

Guernsey

GFSC Finance Sector Code of Corporate Governance, September 2011.

Hungary

Corporate Governance Recommendations, November 2012.

Corporate Governance Recommendations, March 2008.

Corporate Governance Recommendations, Budapest Stock Exchange, February 2002.

Iceland

Guidelines on Corporate Governance (4th edition), December 2012.

Corporate Governance Guidelines, June 2009.

Guidelines on Corporate Governance, Iceland Stock Exchange (ICEX), Iceland Chamber of Commerce,

Confederation of Icelandic Employers, March 2004; 2nd edn, 2005.

Ireland

Corporate Governance Code for Credit Institutions and Insurance Undertakings, December 2013.

Code of Practice for Good Governance of Community, Voluntary and Charitable Organisations in Ireland, March 2012.

Corporate Governance Code for Collective Investment Schemes and Management Companies, December 2011.

Corporate Governance Code for Irish Domiciled Collective Investment Schemes, September 2010.

Code of Corporate Governance for Independent Directors of Investment Funds, January 2010.

Corporate Governance Code for Credit Institutions and Insurance Undertakings, 2010.

Irish Development NGOs Code of Corporate Governance, 2008.

Corporate Governance for Reinsurance Undertakings, December 2007.

Corporate Governance, Share Option and Other Incentive Schemes, Irish Association of Investment Managers, March 1999.

Italy

Codice di Autodisciplina 2014, July 2014.

Codice di Autodisciplina, December 2011.

New Regulation on Banks' Organisation and Corporate Governance, 2008.

Corporate Governance Code (Codice di Autodisciplina), Comitato per la Corporate Governance, Borsa Italiana, March 2006.

Handbook on Corporate Governance Reports, Associazione fra le società italiane per azioni (Assonime), February 2004.

Corporate Governance Code (il Codice di Autodisciplina delle società quotate rivisitato), Committee for the Corporate Governance of Listed Companies, Borsa Italiana, July 2002.

Report and Code of Conduct (The Preda Report), Committee for the Corporate Governance of Listed Companies, Borsa Italiana, October 1999.

Testo Unico sulle disposizioni in materia di intermediazione, based on Draghi Proposals, February 1998.

Kazakhstan

Code on Corporate Governance, July 2007.

Latvia

Principles of Corporate Governance and Recommendations on their Implementation, May 2010.

Principles of Corporate Governance and Recommendations on their Implementation, Riga Stock Exchange, December 2005.

Lithuania

The Corporate Governance Code for the Companies Listed on NASDAQ OMX Vilnius, January 2010.

Corporate Governance Code for the Companies listed on the National Stock Exchange of Lithuania, National Stock Exchange of Lithuania, April 2003.

Luxembourg

ALFI Code of Conduct for Luxembourg Investment Funds, June 2013.

The X Principles of Corporate Governance of the Luxembourg Stock Exchange (3rd edition), May 2013.

The Ten Principles of Corporate Governance of the Luxembourg Stock Exchange, September 2009 (first published April 2006).

Macedonia

Corporate Governance Code for Companies Listed on the Macedonian Stock Exchange, June 2006.

White Paper on Corporate Governance in South-Eastern Europe, June 2003.

Malta

Principles of Good Corporate Governance: Revised Code for Issuers of Listed Securities, Malta Financial Services Authority (MFSA), November 2005.

Principles of Good Corporate Governance for Public Interest Companies, MFSA, November 2005.

Principles of Good Corporate Governance, Malta Stock Exchange, October 2001.

Moldova

Code of Corporate Governance, June 2007.

Montenegro

Corporate Governance Code in Montenegro, May 2009.

The Netherlands

Governance Principles for Insurance Companies, December 2010.

Dutch Corporate Governance Code, December 2008.

Handbook of Corporate Governance, Corporate Governance Research Foundation for Pensionfunds (SCGOP), 2004.

The Dutch Corporate Governance Code (the Tabaksblat Code), Corporate Governance Committee, December 2003.

Handbook of Corporate Governance, The Foundation for Corporate Governance Research for Pension Funds (Stichting Corporate Governance Onderzoek voor Pensioenfondsen: SCGOP), August 2001.

Government Governance; Corporate Governance in the Public Sector, Why and How? The Netherlands Ministry of Finance Government Audit Policy Directorate (DAR), November 2000.

Peters Report: Corporate Governance in the Netherlands, Committee on Corporate Governance, July 1997.

Norway

The Norwegian Code of Practice for Corporate Governance, 23 October 2012 (earlier editions 2011, 2010, 2009, 2007, 2006, 2005, 2004).

Poland

Code of Best Practice for WSE Listed Companies, November 2012.

Code of Best Practice for WSE Listed Companies, May 2010.

Code of Best Practice for WSE Listed Companies, July 2007.

Best Practices in Public Companies, 2005 (draft 2004).

Best Practices in Public Companies in 2002, The Best Practices Committee at Corporate Governance Forum, July 2002.

The Corporate Governance Code for Polish Listed Companies (The Gdansk Code), The Polish Corporate Governance Forum, June 2002.

Portugal

Código de Governo das sociedades, January 2014.

CMVM Corporate Governance Code 2013 (Recommendations), October 2013.

Corporate Governance Code 2012.

CMVM Corporate Governance Code, 2010 (original code 2007).

White Book on Corporate Governance in Portugal, Instituto Português de Corporate Governance, February 2006.

Recommendations on Corporate Governance, Comissão do Mercado de Valores Mobiliários (CMVM), November 2003.

Recommendations on Corporate Governance, Comissão do Mercado de Valores Mobiliários (CNMV), November 1999.

Romania

Bucharest Stock Exchange Corporate Governance Code, January 2009.

Corporate Governance Code in Romania, International Center for Entrepreneurial Studies, University of Bucharest, 24 June 2000.

Russia

Russian Code of Corporate Governance (2014), April 2014.

The Russian Code of Corporate Conduct, April 2002.

Serbia

Corporate Governance Code of the Belgrade Stock Exchange, July 2008.

Slovakia

Corporate Governance Code for Slovakia, January 2008.

Corporate Governance Code (based on the OECD Principles), Bratislava Stock Exchange, September 2002.

Slovenia

Corporate Governance Code, December 2009 (earlier version 2007).

Corporate Governance Code, Ljubljana Stock Exchange, Managers' Association of Slovenia, Association of the Supervisory Board Members of Slovenia, December 2005.

Corporate Governance Code, Ljubljana Stock Exchange, Association of Supervisory Board Members of Slovenia, Managers' Association of Slovenia, March 2004.

Spain

Código Unificado de buen gobierno de las sociedades cotizadas, June 2013.

Unified Good Governance Code, May 2006.

Code of Ethics for Companies, Instituto de Consejeros-Administradores, April 2006.

Draft Unified Code of Recommendations for the Good Governance, Comision Nacional del Mercado de Valores (CNMV), January 2006.

IC-A: Principles of Good Corporate Governance, Instituto de Consejeros-Administradores, December 2004.

Decálogo del Directivo, Instituto Español de Analistas Financieros (IEAF), May 2004.

The Aldama Report, Special Commission, January 2003.

Código de Buen Gobierno, Special Commission, February 1998.

Círculo de Empresarios, October 1996.

Sweden

The Swedish Code of Corporate Governance, January 2010 (previously May 2008 and September 2007).

Swedish Code of Corporate Governance Report of the Code Group, The Codes Group, December 2004.

Corporate Governance Policy, The Swedish Industry and Commerce Stock Exchange Committee (Naringslivets Borskommitte: NBK), October 2001.

Swedish Academy of Directors, Sveriges Aktiesparares Riksförbund (The Swedish Shareholders' Association), 1994.

Switzerland

Swiss Code of Best Practice for Corporate Governance, February 2008.

Governance in Family Firms, December 2006.

Swiss Code of Best Practice for Corporate Governance, Swiss Business Federation, June 2002.

Corporate Governance Directive, SWX Swiss Exchange, June 2002.

Turkey

Corporate Governance Principles, The Capital Markets Board of Turkey, February 2005 (original June 2003).

Ukraine

Ukrainian Corporate Governance Principles, Ukrainian Securities Commission, June 2003.

United Kingdom

(See the list of corporate governance reports and the UK Corporate Governance Code listed in Chapter 5.)

Middle East

Bahrain

Corporate Governance Code of the Kingdom of Bahrain, March 2010.

Israel

The Goshen Report, December 2006.

Jordan

Jordanian Corporate Governance Code, 2012.

Corporate Governance Code for Shareholding Companies Listed on the Amman Stock Exchange, 2008.

Corporate Governance Code for Banks in Jordan, 2007.

Lebanon

Corporate Governance Guidelines for Listed Companies, 2010.

Oman

Code of Corporate Governance for Public Listed Companies, June 2002.

Qatar

Corporate Governance Code for Companies listed in markets regulated by the Qatar Financial Markets Authority, January 2009.

Saudi Arabia

Corporate Governance Regulations in the Kingdom of Saudi Arabia, March 2010.

Corporate Governance Regulations in the Kingdom of Saudi Arabia, November 2006.

United Arab Emirates

Corporate Governance Code for Small and Medium Enterprises Dubai, September 2011.

Ministerial Resolution No. (518) of 2009 Concerning Governance Rules and Corporate Discipline Standards, October 2009.

Corporate Governance Code for Joint-Stock Companies, April 2007.

Yemen

Guidelines on Corporate Governance, March 2010.

North America

Canada

Corporate Governance Guideline, January 2013.

Corporate Governance: Guide to Good Disclosure, January 2006.

Corporate Governance: Guide to Good Disclosure, Toronto Stock Exchange, December 2003.

Beyond Compliance: Building a Governance Culture (Saucier Report), Joint Committee on Corporate Governance, November 2001.

Five Years to the *Dey*, Toronto Stock Exchange and Institute of Corporate Directors, June 1999 [Mr Dey was the author of the 1994 report].

Building on Strength: Improving Governance and Accountability in Canada's Voluntary Sector, Panel for Accountability and Governance in the Voluntary Sector, February 1999.

Where Were the Directors? Guidelines for Improved Corporate Governance in Canada (Dey Report), The Toronto Stock Exchange, December 1994.

Mexico

Código de Mejores Prácticas Corporativas, 2010 (first published 1999).

United States

Full CII Corporate Governance Policies, September 2013.

Principles of Corporate Governance 2012, March 2012.

Report of the New York Stock Exchange Commission on Corporate Governance, September 2010.

Key Agreed Principles to Strengthen Corporate Governance for US Publicly Traded Companies, October 2008.

TIAA–CREF Policy Statement on Corporate Governance, March 2007.

Asset Manager Code of Professional Conduct, Centre for Financial Market Integrity, November 2004.

Enterprise Risk Management: Integrated Framework, Committee of Sponsoring Organizations of the Treadway Commission, New York, 2004.

Amendments to the Corporate Governance Rules, NYSE, August 2004.

Corporate Governance Rules, New York Stock Exchange, November 2003.

Commission on Public Trust and Private Enterprise Findings and Recommendations: Part 2: Corporate Governance, the Conference Board, New York, 2003.

Sarbanes-Oxley Act of 2002.

Corporate Governance Rule Proposals, New York Stock Exchange, August 2002.

Principles of Corporate Governance, the Business Roundtable, May 2002.

Core Policies, Principles of Corporate Governance: Analysis and Recommendations, Council of Institutional Investors, 2002.

General Principles, Positions and Explanatory Notes, American Law Institute, March 2002.

Blue Ribbon Report on Director Professionalism, National Association of Corporate Directors, 2001.

Blue Ribbon Report on Improving the Effectiveness of Corporate Audit Committees, New York Stock Exchange and National Association of Securities Dealers, New York, 1999.

Statement on Corporate Governance, The Business Roundtable, September 1997.

Internal Control Integrated Framework (The COSO Report), Committee of Sponsoring Organizations of the Treadway Commission, American Institute of Certified Public Accountants, New York, 1992.

Report on the National Commission of Fraudulent Reporting (The Treadway Report), American Institute of Certified Public Accountants, New York, 1987.

Commission on Auditors' Responsibilities (The Cohen Commission Report), American Institute of Certified Public Accountants, New York, 1978.

South America

Latin American Corporate Governance, Latin America Corporate Governance Roundtable White Paper, 2003.

Argentina

Código de Mejores Prácticas de Gobierno de las Organizaciones para la República Argentina, January 2004.

Barbados

Corporate Governance Guideline, February 2013.

Brazil

Code of Best Practice of Corporate Governance (4th edition), September 2009.

Code of Best Practice of Corporate Governance, Instituto Brasileiro de Governança Corporativa (IBGC), March 2004.

Recomendações sobre Governança Corporativa, Comissão de Valores Mobiliários, June 2002.

Code of Best Practice of Corporate Governance, Instituto Brasileiro de Governança Corporativa (IBGC), May 1999.

Colombia

Colombian Guide of Corporate Governance for Closed Societies and Family Firms, September 2009.

Colombian Code of Best Corporate Practice, 2007.

Jamaica

Code of Corporate Governance, Private Sector Organization of Jamaica, October 2006 (drafts 2005).

Netherlands Antilles

Corporate Governance: Summary of Best Practice Guidelines, November 2006.

Peru

Principios de Buen Gobierno para las Sociedades Peruanas, July 2002.

Trinidad and Tobago

Trinidad and Tobago Corporate Governance Code 2013, November 2013.

Corporate Governance Guideline, Central Bank of Trinidad and Tobago, May 2007 (original May 2006).

Answers to End-of-Chapter Self-Test Questions

PART ONE Principles

Chapter 1 Corporate Governance: A subject whose time has come

1. Corporate governance is about the exercise of power over corporate entities.

2. The key concept of a joint-stock, limited-liability company, separate from the owners, has many of the legal property rights of a real person—to contract, to sue and be sued, to own property, and to employ. The company has a life of its own, giving continuity beyond the life of its founders, who could transfer their shares in the company. Crucially, the owners' liability for the company's debts is limited to their equity investment.

3. Ownership is the basis of power over the joint-stock, limited-liability company.

4. Berle and Means (1932) drew attention to the growing separation of power between the executive management of major public companies and their increasingly diverse and remote shareholders.

5. The Bullock Report—*The Report of the Committee of Inquiry on Industrial Democracy* (1977)—proposed a continuation of the unitary board, but with worker representative directors.

6. *The Corporate Report* (1975) called for all economic entities to report publicly and to accept accountability to all those whose interests were affected by the directors' decisions.

7. In Australia, Alan Bond, Laurie Connell of Rothwells, and the Girvan Corporation; in Japan, Nomura Securities and The Recruit Corporation; in the United States, Ivan Boesky, Michael Levine, and Michael Milken of Drexal, Burnham, and Lambert; in the United Kingdom, the Guinness cases and Robert Maxwell's companies.

8. The first report on corporate governance in 1992 came from Sir Adrian Cadbury in the United Kingdom and was on the financial aspects of corporate governance. The committee he chaired was set up in response to various company collapses. The report called for:
   - wider use of independent outside, non-executive directors;
   - audit committees as a bridge between board and external auditor;
   - separation of the roles of chairman of the board and chief executive.

9. Bear Stearns, Fannie Mae, and Freddie Mac, AIG (American International Group), and Lehman Brothers.

10. The Hilmer report argued that governance is about performance as well as conformance: 'the board's key role is to ensure that corporate management is continuously and effectively striving for above-average performance, taking account of risk . . . (although) this is not to deny the board's additional role with respect to shareholder protection.'

Chapter 2 Governance and Management

1. To define the rights and duties of members, and to lay down the rules about the way it is to be governed.

2. A private company may not offer its shares for sale to the general public; a public company can.

3. Refer to detailed explanations in the text and the 'governance circle and management triangle' model.

4. Performance (strategy formulation and policy-making) and conformance (supervising executive activities and accountability).

5. See Figure 2.8 and related text in the chapter.

6. Companies House: www.companieshouse.co.uk

7. The great 1929 financial crash in the United States. The mission of the US Securities and Exchange Commission is to protect investors, to maintain fair, orderly, and efficient markets, and to facilitate capital formation. Among the key participants in the securities world that the SEC oversees are securities exchanges, securities brokers and dealers, investment advisers, and mutual funds.

8. This structure can be found in many small, family firms and start-up businesses, where the company has not reached the stage at which it needs non-executive directors. The all-executive director board is also found frequently in the board structures of subsidiary companies operating in corporate groups.

9. The typical board of a company listed in the United States has one or two executive directors—the chairman/CEO, the chief operating officer, and perhaps the chief finance officer—with three or four times that number of independent outside directors.

10. In the two-tier board structure, the supervisory board, which consists entirely of non-executive

outside members, oversees the work of the executives in the management board. In practice, members of the executive board attend meetings of the supervisory board, but have no vote. The executive members present their strategies, management plans, and budgets to the supervisory board for comment and approval. If necessary, the supervisory board refers matters back to the executives for further consideration. The supervisory board can then review and assess subsequent managerial performance. The power of the supervisory board lies in its ability to appoint to and remove members from the executive board.

Chapter 3 Theories and Philosophies of Corporate Governance

1. Agency theory is based on the premise that a director will maximize his or her own personal utility and cannot be expected to act in the best interests of the shareholder. Stewardship theory follows the legal perspective that directors can be trusted to fulfil their fiduciary duty to shareholders.
2. Stewardship theory follows the legal requirement for directors to act solely in the interests of the shareholders. Stakeholder philosophy believes that companies should be accountable to a wide range of stakeholders affected by its activities.

Chapter 4 The Governance Partnership: Investors, companies, and directors

1. Shareholder rights are determined by the company's articles of association and company law, predominantly the Companies Acts.
2. Having elected directors to govern the company, shareholders do not have the right to be involved in the day-to-day management of the business, nor to inspect company records or management accounts.
3. The company must answer any questions relating to the business put by a member, unless it can be shown that it is not in the interests of the company or the question has already been answered on the company's website. Shareholders have the right to have matters included on the agenda of the annual general meeting, if they hold 5% of the voting shares or have the support of 100 members entitled to vote.
4. Institutional investors should have a clear policy on voting and disclosure of their voting activity. They should seek to vote all shares held. They should not automatically support the board. If they have been unable to reach a satisfactory outcome through active dialogue, they should register an abstention or vote against the resolution.
5. An independent non-executive director (INED) is a director with no affiliation or other relationship with the company, other than the directorship,

that could affect, or be seen to affect, the exercise of objective, independent judgement. A connected non-executive director (CNED) is an outside director who does have some relationship with the company.
6. An outside director is another word for non-executive director. Mainly used in the United States, it is often taken to refer to an independent director. A shadow director is a person who, although not formally a member of a board, is able to exert pressure on the decisions of that board.
7. Yes. They are sometimes referred to as associate directors.
8. Chairman of the board of directors.
9. There are different perspectives. Those in favour point out the years of experience, knowledge, and connections that the retiring top executive could bring to the board as its chair—experience that would otherwise be lost. Those questioning the move point out potential difficulties for the new CEO. It is a rare person, having been a successful CEO, who can pass on the managerial reins to a new CEO without interfering in the day-to-day running of the business. Some codes of good practice in corporate governance oppose the appointment of a retiring CEO to the chair of that company's board.
10. No. In most jurisdictions and consistent with most corporate constitutions, the roles and responsibilities of all directors are the same.

Chapter 5 The Regulatory Framework

1. The Cadbury Report called for:
   - the wider use of independent non-executive directors;
   - the introduction of an audit committee of the board with a minimum of three non-executive—directors with a majority of them independent;
   - the division of responsibilities between the chairman of the board and the chief executive—but, should the roles be combined, the board should have a strong independent element;
   - the use of a remuneration committee of the board to oversee executive rewards;
   - the introduction of a nomination committee with independent directors to propose new board members; and
   - adherence to a detailed code of best practice.
2. a. On professional development.
   - All directors should receive induction training.
   - All directors should have regular updates on relevant skills, knowledge, and familiarity with the company.
   b. On boards' performance evaluation
   - Boards should undertake an annual evaluation of their own performance.

- There should also be an annual assessment of the performance of individual directors and of the main board committees.

3. The OECD has produced sets of principles that are intended to assist governments in their efforts to evaluate and improve the legal, international, and regulatory framework for corporate governance in their countries, and to provide guidance and suggestions to stock exchanges, investors, corporations, and others that have a role in the process of developing good corporate governance.

4. Companies should manage effectively relationships with their employees, suppliers, and customers, and with others who have a legitimate interest in the company's activities. Companies should behave ethically and have regard for the environment and society as a whole. (Principle 9)

5. Section 404 of the Act requires management to produce an 'internal control report' as part of each annual Exchange Act report. The report is required to affirm 'the responsibility of management for establishing and maintaining an adequate internal control structure and procedures for financial reporting'.

6. Principle 7: Companies should have and continue to develop coherent strategies for each business unit. These should ideally be expressed in terms of market prospects and of the competitive advantage the business has in exploiting these prospects. The company should understand the factors that drive market growth, and the particular strengths that underpin the competitive position.

   Principle 8: Companies should be able to explain why they are the 'best parent' of the businesses they run. Where they are not best parent, they should be developing plans to resolve the issue.

7. No director qualifies as 'independent' unless the board of directors affirmatively determines that the director has no material relationship with the listed company (either directly or as a partner, shareholder, or officer of an organization that has a relationship with the company).

8. The audit committee must have a minimum of three members. Each member of the audit committee must be financially literate, as such qualification is interpreted by the company's board in its business judgement, or must become financially literate within a reasonable period of time after his or her appointment to the audit committee. In addition, at least one member of the audit committee must have accounting or related financial management expertise, as the company's board interprets such qualification in its business judgement.

9. Listed companies must adopt and disclose a code of business conduct and ethics for directors, officers, and employees, and promptly disclose any waivers of the code for directors or executive officers.

10. The responsibilities of the board include the strategic guidance of the company, the effective monitoring of management by the board, and the board's accountability to the company and the shareholders.

Chapter 6 Models of Corporate Governance

1. Refer to the text.

2.

Country	Individuals	Institutional investors
UK	19%	58%
USA	51%	41%

3. Refer to the text.

4. Studies suggest that overseas Chinese firms:
   - are family-centric with close family control;
   - in listed companies, keep the public in a minority with a controlling equity stake kept within the family, sometimes causing problems of family-related transactions;
   - are entrepreneurial, often with a dominant entrepreneur, centralized decision-making, with close personal links emphasizing trust and control;
   - have a paternalistic management style, in a social fabric dependent on relationships and social harmony, avoiding confrontation and the risk of loss of 'face';
   - see an intuitive strategy formulation in which business is seen as more of a succession of contracts or ventures, relying on intuition, superstition, and tough-minded bargaining rather than quantitative analysis.

5. Listing 'through the back door' involves the acquisition of a Hong Kong-listed company and backing a China business into this shell.

6. Refer to the text.

7. A reliable legal system
   - Stock market with liquidity
   - Financial institutions
   - Regulatory authorities
   - A companies registry
   - Accounting and legal professions
   - Auditing firms that are professional
   - Professional organizations
   - Educational institutions
   - Consulting organizations
   - Financial and corporate governance training, continuous professional development
   - Corporate governance research with academic and professional publications

8. – Corporate governance codes of good practice
   – Securities regulations
   – International accounting standards
   – Global concentration of audit practices

– Raising capital on overseas stock exchanges
– International institutional investors
– Research publications, international conferences, and professional journals

9. – Legal differences
   – Standards in the legal process
   – Stock market differences
   – Ownership structures
   – History, culture, and ethnic

10. Trust

PART TWO Policies

Chapter 7 Functions of the Board

1. Strategy formulation is the process of generating and reviewing alternative longer-term directions for the firm that lead towards the achievement of its purpose.

2. A mission statement is a concrete statement of the company's purpose, aims, and direction, which can inspire employees and inform customers and other stakeholders.

3. In long-range planning, the planner is, conceptually, inside the organization looking out. The approach fails to take a strategic perspective, perpetuating the existing business, rather than recognizing strategic changes in technology, markets, and competition, and ignoring the economic and social context.

4. 1. Who is currently competing in our market?
   2. What strategic powers do our upstream suppliers of goods and services have?
   3. What strategic powers do our downstream distributors and ultimate customers have?
   4. Could our customers' needs be met in other ways—with substitute goods or services?
   5. Could other firms enter the market?

5. Resource-based strategic theory sees a firm as a collection of resources and capabilities that need to be utilized to create a winning strategy. The resources could include access to capital, employee skills, unique products or services, managerial talent and experience, equipment and buildings, or goodwill. This resource-based perspective seeks to find a fit between a firm's internal capabilities and its external market situation that will produce a competitive advantage.

6. Corporate policies can be thought of as the rules, systems, and procedures that are laid down by the board to guide and constrain executive management.

7. Financial accounts—profit and loss account and balance sheet
   – Budgetary control with cost centres
   – Profit performance with profit or profitability centres
   – Multiple performance measures and control systems.

8. In designing a management control system, in which units of the organization are to be held responsible for various performance criteria, in seeking to meet their required performance each unit will tend to take action that is beneficial to achieving its own objectives, but potentially detrimental to the organization as a whole.

9. Universally, the answer is: the members. In the case of a joint-stock, limited-liability company, the members are those shareholders with voting rights. In a co-operative society, the members are those with voting rights under the constitution. In a professional body, the members are those who are paid-up and qualified to vote under the rules of that association.

10. To reduce the reports presented to directors, some firms rely on exception reporting in which only significant variations from planned performance have occurred and board-level action is required.

Chapter 8 The Governance of Corporate Risk

1. The UK Corporate Governance Code; the Sarbanes-Oxley Act, the Basel II agreement.

2. Audit committees tend to be orientated towards the past, involved with audit outcomes, and approving accountability information for publication, while risk assessment needs a proactive, forward-looking orientation.

3. Form a risk assessment or risk management committee as a distinct standing committee of the board.

4. Such a risk management committee might have four or five members, wholly or mainly INEDs with appropriate business experience, meeting, perhaps, four times a year, and reporting to the board as a whole. Members of senior management and external experts in risk might be invited to attend meetings to give advice.

5. In a management-based risk management committee, which might include the CEO, the CFO, profit-responsible division or unit heads, and the CRO, with external experts invited to attend to give advice.

6. See the details in the text.

7. An enterprise risk management system (ERMS) should provide information routinely and regularly for management to take executive decisions and for the board to carry out its monitoring and supervisory function. The ERMS should also generate information to enable the company to communicate externally to auditors, regulators, shareholders, and other legitimate stakeholders, as well as its insurers and brokers.

8. • Risk recognition
   • Risk assessment
   • Risk evaluation
   • Risk management policies
   • Risk monitoring
   • Risk transfer (buying insurance, creating a derivative, or just self-insuring)

9. • A simple tabular approach
   • A questionnaire designed to identify risks and hazards
   • Mind mapping
   • Risk benchmarking by industry, country, or other company
   • Software programs and systems
10. • Avoid the risk. Do not commit to the planned action. Abandon the project.
   • Mitigate the risk by making capital investment or incurring ongoing expenditure.
   • Transfer the risk. Enter derivative agreements. Insure against the risk.
   • Risk retention. Accept the risk. Self-insure.

Chapter 9 Corporate Social Responsibility and Sustainability

1. The stakeholders of a company could include:
   - customers of the end product or service;
   - agents, distributors and others in the downstream supply chain;
   - original suppliers and others in the upstream supply chain;
   - other creditors;
   - bankers and non-equity sources of finance;
   - employees, including managers;
   - self-employed contractors to the company;
   - local and national societal institutions;
   - regulators;
   - government, local and national;
   - society generally.
2. Societal; strategy-driven; stakeholder; ethical; political; philanthropic.
3. A firm's 'socially responsible activities' might include:
   • the contributions of facilities, staff time to local and other organizations;
   • educational and academic contributions:
     - support for local and other academic institutions;
     - contributions to research and similar activities;
   • aesthetic and arts contributions:
     - expenditure on building and landscape design;
     - sponsorship of arts, crafts, and similar activities;
   • sports and leisure contributions.
4. Boards adopting an enlightened shareholder value (ESV) approach believe that the satisfaction of the needs of stakeholders is crucial to corporate success and essential to creating value for shareholders. The ESV concept of corporate governance attempts to overcome apparent conflicts between the shareholder and the stakeholder-focused perspectives.

   Profits can be generated, shareholder value created, and society's wealth increased by satisfying stakeholder interests, rather than through the classical attempts of shareholder theory to maximize shareholder wealth.
5. To be effective, a company's CSR efforts need to be led by the directors. A primary duty of the board is to identify the aims of the company, establish its mission, and set its values. A company's attitude to CSR should be embedded in its corporate strategy.
6. A CSR policy is a summary of the firm's attitudes to relationships with its business stakeholders and the communities in which it operates, and the impact it wants to have on them. To be effective, CSR policies need to be understood, accepted, and applied throughout the organization.
7. A clear CSR policy can influence potential investors looking for socially responsible, ethical, or environmentally friendly enterprises in which to invest.
8. The United Nations Brundtland Report defines sustainable development as 'development that meets the needs of the present without compromising the ability of future generations to meet their own needs'.
9. The Global Reporting Initiative (GRI) is a worldwide, multi-stakeholder network to create and develop the Sustainability Reporting Framework, in which business, civil society, labour, investors, accountants, and others collaborate.
10. The GRI is based on the underlying belief that reporting on economic, environmental, and social performance by all organizations should be as routine and comparable as financial reporting. The principles and guidance section of the GRI framework provides guidance and principles for defining the report content, which helps to determine what should be covered by the sustainability report and where its boundaries should be drawn.

Chapter 10 The Governance of Listed Companies

1. • A *holding company* is a company that holds all or a dominant share of the voting rights in another company.
   • A *subsidiary company* is a company in which another company (its holding company) holds all of its voting shares (a *wholly owned subsidiary*) or a majority of its voting shares (a *partially owned subsidiary*).
   • An *associate company* is a company over which another company exercises dominant power, even though it does not hold a majority of the voting rights in that company, for example where the other shareholdings are widely spread.
2. The primary reason is, typically, low taxation with some businesses exempt from profits tax, and no capital gains or wealth taxes. Additionally, an offshore jurisdiction might have good communications, political and economic stability, no exchange

controls, and offer companies registered there flexibility, corporate privacy and confidentiality, a pool of professional service providers, sound company law, and regulation that is reasonable, but not bureaucratic.

3. Not unless they are managers of the company as well as shareholders.

4. Principally to leverage financial power gained from the gearing. By investing in a chain, the head of the chain is able to exercise more influence over the companies in the chain than would be available by investing in individual companies in the chain.

5. The creation of two or more classes of voting shares in which one class enjoys greater voting rights than the other class.

6. A nominated adviser authorized by the UK AIM market, which all AIM companies are required to appoint. The Nomad's experience provides a quality control mechanism by checking the company's plans and certifying to the Exchange that the company is suitable and ready for listing.

7. A dual-listed company is a group structure in which two listed companies merge but both companies continue to exist and share ownership of a single, operational business. The group then has two stock exchange listings, with different bodies of shareholders, usually in different countries.

8. Many companies use joint ventures with another company to enter markets, transfer technology, procure supplies, obtain finance, share management skills, manufacture products around the world, or share risk on an international scale.

9. Shareholder activism can include communication and negotiation direct with management, but also media campaigns or blogging to change corporate practices, proxy battles advancing shareholder resolutions to force change, calling shareholder meetings, or litigation against companies or their directors. Some shareholder activists use their shareholding to advance their own social, environmental or other agenda, and influence corporate behaviour.

10. Only in some company law jurisdictions. In other jurisdictions, companies are prohibited from investing in themselves through group networks.

Chapter 11 The Governance of Private Companies and other Corporate Entities

1. If disagreements arise that were not envisaged in the initial joint venture (JV) agreement, directors of the JV company can face conflicts between their responsibilities to the JV company and to the JV partner company that employs them. Although many JV companies do appoint the managing director or CEO of the JV to the board, others now appoint only representative directors from the partner companies and have the JV managing director attend meetings in a non-voting, non-partisan way.

2. Basically, in a partnership, the partners are responsible for governing the firm. In a firm with few partners, governance is by a meeting of all of the partners. In larger firms, the partnership may decide to appoint a managing partner and a governing body, perhaps called an executive or management committee, which meets regularly to manage partnership affairs, with a periodic, perhaps annual, meeting of the entire partnership to accept the accounts, to transact business reserved to the meeting and appoint members to the governing body.

3. Some countries have a form of limited-liability partnerships (LLP). This governance vehicle gives the benefits of limited liability to the members, but allows the flexibility of organizing as a traditional partnership. The governance of an LLP is similar to that of a partnership: members provide the capital, contribute personally, and share profits and losses, to give some protection to those dealing with a limited partnership. However, the disclosure requirements tend to be more stringent than those for a traditional partnership, and similar to those of a company.

4. • A holding company is the company at the head of the group pyramid. Its board of directors is often called the 'main board'.
   • A subsidiary company is one in which the holding or parent company holds all or a majority of the voting shares in that company.
   • An associated company is one in which the holding company, although not holding a majority of the shares, has sufficient interests to control it and determine its actions.

5. (1) Subsidiary company self-governance, allowing each company in the group to govern itself and manage its own affairs, subject to overall group-wide policies and resource allocation.
   (2) Group-wide governance, treating the group companies as divisions or departments of the holding company.

6. The opportunity for cross-group coordination, the sharing of expertise, training, and development of future main board directors, management development, and the building of group norms and culture.

7. A family council, consisting of the family members who own shares (management and non-management), meets prior to meetings of the shareholders and the directors to identify issues that affect family members and to resolve them in the best interests of the family.

8. An investment fund that invests a country's financial surpluses in the shares of companies in other countries. Arab and Asian countries' state-owned funds have been used to invest in the United States and Europe.

9. Sovereign-wealth funds have invested in telecoms, technology, real estate, ports, and transport operations, and in the financial sectors.

10. The distinguishing features include:
    - they are working for the public good;
    - their aims reflect community objectives;
    - their legal status is rooted in the law of trusts, charities, co-operatives, or other legal acts;
    - their form can take various legal structures;
    - their underpinning constitution determines their form and purpose;
    - governance is provided by a governing body, which can be known variously as a council, board of trustees, management committee, etc.;
    - their performance is measured by the achievement of multiple goals and is often difficult to measure;
    - their governing body is often large and drawn entirely from outside, non-executive members;
    - their objectives can conflict;
    - nomination to the governing body may come from the members, funding bodies, representative bodies (staff, beneficiaries, funding bodies, the local community, etc.), subject to the constitution;
    - the top executive and the top management team are typically invited to attend meetings of the governing body, make reports, and answer questions, but are seldom voting members of it;
    - membership of the governing body is usually voluntary and unpaid, with no fees, remuneration, or capital gains, subject perhaps to reasonable expenses;
    - trustees are the guardian angels of a voluntary organization, watching over its activities, and need to be competent, informed, but personally disinterested.

PART THREE Practices

Chapter 12 Corporate Governance Around the World

1. A shares—listed in China and available only to Chinese residents
   B shares—listed in China, but available only to foreign investors
   N shares—China-based companies listed in New York
   L shares—China-based companies listed in London
   H shares—China-based companies listed in Hong Kong and Singapore
2. SASAC, the State-owned Assets Supervision and Administration Commission of the State Council, holds the China government's shareholding in all China's listed companies (other than those in the finance sector). CSRC, the China Securities Regulatory Commission of the State Council, is the Chinese government's corporate regulator.
3. - State-owned enterprises (SOEs), which may be large, medium, or small, with state ownership at the national, provincial, or local level.

   - Collectively owned enterprises, including urban collectives and rural township and village entities (TVEs)
   - Privately owned organizations, defined as firms with more than seven employees
   - Small, individually owned enterprises with no more than seven employees
   - Foreign-invested firms
4. Companies in India, both in the public and private sectors including multinationals, are dominated by majority shareholders, with pre-emption rights for minority shareholders frequently ignored. A corporate governance rating by the Asian Corporate Governance Association in 2007 assessed India's corporate governance as 'fair to poor'.
5. The role of the state has expanded and government influence over some companies has increased. Some ownership has been transferred back to the state by expropriation or by acquisition in the market, as in the case of Yukos.
6. Brazilian company law and the code have three unusual corporate governance features—the fiscal council, the family council, and the advisory board.
7. No. Hong Kong has its own corporate governance code, enshrined in the Hong Kong Stock Exchange listing rules.
8. Listed chaebol companies are often still controlled by the dominant owner-family interests. Even though companies attract outside capital, family domination is maintained through insider boards and cross-ownership with subsidiary companies.
9. - Concentrated ownership, with strong family ownership of both private and listed companies or state ownership
   - Dominant family oversight and control, with leadership from the head of the family, entrepreneurial decision-making, opaque communications and relationship-based trading
   - Debt financing in which bank financing is often more than shareholders' equity
   - Banking sector equity investment, with banks holding significant shares in companies
10. Islamic *shariah* law introducing religious rules and interpretations.

Chapter 13 Board Membership: Directors' appointment, roles, and remuneration

1. The remuneration committee is a subcommittee of the main board, consisting wholly or mainly of independent outside directors, which is set up with responsibility for overseeing the remuneration packages of board members, particularly the executive directors and, possibly, members of senior management.
2. Integrity means being able to distinguish right from wrong and judge corporate behaviour accordingly. It means being able to recognize

and declare a conflict of interest. It means acting in the company interest, not self-interest, and resisting the temptation to make an unacceptable personal gain. Essentially, integrity means acting honestly.

3. Integrity and honesty, passion for customers, for our partners, and for technology, openness and respectfulness, taking on big challenges and seeing them through, constructive self-criticism, self-improvement, and personal excellence, and accountability to customers, shareholders, partners, and employees for commitments, results, and quality.

4. They can be summarized as intellect, character, and personality.

5. The essential director-level skills include:
   - strategic reasoning, perception, and vision;
   - a critical faculty capable of quantitative and qualitative analysis and financial interpretation;
   - planning and decision-making capabilities;
   - communication and interpersonal skills;
   - networking and political abilities.

6. Character traits, what some call 'strength of character', include being independently minded, objective, and impartial. A director needs to be capable of moving towards consensus. Yet, from time to time, a director needs to be tough-minded, tenacious, and resilient, with the courage to make a stand. Further, a director needs to have a balanced approach to risk, be results-orientated—neither risk-averse nor rash.

7. - A duty of trust—to exercise a fiduciary responsibility to the shareholders
   - A duty of care—to exercise reasonable care, diligence, and skill

8. Related-party transactions provide a good example of the requirement to disclose personal interests. The listing rules of most stock exchanges and securities regulators require related-party transactions to be disclosed and, often, approved by the other shareholders.

Chapter 14 Board Leadership: The reality of the boardroom

1. The fundamental power of the board is derived from the shareholders who have delegated the running of the company to the directors. This power is reinforced by authority derived from the company's constitution backed up by company law.

2. • By a majority or dominant shareholder putting pressure on the board
   • From the threat of a potential takeover
   • By the prospect of litigation
   • Through the influence of the auditors
   • From the effects of legislation and regulation
   • From media pressure and other external exhortation
   • By a dominant or charismatic leader
   • And, obviously, through the changing business circumstances

3. Knowledge power is power derived from access to information, skills, or experiences not available to the other directors (e.g. the influence on board discussions about international currency rates by the INED who is also a director of an international bank).

4. • Personality power
   • Knowledge power
   • Sanction power
   • Interpersonal power
   • Networking power
   • Ownership power
   • Representative power

5. Professional, representative, rubber-stamp, and country club.

6. See the text.

7. To manage the board.

8. - Management of the board
   - Management of meetings
   - Strategic leadership
   - Linking the board with management
   - Arbitration
   - Figurehead or public face of the company

9. See the text.

10. See the text.

Chapter 15 Board Activities: Corporate governance in practice

1. The remuneration committee is responsible for recommending to the board the remuneration packages of executive directors, and sometimes other top management, including their salary, fees, pension arrangements, options to acquire shares in the company, and other benefits.

2. The role of the nomination committee is to suggest names for board membership, in an attempt to introduce different experience, personalities, and diversity to the board, and to avoid domination of the nomination process by the chairman, CEO, or any other dominant directors.

3. The primary role of the audit committee is to liaise between the board and the independent external auditors.

4. Liaising between the board and the independent external auditors might include:
   • making recommendation to the board on their appointment, reappointment, or removal and replacement;
   • reviewing and approving their terms of engagement;
   • ensuring their objectivity and independence from the company, confirming that no conflicts of interest exist that could affect the auditor's ability to issue an unbiased opinion on the company's financial statements;
   • developing and implementing a policy for their engagement on non-audit work;
   • approving their remuneration;
   • working with them on audit procedures and plans, receiving the auditor's report and management letter about issues that have arisen

during the audit, and reviewing and acting on these issues.

5. See the seventeen items listed in the main text.

6. See the ten items listed in the main text.

7. The directors are responsible for the preparation of the financial statements, and for being satisfied that they give a true and fair view. The auditors' responsibility is to audit and express an opinion on the financial statements in accordance with applicable law and International Auditing Standards.

8. The PCAOB standards require auditors to:
   - obtain reasonable assurance that effective internal control over financial reporting has been maintained;
   - assess the risk that a material weakness exists, testing and evaluating the design, and operating effectiveness of internal control based on the assessed risk;
   - perform such other procedures as are considered necessary in the circumstances.

9. In the United States, the company secretary is typically known as the corporate secretary, and the role is frequently carried out by the corporate lawyer.

10. See the nine items in the main text.

Chapter 16 Board Effectiveness: Building better boards

1. Commitment, character, collaboration, competence, creativity, contribution.

2. See Case study 16.1 in the text.

3. Confidentiality, security, integrity, availability, assurance, cost-effectiveness, flexibility, simplicity, and ease of use.

4. Why, what, when, where, and who.

5. A director cannot opt out of certain items because he or she lacks appropriate knowledge, although he or she may rely on information received and the opinions of fellow directors, given in good faith, unless he or she has any reason to doubt—in which case he or she must pursue the issue to its root.

6. Although, subject to the articles, there are no specific rules governing the content or format of minutes of board or board subcommittee meetings; they should provide a competent and complete record of what transpired, what was decided, and what actions are to be taken by whom and when.

7. A good report with high-quality information is:
   - understandable;
   - reliable;
   - relevant;
   - comprehensive;
   - concise;
   - timely;
   - cost-effective.

8. A newly appointed director needs a proper induction programme to reduce the learning time taken before beginning to make significant contributions to board deliberations.

9. Directors' and officers' insurance.

10. No. Actions can be brought against the company, the board, and/or individual directors. Claims for unlimited amounts can put directors' personal assets at risk.

Chapter 17 Board Evaluation: Reviewing directors and boards

1. See text.

2. In many cases at the moment, director appraisals are being conducted in an informal way, with the chairman personally assessing the performance and commenting privately to the director involved.

3. Yes, the pressure is on for director appraisals to be more formalized. To set up such a process needs a board policy decision, with the full support of all the directors.

4. Typically, the output of an individual director performance assessment will be a confidential report to the chairman and, possibly, the chairman of the board's nomination committee, if involved in the review process. Given the personal nature of the report, most chairmen will not table it at a board meeting, but discuss the relevant portion with each director.

5. The UK Corporate Governance Code calls on the non-executive directors, led by the senior independent director, to be responsible for performance evaluation of the chairman, taking into account the views of executive directors. But in most cases, the chairman's performance is reflected in the performance of the company as a whole. Continued poor performance will bring calls for a change of chairman from major investors, the media, or occasionally from fellow directors who are dissatisfied.

6. Yes and yes.

7. The chairman often assumes the role of:
   - an experienced INED, perhaps the senior INED;
   - an executive director, such as the CEO or the CFO;
   - the internal auditor;
   - the audit committee;
   - a past chairman;
   - a respected chairman or INED from the board of another company not in competition;
   - an independent organization or firm of consultants.

8. Refer to the text.

9. - Ownership structure and external influences
   - Shareholder rights and relations
   - Transparency, disclosure, and audit
   - Board structure and effectiveness

10. - The World Bank and International Monetary Fund Reports on the Observance of Standards and Codes (ROSC) programme
    - The European Bank for Reconstruction and Development (2003) (EBRD) corporate governance assessment project
    - The FTSE ISS CGI company ratings

**Chapter 18 Corporate Governance:
The next thirty years**

1. Refer to the text.
2. The Commission supports the NYSE's listing requirements generally providing for a majority of independent directors, but also believes that companies can have additional non-independent directors so that there is an appropriate range and mix of expertise, diversity, and knowledge on the board.
3. American concepts of corporate governance rely on rules, and the British on principles.
4. The question is which is preferable: a dominant leader, who can provide single-minded leadership and enhance performance, or shared responsibility, which reduces risk?
5. Recognize that good corporate governance is about the effectiveness of the governing body not about compliance with codes.
6. See the text.
7. – The development of new organizational forms
   – The reinforcement of the right of owners to nominate directors
   – Institutional investors exercising more power over their investments
   – The drive for gender diversity on boards
   – The demand for genuine independence of external auditors
   – New theories of corporate governance
8. Board-level information systems that enable directors to search for the information they feel they want, perhaps applying other tools and simulations to explore possible outcomes, while communicating their ideas to other board colleagues online.

Index

Note: non-UK and non-US-based entities and institutions are listed under the names of their countries; e.g. 'Germany, Volkswagen'. All UK/US entries appear alphabetically.